FOREIGN INVESTMENT LAW AND DISPUTES

including

China, Europe, and North America

Ralph H. Folsom

Professor of Law
University of San Diego School of Law
A.B. Princeton University, J.D. Yale Law School,
LLM London School of Economics

CONCISE HORNBOOK SERIES™

WEST
ACADEMIC
PUBLISHING

© 2022 LEG, Inc. d/b/a West Academic
    444 Cedar Street, Suite 700
    St. Paul, MN 55101
    1-877-888-1330

Printed in the United States of America

ISBN: 978-1-68561-006-7

Preface

Foreign investment is commonplace around the globe. Inbound and outbound foreign investment flows are massive. Home country investors merge or acquire existing host nation businesses or establish new companies abroad. Foreign investors also purchase stocks and bonds on numerous exchanges, along with foreign sovereign debt. The sums involved are staggering.

Foreign Investment Law and Disputes examines the law, practice, regulation, and dispute settlement of foreign investment. Unlike international trade law governed significantly by the World Trade Organization, no uniform body of foreign investment law exists. There is no "World Investment Organization". Hence foreign investment rules are predominantly national, occasionally regional, in character and vary considerably.

This Concise Hornbook introduces foreign investment entry and operational control patterns, developing world investment characteristics, expropriation risks and insurance, and investment-related technology transfers across borders. It reviews investing in China, Europe, and North America as "case studies".

The multitude of foreign investment treaties (BITs) and free trade agreement (FTA) investment regimes are explored, with emphasis on the dynamic investment rules and proceedings under NAFTA 1994 and USMCA 2020. Controversial foreign investor-host state arbitration systems for settlement of disputes are closely examined.

This Concise Hornbook can be used in connection with *any* foreign investment or international business course. It can be used on its own as a course book or treatise, notably in conjunction with the documents appended at the end of various chapters.

It has been a genuine pleasure to prepare this first edition of *Foreign Investment Law and Disputes including China, Europe, and North America.* I am indebted to Professor Michael Gordon, Emeritus at the University of Florida Law School, for his prior work on some of the materials appearing in this book and to Professor John Luther Rogers for his China contributions to Chapter 4.

I hope that students, academics, lawyers, government officials and people in business will find it useful. Your comments and suggestions are most welcome.

Ralph H. Folsom
rfolsom@sandiego.edu

February, 2022

About the Author

Ralph H. Folsom has been a Professor at the University of San Diego School of Law since 1975. A graduate of Princeton University, Yale Law School, and the London School of Economics (LLM), Professor Folsom teaches, writes, and consults extensively in the field of international business law.

Folsom has been a Senior Fulbright resident scholar in Singapore and a Visiting Professor at the University of Hong Kong, University of Aix-Marseille, University of Brest, University of Paris, University of Toulouse, University of Puerto Rico, Monash University in Australia, and Tecnológico de Monterrey in México.

Professor Folsom has authored or co-authored a range of books with West Academic Publishing. These include a popular problem-oriented course book on *International Business Transactions*, now in its Thirteenth Edition.

Professor Folsom has also written in the West Concise Hornbook Series:

> *International Litigation and Arbitration;*
>
> *The European Union Beyond BREXIT;*
>
> *Free Trade Agreements;*
>
> *International Trade Beyond Trump;* and
>
> *International Business Transactions* (co-authored).

He is the author of a two-volume *Practitioner Treatise on International Business Transactions* and the nine-volume Eckstrom treatise on *International Joint Ventures*, both published by Thomson Reuters and available on Westlaw.

Ralph Folsom is married to Pixie Haughwout, an avid boater and author of *Canal Cruising in the South of France: The Romantic*

Canal du Midi and *Well-Favored Passage: The Magic of Lake Huron's North Channel*. See www.SeaFeverCruisingGuides.com.

Summary of Contents

Table of Contents

FOREIGN INVESTMENT LAW AND DISPUTES

including

China, Europe, and North America

Introduction

The World Trade Organization (WTO), covered in my Concise Hornbook on *International Trade Beyond Trump,* generated a reasonable degree of harmony among roughly 165 member-nations. In contrast, there is no "World Investment Organization". Hence the law governing foreign investment varies considerably around the globe among approximately 200 countries and other jurisdictions (such as the European Union and the USMCA). Put another way, the law of foreign investment is seriously chaotic. The level of this chaos escalates when both home and host countries decide to regulate foreign investment transactions.

For purposes of this book, "host-nation" identifies the nation in which the investment is made. "Home-nation" designates the nation from which the investment capital, technology and the like comes, often the nation in which a multinational parent is incorporated and has its management center. Foreign investors will regularly encounter laws in the host nation that differ from laws regulating investment in the home nation.

Why Invest Abroad?

There are movements of capital, technology and people associated with foreign investment around the world. These movements are profit-driven, often focusing on lower costs, fewer regulations, less taxation, increased revenues, market penetration, supply chain security, access to natural resources, access to technology, avoidance of trade restraints (Buy America, Buy China, for examples), and leapfrogging over national and regional tariffs.

Rising China is major foreign investor, especially under its global Belt and Road Initiative (BRI). See Chapter 4. The United States and Europe are world leading foreign direct investment partners, often via multinational subsidiaries, each accounting for approximately 60% of all foreign investment in the other's economy. See Chapters 5 and 6. U.S. subsidiaries in Europe typically generate far greater profits than they garner in China or India. The U.S. and EU are also major sources of mergers and acquisitions and securities investments in each other's markets.

Where to invest and evaluating what risks are involved are critical issues for counselors to foreign investors.

Types of Foreign Investment

This Concise Hornbook attempts to bring a degree of understanding to the chaos of foreign investment law. There are distinctions, trends and patterns that repeat. One of the most essential is the difference between direct and indirect (portfolio) foreign investment.

Direct Investment

Direct investment, often referred to as "greenfields investment", typically involves starting from scratch in a host country. Direct investors may be engaged in manufacturing, infrastructure projects, sales and distribution of goods or services, franchising, or other businesses.

Lower labor, taxation, and regulatory costs, expanding consumer markets, and access to natural resources, are often major incentives to invest abroad (so-called "outsourcing"). These incentives may vary over time. In recent years, for example, China's seemingly endless supply of labor has declined, and wages have risen causing a considerable exodus of assembly plant investments to move to Southeast Asia. President Trump's tariffs on Chinese goods fueled this trend as investors re-worked their global supply chains. COVID trade and shipping bottlenecks dramatically taught many foreign investors the risks of globalized supply chains. There is a trend underway to bring home or at least closer to home essential suppliers.

Classic "concession agreements" for development of natural resources generally involved ownership by foreigners for extended periods. In 1901, for example, the Shah of Persia granted 500,000 square miles of exclusive oil rights to a foreign investor for 60 years (the D'Arcy Concession). Gradually, particularly since the end of the colonial era, developing nations have repudiated, re-negotiated or expropriated natural resource concessions, often favoring instead "production sharing" and service contracts with multinational businesses.

Services are the most rapidly growing foreign investment sector, with branches and subsidiaries of banks, insurance companies, brokerage houses, utilities, E-commerce, transport, and telecoms leading the way. Foreign investment in services is facilitated by market openings under the WTO General Agreement on Trade in Services (GATS). See Chapter 1 in my *International Trade Beyond Trump* Concise Hornbook. Multinational legal, accounting, and other service firms have been multiplying, often using a Swiss association called a "Verein", which separates the liability of each independent office from the others.

Foreign goods, capital, technology, machinery, knowhow, components, and management personnel move from one part of the developed world into another. At this point, however, foreign direct investment in developing nations has surpassed investment in developed nations. For example, China and Brazil have been and continue to be major recipients of foreign investment, including notably venture capital.

Developed world direct foreign investment flows have been joined by rising amounts of foreign investment flowing *out* of advanced developing nations. China and India, for example, longstanding recipients of direct foreign investment, are increasingly exporters thereof. Chinese investors alone have huge sums invested around the globe, often focused on natural resources needed to run its powerful economy. Chinese firms have acquired or established numerous companies in the United States, employing many Americans. See Chapter 4. Chinese companies have also bought trophy properties like the Waldorf Astoria Hotel.

Despite increased PRC restraints on capital exports, billions in funds have left China, much of it headed into direct foreign investments. U.S. and European scrutiny of Chinese investments, especially those of state-owned or controlled entities, on "national security" grounds is on the rise. See Chapter 6.

Lastly, there is a growing business and residential foreign direct investment trend driven by individuals and their families seeking permanent residency or citizenship in stable societies. In the Caribbean, for example, citizenship can be obtained for as little as a $200,000 investment in Dominica. Malta and Cyprus proffer residency rights and EU-wide visa-free travel for roughly the same amount. Russians frequently follow this path. The United States "million-dollar" green card, frequently discounted to $500,000, has been popular with Chinese and more recently Vietnamese investors.

Mergers and Acquisitions

A variation on the theme of foreign investment is the purchase of an existing business in the host country. In other words, mergers, and acquisitions (M&A). Such investments avoid the labor-intensive nature of a "greenfields" investment. Trillions of dollars of cross-border mergers and acquisitions occur yearly. Most jurisdictions have M&A controls that must be navigated. See Chapters 4, 5 and 6.

The privatization of state-owned companies by formerly nonmarket economies (for example, the Soviet Union and its satellites) also creates acquisition opportunities. "Tax inversion" mergers and acquisitions with U.S. companies "taken over" by European or Canadian competitors may generate substantial tax savings, though increased U.S. regulation has reduced these benefits.

Securities Investments

Indirect investment involves buying securities, normally stocks or bonds, in host country businesses. This can be done on foreign or U.S. stock exchanges, including funds holding foreign securities. Chinese companies have floated securities on the New York Stock Exchange. For example, Alibaba, China's answer to Amazon, made an initial public offering on the New York Exchange that was the largest in history. Whether this will continue is uncertain ever since the Trump administration mandated compliance with U.S. accounting and auditing standards by U.S. listed Chinese companies. See Chapter 6.

China's stocks and bonds, now included in the MSCI and FTSE Russell stock indexes and Bloomberg Barclays Aggregate Bond Index, have flowed across borders rapidly as funds and ETFs adjust their holdings. U.S. private equity firms have led the way into China's securities markets. Individual buyers of shares in such funds may not think of themselves as foreign investors, but financial crises like that of China's realty companies (notably Evergrande in 2021) wake them up.

The U.S. now bars personal or fund ownership of certain portfolio investments, particularly in Chinese firms linked to its military, some of which have been de-listed from the NYSE and NASDAQ. See Chapter 6. Indirect flows of investment funds, often financed in dollars, as between China and Hong Kong have massively increased.

Any student of securities law will appreciate the regulated nature of financial markets. For example, until 2015 foreigners were not allowed to purchase shares on the Saudi Arabia stock market. Foreign access to China's fledgling stock exchanges has been significantly controlled. When "foreigners" are the buyers, legal scrutiny likely will increase, particularly say if the buyers are perceived to be speculators (hello hedge funds).

Special issues may arise when sovereign bonds or other debt are involved, notably the risk of default, as has been prominently the case with Argentina and Greece. Complex infrastructure projects in the developing world are often financed by international banks and monetary funds. This normally creates foreign ownership of the loans involved and extensive work for international business lawyers.

Risks in Foreign Investment

There are risks, and usually entry and host nation operational restrictions, involved with every foreign investment. Such risks may cause losses of part or all the invested capital and technology. For example, there is a risk of expropriation (see Chapter 3), and there may be restrictions that limit foreign investment to a minority equity position (see Chapter 1). Rule of law risks can be major in many parts of the world, particularly concerning piracy of intellectual property and corrupt legal systems.

There is also a risk of failure due to a lack of understanding of different cultures, although perhaps that is more a challenge than a risk. For example, Venezuela as an investment location has major risks if democratization is not successful and the nation continues to nationalize foreign businesses. India may impose too many restrictions in the form of mandatory joint ventures, data localization or local content requirements. Nigeria may have a corrupt government whose officials constantly demand bribes. Brazil may be unable to control inflation and periodically establish exchange controls that prohibit repatriation of profits.

In contrast, Poland, Thailand, and Kenya may be better from the viewpoint of fewer risks and fewer restrictions on the formation and operation of an investment, even though they may be less favorable when only business issues are evaluated. Their market demographics and profit perspectives may prevail.

Many such risks can be avoided by investing in a developed nation, for example within the European Union (see Chapter 5). While risks and restrictions also exist with respect to developed nations, they tend to be like risks and restrictions in the United States (see Chapter 6). And they tend to be less severe than in developing or nonmarket economy nations in transition.

Some risks at a foreign plant are easily covered by insurance, such as fire or theft, just as they would be in the United States. Risks of injuries to employees may be covered by a state or national plan similar to U.S. workmen's compensation, while liability insurance for injuries to visitors and other individuals may be less expensive because of lower court awards.

Some risks of investing abroad are for the most part unique to foreign investment, such as convertibility of currency, expropriation of the company's property, or damage due to war, revolution, or insurrection. Special insurance, such as that written by the U.S. Development Finance Corporation (DFC, formerly OPIC), the World Bank's Multilateral Investment Guarantee Agency (MIGA), or private insurers may cover those risks (see Chapter 3).

The Role of Lawyers in Foreign
Investment Transactions

Where, why, and how to invest abroad is a complex business decision. Expectations of profitability are a dominant factor. Other issues may influence where and why decisions related to foreign investment. Lawyers tend to be involved in advising on taxation, regulatory rules, political stability, technology and IP issues, rule of law and the like.

U.S. lawyers often play a leading role in foreign investment counseling and negotiation, quite frequently with foreign as well as American clients. U.S. lawyers are generally thought to have foreign investment expertise. In Asia, and elsewhere, lawyers may play a more subsidiary role in foreign investment, perhaps limited to drafting documents for a transaction that business leaders have already negotiated.

Chapters 4, 5 and 6 explore investing in China, Europe, and North America respectively. These jurisdictions provide a representative sampling of legal issues impacting the where, why, and how of foreign investment decisions and the role of lawyers therein.

Chapter 1

ENTRY CONTROLS OVER FOREIGN INVESTMENT

§ 1.1   Introduction

Individuals and multinationals have many reasons to invest abroad. It may be part of an initial overall plan to produce goods or provide services worldwide. It may be the next progression considered after a home market is saturated. Foreign investment abroad often occurs after less extensive contact with the host country in the form of trading goods or transferring production technology. Foreign investment is a major part of the business of many companies chartered in developed nations. Since the early 1980s, multinational enterprises have moved toward global supply chains and global production and division of labor.

A further foreign investment step is to move the state of incorporation to another country where the organizational, tax and regulatory laws are more favorable. This is not an action without critics, especially in the country the corporation is departing. The reality is that poor hosts cause guests to depart. The generally accepted rule that the law of the state of incorporation applies to internal affairs may encourage such moves.

Foreign investment involves ownership and control of the enterprise abroad, whether branch or subsidiary in form. Enterprises which undertake foreign investment are referred to by several names, multinational corporations (MNCs) or enterprises (MNEs). More important than what they are called are the percentages of ownership, and control by the home-nation individual or entity. Share ownership discloses whether the enterprise is a joint venture involving two countries, and which country is likely to assert authority over it. Both the governments of the home nation (place of incorporation) and the foreign host nation (place of the productive part of the business) may attempt to assert such authority, leading to intergovernmental conflicts.

The Decision to Invest Abroad

Whether to invest abroad is a complex, multi-faceted decision driven primarily by profit seeking. Lower labor and production costs are often critical factors. Yet a business of one country may remain, even when some significant advantages suggest investment elsewhere. The business may not wish to risk disturbing its market share at home, even though its sales are increasingly abroad. Avoiding high tariffs may be a factor in deciding whether to stay or move. So may be a perception that the host country is moving away from remaining a market economy.

Foreign investment might be considered when a licensee abroad is creating problems, and the company believes it can make a better product or provide a better service on its own. Poor-quality products or services by licensees, or disappointment with partners, is often a reason for assuming control of production abroad. In China, for example, many foreign investors that commenced as joint venture partners with local companies (frequently state-owned), are now becoming wholly foreign owned enterprises, known as WFOEs. See Chapter 4.

Intra-regional foreign investment is another aspect of this development. The creation in 1957 of the European Economic Community (now European Union) and the adoption of the North American Free Trade Agreement in 1994 (now USMCA) stimulated increased foreign investment within these trading areas. The completion of the Uruguay GATT Round in 1995 added new WTO investment opportunities and rules (TRIMs and GATS), discussed below. These rules encouraged even more foreign investment.

Regulating and Incentivizing Foreign Investment

The composition of the rules that should govern foreign investment has been a subject of frequent debate among developed and developing countries. The North-South dialogue split developed countries in the northern hemisphere from less developed countries generally in the southern hemisphere. The North-South dialogue led in the 1970s to both restrictive United Nations General Assembly Resolutions, and restrictive foreign investment laws in many developing nations. The less developed countries argued that they were poor because the developed countries were rich, and that the development gap was increasing.

The less developed countries made demands that were largely aspirational, and invariably unrealistic. They wanted transfers of the most advanced technology at little or no cost, increased investment capital in companies with majority local control and ownership, and both forgiveness of old debt and assurances of new borrowing with few restrictions as to use. The dialogue was most active in the late 1960s and through the 1970s. It unraveled with sovereign debt defaults in the early 1980s, and the election of more market-oriented leaders in many developing nations who realized that development lay more in local effort than foreign largesse.

Subsequent election of governments more determined to join the developed world than to lead the third world removed impediments to foreign investment. Nationalizations in the 1960s and 1970s gave way to privatizations in the 1980s and 1990s. Investment restrictions gave way to investment incentives as nations that had rejected foreign investment welcomed it. Legal requirements mandating joint ventures were changed to voluntary joint ventures. Even though this liberalization has provided investors with significant opportunities in many foreign nations, obstacles to foreign investment remain, and old ones may be exhumed as governments change.

§ 1.2   Home Nations

Governance of foreign investors may be divided into three spheres: Governance by the home nation, by the host nation, or by multi-nation organizations. One might also wish to add a fourth, governance by international law. Although the latter might constitute an ideal method in an ideal world, international legal norms that govern multinational enterprises are few and contested in status.

Regulation of a U.S. multinational abroad by the home nation is essentially a matter of U.S. federal law. See Chapter 6. These laws tend to fall into one of two classes. First are those laws enacted to deal with domestic issues without serious consideration of their impact on foreign activities of American firms. Examples are the federal securities and antitrust laws. Both can have extraterritorial application, although their potential impact abroad was not seriously debated when these laws were enacted. Second are laws that address specific foreign policy issues and are intended to achieve what are largely political goals. Examples are the Foreign Corrupt Practices Act (FCPA) and U.S. boycott and anti-boycott laws. See my Concise Hornbook, *International Trade Beyond Trump,* Chapter 13.

There are other U.S. laws that affect the actions abroad of U.S. firms, such as tax laws that may encourage investment in friendly nations. Customs provisions allowing assembly of U.S. made parts with duties applied only to the value added abroad when the products re-enter the United States, and the Generalized System of Preferences (GSP) intended to assist development in source countries provide examples. *Id.*

Foreign nations should understand that home nations in which multinationals are registered and usually "seated" tend only to enact laws that are in the best interests of their nations, usually without extensive regard for any special interests of the various possible host nations. As discussed below, it is only the host nations' laws that may effectively regulate foreign investor activity in that country.

§ 1.3   Developing Host Nations

The laws enacted in the 1970s by developing nations, notably in Latin America, to govern foreign investment tended to be very restrictive. In addition to restrictions based on the desire to have host nation nationals participate in equity and management, restrictions were often imposed when foreign investment was believed to infringe upon national sovereignty, contrary to a development plan, unbalanced in favor of the foreign party, environmentally damaging, or violated host nation law.

Mandatory joint ventures were a key element in developing nation restraints on foreign investment during the late 20th century. In theory, and on paper, laws of this nature were mandatory, but as Professor Michael Gordon ably demonstrated, foreign investors were sometimes able to avoid such restrictions under an "operational code" or unwritten law that allowed foreign investment.

Developing nation laws governing foreign investment tended to evolve from two quite different perspectives. One group which enacted restrictive laws mandating joint ventures included nations which already had considerable foreign investment, such as India, Mexico, and Nigeria. These nations viewed the new laws to gain greater control over foreign multinationals and to allow their nationals to participate in the equity and management of the means of production in the nation.

At the same time nonmarket economy nations were beginning to adopt joint venture laws that were used to admit for the first time in decades some limited foreign equity. The reason was usually that the nation needed technology that would not be transferred unless it accompanied an equity investment. Nations adopting such laws included several in Eastern Europe, plus China and Cuba.

Governance by host nations has been a dynamic process. By the 21st century the restrictiveness of the earlier laws had largely been replaced by laws encouraging foreign investment. Written incentives to invest have significantly replaced unwritten policy-based disincentives. Host nations often strongly promote foreign investment and offer diverse incentives to foreign investors. States or provinces within nations may also offer incentives, possibly diverging with federal policy.

These changes were both internally induced after financial crises when foreign national debts could not be paid, and externally induced to participate in regional pacts and the GATT/WTO. Later decades moved to marketization and privatization, rather than nationalization, with some notable exceptions in Latin America.

That said, few developing nations have a completely "open-door" approach to foreign investment. Many continue to restrict foreign investment. Indonesia, for example, has notably expanded its list of no foreign entry industries. In addition to legislation governing foreign investment, there may be constitutional provisions that affect investment. These may reserve areas for national ownership. For example, until recently the Mexican Constitution reserved basic oil and gas rights and production to the nation by vesting ownership in PEMEX, a state-owned monopoly. Mexico retains most subsurface land rights.

Other constitutions allocate regulation to or among specific government agencies. The Indian Constitution outlines government involvement in investment, including the ability to exclude private participation. Still other constitutions outline the form of economy the nation has adopted, often reserving in nonmarket economies the means of production and distribution to the state.

When China initially welcomed foreign investment with the adoption of a law on joint ventures in 1979, it first amended the Constitution of 1978 to sanction foreign investment. If a foreign investment law is inconsistent with the nation's constitution, but not questioned by the current government, problems may arise for the foreign investor with a later government not inclined to view the investment law liberally.

§ 1.4   Restrictions upon Entry

The United States is almost unique in not having a general foreign investment control commission. Except for national security and other limited circumstances (see Chapter 6), U.S. policy on foreign investment is wide open and welcoming. Most of the rest of the world is not so inclined. Canada, for example, scrutinizes mergers and acquisitions of existing Canadian firms in the "national interest." This control system continued to operate under NAFTA 1994 and remains under its USMCA 2020 successor. See Chapter 8.

At what point in the investment process government regulation or law takes effect presents another key distinction. Some nations make *entry* very difficult by mandatory review of proposed investments, requirements of joint ventures or exemptions gained only after long negotiation and concessions, restrictions on acquisitions, and numerous levels of permission from various ministries and agencies. Mexico, until the late 1980s, possessed in its legal structure an example of each such restriction.

By 1994 Mexico had removed many of these restrictions for U.S. and Canadian investors, changes negotiated to facilitate its participation in NAFTA. See Chapter 6. Comparable removals of investment restraints were subsequently granted EU and Japanese investors under their free trade agreements with Mexico.

Restrictions upon entry tend to assume one of two forms. Nations sometimes restrict the maximum foreign equity allowed. Additional rules may also limit foreign management or control to a minority interest. The enterprises resulting from these restrictions are commonly referred to as equity joint ventures.

Those few nonmarket economies that remain do not usually allow private ownership of the means of production and distribution and may not have corporation laws. Their manner of control over permitted foreign investment has typically been by contract. The foreign investor's rights are detailed in what is often referred to as a contractual joint venture. The foreign party receives a percentage of the profits and is granted certain management rights.

As nonmarket nations have converted to market economies, they have adopted corporation laws and shifted from the use of contractual to equity joint ventures. Many have also shifted from mandatory to voluntary joint ventures. In some cases, the shift has involved a change from contractual joint ventures directly to permitting wholly foreign owned corporate entities (WFOEs),

reasons to limit: Nat security, natural resources

without an intermediate stage of mandating equity joint ventures. China made this leap early on, allowing contractual and equity joint ventures as well as WFOEs. See Chapter 4.

§ 1.5   Foreign Ownership Limits

Although foreign investor ownership restrictions may assume a seemingly infinite number of alternatives, there are several forms that continue to appear in the laws of various nations.

Total Prohibition in Certain Sectors

Almost every nation, including the United States, prohibits foreign investment in certain sectors. Both developed and developing nations limit investment where national security is threatened. Aeronautics, high-tech, petroleum, and iron and steel industries also rank high among the key protected sectors, even in countries with generally open investment policies. Developing nations sometimes increase the scope of prohibited investment to a degree that may suggest the nation is really a nonmarket economy—it mandates state ownership of most of the means of production and distribution.

Foreign investment is most often prohibited in the exploitation of a nation's most important natural resources. Until recently, Mexico, for example, has long prohibited nearly all foreign investment in the petroleum industry. Canada's early foreign investment regulations discouraged foreign investment in railroads by limiting ownership of railroads receiving government aid to British subjects. Canada also restricted natural resources, limiting oil and gas leases, mining, and exploration assistance grants to Canadian companies or foreign companies with at least 50 percent Canadian ownership.

Outside of the North American hemisphere, similar restrictions on foreign investment have been imposed by many nations. For example, India reserved some industries to its public sector in its Industrial Policy Resolution of 1948. In the 1970s India took such a strong position about limiting foreign investment that it attempted to force foreign owned corporations in India to reduce ownership to less than 50 percent. IBM and Coca-Cola withdrew.

Additionally, some sectoral barriers through legislation and national monopolies remain impediments to "foreign" (meaning non-EU) investment in the European Union. Transportation, telecommunications, and utilities offer examples, but again intra-EU investors have much less trouble than non-EU investors within the region. See Chapter 5.

Only Domestic Private Investors

A second group of industries may be permitted to be private rather than national ownership, but the private owners must be host-nation nationals. These are industries where the nation believes that public ownership is not necessary, but the country prefers to reserve the areas for their own nationals. The reasons may be no greater than protectionism and the power of lobbying efforts of domestic industry, which does not wish to compete with foreign owned investment.

If the nation admits private ownership in a specific industry, it may have difficulty reserving that industry for its own nationals if it is a member of the GATT/WTO. The current trend under the concept of national treatment is to require that the host nation offer the same investment opportunities to foreigners that it offers to its own nationals. China is nominally moving in this direction. On the other hand, national treatment duties could conceivably cause nations to move these industries not to ownership by nationals or foreigners, but exclusively to state ownership.

Foreign Investment Allowed but. . .

Industries not included in the protected classes mentioned above may have foreign ownership participation. But foreign private ownership may be limited to joint ventures, and possibly only minority interests. In some joint venture laws, it appears at first that all areas are open to foreign investment because the law does not reserve any spheres of activity for the state or its nationals. This was true of the Cuban joint venture law of 1982, but it was clear that foreign investment was to be directed to restoring Cuba's tourist industry, which would help obtain foreign currency.

The Tanzanian law specifically prohibited foreign participation only in petroleum and minerals, but the Investment Promotion Centre could refuse investments in other areas, particularly if they were not joint ventures. The Namibian law referred only to "eligible investment", without defining what areas were open or closed to foreign investment. Notices regarding areas reserved for Namibians were issued broadly defining "services or the production of goods which can be provided or produced adequately by Namibians."

Outright bans on foreign investment appear less frequent than equity limitations, but such laws present the first question a foreigner looking to invest abroad must consider—is the industry in which I am interested open to me?

If the industry is one that is historically sensitive, such as natural resources and transportation, the answer may remain—no, it is not open to foreign investment. Where foreign investment is limited to minority participation in joint ventures, the country is not a very receptive location for foreign investment.

§ 1.6   Mandatory Joint Ventures

The equity percentages allowed to foreign investors have varied with the type of industry and the host nation's goal in applying the restriction. The reason for equity percentage limitations may be to allow the amount to depend on what the investment is perceived to offer the nation, such as needed technology, or an economic/social philosophy that foreign investment is inherently evil and to be prohibited. The former may be overcome by the foreign investor, the latter often may not. For years nonmarket economy nations adopted the latter view but moved to the former when it was apparent that their development levels had remained at best static.

When nations adopt mandatory joint venture rules, they often limit foreign ownership to a minority share, usually 49 percent. The reason is stated to be a preference to keep majority ownership and control in the hands of nationals. If the nation decides to allow majority control to be owned by foreign investors, it often takes the additional step and allows the investment to be *wholly* foreign owned.

If there is one certain characteristic of equity percentage limitations, it is that they are neither likely to remain static over time, nor likely to be enforced absolutely. The host nation may often waive restrictive equity limitations. Mexico, for example, waived its mandatory joint venture rule to facilitate an early computer plant investment in Guadalajara by IBM, subsequently sold to Lenovo of China. Several reasons for such waivers are commonly found in exception provisions in written investment laws, or in the unwritten "operational code" of the government.

Joint Venture Waivers

Waivers of mandatory joint venture rules and equity percentage limits have been characteristically granted for the following reasons:

Technology. Some companies with high technology, such as IBM, have been able to avoid joint venture mandates and retain total ownership. Contrastingly, IBM withdrew from India in the late 1970s when India demanded that IBM convert its wholly foreign parent owned investment in India to a joint venture. Minority shares would have been owned by the parent, with the majority owned by Indian nationals.

What form of technology will gain such a waiver is likely to vary from one nation to another. Where there is a transfer of technology law, it is likely to state several reasons allowing registration of a technology agreement. These reasons include technology that assists import substitution, the most up-to-date technology, high priority areas such as computers, technology intended to enhance job opportunities, and technology viewed as reasonable in cost.

Plant Location. The willingness to locate a production facility away from already saturated areas, such as the most populated cities, will increase chances of gaining a mandatory joint venture waiver. Some countries specify areas that the nation feels are already sufficiently industrialized, others specify areas they have designated for industrial development, or simply mention "less developed" areas.

Education. The willingness to establish training centers in the host nation, especially centers that will teach jobs to function with new technology, is a method of gaining a waiver.

Research and Development. A major criticism of many nations is that multinationals only export their technology while undertaking all the research to develop that technology in their home nation. Being willing to undertake some research and development in a host nation may gain a waiver of maximum equity participation requirements.

Balance Imports with Exports. Because of chronic shortages of hard currencies, many host nations grant waivers of investment restrictions where the investment will require little demand on the host nation's scarce hard currency reserves. Exporting part of the production to earn sufficient hard currency to pay for imports and cover profit and royalty payments may be decisive. The host nation's appreciation will increase as the export earnings continue to exceed the import demand. China initially placed great emphasis on exports; it was often the key to obtaining permission to establish a wholly owned foreign investment.

Sourcing Capital from Abroad. In addition to shortages of foreign currency, some nations have shortages of domestic currency to lend to companies. They often wish to reserve that lending capacity for locally owned business. Thus, commencing an investment with capital from outside the host nation is another possible key to gaining a mandatory joint venture waiver.

Reasons for Accepting Equity Restrictions

Foreign investors generally prefer to have total ownership of their foreign investments. Why would a foreign investor agree to limit participation to a minority interest?

An investment in place at the time of enactment of a government demand to either convert to a joint venture or withdraw from the nation may be less costly to continue as a joint venture with a minority position than to withdraw from the country. A local partner may be an asset if market penetration is difficult or political contacts are critical.

It is unlikely that the parent company will increase its investment or transfer the latest technology to the joint venture enterprise. The foreign entity will become quite unlike other wholly owned foreign investments. It may remain relatively static while other foreign wholly owned company investments receive needed additional capital and the latest technology.

If the host nation offers attractive investment incentives, accepting limitations on equity and management participation may be a fair trade, especially if the incentives are available immediately and the joint venture rules are likely to fade in time. If the market in the host nation has good long-term prospects, it may be appropriate to accept a joint venture and invest.

For example, in Mexico the willingness of Japanese investors to enter joint ventures with minority participation placed pressure on U.S. firms to accept the same limits on ownership, and even to offer better deals because of the growing Mexican desire to lessen reliance on U.S. investment. New investment was never as extensive as it would have been without restrictive Mexican, illustrated by the rapid increase in new foreign investment after such laws were repealed in the 1990s and Mexico entered both GATT/WTO and NAFTA 1994.

Retroactive Effect of Equity Limitations

To force foreign investment already in existence to convert to joint ventures may give rise to claims of expropriation. Consequently, countries usually applied the laws to new investment, but often added provisions that made it very difficult for current investment to continue without conversion. For example, the Mexican 1973 Investment Law was not retroactive on its face, but regulations denied permission to enter new lines of products or establish new locations without conversion to a joint venture.

India's Foreign Exchange Regulation Act of 1975 separately classified existing and new investment, granting the latter favorable treatment because it complied with joint venture mandates. The Indian government began to place pressure on all foreign investment to convert to joint ventures, leading to conflicts with many companies.

§ 1.7   Tech Investment Transfers

Many foreign direct investments include the transfer of technology to a subsidiary or joint venture. Such technology may be patented, copyrighted, a trade secret, or simply "knowhow". Legal protection for knowhow varies from country to country and is, at best, limited. Unlike patents, copyrights, and trademarks, you cannot by registration obtain exclusive legal rights to knowhow.

Knowledge, like the air we breathe, is a public good. Once released in the community, knowhow can be used by anyone and is almost impossible to retrieve. In the absence of exclusive legal rights, preserving the confidentiality of knowhow becomes an important business strategy. If everyone knows it, who will pay for it? If your competitors have access to the knowledge, your market position is at risk.

Typically, if only for tax reasons, there will be a separate transfer of technology agreement, often subject to regulatory review and approval either in conjunction with the investment or independently. It is not unknown for host developing nations, such as China, to require technology transfers. See Chapter 4.

The Indian government of the 1970s did not expressly state that the foreign parent would have to share the secret and very valuable Coke formula. The government did say that such sharing would be the natural consequence of the partnership sense of the mandatory joint venture. Coca-Cola would not disclose its formula, and withdrew from India, not to return until the 1990s, when India had relaxed its previously strict foreign investment rules.

In countries with extensive counterfeiting and intellectual property piracy, again China, foreign investors may not be willing to transfer frontier technology. The transfer of strategic technology may not be permitted by the home nation, as commonly happens in the United States under its export control regulations. See my *International Trade Beyond Trump* Concise Hornbook, Chapter 10.

From the licensee's standpoint, and the perspective of its government, there is the risk that the licensed technology may be old or obsolete, not "state of the art." Goods produced under old technology will be hard to export and convey a certain "second class" status. On the other hand, older more labor-intensive technologies may be sought in the early stages of development. Excessive royalties may threaten the economic viability of the investment and drain hard currencies from the country. The recipient typically is not in a sufficiently powerful position to bargain away restrictive features of standard international licenses.

For all these reasons, and more, developing countries frequently regulate patent and knowhow licensing agreements. See Chapter 9. Royalty levels may be limited, certain clauses prohibited (*e.g.*, export restraints, resale price maintenance, mandatory grant-backs to the licensor of improvements), and the desirability of the technology evaluated. Regulation of licensing is not limited to the developing world. The European Union extensively regulates patent, knowhow, and software licensing. See Chapter 5. In the United States, there is a less direct form of licensing regulation via antitrust law. See Chapter 6.

The home country investor also faces legal risks. The flow of royalty payments may be stopped, suspended, or reduced by currency exchange regulations. The taxation of the royalties, if not governed by double taxation treaties, may be confiscatory. The licensee may abscond with the technology or facilitate unauthorized distribution of "gray market" goods that eventually compete for sales in markets exclusively intended for the source company. In the end, patents expire and become part of the world domain.

Licensing is a kind of partnership. If it succeeds, the parent company's royalties (often based on sales volumes) will increase and a continuing partnership through succeeding generations of technology may evolve. If not, the dispute settlement provisions of the agreement may be called upon as either party withdraws from the partnership. Licensing of patents and knowhow often is combined with, indeed essential to, foreign investments. A foreign subsidiary or joint venture will need technical assistance and knowhow to commence operations. When this occurs, the licensing terms are usually a part of the basic joint venture or investment agreement.

Technology transfers may also be combined with a trade agreement, as where the parent company ships necessary supplies to the joint venture or subsidiary. Such supply agreements have sometimes been used to overcome royalty limitations through a form of "transfer pricing," the practice of marking up or down the price of goods to allocate revenues to preferred parties and jurisdictions (*e.g.*, tax havens).

The Trump administration focused on opposition to "forced technology transfers" associated with making foreign investments in China. The Biden administration has likewise complained of such practices. See Chapter 4.

§ 1.8   Performance Requirements, TRIMs

Trade-oriented foreign investment barriers that individual nations impose are described as "trade-related investment measures" or TRIMs, a title incorporated into the 1995 WTO package of agreements. Led by the United States, the developed nations have tried to limit foreign investor TRIMs through the General Agreement on Tariffs and Trade (GATT)/World Trade Organization (WTO) process.

Developing nations take a less negative view of TRIMs. They believe TRIMs provides a means of host nation control over various aspects of foreign multinational enterprise activity. Specifically, they believe that TRIMs serve as useful policy tools to promote government objectives in furthering economic development and ensuring balanced trade. Additionally, developing nations have quite vigorously defended the use of TRIMs as an aspect of national sovereignty, historically to maintain control over natural resources and more recently to preserve domestic culture.

TRIMs represents one of the very few areas of foreign investment law where a modicum of unity exists. Although many countries impose TRIMs, the developed and developing countries have different views regarding their economic effects. Developed nations argue that TRIMs cause investors to base their decisions on considerations other than market forces. The TRIMs Agreement embraces the core principle of national treatment, mandating that foreign-controlled enterprises receive no less favorable treatment from governments than their domestic counterparts.

It is less than clear exactly what form of practice the term TRIMs encompasses. The Uruguay Round of GATT, leading to the creation of the WTO, defined fourteen practices as TRIMs. United Nations and other commentators have broken these into four categories of host country law imposed on foreign investors: Local content requirements, trade-balancing rules, export requirements, and mandatory technology transfer/local R&D duties. The latter category was a central complaint of the Trump administration regarding China. See Chapter 4.

The term "performance requirements" generally refers to barriers that governments use to condition entry of foreign investors, often through a "permission to invest" regulatory commission. Trade-related investment practices that are deemed inconsistent with TRIMs are listed illustratively in an Annex. These include minimum domestic content rules (say 50% of the value of the foreign investor's products must be sourced locally), limitations on imports used in production, the linkage of allowable imports to export requirements (known as "trade balancing" requirements), export quotas or percentage of production requirements, employment and training duties, and restrictions on foreign exchange designed to limit imports.

Member states may "deviate temporarily" from national treatment principles, thus undermining the impact of TRIMs. There have been about a dozen TRIMs disputes, all centered on automobiles. For example, the United States and others have succeeded in challenging Indian and Indonesian local content and export requirements for autos through strictly intergovernmental WTO proceedings.

On balance, performance requirements, most notably local content rules, continue to be widely present around the globe, especially under pre-investment clearance controls. Sometimes these requirements are literally impossible to fulfill, such as Indonesia's mandate that all tablets and smartphones sold in that country contain at least 30% local components. Of course, such rules incentivize foreign investment to produce such components in Indonesia.

For more on TRIMs, see my *International Trade Beyond Trump* Concise Hornbook, Chapter 1. The text of TRIMs is reproduced in Section 1.16 below.

§ 1.9　Service Investments, GATS

In the United States, services account for over two-thirds of national GDP and provide jobs for nearly two-thirds of the work force. Services account for almost one-third of U.S. exports in sectors such as tourism, education, finance, construction, telecommunications, transport, and health. In contrast, most developing nations are minimal exporters of services, save by means of exporting their people, but migration was not included as a subject under the WTO General Agreement on Trade in Services (GATS). The GATS facilitates foreign investment abroad by selectively enabling the establishment of service-connected foreign branches, offices, and subsidiaries.

Market access for services is a major focus of the GATS. The GATS defines the supply of services broadly to include providing services across borders or inside member states with or without a commercial presence therein. The core GATS Article XVII commitment is to afford most-favored-nation treatment to service providers, subject to country-specific, preferential trade agreement or labor market integration agreement exemptions. One such exemption covers provision of audio-visual services in the EU.

In addition, each WTO member state made under GATS a specific schedule of commitments (concessions) on opening their markets in services' sectors negotiated using the WTO Services Sectoral Classification List. They further agreed under Article XVI to provide national treatment to their services' commitment schedule. Certain mutual recognition of education and training for service-sector licensing occurs. For example, to what degree may foreign banks or foreign economic consultants provide services, and are they entitled to national treatment? The answers to those questions will be found in the specific commitments of each GATS member.

National laws that restrict the number of firms in a market, that are dependent upon local "needs tests", or that mandate local incorporation are regulated by the GATS. Various "transparency" rules require disclosure of all relevant laws and regulations, and these must be administered reasonably, objectively, and impartially.

State monopolies or exclusive service providers may continue but must not abuse their positions. Detailed rules are created in annexes to the GATS on financial, telecommunications and air transport services. Under the Telecommunications Reference Paper (TRP), for example, the United States successfully argued that Telmex had abused its monopoly position in Mexico by charging discriminatory, non-cost-oriented connection fees for foreign calls.

Much to its consternation, the United States was found to have failed to exclude Internet gambling services under its GATS commitments' schedule. This caused Antigua-Barbuda to prevail in a dispute that alleged U.S. gambling laws discriminatorily prohibited its right to export such services (owned by U.S. foreign investors) to the U.S. market. The United States also lost the argument that its Internet gambling services' restraints were justifiable on public morals' grounds. This argument failed as discriminatory under the "chapeau" of the GATS Article XIV general exceptions.

The U.S. Congress approved and implemented the GATS agreement in December of 1994 under the Uruguay Round Agreements Act. Subsequently, early in 1995, the United States refused to extend most-favored-nation treatment to financial services. The European Union, Japan and other GATS nations then entered into an interim 2-year agreement which operated on MFN principles.

Financial services were revisited in 1996–97 with further negotiations aimed at bringing the United States into the fold. These negotiations bore fruit late in 1997 with 70 nations (including the United States) joining in an agreement that covers 95 percent of foreign trade and investment in banking, insurance, securities, and financial information. This agreement took effect March 1, 1999.

For more on GATS, see my *International Trade Beyond Trump* Concise Hornbook, Chapter 1. The text of GATS is reproduced in Section 1.17 below.

§ 1.10   U.N. and World Bank Rules

The principal multi-nation organization that has attempted to regulate multinationals is the United Nations. The United Nations

(UN) and its subsidiary organizations, however, have had little success in developing an effective, widely accepted regulatory scheme. This should not be surprising because the UN is a large organization with diverse cultural, economic, and political norms. The role of the United Nations, especially the Centre on Transnational Corporations, has become somewhat obscure as developing nations and nonmarket economies increasingly adopted less restrictive investment laws.

The aspirations of developing nations of the 1970s to achieve development through transfers (reparations for alleged abuses of colonialism, transfers of technology based on ideas being the patrimony of mankind rather than subject to private ownership, etc.), have been largely subordinated to a desire to achieve development through self-help and encouragement of foreign investment.

Part of the efforts of the developing nations in the 1970s involved the creation of international norms that would control multinationals, such as a UN initiated Code of Conduct. Not only did these efforts fail, the development of international law in general has been disappointing in its failure to establish legal norms for both multinationals and host nations. For example, the most contentious issue, compensation rights after expropriation, was before the International Court of Justice in the *Barcelona Traction* decision (1970 I.C.J. Rep. 3), but the I.C.J. focused on a narrow issue of ownership and did not address compensation.

The earlier focus on investment rules by the United Nations was renewed around the turn of the century, but this time as a joint effort with the International Chamber of Commerce (ICC) in Paris. Rather than the restrictive approach taken by the United Nations in the 1960s and 1970s, the UN-ICC effort sought to produce investment guidelines for the private sector, promoting that sector's involvement in the UN's decision-making processes, and its greater participation in the economic development of the poorest countries. This joint effort has also not been successful. The principal focus of the ICC regarding investment rules by the UN has involved the latter's attempts to control climate, and the former's concern that any such UN controls may harm investment.

The World Bank, home of the successful International Centre for the Settlement of Investment Disputes (ICSID, see Chapter 7), is another organization that has drafted guidelines on foreign investment. They are important to investors seeking World Bank investment assistance. World Bank lending and investment programs have been heavily influenced by U.S. perspectives since its inception post-WWII. As an alternative, China has created and funded the Asian Infrastructure Development Bank (AIDB). The

United States elected not to participate in AIDB, but the EU, Japan, Canada, and others do.

§ 1.11 OECD Multilateral Agreement

The OECD, an organization comprised of about 35 developed nations, also participated in developing rules governing foreign investment. It conducted extensive work on a proposed Multilateral Agreement on Investment (MAI). The United States urged that this Agreement liberalize foreign investment law, and address such issues as national treatment, standstill and roll-back rules, non-discriminatory most favored nation treatment, and transparency. The OECD considered such issues as free movement of executives, foreign investor rights to participate in privatization, state monopolies, intellectual property rights, portfolio investment, restrictions on investment in sensitive areas, relations with regional organizations, authority over investment by sub-federal government (i.e., states and provinces), protection of culture by limitations on investment, and dispute settlement.

Developing nations expressed concern that the MAI might be an attempt by the OECD to monopolize market share by industrialized nation corporations in the developing world. There were expectations that the MAI would be completed by 1998. But the United States would not agree to EU insistence that an exception be created so that it could deny investment benefits granted exclusively within the EU to non-EU investors

The United States further rejected "cultural exception" and "public order" clauses in the proposed MAI. The cultural exception would have allowed nations to limit investment when it had an adverse impact on the host nation's culture (promoted by France and Canada). The public order clause would permit withholding national treatment in industries considered essential to national security, law enforcement, and public order.

The United States tabled many exceptions to the applicability of the proposed Agreement's provisions and pushed hard for NAFTA-like foreign investor rights. In Europe, major concerns were raised by a NAFTA "investor-state" arbitration dispute (see *Ethyl v. Canada* in Chapter 8) that implied rather extraordinary rights of foreign investors to challenge national safety, health, and environmental regulations. France, decrying the proposed "hyper-rights" of foreign investors under the MAI, withdrew in frustration.

During the debate over the MAI, a Canadian study suggested that it would not have eliminated important foreign investment barriers. The report illustrated that when some barriers, such as mandatory joint ventures or local content requirements are removed, others arise. Some such barriers represent deeply rooted and long-established practices never intended as barriers, but which have come to function as such.

The year (1998) ended without completion of the Multilateral Agreement on Investment, and without any expectation that it would ever be concluded. The MAI has since remained dormant, though it remains as close to a Code of foreign investment law rules as has ever been attempted. Its failure returns the focus on foreign investment law to host nations, both developed and developing.

§ 1.12   Mergers and Acquisitions

A frequently used method to invest abroad is to merge or acquire a locally owned company in the host nation. Foreign acquisitions may provide an infusion of needed capital not available at home and bring new management ideas where old management has lacked creativity and been stagnant. Foreign acquisitions have many of the characteristics of an acquisition inside the United States but are regulated by the host state. Foreign M&A may generate the loss of an opportunity to increase the number of competitors in the business if the investing company were to commence a "greenfields investment" from scratch.

A common reason for regulating foreign M&A has been the replacement of a locally owned business by a foreign owned business. The host nation may be particularly concerned where the proposed acquisition is of a large domestic industry that is thought to *be* a domestic industry. For example, a proposed foreign acquisition of General Motors, an American icon would create far more objection than proposed foreign acquisitions of less iconic U.S. firms. That of course did not stop Fiat from acquiring control of Chrysler after the U.S. 2008 meltdown.

One Canadian report noted a range of foreign acquisition barriers:

1. Antitrust policies, such as merger controls, that prohibit takeovers for economic or social reasons.

2. Administrative procedures, such as using required takeover reviews to demand performance requirements.

3. Structuring corporations with voting schemes that permit effective control by a small group representing a small proportion of the shares but with ability to block a takeover.

4. Anti-takeover laws that restrict voting rights of individuals or groups, such as in some American states.

5. Restrictions on privatized government companies such as the U.K. and Italian use of "golden shares" to prevent changes of control.

6. Structures such as the Japanese keiretsu that essentially precludes a hostile takeover, or large bank holdings that block takeovers.

7. The limited role of stock markets with few listings, and high local concentrations of ownership that are hard to dislodge.

Even more sensitive may be proposed acquisitions of enterprises bearing the name of the nation, such as Mexicana Airlines or Canadian Pacific Railway. U.S. incorporated airlines, wishing to merge or have some close linkage with large foreign airlines, have often been rejected in their attempts.

Likewise, many nations will bar or closely examine the acquisition of "national champions". Japan, for example, took this approach regarding the purchase of Sharp Electronics and its valuable technology by Foxconn of Taiwan. European governments are also known to protect their national champions. The objection may be cultural and emotional as well as economic. See Chapter 5.

Restrictions on acquisitions are often based more on the feared *loss* of a domestic company, than the feared *addition* of a new foreign company. This means foreign investors and their lawyers have a different obstacle to overcome to obtain approval of an acquisition as opposed to a new investment. Examples include mergers and acquisitions laws in China (Chapter 4), Europe (Chapter 5) and North America (Chapter 6).

Pre-Merger Clearances

Pre-merger notification and review requirements have long been a feature of United States and European Union law. These requirements, combined with the "extraterritorial" jurisdiction of U.S. antitrust and EU business competition law to parties and activities located outside their territories, have created a broad transatlantic sweep for mergers regulation. They have also created some very real conflicting outcomes, the GE/Honeywell merger coming immediately to mind. See Chapter 5.

To smooth the waters, the U.S. and the EU inked in 1991 an Antitrust Cooperation Agreement that has reduced though not eliminated parallel merger review problems. Mergers of global MNE giants can attract scrutiny in dozens of jurisdictions. For example, the GE/Alstom of France merger required about 20 approvals.

China, Brazil, India, South Africa, Japan, Russia and some 100 other nations and regional entities now have pre-merger review systems. Regrettably, there is no international agreement on what approval standards to use, what fees to charge, and how far "extraterritorial" mergers' jurisdiction should reach. Conflicts abound. For example, Microsoft's acquisition of Nokia required clearance in 17 jurisdictions, all going rather smoothly until Chinese authorities demanded patent concessions, which they obtained. But South Korea (home to Samsung) sought still more IP concessions, so much so that a Nokia factory located there was removed from the acquisition to avoid pre-merger clearance in that country. Clearance of U.S. and Chinese multinational mergers and acquisitions became politicized in the context of the Trump tariff war. See Chapters 4 and 6.

Administrative merger review fees can be stunningly high. COMESA (a regional 19-nation African group), for example, has been known to charge $500,000 to process its pre-merger clearances, commenced in 2013. This roughly double the highest amount possible under U.S. DOJ and FTC procedures. COMESA, moreover, has some of the most minimal "extraterritorial" jurisdiction rules in the antitrust field. Ukraine, likewise, extends its mergers' review very widely beyond its borders. Mergers are intrinsically fragile agreements, and delays in obtaining numerous approvals can kill the deal. There does not appear to be any internationally recognized solution in sight.

§ 1.13 Securities Investments

The purchase of foreign stocks, bonds and similar investments has become widespread, indeed almost mandatory as pension and mutual funds, insurance companies, hedge funds and money managers seek globally balanced or specific foreign portfolios. The risks inherent in such indirect foreign investments vary with the nature of the stocks and bonds, and the exchanges upon which they are traded. For example, the vast liquidity and for the most part orderly running of the U.S. securities markets is commonly seen as a "safe haven", while the governmentally managed character of Chinese exchanges is perceived to be "risky".

As noted in Chapter 6, foreign businesses may make offerings on U.S. exchanges provided they adhere to U.S. securities law, notably its disclosure rules. Such offerings may reduce the perception that Chinese and other stocks and bonds of foreign origin are risky. For example, Alibaba, China's answer to Amazon, made an initial public offering on the New York Exchange that was the largest in history. Whether this will continue is uncertain ever since the Trump administration mandated compliance with U.S. accounting and auditing standards by U.S. listed Chinese companies. In addition, the U.S. now regulates selected foreign investments, particularly by Chinese firms linked to its military, some of which have been de-listed from the NYSE and NASDAQ.

Sovereign Debts and the IMF

Special problems arise when sovereign debt is purchased. Massive movements of stock and bond investments can de-stabilize developing/emerging nations and their markets. Chile and other countries have imposed transaction taxes to manage the flow of "hot money" from abroad. Whereas the securities of private and state-owned or controlled enterprises are normally governed by bankruptcy law, sovereign bonds are not. Sovereign state defaults on debt payments have occurred down through history, most recently by Argentina and Greece. Argentina remains in default on some of its un-renegotiated 2001 debt, bought up by speculators, who succeeded in obtaining a federal court order for payments due, and are now in pursuit of Argentinian assets around the world.

In recent years, with United States support, International Monetary Fund (IMF) loans have rescued sovereign debt issuers and owners, "conditioned" upon adoption of specific reforms by debtor states. This occurred widely in Asia and Latin America during the late 1900s and led to the perception that the IMF is the world's "sheriff", setting the terms for refinancing national debts and protecting the interests of creditors.

The IMF functioned as the first line of negotiation in an international "debt crisis," and commercial and national banks often conformed their loans to IMF conditions. These conditions had dramatic, negative political and social repercussions in debtor nations. From 2006 onwards, nations paid off their IMF debt in record numbers. Argentina did so with an assist from Venezuela. Brazil, Russia, Bolivia, Uruguay, Indonesia, The Philippines, and others joined in the flight from IMF loan conditions.

The IMF's loan portfolio stood at $100 billion in 2003. By 2008, that portfolio was approaching zero, and the IMF was running a budget deficit, cutting staff, and proposing sales of gold reserves. Many commentators wondered aloud what was the role of the IMF without loans?

The global financial and economic crisis that commenced late in 2008 muted this commentary. The IMF "pre-approved" unconditional, short-term loans to nations it deemed sound but facing liquidity problems, such as Mexico, Brazil, and South Korea. Conditional IMF loans were made to Iceland, Pakistan, Ukraine, and Hungary late in 2008, with others, notably Greece, Portugal, Ireland, and Ukraine following. Injections of new capital made it clear that the IMF was back in the loan and loan conditioning business.

For the first time, the IMF joined with the EU and the European Central Bank ("The Troika") to finance a 110 billion rescue of Greece with lots of conditions attached. Indeed, the EU seemed almost grateful that the IMF would enforce dramatic reductions in government spending and employment, improved accounting and anti-corruption measures, privatization, tax increases, monopoly break-ups and structural changes in the Greek economy. The IMF does this through constant monitoring and gradual, contingent release of bailout funds.

Despite large social and political protests, Greece was bailed out *three* times by the Troika under steadily more difficult conditions that make it extremely doubtful Greece will ever be able to pay off its debts without a "haircut" in the total amount due. See my *European Union Beyond BREXIT* Concise Hornbook, Chapter 4.

Sovereign Wealth Funds

The IMF has also drafted a Code of Best Practices for "Sovereign Wealth Funds" (SWFs). Such Funds are said to hold over $3 trillion and are expanding rapidly. Abu Dhabi, Saudi Arabia, Kuwait, Singapore, Russia, China, and Norway all have large SWFs, many of which played an important role in bailing out U.S. banks and securities firms with heavy sub-prime loan exposure. In recent years, developing nations (particularly their central banks) have bought over 50 percent of the net foreign purchases of U.S. government securities.

In a role reversal, the United States has become heavily dependent on SWF and developing world (especially Chinese) capital inflows to finance its large national debt and enormous international trade deficit. The primary concern is that SWFs and developing nations might use their power for political purposes. Their emergence further diminishes the need for IMF loans. The SWFs have not "conditioned" their lending or investment decisions.

§ 1.14   Franchising Investments

One of the easiest ways to invest abroad is franchising. Back in the home country the franchisor has created a "formula for success". Many rightly consider franchising to be a U.S. invention, but foreigners have also rapidly been developing international franchising systems. Exporting that formula, often with adaptations to local laws and culture, requires relatively little capital on either side of the transaction. "Start-up" payments by franchisees can provide a quick infusion of cash to the franchisor, but royalty payments over the life of a profitable franchise are the major goal.

Although patents, copyrights and trademarks may all be involved in international franchising, trademark licensing is at the core of most international franchise agreements. "Famous" trademarks are may be used deceptively, or directly copied, in developing nations. For example, Kentucky "Finger Lickin Good" Fried Chicken became Kenny's "Lip Smackin Good" Fried Chicken, using the same color scheme, in Kenya. Famous marks are granted special status under the 1883 Paris Convention for the Protection of Industrial Property, but the operational reality of such protections may be weak in the legal systems of developing nations.

Distribution (wedding gowns) and service (fast food) franchises may differ in purpose and content. In general, franchising is especially useful to facilitate market entry and brand awareness. For example, a principal joint venture investment in Cuba has been hotel franchises. Most franchisors have established standard contracts and business formulae that are utilized in their home markets and receive counsel on the myriad of laws relevant to their domestic business operations.

Approaches to developing, defining, and managing franchise relationships that have worked domestically may not work abroad. For example, agreements authorizing development of multiple locations within a given territory and sub-franchising by a *master franchisee* are often used overseas while infrequent in the United States.

International franchising confronts the attorney with the need to research and evaluate a broad range of foreign laws that may apply in any particular jurisdiction. Such laws tend to focus on placing equity and control in the hands of local individuals and on regulating the franchise agreement to benefit the franchisees.

The European Union, for example, has a regulation that details permissible, prohibited and "gray area" franchise agreement clauses. See Chapter 5. Many jurisdictions, including in the United States, mandate extensive disclosure by franchisors. See Chapter 6. Antitrust and tax law are important in international franchising. Double taxation treaties, for example, will affect the level of taxation of royalties. Antitrust law will temper purchasing requirements of the franchisor, lest unlawful "tying arrangements" be undertaken. Tying arrangements involve coercion of franchisees to take supplies from the franchisor or designated sources as part of the franchise.

In addition, counsel should be sensitive to the cultural impact of foreign franchising. For example, the appearance of a franchise trademark or symbol may conflict in a foreign setting with traditional architectural forms (such as in European cities) or nationalist feelings hostile to the appearance of foreign trademarks on franchised products (such as in India or Mexico). Cultural conflicts can diminish the value of international franchises. To anticipate and solve legal and cultural problems, foreign counsel is often chosen to assist in the task of franchising abroad.

Franchise Trademarks and Trade Secrets

Because franchising links trademarks with business attributes, there is a broad duty in the law for the franchisor to maintain quality controls over the franchisee, particularly in the business format franchise system. Any failure of the franchisor to maintain such quality controls could cause the trademark in question to be abandoned and lost to the franchisor. To maintain adequate quality controls, the franchisor must typically police the operations of the franchisee. Broadly speaking, the duty to maintain quality controls arises because a trademark is a source symbol. The public is entitled to rely upon that source symbol in making its purchasing decisions to obtain consistent product quality and attributes.

International franchisors operating at a distance from their franchisees must be especially concerned with quality controls. On the other hand, excessive control or the public appearance of such control may give rise to an agency relationship between the franchisor and the franchisee. Such a relationship could be used to establish franchisor liability for franchisee conduct, including international product and other tort liabilities. It may be possible to minimize these risks through disclaimer or indemnification clauses in the franchise agreement.

Franchise formulae often involve utilization of trade secrets and confidential information. This may range from recipes and cooking techniques to customer lists, pricing formulas, market data or bookkeeping procedures. It is extremely difficult to protect such secrets and information. The first problem arises from the concept of what is a trade secret. Abstract ideas or business practices which do not involve an element of novelty are not generally considered trade secrets. Some international clarity for defining trade secrets is provided in the WTO TRIPs agreement, and treaties like NAFTA (the first international agreement to include coverage of trade secrets). The European Union, on the other hand, is still struggling to harmonize trade secret law among its members.

When international franchise trade secrets are involved, maintaining such secrets can be difficult given the wide number of persons who may have access to the confidential information. Terminated employees and terminated franchisees are another fertile source of the loss of trade secrets and confidential information. Even though the franchisees may warrant to protect confidentiality, once released there may not be an effective way to recapture the secret or remedy the harm. This is particularly the case in the Internet age.

§ 1.15 Investment Incentives

The enactment of restrictive investment laws was most prominent in the 1970s. Two important events in the 1980s tended to stop the enactment of restrictive investment laws. The first was the debt crisis in the early 1980s, which caused nations to realize that restrictive investment laws did not contribute to economic growth and exports. The second was the dismantling of the USSR and the commencement of the transition of many nonmarket economies to market economies. Even nonmarket economies outside the Eastern Europe and USSR group were making such changes. Vietnam, for example, first adopted a foreign investment law in 1987, and has since amended it several times. Tanzania and Mongolia both enacted investment laws in 1990, neither of which has any reference to mandatory joint ventures.

The former USSR first adopted joint venture legislation in 1987, with modifications in 1988 and 1989, and a new law in 1990. The law was quite liberal, a direction taken by the nations that were formerly part of the USSR. Poland enacted a series of investment laws, each more liberal than the previous. The 1991 law eliminated the previously required approval process for many investments.

By the turn of the millennium nearly all developing and nonmarket economies had opened their economies to more foreign direct investment, even though their earlier announced reservations about extensive participation in the means of production and distribution by foreign enterprises remained in many existing written laws. There was a reluctance at first to repeal these laws, which were often popular with the citizens, media, and academics. The nations instead began to relax their enforcement of the restrictive laws.

While foreign nations, both developing and nonmarket, previously had brought many, and sometimes all, industries within the ambit of foreign equity limitations or prohibitions, these governments began to administer those laws with increasing flexibility. At times, the way the laws read and the way they were applied seemed quite opposite. Starting in the 1990s, the laws began to be modified to reflect the reality of practice, and to reflect obligations under bilateral and multilateral investment agreements (see Chapter 7).

In the last two decades, foreign investment has increasingly been recruited and offered incentives. This amounts to a vastly different picture of foreign investment than existed in earlier times when it was subject to discouraging restrictions in most developing nations, and even in a few developed nations, such as Canada.

The world of foreign investment has changed markedly. Many developing nations offer substantial benefits, such as property tax holidays, special exchange preferences, and labor incentives such as the absence of labor unions. Incentives vary country-by-country, and within a country over time. Tax rates are sometimes reduced for specified periods of time.

Incentives are now the norm, and not only in developing nations. States or provinces, and counties and cities, offer attractive incentives. BMW autos are being made in South Carolina, and Mercedes-Benz in Alabama, with notable government incentives. Foxconn of Taiwan, maker of many Apple products in China, obtained an incredibly generous incentive package from Wisconsin to commence electronics production in that state. Nevertheless, Foxconn retreated on its Wisconsin investment commitments.

Incentives are typically given for new greenfields investment, but usually not for acquiring a local company. Governments might offer incentives to buy a state-owned company, perhaps in the form of a more favorable price. If the foreign investor plans to export most of production, the likelihood of receiving incentives rises, especially from federal/central governments.

§ 1.16   Text of WTO TRIMs Agreement (1995)

Members,

Considering that Ministers agreed in the Punta del Este Declaration that "Following an examination of the operation of GATT Articles related to the trade-restrictive and distorting effects of investment measures, negotiations should elaborate, as appropriate, further provisions that may be necessary to avoid such adverse effects on trade";

Desiring to promote the expansion and progressive liberalisation of world trade and to facilitate investment across international frontiers so as to increase the economic growth of all trading partners, particularly developing country Members, while ensuring free competition;

Taking into account the particular trade, development and financial needs of developing country Members, particularly those of the least-developed country Members;

Recognizing that certain investment measures can cause trade-restrictive and distorting effects;

Hereby *agree* as follows:

Article 1
Coverage

This Agreement applies to investment measures related to trade in goods only (referred to in this Agreement as "TRIMs").

Article 2
National Treatment and Quantitative Restrictions

1.   Without prejudice to other rights and obligations under GATT 1994, no Member shall apply any TRIM that is inconsistent with the provisions of Article III or Article XI of GATT 1994.

2.   An illustrative list of TRIMs that are inconsistent with the obligation of national treatment provided for in paragraph 4 of Article III of GATT 1994 and the obligation of general elimination of quantitative restrictions provided for in paragraph 1 of Article XI of GATT 1994 is contained in the Annex to this Agreement.

Article 3
Exceptions

All exceptions under GATT 1994 shall apply, as appropriate, to the provisions of this Agreement.

Article 4
Developing Country Members

A developing country Member shall be free to deviate temporarily from the provisions of Article 2 to the extent and in such a manner as Article XVIII of GATT 1994, the Understanding on the Balance-of-Payments Provisions of GATT 1994, and the Declaration on Trade Measures Taken for Balance-of-Payments Purposes adopted on 28 November 1979 (BISD 26S/205-209) permit the Member to deviate from the provisions of Articles III and XI of GATT 1994.

Article 5
Notification and Transitional Arrangements

1.   Members, within 90 days of the date of entry into force of the WTO Agreement, shall notify the Council for Trade in Goods of all TRIMs they are applying that are not in conformity with the

provisions of this Agreement. Such TRIMs of general or specific application shall be notified, along with their principal features.[1]

2.   Each Member shall eliminate all TRIMs which are notified under paragraph 1 within two years of the date of entry into force of the WTO Agreement in the case of a developed country Member, within five years in the case of a developing country Member, and within seven years in the case of a least-developed country Member.

3.   On request, the Council for Trade in Goods may extend the transition period for the elimination of TRIMs notified under paragraph 1 for a developing country Member, including a least-developed country Member, which demonstrates particular difficulties in implementing the provisions of this Agreement. In considering such a request, the Council for Trade in Goods shall take into account the individual development, financial and trade needs of the Member in question.

4.   During the transition period, a Member shall not modify the terms of any TRIM which it notifies under paragraph 1 from those prevailing at the date of entry into force of the WTO Agreement so as to increase the degree of inconsistency with the provisions of Article 2. TRIMs introduced less than 180 days before the date of entry into force of the WTO Agreement shall not benefit from the transitional arrangements provided in paragraph 2.

5.   Notwithstanding the provisions of Article 2, a Member, in order not to disadvantage established enterprises which are subject to a TRIM notified under paragraph 1, may apply during the transition period the same TRIM to a new investment (i) where the products of such investment are like products to those of the established enterprises, and (ii) where necessary to avoid distorting the conditions of competition between the new investment and the established enterprises. Any TRIM so applied to a new investment shall be notified to the Council for Trade in Goods. The terms of such a TRIM shall be equivalent in their competitive effect to those applicable to the established enterprises, and it shall be terminated at the same time.

Article 6
Transparency

1.   Members reaffirm, with respect to TRIMs, their commitment to obligations on transparency and notification in Article X of GATT 1994, in the undertaking on "Notification" contained in the Understanding Regarding Notification, Consultation, Dispute

---

[1]   In the case of TRIMs applied under discretionary authority, each specific application shall be notified. Information that would prejudice the legitimate commercial interests of particular enterprises need not be disclosed.

Settlement and Surveillance adopted on 28 November 1979 and in the Ministerial Decision on Notification Procedures adopted on 15 April 1994.

2.   Each Member shall notify the Secretariat of the publications in which TRIMs may be found, including those applied by regional and local governments and authorities within their territories.

3.   Each Member shall accord sympathetic consideration to requests for information, and afford adequate opportunity for consultation, on any matter arising from this Agreement raised by another Member. In conformity with Article X of GATT 1994 no Member is required to disclose information the disclosure of which would impede law enforcement or otherwise be contrary to the public interest or would prejudice the legitimate commercial interests of particular enterprises, public or private.

Article 7
Committee on Trade-Related Investment Measures

1.   A Committee on Trade-Related Investment Measures (referred to in this Agreement as the "Committee") is hereby established and shall be open to all Members. The Committee shall elect its own Chairman and Vice-Chairman and shall meet not less than once a year and otherwise at the request of any Member.

2.   The Committee shall carry out responsibilities assigned to it by the Council for Trade in Goods and shall afford Members the opportunity to consult on any matters relating to the operation and implementation of this Agreement.

3.   The Committee shall monitor the operation and implementation of this Agreement and shall report thereon annually to the Council for Trade in Goods.

Article 8
Consultation and Dispute Settlement

The provisions of Articles XXII and XXIII of GATT 1994, as elaborated and applied by the Dispute Settlement Understanding, shall apply to consultations and the settlement of disputes under this Agreement.

Article 9
Review by the Council for Trade in Goods

Not later than five years after the date of entry into force of the WTO Agreement, the Council for Trade in Goods shall review the operation of this Agreement and, as appropriate, propose to the Ministerial Conference amendments to its text. In the course of this review, the Council for Trade in Goods shall consider whether the

Agreement should be complemented with provisions on investment policy and competition policy.

ANNEX

Illustrative List

1.   TRIMs that are inconsistent with the obligation of national treatment provided for in paragraph 4 of Article III of GATT 1994 include those which are mandatory or enforceable under domestic law or under administrative rulings, or compliance with which is necessary to obtain an advantage, and which require:

(a)   the purchase or use by an enterprise of products of domestic origin or from any domestic source, whether specified in terms of particular products, in terms of volume or value of products, or in terms of a proportion of volume or value of its local production; or

(b)   that an enterprise's purchases or use of imported products be limited to an amount related to the volume or value of local products that it exports.

2.   TRIMs that are inconsistent with the obligation of general elimination of quantitative restrictions provided for in paragraph 1 of Article XI of GATT 1994 include those which are mandatory or enforceable under domestic law or under administrative rulings, or compliance with which is necessary to obtain an advantage, and which restrict:

(a)   the importation by an enterprise of products used in or related to its local production, generally or to an amount related to the volume or value of local production that it exports;

(b)   the importation by an enterprise of products used in or related to its local production by restricting its access to foreign exchange to an amount related to the foreign exchange inflows attributable to the enterprise; or

(c)   the exportation or sale for export by an enterprise of products, whether specified in terms of particular products, in terms of volume or value of products, or in terms of a proportion of volume or value of its local production.

§ 1.17 Text of GATS Agreement (1995)

GENERAL AGREEMENT ON TRADE
IN SERVICES, PARTS I–IV
PART I
SCOPE AND DEFINITION

Article I
Scope and Definition

1.   This Agreement applies to measures by Members affecting trade in services.

2.   For the purposes of this Agreement, trade in services is defined as the supply of a service:

(a)   from the territory of one Member into the territory of any other Member;

(b)   in the territory of one Member to the service consumer of any other Member;

(c)   by a service supplier of one Member, through commercial presence in the territory of any other Member;

(d)   by a service supplier of one Member, through presence of natural persons of a Member in the territory of any other Member.

3.   For the purposes of this Agreement:

(a)   "measures by Members" means measures taken by:

(i)   central, regional or local governments and authorities; and

(ii)   non-governmental bodies in the exercise of powers delegated by central, regional or local governments or authorities;

In fulfilling its obligations and commitments under the Agreement, each Member shall take such reasonable measures as may be available to it to ensure their observance by regional and local governments and authorities and non-governmental bodies within its territory;

(b)   "services" includes any service in any sector except services supplied in the exercise of governmental authority;

(c)   "a service supplied in the exercise of governmental authority" means any service which is supplied neither on a commercial basis, nor in competition with one or more service suppliers.

PART II
GENERAL OBLIGATIONS AND DISCIPLINES

Article II
Most-Favoured-Nation Treatment

1. With respect to any measure covered by this Agreement, each Member shall accord immediately and unconditionally to services and service suppliers of any other Member treatment no less favourable than that it accords to like services and service suppliers of any other country.

2. A Member may maintain a measure inconsistent with paragraph 1 provided that such a measure is listed in, and meets the conditions of, the Annex on Article II Exemptions.

3. The provisions of this Agreement shall not be so construed as to prevent any Member from conferring or according advantages to adjacent countries in order to facilitate exchanges limited to contiguous frontier zones of services that are both locally produced and consumed.

Article III
Transparency

1. Each Member shall publish promptly and, except in emergency situations, at the latest by the time of their entry into force, all relevant measures of general application which pertain to or affect the operation of this Agreement. International agreements pertaining to or affecting trade in services to which a Member is a signatory shall also be published.

2. Where publication as referred to in paragraph 1 is not practicable, such information shall be made otherwise publicly available.

3. Each Member shall promptly and at least annually inform the Council for Trade in Services of the introduction of any new, or any changes to existing, laws, regulations or administrative guidelines which significantly affect trade in services covered by its specific commitments under this Agreement.

4. Each Member shall respond promptly to all requests by any other Member for specific information on any of its measures of general application or international agreements within the meaning of paragraph 1. Each Member shall also establish one or more enquiry points to provide specific information to other Members, upon request, on all such matters as well as those subject to the notification requirement in paragraph 3. Such enquiry points shall be established within two years from the date of entry into force of the Agreement Establishing the WTO (referred to in this Agreement

as the "WTO Agreement"). Appropriate flexibility with respect to the time-limit within which such enquiry points are to be established may be agreed upon for individual developing country Members. Enquiry points need not be depositories of laws and regulations.

5.   Any Member may notify to the Council for Trade in Services any measure, taken by any other Member, which it considers affects the operation of this Agreement.

Article III bis
Disclosure of Confidential Information

Nothing in this Agreement shall require any Member to provide confidential information, the disclosure of which would impede law enforcement, or otherwise be contrary to the public interest, or which would prejudice legitimate commercial interests of particular enterprises, public or private.

Article IV
Increasing Participation of Developing Countries

1.   The increasing participation of developing country Members in world trade shall be facilitated through negotiated specific commitments, by different Members pursuant to Parts III and IV of this Agreement, relating to:

(a)   the strengthening of their domestic services capacity and its efficiency and competitiveness, *inter alia* through access to technology on a commercial basis;

(b)   the improvement of their access to distribution channels and information networks; and

(c)   the liberalization of market access in sectors and modes of supply of export interest to them.

2.   Developed country Members, and to the extent possible other Members, shall establish contact points within two years from the date of entry into force of the WTO Agreement to facilitate the access of developing country Members' service suppliers to information, related to their respective markets, concerning:

(a)   commercial and technical aspects of the supply of services;

(b)   registration, recognition and obtaining of professional qualifications; and

(c)   the availability of services technology.

3.   Special priority shall be given to the least-developed country Members in the implementation of paragraphs 1 and 2. Particular account shall be taken of the serious difficulty of the least-developed countries in accepting negotiated specific commitments in view of

their special economic situation and their development, trade and financial needs.

Article V
Economic Integration

1.   This Agreement shall not prevent any of its Members from being a party to or entering into an agreement liberalizing trade in services between or among the parties to such an agreement, provided that such an agreement:

(a)   has substantial sectoral coverage[1], and

(b)   provides for the absence or elimination of substantially all discrimination, in the sense of Article XVII, between or among the parties, in the sectors covered under subparagraph (a), through:

(i)   elimination of existing discriminatory measures, and/ or

(ii)   prohibition of new or more discriminatory measures,

either at the entry into force of that agreement or on the basis of a reasonable time-frame, except for measures permitted under Articles XI, XII, XIV and XIV bis.

2.   In evaluating whether the conditions under paragraph 1(b) are met, consideration may be given to the relationship of the agreement to a wider process of economic integration or trade liberalization among the countries concerned.

3.   (a)   Where developing countries are parties to an agreement of the type referred to in paragraph 1, flexibility shall be provided for regarding the conditions set out in paragraph 1, particularly with reference to subparagraph (b) thereof, in accordance with the level of development of the countries concerned, both overall and in individual sectors and subsectors.

(b)   Notwithstanding paragraph 6, in the case of an agreement of the type referred to in paragraph 1 involving only developing countries, more favourable treatment may be granted to juridical persons owned or controlled by natural persons of the parties to such an agreement.

4.   Any agreement referred to in paragraph 1 shall be designed to facilitate trade between the parties to the agreement and shall not in respect of any Member outside the agreement raise the overall level of barriers to trade in services within the respective sectors or

---

[1]   This condition is understood in terms of number of sectors, volume of trade affected and modes of supply. In order to meet this condition, agreements should not provide for the *a priori* exclusion of any mode of supply.

subsectors compared to the level applicable prior to such an agreement.

5.   If, in the conclusion, enlargement or any significant modification of any agreement under paragraph 1, a Member intends to withdraw or modify a specific commitment inconsistently with the terms and conditions set out in its Schedule, it shall provide at least 90 days advance notice of such modification or withdrawal and the procedure set forth in paragraphs 2, 3 and 4 of Article XXI shall apply.

6.   A service supplier of any other Member that is a juridical person constituted under the laws of a party to an agreement referred to in paragraph 1 shall be entitled to treatment granted under such agreement, provided that it engages in substantive business operations in the territory of the parties to such agreement.

7.   (a)   Members which are parties to any agreement referred to in paragraph 1 shall promptly notify any such agreement and any enlargement or any significant modification of that agreement to the Council for Trade in Services. They shall also make available to the Council such relevant information as may be requested by it. The Council may establish a working party to examine such an agreement or enlargement or modification of that agreement and to report to the Council on its consistency with this Article.

(b)   Members which are parties to any agreement referred to in paragraph 1 which is implemented on the basis of a time-frame shall report periodically to the Council for Trade in Services on its implementation. The Council may establish a working party to examine such reports if it deems such a working party necessary.

(c)   Based on the reports of the working parties referred to in subparagraphs (a) and (b), the Council may make recommendations to the parties as it deems appropriate.

8.   A Member which is a party to any agreement referred to in paragraph 1 may not seek compensation for trade benefits that may accrue to any other Member from such agreement.

Article V bis
Labour Markets Integration Agreements

This Agreement shall not prevent any of its Members from being a party to an agreement establishing full integration[2] of the labour markets between or among the parties to such an agreement, provided that such an agreement:

---

[2]   Typically, such integration provides citizens of the parties concerned with a right of free entry to the employment markets of the parties and includes measures concerning conditions of pay, other conditions of employment and social benefits.

(a) exempts citizens of parties to the agreement from requirements concerning residency and work permits;

(b) is notified to the Council for Trade in Services.

Article VI
Domestic Regulation

1.   In sectors where specific commitments are undertaken, each Member shall ensure that all measures of general application affecting trade in services are administered in a reasonable, objective and impartial manner.

2.   (a) Each Member shall maintain or institute as soon as practicable judicial, arbitral or administrative tribunals or procedures which provide, at the request of an affected service supplier, for the prompt review of, and where justified, appropriate remedies for, administrative decisions affecting trade in services. Where such procedures are not independent of the agency entrusted with the administrative decision concerned, the Member shall ensure that the procedures in fact provide for an objective and impartial review.

(b) The provisions of subparagraph (a) shall not be construed to require a Member to institute such tribunals or procedures where this would be inconsistent with its constitutional structure or the nature of its legal system.

3.   Where authorization is required for the supply of a service on which a specific commitment has been made, the competent authorities of a Member shall, within a reasonable period of time after the submission of an application considered complete under domestic laws and regulations, inform the applicant of the decision concerning the application. At the request of the applicant, the competent authorities of the Member shall provide, without undue delay, information concerning the status of the application.

4.   With a view to ensuring that measures relating to qualification requirements and procedures, technical standards and licensing requirements do not constitute unnecessary barriers to trade in services, the Council for Trade in Services shall, through appropriate bodies it may establish, develop any necessary disciplines. Such disciplines shall aim to ensure that such requirements are, *inter alia*:

(a) based on objective and transparent criteria, such as competence and the ability to supply the service;

(b) not more burdensome than necessary to ensure the quality of the service;

(c) in the case of licensing procedures, not in themselves a restriction on the supply of the service.

5. (a) In sectors in which a Member has undertaken specific commitments, pending the entry into force of disciplines developed in these sectors pursuant to paragraph 4, the Member shall not apply licensing and qualification requirements and technical standards that nullify or impair such specific commitments in a manner which:

(i) does not comply with the criteria outlined in subparagraphs 4(a), (b) or (c); and

(ii) could not reasonably have been expected of that Member at the time the specific commitments in those sectors were made.

(b) In determining whether a Member is in conformity with the obligation under paragraph 5(a), account shall be taken of international standards of relevant international organizations[3] applied by that Member.

6. In sectors where specific commitments regarding professional services are undertaken, each Member shall provide for adequate procedures to verify the competence of professionals of any other Member.

Article VII
Recognition

1. For the purposes of the fulfilment, in whole or in part, of its standards or criteria for the authorization, licensing or certification of services suppliers, and subject to the requirements of paragraph 3, a Member may recognize the education or experience obtained, requirements met, or licenses or certifications granted in a particular country. Such recognition, which may be achieved through harmonization or otherwise, may be based upon an agreement or arrangement with the country concerned or may be accorded autonomously.

2. A Member that is a party to an agreement or arrangement of the type referred to in paragraph 1, whether existing or future, shall afford adequate opportunity for other interested Members to negotiate their accession to such an agreement or arrangement or to negotiate comparable ones with it. Where a Member accords recognition autonomously, it shall afford adequate opportunity for any other Member to demonstrate that education, experience,

---

[3] The term "relevant international organizations" refers to international bodies whose membership is open to the relevant bodies of at least all Members of the WTO.

licenses, or certifications obtained or requirements met in that other Member's territory should be recognized.

3.   A Member shall not accord recognition in a manner which would constitute a means of discrimination between countries in the application of its standards or criteria for the authorization, licensing or certification of services suppliers, or a disguised restriction on trade in services.

4.   Each Member shall:

(a)   within 12 months from the date on which the WTO Agreement takes effect for it, inform the Council for Trade in Services of its existing recognition measures and state whether such measures are based on agreements or arrangements of the type referred to in paragraph 1;

(b)   promptly inform the Council for Trade in Services as far in advance as possible of the opening of negotiations on an agreement or arrangement of the type referred to in paragraph 1 in order to provide adequate opportunity to any other Member to indicate their interest in participating in the negotiations before they enter a substantive phase;

(c)   promptly inform the Council for Trade in Services when it adopts new recognition measures or significantly modifies existing ones and state whether the measures are based on an agreement or arrangement of the type referred to in paragraph 1.

5.   Wherever appropriate, recognition should be based on multilaterally agreed criteria. In appropriate cases, Members shall work in cooperation with relevant intergovernmental and non-governmental organizations towards the establishment and adoption of common international standards and criteria for recognition and common international standards for the practice of relevant services trades and professions.

Article VIII
Monopolies and Exclusive Service Suppliers

1.   Each Member shall ensure that any monopoly supplier of a service in its territory does not, in the supply of the monopoly service in the relevant market, act in a manner inconsistent with that Member's obligations under Article II and specific commitments.

2.   Where a Member's monopoly supplier competes, either directly or through an affiliated company, in the supply of a service outside the scope of its monopoly rights and which is subject to that Member's specific commitments, the Member shall ensure that such a supplier does not abuse its monopoly position to act in its territory in a manner inconsistent with such commitments.

3.   The Council for Trade in Services may, at the request of a Member which has a reason to believe that a monopoly supplier of a service of any other Member is acting in a manner inconsistent with paragraph 1 or 2, request the Member establishing, maintaining or authorizing such supplier to provide specific information concerning the relevant operations.

4.   If, after the date of entry into force of the WTO Agreement, a Member grants monopoly rights regarding the supply of a service covered by its specific commitments, that Member shall notify the Council for Trade in Services no later than three months before the intended implementation of the grant of monopoly rights and the provisions of paragraphs 2, 3 and 4 of Article XXI shall apply.

5.   The provisions of this Article shall also apply to cases of exclusive service suppliers, where a Member, formally or in effect, (*a*) authorizes or establishes a small number of service suppliers and (*b*) substantially prevents competition among those suppliers in its territory.

Article IX
Business Practices

1.   Members recognize that certain business practices of service suppliers, other than those falling under Article VIII, may restrain competition and thereby restrict trade in services.

2.   Each Member shall, at the request of any other Member, enter into consultations with a view to eliminating practices referred to in paragraph 1. The Member addressed shall accord full and sympathetic consideration to such a request and shall cooperate through the supply of publicly available non-confidential information of relevance to the matter in question. The Member addressed shall also provide other information available to the requesting Member, subject to its domestic law and to the conclusion of satisfactory agreement concerning the safeguarding of its confidentiality by the requesting Member.

Article X
Emergency Safeguard Measures

1.   There shall be multilateral negotiations on the question of emergency safeguard measures based on the principle of non-discrimination. The results of such negotiations shall enter into effect on a date not later than three years from the date of entry into force of the WTO Agreement.

2.   In the period before the entry into effect of the results of the negotiations referred to in paragraph 1, any Member may, notwithstanding the provisions of paragraph 1 of Article XXI, notify

the Council on Trade in Services of its intention to modify or withdraw a specific commitment after a period of one year from the date on which the commitment enters into force; provided that the Member shows cause to the Council that the modification or withdrawal cannot await the lapse of the three-year period provided for in paragraph 1 of Article XXI.

3.   The provisions of paragraph 2 shall cease to apply three years after the date of entry into force of the WTO Agreement.

Article XI
Payments and Transfers

1.   Except under the circumstances envisaged in Article XII, a Member shall not apply restrictions on international transfers and payments for current transactions relating to its specific commitments.

2.   Nothing in this Agreement shall affect the rights and obligations of the members of the International Monetary Fund under the Articles of Agreement of the Fund, including the use of exchange actions which are in conformity with the Articles of Agreement, provided that a Member shall not impose restrictions on any capital transactions inconsistently with its specific commitments regarding such transactions, except under Article XII or at the request of the Fund.

Article XII
Restrictions to Safeguard the Balance of Payments

1.   In the event of serious balance-of-payments and external financial difficulties or threat thereof, a Member may adopt or maintain restrictions on trade in services on which it has undertaken specific commitments, including on payments or transfers for transactions related to such commitments. It is recognized that particular pressures on the balance of payments of a Member in the process of economic development or economic transition may necessitate the use of restrictions to ensure, *inter alia,* the maintenance of a level of financial reserves adequate for the implementation of its programme of economic development or economic transition.

2.   The restrictions referred to in paragraph 1:

(a)   shall not discriminate among Members;

(b)   shall be consistent with the Articles of Agreement of the International Monetary Fund;

(c)   shall avoid unnecessary damage to the commercial, economic and financial interests of any other Member;

(d)   shall not exceed those necessary to deal with the circumstances described in paragraph 1;

(e)   shall be temporary and be phased out progressively as the situation specified in paragraph 1 improves.

3.   In determining the incidence of such restrictions, Members may give priority to the supply of services which are more essential to their economic or development programmes. However, such restrictions shall not be adopted or maintained for the purpose of protecting a particular service sector.

4.   Any restrictions adopted or maintained under paragraph 1, or any changes therein, shall be promptly notified to the General Council.

5.   (a)   Members applying the provisions of this Article shall consult promptly with the Committee on Balance-of-Payments Restrictions on restrictions adopted under this Article.

(b)   The Ministerial Conference shall establish procedures[4] for periodic consultations with the objective of enabling such recommendations to be made to the Member concerned as it may deem appropriate.

(c)   Such consultations shall assess the balance-of-payment situation of the Member concerned and the restrictions adopted or maintained under this Article, taking into account, *inter alia,* such factors as:

(i)   the nature and extent of the balance-of-payments and the external financial difficulties;

(ii)   the external economic and trading environment of the consulting Member;

(iii) alternative corrective measures which may be available.

(d)   The consultations shall address the compliance of any restrictions with paragraph 2, in particular the progressive phaseout of restrictions in accordance with paragraph 2(e).

(e)   In such consultations, all findings of statistical and other facts presented by the International Monetary Fund relating to foreign exchange, monetary reserves and balance of payments, shall be accepted and conclusions shall be based on the assessment by the Fund of the balance-of-payments and the external financial situation of the consulting Member.

---

[4]   It is understood that the procedures under paragraph 5 shall be the same as the GATT 1994 procedures.

6.   If a Member which is not a member of the International Monetary Fund wishes to apply the provisions of this Article, the Ministerial Conference shall establish a review procedure and any other procedures necessary.

Article XIII
Government Procurement

1.   Articles II, XVI and XVII shall not apply to laws, regulations or requirements governing the procurement by governmental agencies of services purchased for governmental purposes and not with a view to commercial resale or with a view to use in the supply of services for commercial sale.

2.   There shall be multilateral negotiations on government procurement in services under this Agreement within two years from the date of entry into force of the WTO Agreement.

Article XIV
General Exceptions

Subject to the requirement that such measures are not applied in a manner which would constitute a means of arbitrary or unjustifiable discrimination between countries where like conditions prevail, or a disguised restriction on trade in services, nothing in this Agreement shall be construed to prevent the adoption or enforcement by any Member of measures:

(a)   necessary to protect public morals or to maintain public order;[5]

(b)   necessary to protect human, animal or plant life or health;

(c)   necessary to secure compliance with laws or regulations which are not inconsistent with the provisions of this Agreement including those relating to:

(i)   the prevention of deceptive and fraudulent practices or to deal with the effects of a default on services contracts;

(ii)   the protection of the privacy of individuals in relation to the processing and dissemination of personal data and the protection of confidentiality of individual records and accounts;

(iii)   safety;

---

[5]   The public order exception may be invoked only where a genuine and sufficiently serious threat is posed to one of the fundamental interests of society.

(d)   inconsistent with Article XVII, provided that the difference in treatment is aimed at ensuring the equitable or effective[6] imposition or collection of direct taxes in respect of services or service suppliers of other Members;

(e)   inconsistent with Article II, provided that the difference in treatment is the result of an agreement on the avoidance of double taxation or provisions on the avoidance of double taxation in any other international agreement or arrangement by which the Member is bound.

Article XIV bis
Security Exceptions

1.   Nothing in this Agreement shall be construed:

(a)   to require any Member to furnish any information, the disclosure of which it considers contrary to its essential security interests; or

(b)   to prevent any Member from taking any action which it considers necessary for the protection of its essential security interests:

(i)   relating to the supply of services as carried out directly or indirectly for the purpose of provisioning a military establishment;

(ii)   relating to fissionable and fusionable materials or the materials from which they are derived;

---

[6]   Measures that are aimed at ensuring the equitable or effective imposition or collection of direct taxes include measures taken by a Member under its taxation system which:

(i)   apply to non-resident service suppliers in recognition of the fact that the tax obligation of non-residents is determined with respect to taxable items sourced or located in the Member's territory; or

(ii)   apply to non-residents in order to ensure the imposition or collection of taxes in the Member's territory; or

(iii)   apply to non-residents or residents in order to prevent the avoidance or evasion of taxes, including compliance measures; or

(iv)   apply to consumers of services supplied in or from the territory of another Member in order to ensure the imposition or collection of taxes on such consumers derived from sources in the Member's territory; or

(v)   distinguish service suppliers subject to tax on worldwide taxable items from other service suppliers, in recognition of the difference in the nature of the tax base between them; or

(vi)   determine, allocate or apportion income, profit, gain, loss, deduction or credit of resident persons or branches, or between related persons or branches of the same person, in order to safeguard the Member's tax base.

Tax terms or concepts in paragraph (d) of Article XIV and in this footnote are determined according to tax definitions and concepts, or equivalent or similar definitions and concepts, under the domestic law of the Member taking the measure.

(iii) taken in time of war or other emergency in international relations; or

(c) to prevent any Member from taking any action in pursuance of its obligations under the United Nations Charter for the maintenance of international peace and security.

2.   The Council for Trade in Services shall be informed to the fullest extent possible of measures taken under paragraphs 1(b) and (c) and of their termination.

Article XV
Subsidies

1.   Members recognize that, in certain circumstances, subsidies may have distortive effects on trade in services. Members shall enter into negotiations with a view to developing the necessary multilateral disciplines to avoid such trade-distortive effects.[7] The negotiations shall also address the appropriateness of countervailing procedures. Such negotiations shall recognize the role of subsidies in relation to the development programmes of developing countries and take into account the needs of Members, particularly developing country Members, for flexibility in this area. For the purpose of such negotiations, Members shall exchange information concerning all subsidies related to trade in services that they provide to their domestic service suppliers.

2.   Any Member which considers that it is adversely affected by a subsidy of another Member may request consultations with that Member on such matters. Such requests shall be accorded sympathetic consideration.

PART III
SPECIFIC COMMITMENTS

Article XVI Market Access

1.   With respect to market access through the modes of supply identified in Article I, each Member shall accord services and service suppliers of any other Member treatment no less favourable than that provided for under the terms, limitations and conditions agreed and specified in its Schedule.[8]

---

[7]   A future work programme shall determine how, and in what time-frame, negotiations on such multilateral disciplines will be conducted.

[8]   If a Member undertakes a market-access commitment in relation to the supply of a service through the mode of supply referred to in subparagraph 2(a) of Article I and if the cross-border movement of capital is an essential part of the service itself, that Member is thereby committed to allow such movement of capital. If a Member undertakes a market-access commitment in relation to the supply of a service through the mode of supply referred to in subparagraph 2(c) of Article I, it is thereby committed to allow related transfers of capital into its territory.

2.   In sectors where market-access commitments are undertaken, the measures which a Member shall not maintain or adopt either on the basis of a regional subdivision or on the basis of its entire territory, unless otherwise specified in its Schedule, are defined as:

(a)   limitations on the number of service suppliers whether in the form of numerical quotas, monopolies, exclusive service suppliers or the requirements of an economic needs test;

(b)   limitations on the total value of service transactions or assets in the form of numerical quotas or the requirement of an economic needs test;

(c)   limitations on the total number of service operations or on the total quantity of service output expressed in terms of designated numerical units in the form of quotas or the requirement of an economic needs test;[9]

(d)   limitations on the total number of natural persons that may be employed in a particular service sector or that a service supplier may employ and who are necessary for, and directly related to, the supply of a specific service in the form of numerical quotas or the requirement of an economic needs test;

(e)   measures which restrict or require specific types of legal entity or joint venture through which a service supplier may supply a service; and

(f)   limitations on the participation of foreign capital in terms of maximum percentage limit on foreign shareholding or the total value of individual or aggregate foreign investment.

Article XVII
National Treatment

1.   In the sectors inscribed in its Schedule, and subject to any conditions and qualifications set out therein, each Member shall accord to services and service suppliers of any other Member, in respect of all measures affecting the supply of services, treatment no less favourable than that it accords to its own like services and service suppliers.[10]

2.   A Member may meet the requirement of paragraph 1 by according to services and service suppliers of any other Member,

---

[9]   Subparagraph 2(c) does not cover measures of a Member which limit inputs for the supply of services.

[10]   Specific commitments assumed under this Article shall not be construed to require any Member to compensate for any inherent competitive disadvantages which result from the foreign character of the relevant services or service suppliers.

either formally identical treatment or formally different treatment to that it accords to its own like services and service suppliers.

3.   Formally identical or formally different treatment shall be considered to be less favourable if it modifies the conditions of competition in favour of services or service suppliers of the Member compared to like services or service suppliers of any other Member.

Article XVIII
Additional Commitments

Members may negotiate commitments with respect to measures affecting trade in services not subject to scheduling under Articles XVI or XVII, including those regarding qualifications, standards or licensing matters. Such commitments shall be inscribed in a Member's Schedule.

PART IV
PROGRESSIVE LIBERALIZATION

Article XIX
Negotiation of Specific Commitments

1.   In pursuance of the objectives of this Agreement, Members shall enter into successive rounds of negotiations, beginning not later than five years from the date of entry into force of the WTO Agreement and periodically thereafter, with a view to achieving a progressively higher level of liberalization. Such negotiations shall be directed to the reduction or elimination of the adverse effects on trade in services of measures as a means of providing effective market access. This process shall take place with a view to promoting the interests of all participants on a mutually advantageous basis and to securing an overall balance of rights and obligations.

2.   The process of liberalization shall take place with due respect for national policy objectives and the level of development of individual Members, both overall and in individual sectors. There shall be appropriate flexibility for individual developing country Members for opening fewer sectors, liberalizing fewer types of transactions, progressively extending market access in line with their development situation and, when making access to their markets available to foreign service suppliers, attaching to such access conditions aimed at achieving the objectives referred to in Article IV.

3.   For each round, negotiating guidelines and procedures shall be established. For the purposes of establishing such guidelines, the Council for Trade in Services shall carry out an assessment of trade in services in overall terms and on a sectoral basis with reference to the objectives of this Agreement, including those set out in paragraph

1 of Article IV. Negotiating guidelines shall establish modalities for the treatment of liberalization undertaken autonomously by Members since previous negotiations, as well as for the special treatment for least-developed country Members under the provisions of paragraph 3 of Article IV.

4.   The process of progressive liberalization shall be advanced in each such round through bilateral, plurilateral or multilateral negotiations directed towards increasing the general level of specific commitments undertaken by Members under this Agreement.

Article XX
Schedules of Specific Commitments

1.   Each Member shall set out in a schedule the specific commitments it undertakes under Part III of this Agreement. With respect to sectors where such commitments are undertaken, each Schedule shall specify:

  (a)   terms, limitations and conditions on market access;

  (b)   conditions and qualifications on national treatment;

  (c)   undertakings relating to additional commitments;

  (d)   where appropriate the time-frame for implementation of such commitments; and

  (e)   the date of entry into force of such commitments.

2.   Measures inconsistent with both Articles XVI and XVII shall be inscribed in the column relating to Article XVI. In this case the inscription will be considered to provide a condition or qualification to Article XVII as well.

3.   Schedules of specific commitments shall be annexed to this Agreement and shall form an integral part thereof.

Article XXI
Modification of Schedules

1.   (a) A Member (referred to in this Article as the "modifying Member") may modify or withdraw any commitment in its Schedule, at any time after three years have elapsed from the date on which that commitment entered into force, in accordance with the provisions of this Article.

  (b) A modifying Member shall notify its intent to modify or withdraw a commitment pursuant to this Article to the Council for Trade in Services no later than three months before the intended date of implementation of the modification or withdrawal.

2.   (a) At the request of any Member the benefits of which under this Agreement may be affected (referred to in this Article as an

"affected Member") by a proposed modification or withdrawal notified under subparagraph 1(b), the modifying Member shall enter into negotiations with a view to reaching agreement on any necessary compensatory adjustment. In such negotiations and agreement, the Members concerned shall endeavour to maintain a general level of mutually advantageous commitments not less favourable to trade than that provided for in Schedules of specific commitments prior to such negotiations.

(b) Compensatory adjustments shall be made on a most-favoured-nation basis.

3. (a) If agreement is not reached between the modifying Member and any affected Member before the end of the period provided for negotiations, such affected Member may refer the matter to arbitration. Any affected Member that wishes to enforce a right that it may have to compensation must participate in the arbitration.

(b) If no affected Member has requested arbitration, the modifying Member shall be free to implement the proposed modification or withdrawal.

4. (a) The modifying Member may not modify or withdraw its commitment until it has made compensatory adjustments in conformity with the findings of the arbitration.

(b) If the modifying Member implements its proposed modification or withdrawal and does not comply with the findings of the arbitration, any affected Member that participated in the arbitration may modify or withdraw substantially equivalent benefits in conformity with those findings. Notwithstanding Article II, such a modification or withdrawal may be implemented solely with respect to the modifying Member.

5. The Council for Trade in Services shall establish procedures for rectification or modification of Schedules. Any Member which has modified or withdrawn scheduled commitments under this Article shall modify its Schedule according to such procedures.

Chapter 2

OPERATIONAL CONTROLS OVER FOREIGN INVESTMENT

Some nations allow entry with comparative ease. Once established, however, the *operation* of the enterprise may be subject to various restrictions that divert time and resources from the main purpose of the investment. Government oversight may be extensive, with frequent visits from different officials to the degree that it becomes more harassment than regulation. Another form of restriction on operations is performance requirements that mandate minimum local content, specify use of local labor, and require levels of technology used in production. The elimination of performance requirements has been a focus of multinational negotiations, especially in the WTO TRIMs Agreement (see Chapter 1) which targets diminished use of such restrictions.

Worldwide economic declines after 2008 brought more demands for corporate regulation, especially in the financial sector. Most of the discussion was focused on such financial issues as lending practices, hedges, and especially executive compensation that is not linked to performance. The European Union, for example, has legislated pay restraints for business executives, be they foreign or not.

Restrictions are often imposed on repatriating capital or sending profits or royalties abroad or receiving hard currency to pay for needed imports. Currency restrictions have long been associated with foreign investment in developing nations such as Brazil, less so with Mexico, and have been prominent in China.

§ 2.1   Currency Issues

Currencies of developing nations are frequently considered "soft" currencies, meaning their values tend to be less stable and less desired than market-driven floating "hard" currencies such as the U.S. and Canadian dollars, the Japanese Yen, the Euro and Swiss Franc. Even market-driven, floating currency issues complicate foreign investment by changing costs, revenues, and profits. They do not to halt it unless they become so extreme that they overwhelm principal investment objectives.

Few developing nations have the kind of controls formerly used in nonmarket economies, where entering persons were required to convert so much hard currency for the soft local currency, and where no currency could be taken out of the nation. Every transaction by foreigners had to be accounted for upon exiting the country, and what local currency had not been spent had to be left within the country, often used to purchase tourist items in a shop at the point of departure. Common as such practices were three to four decades ago, they were largely dismantled as part of the transitional process to market economies.

Soft currencies generate significant currency risks as do the super-soft currencies of nonmarket economies. But within the developing world there are soft currencies and there are softer currencies. One way to deal with the impact on costs, revenues and profits of currency risk is to hedge in the vast currency markets of the world. Another is to contract for and receive payments in hard currencies. A third is to engage in "transfer pricing", outlined below.

Currency controls in developing nations often amount to attempts to fix or manage the rate of exchange rather than allow it to freely float, or to link the currency to a hard currency. Hong Kong, for example, linked its dollar to the U.S. dollar for decades. Mexico for many years linked the Mexican peso to the dollar, and sometimes adjusted the peso daily, often with a slight daily slippage or decline in the peso against the dollar. Denmark and Bulgaria peg their currencies to the Euro.

When the local currency is formally linked to a hard currency, or a hard currency is adopted as the national currency (Ecuador and El Salvador have adopted the U.S. dollar), the local currency has two problems. First, the country's monetary policy effectively is transferred to the linked nation. For example, if the dollar falls against other hard currencies, such as the yen or Euro or Pound Sterling, the linked nation's currency also falls. Seeking to escape this problem, El Salvador in 2021 became the first country in the world to make Bitcoin a national currency.

Second, the linking may prove to be artificial and cause a parallel free market rate to arise. The parallel market may be allowed to exist, or be suppressed to the extent possible, and become a black-market currency. The country may use the parallel free market rate as a guide against which to devalue the fixed official rate.

Many developing nations compound currency problems with high inflation. A nation with high inflation cannot long keep its currency pegged to that of a low inflation developed nation. There must be periodic devaluations, or the developing nation currency will be highly overvalued. This will cause a parallel market at market rates to develop, will encourage nationals to move currency abroad, and may cause the economy to unofficially "dollarize." The latter occurs when there is little faith in the local currency and nationals begin to deal in a hard foreign currency. This is what Venezuela is currently experiencing.

Most transitional nations have attempted to stabilize their currencies. The transitional process has brought some "hardness" to these currencies. One intermediate measure for Eastern European nations in transition from nonmarket to market economies was to peg the domestic currency at a floating rate to a Western hard currency, initially the German Deutschmark, and subsequently the Euro. With later entry into the European Union, the Euro became in most instances the nation's official currency.

§ 2.2   Management and Tech Rules

A limitation on the permitted foreign equity may not mean an inability to control the investment. Host nation majority owners may elect foreign management. Some host nation laws, however, stipulate that the percentage of foreign management may be no greater than the permitted equity participation, a feature of the now repealed 1973 Mexican law. Even this limitation may be unimportant if the local board is dominated by host nation nationals who are all profit motivated entrepreneurs with goals far more aligned with the foreign affiliate than with local government officials who focus on pursuing national social goals.

With the arrival of the digital age, data, e-commerce, and privacy restraints have emerged in a manner that impacts foreign investment. "Data localization" (storage) rules have emerged in Europe and Asia particularly. China for example required Apple to shift iCloud accounts of Chinese customers to the servers of local Apple partners, presumably within reach of PRC authorities. See Chapter 4. India has restricted online sales of foreign retailers like Amazon and Wal-Mart through local companies, thus limiting competition in retail markets.

The European Union has adopted a stringent General Data Protection Regulation broadly requiring consumer consent and controlling data transfers across EU and international borders. See Chapter 5. The United States has pushed back against foreign tech restraints, notably in its revised NAFTA agreement, the USMCA of 2020. See Chapter 6. For overseas tech investors and their shareholders, these operational issues have come of age.

§ 2.3   Monetary Transfer Limits

One aspect of an import/export performance requirement is to alleviate trade imbalances, reflected in part by the flow of capital in or out of a country. Some countries have no systematic restrictions on movements of capital such as foreign exchange controls, limits on borrowing, transfer pricing, as well as repatriation of earnings. Ironically, restricting remittance of earnings does not always solve balance-of-payments problems. It may rather cause companies to maintain a static position with respect to their capital, and freeze the flow of currency, both inbound and outbound, to the host nation.

Repatriation of assets, profits, or royalties may have to be reviewed by a national bank. This is often the case even where the general policy is to allow relatively free transfer of currencies. Similar approval may be needed to pay for necessary imports. Some countries have been notorious for demanding that all receipts in foreign currencies be converted to the host nation (usually soft) currency. Any foreign currency thereafter needed to pay for imports or to remit home as profits must be approved. This restrictive policy often leads to double billing for exports, with part of the price going directly to the home nation. Such "transfer pricing" (see below) is as commonly practiced as it is commonly deemed unlawful.

Brazil and Argentina are examples of nations that have relied heavily on currency restrictions. The restrictions have been government responses to a frustrating inability to control inflation and indexation. Argentina even partly linked the Argentine currency with the U.S. dollar, which constituted a form of official dual currency in Argentina. Such currency linkages rarely last.

Brazil has relatively little in the way of pre-investment clearance procedures, but its Profits Remittance Law requires registration of foreign capital, reinvestment and regulates outgoing payments for dividends, royalties, and profits. This Law operates in tandem with Brazilian taxation. Brazil has reduced restrictions on capital and profit repatriations, but it has a history of currency restrictions and investors are always concerned that restrictions will be restored.

Mexico, contrastingly, imposed currency restrictions only during a brief four-month period in 1982. As a result of considerable inflation, capital flight from Mexico increased dramatically in the early 1980s. To conserve remaining hard currency, the government nationalized banks and imposed exchange controls in 1982. The elected but not yet inducted president terminated the controls a few months later. The banking industry was partially opened to foreign investment several years later. Mexico's 1994 entry into NAFTA a decade later accelerated Mexico's return to private ownership of and foreign participation in banking.

India seems to have stood somewhere between Mexico and Brazil. While repatriations were generally freely allowable, they were controlled by the Reserve Bank of India and subject to numerous restrictions. Yet the Indian practice was generally thought to be accommodating to foreign investment. If a repatriation or divestment was particularly large, the Indian government might stagger it over several years to cushion its impact on India's persistent foreign exchange difficulties.

China, as part of obtaining export oriented or technologically advanced status, encourages investors to reinvest profits in China rather than remitting them abroad. Such encouragement is generally present in most nations, both because it reduces demand on foreign currency reserves and adds to the industrial base of the nation. Reinvestment may be the only real choice for a foreign investment since idle funds may be taxed or diminished in value if there is indexation that does not apply to such funds.

§ 2.4   Investment Taxation

A major consideration of any company considering foreign investment is taxation. If a desirable location has exceptionally high corporate income and other taxes (social security, real property, etc.), that desirability may diminish to the point where the nation is rejected as a possible site. Many international business lawyers are uncomfortable with rendering tax advice and are likely to add the services of a tax specialist. That may include both a specialist on the taxation rules in the foreign nation, as well as a U.S. lawyer familiar with the U.S. tax rules covering such areas as the taxation of income of the foreign investment repatriated (or deemed repatriated) from abroad, income taxation of U.S. employees working abroad in the foreign investment, and the like. As in so many domestic instances, such as mergers, business reasons suggest certain actions, but tax rules often determine how each action may be carried out.

Many developed nations have concluded *tax treaties* with nations in which their multinationals invest, essentially to avoid double taxation. The U.S. has about 40 such "double tax treaties". Even though a nation may have a liberal foreign investment law, unless there is a reasonably clear expression of the form of taxation facing the investment, investors will be slow to enter. Some nations offer tax incentives to foreign investment, such as tax holidays that defer tax for a certain number of years, or rebates when profits are reinvested rather than repatriated. These tax benefits are often linked to investment in high priority areas, such as those that generate foreign exchange for the host country.

Tax benefits may extend beyond a tax on profits to taxation of royalties, taxes on imports and exports, sales and consumption taxes, and taxes on personal income of expatriates. One problem for foreign investors is the dynamics of taxation in foreign nations. Tax burdens change frequently, and incentives received one year may be far less valuable in another.

Tax units, whether nations, states, or provinces, are always concerned when reporting methods tend to diminish income expectations. Two issues relate to transfer pricing and the unitary tax. If a foreign company reduces its taxable income in a host nation by intracompany transfers at prices which do not reflect arms-length transactions, the host nation may respond with methods to restructure the transfers, and possibly impose sanctions.

Secondly, when the subsidiary reports an income that as a percentage of the world-wide corporate entity's income is considerably lower than the percent of assets, employees, and sales within the host nation, the host nation may adopt a unitary tax. Such a tax replaces a tax based on reported income by adjusting that income to parallel the percent of assets, employees, and sales in the jurisdiction.

§ 2.5   Transfer Pricing

"Transfer pricing" is a chronic tax issue associated with foreign investment. Parent companies adjust the price of goods, services, technology, or intellectual property rights charged to their foreign subsidiaries or joint ventures in a manner that is "tax efficient". Such adjustments primarily transfer profits as between affiliated business entities. In other words, they are not the product of arms-length negotiations. Transfer pricing can be used to avoid or minimize host nation business taxation, host nation limits on technology and IP royalties, and host nation currency controls. To some degree, transfer pricing issues may be resolved in "double taxation" treaties between developed nations when the flow of foreign investment is two-way.

Section 482 of the U.S. Internal Revenue Code authorizes the IRS to re-allocate gross income, deductions, credits, or allowances among entities owned or controlled directly or indirectly by the same interests to prevent evasion of taxes or to clearly reflect income. This is easier said than done, and the IRS almost always has numerous "transfer pricing" tax disputes in progress. For example, the IRS once served a $3.3 *billion* dollar tax liability notice on Coca-Cola for transfer pricing related to sales of its syrup.

Not surprisingly, transfer pricing has been widely used to avoid U.S. corporate taxation by transferring royalties and revenues to tax haven entities. California employs "unitary tax rules" to deal with transfer pricing. It taxes foreign subsidiaries, not on earnings, but on the average amount of the subsidiary's employees, assets, and sales in California. Minority shareholders who lose earnings because of transfer pricing may want to consider whether transfer pricing involves a breach of fiduciary duties by Boards of Directors.

Other jurisdictions have also followed the IRS re-allocation approach, but the complexity of the issues and accountings mandates a reasonably sophisticated tax service, not always found in the developing world. Developing nations are particularly interested in ensuring that local joint venture partners get their proper share of profits. India has sent transfer pricing tax notices to Microsoft, Shell, GE, and others alleging payment of low prices for shares in their respective Indian subsidiaries, a financing technique used by MNE.

The EU has challenged very favorable transfer price deals obtained from national tax authorities by Starbucks in the Netherlands, Fiat/Chrysler, Amazon, and McDonald's in Luxembourg, Apple in Ireland, and Anheuser-Busch InBev in Belgium. The EU Commission considers them unlawful state subsidization. Appeals by the companies and national governments involved before EU courts have resulted in reversals in some cases.

In Mexico, "maquiladoras" (assembly plants) were run by foreign investors for decades as break-even cost centers using transfer pricing techniques. This practice avoided relatively high rates of Mexican corporate taxation, and in the early years of maquiladoras, Mexican currency controls and royalty limits. Mexico eventually established "safe harbors" in their tax regulations indicating that minimum, low levels of maquiladora profits were unlikely to attract "arms-length" tax audits. Bingo! Maquiladoras suddenly showed profits slightly higher than needed to take advantage of the safe harbors.

§ 2.6   Withdrawal, Bankruptcy Shopping

The withdrawal of foreign investment may be subject to restrictions. These restrictions may affect the ability to repatriate capital, the liability of the foreign parent or other subsidiaries in the country for debts of the withdrawing entity, and the removal of physical assets from the country. Potential investors should evaluate the restrictiveness at each level in determining whether to invest.

Termination of an investment by bankruptcy may introduce the foreign investor to different theories of bankruptcy, including liability of the parent for debts of the foreign subsidiary. Chapter 11 of U.S. bankruptcy law provides a form of reorganizing a corporation. Few other nations have such proceedings. Where a corporation has assets in the United States but is principally a foreign corporation, Chapter 11 may be attractive.

For example, the Russian oil giant Yukos filed for Chapter 11 protection in Houston, where the company claimed it had assets and where its chief financial officer had a residence. The petition asked the U.S. court to stop an auction planned in Russia a few days later of a Yukos gas company. The Russian government scheduled the auction to collect on a tax claim that some officers of Yukos viewed as expropriation. An injunction was issued by a U.S. court prohibiting Gazprom, the huge Russian natural gas company, from participating in the auction.

The injunction was ignored in Russia and the auction was held as scheduled. However, Gazprom apparently was concerned that its gas exports could be threatened by legal actions in Europe. It did not bid. At the auction an unidentified buyer purchased the Yukos gas company in a six-minute auction. The buyer was believed to be a group of individuals who would quickly sell the company to another Russian oil giant with Kremlin approval. The secrecy of the proceeding illustrates the lack of transparency in Russia in insolvency proceedings, and the need for global bankruptcy rules.

Firms sometimes file for bankruptcy under laws more favorable to restructure the company, and this practice is increasing. For example, an auto parts maker in Germany (Schefenacker) was facing default on a bond debt and moved its headquarters to London. It filed for bankruptcy in the UK and restructured the company in a manner not permitted under German law. A small group of bondholders in Germany might have been able to force a liquidation in German courts but could not do so in London. Schefenacker already had a plant in the United Kingdom, thus providing a link with Britain.

That can be important because EU law limits the filing of insolvency petitions to the "center of a debtor's main interests." Sometimes bonds held in the country from which the company moves are converted into shares, reducing the vote of bondholders in that departed nation. Management is retained as before. In a case involving Parmalat of Italy the Bank of America was able to file to wind up the proceedings of a Parmalat Irish entity located in Dublin. Such global bankruptcy shopping has resulted in revisions to the laws in France, Germany, and Italy.

Protocols between governments sometimes can sort out bankruptcy across borders. In 1991–1992 the first significant protocol was used in the Maxwell communications empire insolvency. The protocol was between courts in the United States and the United Kingdom. The function of a protocol is to agree upon how the insolvency will proceed, and avoid the problems discussed above.

The Maxwell protocol is an exemplary case and other protocols have followed. Several have involved U.S.-Canadian cases. Some have used satellite television for hearings. Protocols increased after the International Bar Association adopted in 1995–96 its Cross-Border Insolvency Concordat. The Concordat is a set of principles intended to encourage and assist insolvency administration involving more than one country. Protocols have filled an important gap.

In 2000, Mexico was the first major nation to adopt the UNCITRAL Model Bankruptcy Law. Canada has also now adopted the essence of the UNCITRAL Model Law, as has the United States, thus making it effective throughout NAFTA/USMCA. Japan and South Africa have adopted legislation based on the Model Law. UNCITRAL has also developed a Legislative Guide on Insolvency as an assist to the many countries in the process of adapting their insolvency laws to the Model Law.

§ 2.7   Corruption

Bribery in some nations has reached epidemic proportions. Visit the Transparency International website, https://www.transparency. org, for their global maps graphically displaying a Corruption Index for the world's nations.

A UK organization, Control Risks, suggests three classes of corruption. First is the payment of bribes to officials and businesses for favorable treatment. Second is nepotism carried to a level of domination of business by clans and families. Third is the evolution of corruption into organized crime, with the participation of officials at the highest levels of government. This last class seems the case with Russia, creating a potentially serious risk of extortion and kidnaping to all persons transacting business in the country.

Disclosures of corruption in China frequently appear to involve government officials. For example, the Chinese People's Procuratorate reported in one year 34,070 cases of economic crimes (bribes, embezzlement, graft, etc.) involving more than 7,000 officials, including 3,017 managers of state-owned industries and 2,141 involved with banking and negotiable securities. The current, vigorous anti-corruption campaign of President Xi Jinping has netted an unprecedented number of high-ranking government and military officials.

The regulated nature of foreign investments and the large sums involved invite corruption, be it extortion by government officials or payments made to obtain, maintain, or influence business interests. Laws against bribery, starting prominently with the U.S. Foreign Corrupt Practices Act in 1977 (FCPA), have proliferated. Individual and corporate sanctions are severe and sanctioning under several legal regimes for the same practices is not infrequent.

§ 2.8   U.S. Foreign Corrupt Practices Act

Back in the 1970s, as a spin-off of Watergate, secret slush funds used by U.S. companies to pay foreign officials to advance business interests were revealed. There was an outcry by the press within the United States and abroad about the disclosed payments, especially by U.S. aircraft corporations to Japanese and Dutch officials. The response of Congress was the FCPA. There was almost no legislative response from other nations individually, and only a very modest response internationally.

The United States stood nearly alone for decades in responding to the general condemnation of payments to foreign officials by enacting the FCPA. Many U.S. businesses objected to the United States adopting a law prohibiting foreign payments. These businesses had to compete abroad for contracts with enterprises from nations that had no such laws, and which in some cases, even allowed foreign bribes to be considered tax deductible ordinary and necessary business expenses.

The current, twice-amended FCPA remains relatively concise. It establishes stringent accounting and disclosure standards supervised by the SEC. The FCPA prohibits payments to foreign officials or political parties directly, or "while knowing" by way of third persons or subsidiaries, when such payments are for influencing any act or decision of a foreign official. Such influence includes inducing the foreign official to act or refrain from acting in violation of the official's duty, inducing the foreign official to use influence with a foreign government *or an instrumentality* of that government (interpreted as including state-owned or state-controlled enterprises) to influence a government or instrumentality act or decision, or to secure "any improper advantage". For example, procurement contracts, tax benefits, customs preferences, and foreign investment privileges fall within its scope.

The Justice Department enforces the illegal payments prohibitions. Sanctions can include felony criminal penalties for willful violations, civil penalties, and jail terms, and even the threat of being denied contracting rights with the U.S. government. Any criminal fine imposed on a person under the FCPA may not be paid or indemnified by the company directly or indirectly. There is an important exception for routine government action ("grease payments"), further defined in a separate section.

The Act establishes as an affirmative defense, cases where the payment was lawful under the *written* laws of the foreign country (this defense has never successfully been invoked) or was a "reasonable and bona fide expenditure" for business purposes. Anyone dealing with the FCPA should read the Department of Justice and SEC Resource Guide to the U.S. Foreign Corrupt Practices Act (2020).

Other "sanctions" are less formal, but potentially no less severe. Reputational damage, procurement exclusion, shareholder lawsuits and higher capital costs may follow. FCPA settlements typically also impose ongoing compliance costs. For example, a small Florida company (IAP) paid over $7 million to settle criminal charges regarding procurement payments to Kuwaiti officials made via a consultant. In addition, IAP promised high-level commitment against corruption, a clear corporate policy against corruption and regular corruption risk reviews, assignment of compliance responsibilities to a senior executive reporting to independent monitoring bodies, extensive training, reporting and investigation systems, disciplinary procedures, and corruption due diligence in mergers and acquisitions.

When the FCPA was first enacted the U.S. government denied that U.S. businesses would suffer. But that view changed as other nations were urged but failed to adopt similar laws. One argument in favor of the law was that foreign officials would become aware that they should not talk about payments to U.S. businesspersons, since such payments were prohibited. But that presumed a more perfect world than existed. Some observers believe that payments by U.S. companies to foreign officials have continued but are made with much greater care and with less of a paper or electronic trail than before.

§ 2.9   Global FCPA Prosecutions

FCPA prosecutions have risen dramatically in the past 10 years. Most are settled under deferred or non-prosecution agreements. This explains the absence of FCPA case law and reinforces the wide discretion to the SEC and DOJ to interpret the Act as they see fit.

Here are a variety of FCPA settlement examples:

The FCPA can apply to extraterritorial activities of foreign as well as U.S. firms. For example, Petrobas of Brazil paid a record $1 billion in FCPA fines. Siemens AG paid bribes in numerous countries and an agreed to an FCPA fine of $800 million. German and 20 other anti-bribery law enforcement authorities also pursued Siemens, which is reported to have spent over $1 billion in legal and accounting fees. The Siemens cases involved the Oil-for-Food program, which resulted in four other settlements against Akzo Nobel of the Netherlands for $3 million in penalties, against Flowserve Corporation for $10.55 million, against AB Volvo for $12.6 million, and against Fiat for $17.8 million in civil and criminal penalties.

The French engineering giant, Alstom, pleaded guilty and agreed to pay $772 million in FCPA criminal fines. Alstom failed to disclose its misconduct or cooperate with U.S. authorities concerning its corrupt payments via consultants in Indonesia, Egypt, Saudi Arabia, and the Bahamas. The total fines amounted to over 2.5 times Alstom's profits from its corrupt activities. A high-ranking Alstom officer spent some 18 months in a U.S. prison pending this settlement. At the same time GE's acquisition of Alstom was delayed, raising concerns of linkage between the imprisonment and the FCPA investigation. Alstom also faced criminal charges before Britain's Serious Fraud Office.

Odebrecht/Braskem of Brazil paid $632 million in FCPA fines along with additional sums to Switzerland and Brazil in the "Car Wash" investigation focusing on Petrobras and corrupt practices throughout Latin America involving construction work order addenda. The Presidents of Brazil and Peru subsequently fell from office.

Significant settlements in the half-billion $ range were imposed Societé Génerale of France, Teva Pharmaceutical of Israel, and Telia of Sweden. Och-Ziff Capital of the USA was penalized over $400 million under the FCPA. KBR/Halliburton settled for $579 million,

BAE Systems of Britain, Total of France, and VimpelCom of Russia for about $400 million. Daimler settled with the SEC, agreeing to pay $185 million in FCPA fines ($96.3 million criminal and $91.4 million civil). Johnson & Johnson for $70 million. Avon voluntarily reported itself concerning illegal payments in China leading to a "moderate" FCPA settlement of $135 million along with the placement of an independent FCPA "monitor" inside the company.

Hitachi of Japan agreed to pay $19 million to settle FCPA charges concerning payments made to South Africa's ruling party regarding power station construction contracts. Payments by Lucent Technologies to Chinese officials resulted in penalties of $137 million. J. P. Morgan paid $264 million in fines under a FCPA settlement for hiring "Sons and Daughters" of influential Chinese officials to secure business. The firm even maintained spread sheets showing the costs and revenues of their program.

A New York Times article covered more than three full pages describing bribes allegedly made by Wal-Mart in Mexico. The payments led to a Department of Justice investigation, an expensive *global* in-house review of payments' practices by Wal-Mart (reportedly costing over a million dollars a day!), and a dramatic drop in the value of Wal-Mart stock. Wal-Mart eventually settled with the DOJ for about 283 million.

The list of corporate FCPA settlements goes on: Embraer, Novartis, Nordion, AB InBev, SciClone Pharmaceuticals, Bilfinger, Parker Drilling, Diebold, Pfizer, Eli Lilly, Alcoa, Total, Stryker, Hewlett-Packard, Philips, Weatherford, Ralph Lauren, and Brazil's Odebrecht ($3.5 billion).

Then, in 2020, *Airbus broke all bribery sanction records* by settling collectively under a deferred prosecution agreement with French, UK, and U.S. authorities for the monumental sum of $4 billion. Airbus allegedly paid middlemen and utilized tax haven shell companies to make payments (sometimes falsely invoiced as medical prescriptions, training funds or paintings) in China, South Korea, Russia, Japan, Colombia, Malaysia, and other countries to obtain sales. The payments were made through Airbus' Strategy and Marketing Organization staffed with 150 people. In its settlement, Airbus agreed to appoint an external compliance officer regarding defense-related sales and disclosures, and to conduct two mandatory audits over the following three years.

There has also been a significant rise in individual prosecutions of officers and managers, often following corporate settlements, assuming personal jurisdiction can be had. Individual prosecutions have for example, included some high-profile persons. Albert Stanley,

CEO of KBR, a subsidiary of Halliburton, agreed to serve seven years in prison and pay $10.8 million in restitution. In 2010, the FBI conducted its first FCPA sting operation ("Shot Show"), resulting in the arrest of 22 executives from military and law enforcement products companies. The government has also seized personal assets (pensions, cars, and homes) of violators as forfeited proceeds of bribery.

§ 2.10 FCPA Compliance Programs

The dramatic increase in FCPA proceedings during recent years, combined with minimal jurisdictional requirements and major reputational and corrective action costs (not to mention share price declines), have caused widespread adoption of company compliance policies and programs. Training of all employees, especially foreign employees, in contact with foreign officials has become routine. Such training is repeated regularly and recorded in personnel files.

A policy will not assure that illegal payments are not made in an investment context. Even if illegal payments are later found to have been made, a written policy, acknowledged by employees' signatures, will help to establish the company's good intentions, and should help in minimizing penalties. Morgan Stanley is thought to have avoided penalties completely when one of their Chinese employees "went rogue" despite major repeated training and compliance efforts.

Vendors, customs brokers, transport carriers, construction and other service providers of U.S. corporations engaged are being required to undergo FCPA training. Such third parties must also complete FCPA audits, and sign contract clauses and affidavits as to compliance and awareness of FCPA risks. Some firms decline absolutely to make any grease payments. Dealing with agents and consultants creates special problems. They should be asked for details about the existence of any relatives or business associates who are in the government.

The company should contact various persons in the U.S. government, Chambers of Commerce, local counsel, and the like to check on their reputation, and conduct a Google search. All this "due diligence" might help to later establish that the company did not act "while knowing" (the FCPA standard) that payments to third parties would end up going corruptly to officials. Finally, the agreement with the agent or consultant should contain a clause that none of the funds paid to the agent will be used in any manner which might violate the FCPA.

FCPA due diligence in connection with international mergers and acquisitions has become the norm. The resulting business assumes FCPA liabilities, though it may seek indemnification. Record keeping and internal control compliance programs are mandatory and critical to adhering to the strict FCPA accounting and disclosure rules, which require a bribe to be declared a bribe.

For more detailed coverage of the FCPA, see my *International Trade Beyond Trump* Concise Hornbook, Chapter 13.

§ 2.11 OECD and UN Bribery Conventions

The 1997 OECD Convention

There was an outcry in the 1970s by the press within the United States and abroad about the disclosed payments made by U.S. corporations. Except for Sweden, there was almost no legislative response from other nations. The United States thus stood nearly alone for two decades in responding to the general condemnation of payments to foreign officials by enacting the FCPA.

Pushed hard by the United States, the 35 industrial nations of the Organization for Economic Cooperation and Development (OECD) addressed corruption by adopting in 1997 the OECD Convention on Combatting Bribery of Foreign Officials in International Business Transactions, some 20 years after the FCPA. The OECD Convention obligates signatories and other subscribing countries to *criminalize* bribery of foreign "public officials" (including those to whom public functions are delegated), and sanction inaccurate accounts. It is a floor not a ceiling. The OECD also recommended prohibiting tax deductions for bribes, a recommendation that Canada, France and others have followed.

Enactment of anti-bribery laws in OECD countries followed slowly, indeed Britain's Bribery Act did not arrive until 2010 (see below). Enforcement of anti-bribery policies has been decidedly uneven within the OECD. Active enforcers include the United States, United Kingdom, Germany, Italy, Switzerland, Norway, and Israel. At the other end of the spectrum, China, Japan, South Korea, Singapore, India, Spain, Mexico, Russia, Belgium, Ireland, and Turkey have undertaken little or no anti-bribery enforcement.

One of the overlooked features of the OECD Convention is the agreement to provide Mutual Assistance to enable government enforcement. Such assistance has led, for example, to cooperative anti-corruption investigations, and to the extradition of individual violators. Also overlooked is the impact on the FCPA of U.S. implementation of the Convention via the International Anti-Bribery Act of 1998. For example, FCPA coverage of payments made to "any person" to secure "any improper advantage" derives directly from the OECD Convention. The Act further expands FCPA jurisdiction over unlawful acts by U.S. businesses and nationals that take place entirely outside the USA. In 2021, the OECD Convention was supplemented with additional recommendations.

Federal courts have ruled that the impact of U.S. implementation of the OECD Convention is pervasive, even as to provisions of the FCPA that were not specifically modified in 1998. For example, the Eleventh Circuit notably upheld a broad definition of "instrumentalit[ies]" of foreign countries as going beyond core public functions, citing the OECD Convention for authority *See United States v. Esquenazi*, 752 F.3d 912 (11th Cir. 2014).

The 2005 UN Convention

The United Nations finally came into the game in 2005, after years of inability to agree and failure to acknowledge that perhaps some governments were responsible for their officials' actions in receiving bribes from foreign entities. The UN Convention against Corruption went beyond the scope of the FCPA and OECD enactments to focus on making bribery and receipt of bribes illegal under national laws. It also notably included procedures for recouping bribes "hidden" abroad by the officials who received them. Some 170 nations have subscribed to the U.N. Convention, but many of the worst offending nations have acted to make it just so many words. Some $20 to $40 billion a year are reportedly lost by developing nations to corruption.

The UN and World Bank are collaborating on a Stolen Assets Recovery Initiative. They are joined by the U.S. Department of Justice's Kleptocracy Initiative. Recoveries of corruptly derived assets are few and far between, and in some countries, graft has become openly brazen. While the UN Convention against Corruption is welcome, the OECD appears to have largely preempted the field with respect to serious attention.

§ 2.12 British Bribery Act (2010)

The British Bribery Act of 2010 (BBA) may have been late in arriving but is now widely perceived to be one of the most rigorous. It extends not just to payments to foreign officials, but also to *private* parties. The Act applies to solicitation as well as *receipt of bribes* and appears to have no statute of limitations. Its coverage is broad in scope (for example, "grease payments" are not exempted) and its criminal and civil *liability is strict* with no need to prove corrupt intent.

Formal criminal charges were commenced for the first time by the Serious Fraud Office in 2013 against individuals associated with a bio-fuel investment fund, and the first criminal corporate conviction secured in 2016. It is also a crime under the BBA to fail to prevent bribery. Deferred prosecution agreements (DPA) with corporate offenders have been authorized and undertaken with cooperating parties since 2014. A record fine of nearly 500 Pounds Sterling was paid by Rolls Royce under a DPA in 2017. Rolls-Royce also paid FCPA and Brazilian corruption penalties.

The BBA extends to essentially all firms doing business in the UK. Hypothetically, therefore, the BBA reaches U.S. firms with U.K. stock listings or sales offices, and perhaps those processing illegal payments via British banks. The BBA governs the activities of such firms around the world, say bribes in India. It is tempered by a defense if "adequate procedures" to prevent offenses were in place. It can be argued that a serious, effective anti-bribery compliance system (see above) may constitute "adequate procedures".

In the Skansen Interiors prosecution of 2018, a jury found inadequate procedures in a corporate criminal prosecution because the self-reporting defendant did not have a specific policy against Bribery Act violations, nor a dedicated compliance officer, nor BBA training for staff, who were not asked to agree to comply with the Act.

In sum, neither the OECD or UN Convention, nor the British Bribery Act, is a clone of the FCPA, but the lonely U.S. position on foreign corrupt practices law now has allies.

§ 2.13   Tort Litigation Investor Risks

Foreign investors have always faced possible litigation in the host nation. Jurisdiction in the host nation, say for products liability, is rarely a problem because the company is clearly there and doing business. But a subsidiary in the host nation often has few assets. While they may be sufficient to satisfy judgments dealing with such common issues as a job-related injury to an employee, or a contract breach, they are insufficient when multiple plaintiff actions are brought for alleged large-scale injury such as environmental damage or labor abuses. In such actions the defendants typically include both the parent and the host nation subsidiary, leading to jurisdiction issues over the parent if the suit is brought in the host nation.

Such suits are also brought in the United States, often in state courts where juries are perceived as hostile to multinational corporations, such as South Texas or Mississippi. Initiated by attorneys with contingent fee contracts and who demand punitive damages, human rights abuses, environmental damages, and even cultural genocide have been the charges in an increasing number of suits against some of the largest corporations in the United States, including Del Monte, DuPont, Exxon Mobil Corp., Ford Motor Company, Texaco, Union Carbide, and United Technologies.

The principal basis for these suits has been alleged violations of international law and specifically of the Alien Tort Claims Act (ATCA) of 1789 (28 U.S.C.A. 1350). The Act gives U.S. courts jurisdiction over "any civil action by an alien for a tort only, committed in violation of the law of nations or a treaty of the United States."

Early U.S. Supreme Court ATCA Case Law

Much of the ACTA litigation has evolved since the *Filártiga v. Peña-Irala* decision (630 F.2d 876) by the Second Circuit Court of Appeals in 1980. *Filártiga* did not involve a corporate defendant. It was brought by a Paraguayan citizen, Filártiga, residing in the United States, against one Peña, another Paraguayan citizen in the United States on a tourist visa. Peña had been the Inspector General of the Police in Asunción, Paraguay, and allegedly tortured and killed the son of Filártiga.

The case was based principally on violations of the Alien Tort Claims Act, a 1789 enactment of Congress addressing quite different concerns, such as acts of piracy. It was rarely used until *Filártiga*. Its brevity and breadth provided the court a foundation to find Peña in violation. The court had little trouble in holding that death by torture constituted a violation of international law.

The Court indicated that private claims under federal common law should not be recognized for violations of international law norms with "less definite content and acceptance among civilized nations than the historical paradigms familiar when the ATCA was enacted." Nevertheless, when the court rendered its opinion in 1980 the floodgates opened for many suits that tried to enlarge upon the scope of violations of international law.

How expansive an interpretation should be given the ATCA's "violation of the law of nations" language is yet undetermined. Torture and extra-judicial killing are certainly such violations. So perhaps are hostage taking and aircraft sabotage and acts of terrorism. The cases have tested the ATCA's language in two ways. One is the scope of acts within a category that appear at first glance to constitute international law violations but may encompass uncertain violations, such as torture (*e.g.*, cutting off hands versus sleep deprivation) and human rights (extra-judicial killing of political dissidents versus "cultural genocide" relocating indigenous people to build a dam).

The second debate is whether to bring within violations of international law areas where there is uncertainty about whether acts violate treaties or customary international law. The most frequently litigated may be violations of environmental laws. While there are many domestic environmental laws, there is considerable debate as to whether there is any international environmental law, especially customary law. Several federal Circuit courts have rejected environmental ATCA claims.

Sosa v. Alvarez-Machain, a 2004 U.S. Supreme Court decision (542 U.S. 692), limited ATCA. *Sosa* involved an individual claiming that his abduction in Mexico by U.S. federal authorities constituted a violation of international law under the ATCA. The case brought the U.S. Supreme Court into the debate over the limits of the ATCA. The Court rejected the defendant's argument that the ATCA does not provide a cause of action but found that the abduction of Alvarez-Machain in Mexico and his transportation to the United States for trial did not violate the law of nations. The Court urged judicial caution in applying too broad an interpretation of the ATCA.

While these issues could be debated and litigated in cases against foreign officials subject to jurisdiction in U.S. courts the far deeper pockets are those of multinational corporations. It was inevitable that suits would be brought against corporate defendants. The first to establish corporate liability was *Doe v. Unocal*, 395 F.3d 932 (9th Cir. 2002), brought by Burmese nationals charging human rights violations by the defendant for complicity with the government in using forced labor in the construction of an oil pipeline. Subsequent Federal Circuit opinions stress the need to prove that corporations share the intent of government acts causing harm to ATCA plaintiffs.

U.S. Supreme Court ATCA Case Law

In 2012, the Supreme Court held that only natural persons could be liable under the federal Torture Victim Protection Act of 1992. The issue of corporate liability under the ATCA was raised but not decided by the U.S. Supreme Court in *Kiobel v. Royal Dutch Petroleum Co.*, 569 U.S. 108 (2013). This opinion involved human rights claims by Nigerian refugees against British and Dutch oil companies and their Nigerian subsidiaries for allegedly aiding and abetting human rights violations by the government in Nigeria.

Declining to rule on a Second Circuit decision that corporations are not subject to ATCA as a matter of customary international law, the Supreme Court instead ruled unanimously that the ATCA could not be used because there is a presumption against extraterritorial application of U.S. law. That presumption is not easily displaced, and the mere presence of a corporation in a foreign country is not a sufficient reason.

The Court held: "And even where the claims touch and concern the territory of the United States, they must do so with sufficient force to displace the presumption against extraterritorial application." While the decision was unanimous, four justices believed that corporations may be "today's pirates." The decision notably reduced ATCA litigation by foreign plaintiffs based on nothing more than a U.S. corporation's presence in a foreign nation.

The Supreme Court ruled in 2018 that foreign corporations are exempt from suit under ATCA. *See Jesner v. Arab Bank PLC*, 138 S.Ct. 1386 (2018). Jesner was an action brought by 6,000 plaintiffs against a Jordanian bank for injuries perpetrated by Hamas and other terrorists in Israel. In 2021, the Supreme Court rejected ACTA claims against major U.S. agribusinesses based on alleged child slave plantation labor in Africa. The Court found only general U.S. corporate decision-making that did not "touch and concern" the United States. *See Nestlé USA v. Doe*, 141 S.Ct. 1931 (2021).

Forum Non Conveniens

Motions for *forum non conveniens (fnc)* rulings are often presented by U.S. defendants as part of mass tort litigation strategy. If they are successful, the case is sometimes moved to a remote foreign forum where the case often dies. The death is because the U.S. attorneys no longer have visions of large punitive damage awards. Indeed, they may have little involvement as attorneys in the foreign forum.

For example, an airplane crash affirmative *fnc* ruling never went to trial in Scotland. The notorious Bhopal gas explosion *fnc* resulted in a settlement in India far less than what might have been a jury's award in the United States, and little of the settlement funds ever reached the injured plaintiffs. Moreover, *forum non conveniens* dismissals can be granted prior to consideration of personal and subject matter jurisdiction, convenient for the court and the litigants.

The law of *forum non conveniens* seems sufficiently elastic that it is hard to predict the outcome, and additionally hard to predict possible conditions that the court may impose upon the defendant in return for granting the *fnc* motion. The law is a product of equity and is somewhat amorphous. U.S. Courts have thus increasingly asked about the nature of the proceeding in the foreign forum, especially about the nature of the process. If there is a viable legal system that provides for the resolution of disputes of the form presented, the *forum non conveniens* motion may be granted.

One problem for defendants and their attorneys in obtaining a successful *forum non conveniens* ruling is that control over the case may be diminished or lost. If the case is actively pursued abroad, the attorneys likely will not be able to appear before the foreign court, and foreign counsel must be hired. The U.S. defendant will have to learn about the foreign law and legal system. Chevron's successful invocation of *fnc* in an environmental pollution dispute resulted in a multi-billion-dollar 2013 judgment against it in Ecuador.

A federal district court opinion found the Ecuadorean judge had been bribed and his opinion fraudulently "ghost-written" by plaintiffs' U.S. attorneys. Chevron successfully utilized arbitration proceedings to obtain an interim award ordering Ecuador not to seek enforcement of the judgment until a final decision was reached. But Chevron failed to persuade U.S. courts to enjoin enforcement globally in the absence of enforcement proceedings in the United States. Chevron spent a small fortune defending itself against collection of the Ecuadorean judgment around the world.

As *Chevron* suggests, the better choice for a mass tort defendant may be to keep the matter in the U.S. court, but to seek application of foreign law. Many such cases merit the application of foreign law, and when a court so rules, the difficulty of proving foreign law may be an impossible burden for the plaintiff.

In an analogous instance also suggesting "be careful what you wish for", a U.S. helicopter firm succeeded in obtaining a *forum non conveniens* dismissal against Chinese parties alleging damages from a helicopter crash inside China. This dismissal led to a default judgment of about $650,000 against the firm in Chinese court proceedings. The Chinese judgment was ultimately held enforceable in California under the Uniform Foreign Money Judgments Recognition Act.

For considerably more extensive coverage of international business litigation issues affecting foreign investment, see my *International Litigation and Arbitration 3d* Concise Hornbook.

§ 2.14 Text of the U.S. Foreign Corrupt Practices Act

(Selected Provisions)

Public Law 95–213, 91 Stat. 1494, Dec. 19, 1977 (amending The Securities Exchange Act of 1934, 15 U.S.C.A. §§ 78q(b), 78dd, 78ff(a) (1976)); as amended by Public Law 100–418, 102 Stat. 1107, Aug. 23, 1988; as amended by Public Law 105–366, Nov. 10, 1998 (International Anti-Bribery & Fair Competition Act)

15 U.S.C.A. § 78m(b)
Periodical and other reports

* * *

(2) Every issuer which has a class of securities registered pursuant to section 78*l* of this title and every issuer which is required to file reports pursuant to section 78*o*(d) of this title shall—

(A) make and keep books, records, and accounts, which, in reasonable detail, accurately and fairly reflect the transactions and dispositions of the assets of the issuer; and

(B) devise and maintain a system of internal accounting controls sufficient to provide reasonable assurances that—

(i) transactions are executed in accordance with management's general or specific authorization;

(ii) transactions are recorded as necessary (I) to permit preparation of financial statements in conformity with generally accepted accounting principles or any other criteria applicable to such statements, and (II) to maintain accountability for assets;

(iii) access to assets is permitted only in accordance with management's general or specific authorization; and

(iv) the recorded accountability for assets is compared with the existing assets at reasonable intervals and appropriate action is taken with respect to any differences.

* * *

15 U.S.C.A. § 78dd–1
Prohibited foreign trade practices by issuers

(a) **Prohibition.** It shall be unlawful for any issuer which has a class of securities registered pursuant to section 78*l* of this title or which is required to file reports under section 78*o*(d) of this title, or for any officer, director, employee, or agent of such issuer or any stockholder thereof acting on behalf of such issuer, to make use of the mails or any means or instrumentality of interstate commerce corruptly in furtherance of an offer, payment, promise to pay, or authorization of the payment of any money, or offer, gift, promise to give, or authorization of the giving of anything of value to—

(1) any foreign official for purposes of—

(A) (i) influencing any act or decision of such foreign official in his official capacity, (ii) inducing such foreign official to do or omit to do any act in violation of the lawful duty of such official, or (iii) securing any improper advantage; or

(B) inducing such foreign official to use his influence with a foreign government or instrumentality thereof to affect or influence any act or decision of such government or instrumentality,

in order to assist such issuer in obtaining or retaining business for or with, or directing business to, any person;

* * *

(3) any person, while knowing that all or a portion of such money or thing of value will be offered, given, or promised, directly or indirectly, to any foreign official, to any foreign political party or official thereof, or to any candidate for foreign political office, for purposes of—

(A) (i) influencing any act or decision of such foreign official, * * * in his or its official capacity, (ii) inducing such foreign official, * * * to do or omit to do any act in violation of the lawful duty of such foreign official, * * *, or (iii) securing any improper advantage; or

(B) inducing such foreign official * * * to use his or its influence with a foreign government or instrumentality thereof to affect or influence any act or decision of such government or instrumentality,

in order to assist such issuer in obtaining or retaining business for or with, or directing business to, any person.

(b) Exception for routine governmental action. Subsections (a) and (g) shall not apply to any facilitating or expediting payment to a foreign official, political party, or party official the purpose of which is to expedite or to secure the performance of a routine governmental action by a foreign official, political party, or party official.

(c) Affirmative defenses. It shall be an affirmative defense to actions under subsection (a) or (g) that—

(1) the payment, gift, offer, or promise of anything of value that was made, was lawful under the written laws and regulations of the foreign official's * * * country; or

(2) the payment, gift, offer, or promise of anything of value that was made, was a reasonable and bona fide expenditure, such as

travel and lodging expenses, incurred by or on behalf of a foreign official * * * and was directly related to—

(A) the promotion, demonstration, or explanation of products or services; or

(B) the execution or performance of a contract with a foreign government or agency thereof.

(d) Guidelines by the Attorney General. Not later than one year after August 23, 1988, the Attorney General, after consultation with the Commission, the Secretary of Commerce, the United States Trade Representative, the Secretary of State, and the Secretary of the Treasury, and after obtaining the views of all interested persons through public notice and comment procedures, shall determine to what extent compliance with this section would be enhanced and the business community would be assisted by further clarification of the preceding provisions of this section and may, based on such determination and to the extent necessary and appropriate, issue—

(1) guidelines describing specific types of conduct, associated with common types of export sales arrangements and business contracts, which for purposes of the Department of Justice's present enforcement policy, the Attorney General determines would be in conformance with the preceding provisions of this section; and

(2) general precautionary procedures which issuers may use on a voluntary basis to conform their conduct to the Department of Justice's present enforcement policy regarding the preceding provisions of this section.

* * *

(e) Opinions of the Attorney General. (1) The Attorney General, after consultation with appropriate departments and agencies of the United States and after obtaining the views of all interested persons through public notice and comment procedures, shall establish a procedure to provide responses to specific inquiries by issuers concerning conformance of their conduct with the Department of Justice's present enforcement policy regarding the preceding provisions of this section. * * *

(f) Definitions. For purposes of this section:

(1)(A) The term "foreign official" means any officer or employee of a foreign government or any department, agency, or instrumentality thereof, or of a public international organization, or any person acting in an official capacity for or on behalf of any such government or department, agency, or instrumentality, or for or on behalf of any such public international organization.

(B) For purposes of subparagraph (A), the term "public international organization" means—

(i) an organization that is designated by Executive Order pursuant to section 1 of the International Organizations Immunities Act (22 U.S.C.A. § 288); or

(ii) any other international organization that is designated by the President by Executive order for the purposes of this section, effective as of the date of publication of such order in the Federal Register.

(2)(A) A person's state of mind is "knowing" with respect to conduct, a circumstance, or a result if—

(i) such person is aware that such person is engaging in such conduct, that such circumstance exists, or that such result is substantially certain to occur; or

(ii) such person has a firm belief that such circumstance exists or that such result is substantially certain to occur.

(B) When knowledge of the existence of a particular circumstance is required for an offense, such knowledge is established if a person is aware of a high probability of the existence of such circumstance, unless the person actually believes that such circumstance does not exist.

(3)(A) The term "routine governmental action" means only an action which is ordinarily and commonly performed by a foreign official in—

(i) obtaining permits, licenses, or other official documents to qualify a person to do business in a foreign country;

(ii) processing governmental papers, such as visas and work orders;

(iii) providing police protection, mail pick-up and delivery, or scheduling inspections associated with contract performance or inspections related to transit of goods across country;

(iv) providing phone service, power and water supply, loading and unloading cargo, or protecting perishable products or commodities from deterioration; or

(v) actions of a similar nature.

(B) The term "routine governmental action" does not include any decision by a foreign official whether, or on what terms, to award new business to or to continue business with a particular party, or any action taken by a foreign official involved in the decision-making process to encourage a decision to award new business to or continue business with a particular party.

(g) Alternative Jurisdiction

(1) It shall also be unlawful for any issuer organized under the laws of the United States, or a State, territory, possession, or commonwealth of the United States or a political subdivision thereof and which has a class of securities registered pursuant to section 12 of this title or which is required to file reports under section 15(d) of this title, or for any United States person that is an officer, director, employee, or agent of such issuer or a stockholder thereof acting on behalf of such issuer, to corruptly do any act outside the United States in furtherance of an offer, payment, promise to pay, or authorization of the payment of any money, or offer, gift, promise to give, or authorization of the giving of anything of value to any of the persons or entities set forth in paragraphs (1), (2), and (3) of this subsection (a) of this section for the purposes set forth therein, irrespective of whether such issuer or such officer, director, employee, agent, or stockholder makes use of the mails or any means or instrumentality of interstate commerce in furtherance of such offer, gift, payment, promise, or authorization.

(2) As used in this subsection, the term "United States person" means a national of the United States (as defined in section 101 of the Immigration and Nationality Act (8 U.S.C.A. § 1101)) or any corporation, partnership, association, joint-stock company, business trust, unincorporated organization, or sole proprietorship organized under the laws of the United States or any State, territory, possession, or commonwealth of the United States, or any political subdivision thereof.

15 U.S.C.A. § 78dd–2
Prohibited foreign trade practices by domestic concerns

(a) **Prohibition.** It shall be unlawful for any domestic concern, other than an issuer which is subject to section 78dd–1 of this title. [At this point, the language for the most part follows that of section 77dd–1, except injunctive relief is specifically allowed. Domestic concerns include individuals who are citizens, nationals or residents of the United States, or essentially any form of business with a principal place of business in the United States, or organized in one of the United States, or a territory, possession or commonwealth of the United States.]

* * *

(g) Penalties

(1) (A) Any domestic concern that is not a natural person and that violates subsection (a) or (i) [alternative jurisdiction] of this section shall be fined not more than $2,000,000.

(B) Any domestic concern that is not a natural person and that violates subsection (a) or (i) of this section shall be subject to a civil penalty of not more than $10,000 imposed in an action brought by the Attorney General.

(2) (A) Any natural person that is an officer, director, employee, or agent of a domestic concern, or stockholder acting on behalf of such domestic concern, who willfully violates subsection (a) or (i) of this section shall be fined not more than $100,000 or imprisoned not more than 5 years, or both.

(B) Any natural person that is an officer, director, employee, or agent of a domestic concern, or stockholder acting on behalf of such domestic concern, who violates subsection (a) or (i) of this section shall be subject to a civil penalty of not more than $10,000 imposed in an action brought by the Attorney General.

(3) Whenever a fine is imposed under paragraph (2) upon any officer, director, employee, agent, or stockholder of a domestic concern, such fine may not be paid, directly or indirectly, by such domestic concern.

* * *

15 U.S.C.A. § 78dd–3
Prohibited foreign trade practices by persons other than issuers or domestic concerns

(a) **Prohibition.** It shall be unlawful for any person other than an issuer that is subject to section 30A of the Securities Exchange Act of 1934 or a domestic concern, (as defined in section 104 of this Act), or for any officer, director, employee, or agent of such person or any stockholder thereof acting on behalf of such person, while in the territory of the United States, corruptly to make use of the mails or any means or instrumentality of interstate commerce or to do any other act in furtherance of an offer, payment, promise to pay, or authorization of the payment of any money, or offer, gift, promise to give, or authorization of the giving of anything of value to—[At this point, the language follows that of active 78dd–1, except injunctive relief similar to that in section 78dd–2.]

* * *

(e) Penalties

(1)(A)   Any juridical person that violates subsection (a) of this section shall be fined not more than $2,000,000.

(B) Any juridical person that violates subsection (a) of this section shall be subject to a civil penalty of not more than $10,000 imposed in an action brought by the Attorney General.

(2)(A)   Any natural person who willfully violates subsection (a) of this section shall be fined not more than $100,000 or imprisoned not more than 5 years, or both.

(B) Any natural person who violates subsection (a) of this section shall be subject to a civil penalty of not more than $10,000 imposed in an action brought by the Attorney General.

(3) Whenever a fine is imposed under paragraph (2) upon any officer, director, employee, agent, or stockholder of a person, such fine may not be paid, directly or indirectly, by such person.

(f) Definitions. For purposes of this section:

(1) The term "person," when referring to an offender, means any natural person other than a. national of the United States (as defined in 8 U.S.C.A. § 1101) or any corporation, partnership, association, joint-stock company, business trust, unincorporated organization, or sole proprietorship organized under the law of a foreign nation or a political subdivision thereof.

* * *

15 U.S.C.A. § 78ff
Penalties

(a) Willful violations; false and misleading statements. Any person who willfully violates any provision of this chapter (other than section 78dd–1 of this title), or any rule or regulation thereunder the violation of which is made unlawful or the observance of which is required under the terms of this chapter, or any person who willfully and knowingly makes, or causes to be made, any statement in any application, report, or document required to be filed under this chapter or any rule or regulation thereunder or any undertaking contained in a registration statement as provided in subsection (d) of section 78o of this title, or by any self-regulatory organization in connection with an application for membership or participation therein or to become associated with a member thereof, which statement was false or misleading with respect to any material fact, shall upon conviction be fined not more than $1,000,000, or imprisoned not more than 10 years, or both, except that when such person is a person other than a natural person, a fine not exceeding

$2,500,000 may be imposed; but no person shall be subject to imprisonment under this section for the violation of any rule or regulation if he proves that he had no knowledge of such rule or regulation.

* * *

(c) Violations by issuers, officers, directors, stockholders, employees, or agents of issuers

(1) (A) Any issuer that violates subsection (a) or (g) of Section 30A of this title shall be fined not more than $2,000,000.

(B) Any issuer that violates subsection (a) or (g) of Section 30A of this title shall be subject to a civil penalty of not more than $10,000 imposed in an action brought by the Commission.

(2) (A) Any officer, director, employee, or agent of an issuer, or stockholder acting on behalf of such issuer, who willfully violates subsection (a) or (g) of Section 30A of this title shall be fined not more than $10,000, or imprisoned not more than 5 years, or both.

(B) Any officer, director, employee, or agent of an issuer, or stockholder action on behalf of such issuer, who violates subsection (a) or (g) of Section 30A of this title shall be subject to a civil penalty of not more than $10,000 imposed in an action brought by the Commission.

(3) Whenever a fine is imposed under paragraph (2) upon any officer, director, employee, agent or stockholder of an issuer, such fine may not be paid, directly or indirectly, by such issuer.

§ 2.15 Table of Contents of DOJ and SEC Resource Guide to the FCPA (2020)*

By the Criminal Division of the U.S. Department of Justice and the Enforcement Division of the U.S. Securities and Exchange Commission

A Resource Guide to the U.S. Foreign Corrupt Practices Act. Second Edition.

FOREWORD

We are pleased to announce the publication of the Second Edition of A Resource Guide to the U.S. Foreign Corrupt Practices Act. The Guide was originally published by the Department of Justice (DOJ) and the Securities and Exchange Commission (SEC) in November 2012 to provide companies, practitioners, and the public with detailed information about the statutory requirements of the

---

*   https://www.justice.gov/criminal-fraud/file/1292051/download.

Foreign Corrupt Practices Act (FCPA) while also providing insight into DOJ and SEC enforcement practices through hypotheticals, examples of enforcement actions and anonymized declinations, and summaries of applicable case law and DOJ opinion releases. Then and now, the Guide represents one of the most thorough compilations of information about any criminal statute and remains relevant to this day.

Although many aspects of the Guide continue to hold true today, the last eight years have also brought new cases, new law, and new policies. The Second Edition of the Guide reflects these updates, including new case law on the definition of the term "foreign official" under the FCPA, the jurisdictional reach of the FCPA, and the FCPA's foreign written laws affirmative defense. It addresses certain legal standards, including the mens rea requirement and statute of limitations for criminal violations of the accounting provisions. It reflects updated data, statistics, and case examples. And it summarizes new policies applicable to the FCPA that have been announced in the DOJ's and SEC's continuing efforts to provide increased transparency, including the DOJ's FCPA Corporate Enforcement Policy, Selection of Monitors in Criminal Division Matters, Coordination of Corporate Resolution Penalties (or Anti-Piling On Policy), and the Criminal Division's Evaluation of Corporate Compliance Programs.

Foreign bribery is a scourge that must be eradicated. It undermines the rule of law, empowers authoritarian rulers, distorts free and fair markets, disadvantages honest and ethical companies, and threatens national security and sustainable development. This updated Guide is meant not only to summarize the product of the dedicated and hardworking individuals who combat foreign bribery as part of their work for the U.S. government, but also to help companies, practitioners, and the public—many of whom find themselves on the front lines of this fight—prevent corruption in the first instance. We hope that the Guide will continue to be an invaluable resource in those efforts.

CONTENTS

Chapter 1: INTRODUCTION

The Costs of Corruption
Historical Background
National Landscape: Interagency Efforts
 Department of Justice
 Securities and Exchange Commission

§ 2.16   Text of OECD Convention on Combating Bribery of Foreign Public Officials in International Business Transactions (1997)

Article 1
The Offence of Bribery of Foreign Public Officials

1.   Each Party shall take such measures as may be necessary to establish that it is a criminal offence under its law for any person

intentionally to offer, promise or give any undue pecuniary or other advantage, whether directly or through intermediaries, to a foreign public official, for that official or for a third party, in order that the official act or refrain from acting in relation to the performance of official duties, in order to obtain or retain business or other improper advantage in the conduct of international business.

2.   Each Party shall take any measures necessary to establish that complicity in, including incitement, aiding and abetting, or authorisation of an act of bribery of a foreign public official shall be a criminal offence. Attempt and conspiracy to bribe a foreign public official shall be criminal offences to the same extent as attempt and conspiracy to bribe a public official of that Party.

3.   The offences set out in paragraphs 1 and 2 above are hereinafter referred to as "bribery of a foreign public official".

4.   For the purpose of this Convention:

    a)   "foreign public official" means any person holding a legislative, administrative or judicial office of a foreign country, whether appointed or elected; any person exercising a public function for a foreign country, including for a public agency or public enterprise; and any official or agent of a public international organisation;

    b)   "foreign country" includes all levels and subdivisions of government, from national to local;

    c)   "act or refrain from acting in relation to the performance of official duties" includes any use of the public official's position, whether or not within the official's authorised competence.

Article 2
Responsibility of Legal Persons

    Each Party shall take such measures as may be necessary, in accordance with its legal principles, to establish the liability of legal persons for the bribery of a foreign public official.

Article 3
Sanctions

1.   The bribery of a foreign public official shall be punishable by effective, proportionate and dissuasive criminal penalties. The range of penalties shall be comparable to that applicable to the bribery of the Party's own public officials and shall, in the case of natural persons, include deprivation of liberty sufficient to enable effective mutual legal assistance and extradition.

2.   In the event that, under the legal system of a Party, criminal responsibility is not applicable to legal persons, that Party shall

ensure that legal persons shall be subject to effective, proportionate and dissuasive non-criminal sanctions, including monetary sanctions, for bribery of foreign public officials.

3.   Each Party shall take such measures as may be necessary to provide that the bribe and the proceeds of the bribery of a foreign public official, or property the value of which corresponds to that of such proceeds, are subject to seizure and confiscation or that monetary sanctions of comparable effect are applicable.

4.   Each Party shall consider the imposition of additional civil or administrative sanctions upon a person subject to sanctions for the bribery of a foreign public official.

Article 4
Jurisdiction

1.   Each Party shall take such measures as may be necessary to establish its jurisdiction over the bribery of a foreign public official when the offence is committed in whole or in part in its territory.

2.   Each Party which has jurisdiction to prosecute its nationals for offences committed abroad shall take such measures as may be necessary to establish its jurisdiction to do so in respect of the bribery of a foreign public official, according to the same principles.

3.   When more than one Party has jurisdiction over an alleged offence described in this Convention, the Parties involved shall, at the request of one of them, consult with a view to determining the most appropriate jurisdiction for prosecution.

4.   Each Party shall review whether its current basis for jurisdiction is effective in the fight against the bribery of foreign public officials and, if it is not, shall take remedial steps.

Article 5
Enforcement

Investigation and prosecution of the bribery of a foreign public official shall be subject to the applicable rules and principles of each Party. They shall not be influenced by considerations of national economic interest, the potential effect upon relations with another State or the identity of the natural or legal persons involved.

Article 6
Statute of Limitations

Any statute of limitations applicable to the offence of bribery of a foreign public official shall allow an adequate period of time for the investigation and prosecution of this offence.

Article 7
Money Laundering

Each Party which has made bribery of its own public official a predicate offence for the purpose of the application of its money laundering legislation shall do so on the same terms for the bribery of a foreign public official, without regard to the place where the bribery occurred.

Article 8
Accounting

1.   In order to combat bribery of foreign public officials effectively, each Party shall take such measures as may be necessary, within the framework of its laws and regulations regarding the maintenance of books and records, financial statement disclosures, and accounting and auditing standards, to prohibit the establishment of off-the-books accounts, the making of off-the-books or inadequately identified transactions, the recording of non-existent expenditures, the entry of liabilities with incorrect identification of their object, as well as the use of false documents, by companies subject to those laws and regulations, for the purpose of bribing foreign public officials or of hiding such bribery.

2.   Each Party shall provide effective, proportionate and dissuasive civil, administrative or criminal penalties for such omissions and falsifications in respect of the books, records, accounts and financial statements of such companies.

Article 9
Mutual Legal Assistance

1.   Each Party shall, to the fullest extent possible under its laws and relevant treaties and arrangements, provide prompt and effective legal assistance to another Party for the purpose of criminal investigations and proceedings brought by a Party concerning offences within the scope of this Convention and for non-criminal proceedings within the scope of this Convention brought by a Party against a legal person. The requested Party shall inform the requesting Party, without delay, of any additional information or documents needed to support the request for assistance and, where requested, of the status and outcome of the request for assistance.

2.   Where a Party makes mutual legal assistance conditional upon the existence of dual criminality, dual criminality shall be deemed to exist if the offence for which the assistance is sought is within the scope of this Convention.

3.   A Party shall not decline to render mutual legal assistance for criminal matters within the scope of this Convention on the ground of bank secrecy.

Article 10
Extradition

1.   Bribery of a foreign public official shall be deemed to be included as an extraditable offence under the laws of the Parties and the extradition treaties between them.

2.   If a Party which makes extradition conditional on the existence of an extradition treaty receives a request for extradition from another Party with which it has no extradition treaty, it may consider this Convention to be the legal basis for extradition in respect of the offence of bribery of a foreign public official.

3.   Each Party shall take any measures necessary to assure either that it can extradite its nationals or that it can prosecute its nationals for the offence of bribery of a foreign public official. A Party which declines a request to extradite a person for bribery of a foreign public official solely on the ground that the person is its national shall submit the case to its competent authorities for the purpose of prosecution.

4.   Extradition for bribery of a foreign public official is subject to the conditions set out in the domestic law and applicable treaties and arrangements of each Party. Where a Party makes extradition conditional upon the existence of dual criminality, that condition shall be deemed to be fulfilled if the offence for which extradition is sought is within the scope of Article 1 of this Convention.

Article 11
Responsible Authorities

For the purposes of Article 4, paragraph 3, on consultation, Article 9, on mutual legal assistance and Article 10, on extradition, each Party shall notify to the Secretary-General of the OECD an authority or authorities responsible for making and receiving requests, which shall serve as channel of communication for these matters for that Party, without prejudice to other arrangements between Parties.

Article 12
Monitoring and Follow-up

The Parties shall co-operate in carrying out a programme of systematic follow-up to monitor and promote the full implementation of this Convention. Unless otherwise decided by consensus of the Parties, this shall be done in the framework of the OECD Working Group on Bribery in International Business Transactions and according to its terms of reference, or within the framework and terms of reference of any successor to its functions, and Parties shall bear the costs of the programme in accordance with the rules applicable to that body.

Article 13
Signature and Accession

1.   Until its entry into force, this Convention shall be open for signature by OECD Members and by Non-Members which have been invited to become full participants in its Working Group on Bribery in International Business Transactions.

2.   Subsequent to its entry into force, this Convention shall be open to accession by any non-signatory which is a member of the OECD or has become a full participant in the Working Group on Bribery in International Business Transactions or any successor to its functions. For each such non-signatory, the Convention shall enter into force on the sixtieth day following the date of deposit of its instrument of accession.

Article 14
Ratification and Depositary

1.   This Convention is subject to acceptance, approval or ratification by the Signatories, in accordance with their respective laws.

2.   Instruments of acceptance, approval, ratification or accession shall be deposited with the Secretary-General of the OECD, who shall serve as Depositary of this Convention.

Article 15
Entry into Force 1

1.   This Convention shall enter into force on the sixtieth day following the date upon which five of the ten countries which have the ten largest export shares set out in DAFFE/IME/BR(97)18/ FINAL (annexed), and which represent by themselves at least sixty per cent of the combined total exports of those ten countries, have deposited their instruments of acceptance, approval, or ratification. For each signatory depositing its instrument after such entry into force, the Convention shall enter into force on the sixtieth day after deposit of its instrument.

2.   If, after 31 December 1998, the Convention has not entered into force under paragraph 1 above, any signatory which has deposited its instrument of acceptance, approval or ratification may declare in writing to the Depositary its readiness to accept entry into force of this Convention under this paragraph 2. The Convention shall enter into force for such a signatory on the sixtieth day following the date upon which such declarations have been deposited by at least two

signatories. For each signatory depositing its declaration after such entry into force, the Convention shall enter into force on the sixtieth day following the date of deposit.

Article 16
Amendment

Any Party may propose the amendment of this Convention. A proposed amendment shall be submitted to the Depositary which shall communicate it to the other Parties at least sixty days before convening a meeting of the Parties to consider the proposed amendment. An amendment adopted by consensus of the Parties, or by such other means as the Parties may determine by consensus, shall enter into force sixty days after the deposit of an instrument of ratification, acceptance or approval by all of the Parties, or in such other circumstances as may be specified by the Parties at the time of adoption of the amendment.

Article 17
Withdrawal

A Party may withdraw from this Convention by submitting written notification to the Depositary. Such withdrawal shall be effective one year after the date of the receipt of the notification. After withdrawal, co-operation shall continue between the Parties and the Party which has withdrawn on all requests for assistance or extradition made before the effective date of withdrawal which remain pending.

Chapter 3

THE LAW OF AND INSURANCE AGAINST EXPROPRIATIONS

Absent any applicable investor-state treaty rules and remedies, for example arbitration proceedings like those found in BITs or NAFTA/USMCA (see Chapters 7 and 8), if a taking occurs, there are several issues that will face the expropriated foreign investor.

What law will apply: The law of the place of the taking, international law, or the law of the forum? Was the taking for a public purpose, or was it retaliatory or discriminatory? Was proper compensation forthcoming? Must remedies be exhausted in the taking nation? If the investor whose property has been taken attempts to sue the taking government in courts in the United States, or in third nations, what are the likely defenses?

Assuming international law applies or is to be considered, what is the content of that law? For example, the Mexican expropriation of foreign petroleum interests in 1938 commenced a dialogue between Mexico and the United States regarding applicable law. Mexico insisted that Mexican domestic law applied, which required compensation. The United States insisted that international law applied, which also required compensation. The United States argued that compensation had to be made in accordance with an alleged "prompt, adequate, and effective" international law standard. Mexico disagreed that such a standard existed under international law. A vigorous debate over what is the international law of expropriation continues.

Avoiding or insuring against the risk of expropriation may depend upon its form. Most attention focuses on direct expropriation, when part or all the investment is taken by decree of the host nation government. Indirect or "creeping" expropriations involve various governmental actions that may make continuation of the investment impossible. These actions can include excessively high tax rates, forced joint ventures, extensive government control, mandatory use of domestic inputs, and mandatory export levels.

The risk of expropriation cannot be fully avoided, and insurance should be considered, especially that provided either by the U.S. Development Finance Corporation (DFC), established in 2018 under the BUILD Act and replacing the Overseas Private Investment Corporation (OPIC), or the World Bank's Multilateral Investment Guarantee Agency (MIGA), discussed below. The BUILD Act stands for Better Utilization of Investments Leading to Development Act of 2018 enacted as part of the FAA Reauthorization Act of 2018 Sections 1401 et seq.

Taking measures to avoid the risk of expropriation cannot assure a foreign investor that expropriation will not occur. Many of the expropriations of the last century resulted from revolutions (USSR, Cuba, Mexico, Nicaragua) or very significant alterations in the government through elections (Chile), or in post-independence nationalism (Indonesia). More recently, expropriations have tended to be ideologically driven, *e.g.*, in Venezuela, Bolivia and Ecuador. Venezuelan expropriations have hit virtually every major oil company, Cargill, Cemex, Banco Santander and many others.

§ 3.1   Law of the Taking Nation

While there does seem to be agreement that international law is applicable to takings of foreign property, this principle has been challenged in two ways. First, the U.N. Charter of Economic Rights and Duties of States affirms the right of nations to expropriate property, and states that compensation issues are to be settled by "domestic law of the nationalization State", unless otherwise agreed.

This Charter, which does not constitute international law, was passed over the objection to this provision by 16 nations, mostly the largest industrialized nations, including the United States. The Charter illustrates the diversity of opinion regarding expropriation arising with the achievement of independence by many former colonies of the industrialized nations.

Second, when a nation expropriates foreign property, it tends to find greater comfort in arguing the applicability of its own law, which invariably is less demanding in requiring compensation than whatever standard the international community has approved.

§ 3.2   International Law

Even if the parties agree that international law is applicable, it may be difficult to determine what international law requires. It may be "prompt, adequate and effective" compensation, as the United States argues, or "just" compensation, as the Restatement of Foreign Relations suggests, or "appropriate" compensation, as U.N. Resolution 1803 proposed in 1962, and which seems to have been adopted by tribunals and courts more than any other standard.

A sovereign nation has full and permanent sovereignty over its natural resources and economic activities. That principle is clearly stated in the U.N. Resolution on Permanent Sovereignty over Natural Resources (1962). Sovereignty gives the nation the right to take privately-owned property, whether that property is owned by the country's nationals or foreigners.

These are long held concepts that exist on both an international and domestic level. Most national (and state or provincial) constitutions express this right. But the theory of taking does not allow the taking for any reason or upon any whim of the prevailing government. There must be a public purpose. There are two problems with the public purpose, however. First is its definition, and second is determining who is to measure public purpose in an international expropriation.

§ 3.3   Public Purpose

There has never been a very clear definition of public purpose. It is often expressed in such broad words as "improvement of the social welfare or economic betterment of the nation." Does this mean such specific goals as improved infrastructure, better medical care, lower rates for basic services such as electricity, more adequate housing, or a lower infant-mortality rate?

Or does it mean something more general, such as a shift to a different fundamental economic theory, by increasing or making exclusive the state ownership of the means of production and distribution. The proper definition may be what the taking nation says it is, but at least there seems to be agreement that some legitimate public purpose is a necessary component of a lawful expropriation, and the taking nation must offer some rational purpose for the taking.

Defining public purpose does not end the problem. When one state has taken the property of nationals of another, what court should sit in judgment of the public purpose issue, both to define it and to determine whether it is likely to be or already has been met? A court in the taking nation is not likely to overrule the taking for lack of public purpose justifications. The ideal setting for establishing these rules is the International Court of Justice. But that court has not yet proven to be an effective body to develop an international law of expropriation.

Such development is thus left to national courts and various tribunals, which have tended to shy away from addressing the public purpose issue. That has been because of both the conceptual difficulty with the issue and the fact that foreign investors whose properties have been expropriated usually are not interested in restitution of their property when the taking government is in office. The foreign investors are interested in receiving compensation. Consequently, while the public purpose element of expropriation is present and should be considered, there are other elements of expropriation more likely to be the subject of investor concern.

§ 3.4   Retaliation

In addition to lacking a public purpose, an expropriation may be unlawful if it was in retaliation for acts of the government of the person who owned the property, or if it discriminated against a particular person or government. Proof of a retaliatory purpose may constitute proof of the absence of a public purpose. If an expropriation is undertaken solely to discriminate against a foreign nation, it may constitute proof of both a lack of a public purpose and retaliation. The three elements of public purpose, retaliation, and discrimination are often quite interrelated.

The Cuban expropriations were examples of both. The first expropriations were exclusively of U.S. property (i.e., discrimination), and were in response to the United States eliminating the Cuban sugar quota (i.e., retaliation). Both were reasons for U.S. courts holding the expropriations to have been unlawful.

The taking of some property of only one nation's nationals is not necessarily discriminatory. A country may decide to nationalize one sector, such as mining. That sector might be owned exclusively by nationals of one foreign nation. It could be difficult in such case to conclude whether the taking was based on the desire to have the state own all mining interests. Perhaps the taking nation believed it was sound economically or preferable for national security reasons. The taking could be based on an intention to discriminate against one nation and take all or most of its foreign invested property, whether mining properties or hotels or anything else.

However important it may be to understand the issues of public purpose, retaliation and discrimination, the most critical issue is likely to be the payment of compensation. If a foreign investor is compensated satisfactorily, there is likely to be little concern with the technicalities of lawfulness or unlawfulness of the taking under international law because of the public purpose, retaliation, or discrimination characteristics of the taking. The investor may be concerned with the loss of future business, however, and may wish to consider the prospects of a return of the property after the new, hostile government is either replaced or adopts a different attitude toward foreign investment or the foreign investor.

§ 3.5   Uncertain Law

As noted above, if the expropriated foreign property owner is satisfactorily compensated, that is likely to end the matter. A ruling by any dispute settling entity, court, or tribunal, domestic or international, that the expropriation was unlawful, is a purely pyrrhic victory if there is no satisfactory compensation. What, therefore, is the proper measure of compensation?

The U.S. government's repeatedly stated position regarding compensation is that it is (1) required under international law, and it (2) must be prompt, adequate, and effective. The first view, that international law requires compensation, is generally shared by jurists within the United States and abroad. The second view, the prompt, adequate, and effective standard, is the subject of vigorous debate and is rejected by many U.S. and foreign jurists. The two parts are often discussed as one issue.

The first international court case usually referred to that discussed expropriation is the 1928 *Chorzów Factory* decision of the Permanent Court of International Justice (PCIJ Ser. A No. 17). That case referred only to a duty of the "payment of fair compensation." That seems less stringent than the "prompt, adequate, and effective" standard alleged to be the prevailing international law by U.S. Secretary of State Hull in 1938 in his notes to the Mexican government. There has been little further guidance from the PCIJ or its successor the International Court of Justice. The narrow focus in the latter's *Barcelona Traction* decision (1970 I.C.J. Rep. 3) added very little, if anything, to the international law of expropriation compensation.

A subsequent dispute involving an intervention that allegedly caused the company to file for bankruptcy was decided by a chamber of the International Court of Justice (the ELSI Judgment, 1989 I.C.J. Rep. 15). It involved the interpretation of the Treaty of Friendship, Commerce, and Navigation between the United States and Italy, most specifically issues regarding interference with the U.S. company's right to "control and manage" its operation in Italy.

The measure of damages became an issue, and was not dealt with very clearly, partly because of the uncertainty of the company's ability to function during the period of intervention and the appropriateness of damages after filing bankruptcy. The ruling was that Italy had not violated international law in its requisition or intervention. Furthermore, since the damages were conditioned upon liability, there was no final decision as to their measure.

Debate over the proper level of compensation continues without anything resembling a consensus. But some standards have developed that might be applied by a court or tribunal. The alternatives seem to use elastic words or terms, but when further defined, there may be less difference than is at first thought to exist.

§ 3.6   Compensation

The "prompt, adequate and effective" standard is likely to be applied by U.S. courts or tribunals applying a U.S. norm of compensation theory, or searching for an international standard, or U.S. courts or tribunals applying an agreement between the parties or nations that calls for the application of the prompt, adequate, and effective standard, such as a bilateral investment treaty.

There is no assurance, however, that a U.S. court or tribunal searching for "the" international law will arrive at a prompt, adequate, and effective standard. For example, the 1981 *Banco Nacional v. Chase Manhattan Bank* decision (658 F.2d 875, 2d Cir.) suggested that the consensus of nations was to apply an "appropriate" standard, quoting one highly regarded American author who rejected the prompt, adequate, and effective standard as a norm of international law.

Because of the very limited number of judicial decisions discussing the compensation issue, decisions of arbitration panels are often useful to compare with cases. In the 1981 *LIAMCO* arbitration

(20 Int'l Legal Mat. 1), the arbitrator suggested that the prompt, adequate, and effective standard was not the only standard, and interpreted the contract to conclude that under general principles of law only "equitable" compensation was required. But the arbitrator included in the award a substantial amount for lost profits, a conclusion suggesting the adoption of a *full* compensation standard.

"Appropriate" compensation norm is the standard in U.N. Resolution 1803 of 1962, which in the view of many jurists, remains the most likely norm to be applied. It has been suggested as the standard in the *Banco Nacional* decision noted above, and in at least two other important international arbitrations, the *TOPCO/CALASIATIC* and *AMINOIL* cases (17 Int'l Legal Mat. 1 (1978) and 21 Int'l Legal Mat. 976 (1982)).

A "fair" compensation standard was used in the much discussed but little followed *Chorzów Factory* PCIJ decision noted above. However, fair compensation has not generally been accepted as the proper standard and has not become an accepted norm of international law. That is at least partly due to the broad sense of what fair might include. A legal norm deserves greater definition.

The Restatement (Third) of the Foreign Relations Law of the United States adopted "just" in place of "appropriate", largely to avoid a possible inclusion of host nation demanded deductions under an "appropriate" standard. Several expropriating nations had calculated compensation by taking the company's value of the property and deducting what were called "excess profits" or "improper pricing" of resources to arrive at a conclusion that either no compensation was due, or that the company owed the expropriating nation. But it is hard to envision a taking nation agreeing that while such deductions could be allowed under an "appropriate" standard, they could not under a "just" standard.

The expropriated foreign investor may prefer to have the property returned rather than receive compensation. This is not likely to be the case where there has been a revolution with an investment-hostile government, such as Cuba, but may be appropriate where a counter-revolution has soon restored an investment welcoming government.

There is some precedent for restitution. In the *TOPCO/CALASIATIC* arbitration, following expropriations of Texas Overseas Petroleum Corporation and California Asiatic Oil Company by Libya, the sole I.C.J. arbitrator, Professor Dupuy (Secretary General of The Hague Academy of International Law), noted that the *Chorzów Factory* decision suggested that *restitutio in integrum* remains international law, and ordered Libya to resume performance of the agreement. Libya settled the claims of U.S. oil companies by giving them oil. But in the *BP Arbitration* (53 ILR 297, 1953) the arbitrator, Swedish Judge Lagergren, stated that the *Chorzów Factory* rule of *restitutio in integrum* was meant only to be used to calculate compensation, suggesting adherence to a full compensation theory.

§ 3.7   Compensation Questions

Whatever legal standard is applicable, three questions must be asked. First, *how much* is to be paid? Second, in *what form* is it to be paid? And third, *when* must it be paid?

If the answers to these questions are the full value of the property, in convertible currency, and immediately or very soon, then the standard that is being applied seems to be the "prompt, adequate, and effective" standard argued by the United States to constitute international law. The Iran-United States Claims Tribunal, meeting in The Hague for over three decades, never formally applied a "prompt, adequate, and effective" standard.

The Tribunal used a "just" standard, which is stated in the U.S.-Iran Treaty of Amity, Economic Relations and Consular Rights. The standard is stated as "prompt payment of just compensation." It goes on to state that it must be paid in "an effectively realizable form" and must be for the "full equivalent of the property taken", thus becoming nearly a prompt, adequate, and effective standard.

Claims approved by the tribunal have been paid *promptly* from the funds established for the purpose, they have been paid in dollars (that surely constitutes *effective* payment), and the methods of valuation used seem to satisfy any reasonable *adequacy* standard. All that said, the Iran-United States Tribunal is quite unique, however, because of the initial agreement to deposit considerable funds to meet approved claims.

If the consensus is an "appropriate" standard, tribunals that have gained the respect of most of the international community, including the main industrialized nations, seem to be applying a standard that is "fair, just, and appropriate" as well as "prompt, adequate, and effective". For now, and perhaps until or unless the investment restrictiveness of the 1970s returns, the demand for a norm allowing only partial compensation has little backing.

§ 3.8   Local Remedies

Seeking compensation from the expropriating government is not only appropriate but may be a precondition for initiating an insurance claim. It is reasonable to first seek compensation from the one who has committed the wrong. That idea makes sense when the expropriation is not part of a total change in economic theory following a revolution that includes the expropriation of all private property.

The taking nation may be prepared to compensate properties taken in a selective nationalization, such as a taking of all telecommunications or air transportation enterprises. When a nationalization occurs of the dimensions of those in the former Soviet Union, China, Eastern Europe, and Cuba, there is little reason either for the expropriated property owner to attempt to exhaust local remedies, or for that party to be forced to do so before the presentation of insurance claims.

Nevertheless, it is probably appropriate for the expropriated party to make some attempt against the taking government if nothing more than a formal written protest of the taking and a demand for compensation. The problem arises when the nation expresses a willingness to hear such claims, but the circumstances and unfolding facts seem clearly to suggest that the willingness to discuss compensation is illusory. Cuba, for example, offered compensation in the form of bonds that deserved the term "junk bonds" long before Wall Street popularized these words decades later.

The expropriated property owner may have to be prepared to establish that local remedies are inadequate before seeking remedies at home or in third party nations. Adequate proof justifying the futility of pursuing local remedies may take time to accumulate. The proof should illustrate deficiencies with the court or tribunal system of the taking nation, the method of valuation, the ability of the country to pay settled claims, and the appropriateness of the form of any payment the taking nation can afford.

The experience with taking nations where the taking is part of a major economic, political, and social revolution clearly suggests that local remedies are likely to very unsatisfactory to the expropriated property owners, and that they will have to seek assistance outside the taking nation.

§ 3.9   The "Calvo Clause"

Expropriated U.S. investors usually report the expropriation to the U.S. Department of State. Diplomatic pressure may be essential to success in dealing with the taking nation. The U.S. executive has frequently intervened after foreign nationalizations of U.S. property. While diplomatic intervention may be helpful and may lead to government sanctions against the taking nation, there is one concern that frequently faces the U.S. investor abroad—the application by the taking nation of the "Calvo Clause", or something comparable.

The Calvo Clause espouses a theory, sometimes expressed in an agreement signed by the foreign investor, that a foreign investor is entitled to treatment no different from domestic investors. This part of the concept means that the foreign investor is entitled to no better treatment than a national, and thus is left exclusively to local remedies. It is consequently interrelated with the exhaustion of local remedies concept and recourse to one's diplomatic channels may result in a *forfeiture* of the property.

The Calvo Clause was included in Article 3 of the restrictive 1973 Mexican Investment Law, but there is no instance of any property forfeiture in Mexico, or in other nations that have either adopted the Calvo Clause concept formally in investment legislation or made it a part of investment rhetoric. The concept was not included in the 1993 Mexican Investment Law, which is more investor friendly than the 1973 law. The NAFTA/USMCA foreign investment provisions eliminate the Calvo Clause as a threat to a Canadian or U.S. investor, a major concession by Mexico.

The concept of the Calvo Clause improperly frustrates the right of a nation to diplomatic intervention to protect property of its citizens. If a government does intervene, it may not be clear whether it does so at the request of the expropriated foreign investor, or on its own initiative. If the latter, it is unfair to conclude that the property is forfeited because of any act of the investor.

While the idea that foreign investors ought to be entitled to no better treatment than nations may seem sensible, the real world does give foreign investors alternatives not available to nationals. One is diplomatic negotiations. When the Calvo Clause goes beyond being a statement of exhaustion of local remedies to being an exclusionary rule precluding any other subsequent remedies, it loses much of its respect and viability.

§ 3.10   U.S. Claims Commissions

A mixed U.S. and British commission to settle claims was created following the U.S. revolutionary war primarily to settle claims of British sympathizers whose lands were seized by the States. It was not effective and was followed by a *national* commission to determine claims after a lump-sum settlement agreement was concluded in 1803. For over 150 years, the United States established national commissions to distribute funds received in settlements with Great Britain, Brazil, China, Denmark, France,

Mexico, Peru, the Two Sicilies, Spain and the Soviet Union (The Litvinov Assignment).

The U.S. Foreign Claims Settlement Commission was established in 1954 as a separate entity when the earlier International Claims Commission was abolished. Its function is essentially judicial, and the benefit of its existence (as opposed to using the district courts, for example) is its ability to acquire expertise in the narrow area of adjudication of foreign claims. Evidence of valuation of property lost abroad is difficult to obtain, and that form of evidence demanded in the courts is rarely available.

In 1980, after years of relative inactivity, the FCSC was transformed into a separate and independent agency within the Department of Justice. Any sums obtained by the United States are distributed according to the statute.

Special funds have been created in the Treasury for specific claims, relating to claims and agreements with Yugoslavia and the People's Republic of China. Each real or expected settlement with an expropriating nation must necessarily be kept separate from another, thus the statutes have titles covering special procedures for various specific takings.

These include claims against: (1) Bulgaria, Hungary, Romania, Italy, and the Soviet Union; (2) Czechoslovakia, Cuba, and China; (3) The German Democratic Republic; and (4) Vietnam. Each is related to takings following significant disturbances, principally war and revolution. The statute illustrates a pattern of procedural provisions which will likely be adopted for any future losses by U.S. citizens abroad where the takings are of all the property of U.S. citizens.

Post WWII, when there has been an extensive nationalization of foreign property, such as by China and Cuba, the most frequent settlement has been by a lump-sum under the terms of a binational agreement. Lump-sum settlements are common, but they remain questionable as a part of the jurisprudence of the international law of compensation.

Any agreed upon lump sum is subsequently divided among claimants who have quite likely filed claims years earlier, soon after the expropriations occurred. For example, the Cuban nationalizations occurred between 1959 and the early 1960s. The Cuban Claims Act was passed in 1964, providing for claims to be filed between 1965 and 1967, extended later to 1972. The valuation method ranged from strict reliance on book value to a usually much higher going concern value.

The Cuban Claims Act process is part of the larger U.S. Foreign Claims Settlement Commission. If Cuba is willing to negotiate the claims, it will not likely agree that the amount as determined by the United States is correct, partly because there was never any Cuban representation at the claim hearings. Cuba will not be able to afford to pay the some $2 billion (and counting) in claims, and the experience of U.S. claims commissions is the ultimate payment of a substantially lower negotiated amount than the full value of previously documented claims.

The Iran-United States Claims Tribunal

Foreign countries often prefer the use of a national claims commission to distribute an agreed upon total sum as the country prefers. The Iran-United States Claims Tribunal is quite unique in this respect, it varies from the norm at least partly because the U.S. hostages were involved, and there was no time to conduct a lengthy process to determine how much money to demand from Iran. The Iran-United States Claims Tribunal was created in 1981 as part of the settlement of the crisis between Iran and the United States arising from the 1979 hostage taking at the U.S. Embassy in Tehran.

The only reason Iran agreed to the tribunal was because the United States had frozen Iranian assets. Claims had to be filed by January 19, 1982, and approximately 1,000 were filed for amounts of $250,000 or more, and 2,800 were filed for smaller claims. Most claims have been satisfied but a few large and complex claims remain.

The Iran-U.S. Tribunal tended to interpret its obligation to provide full compensation to mean something closer to going concern value than book value. Arguing for acceptance of a claim under a going concern value does not assure that one will receive that higher amount, but it may mean a claim accepted for an amount higher relative to other U.S. claimants, and thus ultimate receipt of a higher amount in the pro rata apportioning of any agreed settlement.

Claimant Lawsuits

Some claimants might prefer bringing their own suits against the foreign government if they are able to locate property owned by that foreign government situated in the United States. That has not proven very successful in most cases. When a nation undertakes a massive expropriation of the property of a foreign nation it usually removes as much property as possible from that nation. The inability of Iran to do so motivated Iran to agree to the Iran-United States Claims Tribunal. Cuba successfully transferred large sums out of the United States before remaining assets were frozen by the Congress.

There may be little sense in seeking a judgment in a U.S. court if there is no property to attach and it is evident that the hostile taking nation will reject any attempt to enforce the judgment in the taking nation. Furthermore, the United States may make filing claims before a national commission the only available procedure. Many investors who were in the process of suing Iran at the time of the resolution of the hostage dispute and the establishment of the claim tribunal were angered that the agreement included removal of their claims from courts to the tribunal.

Requiring all U.S. claimants to use this same process may benefit relations between the nations but may not satisfy some claimants who were able to attach specific property of the foreign government, and who believe they might receive a greater share of their claim by separate litigation.

Separate litigation will often be attempted by expropriated investors, perhaps more successfully when the expropriations have not been massive takings as discussed above, but more selective takings of only certain property. For example, owners of Chilean copper mines expropriated under the Allende regime were compensated after they attached the proceeds of sales by the successor state-owned copper company. Some thought should also be given to individual suits against foreign governments for expropriation.

For immunity and act of state reasons, collecting on judgments against foreign sovereigns is extremely difficult. See my *International Litigation and Arbitration 3d* Concise Hornbook, Chapter 7.

§ 3.11 DFC Insurance

The U.S. Development Finance Corporation (DFC) mandate, like that of its predecessor OPIC, is to mobilize and facilitate the participation of U.S. private capital and skills in the economic and social development of less developed friendly countries and areas, thereby complementing the development assistance objectives of the United States. Guided by the expected economic and social development impact of a project, and its compatibility with other U.S. projects, preferential consideration is given to investment projects in countries having low per-capita income.

The replacement of OPIC with the DFC in 2018 came with a large investment cap ($1 billion), and increased flexibility to offer loans, equity financing, grants, and insurance. Under the Biden administration, the DFC has focused on health, technology, climate change, and gender equality projects. For example, DFC financed the production of U.S.-owned First Solar panels in India, an alternative to the world leader, China. Critics maintain that that OPIC and now the DFC resemble corporate welfare.

The President may designate countries as beneficiaries. Countries may be denied DFC insurance if they do not extend internationally recognized workers' rights to workers in that country, but the President may waive this prohibition on national economic interest grounds.

The DFC is a government entity to insure U.S. investment abroad against:

(1) Inconvertibility of local currency;

(2) Expropriation or confiscation of U.S. owned property; or

(3) War, revolution, insurrection, or civil strife.

All are subject to definition, generally left to principles of U.S. or international law. Claims paid by the DFC to insured investors are subrogated to U.S. government, which has far more leverage in exacting compensation from host countries than investors.

The DFC operates with a Board of Directors that includes persons appointed by the President from outside the government. Other Board members include the Administrator of the U.S. Agency for International Development, the U.S. Trade Representative or the Deputy, the President of the DFC, and four members who are senior officials of such entities as the Department of Labor. The DFC President and CEO are appointed by the President. It is this composition that causes the DFC to be referred to as a "quasi-private/quasi-public" organization.

The DFC runs programs for U.S. business. Eligibility is limited to U.S. citizens, U.S. corporations, partnerships, or other associations "substantially beneficially owned" by U.S. citizens. "Substantial beneficial ownership" ordinarily means that more than 50 percent of each class of issued and outstanding stock must be directly or beneficially owned by U.S. citizens. Foreign corporations, partnerships and other associations are also eligible if they are 95 percent owned by U.S. citizens. If it appears from all the circumstances that foreign creditors can exercise effective control over an otherwise eligible corporation, no insurance will be written.

As is the case of many organizations formed for a specific purpose, OPIC (now DFC) began to assume roles sometimes unrelated to its original mandate. The DFC has become a broader "development" agency. For example, building upon its guarantees and political risk insurance OPIC assumed a lending role (with loan guarantees) for such projects as the Kenya Women's Finance Trust, a water desalination plant in Algeria, and constructing four solar power plants in Peru. The role of risk insurance has continued under the DFC and has become at least partially shared with the successful Multilateral Investment Guarantee Agency (MIGA) discussed below.

The DFC has broad power to engage to insure, reinsure, cooperate in insuring, enter into pooling or risk-sharing agreements, and hold ownership in investment insurance entities. But its role is not limited to insurance. In addition to insuring investment risks, the DFC has some financing authority. It provides loans that are sponsored by or significantly involve U.S. small businesses. The DFC may also guarantee loans, regardless of the size of the company. Although the DFC currently provides financing worldwide, much of OPIC's initial focus was for investments in Latin America.

§ 3.12 DFC Programs, Terms

The three principal investment risks noted above (1) inconvertibility of currency, (2) expropriation or confiscation of property, and (3) property loss caused by war, revolution, insurrection, or civil strife were the initial reason for the existence of OPIC. A fourth class was added called "business interruption" due to any of the principal three risks. DFC insurance for these reasons is limited to 90% of the book value of the investment. Its premiums are not cheap, commonly 1.5% to cover all these risk categories.

Inconvertibility

Before insurance against inconvertibility of currency is approved, the investor must obtain assurance from the host country that investor earnings will be convertible into dollars and that repatriation of capital is permitted. If the currency thereafter becomes inconvertible by act of the government, DFC will accept the foreign currency, or a draft for the amount, and will provide the investor with U.S. dollars.

Expropriation

Expropriation is broadly defined and "includes, but is not limited to, any abrogation, repudiation, or impairment by a foreign government of its own contract with an investor with respect to a project, where such abrogation, repudiation, or impairment is not caused by the investor's own fault or misconduct, and materially adversely affects the continued operation of the project." OPIC and DFC contracts have followed a more specific and enumerative approach because the law does not define specifically what actions constitute expropriation.

The DFC's standard insurance contract contains a lengthy description of what is considered expropriatory action sufficient to require payment. That definition may help an investor in drafting a contract with the foreign host government, because that government will have to deal with the DFC once the investor's claim has been paid.

The DFC insured U.S. investor must exhaust local remedies before DFC is obligated to pay any claim. All reasonable action must be taken by the investor. These include pursuing administrative and judicial claims to prevent or contest the challenged action by the host government.

War, Revolution, Insurrection or Civil Strife

The third form of coverage, "war, revolution, insurrection, or civil strife," (political violence) is not defined by the statute. A usual DFC contract provides protection against:

> injury to the physical condition, destruction, disappearance or seizure and retention of Covered Property directly caused by war (whether under formal declaration) or by revolution or insurrection and includes injury to the physical condition, destruction, disappearance or seizure and retention of Covered Property as a direct result of actions taken in hindering, combating, or defending against a pending or expected hostile act whether in war, revolution, or insurrection.

Civil strife is politically motivated violence (*e.g.*, civil disturbances, riots, acts of sabotage, terrorism). Added to the OPIC/DFC statute in 1985 was a provision providing:

> Before issuing insurance for the first time for loss due to business interruption, and in each subsequent instance in which a significant expansion is proposed in the type of risk to be insured under the definition of "civil strife" or "business interruption", the Corporation shall . . . submit to [Senate and House Committees] . . . a report with respect to such insurance, including a thorough analysis of the risks to be covered, anticipated losses, and proposed rates and reserves and, in the case of insurance for loss due to business interruption, an explanation of the underwriting basis upon which the insurance is to be offered.

Since its inception, OPIC/DFC has funded, guaranteed, or insured billions worth of investments, not all of them in accordance with standard insurance risk management principles. For example, OPIC insured a GE Hungarian investment for $141 million, but the

World Bank's MIGA reinsured $50 million of this project, thus lessening the full exposure of OPIC.

§ 3.13 DFC Eligibility

Upon payment of a claim, DFC is subrogated to all rights to the investor's claim against the host government. Because the United States must deal with the foreign government, DFC will not write any insurance in a foreign country until that country agrees to accept DFC insurance and thus to negotiate with DFC after claims have been paid.

Legislation authorizes DFC to carry out its functions "utilizing broad criteria". DFC must consider investment eligibility in accordance with extensive guidelines that provide that DFC conduct operations on a self-sustaining basis.

For example, it must consider: The economic and financial soundness of the project; use private credit and investment institutions along with DFC's guarantee authority; and broaden private participation and revolve its funds by selling its direct investments to private investors. The DFC must also apply principles of risk management; provide preferential consideration to projects involving small business (at least 30 percent of all projects); and consider less developed nation receptiveness to private enterprise.

The DFC must consider whether projects foster private initiative and competition and discourage monopolistic practices; further balance of payment objectives of the United States; and support projects with positive trade benefits to the United States. Furthermore, the DFC is required to advise and assist agencies of the United States and other public and private organizations interested in projects in less developed nations. It must avoid projects that diminish employment in the United States and refuse projects that do not have positive trade benefits to the United States. Further, it must refuse projects that pose an unreasonable or major environmental, health, or safety hazard, or result in significant degradation of national parks and similar protected areas.

DFC must operate consistently with the goals of U.S. law relating to protection of environment and endangered species in less developed nations. Additionally, it must limit operations to nations that provide or are in the process of providing internationally recognized rights for workers. That includes right of association, right to organize and bargain collectively, prohibition of forced or compulsory labor, minimum age for employment, and acceptable conditions of work. Such requirement is often observed more on paper than in practice in many of the countries listed as acceptable for DFC assistance. Finally, DFC must consider the host nation's observance of and respect for human rights.

The DFC participates only in *new* investments via loans or insurance. Its role is to encourage new investment, not facilitate existing investment. Each proposed investment is evaluated by DFC to consider in addition to the above eligibility requirements the extent to which the U.S. participant has long-term management arrangements with the new enterprise, the extent of private participation, and whether the project is likely to assist further development of the host nation's private sector.

Loans or the contribution of goods or services to foreign governments will not be insured unless they are part of a construction contract. Nor will DFC insure the credit or solvency of the foreign government.

§ 3.14   DFC Claims and Disputes

Claims presented by insured investors are typically settled, and disputes arising as a result thereof may be arbitrated with the consent of the parties, on such terms and conditions as the DFC may determine. OPIC/DFC insurance contracts have stated that "any controversy arising out of or relating to this Contract or the breach thereof shall be settled by arbitration in accordance with the then prevailing Commercial Arbitration Rules of the American Arbitration Association." OPIC/DFC has arbitrated claims presented to it by U.S. companies claiming to have lost property through expropriations.

From 1966 to 1970, $3.5 million was paid to settle eight claims. From 1971 through most of 2012, OPIC agreed to 292 insurance claim settlements which totaled $970.8 million, constituting either cash settlements to investors or guaranties of host nation obligations. During this period, OPIC denied twenty-eight claims, fourteen of which had been submitted to arbitration by the investors.

Since 1978, OPIC/DFC has had the authority to deny loss claims if the investor, a controlling shareholder, or any agent of the investor has engaged in any act which resulted in a conviction under the 1977 Foreign Corrupt Practices Act, and such act has been the "preponderant" cause of the loss. There have been relatively few convictions under the FCPA, however, since most charges lead to a consent decree involving a fine. See Chapter 2.

§ 3.15   World Bank Insurance

The concept of offering insurance for various investment risks which led to the creation of OPIC in the United States, and to similar programs in several other nations, has been built upon on an international level by the World Bank's 1988 creation of the Multilateral Investment Guarantee Agency (MIGA). This organization, part of the World Bank, was intended to encourage increased investment to the developing nations by offering investment insurance and advisory services. Voting power is equally divided between the industrial and developing nation groups. Shares are proportional to member nations' shares of World Bank capital. Unlike OPIC/DFC, MIGA is not a lending agency, but its parent organization the World Bank serves principally as a lender.

Creating MIGA within the World Bank structure offers benefits a separate international organization lacks. MIGA has access to World Bank data on nations' economic and social status. This gives considerable credibility to MIGA and encourages broad participation.

A U.S. based company may prefer dealing with DFC because of greater confidence of claims being paid, of maintaining information confidentiality, and benefiting from legal processes established in bilateral investment treaties. U.S. companies may find MIGA insurance available where DFC is not. Rather than being an alternative to DFC, MIGA should be viewed as compatible with it. For example, International Paper Investments of the United States obtained MIGA insurance for risks of currency transfer, expropriation, and war and civil disturbance, plus additional political risk insurance from OPIC/DFC.

Banks have found MIGA attractive because bank regulators in some countries have exempted commercial banks from special requirements for provisioning against loss where loans or investments are insured by MIGA. Furthermore, investors in nations without adequate national insurance programs have very much welcomed MIGA's creation. But even some of the newly industrializing nations, such as India and South Korea, have adopted national programs.

. MIGA is not intended to replace national programs, but to extend the availability of investment insurance to many areas where it was not previously available, which in turn is expected to assist economic development in those areas. MIGA's success will likely be where it fills gaps rather than where it competes with established and successful national insurance programs. Those gaps are substantial and MIGA has a major role to play in the world.

Unlike national programs, such as DFC, MIGA has the leverage of a large group of nations behind it when it presses a claim. The clear intention of MIGA is to avoid political interference and consider the process solely as creating legal issues. Recent decades have been quiet times for foreign investment regarding the risks insured against by OPIC/DFC and MIGA. The risks are perceived as sufficiently likely that DFC and MIGA have been quite busy writing new insurance.

§ 3.16 MIGA Insurance Programs

Risks covered by MIGA are noncommercial and include risks of currency transfer; expropriation; war, terrorism, and civil disturbance; breach of contract; and failure to honor sovereign financial obligations, all actions by the host government. Only developing nations are eligible locations for insured investments.

Currency Transfer

This insurance is similar to that offered by DFC. It covers losses incurred when an investor is unable to convert host nation currency into foreign exchange and transfer that exchange abroad. Host nation currency may be that obtained from profits, principal, interest, royalties, capital, etc. The insurance covers refusals and excessive delays where the host government has failed to act, where there have been adverse changes in exchange control laws or regulations, or where conditions in the host nation that govern currency transfer have deteriorated.

Currency devaluations are *not* covered. Such devaluations are often the cause of substantial losses, but these are commercial losses attributed to changes that are to some extent predictable and are not carried out by host nations to harm investment. Indeed, currency devaluations are usually extreme measures to address changing demand for the nation's currency.

Expropriation

This is insurance for partial or total loss from acts that reduce ownership control over, or rights to, the insured investment. Included is "creeping" expropriation, where a series of acts has the same effect as an outright taking. Not covered are nondiscriminatory actions of the host government in exercising its regulatory authority.

Valuation for compensation is net book value; that may mean inadequate compensation where book value reflects historic costs. Loans and loan guarantees are compensated to the extent of the outstanding principal and interest. Compensation is paid at the same time as the insured assigns its rights in the investment to MIGA, which then may act against the expropriating government.

War, Terrorism, and Civil Disturbance

This insurance covers losses for damage, disappearance, or destruction to tangible assets by politically motivated acts of war or civil disturbance, such as revolution, insurrection, *coups d'état*, sabotage, and terrorism. Compensation is for the book value or replacement cost of assets lost, and for the repair of damaged assets.

This insurance also covers losses attributable to an interruption in a project for a period of one year. This is business interruption coverage and becomes effective when the investment is considered a total loss. Book value is the measure of compensation.

Breach of Contract

This special insurance covers losses caused by the host government's breach or repudiation of a contract. When there is an alleged breach or repudiation, the foreign investor must be able to invoke an arbitration clause in the contract and obtain an award for damages. If that award is not paid by the host government, MIGA provides compensation.

Failure to Honor Sovereign Financial Obligations

More recently added, this insurance is for losses from the failure of a government to make payments when due where there is an unconditional (not subject to defenses) obligation or guarantee related to an eligible investment. The investor does not need to obtain an arbitral award.

§ 3.17 MIGA Eligibility

MIGA insurance may cover, to a maximum of U.S. $220 million per project and usually for a maximum of fifteen years, new equity investments, shareholder loans or guaranties, and non-shareholder loans. Also covered are technical assistance and management contracts, asset securitization, capital market bond issues, leasing, services, and franchise and licensing agreements. MIGA will insure acquisitions under a state privatization program, an important program.

Two member countries are involved. First, investors must be from a member country, and only foreign investors qualify. With Agency approval, however, domestic investors may receive coverage for projects where they bring assets back to their nation. This special allowance is intended to promote the return of capital transferred to safe havens during times of political or economic uncertainty. Second, the location of approved investments must be in developing member nations that approve the insurance.

There was considerable discussion regarding insuring only in developing nations which adopted standards for protecting foreign investment, but the final Convention did not include any such standards. Member nation standards for protecting foreign investment may nevertheless be a factor in writing insurance, if any measure of risk management principles is to be followed. Since the viability of MIGA is dependent both on its care in selecting risks, and on its ability to negotiate settlements after paying claims, the right of subrogation is extremely important.

An investor seeking MIGA insurance must be a national or member country *other than* the country in which the investment is to be made. The test of nationality for corporations is incorporation and having its principal place of business in the member nation, *or* being majority owned by nationals of the member nation. Commercially operated state-owned corporations are eligible if it operates on a commercial basis. Even non-profit organizations are eligible if they operate on a commercial basis.

§ 3.18 MIGA Coverage

MIGA covers investments under a standard term of fifteen years, which may be increased to twenty years if MIGA determines that the longer term is justified by the nature of the project. If the insurance is for a loan, the term follows the duration of the loan agreement. Once written, MIGA is not able to terminate the coverage except for default by the investor. The insured investor, however, is entitled to cancel the insurance on any anniversary date after the third.

Premiums are based on a risk assessment which includes consideration of the political and economic conditions in the host nation. They average about one percent of the insured amount per year. Rates vary, however, depending on the industry and type of coverage. MIGA can insure equity investments to ninety percent of the initial contribution, plus 180 percent to cover earnings. Contracts such as for technical assistance are covered to ninety percent of the value of the payments due under the agreement. Loans and loan guarantees are also insured to ninety percent of the principal and interest that will accrue over the term of the loan.

These figures are maximum available guarantees. The *current* amount is that in force for the given year. The difference between the maximum and current amount is referred to as the *standby* amount of guarantee and constitutes a reserve coverage that the investor may place in effect each year to cover changes in the value or amount of investment at risk.

§ 3.19 MIGA Claims

In all but two cases, MIGA has resolved disputes that would have led to claims. It has paid additional claims related to damage from war and civil disturbance. The first was for an equity investment in a power corporation in Indonesia, which was suspended by a presidential decree due to an economic crisis. The second was for war and civil disturbance, a guerilla attack in Nepal had damaged a hydroelectric plant and dealt with a power project. The third claim involved a toll road project in Argentina when the nation faced yet another financial crisis.

MIGA's success lies in finding a resolution without the investor resorting to the claims process. MIGA appears to be a successful entity and a welcome addition to DFC for U.S. investors.

Choosing MIGA or DFC for a U.S. investor planning an investment abroad is *not* a coin toss. In one case MIGA may be the better or only choice. In another DFC may be better. In still other cases, either DFC or MIGA may be appropriate. Finally, there may be instances when a project has several aspects that call for use of both MIGA and DFC.

Chapter 4

INVESTING IN CHINA

§ 4.1 Introduction

China, in its rise as one of the world's leading economies, has relied heavily upon investment of money and technology from foreigners. The importance of investing in China—both for the country and the investors—is dramatically underscored by the extraordinary number of foreign companies operating in China and the enormous volume of monies invested to date.

According to Xinhua, the official Chinese government news agency, the number of foreign investors in the PRC is estimated at well over 500,000. Over the past 40 years since China opened its doors to global investment, foreign companies have contributed several trillions of dollars to the stock of direct investment in China. China now has the fourth largest stock of foreign direct investment (FDI) in the world following only the European Union, the United States and Hong Kong. The investment flow into China continues. For the past decade, China has been in competition with the United States to be the top recipient of FDI.

Initially many foreign companies invested heavily in China seeking a source of low-cost goods. Clothing, shoes, and other labor-intensive goods were sourced extensively by western retailers. Consequently, the real cost of items such as clothing in the U.S., adjusted for inflation, declined. As China grew wealthier with a growing middle class, foreign companies were quick to recognize the untapped potential of 1.4 billion customers as a must-have market, and these companies have flocked to China.

Household American names such as McDonald's, KFC and Starbucks are on every corner, and many consider China to be their most important growth market. McDonalds has over 2,000 outlets and KFC has more than 4,800 stores throughout China. Starbucks has experienced similar growth and success. In January 1999, Starbucks opened its first store in Beijing, and has since gone on to expand its fleet there to over 2000 outlets. China has the third largest number of Starbucks stores worldwide, following the United States and Canada.

Some companies have utilized China both as a source of product and as a market. Wal-Mart is an excellent example of this dual strategy. It is estimated that at one time Wal-Mart was responsible for 10% of total China exports to the U.S. that contributed greatly to its low prices. The company has also expanded its retail store concept and capitalized on China as a market, opening in hundreds of retail stores. As this book went to print, Wal-Mart was losing sales under a PRC-orchestrated campaign chastising it for not carrying products from Xinjiang Province (where Muslim Uyghurs and the U.S. assert gross human rights abuses).

And, in an interesting strategy twist, General Motors, which initially accessed the China market for internal automobile sales potential, has successfully exported China-made Buicks to the U.S. GM now derives about a notable percentage of its global revenues from China and sells more Cadillacs there than in the USA. Ford came late to the party and is doing its best to catch up. Virtually all the world's leading auto companies are making vehicles in China, very often via joint ventures with local firms. Tesla was the first foreign company to gain permission to wholly own its Shanghai subsidiary. In recent years, PRC auto sales by most foreign manufacturers have noticeably declined, even for Tesla. Chinese auto manufacturers, especially EV vehicles, have become leaders in the PRC market.

To borrow the insightful words of Jim McGregor in his book *One Billion Customers*: "There are two kinds of foreign companies in China. One is the kind that China needs. The other kind needs China."

Sorting out which kind of investor you are is essential. Your category may shift, sometimes dramatically, as some foreign auto producers in the PRC have learned the hard way. In 2021, spurred by the PRC's new Personal Information Protection Law (modeled on the EU General Data Protection Regulation (see Chapter 5), the shift caused Yahoo to follow Microsoft's LinkedIn out of China.

Meanwhile, under liberalized foreign investment rules, virtually all the major U.S. investment banks were piling into China, many converting their joint ventures into wholly owned subsidiaries. U.S. wealth management funds (for example, Vanguard) likewise enabled by changes in PRC law also joined the investment influx, as have many U.S.-based venture capital funds or partnerships focused primarily on heavily subsidized semiconductor production and development in China. Such funds sometimes use existing Chinese affiliates to make such venture capital investments, an approach that obscures the origin of U.S. capital. Even Intel, the leading U.S. chip producer, reportedly does so.

Foreign investment in China generally avoids extensive U.S. controls over exports of goods and technology to the PRC. The U.S. has tightened up foreign subsidiary and technology loopholes in its control system governing exports of semiconductor chips to the PRC. Notable restraints bar foreign chipmakers using U.S.-designed tools in Japan, Korea, and Taiwan (a world leader in semiconductors) from exporting to the PRC. See my Concise Hornbook on *International Trade Beyond Trump*, Chapter 10.

Currently, the United States lacks national security controls over outbound foreign investments by U.S. firms. China has a track record of enticing foreign investment in critical industries (telecommunications, high speed rail) then subtly shifting knowhow and market access to local champions.

China's New Normal

For years, the headlines have trumpeted the unparalleled growth of the Chinese economy. China achieved a growth rate of approximately 10% for three decades and became the 2nd largest economy in the world. For the last several years, the headlines have proclaimed that China is slowing economically and that 10% growth rates are clearly unsustainable. Indeed, the GDP growth of late has been coming in around 6%, large by world standards yet substantially reduced by Chinese standards.

In acknowledging these changes, the Chinese government has adopted the slogan 'New Normal' as descriptive of expected growth and coupled with the myriad of economic reforms needed to take China forward. China's transition from an export-led economy to one based on domestic consumption is a leading global economic theme today, especially given the outsized importance of the country's economy.

China's growth since the 1980s was driven largely by exports and high levels of investment. Today, the government is increasingly working to manage economic growth and expectations while emphasizing a New Normal focused on sustainable development as the country rebalances to a model involving a greater role for services and consumption.

As China seeks to rebalance its economy and achieve sustainable growth, the potential for foreign investment is significant. Slower growth does not necessarily mean slower opportunities. Rather, foreign investors need to think differently and adapt their strategies to a changing environment. Changes in demographics, market forces and investment regulations are opening new sectors and opportunities that would never have been thought possible a few years ago, much less open to foreign investment.

PRC State, Private and Foreign Investment Sectors

According to the 1982 Constitution, the state sector is the leading force in the economy of the People's Republic of China. Starting in the early 1980s, there was a quiet retreat from this position. The amount of China's industrial output produced by state enterprises steadily dropped. Correspondingly, during the 1980s, there was rapid growth in the number and economic significance of foreign, private, and collective enterprises.

These enterprises accounted for over half of the gross domestic product (GDP) of the People's Republic by the late 1980s. They were an engine of economic growth and jobs. In 1988 and again in 1993, the Constitution of the PRC was amended to affirm the development of these sectors as a supplement to the state economy.

Ever since Mao died in the 1970s, and a receptive environment was created, China has been taking in foreign investment at a phenomenal pace. Initially, many investors chose the equity joint venture (EJVs) format, though wholly owned subsidiaries (WFOEs) were also an option. The arrival of foreign investors brought a wave of capital, technology, and talent in a policy retreat from state-owned enterprise. Wal-Mart, KFC (Yum Brands), Volkswagen, General Motors and GE exemplify China investment success stories. Revlon and Best Buy came and then left China as strong local brands emerged.

A significant number of EJVs have been undertaken in partnership with Chinese governmental entities, particularly local governments. Such entities often provided *"guanxi"*, connections necessary to China's foreign investment approval and implementation process. In more recent years, foreign investors have tended to favor WFOEs, more confident of their ability to navigate China's bureaucratic and cultural maze. In addition, some EJVs have converted to WFOEs.

In 2021, however, China began to reign in its private sector, especially in the technology field. Alibaba, for example, was denied a major listing on the Hong Kong and Shanghai exchanges. Its famous founder, Jack Ma, was no longer celebrated. Tencent, ByteDance, Baidu, Didi and other prominent private sector Chinese companies and their leaders were similarly constrained, often in the name of Xi Jinping's "Common Prosperity" wealth-sharing goals and national data security. Substantial donations to government priorities from China's private sector have been undertaken.

Some foreign investors moved away from greater activities in the PRC. For example, mega-U.S. property investor Blackstone withdrew from a major deal as the China property giant Evergrande teetered on the edge of bankruptcy. Large well-entrenched state-owned or state-controlled enterprises continue to dominate certain sectors, such as banking. State banks in turn have lent copiously to state manufacturing "dinosaurs," such as steel and shipbuilding. The market viability of these loans and the state enterprises they support, absent further underwriting, is doubtful.

§ 4.2　A Planned Economy

China continues its tradition of engaging in long-range planning seeking to set goals for development. In March 2016 and again in March 2021, the National People's Congress adopted the government's blueprint for the country. Known as the 13th and 14th Five-Year Plans, these documents signal the general direction of key economic, social, environmental, and industrial policies, setting out clear goals such as achieving an innovation-driven development strategy and an average annual growth rate of 6.5% to 7%. While substantially below growth goals set forth in previous Five-Year plans, this rate of growth is consistent with the New Normal and the new Chinese economy.

These road maps have important considerations for foreign investors and how companies will conduct their businesses and plan market strategies. Notably important for foreign investors is the changed focus and how this impacts investment decisions. The key themes of the 13th and 14th Five-Year Plans indicate that there is set to be a shift in economic focus to compensate and rebalance to address the current pressures facing China as it seeks economic adjustment. This shift will see an economy largely fired previously by heavy industry and manufacturing moving towards more sustainable economic forms through innovation, service, retail, infrastructure, and overseas expansion.

This means that there will be significant opportunities for both Chinese domestic and foreign businesses operating in the PRC. The 13th and 14th Five-Year Plans have been formulated based upon the following Five Tenets:

(i) Innovation as a primary driver of economic development to shift China's economic structure into higher-quality growth pattern, moving away from mass manufacturing model;

(ii) Coordination to utilize both global and domestic markets;

(iii) Green growth to combat the environmental issues resulting from China's rapid development;

(iv) Balanced development among both rural and urban areas, and across different industries; and

(v) Sharing of the benefits to the wider Chinese population to ensure that prosperity is shared with the whole nation and delivers improved social services.

To survive and sustain effective operations under these Plans, international investors must align with the policy direction of China and the government's motivations by developing business strategies around these tenets. China as a market continues to evolve and foreign businesses will need to adapt if they are to survive and prosper under the Plan criteria.

§ 4.3   Cartel and Regulatory Law

A broad trend towards free market economics (taking goods off "the plan") was apparent in the People's Republic commencing in the 1980s. The number of products allocated through central planners and the share of industrial output and retail sales subject to state planning dropped. Nevertheless, China's economy remains regulated. The government's central administration fixes prices for important consumer and producer goods, and local economic bureaucrats also set prices and control supplies. The fixed price has little to do with actual costs.

The tensions inherent in moving China's planned economy into the marketplace are evident in its regulatory law. China has, for example, an unusual collection of laws supporting competition and encouraging collaboration. Regulations Concerning the Promotion of Economic Combinations were first adopted in 1980. These regulations encourage state enterprises to voluntarily participate in economic combines by signing a contract. Producers and processors of raw materials might, for example, execute such a cartel agreement. Combines can enjoy incentives in the marketing and supply of products.

Regulations Concerning Development of Socialist Competition were also initially issued. Under these regulations, state enterprises are given more power to decide on production, marketing, finance, and the like without interference from local authorities. No monopoly of any commodity is allowed other than those (such as the state tobacco monopoly) designated by the government. Although these regulations give priority to the government's economic plans, state enterprises may produce over plan quotas. In addition, authorities cannot create local monopolies, or forbid the sale locally of products that are made elsewhere. These regulations were incorporated into the Anti-Improper Competition Law of December 1993. This Law does not address abuses of market power by state enterprises.

The government is thus in a legal position which allows it to choose between economic combines or socialist competition. Prior to 1989, the trend was clearly in the direction of more competition and fewer state-authorized cartels. Indeed, as market forces increasingly came into play the capitalist phenomenon of "multifarious monopolies" reared its head. New regulations were adopted by the State Council to combat these practices. No enterprises or trade associations may establish a "monopoly price," regardless of whether the state has set a ceiling price for the relevant product or decreed that it is subject to a floating or free market price. The state will punish offenders and replace monopoly prices with "reasonable" ones.

China's answer to monopoly pricing is thus in part re-regulation of markets, not a greater promotion of competitive alternatives. This is a step backwards from the development of a market economy, one that the Chinese explain by reference to the infant state of their economic system. There may be some legitimacy to this explanation, but monopoly pricing controls could undercut the progress toward deregulation of markets and attraction of foreign investors.

While there is certainly movement to support competition, the Chinese government retains extensive power over industries. For example, the government has ordered the consolidation of steel and auto companies and ordered the combination of the country's two largest high-speed rail equipment manufacturers so that a single entity could compete more effectively on the world stage.

§ 4.4   From Isolation to Open Entry and Exit

Under Mao Zedong, China followed trade and investment policies of economic isolation and self-sufficiency. These policies were partly a response to past economic exploitation of the country by foreigners. They also reflected communist ideology and a rejection of the economic tenets of modern capitalism. Since the Cultural Revolution, the People's Republic has opened its doors and law to world trade and investment as part of its modernization and development strategy. This reversal is most evident in its relations with Hong Kong, Japan and the United States, China's three leading trade partners. Roughly one-fifth of China's GDP is now involved in foreign trade, a declining percentage as its economy grows internally.

Even after the 1989 resurgence in the power of economic traditionalists, the PRC continued to be receptive to world trade and investment. Following Tiananmen Square once enthusiastic foreign investors became cautious and were constrained by their banks and governments. Recentralization, austerity, and contractions in China's economy hurt their existing investments. Though the doors remained open, many though not all foreigners hesitated to enter. The Taiwanese, Singaporeans, South Koreans and (more deliberately) the Japanese led the return to trading and investing in China.

Until the relatively recent "normalization" of PRC-Taiwan (Chinese Taipei) relations, Taiwanese investors often set up shell companies in Hong Kong to funnel investments into China, principally in Fujian province across the straits from Taiwan. By 2014, Taiwanese firms based in China were employing over 15 million workers, Japanese companies about 11 million, and South Korean enterprises had approximately 2 million Chinese employees. Broadly speaking, this reflects a growing trend, the "Asianization" of

China's international economic relations. It portends diminished influence for the United States in Chinese trade and investment policies.

PRC Belt and Road Initiative

By far, China's biggest and most ambitious outbound foreign investment endeavor is the Belt and Road Initiative (BRI) (formerly known as One Belt, One Road). This Initiative seeks to build megaprojects along the ancient land route of the Silk Road and throughout Southeast Asia and eastern Africa on a Maritime Silk Road. These projects consist of dozens of road, rail, port, and power generation plants along corridors that span at least 65 countries with a combined population of 4.4 billion and about a third of the world's economic output.

The transportation links are especially important as this facilitates the movement of goods connecting China and Europe. In 2017, China dispatched the 'East Wind' train on a 12,000-kilometer (7,500 mile) journey across Kazakhstan, Russia, Belarus, Poland, Germany, Belgium, and France on its way to the UK. Thirteen of the EU member states have formally signed on to China's BRI program, notably Italy in 2019.

The BRI is notable not just for its scale, but for its timeframe. Its first phase focuses on infrastructure development, specifically in transportation, communications, and power. The second phase will involve softer sectors such as e-commerce, healthcare, education, and financial services. By 2021, China had created over two dozen economic and trade cooperation zones in numerous African countries investing over $735 billion therein. China is easily Africa's largest trade and investment partner. Early projects are up and running now and the whole Initiative is not expected to conclude until at least 2050.

Financing for many of the BRI projects comes from the Asia Infrastructure Investment Bank (AIIB) created by China to compete with the World Bank and the Asia Development Bank. The AIIB has as its members every major country of the world except the United States and Japan. In addition to the AIIB, China had dedicated large sums in a 'Silk Road Fund' and instructed its state-controlled bank to issue loans for various BRI projects. Most of these projects are built by Chinese firms largely employing Chinese staff. Foreign investment options are limited.

§ 4.5   Early U.S.-China Investment Disputes

Since 1980, Chinese imports and exports have benefited from U.S. Export-Import Bank financial support, although this was slow in forthcoming after Tiananmen Square. Because the United States and China exchanged diplomatic notes in 1980 on investment guarantees, U.S. Overseas Private Investment Corporation (OPIC, now FDC) loans, insurance and guarantees have also been extended to China. See Chapter 3. Should the FDC make payment to any U.S. investor or trader in China the PRC will recognize its rights to the claims of that person.

Trade and investment disputes between the United States and the People's Republic regularly emerged prior to 2001 when the PRC joined the WTO. For example, private U.S. investors owning property in prerevolutionary China or holding imperial government bonds commenced litigation in the early 1980s against the PRC in the federal courts. This litigation threatened to undermine the lump-sum claims settlement agreed upon in 1979 by the U.S. and the PRC. That settlement released assets frozen by both governments since 1949 for the purpose of paying claimants. U.S. litigants were disgruntled with their return of only 40 cents on each dollar of their investments. One default judgment was entered against the PRC, which has always disclaimed liability for the "odious debts" of prerevolutionary China. The lump-sum claims settlement was eventually upheld by the U.S. federal courts, but not before economic relations were frayed.

In addition to pressures from the U.S. and other partners regarding its trade practices, there has also been continuing debate within the Chinese leadership on the extent to which the country should remain open to foreign trade and investment. The position of the Chinese government is to continue to open to the outside world to absorb capital and technology that will continue to help the PRC grow, thus reinforcing Chinese Communist party rule. However, a more conservative minority element within the Chinese leadership advocates greater caution in dealing with foreigners to protect the PRC from "spiritual pollution" and possible exploitation.

There are additional gaps in China's foreign investment relations with the United States. One notable omission is the absence of a bilateral investment treaty (BIT) with the United States. Negotiations on such a treaty have been ongoing for years. In sum, U.S. trade and investment relations with the PRC, prior to the arrival of President Trump, more closely resembled those of an ally than an enemy.

§ 4.6   Rule of Law?

The seemingly simple concept of Rule of Law gets much attention and following many years of investment into China this remains one of the most problematic and on-going priority issues for foreigners. At its simplest, the Rule of Law may be perceived as the restriction of the arbitrary exercise of power by subordinating it to well-defined and established laws.

A clear statement of the concerns for foreign investors is well summarized by an American Chamber of Commerce of China (AmCham) White Paper: "We believe that China's legal and regulatory framework can be improved through development of a more robust rule of law." It further explains the shortcomings of the current situation and their importance to foreigner investors:

- AmCham China believes that the commitments from China's Third and Fourth Plenums to further open and reform the economy and to implement the rule of law throughout the country represent positive steps forward. Non-transparent, unclear, and inconsistent rulemaking were identified by 65 percent of our members as limiting their ability and willingness to invest in China and have remained as top challenges to business for the last four years in a row. Effective rule of law is essential to ensuring that China's market remains open to foreign business, and that foreign investments will be treated fairly.

- We believe that China's regulatory and legal system should be transparent, predictable, stable, accountable, and have legal due process for all involved. While we recognize that rule of law in China at this time will likely be more in the nature of rule by law than rule of law, we nevertheless believe that substantial progress can be made in these areas such that outcomes are less likely to be affected by nationality of the shareholder.

- We encourage the Chinese government to facilitate more robust sharing of international rulemaking best practices by fully and consistently implementing a minimum 30-day notice and comment period on draft laws and regulations across all agencies. We encourage the publication of internal guidelines that govern the administration of both domestic and foreign companies in China and of judicial decisions to facilitate compliance. We also urge the application of due process in investigations of, and non-discriminatory enforcement against, foreign companies and FIEs.

Closely related to the transparency and certainty afforded by Rule of Law is how this concept affects the ease of the ease of doing business in China as well as the perception of corruption. While there are many changes in adherence to the rule of law concepts and lessons learned from those who have gone before, China can still be a place of difficulty in doing business.

The World Bank ranks 190 economies on a scale reflecting the ease of doing business. With detailed explanation it uses criteria on starting a business, dealing with construction permits, getting electricity, registering property, getting credit, protecting minority investors, paying taxes, trading across borders, enforcing contracts, and resolving insolvency. Overall, China is in the middle of the pack ranking 78 out of 190 (2018) up slightly from previous reports. It is important to note however wide range for different criteria as the country ranks a very high 5/190 in enforcement of contracts, while at the same time protection of minority investors was 119/190.

Investors are and should also be concerned about corruption and the anti-corruption campaign by the current administration is notable in its intensity. One measure of a country's corruption is the annual report of Transparency International, based upon opinion and perception of corruption from business executives. In a recent survey, China again is in the middle ranking at 77th place of 180 countries.

§ 4.7   Foreign Investment Entry and Operational Controls

The foreign investment climate in the People's Republic of China changed dramatically after the Cultural Revolution. The country moved from a position of outright hostility and suspicion of foreign investors to an open, selective embracement of their capital, talent, and technology.

At the central government level, MOFCOM (China's Ministry of Commerce) is typically the gatekeeper. Local entry controls may also apply. In recent years, controversial VIEs ("variable interest entities", discussed below) have been used to circumvent China's regulatory restraints on foreign investment.

Political and economic stability has always been a basic premise upon which most China investment is undertaken. With this premise in doubt after Tiananmen Square, the investment climate was initially perceived by foreigners as risky. Some new foreign investments and loans were delayed, cancelled, or made prohibitively expensive. Nevertheless, while North American and European investment in China at first declined or plateaued, capital and technology imports from Hong Kong, South Korea, Taiwan, and Singapore (the "Four Dragons") increased.

Since South Korea and Taiwan were not officially recognized by the PRC, much of this trade and investment was channeled through Hong Kong companies. From China's perspective, the Four Dragons of East Asia represent an increasingly desirable alternative for foreign investment resources, an alternative that brings with it far less criticism of domestic policies.

Time has also brought North Americans, Europeans, and the Japanese actively back into the Chinese market. Early in 1992, for example, General Motors announced a new joint venture to make pickup trucks in the PRC. GM is now heavily invested in auto production in China, and exports Buicks to America, though Volkswagen remains China's top seller of cars.

The embracement by the People's Republic of foreign investors is mirrored in the progression of laws, regulations, and treaties on foreign direct investment since the Cultural Revolution. For example, State Council regulations adopted in 1986 (known as the "22 Articles"), favored "export" and "technologically advanced" enterprises with reduced land use fees, more independence from the state, the right to hire and fire at will, lower labor and utility costs and less taxation. Many existing investments were certified by local authorities as qualifying for such benefits. Indeed, cities and provinces have competed for foreign investment in offering these types of incentives.

They also compete among themselves in enacting liberal investment regulations. Guangdong Province and the Shenzhen SEZ adjacent to Hong Kong have attracted the most foreign investment using these techniques. However, Shanghai issued new regulations that subject foreign enterprises to more government controls over price, transport, labor, supplies, and sales. The main thrust of these regulations was to remove the preferential treatment once accorded foreign investment and subject it to "equal treatment" with domestic enterprises.

The central government also announced an important policy change; all foreign investment enterprises (like their domestic counterparts) must have unions to represent their work forces. They are also required to have an internal "Chinese Communist Party Committee" whose task is to monitor compliance with CCP policies.

§ 4.8   The Investment Catalogue System—the Negative List

As a matter of government policy and to comply with its requirement under the WTO China has opened its economy considerably to investment by foreign companies. However, not all industrial sectors are open to foreign investment. Foreign investment in China is currently governed by the "Catalogue for Guiding Foreign Investment in Industries" and the Catalogue system is one of the most fundamental legal documents in the regulatory scheme of foreign investment in China.

The Catalogue is viewed as guidance from the PRC government to direct foreign investment and classified industry sectors into three categories, namely:

(i)   Encouraged,

(ii)   Restricted, and

(iii) Prohibited.

Foreign investments not falling within these categories are "Permitted."

The National Development and Reform Commission (NDRC) and Ministry of Commerce (MOFCOM) released the 2017 version of the *Catalogue for the Guidance of Foreign Investment Industries,* the seventh version of this regulatory tool. The Catalogue, which took effect in July 2017, introduces a national negative list to guide foreign investment, and cuts the number of special administrative measures restricting foreign investment.

Industries with foreign investment restrictions eased or removed in the new Catalogue include rail transportation equipment, motorcycles, new energy vehicle batteries, civil satellites, unconventional oil and gas development, and credit investigation and rating services. Additionally, a handful of high-tech industries, such as virtual reality (VR) and augmented reality (AR) devices, have been given special incentives to encourage foreign investment.

Although the new Catalogue opens a variety of new industries to foreign investment, several key industries such as banking and securities, healthcare, and telecommunications remain highly restricted, leading to ongoing criticism from the foreign business community over China's closed markets. However, while differences may remain in the treatment of domestic and foreign investments, those operating in the Catalogue's freshly opened sectors will find appealing new opportunities for investment.

The Negative List specifies the industries in which foreign investment is restricted or prohibited. Those falling under the "restricted" category are subject to restrictions such as shareholding limits and must receive prior approval from MOFCOM. Industries in the prohibited category are closed completely to foreign investment. For example, at the time of issuance foreign automobile companies were limited to 50% ownership with the requirement of a Chinese partner.

For any industry not listed on the Negative List, foreign investors are given equal treatment to domestic Chinese investors. Domestic investors still face restrictions in certain industries, like telecommunications and education but foreign firms are treated in a similar fashion. Although foreign investors do not require prior approval from MOFCOM in industries outside the list, they are still subject to record-filing requirements.

The Catalogue also has an "encouraged" category, which lists industries specifically encouraged for foreign investment. Encouraged industries benefit from special incentives, such as reduced tax rates. Encouraged industries can still be subject to certain restrictions on foreign investment if they are also on the negative list, however. For example, design, manufacturing, and repair of general-purpose airplanes is encouraged, but also restricted to joint ventures (JVs) with a Chinese partner entity.

The Negative List clarifies which industries need prior approval from MOFCOM. Previously, some industries under the "encouraged" category required MOFCOM approval but did not appear under the "restricted" category. Now, every industry that requires MOFCOM approval is clearly listed on the Negative List.

The easing of restrictions in emerging industries, such as blade energy, vehicle manufacturing and batteries for new energy vehicles is significant and could be a precursor to further liberalizations in China's automobile industry. Greater access for foreign accounting and auditing firms and credit investigation and rating services has also been long awaited and could provide China with more accurate risk assessments in its enormous debt market. Meanwhile, foreign investors can benefit from strong government support in emerging tech industries.

While the relaxations are welcomed by foreign investors, they are not as ambitious as many in the foreign business community have anticipated and the program has been criticized by the foreign Chambers of Commerce as falling short. Many of the relaxed industries are already dominated by domestic Chinese companies, such as rail transport technology and motorcycle manufacturing. Although several high-tech industries are encouraged, China's treatment of foreigners in these sectors can be controversial.

In 2018, the Negative List program was amended significantly for foreign automobile manufacturers. As noted, such companies previously were restricted to a 50% ownership and required to have a Chinese partner. That restriction was lifted and foreign companies producing electric vehicles can be wholly owned starting in 2019 and in 2022 for internal combustion vehicles. This change is, in part, a reaction to on-going trade and investment disputes.

Use of the Negative List is retained under China's 2020 Foreign Investment Law, discussed below.

§ 4.9   Preferential Trade and Investment Zones

Businesses are treated preferentially in China's Special Economic Zones (SEZs), Economic and Technological Development Zones (ETDZs), Free Trade Zones (FTZ) and selected "open" coastal cities. In these zones and cities, enterprises are granted preferences and subsidies concerning employment of workers, taxation, utilities, land use, export permits and such. Four rural SEZs were created in 1979.

Fourteen coastal cities the government hoped to industrialize with foreign capital were "opened" in 1984. In addition, thirteen ETDZs were authorized in 1985 and an additional SEZ, Hainan Island, was established in 1987. In 2013, the Shanghai Free Trade Zone was established with much publicity intended to become a "shining example of market reform," especially financial reform.

One of the most important of these areas is the Shenzhen SEZ in Guangdong Province located directly across the border from Hong Kong. This is where considerable growth and development within China's enterprise zones has taken place. Substantial investment and trading in Shenzhen comes from Hong Kong sources. The Hong Kong dollar is accepted as currency there.

There has also been a substantial surge in Taiwanese investment in the Xiamen SEZ in Fujian Province on the mainland just across from Quemoy. Smaller sums are being invested in the Zhuhai SEZ adjacent to Macao and the Shantou SEZ in Guangdong Province. Shenzhen and Zhuhai were set up as multipurpose zones incorporating a variety of economic activities such as industry, commerce, housing, agriculture, and tourism. Shantou and Xiamen were to focus on the processing of exports.

Some of the commerce in the zones is "compensation trade." As applied to the PRC, compensation trade refers principally to a contract whereby a foreigner supplies capital equipment (*e.g.*, textile machinery) which is paid for in installments with goods produced by that equipment. The great advantage of such contracts is their avoidance of foreign exchange and debt problems. A variation on the compensation trade theme involves "assembly operations." Here the foreigner supplies component parts (*e.g.*, electronics) processed or assembled in China for a fee.

In 2013 a large area of Shanghai's Pudong was designated as a Free Trade Zone (FTZ), again with the goal of recapturing some of the innovative approaches of the early SEZs. Foreign investors are faced with the Negative List Catalogue system (noted above), listing business activities that are encouraged, permitted, restricted, and prohibited for foreign investors. However, foreign investors in Free Trade Zones (FTZs) are permitted greater latitude. It is in Pudong that Elon Musk built a Tesla auto plant as a wholly owned subsidiary.

An example of the more permissive FTZ Negative List approach is its application to foreign law firms. The practice of law in China for foreign law firms has been a prohibited activity and the Chinese legal profession is open only to Chinese citizens who have passed the PRC judicial examination and satisfied certain other admission criteria. Under current rules, the right of individuals to practice as a lawyer is suspended if they work for a non-Chinese organization (*e.g.*, a non-Chinese owned law firm).

While there are many foreign law firms in China these firms are not allowed to opine on Chinese law and not allowed to formally represent clients in litigation. Because law firms are not on the Shanghai FTZ Negative List, Baker & McKenzie was able to form a Joint Operation arrangement with the Chinese law firm FenXun Partners to offer integrated service covering international and PRC law.

In theory, the PRC's preferential economic zones are to be used principally to attract foreign commerce and to serve as "bridges" for introducing foreign capital and advanced technology into the rest of China. In addition, they are classrooms for training Chinese personnel in management techniques and in the use of advanced technology. Deng Xiaoping referred to the Shenzhen SEZ as a "bold experiment" which he hoped would succeed but "if it fails, we can draw lessons from it." These words reflect the negative side of Shenzhen and other SEZs as they have become shopping and employment centers for well-connected Chinese.

For example, considerable Shenzhen SEZ production is sold to Chinese buyers, leading to a net outflow of money from the rest of the country to the SEZ. Shenzhen has succeeded in attracting domestic capital to purchase imported or SEZ consumer goods. A fence has been constructed to isolate Shenzhen from the rest of Guangdong Province. Hainan Island was so consumed with illegal trading of foreign goods and illegal currency exchanges that the Party leadership released details of multimillion dollar scandals involving local officials, including the People's Army and Navy.

Crackdowns followed, but the general pattern of opportunistic abuse of the zones by those with connections (*guanxi*) continues. Despite these and other problems with China's preferential zones, the Chinese government has re-endorsed its support for their continuation.

Investment, licensing, and trading in preferential PRC zones are subject to zone regulations. An early example was the Shenzhen SEZ Regulations for Foreign Economic Contracts (1984) issued by Guangdong Province. These regulations govern joint ventures, cooperative ventures, compensation trade, and assembly agreements in Shenzhen. The regulations require certain clauses for each type of SEZ contract, including dispute settlement clauses. The Guangdong government has also adopted Importation of Technology, Bankruptcy, and Shareholding Company Regulations for Shenzhen. Regulations of this type have often preceded national laws covering the same subjects.

The zones are not only economic experiments they are also legal experiments. Some of the lessons drawn from such experiments found their way into the Foreign Economic Contract Law of 1985 (FECL). For example, the Shenzhen contract regulations emphasize formalities, whereas the FECL did not. The Shenzhen regulations mandate that the Chinese language version of the contract govern. The FECL left that issue to the parties' choice.

The announcement in 2016 of the seven new FTZs signified an attempt by Chinese authorities to open China's lesser developed central and western regions to foreign investment. Each of these new FTZs aims to stimulate different aspects of the Chinese economy. The investment environments of China's FTZs—as testing grounds for new economic policies—can change rapidly as policies are developed and implemented. Indeed, President Xi Jinping called for a more coherent understanding of what each FTZ seeks to achieve, and more creativity in bringing about well-defined goals.

§ 4.10   Foreign Investment Options: Joint Ventures, Subsidiaries, and VIEs

Early in the post-Mao era China created three basic foreign direct investment options. These are equity joint ventures (EJVs), contractual joint ventures (partnerships, CJVs) and wholly owned foreign owned subsidiaries (WFOEs).

The form of the investment is often dictated by the business activity, that is, the Catalogue system may dictate whether there must be a Chinese partner or whether the foreign investor may own the entity. Separate laws govern each of these three structures, which collectively are referred to as foreign invested enterprises (FIEs).

All FIEs are subject to a strict regulatory regime, built on a case-by-case approval system if the activity is on the Negative List. In practice, this means that both the establishment of an FIE and any subsequent material changes—capital increase or reduction, amendment of articles of association, mergers, and acquisitions, etc.—require prior government approval, regardless of the FIE's size, nature, or industry. FIE regulations are currently scattered and sometimes inconsistent. Each investment option is discussed below along with its governing law and implementing regulations.

Variable Investment Entities (VIEs)

An important consideration is whether to utilize a Variable Investment Entity (VIE) to circumvent foreign investment regulatory controls. VIEs involve setting up a WFOE which contracts with a Chinese-owned VIE operating company (often shell companies in a tax haven) that invests in sectors where foreign ownership is restricted. The contracts give the WFOE effective control of the operating company, but not ownership. Amazon, CBS, Pearson, and others are said to operate in China under VIEs.

The most visible use of the VIE structure was the Alibaba IPO on the New York stock exchange in 2014, the largest IPO in history. In its filing with the US Securities and Exchange Commission, Alibaba stated that the licenses to operate various websites in China are held by VIEs that are 100% owned by Chinese citizens and are not owned by the Alibaba filing for the IPO. The licenses the VIEs hold are critical to its business and its contracts with the vehicles "give us effective control over each" of the VIEs. Alibaba relies on VIE equity holders to perform their contractual obligations to the company.

Chinese companies must adopt the VIE structure if they want to list overseas and comply with the letter of Chinese regulations. Some 200 Chinese companies are listed on U.S. stock exchanges. The uncertainty is obvious in an environment of constantly changing regulations. By 2022, the China had made it clear that Chinese companies listed outside the PRC remain subject to its national security, data security (new 2021 law) and foreign investment rules.

The controversy surrounding the VIE model stems from significant legal risks inherent in its structure. No Chinese regulatory body has officially approved a VIE structure and controls have tightened over VIE structured candidates wishing to list on the Hong Kong Stock Exchange. In recent years there have been several challenges by regulators based on allegations that VIE structures were used to circumvent industry investment regulations and restrictions.

In 2021, the SEC commenced an investigation into VIEs related to U.S. listed Chinese firms. It is said that some such firms have failed to remit profits generated by their VIEs.

§ 4.11   Foreign Investment Law 2020

A draft of a new Foreign Investment Law containing 1700 Articles was released for public comment in 2015. This Draft Law suggested consolidated coverage of Chinese investment options into one law, and abandonment of the case-by-case approval system for foreign investments not on the Negative List of prohibited and restricted sectors. Use of viable interest entities (VIEs) to circumvent foreign investment regulatory controls would possibly be circumscribed.

In 2019, the PRC adopted a new Foreign Investment Law with only 170 Articles, effective in 2020 (FIL 2020). Its coverage extends to investments from Hong Kong, Macau, and Taiwan. *After five years,* this Law eliminates the traditional three foreign investment categories in favor of an omnibus legal regime retaining the Negative List system outlined above. The FIL 2020 removed the requirement that the PRC Ministry of Commerce (MOFCOM) approve the investment.

While there is broad language emphasizing equal treatment for FIEs under Chinese law and procedures (including expropriation), the language of FIL 2020 is opaque, leaving plenty of room for local authorities to construe it differently. Certainly, the new Law will need to be filled by detailed implementing guidelines and regulations. One particularly opaque area is the new Law's coverage (if any) of VIEs.

Under pressure from the Trump administration, FIL 2020 explicitly bars forced technology transfers and the theft of IP and commercial secrets. Foreign firms have longed complained that officials conducting Chinese law conformity assessments and security reviews frequently pass along technology and secrets to local competitors. The new Law indicates that officials who use administrative measures to violate FIL 2020 rules can be criminally prosecuted. However, national security (a broad concept in China) can override the Law.

An excerpt from the FIL 2020 appears at the end of this chapter.

§ 4.12 *Guanxi* Trading and Investing

There is a difference between PRC trade and investment law on the books and in operation. This difference is most evident in the practice known as "trading or investing through the back door." Such practices constitute a return to the venerable *guanxi* system of private "relationships." The *guanxi* system breeds corruption, inefficiency, and illegal behavior. Some instructive examples of trading and investing through the back door are given by Walter Keats writing in the *China Business Review*:

> How does *guanxi* manifest itself today in China trade? It can be seen in high officials who pass the word to favor certain vendors with whom they have a special "relationship." It reveals itself in the way some overseas Chinese agents represent Chinese units that are perfectly capable of dealing with foreign companies on their own— simply because the agent has a "relationship" with one of the Chinese officials. It can be seen in the willingness of officials in Guangdong Province to permit the import of agricultural material in violation of Chinese quarantine restrictions because of their "relationship" with the vendor or vendor's agent.
>
> Sometimes the price asked in exchange for buying your product or service is sponsoring an official's child to attend college overseas. Or a foreign business partner may be asked not only to invite certain officials in his country but expected to give them special favors including "gifts", such as stereos, TVs, washing machines, refrigerators, cars and even money. All too often, the abuses are even more blatant. A financial official may delay approval of a contract or letter-of-credit until he or she is invited to join a delegation going overseas. Or a visiting delegation may demand that each of its members receive a percentage of the value of a contract in US dollars. And worst of all for China, certain projects receive approval or foreign exchange allocations based on who knows whom, not the true merits of the project.

Guanxi practices, combined with the cumbersome bureaucracy the Chinese have been cultivating for generations, create major problems for foreigners (particularly United States attorneys and executives who face severe penalties under the U.S. Foreign Corrupt Practices Act). *Guanxi* practices challenge the very idea of a rule of Chinese law governing trade and investment relations. Much of the progress represented by the PRC investment laws could be undermined if *guanxi,* not law, prevails.

§ 4.13 Equity Joint Ventures

The first major step taken by the Chinese to open their economy to foreign investors was the passage of joint venture legislation in 1979. The Law on Joint Ventures Using Chinese and Foreign Investment ("JVL") and its successors allows joint ventures, known as "equity joint ventures," to be established between foreign corporations and Chinese enterprises. The JVL is accompanied by its own income tax law and implementing regulations. Equity joint ventures must be approved by the central government.

Prior to 1988, this power had been increasingly delegated to local government organizations. Such delegation was part of the general trend toward decentralization of economic controls in China, a trend reversed as the government's central planners get a stronger grip on foreign investment decisions.

The most distinguishing features of Chinese law on equity joint ventures have traditionally been:

- 10- to 30-year terms

- Profit and risk sharing proportionate to share capital

- Limited access to sales in the Chinese market

- Arbitration of labor disputes

- Non-negotiable shareholdings

- Regulated debt-equity ratios

- Flexibility in terms of types of capital contributions (technology included)—25% foreign capital minimum

- Priority to Chinese sources of materials

- Foreign currency account must be balanced, including remission of profits

- Foreigners could not (prior to 1990) serve as chairs of boards of directors

- 33% maximum tax rate

Amendments to the Equity Joint Ventures Law were adopted in 1990 that reduced the differences between it and the Contractual Joint Ventures Law (*infra*). No "nationalization" may take place. But any "requisition. . .when the public interest requires" is subject to a duty to pay "appropriate compensation." One suspects that the difference between "nationalizations" and "requisitions" may be lost on foreign partners to PRC joint ventures.

Foreigners may now serve as chairs of the board of directors. Joint ventures may run beyond their original term with special permission and may bank at any approved foreign exchange institution.

Equity joint ventures, as the oldest form of foreign investment in the PRC, have the longest track record. Partly because of the early adoption of the JVL and the legal security it created equity joint ventures became the most popular Chinese investment vehicle of multinational corporations. Thousands of well-known firms have agreed to equity ventures in the PRC. One can find the label "Made in The People's Republic of China" on such diverse products as Camel cigarettes, Nike shoes, Kodak film, Otis elevators, Jeep trucks, Xerox copiers, Singer sewing machines and Heinz baby foods.

Within the limits of the JVL and its implementing regulations and taking into consideration the model contracts the Chinese have developed, the terms of these joint ventures are negotiable. The regulated nature of joint venture investments in China often requires that local government representatives be brought into the negotiations. Although various central investment authorities will be involved, local officials typically hold important keys to approval of the venture, and most critically, its successful operation in the future. They will for example heavily influence such variables as taxation, labor supply, utilities, land use permits and the like.

The equity joint venture bargain thus determines much of its future viability. As many foreign investors have discovered, reaching agreement is just the beginning of an equity venture in the PRC. The Chinese often perceive that the agreement merely provides a framework within which negotiations are ongoing. Foreign investors tend to be less flexible and are more likely to want to stick to the terms of the deal and accompanying government representations. These differing perspectives frequently produce disputes.

In addition, the PRC is simply a difficult place to invest. The abruptness of the change in China's investment outlook and laws since the Cultural Revolution has left some uneven edges. Governmental interference with joint ventures is common, quality control problems with inputs and outputs endemic, the necessary infrastructure, managerial talent, skilled labor, and hard currency absent, and so on.

Repatriating profits (if there are any) is an art form. Government credit squeezes, combined with rising inflation and corruption, remain particularly painful to many joint ventures.

Government insistence since 1989 upon adding a Communist Party member responsible for Party organization and loyalty to the management team at joint ventures has increased the discomfort level of foreign investors. When these general "environmental" difficulties are combined with differing contract perspectives, it is not surprising that serious disruptions can occur. To borrow a Chinese saying, the joint venture partners may be in the "same bed, with different dreams".

§ 4.14 Problems at the Jeep Joint Venture

One of the most publicized disruptions was that of the highly favored American Motors Corporation (now owned by Chrysler/Fiat) "model" equity joint venture in Beijing. It is representative of the problems encountered by many other investors in the People's Republic of China. This excerpt appeared in a 1986 edition of the *Shanghai World Economic Herald*:

> The original contract called for the Chinese and American sides to jointly design a new jeep using only Chinese components. However, according to the Beijing Review, 'after several months of work by Chinese and American engineers . . . it was found that the vehicle designed was defective in such areas as its exhaust system, noise, visibility, and speed, none of which could match international standards . . . AMC suggested that the idea of joint design be postponed . . . The Chinese, however, took AMC's suggestions as a symbol of the Americans' unwillingness to cooperate on a jointly designed vehicle and . . . of AMC's desire to control China's market.' Ultimately, the Chinese agreed to build AMC's XJ model series, including the Cherokee jeep, using imported components— but clearly in a suspicion-marred environment that foreshadowed the more serious troubles that arose later.
>
> . . .
>
> In mid-1985 the Beijing International Trust and Investment Corporation—an arm of the Beijing city government—reportedly loaned the venture $8.5 million to buy equipment for a new Cherokee jeep assembly line and to import kits. At that time, AMC chipped in an additional $6 million for the assembly line. But recent indications are that the loan was made under the assumption that the vehicles could be sold to end-users in China for foreign exchange. Since December 1985, these end-users have proven unwilling or unable to buy the vehicles with foreign exchange—chiefly because foreign exchange allocations to

enterprises have been slashed across the board, but perhaps also because a 60 percent duty on imported parts makes the Beijing price considerably higher than the North American price. During the first part of 1986, local authorities were unwilling to renew foreign exchange allocations or loans to the venture, since the venture's expected foreign exchange earnings were not forthcoming.

This forced a major showdown in which AMC allowed its grievances to leak into American newspapers and, according to numerous reports, threatened to pull out of the venture. The gesture aroused enough high-level concern in China to guarantee the venture renewed foreign exchange for kit purchases, at least for the time being. According to Chinese press reports, the central government has offered $2 million for jeeps already assembled, in addition to an unspecified amount for further kit imports. But the venture's Cherokee jeep production will almost certainly fall well short of the earlier 4000-unit target.

. . .

The Chinese argue that AMC should also take some responsibility for maintaining the venture's foreign exchange flow. And a number of foreign observers point out that AMC's initial cash contribution—$8 million—was very small in relation to its goal of building an export-quality jeep in China. The corporation has apparently agreed to increase equipment supplies to the joint venture as part of the settlement of the foreign exchange dispute.

Despite such obstacles, foreign firms continue to invest in the PRC in record numbers. Surprisingly, many of these investments are *not* covered by political risk insurance against expropriation, civil unrest, and other such contingencies. See Chapter 3. United States' investors, for example, have channeled billions into uninsured Chinese equity joint ventures. This response may have more to do with evaluations of China's market potential than its investment laws. Nevertheless, the sustained, substantial effort on the part of PRC lawmakers to improve the legal environment within which equity joint ventures function is noteworthy.

§ 4.15 Wholly Foreign Owned Subsidiaries

Joint ventures with foreign investors are often found in developing countries like the PRC. Such joint ventures were reasonably common in Eastern Europe before the Iron Curtain came down and were permitted in the former Soviet Union. There is a sense therefore in which China's 1979 equity joint venture law was merely catching up to world trends. The 1986 law allowing wholly foreign owned enterprises (WFOEs) was another matter. With this law, China leaped ahead of other socialist countries and many developing nations as well. WFOEs are indicative of just how open and embracing the country can be to foreign investment.

Beginning in 1980, wholly owned enterprises were allowed in a few preferential economic zones, such as the Shenzhen near Hong Kong. These were often small companies established in Shenzhen by Hong Kong Chinese. Success with this experiment led, in 1983, to the designation of coastal cities where wholly foreign owned enterprises could be established. The first wholly owned enterprise outside a SEZ was that of 3M in Shanghai. For 3M in China, the need to balance foreign exchange receipts, uncertainty over applicable tax law, and labor relations proved troublesome.

From the Chinese perspective, the march forward was not to be denied. In 1986, a general law was passed permitting WFOEs *anywhere* in the PRC. WFOEs can also be used by foreigners with more than one investment in the PRC to unite the management and operations of those enterprises.

The Law on Wholly Foreign-Owned Enterprises and its implementing regulations (particularly those issued in 1990) and their successors create the most restrictive of all the PRC's foreign investment rules. These rules reflect caution and concern about total foreign ownership of enterprises located in China. The main legal features of the law on WFOEs have been as follows:

- Foreigners may serve as chairs of boards of directors
- Importation of advanced technology and equipment and substantial exportation of products (these rules have recently been relaxed)
- Protection of investment, profits, and other rights "under Chinese law"
- Expropriation in "special circumstances," with "commensurate compensation"
- "For the record" submission of production and operational plans to the government—noninterference is to be the rule
- Chinese tax and financial supervision, 50% maximum tax
- Chinese insurance required

- Priority to local sourcing if terms are competitive with international market

- Foreign exchange account must be balanced

- Mandatory trade union facilities

- General supervision by approving authorities

To some extent, the restrictive terms of Chinese law on WFOEs have deterred multinational foreign investors. In general, their preference for equity joint ventures is primarily based upon a desire to have a Chinese partner escort them through the bureaucratic and political maze that foreign investors encounter. Lately, however, the "carrying costs" of a Chinese partner and growing familiarity with doing business in China has led many foreign investors to switch to WFOEs.

§ 4.16 Contractual Joint Ventures (Partnerships)

Hong Kong, Overseas Chinese and other foreign investors have often preferred "contractual joint ventures." Historically, this has been a less regulated form of doing business in China. Such enterprises (many of them hotel investments) have been established since the Cultural Revolution. Because there are no equity shares, contractual joint ventures resemble partnership agreements. Prior to 1988 a principal attraction of such agreements was the *absence* of a basic law governing them. Even after the adoption in 1988 of a contractual joint venture law, flexibility is still their chief attraction.

The Chinese are shrewd trade negotiators, as many a foreign executive has learned the hard way. They deal from a fundamentally different perspective on time and its value. To them, quite literally, time is not money, and they exploit the advantages of delay in negotiations. In addition, the Chinese often deliberately cultivate a sense of friendship and obligation in their negotiating opposites, relationships that can promote guilt or dependence to their advantage. Many a foreign trader or investor has been "shamed" into a contract term it later regrets.

Fundamental cultural clashes about the meaning of a contract can also serve to undermine the significance of concluding a China trade agreement. For many foreigners, the signing of a contract culminates the negotiations—they have a deal. The terms of the deal are found strictly within the four corners of the agreement. To many Chinese, the same event merely signals that the two parties have established "a relationship," one that allows either to call upon the other for tolerance, flexibility, and favors.

Much to the surprise of foreign parties, these calls often run counter to the very heart of their hard-won agreement. They find themselves involved in endless rounds of frustrating negotiations. They get worn down, tired of losing money and skeptical of the wisdom of doing business in China. Some pull out, but many hang on—waiting for that pot of gold that surely must be at the end of their Chinese rainbow.

Many Chinese companies have developed standardized international contracts with which they usually commence negotiations and from which they are often unwilling to deviate significantly. Use of standard form contracts provides uniformity of terms and perhaps more importantly, security for the Chinese negotiators. Deviations from the standard form run the risk of sanctions later should the deal turn sour

The 1988 Law on Chinese-Foreign Contractual Joint Ventures (CJV) and its successors were promulgated after years of experience with cooperative enterprise agreements. Viewed together with the 1986 General Principles of Civil Law, the most notable features of the law on CJVs have been as follows:

- Any split of profits may be chosen
- Limited liability is available to CJVs qualifying as legal persons under the Civil Law
- Protection of the rights and interests of the CJV and its parties "according to the law"
- Noninterference with operational and managerial decisions
- Trade unions required
- Balance in foreign exchange receipts required, subject to state assistance
- No minimum percentage of foreign capital
- Foreigners may serve as chairs of boards of directors
- No limit on duration of contractual agreement

Contractual joint ventures are the principal form of small business investment in the PRC. Until 1986, they easily outnumbered equity joint ventures. The return of sovereignty over Hong Kong and Macao by the end of the century caused Chinese investors from those cities to want to be on friendly terms with the mainland. The most common means for such investments is the CJV.

§ 4.17 Mergers and Acquisitions

Another avenue available to foreign investors for China market entry is to acquire existing businesses in China. China has a sophisticated regulatory framework for mergers and acquisitions involving foreign investors and the primary governing legislation is the Regulations on the Merger and Acquisition of Domestic Enterprises by Foreign Investors ('Foreign M&A Regulations') which is supplemented by a number of departmental rules governing specific industries or target groups.

Like Permitted Activities for initial or "greenfield" investors, those seeking to acquire Chinese companies are subject to foreign investment Negative List restrictions noted above. The classifications set forth in the Catalogue affect the maximum percentage of foreign ownership allowed, as well as the level of Chinese government authorities from which approvals would be required.

The Foreign M&A Regulations also introduced the concepts of "industries affecting national economic security" and "companies owning well-known trademarks and old Chinese trade names," a change of control in which will require approval from central MOFCOM regardless of the transaction value. The level of the approval authorities is determined in other cases by the transaction value, or the total investment amount set for the target entity.

The State Council and MOFCOM issued regulations in 2011 fleshing out a national security review procedure already referred to in general terms in the Foreign M&A Regulations. A joint committee led by NDRC and MOFCOM is responsible for carrying out a review to determine whether a transaction will have a major impact on national security and if that impact cannot be mitigated the transaction will not be permitted to go forward.

A filing is required if the acquisition would give a foreign investor actual control of a domestic defense enterprise, or a non-defense enterprise which (1) has a bearing on national security and (2) involves industries such as major agricultural products, major energy sources and resources, major infrastructure facilities, major transportation services, key technologies, and the manufacture of major equipment. The determination of when such a filing must be made can be problematic as there is no "bright-line" standard and the consequences for not seeking approval are substantial.

In a manner similar in other jurisdictions, potential acquirers have strategic reasons for structuring a transaction either as acquisition of equity or assets. A foreign investor can acquire equity in a wholly Chinese-owned enterprise and convert it into a foreign-invested enterprise or, when acquiring assets, the investors will first establish its own FIE. There are some requirements equally applicable to both equity and asset acquisitions. For instance, the parties are required to have the value of the equity appraised before transfer. In the approval process, prices considerably lower than the appraisal result are not permitted.

Asset acquisitions may have some advantages over equity acquisitions as the buyer can pick and choose which parts of the company it wishes to buy. Much like other jurisdictions, existing obligations, liabilities, or restrictions will remain the sole responsibility of the acquired company. PRC laws recognize two forms of merger: "merger by absorption" and "merger by new establishment." A "merger by absorption" involves the absorption by one company of another pursuant to which the absorbed company is dissolved, and its registered capital and assets merged into the surviving entity. In a "merger by new establishment," each of the pre-merger companies is dissolved and a new company established holding an aggregate of the pre-merger companies' assets and registered capital. As a practical matter, mergers are rare, acquisitions common.

Due Diligence and Approvals

By far the biggest issue for foreign investors in attempting a PRC acquisition is that of due diligence. Transparency is not the norm and opacity reigns in areas of business operations subject to review. There is no better illustration of the difficulty of due diligence and the following disastrous outcome than that of Caterpillar Inc's $677 million purchase of ERA Mining Machinery Ltd. ERA was the holding company for Zhengzhou Siwei Mechanical & Electrical Equipment Manufacturing Co Ltd, one of China's biggest makers of hydraulic coal-mine roof supports. Siwei would help Caterpillar gain traction in the world's largest coal industry.

While the transaction was feted as the "Deal of the Year" for 2012, Caterpillar announced on January 18, 2013, that it had discovered "deliberate, multi-year, coordinated accounting misconduct" at Siwei in January 2013. Thereafter, Caterpillar took a non-cash goodwill impairment charge of $580 million—86% of the value of the deal. The company says it was caught unaware by the problems at Siwei and only discovered them in November 2012, five months after the deal closed.

An Anti-Monopoly Law emerged in 2008. Coca-Cola's attempted acquisition of a leading Chinese soft drinks company was blocked under this law in 2009. Microsoft's acquisition of Nokia in 2013 was delayed by Chinese authorities fearing IP losses. The merger of global mining giants Glencore and Xstrata was conditioned upon sale of a Peruvian mine that was quickly purchased by a consortium of state-owned Chinese firms. Chinese regulators may require the maintenance of prices post-merger, market exclusivity, and "hold separate" delays for the merging parties, all to the benefit of Chinese competitors.

In the Trump era, China increased its review of mergers and acquisitions to stall or block M&A investments. For example, China asserted its anti-monopoly regulatory power in denying approval to the U.S. company Qualcomm. Qualcomm, which receives approximately 2/3 of its revenue from China, received a disapproval for its proposed purchase of the Dutch tech company NXP—this notwithstanding that Qualcomm had secured permission from the eight other major antitrust regulators around the world. It is unclear whether this disapproval was for competition reasons or retaliation in connection with U.S.-China trade disputes noted below.

§ 4.18   Dispute Resolution

The best laid plans of foreign investors often go awry for terms and items not considered or actors not considerate. Related closely to the Rule of Law issue is the need for a consistent and transparent system to resolve inevitable disputes. While China has made advancement in this area there remains suspicion by foreign investors whether disputes can be fairly resolved notwithstanding their foreign status.

While conducting business in China, foreign companies occasionally find themselves embroiled in disputes with Chinese individuals, companies, or even the Chinese Government Like in many other jurisdictions, litigation, and Alternative Dispute Resolution (ADR) (negotiation, mediation, and arbitration) are the main methods to settle commercial disputes. *Mediation and arbitration are the most popular dispute resolution method among foreign firms that conduct business in China or with Chinese parties.*

Friendly Consultations, Mediation

Simple negotiation with your partner, which the Chinese will insist upon and call "friendly consultations," is usually the best method of dispute resolution. It is the least expensive and it can preserve the working relationship of the parties involved. Many business contracts in China include a clause stipulating that negotiation should be employed before other dispute settlement mechanisms are pursued. When a foreign firm has difficulty directly negotiating a solution to a dispute with its Chinese partner, companies sometimes seek assistance from Chinese government officials who can encourage the Chinese party to honor the terms of the contract. Unfortunately, negotiations do not always lead to resolution.

Another option is mediation. The principle of mediation is that the parties may present their proposals to the mediator (the Chinese prefer joint mediation with each side selecting a mediator) who suggests a solution based on those proposals. Mediation is non-binding and has substantial success as a means of settling commercial disputes between foreign and Chinese parties. In both the arbitration and litigation contexts, mediation represents an early step in the resolution of the dispute.

Whether in arbitration or in litigation before the Chinese courts, parties are encouraged to participate in mediation with mediators selected by the panel or during an in-court session. The less confrontational nature of mediation may also help preserve the commercial relationship.

Arbitration

Arbitration is considered confrontational and is a less preferred method of dispute resolution in China. Since it is rare for the parties to agree on arbitration after the dispute has arisen, the underlying contract or separate agreement must expressly provide that disputes will be resolved through arbitration. In China, a valid arbitration agreement must reflect a clear intent to arbitrate and clearly identify the arbitration institute that will administer the case. If so, arbitration will be the only available binding means of dispute resolution available under the contract; otherwise, the dispute must be resolved by the courts.

There are important differences in arbitration in China versus arbitration in other countries. For example, ad hoc arbitration is not recognized in Chinese law when it takes place within China. Rather, arbitration may be conducted only by officially recognized arbitration institutions. As a result, parties selecting China as their arbitration location will be constrained in their choice of applicable procedural and substantive rules, and, if an arbitration is necessary, will be required to choose arbitrators from lists maintained by the arbitration institution they select.

In China, arbitration offers many advantages over litigation. A major advantage is the finality of the rulings. Court rulings are subject to appeal, which means litigation may continue for years. Judges in China are often poorly qualified, while arbitration panels are made up of a panel of experts, which improves the quality of the hearing. In addition, the proceedings and rules of arbitration are often more transparent than litigation.

CIETAC et al.

The best-known arbitration institution originally designated to hear "foreign-related" disputes is the China International Economic and Trade Arbitration Commission (CIETAC). Chinese arbitration institutions were traditionally divisible into those handling "foreign related" disputes and those handling purely domestic disputes. "Foreign-related" disputes are those in which at least one party is a foreign person or entity, the contract was formed, modified or terminated in a country other than China, or the object of the action is in a foreign country. Note that a foreign-invested enterprise (FIE) in China is not a foreign entity for these purposes, and as an organization established under Chinese law, it is considered a domestic entity.

In addition to CIETAC, there are over 140 local arbitration commissions that have been established in most major cities, including Beijing, Shanghai, Guangzhou, and Shenzhen. Originally designed to hear purely domestic disputes only, these commissions hear "foreign-related" disputes as well. The most active of these in "foreign-related" arbitration is Beijing Arbitration Commission (BAC).

While the local arbitration commissions are in principle civil institutions and not government units, they remain closely tied to government in several ways, including financing and personnel appointments. Despite initial misgivings in the foreign investment community about the quality of arbitration by local commissions as opposed to CIETAC, experience thus far indicates that at least some commissions, such as the BAC, are performing better than expected.

There is the contractual option to specify international arbitration and utilize the services of institutions such as ICC, the Hong Kong International Arbitration Center (HKIAC), the Singapore International Arbitration Centre and the American Arbitration Association (AAA) among others. They provide an international alternative to Chinese arbitration at CIETAC or the local commissions.

Convincing a Chinese party to agree to offshore arbitration, however, may be difficult at best. Early on Danone obtained agreement with its Chinese equity joint venture partner to arbitrate disputes before the Stockholm Chamber of Commerce. Taking a dispute to that tribunal resulted in a settlement that caused Danone to give up its China investment, a source of over 5% of its worldwide profits.

Award Enforcement

Moreover, gaining a Chinese party's participation in an offshore arbitration is also problematic because of actual or perceived foreign travel restrictions or other concerns. One of the most frequently cited difficulties of arbitration in China is enforcement. Once a domestic arbitral award is issued, securing payment is beyond the powers of the arbitration commission. As a result, the prevailing party most often must apply to a court to have the award recognized and enforced. Foreign awards that are not paid voluntarily also may be filed with a court to compel enforcement.

Because China has acceded to the 1958 UN Convention on Recognition and Enforcement of Foreign Arbitral Awards, commonly referred to as the New York Convention, CIETAC and local commission awards are enforceable in other signatory countries based on reciprocity. While in principle the same should apply in China, in practice, enforcement is problematic. CIETAC and local commission awards are not enforceable in China under the New York Convention, but rather under Article 260 of China's own Civil Procedure Law, which, much like the New York Convention, allows courts to refuse enforcement only for a limited number of procedural reasons.

Arbitral enforcement in Chinese courts is complicated by the same factors that make parties unwilling to litigate disputes in these same courts. Court officials often lack sufficient legal training and, according to reports, inadequate training has led to delays of more than one year in accepting or processing an application for arbitral enforcement. Local protectionism, the influence of party officials, lack of professional ethics, and inadequate authority may complicate enforcement even when the staff is well-trained.

Litigation

A final way to resolve a business dispute in China is through litigation in Chinese courts. In China, foreign individuals and companies have the same ability to bring action in court as Chinese citizens and companies. There are four levels of courts in China. Every major city has basic courts and intermediate courts. Supervising these courts are the provincial high courts. The Supreme People's Court, located in Beijing, has appellate jurisdiction over all courts in China. Cases involving foreign interests can be filed in either the basic-level courts or intermediate courts, depending on their nature.

Most observers agree that Chinese courts are not up to international standards. For instance, most judges have minimal legal training and observers have stated those poorly trained court officials are susceptible to corruption and regional protectionism. Also, courts are funded by local governments, undermining their independence. Their activities are actively monitored, and outcomes are sometimes directed by the Party. President Xi Jinping has openly stated that China will not embrace principles of judicial independence.

§ 4.19   PRC Intellectual Property Law

China's legal framework for the protection of intellectual property is comprehensive, but the challenge is for China to enforce the legislation effectively and transparently. The complaints from foreign investors in this area are universal and ongoing. China is a member of the WTO and consequently a party to all major intellectual property conventions of the organization, as well as others, including the Paris Convention, Patent Cooperation Treaty, Berne Convention, Universal Copyright Convention, Geneva Convention and Madrid Agreement on International Registration of Marks.

Patents

The Patent Law of the People's Republic of China (the "Patent Law") was amended in 2008. The revision came into effect on October 1, 2009, and was supplemented in 2010 with revised Implementing Regulations (the "Implementing Regulations

There are three types of PRC patents: Patents for inventions of 20 years duration from the application filing date; patents for utility models of 10 years duration; and design patents of 10 years duration. The system is compliant with the WTO Agreement on Trade-Related Aspects of Intellectual Property Rights ("TRIPs Agreement"). China has adopted a "first-to-file" rather than "first-to-invent" system and foreign applicants are required to submit patent applications in China through an officially designated patent agent.

Trademarks

The Trademark Law of the People's Republic of China (the "Trademark Law") was amended for the third time in 2014. Revisions to the Implementing Regulations of the Trademark Law (the "Implementing Regulations") were issued. A trademark registration is valid for 10 years from the final date of approval (i.e., upon expiration of the three-month opposition period or, for international trademark registrations extended to the PRC under the Madrid Agreement or the Madrid Protocol, the date of filing), with further 10-year renewal terms available.

The law imposes a strict first-to-file rule for obtaining trademark rights, whereby the first party to file for registration of a mark pre-empts later applicants. Prior use of an unregistered mark is generally irrelevant for trademark registration purposes, unless the prior mark in question is a well-known mark, or the later filing is a bad-faith pre-emption of the prior mark that has achieved a certain degree of fame through use.

Copyright

The Copyright Law of the People's Republic of China (the "Copyright Law") was amended in 2001 and again in 2010, followed by Implementing Regulations. The 2010 Amendment was in response to a 2009 WTO dispute and attempts to confirm that "illegal" works can obtain copyright protection.

The current Copyright Law introduces protection for (1) written works, (2) oral works, (3) musical, dramatic, Chinese folk art, choreographic and acrobatic works, (4) works of fine art and architectural works, (5) photographic works, (6) cinematographic works, (7) graphic works, (8) model works and (9) computer software. The Copyright Law does not protect databases, i.e., collections of original information that do not qualify for copyright protection. However, if the means of compilation satisfies the requirement of originality, then such compilation can be protected.

Under the Copyright Law, an author's moral rights of attribution, revision and integrity are perpetual. A citizen's right of publication and the various economic rights are protected for the duration of the life of the author plus 50 years. For works of a legal person or other organization or works for hire vested in a legal person or other organization, as well as for photographic works and cinematographic works, the right of publication and other economic rights are protected for a period of 50 years from the date of first publication. Registration is not a precondition to copyright enforcement but can provide prima facie evidence of ownership in enforcement actions.

Trade Secrets

A trade secret is defined in both the Law of the PRC against Unfair Competition ("Unfair Competition Law") and the PRC Criminal Code as technical and business information that is private, able to bring economic benefits to the rightful party, is practical, and for which that party has adopted measures to maintain its confidentiality. A non-exhaustive list of measures to maintain confidentiality is set forth in the Several Provisions on the Prohibition of Acts of Infringement of Trade Secrets (the "Trade Secrets Provisions"), effective from November 23, 1995, and amended on December 3, 1998.

Such measures include disclosing secrets on a need-to-know basis only, adopting physical preventive measures such as locking, marking information "confidential," requiring access codes and passwords, and requiring confidentiality agreements.

Trade secrets are protected under the Unfair Competition Law. Under that legislation, business operators are prohibited from infringing upon commercial secrets by obtaining the commercial secrets of others by theft, inducement, coercion, or other illicit means. Also prohibited is the revealing, using, or allowing others to use commercial secrets obtained by such means or possessed by violation of agreements or other requests for confidentiality by the owners concerned. If a third party knows or should have known of such acts violating the law, but obtains, uses, or reveals commercial secrets of others, this will also constitute infringement.

Under a Supreme People's Court Interpretation on intellectual property crimes issued in 2004, the infringement of a trade secret causing loss of more than RMB 500,000 is regarded as serious and will trigger criminal prosecution under the PRC Criminal Code.

§ 4.20   Technology Transfers to the PRC

Major changes have been undertaken in the licensing and intellectual property law of the People's Republic of China since the Cultural Revolution. These changes reflect China's desire to create a modern economy by importing technology and by fostering its development. According to a report issued by central authorities in Beijing, the importation of technology augments China's modernization program in four ways:

(1)   By decreasing the gap on product quality and standards between China and the developed world;

(2)   By helping to promote the technological upgrading of Chinese enterprises;

(3)   By enhancing the ability of Chinese enterprises to independently develop their own new products and technology; and

(4)   By improving enterprise management.

China's desire to modernize its economy through technological imports is most evident in PRC patent and licensing law. A host of technology import regulations authorizing license agreements with foreign sources has been enacted. These regulations are not a blank check permitting technology importation at any cost. Rather, they are carefully constructed rules intended to promote technology transfers to China under acceptable terms and conditions.

Forced technology transfers are the subject of the on-going dispute between the U.S. and China wherein many companies are required to provide technology to their Chinese partners or state regulators. See Trump and China below. The resolution of this issue will be critical to the success of many foreign companies in the Peoples Republic.

§ 4.21 Technology Piracy in the PRC

Despite the adoption of major PRC patent, trademark, copyright, and technology transfer laws and their implementing regulations, a dark shadow hangs over much of Chinese intellectual property practice. Counterfeiting of goods and unlicensed use of technology is approaching epidemic proportions. Computer software is perhaps the most prominent victim. The official remedies discussed below, however diligently applied, seem inadequate to the task of dealing with this problem. Partly, one suspects, there are cultural forces at work. To copy another's work is traditionally a compliment in China.

Partly also, the economics of development fuel piracy in the PRC. It is simply much less expensive to "borrow" from foreigners and (increasingly) domestic entities whatever can be reverse-engineered and imitated. Even "Beijing Jeeps" have reportedly been knocked off by township enterprises.

Responding to domestic and foreign criticism about piracy, the PRC created a new Supreme People's Court IP Tribunal. This Tribunal reviews *all* lower court IP decisions, and remedies, under speedy procedures with livestream transparency. Remarkable! And IP owners, foreign and domestic, are often prevailing over local court bias and protectionism.

Although there have been advances in protection of intellectual property and foreigners have successfully availed themselves of Chinese courts, the PRC has long been a hostile environment for intellectual property. Foreign investors in the PRC take serious piracy risks. China is by far the number one source of counterfeit goods entering the USA. See my *International Trade Beyond Trump* Concise Hornbook, Chapter 8. In this area, Chinese law will likely take time to mature.

§ 4.22 Made in China 2025

China is already a major technology leader. It has, for example, more supercomputing power than the USA. It is ahead in the production of drones for consumers, possesses huge online innovators (Alibaba, Tencent, Baidu), leads the world in mobile payments systems (We-Chat Pay, Alipay), and has outstanding facial recognition systems. China exports high-speed rail systems (which can be found all over the PRC), has developed nuclear power plants in China and other countries, and now attracts more high-tech venture capital than Silicon Valley.

The PRC "Made in China 2025" program seeks to make China a global leader in strategic manufacturing and technology industries, specifically:

- Aviation and Aerospace
- Agriculture
- Electrical Power
- New Energy Automotive
- High-End Robotics
- Next Gen Information Technology
- New Materials & Composites
- Rail Transportation
- Maritime Engineering
- Biomedical & Advanced Medical Equipment

Made in China 2025 focuses on developing semiconductors, advanced machine tools, medical devices, biopharma, aerospace and aeronautics, advanced information technology, artificial intelligence, green and driverless autos, and robotics. Unhackable quantum computing, said by some capable of transforming the world, is also a major goal.

To achieve these goals, local content Buy China rules are set at 40% for 2020 and expected to rise to 70% by 2025, abundant state subsidies are upward bound, and protection from foreign competition is anticipated. As a matter of policy, much tech development in China is in service of its massive cyber state.

China takes pride in allocating $300 billion for low-cost loans to underwrite the Made in China 2025 program. Part of this program also includes pressuring foreign and Chinese companies to provide their leading technology. The principal pressure is access to China's large, lucrative, and growing domestic market. In other words, this is the price to pay to make investments and do business in the PRC. One way to force technology transfers is to *mandate use of joint ventures* with a Chinese partner. This has been done in approximately 35 sectors, including autos, insurance, cloud computing and telecommunications.

Another way is to mandate research and development inside China, with improvements in licensed technology passing to or "shared" with a Chinese partner and/or government regulators and auditors. Microsoft, DuPont, and Huntsman (chemicals), GE (avionics), Apple (iCloud) and chipmaker Qualcomm, for example, have "voluntarily" set up joint ventures in China under pressure to make technology transfers.

Pursuit of Made in China 2025 also involves acquiring foreign technology by buying tech companies and supporting tech start-ups in the USA, Europe, Japan and elsewhere. China's strategic asset seeking behavior includes sending numerous STEM PhD students to U.S. universities, and even paying to have PRC government employees audit U.S. courses. Much of China's success with artificial intelligence, for example, is thought to be a byproduct of Chinese owned, controlled, or financed U.S. start-ups. Such investments, until recently, have mostly escaped U.S. regulatory controls.

Many foreign businesses are worried about longer-term access to the market, particularly after technical knowledge has been transferred to domestic firms. After that happens, foreign players may become less relevant in the Chinese market, while local players may become global competitors, edged on by favorable government policies.

§ 4.23 Responses to Made in China 2025

Host jurisdictions have woken up and are increasingly active in regulating tech-driven Chinese mergers, acquisitions, and relationships. In 2018/19, for example, the United States beefed up its CFIUS controls over foreign investment in critical technologies and expanded U.S. export controls over emerging and foundational technologies. These controls now cover biotech, advance computing, artificial intelligence and machine learning, position-navigation, and timing (PNT) technology, microprocessors, robotics, brain-machine interface, advanced materials, advanced surveillance, data analytics, quantum information and sensing, logistics technology, additive manufacturing, and hyper-sonics, with additional categories to follow. See Chapter 6.

China has had policies favoring indigenous technology development for several decades and is increasingly tech innovative versus adaptive. The sheer volume of data available in China, and the absence of privacy restraints, has fueled its artificial intelligence gains to a point that some analysts believe it is now the world leader in AI.

As investor/author Kai-Fu Lee put it: "If data is the new oil, China is the new Saudi Arabia". That said, tech imports and foreign investor tech developments inside China remain important to Made in China 2025.

§ 4.24 Trump, Biden, and China

Few countries took more abuse than China in the U.S. Presidential election race of 2016, particularly for its massive trade surplus in goods and services with the United States, $337 billion in 2017. Roughly 20% of all U.S. imports come from China, and several studies affirm China's adverse impact since joining the WTO in 2001 on U.S. manufacturing jobs.

For more on Trump and his multi-faceted tech-driven trade war with China, and Biden on trading with China, see my *International Trade Beyond Trump* Concise Hornbook, Chapter 18.

USTR Section 301 Study of China's Tech Transfer and IP Practices

Acting under Section 301 of the Trade Act of 1974, the USTR completed in March of 2018 a lengthy study of China's intellectual property and technology acquisition practices. The Report was divided into three major arguments:

> (1) China's Unfair Technology Transfer Regime for U.S. Companies in China;

> (2) China's Discriminatory Licensing Restrictions; and

> (3) China's Outbound Investment and Technology Acquisition Policies.

Apart from outright IP, trade secret and confidential business information theft, often via state-sponsored hacking, the USTR Report zeroed in on forced or pressured technology transfers (TT) inside China. One such technique is associated with China's mandatory joint venture rules (autos, insurance, cloud computing, telecommunications) as a condition of access to China's vast market.

Forced disclosure of software source codes and data localization rules under China's recent Cybersecurity Law were noted in the USTR report, as were mandatory R&D in China, technology R&D and acquisition inside the USA, Europe and elsewhere, the Made in China 2025 ultra-high-tech program, and Chinese administrative control of licensing and improvement technology. The USTR Report also cited technology transfers undertaken "voluntarily" by Microsoft, Qualcomm, Apple, and others.

§ 4.25   Recent China Investment Patterns

China's WTO-negotiated 25% tariff on cars combined with the world's fasting growing auto market makes the PRC a must-be-there market. Virtually all major auto producers have invested in China, with Volkswagen and General Motors leading in sales, and China's Geely rising rapidly after its purchase of Volvo and its owner's personal acquisition of nearly 10% of the shares of Daimler. Until recently, having abandoned India and Europe, about 40% of GM's global auto sales were in China, with Ford roughly making 20% of its world-wide sales in the PRC.

Chinese investments in the USA, which had been growing rapidly, have tightened under Chinese capital export controls and aggressive U.S. national security CFIUS reviews. See Chapter 6. This has been especially the case when state-owned Chinese enterprises are involved, and even resulted in the blocking of the hostile purchase attempt by Singapore's Broadcomm of San Diego-based Qualcomm (a high-tech 5G chip wizard). Broadcomm's connection to China was not obvious.

China, in turn, delayed its review of Qualcomm's proposed acquisition of NXP, an auto and security chip leader. The NXP deal was thought to be critical to Qualcomm's future, and would reduce its heavy dependence on China revenues. The Trump Administration also blocked the acquisition of MoneyGram by China's Ant Financial. Meanwhile, Boeing opened its first airplane finishing plant in the PRC in 2019, and EXXON constructed a major refinery in Southeast China.

U.S. gaming stars from Las Vegas, including The Sands, and Wynn and MGM Resorts (but not Caesars), are heavily invested in Macau, a former Portuguese colony not far from Hong Kong. Macau is China's gaming capital, where VIPs and others are well entertained. The washing of corrupt funds sourced in the PRC, and even North Korean funds, is apparently possible. The U.S. investors have 20-year licenses that expire in 2022. Whether they will be renewed is unclear, particularly in the face of Xi Jinping's anti-corruption and "common prosperity" campaigns.

Tech Investment Issues

Under Phase One trade truce agreement with President Trump covering 2020–2022, China promised greater protection for intellectual property. notably patented pharmaceutical and trade secret rights. Also promised were greater administrative and judicial controls over forced technology transfers by U.S. investors in the PRC, and greater market openings in its financial sector (notably life insurance, e-payments, futures, securities, banks, and mutual funds, think Vanguard paired with Ant Financial). The latter promised repeated changes to a significant degree already adopted into PRC law.

For more on the Phase One PRC-U.S. truce agreement, see my *International Trade Beyond Trump* Concise Hornbook, Chapter 18.

In sum, little in the Trump administration's "managed trade" Phase One accord impacted core U.S. complaints regarding industrial and tech subsidies, cyber-theft, state-owned enterprises, and China's strategic high-tech goals under its Made in China 2025 program (above). Meanwhile China continues to pour funds into tech innovators as an end-run around U.S. dependency. China was the largest investor in the world in 2020, notably investing in small tech start-ups, often generously subsidized. Many U.S.-based venture capital firms have also been supporting PRC tech production, notably of semiconductor chips. Even Intel has also done.

§ 4.26 Text of the 2020 PRC Foreign Investment Law (Excerpt)

Chapter I. General Provisions

Article 1. The Foreign Investment Law of the People's Republic of China (hereinafter referred to as "the Law") is hereby formulated in accordance with the Constitution of the People's Republic of China in a bid to further expand opening-up, vigorously promote foreign investment, protect the legitimate rights and interests of foreign investors, standardize the management of foreign investment, impel the formation of a new pattern of all-round opening-up and boost the sound development of the socialist market economy.

Article 2. The Law shall be applicable to the foreign investment within the territory of the People's Republic of China ("the territory of China").

For the purpose of the Law, foreign investment refers to the investment activity directly or indirectly conducted by a foreign natural person, enterprise or other organization (the "foreign investors"), including the following circumstances:

1. A foreign investor establishes a foreign-funded enterprise within the territory of China, independently or jointly with any other investor;

2. A foreign investor acquires shares, equities, property shares or any other similar rights and interests of an enterprise within the territory of China;

3. A foreign investor makes investment to initiate a new project within the territory of China, independently or jointly with any other investor; and

4. A foreign investor makes investment in any other way stipulated by laws, administrative regulations or provisions of the State Council.

For the purpose of the Law, a foreign-funded enterprise refers to an enterprise that is incorporated under the Chinese laws within the territory of China and is wholly or partly invested by a foreign investor.

Article 3. The State shall adhere to the basic state policy of opening-up and encourage foreign investors to make investments within the territory of China.

The State shall implement policies on high-level investment liberalization and convenience, establish and improve the mechanism to promote foreign investment, and create a stable, transparent, foreseeable, and level-playing market environment.

Article 4. The State shall implement the management systems of pre-establishment national treatment and negative list for foreign investment.

For the purpose of the preceding paragraph, pre-establishment national treatment refers to the treatment given to foreign investors and their investments during the investment access stage, which is not lower than that given to their domestic counterparts; negative list refers to special administrative measures for the access of foreign investment in specific fields as stipulated by the State. The State shall give national treatment to foreign investment beyond the negative list. The negative list will be issued by or upon approval by the State Council. If more preferential treatment concerning access is offered to a foreign investor under any international treaty or agreement that the People's Republic of China concludes or joins in, relevant provisions in such treaty or agreement may prevail.

Article 5. The State shall protect foreign investors' investment, earnings and other legitimate rights and interests within the territory of China in accordance with the law.

Article 6. Foreign investors and foreign-funded enterprises carrying out investment activities within the territory of China shall observe the Chinese laws and regulations and shall not impair China's security or damage any public interest.

Article 7. The competent departments for commerce and investment under the State Council shall, pursuant to the division of duties, promote, protect and manage foreign investment; other relevant departments under the State Council shall take charge of the relevant work in the promotion, protection and management of foreign investment within the scope of their respective duties.

The relevant department under the local people's government at or above the county level shall carry out the work relating to promotion, protection and management of foreign investment in accordance with laws and regulations and in line with the division of duties determined by the people's government at the same level.

Article 8. Employees of a foreign-funded enterprise shall, pursuant to the law, establish trade union, carry out trade union activities, and safeguard their legitimate rights and interests. A foreign-funded enterprise shall provide necessary conditions for its trade union to carry out relevant activities.

* * *

Chapter III. Investment Protection

Article 20. The State is not to expropriate any investment made by foreign investors.

Under special circumstances, the State may expropriate or requisition an investment made by foreign investors for public interests in accordance with the law. Such expropriation or requisition shall be made pursuant to statutory procedures and fair and reasonable compensation will be given in a timely manner.

Article 21. A foreign investor may, in accordance with the law, freely transfer inward and outward its contributions, profits, capital gains, income from asset disposal, royalties of intellectual property rights, lawfully obtained compensation or indemnity, income from liquidation and so on within the territory of China in CNY or a foreign currency.

Article 22. The State shall protect the intellectual property rights of foreign investors and foreign-funded enterprises, and protect the legitimate rights and interests of holders of intellectual property rights and relevant right holders; in case of any infringement of intellectual property right, legal liability shall be investigated strictly in accordance with the law.

During the process of foreign investment, the State shall encourage technology cooperation on the basis of free will and business rules. Conditions for technology cooperation shall be determined by all investment parties upon negotiation under the principle of equity. No administrative department or its staff member shall force any transfer of technology by administrative means.

Article 23. Administrative departments and their staff members shall keep confidential any trade secret of foreign investor or foreign-funded enterprise they are aware of during the performance of their duties and shall not divulge or illegally provide to others the secret.

* * *

Chapter IV. Investment Management

Article 28. Foreign investors shall not invest in any field forbidden by the negative list for access of foreign investment (hereinafter referred to as the "negative list").

For any field restricted by the negative list, foreign investors shall conform to the investment conditions provided in the negative list.

Fields not included in the negative list shall be managed under the principle that domestic investment and foreign investment shall be treated uniformly.

Article 29. During the process of foreign investment, where verification and record-filing of a foreign investment project are required, relevant provisions of the State shall be followed.

Article 30. If a foreign investor invests in an industry or field where license is required in accordance with the law, relevant licensing formalities shall be handled as stipulated by law.

Unless otherwise provided by laws or administrative regulations, relevant competent department shall review the application for license filed by the foreign investor based on the same conditions and procedures as those for domestic investment.

Article 31. The organization form, institutional framework and standard of conduct of a foreign-funded enterprise shall be subject to the provisions of the Company Law of the People's Republic of China, the Partnership Enterprise Law of the People's Republic of China, and other laws.

Article 32. In carrying out production and operation activities, foreign-funded enterprises shall conform to relevant provisions on labor protection and social insurance stipulated in laws and administrative regulations, handle tax, accounting, foreign exchange and other matters in accordance with laws, administrative regulations and relevant provisions of the State, and shall be subject to the supervision and inspection conducted by relevant competent departments in accordance with the law.

Article 33. Foreign investors who acquire a company within the territory of China through mergers and acquisitions or participate in the concentration of undertakings by other means shall be subject to the examination for concentration of undertakings as stipulated by the Anti-Monopoly Law of the People's Republic of China.

Article 34. The State shall establish a foreign investment information reporting system. Foreign investors or foreign-funded enterprises shall submit the investment information to competent departments for commerce through the enterprise registration system and the enterprise credit information publicity system.

The contents and scope of foreign investment information to be reported shall be determined under the principle of necessity; investment information that is available through interdepartmental information sharing will not be required to be submitted again.

Article 35. The State shall establish a security review system for foreign investment, under which the security review shall be conducted for any foreign investment affecting or having the possibility to affect national security.

The decision made upon the security review in accordance with the law shall be final.

Chapter 5

INVESTING IN EUROPE

Sec.

With 28/27 member states and over 500 million residents, and approximately 70 free trade partners for its exports, the European Union is a strong investment magnet containing enormous wealth and purchasing power. Investing in the EU jumps over tariff and other trade barriers exporters typically face when shipping goods into the Common Market. This chapter focuses upon investing in Europe.

This chapter is written primarily for an audience located outside Europe. The underlying assumption is that foreign investors will treat Europe as a regional market, not a series of individual national markets. Although the relevant laws and bilateral investment treaties (BITs, see Chapter 7) of the European country where the investment will be made always need to be consulted and can vary greatly, this chapter primarily covers European Union investment and trade law. This body of law that governs the operational realities of the market called Europe. It is the EU market potential that so attracts foreign investors to the world's largest common market.

Business executives tend to think in terms of markets. Lawyers tend to think in terms of jurisdictions. From either perspective, Europe since 1950 has been a puzzle whose pieces sometimes change shape or fracture, sometimes disappear, or reappear, and are generally hard to fit together. The timeline that follows takes an historical approach to understanding the European puzzle. This approach helps to answer the most basic of investment decisions: Where in Europe shall we invest?

For much broader EU law coverage, see my Concise Hornbook on *The European Union Beyond BREXIT.*

§ 5.1   EU Timelines

1951—European Coal and Steel Community ("Treaty of Paris")

1957—European Economic Community (EEC) ("Treaty of Rome"), European Atomic Energy Community Treaty (EURATOM)

1959—European Free Trade Area Treaty (EFTA)

1968—EEC Customs Union fully operative

1973—Britain and Denmark switch from EFTA to EEC; Ireland joins EEC; Norway rejects membership; remaining EFTA states sign industrial free trade treaties with EEC

1979—Direct elections to European Parliament

1981—Greece joins EEC

1983—Greenland "withdraws" from EEC

1986—Spain and Portugal join EEC, Portugal leaves EFTA

1987—Single European Act amends Treaty of Rome to initiate campaign for a Community without internal frontiers by 1993

1990—East Germany merged into Community via reunification process

1993—Maastricht Treaty on European Union (TEU), EEC officially becomes EC

1995—Austria, Finland, and Sweden join EU, Norway votes no again

1999—Amsterdam Treaty

1999—Common currency (EURO) managed by European Central Bank (ECB) commences with 11 members

2003—Treaty of Nice, draft Constitution for Europe released

2004—Cyprus, Estonia, Slovenia, Poland, Hungary, the Czech Republic, Slovakia, Latvia, Lithuania, Malta join EU

2005—Constitution for Europe overwhelmingly defeated in France and Netherlands

2007—Accession of Bulgaria and Romania

2009—Reform Treaty of Lisbon takes effect. Treaty of Rome becomes Treaty on the Functioning of the European Union

2010—Greece and Ireland bailed out; 1 trillion EURO safety net created for financial crises

2011—Portugal bailed out, EURO in crisis

2012—Spanish and Italian banks bailed out, Greece bailed out again, EURO in extreme crisis, Treaty on Stability, Coordination and Governance (TSCG) adopted by 25 member states creating permanent European Stability Mechanism crisis loan fund and a Fiscal Compact with balanced budget rules, ECB agrees to buy unlimited short-term national bonds

2013—Croatia joins EU, Cyprus bailed out

2014—Latvia joins EURO zone, Scotland votes against independence from the U.K.

2015—Lithuania joins EURO zone, ECB commences bond buying ("quantitative easing"), Greece bailed out a third time, massive waves of migrants enter Europe

2016—U.K. votes to leave EU (BREXIT); migrant and terrorist waves escalate

2017—BREXIT negotiations commence

2020—BREXIT finalized, COVID virus arrives

2021—EU and UK agree on Trade and Cooperation future relations

CHRONOLOGY OF EUROPEAN UNION MEMBERSHIP

1957—France, Germany, Italy, Belgium, Netherlands, and Luxembourg create EEC (6)

1973—United Kingdom, Eire, and Denmark (9)

1981—Greece (10)

1986—Spain and Portugal (12)

1995—Austria, Finland, and Sweden (15)

2005—Cyprus, Estonia, Slovenia, Poland, Hungary, Czech Republic, Slovakia, Latvia, Lithuania, and Malta (25)

2007—Bulgaria and Romania (27)

2013—Croatia (28)

2020—Britain exits EU (27)

EURO ZONE PARTICIPANTS (19)

1999—Germany, France, Ireland, Spain, Portugal, Austria, Italy, Netherlands, Luxembourg, Belgium, Finland

2001—Greece

2007—Slovenia

2008—Cyprus, Malta

2009—Slovakia

2011—Estonia

2014—Latvia

2015—Lithuania

§ 5.2   Where to Invest in the EU

The timeline, chronology and EURO Zone listings presented above suggest where and where not to invest in Europe. Consider the following investment issues:

1. Would you invest in Norway, a country whose 3–4 million people have twice voted against membership in the EU? Would you invest in Switzerland, which is an equally small market that is not part of the European Union? FYI, some firms manufacturing in Switzerland have "disinvested" and relocated their operations inside the EU.

2. Inside the EU, would you invest in bailout prone Greece, a country that may not remain in the EURO zone ("GREXIT")? What about the U.K. after BREXIT? Just the possibility of Britain exiting the EU caused foreign investors to postpone additional or new investments in that nation.

3. What about the EURO crisis? Many U.S. investors have traditionally favored EURO zone countries like Ireland, saving considerable sums trading in a zone that does not require currency exchanges. It does not hurt that Ireland is English speaking, a short plane ride, and has one of the very lowest corporate taxation rates (12.5%) in the EU as well as reduced taxation of patent income (known as "patent box" taxation).

4. Modest *flat* taxation rates on corporate and personal income as well as VAT transactions exist in some of the states formerly behind the Iron Curtain, Slovakia, and Estonia for example. Slovakia has attracted substantial foreign and EU auto industry investments.

5. High tax EU countries such as Germany and France have seen foreign and domestic investment exit their markets in favor of lower tax and lower wage Eastern European member-states. Costs of operation and prices of goods and services in member states, which are not part of the EURO zone, such as Hungary and Poland, are reduced when national currencies float down against the EURO. Is investing in the EU outside the EURO zone is a plus or minus?

6.   A series of "right of establishment" decisions by the European Court of Justice indicate that investors can incorporate almost anywhere they wish regardless of where their principal place of operations is located inside the EU. Careful evaluation of corporate law questions concerning capital requirements, capacity to sue, liability risks and the like, as well as taxation, needs be undertaken. Thousands of U.K. companies when Britain was an EU member were set up to avoid German paid-in capital requirements.

7.   Would you be willing to invest in the EU without investor-state arbitration protections? See Section 5.7 below.

Where to invest may be influenced by less tangible factors, such as the preference of executives for an EU location and lifestyle. Access to major financial markets, such as the City of London, has become more difficult post-BREXIT.

§ 5.3   The EU Common Market

Investors in the European Union have a great interest in how well its common market works. Their basic goal is to sell in a regional (not a national) market. This section highlights the law governing free movement of goods, workers, capital, and services. It also very selectively focuses upon the development of common policies of particular concern to foreign investors (with emphasis on U.S. interests).

Space does not permit treatment of European law governing:

Medical and food products, free movement of people, worker and professional rights, banking insurance, investment advisors, transportation, value-added and excise taxation, broadcasting and media products, computer software, commercial agents, corporate taxation, subsidies, industrial and intellectual property, procurement, products liability, consumer protection, advertising, companies, the environment, energy, telecommunications, agricultural and fisheries policy, customs, trade, distribution agreements and antitrust.

All these topics, which may well influence investment in Europe decisions, are covered in my *European Union Beyond BREXIT* Concise Hornbook.

A Single Market

The campaign for a European Community without internal frontiers was the product of Commission studies in the 1980s, which concluded that a hardening of the trade arteries of Europe had occurred. The Community was perceived to be stagnating relative to the advancing economies of North America and East Asia. Projections of the wealth that could be generated from a truly common market for Western Europe suggested the need for revitalization. A "white paper" drafted under the leadership of Lord Cockfield of Britain and issued by the Commission in 1985 became the blueprint for the campaign.

The Commission's white paper identified three types of barriers to a Europe without internal frontiers—physical, technical, and fiscal. Physical barriers occur at the borders. For goods, they include national trade quotas, health checks, agricultural monetary compensation amount (MCA) charges, statistical collections, and transport controls. For people, physical barriers involve clearing immigrations, security checks and customs.

Technical barriers mostly involve national standards and rules for goods, services, capital, and labor, which operate to inhibit trade among the member states. Boilers, railway, medical and surgical equipment, and pharmaceuticals provide traditional examples of markets restrained by technical trade barriers. Fiscal barriers centered on different value-added and excise taxation levels and the corresponding need for tax collections at the border. There were, for example, wide value-added tax (VAT) differences on auto sales within the Common Market.

The Commission (Cecchini Report) estimated that removal of all these barriers could save the Community upwards of 100 billion ECUs (European Currency Units) in direct costs. In addition, another roughly 100 billion ECUs could be gained as price reductions and increased efficiency and competition take hold. Overall, the Commission projected an increase in the Common Market's gross domestic product (GDP) of between 4.5 to 7 percent, a reduction in consumer prices of between 6 to 4.5 percent, 1.75 to 5 million new jobs, and enhanced public sector and external trade balances. These figures were thus said to represent "the costs of non-Europe."

Major amendments to the Treaty of Rome (now the Treaty on the Functioning of the European Union, TFEU) were undertaken in the Single European Act (SEA) effective in 1987. Amendments to the Treaty can occur by Commission or member state proposal to the Council. The amendments are not effective until ratified by all the member states in accordance with their respective constitutional requirements. Proposals originating in the Commission's 1985 white paper on a Europe without internal frontiers were embodied in the Single European Act.

The SEA amendments not only expanded the competence of the European institutions, but also sought to accelerate the speed of integration by relying more heavily on qualified majority (not unanimous) legislative voting principles in Council decision-making. The Single European Act envisioned the adoption of hundreds of new legislative measures designed to fully integrate the Common Market by the end of 1992. Nearly all these measures were adopted by the Council. They increased the power of the EU to attract foreign investment.

The EU Customs Union

North American traders and investors should understand that the free movement of goods within Europe is based upon the creation of a customs union. Under this union, the member states have eliminated customs duties among themselves. They have established a common customs tariff for their trade with the rest of the world. Quantitative restrictions (quotas) on trade between member states are prohibited, except in emergency and other limited situations. The right of free movement applies to goods that originate in the Common Market *and* to those that have lawfully entered it and are in "free circulation." In other words, all goods lawfully inside the EU may be freely traded. In contrast, NAFTA/USMCA has no such universal rule.

The establishment of the customs union has been a major accomplishment, though not without difficulties. The member states not only committed themselves to the elimination of tariffs and quotas on internal trade, but also to the elimination of "measures of equivalent effect." The elastic legal concept of measures of equivalent effect has been interpreted broadly by the European Court of Justice, and the Commission, to prohibit a wide range of trade restraints, such as administrative fees charged at borders which are the equivalent of import or export tariffs.

Charges of equivalent effect to a tariff should be distinguished from internal taxes that are applicable to imported and domestic goods. The latter must be levied in a nondiscriminatory and non-protective manner while the former is prohibited entirely. There has been a considerable amount of litigation over this distinction.

The elasticity of the concept of measures of an equivalent effect is even more pronounced in the Court's judgment relating to quotas. This jurisprudence draws upon an early Commission directive (no longer applicable) of extraordinary scope. In this directive, the Commission undertook a lengthy listing of practices that it considered illegal measures of effect equivalent to quotas. It is still occasionally referenced in Commission and Court of Justice decisions. Its focus is on national rules that discriminate against imports or simply restrain internal trade.

Effects Test

This "effects test" soon found support from the ECJ. In a famous case, the Court of Justice ruled that Belgium could not block the importation of Scotch whiskey via France because of the absence of a British certificate of origin as required by Belgian customs law.

The Court of Justice has held that any national rule directly or indirectly, or potentially capable of hindering internal trade is generally forbidden as a measure of equivalent effect to a quota. However, *if* European law has not developed appropriate rules in the area concerned (here designations of origin), the member states may enact "reasonable" and "proportional" (no broader than necessary) regulations to ensure that the public is not harmed. *See Rewe Zentral v. Branntwein*, (1979) Eur. Comm. Rep. 649. This is often referred to as the "*Cassis* formula".

Products meeting reasonable national criteria, the *Cassis* opinion continues, may be freely traded. This is the origin of the innovative "mutual reciprocity" principle used in significant parts of the legislative campaign for a Europe without frontiers.

The *Cassis* decision suggests use of a Rule of Reason analysis for national fiscal regulations, public health measures, laws governing the fairness of commercial transactions and consumer protection. Environmental protection and occupational safety laws of the member states have been similarly treated. Under this approach, for example, a Danish "bottle bill" requiring use of approved containers was therefore unreasonable. However, the Danes' argument that a deposit and return system was environmentally necessary prevailed. This was a reasonable restraint on internal trade recognized by the Court under the *Cassis* formula.

Under *Cassis*, national rules requiring country of origin or "foreign origin" labels have fallen as measures of effect equivalent to quotas. So have various restrictive national procurement laws, including a "voluntary" campaign to "Buy Irish." Minimum and maximum retail pricing controls can also run afoul of the Court's expansive interpretations. Compulsory patent licensing can amount to a measure of equivalent effect nullified by operation of regional law. The U.K. could not compulsorily require manufacturing within its jurisdiction.

Member states may not impose linguistic labelling requirements to block trade and competition in foodstuffs. In this instance, a Belgian law requiring Dutch labels in Flemish areas was nullified as in conflict with the Treaty. These cases vividly illustrate the extent to which litigants are invoking the Treaty and the *Cassis* formula in attempts at overcoming commercially restrictive national laws.

There are cases which suggest that "cultural interests" may justify national restrictions on European trade. For example, British, French, and Belgian bans on Sunday retail trading have survived initial scrutiny under the *Cassis* formula. French legislation prohibiting the sale or rental of cassettes within one year of a film's debut also survived such scrutiny. British prohibitions of sales of sex articles except by licensed sex shops are compatible. National laws prohibiting sales below cost, when applied without discrimination as between imports and domestic products, are not considered to affect trade between the member states.

Selling Arrangements

In *Keck*, a remarkable decision signaling a jurisprudential retreat, the ECJ ruled that such laws may not be challenged under the traditional *Cassis* formula. *See Keck and Mithouard* (1993) Eur. Comm. Rep. I-6097. Deceptive trade practices laws ordinarily do not amount to "selling arrangements," but national laws regulating outlets and advertising may.

In recent years, member state regulations capable of being characterized as governing "marketing modalities" or "selling arrangements" have sought shelter under *Keck*. For example, the French prohibition of televised advertising (intended to favor printed media) of the distribution of goods escaped the rule of reason analysis of *Cassis* in this manner. Some commentators see in *Keck* and its progeny an unarticulated attempt by the Court to take subsidiarity seriously. Others are just baffled by its newly found tolerance for trade distorting national marketing laws. The Court of Justice has poignantly refused to extend *Keck* to the marketing of services.

The Court has made it clear that all Rule of Reason justifications for national regulatory laws are temporary. Adoption of Common Market legislation in any of these areas would eliminate national authority to regulate trading conditions under *Cassis* and (presumably) *Keck*. These judicial mandates, none of which are specified in the TFEU vividly illustrate the powers of the Court of Justice to expansively interpret the Treaty and rule on the validity under European law of national legislation affecting internal trade *in goods*.

Nontariff Trade Barriers (NTBs)

The provisions of the Treaty on the Functioning of the European Union (TFEU) dealing with the establishment of the customs union do not adequately address the problem of nontariff trade barriers NTBs. As in the world community, the major trade barrier within Europe has become NTBs. To some extent, in the absence of a harmonizing directive completely occupying the field, this is authorized. Article 36 TFEU permits national restraints on imports and exports justified on the grounds of:

(1)   Public morality, public policy ("ordre public") or public security;

(2)   The protection of health and life of humans, animals or plants;

(3)   The protection of national treasures possessing artistic, historical, or archeological value; and

(4)   The protection of industrial or commercial property.

Article 36 amounts, within certain limits, to an authorization of nontariff trade barriers among the member nations. This "public interest" authorization exists in addition to, but somewhat overlaps with, the Rule of Reason exception formulated in *Cassis* above. However, in a sentence much construed by the European Court of Justice, Article 36 continues with the following language: "Such prohibitions or restrictions shall not, however, constitute a means of arbitrary discrimination or a disguised restriction on trade between member states."

In a wide range of decisions, the Court of Justice has interpreted Article 36 in a manner which generally limits the ability of member states to impose NTB barriers to internal trade. Britain, for example, could use its criminal law under the public morality exception to seize pornographic goods made in Holland that it outlawed, but not inflatable sex dolls from Germany which could be lawfully produced in the United Kingdom.

Germany could not stop the importation of beer (*e.g.*, Heineken's from Holland) which fails to meet its purity standards. *Commission v. Germany*, (1987) Eur. Comm. Rep. 3795. This case makes wonderful reading as the Germans, seeking to invoke the public health exception of Article 36, argue all manner of ills that may befall their populace if free trade in beer is allowed. Equally interesting are the unsuccessful Italian health protection arguments against free trade in pasta made from common (not durum) wheat (*Re Drei Glocken GmbH*, (1988) Eur. Comm. Rep. 4233) and French failures to block free trade in foie gras (*Commission v. France*, (1998) Eur. Comm. Rep. I-06197).

A state may obtain whatever information it requires from importers to evaluate public health risks associated with food products containing additives that are freely traded elsewhere in the Common Market. This does not mean that an importer of muesli bars to which vitamins have been added must prove the product healthful, rather that the member state seeking to bar the imports must have an objective reason for keeping them out of its market. Assuming such a reason exists, the trade restraint may not be disproportionate to the public health goal.

A notable 2002 ECJ opinion invalidated a French public health ban on U.K. beef imports maintained after a Commission decision to return to free trade following the "mad cow" outbreak. *National Farmers Union v. Secretariat General*, (2002) Eur. Comm. Rep. I-9079.

Public security measures adopted under Article 36 can include external as well as internal security. An unusual case under the public security exception contained in Article 36 involved Irish petroleum products' restraints. *Schmidberger v. Austria*, (2003) Eur. Comm. Rep. I-5659. The Irish argued that oil is an exceptional product always triggering national security interests. Less expansively, the Court acknowledged that maintaining minimum oil supplies did fall within the ambit of Article 36.

The public policy exception under Article 36 has been construed along French lines (ordre public). Only genuine threats to fundamental societal interests are covered. Consumer protection (though a legitimate rationale for trade restraints under *Cassis*), does not fall within the public policy exception.

Intellectual Property Rights as Trade Barriers

A truly remarkable body of case law has developed around the authority granted national governments in Article 36 to protect industrial or commercial property by restraining imports and exports. These cases run the full gamut from protection of trademarks and copyrights to protection of patents and knowhow. There is a close link between this body of case law and that developed under Article 101 concerning business restraints on competition (antitrust).

Trade restraints involving intellectual property arise out of the fact that such rights are nationally granted. As an alternative national IP rights, late in 1993 the Council reached agreement on a Common Market trademark regime that has been widely used, especially by U.S. firms. The Council also adopted Directive 89/104, which seeks to harmonize member state laws governing trademarks. Decades were spent by the Commission on developing Common Market patents to provide an alternative to national intellectual property rights.

These proposals finally matured in 2014 with the creation of the EU Unitary Patent regime (not applicable in Spain and Italy). In the copyright field, several directives have harmonized European law, perhaps most importantly on copyrights for computer software. All these efforts have helped reduce the potential for trade restraining impact of national IP rights.

Perhaps more importantly, the European Court of Justice has directly addressed Article 36 and generally resolved against the exercise of national intellectual property rights in ways that inhibit free internal trade. In many of these decisions, the Court acknowledges the existence of the right to block trade in infringing goods but holds that the *exercise* of that right is subordinate to the TFEU.

Exhaustion Doctrine

The Court has fashioned a doctrine that treats national intellectual property rights as having been *exhausted* once the goods to which they apply are freely sold on the market. One of the few exceptions to this doctrine is broadcast performing rights, which the Court treats as incapable of exhaustion. CDs and the like embodying such rights are, however, subject to the exhaustion doctrine once released into the market. Such goods often end up in the hands of third parties who then ship them into another member state.

The practical effect of many of the rulings of the Court of Justice is to remove the ability of the owners of the relevant intellectual property rights from successfully pursuing infringement actions in national courts. When intellectual property rights share a common origin and have been placed on goods by consent, as when a licensor authorizes their use in other countries, then infringement actions to protect against trade in the goods to which the rights apply are usually denied. It is only when intellectual property rights do not share a common origin, or the requisite consent is absent, that they stand a chance of being upheld to stop trade in infringing products.

Compulsory licensing of patents, for example, does not involve consensual marketing of products. Patent rights may therefore be used to block trade in goods produced under such a license. But careful repackaging and resale of goods subject to a common trademark may occur against the objections of the owner of the mark.

Centrafarm Case

An excellent example of the application of the judicial doctrine developed by the Court of Justice in the intellectual property field under Article 36 can be found in its *Centrafarm* opinion. *Centrafarm BV v. Sterling Drug*, (1974) Eur. Comm. Rep. 1147. The United States pharmaceutical company, Sterling Drug, owned the British and Dutch patents and trademarks relating to "Negram." Subsidiaries of Sterling Drug in Britain and Holland had been assigned the British and Dutch trademark rights to Negram.

Owing in part to price controls in the UK, a substantial difference in cost for Negram emerged as between the two countries. Centrafarm was an independent Dutch importer of Negram from the UK and Germany. Sterling Drug and its subsidiaries brought infringement actions in the Dutch courts under their national patent and trademark rights seeking an injunction against Centrafarm's importation of Negram into The Netherlands.

The Court of Justice held that the intellectual property rights of Sterling Drug and its subsidiaries could not be exercised in a way which blocked trade in "parallel goods." In the Court's view, the exception established in Article 36 for the protection of industrial and commercial property covers only those rights that were specifically intended to be conveyed by the grant of national patents and trademarks.

Blocking trade in parallel goods after they have been put on the market with the consent of a common owner, exhausting the rights in question, was not intended to be part of the package of benefits conveyed. If Sterling Drug succeeded, an arbitrary discrimination or disguised restriction on Union trade would be achieved in breach of the language which qualifies Article 36. The European Court of Justice ruled upheld in *Centrafarm* the free movement of goods within the Common Market even when that negates clearly existing national legal remedies.

Only in the unusual situation where the intellectual property rights in question have been acquired by independent proprietors under different national laws may such rights inhibit internal trade. While the goal of creation of the Common Market can override national intellectual property rights when internal trade is concerned, these rights apply fully to the importation of goods (including gray market goods) from outside the European Union.

North American exporters of goods subject to rights owned by Europeans may therefore find entry challenged by infringement actions in national courts. This is notably true regarding unauthorized trade in gray market goods and can benefit U.S. companies. Using its UK trademark rights, Levi Strauss, for example, successfully kept low-price (Made in the USA) Levi's out of the EU.

Legislative Solutions to NTBs

Nontariff trade barrier problems were the principal focus of the campaign for a fully integrated Common Market. Many legislative acts have been adopted which target NTB trade problems. There are basically two different methodologies being employed.

Harmonization

When possible, a common European standard is adopted. For example, legislation on auto pollution requirements adopts this methodology. Products meeting these standards may be freely traded in the Common Market. Traditionally, this approach (called "harmonization") has required the formation of a consensus as to the appropriate level of protection.

Once adopted, harmonized standards must be followed. This approach can be deceptive, however. Some harmonization directives contain a list of options from which member states may choose when implementing those directives. In practice, this leads to differentiated national laws on the same so-called harmonized subject. Furthermore, in certain areas (notably the environment and occupational health and safety), the TFEU expressly indicates that member states may adopt laws that are more demanding. The result is, again, less than complete harmonization.

Many efforts at the harmonization of European environmental, health and safety, standards and certification, and related law have been undertaken. Nearly all of these are supposed to be based upon "high levels of protection." Many have criticized what they see as the "least common denominator" results of harmonization of national laws under the campaign for a Europe without internal frontiers.

One example involves the safety of toys. Directive 88/378 permits toys to be sold throughout the Common Market if they satisfy "essential requirements." These requirements are broadly worded in terms of flammability, toxicity, etc. There are two ways to meet these requirements: (1) produce a toy in accordance with CEN standards (drawn up by experts); or (2) produce a toy that otherwise meets the essential safety requirements.

Mutual Reciprocity

The least common denominator criticism may be even more appropriate to the second legislative methodology utilized in the internal market campaign. The second approach is based on the *Cassis* principle of mutual reciprocity. Under this "new" minimalist approach, European legislation requires member states to recognize the standards laws of other member states and deem them acceptable for purposes of the operation of the Common Market.

However, major legislation has been adopted regarding professional services. By mutual recognition of higher education diplomas based upon at least three years of courses, virtually all professionals have now obtained legal rights to move freely in pursuit of their careers. This is a remarkable achievement.

Services Across Borders

Bankers, investment advisors and insurance companies have long awaited the arrival of a truly common market. Their right of establishment in other member states has existed for some time. The right to provide services across borders without establishing local subsidiaries was forcefully reaffirmed by the Court of Justice in 1986. This decision largely rejected a requirement that all insurers servicing the German market be located and established there.

One-Stop Licensing

Legislative initiatives undertaken in connection with the single market campaign promise to create genuinely competitive cross-border European markets for banking, investment, and insurance services. Licensing of insurance and investment service companies and banks meeting minimum capital, solvency ratio and other requirements as implemented in member state law is done on a "one-stop" home country basis. Banks, for example, cannot maintain individual equity positions in non-financial entities over 15 percent of their capital funds, and the total value of such holdings cannot exceed 50 percent of those funds. They can participate and service securities transactions and issues, financial leasing, and trade for their own accounts. The proposed investment services directive requires home country supervision of the "good repute" and "suitability" of managers and controlling shareholders.

Member states must ordinarily recognize home country licenses and the principle of home country control. For example, Council Directive 89/646 ("the Second Banking Directive") employs the home country single license procedure to liberalize banking services throughout the region. However, host states retain the right to regulate a bank's liquidity and supervise it through monetary policy and in the name of the "general good."

Similarly, no additional insurance permits or requirements may be imposed by host countries when large industrial risks (sophisticated purchasers) are involved. However, when the public at large is concerned (general risk), host country rules still apply. Major auto and life insurance directives employing one-stop licensing principles were adopted in 1990. The auto insurance directive reproduces the large versus general risk distinctions found in the Second Non-Life Insurance Directive. Host country controls over general risk auto insurance policies were retained until 1995. Host country permits are also required when life insurers from other member states actively solicit business.

Foreign Service Providers

There was a rush by foreign bankers, investment advisors and insurers to get established before January 1, 1993 to qualify for home country licenses. North Americans and others have been particularly concerned about certain features of the legislation mandating effective access in foreign markets for European companies before outsiders may benefit from the liberalization of services within the Common Market.

This problem is generally referred to as the "reciprocity requirement." It is this kind of requirement that gave the campaign for a Europe without internal frontiers the stigma of increasing the degree of external trade barriers. Many outsiders, in rhetoric which sometimes seems excessive, refer to the development of a "Fortress Europe" mentality and threat to world trading relations.

Since state and federal laws governing banking, investment services and insurance are restrictive, and in no sense can it be said that one license permits a company to operate throughout the United States, one result of European integration has arguably been reform of United States regulatory legislation. Since 1994, the U.S. has noticeably relaxed its rules on interstate banking, and largely repealed the Depression-era Glass-Steagall Act limitations on universal banking.

Equal Pay and Equal Treatment

Once invested inside the European Union, the law of equal pay and equal treatment of men and women in the workforce is perhaps the most startling "operational reality" foreign investors encounter. This area is a prominent element in wide-ranging European social policies. It is derived from International Labor Organization Convention No. 100 which three states, including France, had adopted by 1957.

The French were rightfully proud of this tradition of nondiscrimination between the sexes on pay. They also appreciated that gender-based inequality in pay in other member states could harm the ability of their companies to compete. EU law thus enshrines a rough equivalent to what is termed "comparable worth" in the United States and a brave new world for investors in Europe.

Equal Pay

EU equal pay rules have been the subject of voluminous legislation and litigation. They apply, quite appropriately, to the

European Community as an employer. Early on, the Court of Justice decided that equal pay for equal work is directly effective EU law. This decision allows individuals to challenge pay discrimination in public and private sector jobs. The ruling was applied prospectively by the Court of Justice to avoid large numbers of lawsuits for back pay.

In an early case, a flight attendant for Sabena Airlines was able to allege illegal discrimination in pay and pension benefits (as a form of deferred pay) to stewards and stewardesses before a Belgian work tribunal. European law in this area enshrines the principle of "comparable worth," a most controversial issue in United States employment law. Furthermore, women who are paid less than men performing work of less worth may claim relief. The hard questions are how to determine what constitutes "equal work" requiring equal pay or what "women's work" is worth more than that being done by men (again requiring pay adjustments). For example, does secretarial work equal custodial work? Is the work of an airline attendant worth more than that of an airline mechanic?

Council Directive 75/117 (now Directive 2006/54) makes the principle of equal pay apply to work of *equal value* (to the employer). This mandates establishment of nondiscriminatory job classifications to measure the comparable worth of one job with another. The Commission successfully enforced Directive 75/117 in a prosecution before the European Court of Justice against the United Kingdom. The Sex Discrimination Act of 1975, adopted expressly to fulfill Article 157 obligations, did not meet European standards because employers could block the introduction of job classification systems.

Danish law's failure to cover nonunionized workers also breached the equal pay directive. But its implementation under German law, notably by constitutional provisions, sufficed to meet regional standards.

In determining equal or greater values, most states favor a job content approach. Content is determined through job evaluation systems which use factor analysis. For example, in Great Britain a job is broken down into various components such as skill, responsibility, physical requirements, mental requirements, and working conditions. Points or grades are awarded in each of these categories and totaled to determine the value of the job.

Different factors may be balanced against each other. In Ireland, the demand of physical work can be balanced against the concentration required for certain skills. This is known as the "total package" approach. The equal job content approach relies on comparisons.

This raises the question of which jobs should be deemed to be suitable for comparison. The member states have taken different approaches to this question. In Britain the comparison must be drawn from the same business establishment. In contrast, the Irish Anti-Discrimination Pay Act provides for "comparisons in the same place," and "place" includes a city, town, or locality. This approach is designed to ensure that legitimate regional differences in pay are not disturbed.

Employer defenses also vary from member state to member state. In Ireland, employers may justify a variation if they can show "grounds other than sex" for a disputed variation in pay. In Britain, employers will succeed if they can prove a "genuine material factor which is not the difference of sex." In Germany, the employer can prove that "material reasons unrelated to a particular sex" justify the differential. A further consideration in the implementation of equal pay laws has been the existence of pre-existing wage schedules set by collective agreement. In Britain and Italy, courts have held that collective agreements relating to pay cannot be changed or altered except where direct discrimination can be shown.

The burden of proving "objectively justified economic grounds" to warrant pay differentials is on the employer. When a woman succeeds a man in a particular position within a company (here a warehouse manager), she is entitled to equal pay absent a satisfactory explanation not based upon gender. The same is true of part-time (female) workers doing the same job as full-time (male) workers. Free travel to railway employees upon retirement cannot go only to men.

And "pay" includes retirement benefits paid upon involuntary dismissal, which cannot be discriminatory. But a protocol adopted at the 1991 Maastricht Summit makes this ruling prospective only. Pay also includes employer-paid pension benefits which cannot be for men only. In this decision the Court refused to remove the retroactive effect of its judgment. Mobility, special training, and seniority may be objectively justifiable grounds for pay discriminations.

Equal Treatment

The principle of equal pay for equal work has been extended by Council Directive to *equal treatment* regarding access to employment, vocational training, promotions, and working conditions (*e.g.*, retirement deadlines). This directive (now 2006/54) prohibits discrimination based upon sex, family, or marital status. The Equal Treatment Directive is limited by three exceptions. Member states may distinguish between men and women if: (1) sex is a determining factor in ability to perform the work; (2) the provision protects women; or (3) the provision promotes equal opportunity for men and women. Equal treatment must be extended to small and household businesses.

Dutch Law compulsorily retiring women at age 60 and men at age 65 violated the directive. Women cannot be refused employment because they are pregnant even if the employer will suffer financial losses during maternity leave. Maternity and adoption leave benefits for women, however, need not be extended to men. The dismissal of a woman because of repeated absences owing to sickness is lawful provided the same absences would lead to the dismissal of men. General prohibitions against night work by women but not men violate equal treatment Directive 76/207. The French government failed to justify this criminal law on any special grounds.

Equality also governs social security entitlements such as disability or caring for the disabled pay. Social security benefits cannot be based upon marital status. Women police officers cannot be denied arms when men are not, even in the interest of "public safety" and "national security." Equal treatment requires the elimination of preferences based upon gender in laws governing collectively bargained employment agreements. The Council adopted a declaration in December 1991 endorsing the Commission's recommended Code of Practice on sexual harassment. This Code rejects sexual harassment as contrary to equal treatment law, specifically Council Directive 76/207. But the equal pay and equal treatment directives fail to cover significant categories of women workers; part-time, temporary, and home workers. Additional legislation in these areas can be expected.

Although Article 157 on equal pay is directly effective law binding upon public and private employers, it is not yet clear to what degree the equal treatment directives discussed above have that effect. Clearly these directives are binding on the member states and public corporations as employers. The private sector must comply after national implementing legislation is adopted, but if that legislation is deficient the only remedy is a prosecution of the member state by the Commission.

There is a trend within the jurisprudence of the Court of Justice towards recognition of a broad human right of equality before the law. This is evidenced in some cases, which suggests that the private sector will eventually be bound by all European legislation on equal pay and equal treatment even in the absence of or despite national implementing law.

Predictably, questions of "affirmative action" have arisen. A controversial decision of the Court of Justice invalidated a Bremen regulation giving women of equal qualifications priority over men where women made up less than half the relevant civil service staff. While not strictly a quota, the Court found that Bremen had exceeded the limits of the equal treatment directive in promoting equality of opportunity.

Article 157(4) attempts to address such issues. It allows member states to maintain or adopt "measures for specific advantages" to make it "easier" for the "under-represented sex" to pursue vocational activity or to prevent or compensate for "disadvantages" in professional careers. Specific reservation of University professorships for women in Sweden likewise fell upon ECJ review. Sweden now uses increasing targets for women in full professorships.

Transsexuals and homosexuals have begun to benefit from this trend. But the Court notably refused to require equal employer travel benefits for same sex partners. Likewise, the Court of First Instance refused to recognize homosexual partnerships as the equivalent of marriage for household allowance purposes. Revisions of the 1976 equal treatment directive emphasizing an approach called "gender mainstreaming" have been adopted.

Directive 2000/43 broadly provides for equal treatment irrespective of racial or ethnic origin. Directive 2000/78 more narrowly prohibits employment discrimination on the grounds of religion or belief, disability, age, or sexual orientation.

§ 5.4   The EURO Zone

Admission

One critical element to foreign investors in the European Union is the status and stability of its currency, the EURO. All member states wishing to join the EURO Zone at its creation in 1999 had to meet strict economic convergence criteria on inflation rates, government deficits, long-term interest rates and currency fluctuations. To join the third stage, a country was supposed to have an inflation rate not greater than 1.5% of the average of the three lowest member state rates, long-term interest rates no higher than 2% above the average of the three lowest, a budget deficit less than 3% of gross domestic product (GDP), a total public indebtedness of less than 60% of GDP, and no devaluation within the ERM during the prior two years.

These criteria continue to govern admission of other member states into the EURO zone. They have been honored more in the breach than conformity, particularly so in the COVID era.

The economic performance of member states in 1997 became the test for admission to the economic and monetary union. Since both

France and Germany had trouble meeting the admissions criteria, this opened a window for much more marginal states such as Belgium, Italy, and Spain to join immediately in 1999. Eleven of the then fifteen EU members commenced the EURO Zone. Greece subsequently in 2001 was deemed "qualified" for the EURO Zone based upon (as we now know) dubious financial data.

As expected, Denmark, Britain and Sweden opted out of initial participation in the common currency. The Danes did so by voting No in a year 2000 national referendum. The Swedes voted similarly in 2003. By 2015, Slovenia, Malta, Latvia, Estonia, Lithuania, Cyprus, and Slovakia had joined the EURO zone, for a total of 19 out of 28 member-states of the Union. The world financial crisis of 2008–09 initially increased the interest of some outside the EURO zone, notably Iceland, to partake of its relative stability. Denmark and Bulgaria have pegged their national currencies to the EURO.

On January 1, 1999, the participating states fixed the exchange rates between the EURO and their national currencies. National notes and coins were removed from the market by July 2002 as the EURO was installed. The EURO has been used for most commercial banking, foreign exchange, and public debt purposes since 1999. It has also been adopted (voluntarily) by the world's securities markets, and by Monaco, San Marino, the Vatican, Andorra, Montenegro, and Kosovo.

The arrival of the EURO had important implications for United States investors and the dollar. For decades, the dollar had been the world's leading currency, although its dominance has been declining since the early 1980s. Use of the Deutsche Mark and Yen in commercial and financial transactions, and in savings and reserves, had been steadily rising. The EURO was expected to continue the dollar's decline in all these markets. It was certainly the hope of many Europeans that they had successfully created a rival to the dollar.

The European Central Bank

It was also agreed at Maastricht that in the third stage the European Central Bank (ECB) and the European System of Central Banks would start operations. The ECB and ECSB are governed by an executive board of six persons appointed by the member states and the governors of the national central banks. The ECB and the ECSB are independent of any other European institution and in theory free from member state influence. Their primary responsibility is to maintain price stability, specifically keeping price inflation below two percent per year. In contrast, the U.S. Federal

Reserve has two primary responsibilities: maximum employment and stable prices.

The main functions of the ECB and ECSB are: (1) define and implement regional monetary policy; (2) conduct foreign exchange operations; (3) hold and manage the official foreign reserves of the member states; and (4) supervise the payments systems. The ECB has the exclusive right to authorize the issue of bank notes within the Common Market and must set interest rates to principally achieve price stability. The Court of Justice may review the legality of ECB decisions.

Under the EURO's founding rules, the ECB worked closely with the Ecofin Council's broad guidelines for economic policy, such as keeping national budget deficits below 3% of GDP in all but exceptional circumstances (2% decline in annual GDP). If the Ecofin considered a national government's policy to be inconsistent with that of the region, it could recommend changes including budget cuts. If appropriate national action did not follow such a warning, the Ecofin could have required a government to disclose the relevant information with its bond issues, blocked European Investment Bank credits, mandated punitive interest-free deposits, or levied fines and penalties.

Regrettably, the fiscal enforcement system established when the EURO was created did not work. Sanctions for failure to comply with the 3% budget deficit rule were held unenforceable by the Court of Justice. Since 1999, many EURO states have been under threat of sanctions for failure to comply with the 3% budget deficit rule, most notably Greece, Portugal, Spain, Italy, and Ireland after the global financial meltdown of 2008–09. Yet no EURO Zone member state was ever sanctioned, suggesting this system for controlling national deficits is toothless. It has essentially been replaced by the 2012 Treaty on Stability, Coordination and Governance, discussed below.

Financial Bailouts

The global meltdown also caused financial markets to finally realize that national debt issued in EUROs by different Zone members came with different levels of risk. Interest rates rose on Greek, Portuguese, Irish and other bonds, while German, and to a lesser extent French, EURO bonds held firm. Despite a specific TFEU Article 125 prohibition against Union bailouts of member state governments, as the market-driven European financial crisis of 2010/11 demonstrated, bailouts of debt-ridden EURO zone members may occur. Joining with the IMF, a 110 billion EURO rescue package for Greece was organized over German laments.

Fearing a cascade of financial crises in Spain, Portugal, Italy and Ireland, a 1 trillion EURO liquidity safety net (EFSF) was devised using EU-backed bonds, special purpose EU-guaranteed investment loans, and more IMF funds. In addition, the ECB for the first time began buying EURO zone national government bonds in the open market.

All this caused Germany to publicly re-think its traditional role as paymaster and proponent of the European Union and EURO. Clearly the EURO was not as good as the fondly remembered Deutschemark. Sure enough, Ireland tapped into this safety net for over 100 billion EUROs late in 2010, followed by Portugal in 2011. In 2012, massive loans to Spanish and Italian banks and their governments staved off bailouts and moderated interest rates, and Greece was bailed out a second time. In 2013, Cyprus was bailed out under a plan that "bailed in" some bank depositors and creditors. In 2015, Greece was bailed out for a third time. These actions ran down the safety net and ECB resources.

Most private holders of Greek debt have been pushed into a renegotiated deal with roughly a 50% "haircut" in the value of their holdings. Since 2013, EU bailouts require sovereign bond holders to take losses under "collective action clauses" designed to keep individual investors from blocking restructured debt deals. Mandatory losses can be imposed when Euro-zone nations are deemed insolvent by the European Central Bank, the European Commission, and the IMF ("The Troika"), acting somewhat like a "bankruptcy court," and the Euro-zone finance ministers unanimously are in accord. This has yet to occur.

Treaty on Stability, Coordination and Governance (TSCG), ECB Bond Buying

In March of 2012, with market pressures and threats of a Greek default or exit from the EURO Zone escalating, 25 of the 27 EU members (minus Britain and the Czech Republic) adopted a Treaty on Stability, Coordination and Governance (TSCG) to provide a "permanent" solution to the EURO crisis. Only Ireland allowed its voters a referendum on this Treaty, which was negotiated outside the regular TFEU framework. The Irish, their bailout in progress, voted in favor of ratification by approximately a 60% margin. Ratification by the German Parliament was upheld by Germany's Constitutional Court under that country's eternal democracy" clause.

The TSCG has two principal components: The European Stability Mechanism (ESM) and a "Fiscal Compact."

Effective in 2013, the ESM created a permanent 900 billion EURO loan fund, 27% of which is financed by Germany. Any increase in the ESM fund must be approved by the German Parliament. EURO Zone countries may apply for bailout loans conditioned upon fiscal and economic reforms. All EURO Zone national parliaments must ordinarily approve of any ESM rescue package. Finland has indicated its approval may require loan collateral. The "Fiscal Compact" incorporates a "balanced budget" rule. "Automatic corrective measures" apply if excessive budgets are reached. The EU Commission monitors national budget deficits and breach of the Compact can result in enforcement actions before the European Court of Justice with penalties payable to the ESM.

In addition, since 2012, the European Central Bank has demonstrated its willingness to buy national government and even corporate bonds under "quantitative easing" programs. Germany's revered Bundesbank has openly opposed these developments, which have the support of the Merkel government. Like ESM loans, such purchases will be conditioned upon fiscal and economic austerity commitments with the ECB serving as the regulator of Zone banks. The extent of the ECB's regulatory powers was much debated, though ECB licensing and penalty powers over large banks represented a regulatory base line.

In sum, there is a three-part attempt at "permanently" solving the EURO crisis: The ESM, the Fiscal Compact and ECB bond buying. This attempt once again seeks to come to grips with systemic flaws that have haunted the EURO since its creation. . .Can national spending policies be stabilized, coordinated, and governed in support of a common currency? Since all EURO Zone countries are jointly liable for ESM and ECB monies, this amounts to a partial mutualization of national debt risk. It is not, however, as some have suggested is needed, EURO bonds backed by the EURO Zone. That said, the ESM was certainly a step in that direction.

The EURO Crisis Continues . . .

The EURO was conceived as a unifier for Europe. It has become instead a divisive wedge among creditors and austerity weary debtor nations. That said, by 2014 Ireland and Portugal had refinanced and exited their bailouts without credit line safety nets, taken to be "success" stories. Cyprus did likewise in 2016. But Greece, Italy and Spain remain troubled, and the EURO Zone crisis is anything but over.

No ESM in sight, but with deflation and economic stagnation apparent, the ECB undertook starting in 2015 a massive, unprecedented, and controversial "quantitative easing (QE)" program buying up national government debt. This program resembled that which the U.S. Federal Reserve had been pursuing for some time. In 2016, the ECB extended its bond buying program to selected corporate debt and reduced bank loans to zero interest for up to four years.

These QE policies have reduced European government borrowing costs, tended to reinforce European equity prices, and weakened the EURO (thus enhancing exports). But they appear to have diminishing returns, pushing ECB bank deposit interest rates into negative territory for example.

Meanwhile, Greece elected a government strongly opposed to the austerity conditions attached to its bailouts, lowering the Grexit threshold. There is cause for opposition to the austerity loan conditions. Over the first six years, Greece received over 240 billion Euros in bailout funds, plus the private sector debt restructuring, yet its economy has shrunk by at least 25%, and its debt to GDP ratio has risen dramatically to over 175%. In short, the bailouts and their conditions have proven self-destructive, making it less (not more) likely that Greece can ever repay its debts.

Greek society pays a very heavy price. Unemployment is widespread, poverty is growing, young people and bank deposits are fleeing, property values are speedily descending, authoritarian rule raised its ugly head, and disillusionment is pervasive. Corruption and tax evasion remain entrenched.

Amidst another Greek crisis in 2015, the EURO initially plunged in value, but rallied somewhat by mid-2015, just in time for a third bailout of Greece by the Troika. This bailout, like its predecessors and over IMF objections, did not reduce the amount of Greek national debt.

One year later in 2016, it was déjà vu all over again. Greece needed more financial support to avoid default, and the IMF, after a somewhat scathing internal review of its participation in the second Greek bailout, pushed hard for debt reductions. Germany and the EU limited their support to extending Greek debt maturities, along with interest rate and debt repayment caps. This support was notably contingent upon pension and tax collection reforms in Greece.

By 2022, relatively little had had changed: The IMF was still unwilling to participate in the third bailout, Germany unwilling to write off Greek debt, and the Greek government and its suffering people remain at risk, particularly so since COVID arrived.

Default Risks

An essential question is whether a Greek default can be absorbed without taking down other EURO Zone states and the EURO itself? In other words, whether a Greek default would prove contagious is the key systemic question. Portugal and Ireland, the bailout "success" stories, remain deeply indebted. Spain and Italy have survived on cash infusions that make the debt of Greece look miniscule, and major Italian banks appear insolvent.

Years later, the 2012 ESM mechanism has yet to be invoked, and Commission review of Fiscal Compact compliance has been "flexible". Hence the "permanent" solution to the EURO crisis created in 2012 remains in doubt. Even some of the world's best financial market wizards say there is no clear-cut answer to the question of what happens in Europe or globally if Greece defaults or a EURO member withdraws from the Zone.

§ 5.5   EU Foreign Investment Controls

Surprisingly, the European Union has little tradition of regionalized foreign investment controls over direct "greenfields" investments. Diverse national laws still largely prevail, and most EU jurisdictions have direct foreign investment control regimes. France and Britain, for example, have no minimum threshold to trigger foreign direct investment review. The same is true for Germany, but mergers and acquisitions by foreign investors obtaining 10 to 25% holdings may be reviewed. Italy focuses on reciprocity in the source country when evaluating foreign investment.

Private and state-owned Chinese investments in Europe have been steadily rising, particularly in the tech field. Some acquisitions have been undertaken using Chinese-owned EU subsidiaries to escape national security reviews.

In 2016, Kuka, a leading German robotics company, was sold to a Chinese investor. Subsequently, an EU framework directive encourages tightening national scrutiny of foreign investment and acquisitions, especially those that are tech related. EU member states have generally done so, but in 2018 Alibaba bought Data Artisans, a Berlin specialist in managing large quantities of data, and an individual Chinese investor quietly acquired nearly 10% of Daimler, a German national champion.

In 2018, a state-controlled Chinese firm avoided Italian investment controls using nominally private Hong Kong shell companies to acquire a military drone manufacturer. Soon thereafter, Italian drone tech and knowhow made its way to a new PRC production site.

Chinese firms now also control Volvo, Pirelli (tires), the Greek port of Piraeus, and the Swiss agrochemical giant Syngenta. Chinese acquisitions of small European firms, especially in the tech sector, have multiplied in recent years. Using European subsidiaries, many of the acquisitions evade EU or national scrutiny as foreign investments. In April of 2019, the EU Foreign Direct Investment "Framework" Regulation took effect. This Regulation authorizes the EU to issue *non-binding* opinions on foreign investments likely to affect EU projects or programs, or which are likely to impact public order or security in in other member states.

Smaller, capital hungry EU member states, such as those in Eastern Europe, are generally quite welcoming as are Spain, the United Kingdom and Ireland. Germany and France, on the other hand, typically undertake scrutiny of direct foreign investments and may impose conditions thereon. Germany, for example, has "co-determination" laws that require worker (normally union) representatives on corporate Boards of Directors of sizeable companies. Germany tried hard to persuade its EU partners to enact similar rules that would have applied throughout the Union.

The European Human Rights Convention of 1950, to which all EU nations plus Russia and others subscribe, protects foreign investors from arbitrary or uncompensated expropriations. This protection has been construed by the European Court of Human Rights to also apply to domestic investors.

In the absence of U.S. trade and investment leadership under President Trump, the EU moved on. Having endured trade disruptions caused by the Trump administration and witnessing the bilateral approach of President Trump's "Phase One" truce agreement with China, the EU advanced their interests without U.S. participation. Prime examples of the EU's "strategic autonomy" policy in action include EU free trade agreements covering foreign investment with Canada, Mexico, and MERCOSUR noted in this chapter

§ 5.6   European Union FTAs

Since the Reform Treaty of 2009, foreign investment law has become an exclusive competence of the European Union.

By 2022, the EU had 40 free trade agreements covering some 70 trade partners, including with Algeria, Chile, Egypt, Iceland, Israel, Jordan, Lebanon, Mexico, Morocco, Norway, Serbia, South Africa, Vietnam, Singapore, Japan, Canada, Tunisia, and a customs union agreement with Turkey.

Traditionally, EU FTAs included foreign investment law rules and dispute settlement exclusively by investor-state arbitrations (ISDS). See Chapter 7. Recent FTAs with Vietnam, Singapore, Mexico, and MERCOSUR adopt the EU's "new generation" policy for foreign investment dispute settlement. This policy anticipates using an Investment Court to oversee ISDS arbitrations.

Mexico and the European Union reached a free trade agreement in 2000, expanded and re-negotiated in 2020. Mexico, with its NAFTA/USMCA membership, becomes a production center with duty free access to the world's two largest consumer markets.

The Union has been aggressively pursuing other free trade agreements. Southern Africa, Peru, Colombia, Central America (six nations), Chile, South Korea, Singapore, and Vietnam have signed on. Canada and the EU inked an historic Comprehensive Economic and Trade Agreement (CETA, below) in 2013 that, after much debate focusing primarily on investor-state dispute settlement, finally reached fruition in 2017.

In 2018, Japan and the EU also reached agreement on a free trade, which took effect in 2019. Perhaps even more remarkably, after 20 years of negotiation, the EU and MERCOSUR (Brazil, Argentina, Uruguay, and Paraguay) signed a free trade deal in 2019. Overcoming protective CAP trade barriers, this FTA contains unprecedented provisions allowing expanded export of MERCOSUR agricultural and meat products to the EU. Ratification of this agreement has stalled over criticism of Brazil's exploitation of Amazon natural resources.

India, Australia, New Zealand, ASEAN, and the Gulf Council may follow. One notable feature of EU free trade agreements is the inclusion of a Human Rights and Democracy Clause backed up by potential trade sanctions.

Canada-EU Comprehensive Economic and Trade Agreement (CETA 2017)

Given the withdrawal of the United States from the TPP, the uncertain future of TTIP negotiations between the U.S. and the EU, and the onslaught of FTAs Britain has sought after BREXIT, one free trade agreement that now stands out in the developed world is CETA, the Comprehensive Economic and Trade Agreement between Canada and the EU, operational since 2017. CETA was cited by many as a model for future UK-EU trade and investment relations post BREXIT, but the final EU-UK 2021 Trade and Cooperation Agreement is less extensive that CETA.

Upon CETA's ratification, 98% of the tariffs on trade between the parties were eliminated, with tariffs on autos phasing out over seven years, subject to 50 to 55% Canadian content rules of origin except for a generous 20% content rule applicable to the first 100,000 Canadian auto exports. Considerable agreement on product standards and testing in the country of export was reached, and Canadian firms get to bid on EU contracts on the same footing as EU companies.

Free trade in services is based on a "negative list", a first for the EU, and will rachet up if either party grants broader entry in any other subsequent free trade agreement. Mobility for service providers and persons in business is extensive, and mutual recognition of professional diplomas and licensing is anticipated.

Both parties have a history of protecting their agricultural and fish/seafood markets. After various transition periods, CETA renders nearly 95% of these markets duty-free. There are exceptions for meat quotas on both sides and EU cheese export quotas. The EU obtained greater protection for geographic origin of products (Feta cheese, Parma ham), and increased pharmaceutical patent protection. Healthcare and education, along with cultural industries, are excluded under CETA, and Canada continues to control development of its natural resources.

Foreign investor rights and arbitral protections cover the entire EU, another first. Investor-state dispute settlement procedures, like those of NAFTA 1994, were tuned up in response to numerous criticisms. Third party amicus briefs are allowed, frivolous complaints may be dismissed, biased arbitrators challenged, and there is considerably more transparency. After much debate and controversy, an Investment Dispute Court comprised of EU and Canadian members will be created to review investor-state disputes. Canada still gets to apply its Investment Act to EU nationals, subject to the "net benefit" to Canada test, but EU investments under $1.5 billion CDN escape review.

Japan/China-EU Trade

Europe's trade relations with Japan and China are less voluminous, less in balance and (at least superficially) less fractious than with the United States. Japan and China run growing surpluses, but the amounts are smaller than the huge surpluses they accumulate in trading with the States.

Many Europeans speak quietly and with determination about their intent to avoid the "United States example" in their trade relations with Japan and China. Less quietly, some national governments have imposed quotas on the importation of Japanese autos and instituted demanding local content requirements for Japanese cars assembled in Europe. The Commission, for its part, has frequently invoked antidumping proceedings against Japanese and especially Chinese goods. It has also demonstrated a willingness to create arcane rules of origin that promote its interests at the expense of Japan and China.

At the GATT/WTO level, however, Japan and the EU share common concerns about retaining their agricultural support systems. These concerns place them in opposition to the U.S. and others who seek to liberalize world trade in agricultural products.

The meteoric economic rise of China, combined with U.S. withdrawal from the Trans-Pacific Partnership (TPP) under President Trump, pushed Japan and the European Union into an historic free trade agreement in 2019. Each is expected to get greater (but not 100%) access to the other's markets, notably for Japanese autos to Europe and EU agricultural goods to Japan.

The Japan-EU Economic Partnership Agreement (2019)

Like CETA, the Japan-EU Economic Partnership Agreement of 2019 is a major example of free trade alternatives to America First trade policy. The agreement anticipates nearly full tariff removals on goods, notably reducing the 10% EU auto tariff to zero over 7 years. Honda, which has a large plant in the UK, announced in 2019 will close production in favor exporting from Japan under its new free trade agreement with the EU.

The EU expects to export more agricultural, textile, chemicals, wood products and leather goods to Japan. Tariff rate quota limitations will protect Japan from EU wheat, dairy, pork, sugar, soft cheese, and beef. Free trade will not apply to rice, Japan's "sacred" food sector, which is protected by a 777% tariff.

Many Japanese nontariff trade barriers (NTBs) will be clarified and relaxed, including those related motor vehicles, medical devices, textile labeling, and beer. In general, technical barriers to trade will be governed by international standards.

Trade in services is expanded beyond WTO commitments, notably in the following fields: Postal and courier services, telecommunications, finance, and international maritime transport. Temporary business and professional visas going beyond anything the EU had previously agreed to are adopted.

State-owned enterprises of either country will receive national treatment when buying or selling on commercial markets. Mutual procurement opportunities are expanded, especially in allowing EU firms to bid on tenders of 54 "core cities" in Japan.

There are obligations to recognize of the eight "fundamental" ILO Conventions, duty free electronic transmissions, and a bar on forced disclosure of source codes. Each side has acknowledged the "adequacy" of the other's data privacy regimes, a priority for the EU operating under its 2018 General Data Protection Regulation. Geographical indicators from Kobe beef to Feta cheese are protected.

In a first for an FTA, the parties reaffirmed their commitment to the Paris Accord on Climate Change. Various provisions promote sustainable development and corporate social responsibility. There is a specific chapter on corporate governance derived from G20/OECD Principles. The EU ban on imports of whale products is retained in the face of continued Japanese whaling practices. General state-to-state dispute settlement procedures are established.

Foreign investment rules and related dispute settlement are being negotiated separately. These are particularly sensitive to Japan, which has never had to defend itself in investor-state arbitration proceedings.

The Japan-EU Economic Partnership Agreement took effect in 2019.

§ 5.7   EU Foreign Investment Treaties

Foreign investment has traditionally been governed by the national laws and treaties of the member states. Hundreds of Bilateral Investment Treaties (BITs) have been negotiated between member states and other, largely developing nations. Germany, for example, has well over 100 BITs, and France nearly as many.

BIT *"treaty shopping"* inside the European Union to avoid the dubious legitimacy of national courts in Poland, Hungary, and quite a few other EU states has been undertaken by making investments in those countries via U.K., Dutch and German companies (typically shell or mailbox companies) benefiting from *intra-EU* BITs. See Chapter 7.

Numerous foreign investors have taken certain European countries (notably Poland, The Czech Republic, Spain, and Hungary) to arbitration concerning cancelled subsidies, changes in regulatory environments, and expropriation.

About 200 *intra-EU* member-state bilateral investment treaty (BIT) arbitration provisions have effectively been invalidated by the European Court of Justice in its landmark 2018 *Slovak Republic v. Achmea* (C-284/16) decision discussed in Chapter 7. The logic of the Court's reasoning is that such provisions interfere with the autonomy, effectiveness, and primacy of the EU legal regime. This reasoning led the ECJ to subsequently rule that Energy Charter Treaty arbitrations (see Chapter 7) are also invalid under EU law. *See Republic of Moldova v. Komstroy LLC* (C-741/19) (2021).

Awards rendered under intra-EU BITs may be unenforceable, but there are arbitral proceedings that continue despite these ECJ rulings. *Achmea* also raises questions as to whether *extra-EU* member state BIT arbitrations, which are numerous, may also be unenforceable. See Chapter 7.

Traditionally, EU BITs have included foreign investment law rules and dispute settlement exclusively by investor-state arbitrations (ISDS). Recent FTAs with Vietnam, Singapore, Mexico, and MERCOSUR adopt the EU's "new generation" policy for foreign investment dispute settlement. This policy anticipates using an Investment Court to oversee ISDS arbitrations.

It is expected that national BITs will in time be replaced by EU BITs. A prime example is the historic China-EU bilateral investment agreement (BIT) finalized New Years' eve in 2020 *despite Biden team requests to hold off for an allied approach.*

The EU-China 2021 Bilateral Investment Treaty (BIT)

China and the European Union finalized very late in December 2020 a bilateral foreign investment agreement, the EU-China Comprehensive Agreement on Investment (CAI). Led by Germany, this agreement was undertaken despite requests by the incoming Biden administration to delay and organize a transatlantic U.S.-EU strategy for dealing with China. Once ratified by the European Parliament, this treaty will replace 26 existing bilateral investment treaties (BITs) between China and individual EU Member States. Ratification remains pending at this writing.

The CAI outlines two-way "rules of the road" for foreign investment between the EU and China. Foreign investors will obtain better access on fairer terms. The CAI opens markets with Beijing making concessions on financial services, manufacturing, real estate, construction, advertising, air transport, maritime services, telecom and, to a limited extent, cloud computing.

In turn, China secured the EU's agreement to open its renewable energy sector to Chinese investment. The CAI also prohibits forced tech transfer by EU firms that establish themselves in China and includes provisions to enhance the transparency of state subsidies for Chinese state-owned companies (which generate about 30% of the PRC's GDP). These subsidy transparency rules notably encompass services. On the human rights side, Beijing pledged to adhere to International Labor Organization's rules against forced labor. The Paris agreement on climate change is affirmed.

Commenced in 2014, the Trump trade war gave Beijing a sense of urgency to cut a deal with Brussels, particularly as U.S.-China BIT negotiations had been going nowhere. Of critical importance to Beijing is a desire to stave off any anti-China alliance. Politically symbolic, CAI represents rejection of the Trump administration's aggressive, disruptive trade policy against both China *and* Europe. Indeed, a U.S.-led containment strategy for China may be the biggest loser.

The CAI demonstrates that Europe can take the lead on negotiations and stand up to China, a position that the U.S. forfeited when it abandoned U.S.-China BIT negotiations and multilateral platforms such as the TPP, TTIP and WTO. Having piled on sanctions against Chinese companies and investors in the USA, the silence on CAI from the outgoing Trump Administration on the deal was deafening.

Some observers feared CAI would tie the hands of the incoming Biden Administration. Other observers believe the Biden administration should not fret over CAI since much of its content aligns with U.S. interests. CAI could possibly turn out to be a foundational document and benchmark for follow-up BIT negotiations by the Biden team with the PRC.

I am indebted to USD Law alumnus Attorney James Zimmerman of the Perkins Coie firm in Beijing for his CAI insights.

§ 5.8   Franchising and Tech Transfers in Europe

Franchising and technology transfer terms associated with foreign investment in the European Union must conform the rules contained in what are called "group exemptions" from EU business competition law (antitrust). Group exemption regulations are largely self-enforced, meaning lawyers drafting franchising and technology transfer provisions typically adhere to them to be sure of their validity and secure an exemption from EU competition law fines and penalties.

Franchising

The EU Commission, following leading European Court of Justice decisions, adopted a "group exemption" (Regulation 4087/88) from EU business competition (antitrust) law for franchise agreements. This 1988 regulation required each franchisee to identify itself as an independent enterprise apart from the trademark/service mark/trade name owner. Disclosure could avoid joint and several franchisor liability for the provision by franchisees of defective goods or services. Regulation 4087/88 defined a "franchise" as a package of industrial or intellectual property rights relating to trademarks, trade names, signs, utility models, designs, copyrights, knowhow, or patents exploited for the resale of goods or the provision of services to customers.

"Franchise agreements" were defined as those in which the franchisor grants the franchisee, in exchange for direct or indirect financial consideration, the right to exploit a franchise to market specified types of goods and/or services. A "*master franchise agreement*" involves the right to exploit a franchise by concluding franchising agreements with third parties. Starting with these basics, Regulation 4087/88 proceeded to detail permitted, permissible and prohibited clauses in EU franchise agreements.

Vertical Restraints Regulation

This approach remained in force until 2000, when the European Union "group exemptions" for exclusive dealing, exclusive purchasing and franchise agreements were replaced by Regulation 2790/99, known as the Vertical Restraints Regulation, accompanied by lengthy vertical restraints Guidelines.

This Regulation and its guidelines are more economic and less formalistic than the predecessors. The efficiency enhancing qualities of intra-brand vertical restraints are recognized. Supply, distribution (including selective distribution) and franchise agreements of firms with less than 30 percent market shares are generally exempt; this is known as a "safe harbor."

Companies whose market shares exceed 30 percent may or may not be exempt, depending upon the results of individual competition law reviews. Since 2004, these may be undertaken by the Commission, national competition authorities and national courts. In either case, no vertical agreements containing so-called "hard core restraints" are exempt. These restraints concern primarily resale price maintenance, territorial and customer protection leading to market allocation, and in most instances exclusive dealing covenants that last more than five years.

In 2010, a new Vertical Restraints Regulation 330/10 (with accompanying Guidelines) was issued. Its content is comparable to that of 1999. Restrictions on the use of the Internet by distributors or franchisees with at least one "brick-and-mortar" store are treated as hard core restraints. For example, distributors and franchisees cannot be required to reroute Internet customers outside their territories to local dealers. Nor can they be forced to pay higher prices for online sales ("dual pricing") or be limited in the amount sales made via the Internet although minimum offline sales can be stipulated.

Distributors and franchisees may typically sell anywhere in the EU in response to customer demand ("passive sales"). Restraints on "actively" soliciting sales outside designated distributor or franchise territories, including by email or banner web advertising, are permissible. *Both* supplier and distributor, and franchisor and franchisee, must have less than 30% market shares to qualify for the 2010 "safe harbor."

Patent, Knowhow, and Software Licensing

The European Union, as befits a major technology center, has a strong intellectual property regime. The EU adheres to the TRIPs agreement and has created regional EU Trademarks and EU Unitary Patents, in addition to traditional national IP rights of the member states.

After major decisions of the European Court of Justice, the EU adopted separate patent licensing and knowhow licensing regulations in 1984 and 1989, which were later merged into the Transfer of Technology Regulations (TT) outlined immediately below. These regulations are called "group exemptions" under EU business competition law, encouraging parties and their lawyers to draft patent and knowhow license agreements that conform to their contents. Failure to do so, can result in Commission prosecutions, fines, and penalties, as well as voiding of the agreement or parts thereof.

Transfer of Technology Regulation 240/96

In 1996 the European Commission enacted Regulation 240/96 on the application of Article 101(3) of the Treaty on the Functioning of the European Union (TFEU) to transfer technology agreements. The intention of this Regulation was to combine existing patent and knowhow business competition law exemptions into a single regulation covering technology transfer agreements, and to simplify and harmonize the rules for patent and knowhow licensing. It contained detailed lists of permitted, permissible, and prohibited clauses.

Regulation 240/96 stated that Article 101(1) of the Treaty did not apply to "pure patent and knowhow licensing agreements and missed patent and knowhow licensing agreements," as well as to agreements with ancillary provisions relating to intellectual property other than patents, when only two undertakings are parties and when one or more of eight listed obligations were included. These were obligations of limitation, such as not to license other undertakings to exploit the technology.

There were time limits (5 years for patents/10 years for knowhow) for the exemption of these eight obligations in certain situations. Article 1 was known as the White-List. Article 2 allowed technology transfers even when certain clauses existed (17 were listed). These clauses were considered generally not restrictive of competition. There were various obligations on the licensee, such as not divulging knowhow communicated by the licensor. Article 2 was known as the Permissible List.

Article 3 of Regulation 240/96 designated that Articles 1 and 2(2) did not apply when any one of seven obligations were present, such as restricting a party in the determination of prices, competition restrictions, limitations on production quantity, licensee improvement grant-back requirements, etc. Article 3 was known as the Black-List. Article 4 carried the scope of the exemption provided for in Articles 1 and 2 to certain other restrictive agreements which were notified to the Commission and received no Commission opposition. Article 4 was known as the Gray List. Regulation 240/96, according to Article 5, did not apply to four classes of agreements, such as most agreements within a joint venture. But under Article 5 it did apply to three forms of agreements, including where the licensor is itself a licensee of the technology and was authorized to grant sub-licenses.

The Commission retained power to withdraw benefits of the Regulation 240/96 if in a specific case the exempted agreement was incompatible with the conditions of Article 101(3). Final articles provided some definitions, a list of what were deemed patents, preservation of confidentiality of information, and the repeal of the two regulations combined in this regulation.

Transfer of Technology Regulation 772/2004

The detailed regulation of technology transfer agreement clauses contained in Regulation 240/96 was replaced by Regulation 772/2004, which generally applies to patent, knowhow, production trademark and software copyright licensing. The new Regulation distinguishes agreements between those of "competing" and "noncompeting" parties, the latter being treated less strictly than the former. Parties are deemed "competing" if they compete (without infringing each other's IP rights) in either the relevant technology or product market, determined in each instance by what buyers regard as substitutes. If the competing parties have a *combined* market share of 20 percent or less, their licensing agreements are covered by group exemption under Regulation 772/2004.

Noncompeting parties, on the other hand, benefit from the group exemption so long as their *individual* market shares do not exceed 30 percent. Agreements initially covered by Regulation 772/2004 that subsequently exceeded the "safe harbor" thresholds noted above lost their exemption subject to a two-year grace period. Outside these exemptions, a "rule of reason" approach applied.

Inclusion of certain "hardcore restraints" causes license agreement to lose their group exemption. For competing parties, such restraints include price fixing, output limitations on both parties, limits on the licensee's ability to exploit its own technology, and allocation of markets or competitors (subject to exceptions). Specifically, restraints on active and passive selling by the licensee in a territory reserved for the licensor are allowed, as are active (but not passive) selling restraints by licensees in territories of other licensees.

Licensing agreements between noncompeting parties may not contain the "hardcore" restraint of maximum price fixing. Active selling restrictions on licensees can be utilized, along with passive selling restraints in territories reserved to the licensor or (for two years) another licensee. For these purposes, the competitive status of the parties is decided at the outset of the agreement.

Other license terms deemed "excluded restrictions" also cause a loss of exemption. Such clauses include:

(1) mandatory grant-backs or assignments of severable improvements by licensees, excepting nonexclusive license-backs;

(2) no-challenges by the licensee of the licensor's intellectual property rights, subject to the licensor's right to terminate upon challenge; and

(3) for noncompeting parties, restraints on the licensee's ability to exploit its own technology or either party's ability to carry out research and development (unless indispensable to prevent disclosure of the licensed knowhow).

Transfer of Technology Regulation 316/2014

Regulation 316/2014 replaced Regulation 772/2004, with a one-year transition period to adapt existing TT agreements. Regulation 316/2014 is valid until 2026 and clarifies that it applies to technology transfers only if other EU regulations concerning research and development (Regulation 2659/2000) and/or specialization agreements (Regulation 2658/2000) are inapplicable.

The distinction between competing and noncompeting parties under Regulation 772/2004 is retained, as are their market share thresholds.

Restrictive changes were made to the TT group exemption regulation as follows:

(1) All *exclusive* grant-back licensee obligations require individual assessment, as do termination clauses triggered by licensee challenges to the validity of the technology. Such clauses are no longer covered by the group exemption.

(2) Purchase requirements from licensors of raw material or equipment are group exempt only if directly related to the production or sale of products made with the licensed technology.

(3) No passive sales restrictions on licensees are group exempt unless objectively necessary for the licensee to penetrate a new market.

(4) Settlement agreements which lead to delayed or limited ability for licensee launch of the product in any market ("pay-for-delay" or "reverse payment" agreements) may be prohibited under certain conditions, as may no-challenge clauses in settlement agreements, particularly if the patent was granted based on incorrect or misleading information.

(5) Technology licensing pools now enjoy a comprehensive, detailed group exemption provided they adhere to Regulation 316/2014.

In all cases, exemption under Regulation 772/2004 or Regulation 316/2014 may be withdrawn where an agreement has effects that are incompatible with Treaty Article 101(3).

For more coverage of EU technology protection and transfer law, see my *European Union Beyond BREXIT* Concise Hornbook, Chapter 15. Regulations 772/2004 and 316/2014 are reproduced in Sections 5.16 and 5.17 below.

§ 5.9   Mergers and Acquisitions

One alternative to direct investment in Europe is to purchase an existing business. Traditionally, the law governing such acquisitions was almost exclusively national. Since 1990, the EU actively regulates sizeable mergers and acquisitions as part of its competition policy. European law in this area is summarized below. Special attention should also be paid to the United States-European Community Antitrust Cooperation Agreement (1991) under which coordinated exchanges of information and review of transnational mergers frequently occur.

In December of 1989, the Council of Ministers unanimously adopted Regulation 4064/89 on the Control of Concentrations between Undertakings ("Mergers Regulation"). This regulation became effective Sept. 21, 1990 and was expanded in scope by amendment in 1997 (Regulation 1310/97). It vests in the Commission the exclusive power to oppose large-scale mergers and acquisitions of competitive consequence to the Common Market and the European Economic Area.

For these purposes, a "concentration" includes almost any means by which control over another firm is acquired. This could be by a merger agreement, stock or asset purchases, contractual relationships, or other actions. Most full function joint ventures creating autonomous economic entities are caught by this test. Thus "control" triggering review can be achieved by minority shareholders, such as when they exercise decisive influence over strategic planning and investment decisions. "Cooperative joint ventures" between independent competitors may also be subject to from the Mergers Regulation.

Pre-Merger Notifications

The control process established by the Mergers Regulation commences when a concentration must be notified to the Commission on Form CO in one of the official languages. This language becomes the language of the proceeding. Form CO resembles second request Hart-Scott-Rodino pre-merger notification filings under U.S. antitrust law. However, the extensive need for detailed product and geographic market descriptions, competitive analyses, and information about the parties in Form CO suggests a more demanding submission. Form CO defines a product market as follows:

> A relevant product market comprises all those products and/or services which are regarded as interchangeable or substitutable by the consumer, by reason of the products' characteristics, their prices, and their intended use.

Meeting in advance of notification with members of the Commission on an informal basis to ascertain whether the "concentration" has a regional dimension and is compatible with the Common Market has become widely accepted. Such meetings provide an opportunity to seek waivers from the various requests for information contained in Form CO. Since the Commission is bound by rules of professional secrecy, the substance of the discussions is confidential.

Merger Jurisdiction and Rules

The duty to notify applies within one week of the signing of a merger agreement, the acquisition of a controlling interest or the announcement of a takeover bid. The Commission can fine any company failing to notify it as required. The duty to notify is triggered only when the concentration involves enterprises with a combined worldwide sales turnover of at least 5 billion Euros (approximately $6 billion) *and* two of them have an aggregate regional turnover of 250 million Euros (approximately $300 million). Additionally, since 1997, mergers with a combined aggregate worldwide turnover of more than 2.5 billion Euros and significant member state and regional turnovers must be notified.

Concentrations meeting these criteria cannot be put into effect and fall exclusively within the Commission's domain. The effort here is to create a "one-stop" regulatory system. However, certain exceptions apply to allow national authorities to challenge some mergers. For example, this may occur under national law when two-thirds of the activities of each of the companies involved take place in the *same* member state. The member states can also oppose mergers by appealing Commission decisions when their public security is at stake, to preserve plurality in media ownership, when financial institutions are involved, or other legitimate interests are at risk.

If the threshold criteria of the Mergers Regulation are not met, member states can ask the Commission to investigate mergers that create or strengthen a dominant position in that state. States that lack national mergers' controls seem likely to do this. Similarly, if the merger only affects a particular market sector or region in a member state, that state may request referral of the merger to it. This is known as the "German clause" reflecting Germany's insistence upon it. It has been sparingly used by the Commission.

Once a concentration is notified to the Commission, it has one month to decide to investigate the merger. If a formal investigation is commenced, the Commission ordinarily then has four months to challenge or approve the merger. During these months, in most cases, the concentration cannot be put into effect. It is on hold.

Effective May 1, 2004, the test for EU merger compatibility was changed to the following: Does the merger "significantly impede effective competition" by creating or strengthening dominant positions? The new test focuses on effects, not dominance. A set of Guidelines on Horizontal Mergers was issued by the Commission in 2004 that elaborate on this approach.

It is thought that this change will bring EU and U.S. mergers law closer together (the U.S. test is "substantial lessening of competition"). During a merger investigation, the Commission can obtain information and records from the parties, and request member states to help with the investigation. Fines and penalties back up the Commission's powers to obtain records and information from the parties.

If the concentration has already taken effect, the Commission can issue a "hold-separate" order. This requires the corporations or assets acquired to be separated and not, operationally speaking, merged. Approval of the merger may involve modifications of its terms or promises by the parties aimed at diminishing its anticompetitive potential. Negotiations with the Commission to obtain such approvals follow. If the Commission ultimately decides to oppose the merger in a timely manner, it can order its termination by whatever means are appropriate to restore conditions of effective competition (including divestiture, fines, or penalties).

Such decisions can be appealed to the General Court. That Court has confirmed that mergers resulting in collective (oligopolistic) dominance of a market fall within European mergers regulation.

Mergers: Case Examples

The first merger blocked by the Commission on competition law grounds was the attempted acquisition of a Canadian aircraft manufacturer (DeHaviland—owned by Boeing) by two European companies (Aerospatiale SNI of France and Alenia e Selenia Spa of Italy). Prior to this rejection in late 1991, the Commission had approved over 50 mergers, obtaining modifications in a few instances. The Commission, in the DeHaviland case, took the position that the merger would have created an unassailable dominant position in the world and the European market for turbo prop or commuter aircraft. If completed, the merged entity would have had 50 percent of the world and 67 percent of the European market for such aircraft.

In contrast, the Commission approved (subject to certain sell-off requirements) the acquisition of Perrier by Nestlé. Prior to the merger, Nestlé, Perrier, and BSN controlled about 82 percent of the French bottled water market. Afterwards, Nestlé and BSN each had about 41 percent of the market. The sell-off requirements were thought sufficient by the Commission to maintain effective competition. The case also presents interesting arguments that the Commission, in granting approval, disregarded fundamental workers' social rights. This issue was unsuccessfully taken up on appeal by Perrier's trade union representative.

In 1997, the Commission dramatically demonstrated its extraterritorial jurisdiction over the Boeing-McDonnell Douglas merger. This merger had already been cleared by the U.S. Federal Trade commission. The European Commission, however, demanded and (at the risk of a trade war) got important concessions from Boeing. These included abandonment of exclusive supply contracts with three U.S. airlines and licensing of technology derived from McDonnell Douglas' military programs at reasonable royalty rates. The Commission's success in this case was widely perceived in the United States as pro-Airbus.

The Commission blocked the MCI Worldcom/Sprint merger in 2001, as did the U.S. Dept. of Justice. For the Commission, this was the first block of a merger taking place outside the EU between two firms established outside the EU. The AOL/Time Warner merger was approved by the Commission after AOL promised to sever links with a German media group, thereby reducing its music publishing rights for delivery online via the Internet.

Much more controversy arose when in 2001 the Commission blocked the GE/Honeywell merger after it had been approved by U.S. authorities. The Commission was particularly concerned about the potential for bundling engines with avionics and non-avionics to the disadvantage of rivals. This bundling theory was rejected in 2005 by the European General Court. Nevertheless, the merger never took place. The United States and the EU, in the wake of GE/Honeywell, have agreed to follow a set of "Best Practices" on coordinated timing, evidence gathering, communication and consistency of remedies in the mergers field.

The EU General Court (GC) overturned a 1999 decision of the European Commission blocking the $1.2 billion merger of Airtours plc and First Choice Holidays plc. The June 2002 GC decision was a notable reversal of an EU merger prohibition. The GC judgment confirmed that transactions can be blocked on collective dominance grounds but found that the Commission had failed to meet the three conditions for proving collective dominance:

> (1) Each member of the dominant group can determine readily how the others are behaving;

> (2) There is an effective mechanism to prevent group members from departing from the agreed-upon policy; and

> (3) Smaller competitors are unable to undercut that policy.

In 2002, acting under "fast track" review procedures, the General Court overturned two additional mergers decisions of the

Commission. The Court found serious errors, omissions, and inconsistencies. Credible evidence, not assumptions or "abstract and detached analysis," must be tendered to prove the strengthening or creation of a dominant position, and the likelihood that the merger will significantly impede competition.

The Commission may be found liable in damages for intervening unlawfully against mergers, notably when making manifest procedural errors. Commission decisions to clear joint ventures or mergers can in rare cases be annulled.

§ 5.10   Hostile Takeovers and National Champions

In June of 2002 the European Court of Justice issued three decisions on the use by member states of so-called "golden shares." Such shares allow governments to retain veto rights with respect to acquisitions of or other significant accumulations in privatized businesses. The Court outlawed a golden share decree allowing France to block a foreign takeover of a privatized oil company. The golden share decree created a barrier to the free movement of capital. The Court also outlawed a law giving Portugal the ability to block the acquisition of controlling stakes in privatized state companies but determined as a matter of public interest that Belgium could retain its golden share in recently privatized canal and gas distribution companies.

Hostile Takeovers

In 2004, the EU adopted a directive on hostile takeover bids. Its two most controversial rules are optional. First, boards of directors are required to obtain shareholder approval before taking defensive measures other than seeking alternative offers. Second, once a bid has been made public, restrictions on share transfers, voting restrictions, and special voting rights are unenforceable.

Hence member state law on hostile takeovers is not uniform. The French, for example, allow use of any defense permitted by the home country of the bidder, and have published a list of strategic sectors that are off-limits to foreign takeovers. In 2007, the ECJ overturned the decades-old "Volkswagen Law." This law had prevented anyone except the government of Lower Saxony from owning more than 20% of the voting rights to Volkswagen. Its invalidation permitted Porsche to complete its hostile takeover of VW.

National Champions

EU countries often pursue policies to prevent "national champions" from falling into the hands of foreign investors, particularly those from outside the Union. If, for example, a U.S. or Chinese firm seeks to acquire a "national champion", state controls and incentives are likely to prevent that outcome, often by arranging a friendly takeover by a national or at least an EU company. Fear of acquisition of major companies has led to novel ideas. France famously indicated that foreign acquisition of Danone, its national champion yogurt maker, would not be tolerated.

Austria discussed the establishment of an Austro-fund to buy controlling interests of major Austrian firms, such as Böhler-Uddeholm (steel), Wienerberger (clay bricks), OMV (oil and gas), Voest (steel), and Lenzing (cellulose fiber). Austria has generally been hostile to major takeovers by foreign forms, while Austrian banks and companies have invested heavily abroad.

Spain has long protested major takeovers, sometimes encouraging instead alternative joint ventures. Spanish politicians, fearing a German takeover of Endesa, Spain's largest electricity company, pushed for an acquisition by Spanish-shareholder owned Gas Natural. Then it pushed for Italy's state-owned energy company Enel, to join with the Spanish firm Acciona, which had already acquired some 20% of Endesa, to make an offer.

Since 2005, France requires government approval of foreign takeovers in 11 key sectors of the economy. Failing "national champions" may present opportunities, which proved to be the case in 2015 when GE, not Germany's Siemens, was finally allowed by the European Commission to purchase the French industrial "crown jewel" Alstom.

Referencing America First and Made in China 2025 and seeking to shield its key industries from foreign takeovers and competition, Germany announced in 2019 creation of a National Industry Strategy 2030 plan. Under this plan, Germany expects to take stakes in strategically significant businesses (such as automobiles, machine tools and chemicals) to protect them from foreign takeovers. Germany is determined to support and retain its national champions.

§ 5.11 COVID-19 Impact

Just as BREXIT was accomplished late in January 2020, the COVID pandemic virus arrived. COVID made negotiating a UK-EU future relations agreement more difficult and raised red flags for foreign investors.

In the following months, the EU and UK responses varied considerably. Important EU rules were relaxed or overwhelmed. Government subsidies, notably regulated by EU law, proliferated as individual countries sought to rescue their economies. For example, France pumped 8 billion Euros into Renault and Germany sent 9 billion Euros into Lufthansa in return for 20% government ownership. Overall, German subsidies cannot be matched by other EU states, threatening to undermine the operation of the EU's Single Market.

Financial controls came under great pressure as Germany for the very first time acquiesced in agreement with France to *collectively backed* "coronabonds". These common EU bonds are intended to raise money for hard-hit Italy, Spain, and southern member states. They are funded in part by new EU taxes on unrecycled plastic waste and digital levies. The EU Central Bank is authorized to buy coronabonds, essentially eliminating risk of default. Resistance by "The Frugals" (Austria, Denmark, the Netherlands, and Sweden) resulted in greater EU budget rebates for them, and possible "emergency brake" limits on COVID bailout funding.

In crisis mode, the ECB resumed substantial purchases of national bonds ("quantitative easing"), even Greek bonds, as the EURO Zone (above) struggled. Border restraints on goods, notably medical equipment, and medicines, emerged. Structural shifts, such as re-shoring, combined with increased supply chain protectionism, diminished economic activity.

EU fiscal controls over national spending were significantly suspended. Different but major national economic contractions emerged as a European recession set in. Doomloop risks rose as shrinking economies made it harder to service national debts.

Perhaps most seriously, extensive border restraints on people essentially negated the Schengen free movement of people regime. See my *European Union Beyond BREXIT* Concise Hornbook, Chapter 4. Early on in 2020 EU nations adopted entry bans against each other, later relaxed selectively among "travel bubble" partners subject to mandatory COVID testing rules. In July 2020, international controls barred persons coming from COVID heavy countries like the USA, Russia, and Brazil. Note that the USA had previously in the pandemic crisis barred entry to many EU residents, and barred entry to the world absent a negative COVID test. The arrival of the Delta and Omicron COVID variants generated similar free movement restrictions in 2021 and 2022.

§ 5.12 BREXIT Impact

BREXIT shook the foundations of the European Union and the United Kingdom as foreign investment magnets. The material that follows examines why and how.

Since 2009, Article 50 of the Treaty on European Union (TEU) permits member states to commence withdrawal negotiations from the European Union. Prime Minister Cameron, wanting badly to be re-elected in 2015 and seeking to appease the hard-core Euroskeptic wing of the Conservative Party, promised in his campaign to re-negotiate Britain's position in the EU and hold a referendum on remaining an EU member state. He won re-election, and after negotiating modest changes in U.K.-EU relations, put the Remain or Leave issue to a public vote.

In a hotly contested campaign, with free movement of people within the EU a prominent issue. Leave supporters made statements that were simply untrue, for example that Britain would save not pay money by leaving and that the National Health Service would directly benefit from these savings. Future Prime Minister Boris Johnson actively participated in promoting this idea.

At no point did the leaders of the Leave movement present a clear plan for or picture of its consequences. Critics maintain that the Leave vote was secured by a campaign riddled with falsehoods that often seemed disconnected from reality. Some Brexiteers even suggested a return to nostalgic Empire glory.

Russia actively supported BREXIT, primarily via divisive Facebook accounts, much as it did in the 2016 U.S. elections in supporting Donald Trump.

After approval by 52% of its voters in a high turnout June 2016 national referendum and strong approval by the House of Commons, Britain commenced two-year withdrawal negotiations on March 29, 2017, nearly the same date as the 60th anniversary of the EU. London, Scotland, and Northern Ireland voted heavily to remain, but the rest of England provided the Leave campaign with victory.

Theresa May, a Minister in David Cameron's Cabinet and a quiet Remain supporter, became Prime Minister shortly after the referendum in the wake of Cameron's resignation. For a considerable period, she simply said "BREXIT means BREXIT".

Two different BREXIT negotiations occurred. The first concerned "divorce" withdrawal terms finalized in 2019. The second negotiation, commenced in 2020, concerned future relations between the UK and the EU. Absent a future relations agreement, Britain and the EU faced a "no deal" hard exit, expected by many to be very damaging. During these negotiations there was a standstill. EU law governed, with no participation by the British in its supranational development.

Rallying around a cry for sovereignty, Britain under Prime Minister May commenced over two years of withdrawal negotiations on March 29, 2017, nearly the same date as the 60th anniversary of the EU.

Prime Minister May's Divorce Agreement

Seeking to raise her bargaining power with the EU under a clear mandate from the British people, Prime Minister May held a snap election in June of 2017. Much to her surprise and that of the pollsters, the Conservative Party lost majority control of the UK Parliament. Many factors were in play during the snap election, but it appeared that at least some British voters had second thoughts about the wisdom of BREXIT, particularly the "hard" version she espoused.

The Conservatives were consequently forced to govern in coalition with a small Protestant-dominated Northern Ireland party, the DUP. This coalition was fragile. The DUP wanted agricultural subsidies post-BREXIT, continued access to EU development funds for poorer regions, and a "frictionless" border with Ireland. The DUP leaned toward remaining in the EU.

Some Brexiteers suggested pursuing the "soft exit" Norwegian or Swiss models for relations with the EU post-BREXIT. But these complicated models for the most part involved acceptance of free movement of people, the EU customs union, cash contributions to the EU budget, and deference to EU/EFTA Court decisions. To what degree would a soft exit really be an exit?

Prime Minister May indicated she would continue to pursue a "hard" exit. Prime Minister May was quoted as saying that "better no deal, than a bad deal," suggesting Britain might walk out of the negotiations. By 2019, despite repeated efforts, she was unable to secure UK Parliamentary approval for the BREXIT deal she had negotiated with the EU.

The core issue was the possibility under "stopgap" provisions, if no future relations agreement was accomplished, that all of the UK would remain inside the EU customs union in order to ensure that the border between Northern Ireland and Ireland would not become "hard". This possibility sparked fears of a return to violence and conflict like that before the Good Friday accords.

Prime Minister Johnson's Divorce Agreement

In July 2019, Prime Minister May resigned and in the ensuing elections Boris Johnson, former mayor of London and a brazen Brexiteer, became Prime Minister. In short order, he re-negotiated the BREXIT divorce deal to remove hard land border risks, essentially creating an internal UK/EU customs and immigration border in the middle of the Irish Sea cooperatively administered by British and EU authorities.

Under this Divorce Agreement, the UK firmly left the EU customs union, thus freeing up Britain to engage in trade agreement negotiations around the world. Northern Ireland remained part of the UK customs regime but obliged to collect VAT taxes and tariffs on goods (but not services) on behalf of the EU. Northern Ireland also remained in the EU's regulated "single market" for goods.

It was agreed that new cooperatively run "trusted traveler" rules on goods moving between Britain and Northern Ireland be established in UK ports. These checks are meant to assure regulatory conformity (especially on agricultural goods and meat) and collect taxes/tariffs on goods "at risk" of being transported or smuggled into the EU via Northern Ireland.

The EU-UK Protocol on Northern Ireland has had a rocky start. Britain wishes to substantially alter it the EU uphold it. Negotiations are underway. Sanctions for its breach are authorized. Unlike all other parts of their BREXIT deal, review of the Protocol by the European Court of Justice is possible.

Money Matters

As a mandatory prerequisite to withdrawal negotiations, early on in Prime Minister May's tenure, the EU presented Britain with an expensive "divorce bill" for what it perceived the UK would owe the Union upon departure. The demand for cash included Britain's liabilities under the generous, entirely unfunded EU pension scheme. It also covered pre-BREXIT and post-BREXIT EU projects under the British-approved EU budget running from 2013 through 2020.

In the end, the "divorce bill" amounted to approximately 35 billion Euros. This bill no doubt stunned many Leave backers, who were led to believe BREXIT would result in a net savings not loss. In addition, Britain lost two well-staffed and well-paid EU agencies, one on Medicines (EMA), the other on banking (EBA).

On the flip side, the EU must adapt to the loss of Britain as a net contributor to its budget.

Done Divorce Deal

The Johnson divorce deal (formally titled the Withdrawal Agreement) was subsequently approved by the EU and the UK Parliaments thereby setting the formal date for BREXIT to occur on Jan. 31, 2020.

§ 5.13 The 2021 EU-UK Trade and Cooperation Agreement (TCA)

The 2021 EU-UK Trade and Cooperation Agreement attempts to repair some of the damage done to both parties post-BREXIT.

Many in the EU felt Britain should "pay a price" to leave. Put another way, to paraphrase one EU leader: "It cannot be the case that Britain ends up better off outside the EU than inside". Overall, the adverse trade consequences of BREXIT for the UK were more significant than for the EU. The UK, for example, sends nearly 50% of its exports to the EU, while less than 10% of EU exports end up in Britain. The UK depends on exports to the EU for approximately 13% of its GDP, while the EU depends on exports to the UK for only 3% of its GDP. All that said, Britain is the largest market for EU exports (notably autos made in Germany) and the fifth biggest economy in the world, considerations which played in the UK's favor.

Bottom line: The independent UK Office for Budget Responsibility forecasts the British economy will be 4% smaller under the TCA than if it had remained.

Nevertheless, after much negotiation and threats of failure, a complex 2,000-page UK-EU Trade and Cooperation Agreement) (TCA) was finally reached on Christmas eve of 2020. It took effect Jan. 1, 2021.

Fundamentally a "thin" free trade in goods (only) agreement, the TCA removes Britain from the EU customs union and the EU single market freedoms for cross-border movement of goods, services, people, and capital. *Unlike most trade deals, the TCA creates more trade and investment restraints than it removes.*

The BREXIT future relations deal needed qualified majority approval by the EU Council, which for these purposes meant 20 out of 27 member states constituting at least 65% of the EU population must affirm the deal. The consent of the European Parliament as well as the UK Parliament was also required.

Specific Divorce and TCA provisions are noted in the topics below, followed by an outline of the TCA.

Fishing

It may seem a bit strange, but the issue that most held up the Trade and Cooperation Agreement (TCA) was fishing. The EU created a Common Fisheries Policy (CFP) just prior to the entrance of the Britain in 1973. It allows EU member states considerable rights to fish in traditionally national waters and regulates levels of catch. Swapping of fish quotas is no longer allowed under the TCA.

Long a thorn in British culture and its economically insignificant fishing industry, the TCA establishes quotas that reduce by 25% over 5.5 years most EU (notably French) rights to fish in UK waters. Thereafter annual negotiations will follow. The irony of this focus is that, for reasons of taste, much of the fish caught or raised in UK waters are exported to the Continent. These exports are expected to continue and are not subject to immediate EU retaliation tariffs if in breach of the TCA, a major concession by the EU that essentially closed the future relations deal.

Early signs under Fishing accord suggest cod catches by British boats (the mainstay of British "Fish n' Chips") have declined. Exports of fish and shellfish to the EU are tied up in new paperwork requirements. Some Scottish trawlers have taken to running their salmon directly to Denmark where prices are double those of the UK.

Free Movement and Residency Rights

Students, retirees, entrepreneurs and workers and their families and pets (with pet passports!) have long enjoyed free movement residency, health care and no roaming cell phone rights throughout the Union, no work permit or visas needed. Existing residency rights (in the UK known as "settled status") were protected under the Divorce Agreement but become subject on both sides after BREXIT to substantial paperwork requirements and fees.

What happens to the nearly 1 million Poles, 350,000 Romanians, 270,000 French citizens, and the other 2 million or so EU nationals working in Britain? What happens to the 1.2 million British retirees and others on the continent? What about EU professionals and restaurant owners who have exercised their EU "right of establishment" to set up shop in the UK, and vice-versa?

One could argue that Britain has obtained a younger, more skilled taxpaying workforce under the EU free movement of people regime. The EU in turn has received a goodly number of higher cost UK seniors.

Future "free movement" rights are eliminated. The TCA enacts visa-controlled movement of people across borders from 2021 forward.

For example, the extensive EU Erasmus Program facilitating hundreds of thousands of cross-border student studies, work experiences and apprenticeships will not be available to students from England, Wales, and Scotland, but (thanks to underwriting by Ireland) will be open to students from Northern Ireland. Mutual recognition of professional qualifications, such as those of doctors, nurses, and architects, will be more limited than under EU rules.

Apart from liberal UK-Ireland travel rules, tourist visas as between the UK and the Schengen area will be good for 90 days of travel during any six-month period. Advance electronic authorizations will be required commencing in 2022. Travel insurance with health care coverage will likely become standard. Mutual emergency health care should generally become available, but not automatic for kidney dialysis and the like.

Fearing the worst, some British citizens began efforts to obtain other EU passports to preserve free movement and other EU rights. Dual nationality in Ireland, Sweden and Germany rank high on this list. A small steady flow of EU nationals out of the UK commenced early in BREXIT's evolution, but most are planning to remain.

Free Internal Trade

Agreeing to tariff free *and quota* free trade was relatively easy for the UK and EU in their TCA negotiations. This was the first time the EU had ever agreed to quota free trade.

On both sides, hundreds of millions of customs and tax forms, fees, import licenses, security checks and certifications must now be regularly filed, a significant and costly trade barrier, especially to the UK. Facing lengthy back-ups, cross-border trucking fees are noticeably up. Early signs suggest some UK importers are reducing and even in some cases eliminating EU imports. Marks & Spencer, for example, dropped hundreds of products from its Northern Ireland stores. During February of 2021, UK exports to the EU were down roughly 50% under new EU customs and COVID regulations.

Complex rules of origin for goods suddenly apply. For example, gas and diesel autos must contain at least 55% UK and EU combined content to be freely traded. For electric and hybrid vehicles, the rule of origin requirement is 40%, but their batterie are limited in the amount of allowable overseas content starting with 70% and running down to 50% by 2026. More red tape is likely to proliferate, particularly as there are no common certification standards on safety, pollution, and the like for autos. Dual production runs for EU and UK compliant vehicles may emerge.

For another example, Britain imports about 25% of its food from the EU while 60% of its agricultural exports head to the continent. No tariffs and quotas apply, but the absence of TCA agreement on common sanitary and phytosanitary standards for food raises UK and in reverse EU certification and paperwork issues galore. Much the same problem and costs could emerge regarding pharmaceutical testing and safety certifications.

Britain in principle escaped the EU's voluminous *"acquis communautaire"*, its vast body of internal trade legislation, regulations, and case law. But many European Union rules seem inescapable since all goods exported from Britain will need to conform to EU law, and extensive cross-border supply chains compel compliance. For example, all auto imports must under the EU End of Life Vehicles Directive be 95% reusable or recyclable.

The EU, recognizing that the two sides will inevitably become competitors, feared that the UK might become a "Singapore-upon-Thames" neighbor with low-cost product standards and taxation. It extracted significant regulatory commitments from the UK not found in its Canada or Japan free trade agreements (below).

The Divorce deal suggested that each side would keep the same standards on state subsidies, competition law, social and employment rules, the environment, climate change and "relevant" tax matters. In addition, the UK agreed to create an independent regulator of government subsidies along the lines of the EU competition authorities.

These "level playing field" regulations were incorporated in the TCA on a "non-regression" basis, meaning the UK promised not to dilute them, but reserved the right to do so subject to possible (but not instant) retaliatory EU trade sanctions. Arbitration procedures were established to resolve disputes in this critical area, notably avoiding the jurisdiction of the European Court of Justice (ECJ).

But if the UK retains EU standards and regulations, will not interpretations of those rules by the ECJ come along with them in arbitrations?

Services and Business Passport Rights

The TCA does not retain the core EU freedom to provide services across borders (see Chapter 5). The British economy relies *very* heavily on its services sector, including IT, legal, accounting, insurance, consultation, audiovisual, and architecture for examples.

Much of the EU services sector operates on "passport" principles under EU law. Bankers, securities firms, insurance companies and the like need only obtain a license in one EU state, which then basically qualifies them to do business in the other member states. Britain, London, and The City comprise the financial center of Europe. Financial firms (including U.S. firms) used British licenses to springboard throughout the EU.

Without passport rights, and if British regulatory rules do not measure up as "equivalent" to those of the EU, British, U.S. and global finance and service companies licensed in the UK could join the BREXIT exodus. Early in the BREXIT saga this started happening, with roughly 7500 financial sector employees and $1.6 trillion in financial assets departing to the benefit of Frankfurt, Paris, Luxembourg, Dublin and even New York.

The EU has made it clear that certain financial operations traditionally done in London will be obliged to be done within its borders. Most clearing house operations, derivatives, EURO bond and direct client services are expected as a matter of EU law to be undertaken inside the Union. Trading of EU stocks shifted almost immediately from London to EU-based exchanges, including the London Stock Exchange's Turquoise platform in Amsterdam.

Even if some British service sector regulations are deemed "equivalent" to the EU, such treatment can be removed by the EU with 30 days' notice.

Foreign Investment

Many foreign, especially Asian and North American, investors set up manufacturing and service centers in Britain. For example, Japanese car companies are notably invested in the United Kingdom. Japan was sufficiently worried about BREXIT that its government delivered a detailed memo of concern to the U.K. soon after the vote to leave in 2016.

British and foreign manufacturers based in the U.K. were especially nervous about going from zero tariff entry into the EU to paying tariffs to gain entry to what will remain the world's largest common market. Autos, for example, are subject to 10% EU import tariffs, agricultural goods subject to 30–40% tariffs. In addition, nontariff regulatory barriers could emerge if British health, safety, subsidy, and environmental standards differ from those of the EU.

British and foreign investors essentially put a hold on investment or expansion of existing operations in the U.K. after the BREXIT vote while negotiations proceeded over four years. Just before the scheduled BREXIT deadline of March 29, 2019, Honda announced it would exit production in the U.K. in favor of USA and Japanese plants. Honda anticipates free trading autos into the EU under the 2019 EU-Japan Economic Partnership Agreement discussed below.

Jaguar Land Rover cut UK employment by thousands of jobs. Dyson, of vacuum cleaner fame, moved its headquarters to Singapore prior to inaugurating an electric vehicle. Nissan too will undertake EV auto production outside the UK. BMW defensively moved its engine plant from the UK to Germany. It seems fair to say, that many investors in the UK perceived that BREXIT in any form represented a clear and present danger. That perspective was not eliminated by the EU-UK Trade and Cooperation Agreement of 2021.

More broadly, late in 2020 the EU completed a bilateral Cooperation Agreement on Investment (CAI, referred to as a "BIT") with China (below). Will the UK follow that path? As noted below, BITs *among* EU members have been invalidated by the European Court of Justice. Britain escapes this ruling via BREXIT.

The UK post-BREXIT quickly legislated a new National Security and Investment Act focused on foreign investment in a range of 17 industries from artificial intelligence to energy. From November 2020 forward, this Act requires notification to the UK government for national security review if a foreign entity is acquiring more than 25% of a British firm in these industries. Companies trying to sell overseas assets used "in connection with activities" in Britain can also be subject to UK review. As under U.S. CFIUS law (see Sections 6.15, 6.16 and 6.17), "national security" is undefined under the British Act.

International Trade Relations

Britain pre-BREXIT derived its trade relations with the world predominantly via the EU. Absent a post-BREXIT agreement with the EU regarding future relations, Britain would likely have reverted to World Trade Organization rules. See my *International Trade Beyond Trump* Concise Hornbook, Chapter 1. How sound that assumption was, and what were its implications for the UK, the EU and WTO partners like the United States was unclear.

The UK had traded under WTO tariffs negotiated under the EU umbrella. Might it have needed to start over as an independent WTO member? Would the EU have needed to compensate WTO members because its tariffs were negotiated on the premise that the UK was included? Since 25% of American exports to the EU go to Britain, these issues mattered to the U.S. and incentivized reaching an agreement on future relations.

"Global Britain" after BREXIT hopes for lots of bilateral free trade and foreign investment deals. Initial dialogues commenced in 2020. Most of the over 70 EU free trade partners (including Korea, Canada, Mexico, Tunisia, Kenya, Southern Africa, Central America, Morocco, Egypt, Ukraine, Norway, Iceland, Japan, Vietnam, Turkey, Singapore) agreed to roll-over their EU deals to maintain "continuity" with the UK. Such free trade agreements raise critical "rules of origin" and costly documentation issues, for example regarding UK-made automobiles such as BMW's Mini-Coopers and Toyota vehicles.

Big deals with the likes of the United States, India, MERCOSUR, and China remain to be negotiated. In 2020, the EU proposed a "New Transatlantic Agenda" with the United States focused on digital supply chain security and data, climate change, product standards and dealing with COVID. In 2021, Australia and the UK signed a free trade agreement, the first for the UK outside of EU rollovers.

The interim year 2020 expanded the scope of UK/EU trade relation issues. Britain and France reversed policy in 2020 by removing participation by China's Huawei in their 5G network. Will the UK and the EU agree on digital revenue taxes, which would notably hit Google, Amazon, Microsoft, Facebook, and other U.S. tech companies? What about data privacy concerning which the EU has been a world leader? These issues remain unresolved.

What about the U.K.'s 2020 global human rights sanctions and blacklists applicable to Russian and Saudi individuals and entities? And the UK's response to the PRC's "national security" rules and repression in Hong Kong? Will the EU support either of these British efforts?

For the first time, in 2020, the EU imposed penalties and asset seizures against Russian, Chinese and North Korean cyberattacks . . . will the UK join them on this cold war trade front? What about EU sanctions against Turkey for its purchase of Russian missile systems and disputed drilling actions in the Eastern Med? And what about EU dual use regulations on technology and goods, subject to a "human rights catch all" . . . will the UK adhere?

On international trade and investment relations, how much EU-UK cooperation will emerge much remains to be seen. Early in 2021, demonstrating its independence, Britain adopted a National Security and Investment Act. This Act creates mandatory pre-notification and review with a wide range of application for merger, acquisition, and other transactions in 17 specific sectors with emphasis on technology. Un-notified deals may be reviewed, conditioned, or rejected by the DBEIS Investment Security Unit within five years of closing. Failure to notify can result in substantial fines and individual criminal sanctions. The unwinding of transactions could be ordered.

Northern Ireland and Scotland

Every political district in Scotland voted in 2016 to remain in the EU. But the Conservatives won 12 districts in the June 2017 snap election. The Scotch voted against leaving the UK several years prior to BREXIT. A second referendum could achieve Scottish independence in search of EU membership. Scotland, as an alternative to leaving the UK, might fairly ask whether special arrangements like those discussed below for Northern Ireland could not be made for it.

Nearly every district in Northern Ireland voted to remain. Peace and border-free transit has been directly linked under the Good Friday Accords to Irish and UK membership in the EU. After BREXIT, the Ireland/Northern Ireland border will be the only land crossing between Britain and the EU. Under the Divorce Agreement, the UK and the EU promised to cooperatively administer byzantine trade rules between Ireland and Northern Ireland to keep this border crossing free of customs and immigration controls.

As a practical matter, this means that Northern Ireland (unlike the UK) is *subject to EU single market regulations and the jurisdiction of the European Court of Justice.* Northern Island will collect VAT and tariffs on behalf of the EU. However, its goods will enter both the EU and the UK duty-free.

This provision was negatively received by Protestants in Northern Island, leading to a threat by the UK Parliament under the Johnson administration to disavow this Divorce Agreement term. It also caused U.S. presidential candidate Joe Biden to warn of his opposition to a return to a hard border. The threat further undermined EU trust in Boris Johnson as a reliable trade partner.

Critics maintain that BREXIT is toxic in the long run for the future of Northern Ireland as part of the UK. Certainly, the TCA pushes the Ireland and Northern Ireland towards eventual unification. The EU-UK agreement on Northern Ireland will be reviewed every four years, opening the door for participation by the Northern Ireland Parliament if it is functioning.

Ireland, a low-tax manufacturing center for many U.S. multinationals, ships substantial goods to the EU using Britain as an inexpensive land-bridge. This is a rat's nest of costly customs law after BREXIT. Already, shippers are using Irish ports and Cherbourg, France as an alternative that entirely avoids Britain. In addition, Ireland's food imports and exports from and to the UK are significant. Ireland has a big stake in BREXIT and the TCA.

Immigration and Free Movement of People

Immigration (mostly by EU nationals) was an issue central to the BREXIT vote. Since Britain does not participate in the Schengen Accord. The UK has always maintained its own external border controls for non-EU migrants. For EU and non-EU persons, Britain is establishing a new merit points-based immigration system, subject to considerable fees.

As noted above, apart from residency benefits existing as of 2021, what will change under the TCA are the extensive rights of UK and EU nationals to freely cross borders in pursuit of employment, education, retirement, or creation of a business.

Cooperation on Foreign Affairs and Security Matters

Administering the TCA will require ongoing trust and cooperation, qualities in short supply after the bruising BREXIT negotiations. The TCA provides for continued UK-EU cooperation on aviation, rail, trucking, defense, foreign affairs, climate change, energy, scientific research (Horizon), intelligence, and national security matters.

UK access to key EU databases will be by request. The UK will not be a member of Europol but will have "a presence" at its headquarters. Euro-Warrant criminal procedures may apply in or for the UK.

The Future of the EU

Britain having made its exit, whatever the price, why not others? In recent years, anti-EU parties have emerged throughout the Union. Marine Le Pen, leader of the National Front Party in France, openly ran on a platform promising a national referendum on leaving the EU (FREXIT). She was resoundingly defeated by Emmanuel Macron, a strong pro-EU candidate.

Does BREXIT signal a decline or even the end of the Union? Or perhaps expansion of a "multi-speed" Union, built around a core of EURO Zone states? Remarkably, the initial BREXIT impact served to unify and harden the EU's negotiating positions on divorce and future relations.

The Future of the UK

Britain, in leaving the world's largest common market, becomes an upper middling economic power, more like Japan for example. Yes, it is an independent nation, and yes it has considerable military and diplomatic resources, but it will struggle economically playing in the Big Leagues with China, the United States, and the European Union.

Even as a more nimble "Free Agent", Britain may ultimately have less power and influence in global economic affairs, particularly as self-sufficiency, nativist trade policies, and heightened national and cyber security emerge as top priorities after COVID and in the wake of China's rise to power.

Who Won?

BREXIT, in this author's opinion, harmed and will continue to harm both Britain and the European Union, more so for the former than the latter. Like the Swiss after Switzerland rejected EU membership, and given the endless joint committees and reviews provided for under the TCA, the UK should expect almost perpetual negotiations with the EU. In those negotiations, Britain (like Switzerland) should expect to generally be the supplicant.

The big BREXIT winner, in this author's opinion, is Vladimir Putin.

§ 5.14   The TCA 2021 in Outline

The TCA is expressly "based on international law, not EU law" (Article 14). Supervision and strategic guidance will be undertaken via a "Partnership Council". The TCA contains seven Parts.

Part I concerns common and institutional provisions. It creates joint cumulative rules of origin for goods (Chapter 2) and rules on technical barriers to trade building on the WTO TBT agreement (Chapter 3). Chapter 4 affirms the right of both sides to maintain their own Sanitary and Phytosanitary (SPS) measures. No mention is made of the WTO SPS Code. Chapter 5 on trade facilitation is based on WTO and WCO principles.

Part II governs trade in services and investment. It "locks in" market access in substantially all sectors along the lines of the EU and UK Free Trade Agreements with Japan. National treatment is a key principle along with temporary entry rights. Telecommunications, delivery services, international maritime, and financial services are detailed. New ground is broken for the provision of legal services by British attorneys advising clients on UK and public international law anywhere in the EU.

Title 3 liberalizes digital trade. Title 4 promotes capital movements. Title 5 focuses on IP rights, Title 6 public procurement, Title 7 small and medium enterprises, Title 8 energy, Title 9 Transparency and Title 10 on good regulatory practices.

Perhaps the most critical controversial area, Title 11 contains extensive provisions on creation of a "level playing field" for open and fair competition and sustainable development. Subsidies, competition law, SOEs, taxation, labor and social standards, the environment and climate all fall within Title 11.

Separate Headings in Part II exist for the rules on aviation, road transport, social security coordination, short-term visas, and fisheries.

Part III covers law enforcement and judicial cooperation in criminal matters. Data exchanges, mutual assistance, money laundering, terrorism, and cooperation with Europol and Eurojust are anticipated.

Part IV is titled "Thematic Cooperation". Health security, cyber security and "migration security" are its focus.

Part V anticipates UK participation in EU programs upon payment of appropriate fees. EU programs such as Horizon Europe, Euratom, Copernicus, and Space Surveillance are specifically named.

Part VI creates dispute settlement procedures and safeguard remedies. The opening language provides: "This Agreement includes dispute resolution mechanisms that are appropriate for a relationship between sovereign equals. This means that there is no role for the Court of Justice of the European Union."

Consultations about asserted breaches of the Agreement precede arbitration. No specific arbitration tribunals or procedures are provided. Rectification by the Party in breach or suitable compensation may follow. If the dispute is not resolved, then the Party not in breach can suspend obligations under the Agreement. Cross-suspension may occur, subject to certain conditions and limitations.

In the event of serious economic, societal or environment difficulties that are likely to persist, the EU or UK may unilaterally undertake strictly proportionate and time-limited remedial safeguard measures.

Part VII indicates that the Agreement is to be reviewed every five years and can be extended to new EU member states. It does not apply to Overseas Territories of the EU or UK. Either Party may terminate the Agreement with 12 months-notice.

§ 5.15 Europe and the United States

At over $1 trillion a year, the trading relationship between the United States and the European Union is the largest in the world, accounting for over one-third of global trade. Europe had a sizeable trade in goods surplus, while the U.S. had a small trade in services surplus. About one-third of the trade involves intra-company transfers between related firms.

The U.S. and EU investment in each other's markets is for both much greater than in all of Asia. EU job and technology creating investment in the U.S. amounts to over $6.5 trillion, and BMW's South Carolina production center is now the number one exporter of autos from the USA. Over four million Americans are employed at facilities owned by European firms. American investment in the Europe, including the UK, exceeds $3 trillion, with corresponding jobs and technology development.

For decades, though not without disputes taken to the WTO, the United States and Europe have maintained a critically important strategic and economic partnership. NATO, for example, counts 22 of the 27 EU states as members. All this suggests that America First policies and tariffs of the Trump administration placed much at risk. The U.S.-EU negotiations for a Transatlantic Trade and Investment Partnership (TTIP) initiated by President Obama disappeared.

President Trump's rejection of the Paris Accord on climate change, the Iran nuclear agreement, the short-range missile agreement with Russia, and his G7 plus Russia goals also signaled the potential for a dramatic shift in European-U.S. trade, security, and investment relations. The EU and others began to see "political risk" in the presidency of Donald Trump, an assessment more commonly associated with foreign investment in developing nations. President Biden has repaired some of the damage by returning to the Paris Accord, opening negotiations with Iran, and limiting the role of Russia in global affairs.

Subjecting the European Union to Trump's national security tariffs on steel and aluminum imports generated equivalent EU retaliation. See my *International Trade Beyond Trump* Concise Hornbook, Chapter 8. President Trump's threat to impose 25% national security tariffs on all U.S. auto imports sparked increased dialogue in 2018–19 between the EU and the United States. This dialogue aimed, a bit unrealistically, at negotiation of a "no subsidies, no nontariff trade barriers, and no tariffs outside industrial goods" agreement that would certainly enhance foreign investment prospects on both sides of the Atlantic. Limited progress has been made toward such an outcome.

President Biden has gradually moved in the direction of greater cooperation and reduced trade and investment tensions with the EU and the UK post-BREXIT. For example, a settlement of the longstanding Boeing-Airbus subsidy dispute has been achieved. Late in 2021, the U.S. agreed to replace Trump steel and aluminum tariffs with tariff rate quotas allowing significant EU avoidance of those tariffs. The EU in return reduced its retaliatory tariffs on U.S. goods. These tariffs remain in place on UK exports.

Biden has largely ignored British hopes for a bilateral trade and investment agreement with the United States.

§ 5.16   Text of EU Technology Transfer Regulation 772/2004

COMMISSION REGULATION (EC) No 772/2004

of 27 April 2004

on the application of Article 81(3) of the Treaty to categories of technology transfer agreements

(Text with EEA relevance)

THE COMMISSION OF THE EUROPEAN COMMUNITIES,

Having regard to the Treaty establishing the European Community,

Having regard to Council Regulation No 19/65/EEC of 2 March1965 on application of Article 85(3) of the Treaty to certain categories of agreements and concerted practices,[1] and in particular Article 1 thereof,

Having published a draft of this Regulation.[2]

After consulting the Advisory Committee on Restrictive Practices and Dominant Positions,

Whereas:

(1) Regulation No 19/65/EEC empowers the Commission to apply Article 81(3) of the Treaty by Regulation to certain categories of technology transfer agreements and corresponding concerted practices to which only two undertakings are party which fall within Article 81(1).

(2) Pursuant to Regulation No 19/65/EEC, the Commission has, in particular, adopted Regulation (EC) No 240/96 of 31 January 1996 on the application of Article 85(3) of the Treaty to certain categories of technology transfer agreements.[3]

(3) On 20 December 2001 the Commission published an evaluation report on the transfer of technology block exemption Regulation (EC) No 240/96.[4] This generated a public debate on the application of Regulation (EC) No 240/96 and on the application in general of Article 81(1) and (3) of the Treaty to technology transfer agreements. The response to the evaluation report from Member States and third parties has been generally in favor of reform of

---

[1] OJ 36, 6.3.1965, p. 533/65. Regulation as last amended by Regulation (EC) No 1/2003 (OJ L 1, 4.1.2003, p. 1).

[2] OJ C 235, 1.10.2003, p. 10.

[3] OJ L 31, 9.2.1996, p. 2. Regulation as amended by the 2003 Act of Accession.

[4] COM(2001) 786 final.

Community competition policy on technology transfer agreements. It is therefore appropriate to repeal Regulation (EC) No 240/96.

(4) This Regulation should meet the two requirements of ensuring effective competition and providing adequate legal security for undertakings. The pursuit of these objectives should take account of the need to simplify the regulatory framework and its application.

It is appropriate to move away from the approach of listing exempted clauses and to place greater emphasis on defining the categories of agreements which are exempted up to a certain level of market power and on specifying the restrictions or clauses which are not to be contained in such agreements. This is consistent with an economics-based approach which assesses the impact of agreements on the relevant market. It is also consistent with such an approach to make a distinction between agreements between competitors and agreements between non-competitors.

(5) Technology transfer agreements concern the licensing of technology. Such agreements will usually improve economic efficiency and be pro-competitive as they can reduce duplication of research and development, strengthen the incentive for the initial research and development, spur incremental innovation, facilitate diffusion and generate product market competition.

(6) The likelihood that such efficiency-enhancing and procompetitive effects will outweigh any anti-competitive effects due to restrictions contained in technology transfer agreements depends on the degree of market power of the undertakings concerned and, therefore, on the extent to which those undertakings face competition from undertakings owning substitute technologies or undertakings producing substitute products.

(7) This Regulation should only deal with agreements where the licensor permits the licensee to exploit the licensed technology, possibly after further research and development by the licensee, for the production of goods or services. It should not deal with licensing agreements for the purpose of subcontracting research and development. It should also not deal with licensing agreements to set up technology pools, that is to say, agreements for the pooling of technologies with the purpose of licensing the created package of intellectual property rights to third parties.

(8) For the application of Article 81(3) by regulation, it is not necessary to define those technology transfer agreements that are capable of falling within Article 81(1). In the individual assessment of agreements pursuant to Article 81(1), account has to be taken of several factors, and in particular the structure and the dynamics of the relevant technology and product markets.

(9) The benefit of the block exemption established by this Regulation should be limited to those agreements which can be assumed with sufficient certainty to satisfy the conditions of Article 81(3). In order to attain the benefits and objectives of technology transfer, the benefit of this Regulation should also apply to provisions contained in technology transfer agreements that do not constitute the primary object of such agreements but are directly related to the application of the licensed technology.

(10) For technology transfer agreements between competitors it can be presumed that, where the combined share of the relevant markets accounted for by the parties does not exceed 20 % and the agreements do not contain certain severely anti-competitive restraints, they generally lead to an improvement in production or distribution and allow consumers a fair share of the resulting benefits.

(11) For technology transfer agreements between non-competitors it can be presumed that, where the individual share of the relevant markets accounted for by each of the parties does not exceed 30 % and the agreements do not contain certain severely anti-competitive restraints, they generally lead to an improvement in production or distribution and allow consumers a fair share of the resulting benefits.

(12) There can be no presumption that above these market share thresholds technology transfer agreements do fall within the scope of Article 81(1). For instance, an exclusive licensing agreement between non-competing undertakings does often not fall within the scope of Article 81(1). There can also be no presumption that, above these market-share thresholds, technology transfer agreements falling within the scope of Article 81(1) will not satisfy the conditions for exemption. However, it can also not be presumed that they will usually give rise to objective advantages of such a character and size as to compensate for the disadvantages which they create for competition.

(13) This Regulation should not exempt technology transfer agreements containing restrictions which are not indispensable to the improvement of production or distribution. In particular, technology transfer agreements containing certain severely anti-competitive restraints such as the fixing of prices charged to third parties should be excluded from the benefit of the block exemption established by this Regulation irrespective of the market shares of the undertakings concerned. In the case of such hardcore restrictions the whole agreement should be excluded from the benefit of the block exemption.

(14) In order to protect incentives to innovate and the appropriate application of intellectual property rights, certain restrictions should be excluded from the block exemption. In particular, exclusive grant back obligations for severable improvements should be excluded. Where such a restriction is included in a licence agreement only the restriction in question should be excluded from the benefit of the block exemption.

(15) The market-share thresholds, the non-exemption of technology transfer agreements containing severely anticompetitive restraints and the excluded restrictions provided for in this Regulation will normally ensure that the agreements to which the block exemption applies do not enable the participating undertakings to eliminate competition in respect of a substantial part of the products in question.

(16) In particular, cases in which the agreements falling under this Regulation nevertheless have effects incompatible with Article 81(3), the Commission should be able to withdraw the benefit of the block exemption. This may occur in particular where the incentives to innovate are reduced or where access to markets is hindered.

(17) Council Regulation (EC) No 1/2003 of 16 December 2002 on the implementation of the rules on competition laid down in Articles 81 and 82 of the Treaty (1) empowers the competent authorities of Member States to withdraw the benefit of the block exemption in respect of technology transfer agreements having effects incompatible with Article 81(3), where such effects are felt in their respective territory, or in a part thereof, and where such territory has the characteristics of a distinct geographic market. Member States must ensure that the exercise of this power of withdrawal does not prejudice the uniform application throughout the common market of the Community competition rules or the full effect of the measures adopted in implementation of those rules.

(18) In order to strengthen supervision of parallel networks of technology transfer agreements which have similar restrictive effects and which cover more than 50 % of a given market, the Commission should be able to declare this Regulation inapplicable to technology transfer agreements containing specific restraints relating to the market concerned, thereby restoring the full application of Article 81 to such agreements.

(19) This Regulation should cover only technology transfer agreements between a licensor and a licensee. It should cover such agreements even if conditions are stipulated for more than one level of trade, by, for instance, requiring the licensee to set up a particular distribution system and specifying the obligations the licensee must

or may impose on resellers of the products produced under the licence. However, such conditions and obligations should comply with the competition rules applicable to supply and distribution agreements. Supply and distribution agreements concluded between a licensee and its buyers should not be exempted by this Regulation.

(20) This Regulation is without prejudice to the application of Article 82 of the Treaty,

HAS ADOPTED THIS REGULATION:

Article 1
Definitions

1.   For the purposes of this Regulation, the following definitions shall apply:

(a) 'agreement' means an agreement, a decision of an association of undertakings or a concerted practice;

(b) 'technology transfer agreement' means a patent licensing agreement, a know-how licensing agreement, a software copyright licensing agreement or a mixed patent, knowhow or software copyright licensing agreement, including any such agreement containing provisions which relate to the sale and purchase of products or which relate to the licensing of other intellectual property rights or the assignment of intellectual property rights, provided that those provisions do not constitute the primary object of the agreement and are directly related to the production of the contract products; assignments of patents, know-how, software copyright or a combination thereof where part of the risk associated with the exploitation of the technology remains with the assignor, in particular where the sum payable in consideration of the assignment is dependent on the turnover obtained by the assignee in respect of products produced with the assigned technology, the quantity of such products produced or the number of operations carried out employing the technology, shall also be deemed to be technology transfer agreements;

(c) 'reciprocal agreement' means a technology transfer agreement where two undertakings grant each other, in the same or separate contracts, a patent licence, a know-how licence, a software copyright licence or a mixed patent, know-how or software copyright licence and where these licences concern competing technologies or can be used for the production of competing products;

(d) 'non-reciprocal agreement' means a technology transfer agreement where one undertaking grants another undertaking a patent licence, a know-how licence, a software copyright licence or a mixed patent, know-how or software copyright licence, or where two undertakings grant each other such a licence but where these licences do not concern competing technologies and cannot be used for the production of competing products;

(e) 'product' means a good or a service, including both intermediary goods and services and final goods and services;

(f) 'contract products' means products produced with the licensed technology;

(g) 'intellectual property rights' includes industrial property rights, know-how, copyright and neighboring rights;

(h) 'patents' means patents, patent applications, utility models, applications for registration of utility models, designs, topographies of semiconductor products, supplementary protection certificates for medicinal products or other products for which such supplementary protection certificates may be obtained and plant breeder's certificates;

(i) 'know-how' means a package of non-patented practical information, resulting from experience and testing, which is:

(i) secret, that is to say, not generally known or easily accessible,

(ii) substantial, that is to say, significant and useful for the production of the contract products, and (iii) identified, that is to say, described in a sufficiently comprehensive manner so as to make it possible to verify that it fulfils the criteria of secrecy and substantiality;

(j) 'competing undertakings' means undertakings which compete on the relevant technology market and/or the relevant product market, that is to say:

(i) competing undertakings on the relevant technology market, being undertakings which license out competing technologies without infringing each other's intellectual property rights (actual competitors on the technology market); the relevant technology market includes technologies which are regarded by the licensees as interchangeable with or substitutable for the licensed technology, by reason of the technologies' characteristics, their royalties and their intended use,

(ii) competing undertakings on the relevant product market, being undertakings which, in the absence of the technology transfer agreement, are both active on the relevant product and geographic market(s) on which the contract products are sold without infringing each other's intellectual property rights (actual competitors on the product market) or would, on realistic grounds, undertake the necessary additional investments or other necessary switching costs so that they could timely enter, without infringing each other's intellectual property rights, the(se) relevant product and geographic market(s) in response to a small and permanent increase in relative prices (potential competitors on the product market); the relevant product market comprises products which are regarded by the buyers as interchangeable with or substitutable for the contract products, by reason of the products' characteristics, their prices and their intended use;

(k) 'selective distribution system' means a distribution system where the licensor undertakes to license the production of the contract products only to licensees selected on the basis of specified criteria and where these licensees undertake not to sell the contract products to unauthorized distributors;

(*l*) 'exclusive territory' means a territory in which only one undertaking is allowed to produce the contract products with the licensed technology, without prejudice to the possibility of allowing within that territory another licensee to produce the contract products only for a particular customer where this second licence was granted in order to create an alternative source of supply for that customer;

(m) 'exclusive customer group' means a group of customers to which only one undertaking is allowed actively to sell the contract products produced with the licensed technology;

(n) 'severable improvement' means an improvement that can be exploited without infringing the licensed technology.

2.   The terms 'undertaking', 'licensor' and 'licensee' shall include their respective connected undertakings.

'Connected undertakings' means:

(a)   undertakings in which a party to the agreement, directly or indirectly:

(i)   has the power to exercise more than half the voting rights, or

(ii)   has the power to appoint more than half the members of the supervisory board, board of management or bodies legally representing the undertaking, or

(iii)   has the right to manage the undertaking's affairs;

(b)   undertakings which directly or indirectly have, over a party to the agreement, the rights or powers listed in (a);

(c) undertakings in which an undertaking referred to in (b) has, directly or indirectly, the rights or powers listed in (a);

(d) undertakings in which a party to the agreement together with one or more of the undertakings referred to in (a), (b) or (c), or in which two or more of the latter undertakings, jointly have the rights or powers listed in (a);

(e) undertakings in which the rights or the powers listed in (a) are jointly held by:

(i) parties to the agreement or their respective connected undertakings referred to in (a) to (d), or

(ii) one or more of the parties to the agreement or one or more of their connected undertakings referred to in (a) to (d) and one or more third parties.

Article 2
Exemption

Pursuant to Article 81(3) of the Treaty and subject to the provisions of this Regulation, it is hereby declared that Article 81(1) of the Treaty shall not apply to technology transfer agreements entered into between two undertakings permitting the production of contract products. This exemption shall apply to the extent that such agreements contain restrictions of competition falling within the scope of Article 81(1). The exemption shall apply for as long as the intellectual property right in the licensed technology has not expired, lapsed or been declared invalid or, in the case of know-how, for as long as the know-how remains secret, except in the event where the know-how becomes publicly known as a result of action by the licensee, in which case the exemption shall apply for the duration of the agreement.

Article 3
Market-share thresholds

1. Where the undertakings party to the agreement are competing undertakings, the exemption provided for in Article 2 shall apply on condition that the combined market share of the parties does not exceed 20% on the affected relevant technology and product market.

2. Where the undertakings party to the agreement are not competing undertakings, the exemption provided for in Article 2 shall apply on condition that the market share of each of the parties does not exceed 30% on the affected relevant technology and product market.

3. For the purposes of paragraphs 1 and 2, the market share of a party on the relevant technology market(s) is defined in terms of the

presence of the licensed technology on the relevant product market(s). A licensor's market share on the relevant technology market shall be the combined market share on the relevant product market of the contract products produced by the licensor and its licensees.

Article 4
Hardcore restrictions

1.   Where the undertakings party to the agreement are competing undertakings, the exemption provided for in Article 2 shall not apply to agreements which, directly or indirectly, in isolation or in combination with other factors under the control of the parties, have as their object:

(a)   the restriction of a party's ability to determine its prices when selling products to third parties;

(b)   the limitation of output, except limitations on the output of contract products imposed on the licensee in a non-reciprocal agreement or imposed on only one of the licensees in a reciprocal agreement;

(c)   the allocation of markets or customers except:

(i)   the obligation on the licensee(s) to produce with the licensed technology only within one or more technical fields of use or one or more product markets,

(ii)   the obligation on the licensor and/or the licensee, in a non-reciprocal agreement, not to produce with the licensed technology within one or more technical fields of use or one or more product markets or one or more exclusive territories reserved for the other party,

(iii) the obligation on the licensor not to license the technology to another licensee in a particular territory,

(iv) the restriction, in a non-reciprocal agreement, of active and/or passive sales by the licensee and/or the licensor into the exclusive territory or to the exclusive customer group reserved for the other party,

(v)   the restriction, in a non-reciprocal agreement, of active sales by the licensee into the exclusive territory or to the exclusive customer group allocated by the licensor to another licensee provided the latter was not a competing undertaking of the licensor at the time of the conclusion of its own licence,

(vi) the obligation on the licensee to produce the contract products only for its own use provided that the licensee is not restricted in selling the contract products actively and passively as spare parts for its own products,

(vii) the obligation on the licensee, in a non-reciprocal agreement, to produce the contract products only for a particular customer, where the licence was granted in order to create an alternative source of supply for that customer;

(d) the restriction of the licensee's ability to exploit its own technology or the restriction of the ability of any of the parties to the agreement to carry out research and development, unless such latter restriction is indispensable to prevent the disclosure of the licensed know-how to third parties.

2. Where the undertakings party to the agreement are not competing undertakings, the exemption provided for in Article 2 shall not apply to agreements which, directly or indirectly, in isolation or in combination with other factors under the control of the parties, have as their object:

(a) the restriction of a party's ability to determine its prices when selling products to third parties, without prejudice to the possibility of imposing a maximum sale price or recommending a sale price, provided that it does not amount to a fixed or minimum sale price as a result of pressure from, or incentives offered by, any of the parties;

(b) the restriction of the territory into which, or of the customers to whom, the licensee may passively sell the contract products, except:

(i) the restriction of passive sales into an exclusive territory or to an exclusive customer group reserved for the licensor,

(ii) the restriction of passive sales into an exclusive territory or to an exclusive customer group allocated by the licensor to another licensee during the first two years that this other licensee is selling the contract products in that territory or to that customer group,

(iii) the obligation to produce the contract products only for its own use provided that the licensee is not restricted in selling the contract products actively and passively as spare parts for its own products,

(iv) the obligation to produce the contract products only for a particular customer, where the licence was granted in order to create an alternative source of supply for that customer,

(v)   the restriction of sales to end-users by a licensee operating at the wholesale level of trade,

(vi)   the restriction of sales to unauthorised distributors by the members of a selective distribution system;

(c)   the restriction of active or passive sales to end-users by a licensee which is a member of a selective distribution system and which operates at the retail level, without prejudice to the possibility of prohibiting a member of the system from operating out of an unauthorised place of establishment.

3.   Where the undertakings party to the agreement are not competing undertakings at the time of the conclusion of the agreement but become competing undertakings afterwards, paragraph 2 and not paragraph 1 shall apply for the full life of the agreement unless the agreement is subsequently amended in any material respect.

Article 5
Excluded restrictions

1.   The exemption provided for in Article 2 shall not apply to any of the following obligations contained in technology transfer agreements:

(a)   any direct or indirect obligation on the licensee to grant an exclusive licence to the licensor or to a third party designated by the licensor in respect of its own severable improvements to or its own new applications of the licensed technology;

(b)   any direct or indirect obligation on the licensee to assign, in whole or in part, to the licensor or to a third party designated by the licensor, rights to its own severable improvements to or its own new applications of the licensed technology;

(c)   any direct or indirect obligation on the licensee not to challenge the validity of intellectual property rights which the licensor holds in the common market, without prejudice to the possibility of providing for termination of the technology transfer agreement in the event that the licensee challenges the validity of one or more of the licensed intellectual property rights.

2.   Where the undertakings party to the agreement are not competing undertakings, the exemption provided for in Article 2 shall not apply to any direct or indirect obligation limiting the licensee's ability to exploit its own technology or limiting the ability of any of the parties to the agreement to carry out research and development, unless such latter restriction is indispensable to prevent the disclosure of the licensed know-how to third parties.

Article 6
Withdrawal in individual cases

1.   The Commission may withdraw the benefit of this Regulation, pursuant to Article 29(1) of Regulation (EC) No 1/2003, where it finds in any particular case that a technology transfer agreement to which the exemption provided for in Article 2 applies nevertheless has effects which are incompatible with Article 81(3) of the Treaty, and in particular where:

(a)   access of third parties' technologies to the market is restricted, for instance by the cumulative effect of parallel networks of similar restrictive agreements prohibiting licensees from using third parties' technologies;

(b)   access of potential licensees to the market is restricted, for instance by the cumulative effect of parallel networks of similar restrictive agreements prohibiting licensors from licensing to other licensees;

(c)   without any objectively valid reason, the parties do not exploit the licensed technology.

2.   Where, in any particular case, a technology transfer agreement to which the exemption provided for in Article 2 applies has effects which are incompatible with Article 81(3) of the Treaty in the territory of a Member State, or in a part thereof, which has all the characteristics of a distinct geographic market, the competition authority of that Member State may withdraw the benefit of this Regulation, pursuant to Article 29(2) of Regulation (EC) No 1/2003, in respect of that territory, under the same circumstances as those set out in paragraph 1 of this Article.

Article 7
Non-application of this Regulation

1.   Pursuant to Article 1a of Regulation No 19/65/EEC, the Commission may by regulation declare that, where parallel networks of similar technology transfer agreements cover more than 50 % of a relevant market, this Regulation is not to apply to technology transfer agreements containing specific restraints relating to that market.

2.   A regulation pursuant to paragraph 1 shall not become applicable earlier than six months following its adoption.

Article 8
Application of the market-share thresholds

1.   For the purposes of applying the market-share thresholds provided for in Article 3 the rules set out in this paragraph shall

apply. The market share shall be calculated on the basis of market sales value data. If market sales value data are not available, estimates based on other reliable market information, including market sales volumes, may be used to establish the market share of the undertaking concerned. The market share shall be calculated on the basis of data relating to the preceding calendar year. The market share held by the undertakings referred to in point (e) of the second subparagraph of Article 1(2) shall be apportioned equally to each undertaking having the rights or the powers listed in point (a) of the second subparagraph of Article 1(2).

2.   If the market share referred to in Article 3(1) or (2) is initially not more than 20 % respectively 30 % but subsequently rises above those levels, the exemption provided for in Article 2 shall continue to apply for a period of two consecutive calendar years following the year in which the 20 % threshold or 30 % threshold was first exceeded.

Article 9
Repeal

Regulation (EC) No 240/96 is repealed. References to the repealed Regulation shall be construed as references to this Regulation.

Article 10
Transitional period

The prohibition laid down in Article 81(1) of the Treaty shall not apply during the period from 1 May 2004 to 31 March 2006 in respect of agreements already in force on 30 April 2004 which do not satisfy the conditions for exemption provided for in this Regulation but which, on 30 April 2004, satisfied the conditions for exemption provided for in Regulation (EC) No 240/96.

Article 11
Period of validity

This Regulation shall enter into force on 1 May 2004. It shall expire on 30 April 2014.

§ 5.17   Text of EU Technology Transfer Regulation 316/2014

COMMISSION REGULATION (EU) No 316/2014

of 21 March 2014

on the application of Article 101(3) of the Treaty on the Functioning of the European Union to categories of technology transfer agreements

(Text with EEA relevance)

THE EUROPEAN COMMISSION,

Having regard to the Treaty on the Functioning of the European Union,

Having regard to Regulation No 19/65/EEC of the Council of 2 March 1965 on application of Article 85(3) of the Treaty to certain categories of agreements and concerted practices,[1] and in particular Article 1 thereof,

Having published a draft of this Regulation,

After consulting the Advisory Committee on Restrictive Practices and Dominant Positions,

Whereas:

(1)   Regulation No 19/65/EEC empowers the Commission to apply Article 101(3) of the Treaty by regulation to certain categories of technology transfer agreements and corresponding concerted practices to which only two undertakings are party which fall within Article 101(1) of the Treaty.

(2)   Pursuant to Regulation No 19/65/EEC, the Commission has in particular, adopted Commission Regulation (EC) No 772/2004.[2] Regulation (EC) No 772/2004 defines categories of technology transfer agreements which the Commission regarded as normally satisfying the conditions laid down in Article 101(3) of the Treaty. In view of the overall positive experience with the application of that Regulation, which expires on 30 April 2014, and taking into account further experience acquired since its adoption, it is appropriate to adopt a new block exemption regulation.

(3)   This Regulation should meet the two requirements of ensuring effective protection of competition and providing adequate

---

[1]   OJ 36, 6.3.1965, p. 533/65.

[2]   Commission Regulation (EC) No 772/2004 of 7 April 2004 on the application of Article 81(3) of the Treaty to categories of technology transfer agreements (OJ L 123, 27.4.2004, p. 11).

legal security for undertakings. The pursuit of those objectives should take account of the need to simplify administrative supervision and the legislative framework to as great an extent as possible.

(4) Technology transfer agreements concern the licensing of technology rights. Such agreements will usually improve economic efficiency and be pro-competitive as they can reduce duplication of research and development, strengthen the incentive for the initial research and development, spur incremental innovation, facilitate diffusion and generate product market competition.

(5) The likelihood that such efficiency-enhancing and pro-competitive effects will outweigh any anti-competitive effects due to restrictions contained in technology transfer agreements depends on the degree of market power of the undertakings concerned and, therefore, on the extent to which those undertakings face competition from undertakings owning substitute technologies or undertakings producing substitute products.

(6) This Regulation should cover only technology transfer agreements between a licensor and a licensee. It should cover such agreements even if the agreement contains conditions relating to more than one level of trade, for instance requiring the licensee to set up a particular distribution system and specifying the obligations the licensee must or may impose on resellers of the products produced under the licence. However, such conditions and obligations should comply with the competition rules applicable to supply and distribution agreements set out in Commission Regulation (EU) No 330/2010.[3] Supply and distribution agreements concluded between a licensee and buyers of its contract products should not be exempted by this Regulation. EN 28.3.2014 Official Journal of the European Union L 93/17.

(7) This Regulation should only apply to agreements where the licensor permits the licensee and/or one or more of its sub-contractors to exploit the licensed technology rights, possibly after further research and development by the licensee and/or its sub-contractors, for the purpose of producing goods or services. It should not apply to licensing in the context of research and development agreements which are covered by Commission Regulation (EU) No 1217/2010[1] or

---

[3]   Commission Regulation (EU) No 330/2010 of 20 April 2010 on the application of Article 101(3) of the Treaty on the Functioning of the European Union to categories of vertical agreements and concerted practices (OJ L 102, 23.4.2010, p. 1).

[1]   Commission Regulation (EU) No 1217/2010 of 14 December 2010 on the application of Article 101(3) of the Treaty on the Functioning of the European Union to certain categories of research and development agreements (OJ L 335, 18.12.2010, p. 36).

to licensing in the context of specialization agreements which are covered by Commission Regulation (EU) No 1218/2010.[2] It should also not apply to agreements, the purpose of which is the mere reproduction and distribution of software copyright protected products as such agreements do not concern the licensing of a technology to produce but are more akin to distribution agreements. Nor should it apply to agreements to set up technology pools, that is to say, agreements for the pooling of technologies with the purpose of licensing them to third parties, or to agreements whereby the pooled technology is licensed out to those third parties.

(8) For the application of Article 101(3) of the Treaty by regulation, it is not necessary to define those technology transfer agreements that are capable of falling within Article 101(1) of the Treaty. In the individual assessment of agreements pursuant to Article 101(1), account has to be taken of several factors, and in particular the structure and the dynamics of the relevant technology and product markets.

(9) The benefit of the block exemption established by this Regulation should be limited to those agreements which can be assumed with sufficient certainty to satisfy the conditions of Article 101(3) of the Treaty. In order to attain the benefits and objectives of technology transfer, this Regulation should not only cover the transfer of technology as such but also other provisions contained in technology transfer agreements if, and to the extent that, those provisions are directly related to the production or sale of the contract products.

(10) For technology transfer agreements between competitors it can be presumed that, where the combined share of the relevant markets accounted for by the parties does not exceed 20 % and the agreements do not contain certain severely anti-competitive restrictions, they generally lead to an improvement in production or distribution and allow consumers a fair share of the resulting benefits.

(11) For technology transfer agreements between non-competitors it can be presumed that, where the individual share of the relevant markets accounted for by each of the parties does not exceed 30 % and the agreements do not contain certain severely anti-competitive restrictions, they generally lead to an improvement in production or distribution and allow consumers a fair share of the resulting benefits.

---

[2] Commission Regulation (EU) No 1218/2010 of 14 December 2010 on the application of Article 101(3) of the Treaty on the Functioning of the European Union to certain categories of specialization agreements (OJ L 335, 18.12.2010, p. 43).

(12) If the applicable market-share threshold is exceeded on one or more product or technology markets, the block exemption should not apply to the agreement for the relevant markets concerned.

(13) There can be no presumption that, above those market-share thresholds, technology transfer agreements fall within the scope of Article 101(1) of the Treaty. For instance, exclusive licensing agreements between non-competing undertakings often fall outside the scope of Article 101(1). There can also be no presumption that, above those market-share thresholds, technology transfer agreements falling within the scope of Article 101(1) will not satisfy the conditions for exemption. However, it can also not be presumed that they will usually give rise to objective advantages of such a character and size as to compensate for the disadvantages which they create for competition.

(14) This Regulation should not exempt technology transfer agreements containing restrictions which are not indispensable to the improvement of production or distribution. In particular, technology transfer agreements containing certain severely anti-competitive restrictions, such as the fixing of prices charged to third parties, should be excluded from the benefit of the block exemption established by this Regulation irrespective of the market shares of the undertakings concerned. In the case of such hardcore restrictions the whole agreement should be excluded from the benefit of the block exemption.

(15) In order to protect incentives to innovate and the appropriate application of intellectual property rights, certain restrictions should be excluded from the benefit of the block exemption. In particular certain grant back obligations and non-challenge clauses should be excluded. Where such a restriction is included in a licence agreement only the restriction in question should be excluded from the benefit of the block exemption.

(16) The market-share thresholds and the non-exemption of technology transfer agreements containing the severely anti-competitive restrictions and the excluded restrictions provided for in this Regulation will normally ensure that the agreements to which the block exemption applies do not enable the participating undertakings to eliminate competition in respect of a substantial part of the products in question.

(17) The Commission may withdraw the benefit of this Regulation, pursuant to Article 29(1) of Council Regulation (EC) No 1/2003 (1), where it finds in a particular case that an agreement to which the exemption provided for in this Regulation applies nevertheless has effects which are incompatible with Article 101(3)

of the Treaty. This may occur in particular where the incentives to innovate are reduced or where access to markets is hindered.

(18) The competition authority of a Member State may withdraw the benefit of this Regulation pursuant to Article 29(2) of Regulation (EC) No 1/2003 in respect of the territory of that Member State, or a part thereof where, in a particular case, an agreement to which the exemption provided for in this Regulation applies nevertheless has effects which are incompatible with Article 101(3) of the Treaty in the territory of that Member State, or in a part thereof, and where such territory has all the characteristics of a distinct geographic market.

(19) In order to strengthen supervision of parallel networks of technology transfer agreements which have similar restrictive effects and which cover more than 50 % of a given market, the Commission may by regulation declare this Regulation inapplicable to technology transfer agreements containing specific restrictions relating to the market concerned, thereby restoring the full application of Article 101 of the Treaty to such agreements,

HAS ADOPTED THIS REGULATION:

Article 1
Definitions

1.   For the purposes of this Regulation, the following definitions shall apply:

(a) 'agreement' means an agreement, a decision of an association of undertakings or a concerted practice;

(b) 'technology rights' means know-how and the following rights, or a combination thereof, including applications for or applications for registration of those rights:

(i)   patents,

(ii) utility models,

(iii) design rights,

(iv) topographies of semiconductor products,

(v)   supplementary protection certificates for medicinal products or other products for which such supplementary protection certificates may be obtained,

(vi) plant breeder's certificates and

(vii) software copyrights;

(c) 'technology transfer agreement' means:

(i)   a technology rights licensing agreement entered into between two undertakings for the purpose of the production of contract products by the licensee and/or its sub-contractor(s),

(ii) an assignment of technology rights between two undertakings for the purpose of the production of contract products where part of the risk associated with the exploitation of the technology remains with the assignor;

(d) 'reciprocal agreement' means a technology transfer agreement where two undertakings grant each other, in the same or separate contracts, a technology rights licence, and where those licences concern competing technologies or can be used for the production of competing products;

(e) 'non-reciprocal agreement' means a technology transfer agreement where one undertaking grants another undertaking a technology rights licence, or where two undertakings grant each other such a licence but where those licences do not concern competing technologies and cannot be used for the production of competing products;

(f) 'product' means goods or a service, including both intermediary goods and services and final goods and services;

(g) 'contract product' means a product produced, directly or indirectly, on the basis of the licensed technology rights;

(h) 'intellectual property rights' includes industrial property rights, in particular patents and trademarks, copyright and neighbouring rights; EN 28.3.2014 Official Journal of the European Union L 93/19

(i) 'know-how' means a package of practical information, resulting from experience and testing, which is:

(i)   secret, that is to say, not generally known or easily accessible,

(ii) substantial, that is to say, significant and useful for the production of the contract products, and

(iii) identified, that is to say, described in a sufficiently comprehensive manner so as to make it possible to verify that it fulfils the criteria of secrecy and substantiality;

(j) 'relevant product market' means the market for the contract products and their substitutes, that is to say all those products which are regarded as interchangeable or substitutable by the buyer, by reason of the products' characteristics, their prices and their intended use;

(k) 'relevant technology market' means the market for the licensed technology rights and their substitutes, that is to say all those technology rights which are regarded as interchangeable or substitutable by the licensee, by reason of the technology rights' characteristics, the royalties payable in respect of those rights and their intended use;

(*l*) 'relevant geographic market' means the area in which the undertakings concerned are involved in the supply of and demand for products or the licensing of technology rights, in which the conditions of competition are sufficiently homogeneous and which can be distinguished from neighboring areas because the conditions of competition are appreciably different in those areas;

(m) 'relevant market' means the combination of the relevant product or technology market with the relevant geographic market;

(n) 'competing undertakings' means undertakings which compete on the relevant market, that is to say:

(i) competing undertakings on the relevant market where the technology rights are licensed, that is to say, undertakings which license out competing technology rights (actual competitors on the relevant market),

(ii) competing undertakings on the relevant market where the contract products are sold, that is to say, undertakings which, in the absence of the technology transfer agreement, would both be active on the relevant market(s) on which the contract products are sold (actual competitors on the relevant market) or which, in the absence of the technology transfer agreement, would, on realistic grounds and not just as a mere theoretical possibility, in response to a small and permanent increase in relative prices, be likely to undertake, within a short period of time, the necessary additional investments or other necessary switching costs to enter the relevant market(s) (potential competitors on the relevant market);

(o) 'selective distribution system' means a distribution system where the licensor undertakes to license the production of the contract products, either directly or indirectly, only to licensees selected on the basis of specified criteria and where those licensees undertake not to sell the contract products to unauthorised distributors within the territory reserved by the licensor to operate that system;

(p) 'exclusive licence' means a licence under which the licensor itself is not permitted to produce on the basis of the licensed technology rights and is not permitted to license the licensed technology rights to third parties, in general or for a particular use or in a particular territory;

(q) 'exclusive territory' means a given territory within which only one undertaking is allowed to produce the contract products, but where it is nevertheless possible to allow another licensee to produce the contract products within that territory only for a particular customer where the second licence was granted in order to create an alternative source of supply for that customer;

(r) 'exclusive customer group' means a group of customers to which only one party to the technology transfer agreement is allowed to actively sell the contract products produced with the licensed technology.

2.   For the purposes of this Regulation, the terms 'undertaking', 'licensor' and 'licensee' shall include their respective connected undertakings.

'Connected undertakings' means:

(a) undertakings in which a party to the technology transfer agreement, directly or indirectly:

(i) has the power to exercise more than half the voting rights, or

(ii) has the power to appoint more than half the members of the supervisory board, board of management or bodies legally representing the undertaking, or

(iii) has the right to manage the undertaking's affairs;

(b) undertakings which directly or indirectly have, over a party to the technology transfer agreement, the rights or powers listed in point (a);

(c) undertakings in which an undertaking referred to in point (b) has, directly or indirectly, the rights or powers listed in point (a);

(d) undertakings in which a party to the technology transfer agreement together with one or more of the undertakings referred to in points (a), (b) or (c), or in which two or more of the latter undertakings, jointly have the rights or powers listed in point (a);

(e) undertakings in which the rights or the powers listed in point (a) are jointly held by:

(i)   parties to the technology transfer agreement or their respective connected undertakings referred to in points (a) to (d), or

(ii)   one or more of the parties to the technology transfer agreement or one or more of their connected undertakings referred to in points (a) to (d) and one or more third parties.

Article 2
Exemption

1.   Pursuant to Article 101(3) of the Treaty and subject to the provisions of this Regulation, Article 101(1) of the Treaty shall not apply to technology transfer agreements.

2.   The exemption provided for in paragraph 1 shall apply to the extent that technology transfer agreements contain restrictions of competition falling within the scope of Article 101(1) of the Treaty. The exemption shall apply for as long as the licensed technology rights have not expired, lapsed or been declared invalid or, in the case of know-how, for as long as the know-how remains secret. However, where know-how becomes publicly known as a result of action by the licensee, the exemption shall apply for the duration of the agreement.

3.   The exemption provided for in paragraph 1 shall also apply to provisions, in technology transfer agreements, which relate to the purchase of products by the licensee or which relate to the licensing or assignment of other intellectual property rights or know-how to the licensee, if, and to the extent that, those provisions are directly related to the production or sale of the contract products.

Article 3
Market-share thresholds

1.   Where the undertakings party to the agreement are competing undertakings, the exemption provided for in Article 2 shall apply on condition that the combined market share of the parties does not exceed 20 % on the relevant market(s).

2.   Where the undertakings party to the agreement are not competing undertakings, the exemption provided for in Article 2 shall apply on condition that the market share of each of the parties does not exceed 30 % on the relevant market(s).

Article 4
Hardcore restrictions

1.   Where the undertakings party to the agreement are competing undertakings, the exemption provided for in Article 2 shall not apply to agreements which, directly or indirectly, in isolation or in

combination with other factors under the control of the parties, have as their object any of the following:

(a)   the restriction of a party's ability to determine its prices when selling products to third parties;

(b)   the limitation of output, except limitations on the output of contract products imposed on the licensee in a non-reciprocal agreement or imposed on only one of the licensees in a reciprocal agreement;

(c)   the allocation of markets or customers except:

(i)   the obligation on the licensor and/or the licensee, in a non-reciprocal agreement, not to produce with the licensed technology rights within the exclusive territory reserved for the other party and/or not to sell actively and/or passively into the exclusive territory or to the exclusive customer group reserved for the other party,

(ii)   the restriction, in a non-reciprocal agreement, of active sales by the licensee into the exclusive territory or to the exclusive customer group allocated by the licensor to another licensee provided the latter was not a competing undertaking of the licensor at the time of the conclusion of its own licence,

(iii) the obligation on the licensee to produce the contract products only for its own use provided that the licensee is not restricted in selling the contract products actively and passively as spare parts for its own products,

(iv)   the obligation on the licensee, in a non-reciprocal agreement, to produce the contract products only for a particular customer, where the licence was granted in order to create an alternative source of supply for that customer;

(d)   the restriction of the licensee's ability to exploit its own technology rights or the restriction of the ability of any of the parties to the agreement to carry out research and development, unless such latter restriction is indispensable to prevent the disclosure of the licensed know-how to third parties.

2.   Where the undertakings party to the agreement are not competing undertakings, the exemption provided for in Article 2 shall not apply to agreements which, directly or indirectly, in isolation or in combination with other factors under the control of the parties, have as their object any of the following:

(a)   the restriction of a party's ability to determine its prices when selling products to third parties, without prejudice to the possibility of imposing a maximum sale price or recommending a sale price, provided that it does not amount to a fixed or minimum sale price as a result of pressure from, or incentives offered by, any of the parties;

(b) the restriction of the territory into which, or of the customers to whom, the licensee may passively sell the contract products, except:

(i) the restriction of passive sales into an exclusive territory or to an exclusive customer group reserved for the licensor,

(ii) the obligation to produce the contract products only for its own use provided that the licensee is not restricted in selling the contract products actively and passively as spare parts for its own products,

(iii) the obligation to produce the contract products only for a particular customer, where the licence was granted in order to create an alternative source of supply for that customer,

(iv) the restriction of sales to end-users by a licensee operating at the wholesale level of trade,

(v) the restriction of sales to unauthorised distributors by the members of a selective distribution system;

(c) the restriction of active or passive sales to end-users by a licensee which is a member of a selective distribution system and which operates at the retail level, without prejudice to the possibility of prohibiting a member of the system from operating out of an unauthorized place of establishment.

3. Where the undertakings party to the agreement are not competing undertakings at the time of the conclusion of the agreement but become competing undertakings afterwards, paragraph 2 and not paragraph 1 shall apply for the full life of the agreement unless the agreement is subsequently amended in any material respect. Such an amendment includes the conclusion of a new technology transfer agreement between the parties concerning competing technology rights.

Article 5
Excluded restrictions

1. The exemption provided for in Article 2 shall not apply to any of the following obligations contained in technology transfer agreements:

(a) any direct or indirect obligation on the licensee to grant an exclusive licence or to assign rights, in whole or in part, to the licensor or to a third party designated by the licensor in respect of its own improvements to, or its own new applications of, the licensed technology;

(b)   any direct or indirect obligation on a party not to challenge the validity of intellectual property rights which the other party holds in the Union, without prejudice to the possibility, in the case of an exclusive licence, of providing for termination of the technology transfer agreement in the event that the licensee challenges the validity of any of the licensed technology rights.

2.   Where the undertakings party to the agreement are not competing undertakings, the exemption provided for in Article 2 shall not apply to any direct or indirect obligation limiting the licensee's ability to exploit its own technology rights or limiting the ability of any of the parties to the agreement to carry out research and development, unless such latter restriction is indispensable to prevent the disclosure of the licensed know-how to third parties.

Article 6
Withdrawal in individual cases

1.   The Commission may withdraw the benefit of this Regulation, pursuant to Article 29(1) of Regulation (EC) No 1/2003, where it finds in any particular case that a technology transfer agreement to which the exemption provided for in Article 2 of this Regulation applies nevertheless has effects which are incompatible with Article 101(3) of the Treaty, and in particular where:

(a)   access of third parties' technologies to the market is restricted, for instance by the cumulative effect of parallel networks of similar restrictive agreements prohibiting licensees from using third parties' technologies;

(b)   access of potential licensees to the market is restricted, for instance by the cumulative effect of parallel networks of similar restrictive agreements prohibiting licensors from licensing to other licensees or because the only technology owner licensing out relevant technology rights concludes an exclusive license with a licensee who is already active on the product market on the basis of substitutable technology rights.

2.   Where, in any particular case, a technology transfer agreement to which the exemption provided for in Article 2 of this Regulation applies has effects which are incompatible with Article 101(3) of the Treaty in the territory of a Member State, or in a part thereof, which has all the characteristics of a distinct geographic market, the competition authority of that Member State may withdraw the benefit of this Regulation, pursuant to Article 29(2) of Regulation

(EC) No 1/2003, in respect of that territory, under the same circumstances as those set out in paragraph 1 of this Article.

Article 7
Non-application of this Regulation

1.   Pursuant to Article 1a of Regulation (EC) No 19/65/EEC, the Commission may by regulation declare that, where parallel networks of similar technology transfer agreements cover more than 50% of a relevant market, this Regulation is not to apply to technology transfer agreements containing specific restrictions relating to that market.

2.   A regulation pursuant to paragraph 1 shall not become applicable earlier than six months following its adoption.

Article 8
Application of the market-share thresholds

For the purposes of applying the market-share thresholds laid down in Article 3 the following rules shall apply:

(a)   the market share shall be calculated on the basis of market sales value data; if market sales value data are not available, estimates based on other reliable market information, including market sales volumes, may be used to establish the market share of the undertaking concerned;

(b)   the market share shall be calculated on the basis of data relating to the preceding calendar year;

(c)   the market share held by the undertakings referred to in point (e) of the second subparagraph of Article 1(2) shall be apportioned equally to each undertaking having the rights or the powers listed in point (a) of the second subparagraph of Article 1(2);

(d)   the market share of a licensor on a relevant market for the licensed technology rights shall be calculated on the basis of the presence of the licensed technology rights on the relevant market(s) (that is the product market(s) and the geographic market(s)) where the contract products are sold, that is on the basis of the sales data relating to the contract products produced by the licensor and its licensees combined;

(e)   if the market share referred to in Article 3(1) or (2) is initially not more than 20% or 30% respectively, but subsequently rises above those levels, the exemption provided for in Article 2 shall continue to apply for a period of two consecutive calendar years following the year in which the 20% threshold or 30% threshold was first exceeded.

Article 9
Relationship with other block exemption regulations

This Regulation shall not apply to licensing arrangements in research and development agreements which fall within the scope of Regulation (EU) No 1217/2010 or in specialization agreements which fall within the scope of Regulation (EU) No 1218/2010.

Article 10
Transitional period

The prohibition laid down in Article 101(1) of the Treaty shall not apply from 1 May 2014 until 30 April 2015 to agreements already in force on 30 April 2014 which do not satisfy the conditions for exemption provided for in this Regulation but which, on 30 April 2014, satisfied the conditions for exemption provided for in Regulation (EC) No 772/2004.

Article 11
Period of validity

This Regulation shall enter into force on 1 May 2014. It shall expire on 30 April 2026.

This Regulation shall be binding in its entirety and directly applicable in all Member States.

Chapter 6

INVESTING IN NORTH AMERICA

Nations have not always welcomed *all* foreign investment. Investment that offers the nation something it lacks, such as technology or sufficient jobs, may be so welcome that it is encouraged by incentives. But foreign investment that competes with domestic firms may face complex obstacles or absolute prohibitions.

Every nation has its own history of foreign investment rules. The respective histories of Canada, Mexico, and the United States in developing each nation's current laws illustrate the struggle with balancing restrictions and incentives.

In some respects, Canada and Mexico have held similar views toward foreign investment, based on their experience with U.S. investment. Both nations remain concerned with dominance by U.S. investment. Both remain concerned they may become the source of foreign (mainly U.S.) investment to extract natural resources for shipment abroad or manufacture. Both remain concerned with the impact on their nation's balance of payments from the return of dividends to parent corporate owners. And finally, both are concerned that having so many foreign centers of decision-making will lead to few professional and managerial positions in Canada and Mexico for host-nation citizens.

This parallel set of concerns is partly why Canadian and Mexican foreign-investment laws, outlined below, have been quite restrictive. That said, the Canadian laws have often addressed more closely acquisitions versus investments commenced from scratch ("greenfields").

There are two schemes of foreign investments rules which must be addressed in North America. The first are the foreign investment laws and regulations of the individual North American countries. The foreign investment laws of Canada, Mexico and the United States are not only very different but have reached their status by means of quite separate histories. The second scheme is that of NAFTA 1994 and its sequel the USMCA of 2020. Both agreements established common foreign investment rules in many areas, though notably less so in 2020 versus 1994. See Chapter 8.

§ 6.1   Foreign Investment in Canada

Although U.S. persons often view Canada in a mirror and see themselves, assuming that the Canadian government will be very receptive to foreign investment, the policies of Canada over the years reflect ambivalence toward investment. Canada has long regulated foreign investment by both federal and provincial laws. Soon after its creation as a federation in 1867, Canada established high tariffs to protect infant industries from imports from the United States. This caused U.S. manufacturers to invest in Canada to surmount the tariff wall, principally through small "branch plants." Soon the United States was the principal source of foreign investment, and for many U.S. companies Canada was a natural location for their first foreign investments.

Most Canadian investment laws have focused on specific sectors, such as financial institutions, transportation, natural resources, and publishing. Oil and gas acquisitions were prohibited until the *Masse Policy*, adopted in 1992, was rescinded. This repeal left regulation to the Investment Canada Act, which allowed greenfields investments but required approval of some oil and gas acquisitions. However, the threshold before approval was required was quite high, making the law less restrictive than it otherwise appeared.

Canada considers publishing to be a cultural industry. Until restrictions in the Canadian *Baie Comeau Policy* on ownership of publishing were relaxed, foreign investment in publishing was very difficult.

Canada was always a natural target for investment from the United States, especially since so much of the industrial development of the United States occurred relatively near the Canadian border. Canada's attitude toward foreign investment remained quite receptive until nationalistic forces in the 1960s began to challenge its open investment policy. The first measure of significance was the creation of the Foreign Investment Review Agency (FIRA) in 1974, which allowed the federal government to review proposed foreign investment, especially acquisitions of Canadian companies, and in some cases deny their development or impose performance requirements. In 1984, a GATT panel notably upheld Canada's right to impose export commitments to obtain foreign investment approvals.

The National Energy Program in 1980 was intended to *reduce* foreign ownership in the oil and gas industry. Most of that foreign ownership was by U.S. companies. A Conservative government replaced the FIRA with the Investment Canada Act (ICA) (1985). This Act continues to govern foreign investment in Canada—especially acquisitions.

Canada's system, like that of Mexico and the U.S. when national security is involved (below), is a pre-investment clearance. Foreign investment review is examined under a "national interest" (including national security) standard. For example, when Burger King bought the iconic Canadian food chain, Tim Hortons, this merger was deemed not a threat to Canadian interests or security.

When Canada and the U.S. signed a bilateral free trade agreement in 1989, and again when NAFTA was adopted in 1994, decisions by Canada following a foreign investment review under the ICA were excluded from NAFTA's dispute settlement provisions. This exclusion continues under the USMCA Agreement of 2020. Hence Canada insisted on retaining some domestic pre-investment control over foreign investment by U.S. and Mexican firms, especially the acquisition of Canadian owned industries, and most especially "cultural" industries.

§ 6.2   Canadian Trade and Investment Restraints on Cultural Industries

Canada has a long history of supporting cultural industries through investment, financial, tax and other governmental acts. The 1989 free trade and foreign investment agreement between Canada and the United States excluded "cultural industries" from its scope. *This exclusion was retained under NAFTA 1994 and USMCA 2020.* The Canadian cultural industry exclusion covers the entire gamut of the USMCA agreement. It applies to goods, services, investment, intellectual property, and dispute settlement.

The argument for this exclusion is not to keep American culture out of the market, but instead to assure a Canadian presence as well. Indeed, Canada maintains that it has neither attempted nor succeeded in keeping out American cultural products and services. That certainly seems right. Over 90 percent of Canada's movie screens and more than 80 percent of its news and TV broadcasts are U.S. controlled. Books of U.S. origin occupy 60 percent of all Canadian shelf space and U.S. magazines take 80 percent of the English-language market.

Cultural industries are defined under the USMCA as those engaged in publishing, distributing, or selling:

- Books, periodicals and newspapers (except their printing or typesetting);

- Films or videos; audio or video music recordings; or printed or machine readable music;

- Public radio communications;

- Radio, television, and cable TV broadcasting; and

- Satellite programming and broadcasting network services (Article 2012).

One practical effect of securing the cultural industries exclusion has been to insulate Canada's broadcasting regulations from regional scrutiny. In Canada, content requirements and airtime rules are an important means by which the Canadian Radio-Television and Telecommunications Commission (CRTC) restricts the amount of foreign broadcast material. Current broadcasting regulations employ a quota system mandating Canadian content for a minimum of 60 percent of all programming and 50 percent of prime time. Comparable quotas apply to films, broadcast TV, cable TV and satellite transmissions.

"Canadian content" is calculated under a points system traditionally requiring that the producer be Canadian and that at least 6 of 10 key creative positions be filled by Canadians. In addition, most production and distribution expenses must be paid to Canadians.

The requirements for radio are similar and focus on the nationality of the composer and performer, and the location and performance of the selection. The government also provides subsidies and tax incentives for national broadcasting enterprises which have financial difficulty in complying with content quotas. Furthermore, investment regulations effectively limit U.S. ownership or control of Canadian cultural enterprises.

For example, Canada refused to permit Borders to open a super-bookstore in Toronto even after securing a Canadian partner as a majority owner. Ironically, although these economically driven rules ensure a national presence in broadcasting, they do not guarantee Canadian cultural content.

All that said, technology has greatly diminished the effectiveness of Canada's audio-visual content rules. Satellite transmission and Internet streaming have made strong inroads. There is a thriving gray market for dishes aimed at U.S. satellites receiving services paid via a U.S. billing address. More broadly, the Internet has undermined Canada's cultural industry trade restraints in ways that mostly avoid even the most determined regulator. Canadian limits on access to Netflix titles, for example, have been widely circumvented by obtaining U.S. Internet addresses via virtual private networks (VPN) installed on Canadian computers and other devices.

In contrast, there was no cultural industry exclusion under NAFTA 1994 or USMCA 2020 applicable to Mexico-United States trade and foreign investment. Integration of U.S.-Mexican cultural industries is occurring. In 1996, for example, the United States and Mexico reached agreement allowing companies in either country to compete for provision of satellite services, including direct-to-home and direct broadcast services. Each country retains the right to impose "reasonable" ownership, content, and advertising regulations, but Mexico (unlike Canada) will not impose local content requirements.

There are exceptions and qualifications to the general exclusion of Canadian cultural industries from free trade and investment. Tariff reductions have been specified under for film, cassettes, records, cameras, musical instruments, and the like. Responding to a United States complaint about Canadian cable TV "pirates," copyright royalties must be paid when U.S.-sourced free transmissions are retransmitted to the Canadian public by cable. In addition, no alteration or non-simultaneous retransmission of such broadcasts is permitted without the permission of the copyright holder. Likewise, no retransmission of cable or pay TV can occur without such authorization.

Occasionally, United States investors may acquire a Canadian cultural industry company by merger or acquisition. If ordered to divest, the U.S. investor must be paid open market value by Canada. Canada, for example, forced Simon & Shuster to divest a Canadian textbook publisher to a Canadian company, which subsequently went bankrupt. No other parties being interested, the Canadian government was obliged to buy the textbook publisher and sold it back to Simon & Shuster.

Canadian Cultural Industries Exclusion—the Sports Illustrated Dispute

Canada's cultural industry exception comes with a price. The United States can unilaterally implement retaliation for cultural industry protection. The U.S. can undertake "measures of equivalent commercial effect" against acts that would have been "inconsistent" but for the cultural industries exclusion. There is no need to utilize designated dispute settlement procedures prior to retaliation, which can be anything except a violation of the free trade agreement. The United States could, for example, pursue "Section 301" investigations and unilateral retaliation under the Trade Act of 1974. See my *International Trade Beyond Trump* Concise Hornbook, Chapter 8. Each year the United States Trade Representative must identify new Canadian acts, policies and practices affecting cultural industries.

Both Canada and the United States have sought to minimize the potential for cultural industry disputes through negotiations. The "successful" resolution of the Country Music Television (CMT) dispute in 1995 is often cited as an example. CMT of Nashville had, in the absence of a Canadian competitor, been licensed as a Canadian cable TV distributor. When a competitor emerged, CMT's license was revoked by the CRTC. CMT then petitioned the USTR for Section 301 relief, and an investigation was commenced. Intergovernmental negotiations resulted in the creation of a partnership of the two competitors, which was then licensed by the CRTC.

Cultural industry disputes have also been diverted from to the World Trade Organization as an alternative forum. In March of 1997, a WTO Dispute Settlement Panel ruled that Canada's taxes, import regulations and postal subsidies concerning magazines (and advertising) violated the GATT 1994 agreement. This longstanding dispute centered on *Sports Illustrated*. Canada was seeking to protect and ensure "Canadian issues" of periodicals and prevent the export of its advertising revenues.

The United States overcame culturally based Canadian policies by electing to pursue WTO remedies, although Canada's compliance was disputed. In May of 1999, a settlement was reached. United States publishers may now wholly own Canadian magazines. In addition, Canada will permit U.S. split-run editions without Canadian editorial content. Such editions may contain Canadian advertisements not above 12 percent by lineage (rising to 18 percent).

Professor Oliver Goodenough has thoughtfully analyzed Canada's preoccupation with culture. *See* 15 *Ariz. J. Int'l & Comp. Law* 203 (1998). He believes that the cultural industry exclusion reflects a weak national identity and that a principal purpose is to rally Canadians around their flag in a "recurring pageant of threat and defense." Professor Goodenough notes that the "war" against Hollywood is primarily protective of Anglophone Canada. Francophone Canada, with a healthy cultural identity, has already demonstrated resilience to U.S. and Anglophonic Canadian influences.

Reaching into the literature on "culture transmission theory," Professor Goodenough finds that most foreign influences will "bounce off" healthy cultures without government intervention or, at the very least, compartmentalize such influences in ways which separate them from hearth and home. He concludes that Canada is "defending the imaginary to death" and if it continues to press its cultural protection policies: "[I]t will indeed be to the death, a death brought about not by 'invasion' from the south, but by the incomparably better claims to culturally-based nationhood possessed by Francophone Quebec and by the First Nation Peoples. Rather than acting as a rallying cry for national preservation, cultural protection provides the intellectual basis for a break-up of Canada."

This author's bottom line: Canada's hard won cultural industries exclusion has been almost completely over-run by technology and the use of WTO remedies. One wonders what truly "cultural" concessions Canada might obtain from the U.S. if it offered to entirely abandon the exclusion.

§ 6.3   Foreign Investment in Mexico

The United States has never viewed Mexico with the same mirror as it does Canada, seeing itself in the reflection. Canada usually has been viewed an equal by the United States. Not so with Mexico. The United States has viewed Mexico as something less than a partner, a rather distant neighbor. The United States views Mexico as needing the United States, but the United States has not seen itself as needing Mexico. Mexico has responded accordingly, with suspicion and deliberation. Canada never really flirted with socialism, as Mexico did in the 1970s by substantially increasing national ownership of the means of production and distribution.

Mexico opened to foreign investment with few restrictions during the *Porfiriato*, the 1876–1911 reign of Porfirio Díaz. But the state assumed a more restrictive role under the 1917 Constitution following revolutionary turmoil begun in 1910. It soon became apparent that the state would begin to intervene in many areas of established foreign investment. After an unsuccessful attempt by Mexico to participate in the foreign owned petroleum industry in 1925, a labor dispute led to the total nationalization of the industry in 1938.

This reduced in the minds of many Mexicans the apparent conflict with Article 27 of the Mexican Constitution, which decreed natural resources owned by the nation. Two years later, the government severely limited foreign participation in the communications sector.

A 1944 Emergency Decree was the first broad attempt to regulate foreign investment and limited certain investments to joint ventures. The joint venture concept was extended by a Mixed Ministerial Commission established in 1947, although it was of limited effectiveness. The 1950s saw the introduction of some limited control of specific industries, and electric power distribution was nationalized in 1960. Foreign investment in mining was subjected to a restrictive 1961 Act.

The Mexican foreign investment, transfer of technology, and trade names and inventions laws, all enacted in the 1970s, were models of restrictive laws of developing nations adopted during the tense, often bitter North-South dialogue. Developing nations argued they were poor because the developed nations were rich, and that there had to be a transfer of wealth from the latter to the former. A strict 1972 Law for the Registration of the Transfer of Technology and the Use and Exploitation of Patents and Marks, forewarned the coming restrictiveness towards foreign investment.

1973 Mexican Foreign Investment Law

The 1973 Law to Promote Mexican Investment and Regulate Foreign Investment to some degree pulled together the policies of encouraging but limiting foreign investment that had been introduced during prior decades and were clearly part of Echeverrían administration policy. The 1973 law classified investments, limiting some to state ownership, some to private ownership exclusively by Mexican nations, and some where minority foreign participation would be allowed. The law did not apply retroactively, but if a company expanded into new lines of products or new locations, it was expected to Mexicanize, meaning to sell majority ownership to Mexicans.

Escape provisions and the operational code in Mexico (the way things really work), resulted in few existing companies converting to Mexican majority ownership. What the 1973 law did accomplish was to significantly curtail foreign investment. A new institution, the National Commission on Foreign Investment, assumed substantial discretionary power to carry out the 1973 rules.

What President Echeverría started, his successor, José Lopez Portillo, continued when he entered office in 1976. His final year in office, 1982, saw first the amendment of the 1972 Transfer of Technology Law, retaining its restrictiveness and extending its scope, and second, the nationalization of the banking industry. His successor, Miguel de la Madrid, assumed control of a nation with a defaulted national debt, a plunging currency, and diminished interest of foreign investors.

Realizing that Mexico must change its policies, de la Madrid issued investment regulations in 1984 that partly relaxed the restrictiveness of the 1970s. Further regulations were issued in the following years, and in 1989, the first year of Carlos Salinas de Gortari's presidency, new regulations were issued that were so inconsistent with the clear philosophy of the restrictive 1973 law that their constitutionality was questioned.

The direction was turned: Mexico's ascension into the stratosphere of developing-nation restrictiveness toward foreign investment had reached its apogee in 1982 and was coming back to earth. Foreign investment was returning. It was further encouraged by Mexico's admission into the GATT in 1986, after years of internal debate. The replacement of the 1973 Investment Law twenty years after its introduction ended an unsettling era of Mexican foreign-investment policy.

1993 Mexican Foreign Investment Law

This 1993 Investment Act was a highlight of the Salinas administration, an encouragement to the many investors who had made commitments to Mexico during his administration, and a stepping-stone to participation in the NAFTA the following year. The 1993 law improved access to investment in Mexico, containing investment-attracting provisions absent from the earlier law. But some significant restrictions remained, including state control over natural resources, reservation of some areas of investment for Mexican nationals, emphasis on joint ventures in the areas of the economy open to foreign investors, and retention of the Calvo doctrine that attempted to limit foreign investors to Mexican remedies in the event of an investment dispute.

The 1993 law nevertheless was a huge reversal of the policies of the 1970s, and it both established a more efficient National Registry of Foreign Investment and allowed proposals to be assumed to have been approved if they were not acted upon within an established time frame. Regulations adopted in 1999 were consistent with both the 1993 law and its investment-encouraging philosophy. Mexico was not yet as open to foreign investment as Canada and the United States, but it had established a sufficiently respectful base from which to participate in the NAFTA foreign-investment framework. It was quite a remarkable transformation and a credit to several of Mexico's leaders.

When NAFTA arrived in 1994, it reduced the some of the restraints on investment remaining in the 1993 law. But only for U.S. and Canadian investors, though foreign owned companies incorporated in either Canada or the USA generally qualified for NAFTA's favorable and preferential investment regime (below).

§ 6.4   Assembly Plants (Maquiladoras)

The United States Tariff Code, various Mexican Decrees, and the economics of assembly plant operations established a growth industry: Maquiladoras. Sometimes called "in-bond" or "border" plants, Mexican maquiladoras enjoyed phenomenal popularity in the 1980s and early 1990s. Maquiladoras provide Mexico with over a million jobs, many of which are filled by women. They are also a major source of foreign currency earnings, second only to oil exports and ahead of tourism.

For the investor, the devaluation and depreciation of the peso in 1982 and again in 1994–95 rendered Mexican labor costs lower than those of Taiwan, Hong Kong, Singapore, and South Korea (the "Four Dragons"), then traditional low-cost assembly plant centers.

As a result, thousands of maquiladoras were established in Tijuana, Ciudad Juarez, Nuevo Laredo, and other border cities. Electronics, apparel, toys, medical supplies, transport equipment, furniture, and sporting goods are examples of the types of industries that have been attracted south of the border. Maquiladoras are being imitated throughout the Caribbean Basin and Central America. Much to the frustration of organized labor, such offshore assembly operations exemplify the internationalization of the United States manufacturing sector.

Complex legal frameworks facilitate maquiladoras. On the United States side, Section 9802.00.80 of the Harmonized Tariff Schedule ("HTS") [formerly Section 807 of the TSUS] allows fabricated United States components to be shipped abroad and returned to the U.S. subject to a customs duty limited to the amount of the value added by foreign assembly operations. This section was first utilized with great success by the Four Dragons and is the same law which facilitates Caribbean and Central American assembly plants.

Mexico initiated its Border Industrialization Program in 1965, which permits wholly owned foreign subsidiaries to escape Mexico's traditional mandatory joint venture rules. This was done partly to compete with East Asian countries taking advantage of Section 9802.00.80 through labor-intensive assembly operations.

The net result of Section 9802.00.80 and the law of an increasing number of developing nations is an interdependent legal framework mutually supportive of assembly plant operations. This can be viewed as a "co-production" or "production-sharing" arrangement between the two countries, an arrangement in which others can participate. Japanese corporations and their U.S. subsidiaries have, for example, become significant investors in such industries. Korean firms have also set up assembly plant operations targeted at the U.S. market. These companies appear to find assembly plants attractive even when they use components that are not from the United States, *e.g.*, Taiwanese electronic parts.

If at least 35 percent of the value of an assembly plant product is of local origin, it may qualify for *duty free* tariff status under the U.S. Generalized System of Tariff Preferences (GSP). Most Caribbean and Central American nations (save those with U.S. free trade agreements) are beneficiary countries under the GSP program, whereas the Four Dragons, India and Malaysia are not.

As a matter of business planning, then, development and use of local components in an assembly plant is a strategy that is now being aggressively pursued. Local suppliers, like their East Asian competitors some years ago, are being pressed to improve the quality and utility of their components. The Four Dragons, by comparative example, suggest that if these suppliers meet this challenge, then fabrication of products of completely local origin may follow.

There is an evolutionary cycle in assembly plants—from cheap raw labor to more skill-oriented operations to capital-intensive manufacturing. One of the most interesting comparative questions is whether there is also an evolutionary process in the applicable laws of these countries. In other words, what legal regimes do developing nations have to adopt in order to first attract assembly operations and do they evolve from extremely accommodating to more demanding as the cycle reaches completion?

Or does the manufacturer's ability to go elsewhere to even cheaper labor markets (*e.g.,* from Mexico to Guatemala to Haiti, or from Hong Kong to the People's Republic of China to Vietnam) constantly temper the legal regimes regulating assembly plants?

NAFTA's Impact on Mexican Maquiladoras

Many export-driven Mexican maquiladoras historically relied on tariff refunds and waivers on inputs. Under NAFTA 1994, starting in 2001, Mexico stopped the beneficial application of tariff refunds and waivers to assembly plants. Full Mexican tariffs apply to imported components, which makes it more difficult for goods assembled with components from outside NAFTA to qualify for NAFTA free trade. However, Mexico subsequently reduced tariffs on some components, notably electronics, as an incentive to continue maquiladora production.

Many Asian manufacturers using Mexican assembly plants were impacted by NAFTA. As the drafters of NAFTA intended, there should be no preferentially tariffed "export platforms" into Canada or the United States. Some such manufacturers switched to North American suppliers for their assembly plant inputs. Others, notably from Japan and Korea, arranged for their home country suppliers to join them in production in Mexico. Components from these loyal affiliates generally avoided the origin problems created under NAFTA when Mexican customs refunds and waivers were eliminated in 2001. They also added to the North American content of the assembled goods, the key to accessing NAFTA/USMCA duty free status.

As the North American content of Asian and other maquiladora operations rose to meet NAFTA's rules of origin governing free trade, greater access to the Mexican market became available. Traditionally, sales of maquiladora products in Mexico had been limited. Starting in 1994, amendments to Mexico's Maquiladora Decree permitted such sales to increase based upon percentages of prior year individual maquiladora exports from Mexico. In 1994, for example, this percentage was 55%, rising 5% annually to 75% in 1998 and 85% in the year 2000. Since 2001, maquiladoras may sell their entire production in Mexico if they choose. This schedule was coordinated with Mexico's phase-out of customs duty drawback and waivers on imported components.

The year 2001 also brought China into the World Trade Organization, effectively guaranteeing its exports MFN "normal" tariff status. Mexico's labor rates were and are low by American standards, but China's wages at the millennium were incredibly low. Labor intensive, portable assembly plants, notably clothing, furniture, and the like, moved almost en masse to China and more generally Asia. Their product prices easily absorbed higher transport and tariff costs compared to Mexican maquiladoras. NAFTA's investment and tariff preferences were just not enough to retain these investments.

By 2022, some assembly plants withdrawn from Mexico were returning due to rising Chinese wages and higher fuel/transport costs. Mexico took a hit, but of late has been bouncing back, particularly as a producer of auto parts and vehicles, a less mobile investment. There is hardly any American, European, Japanese, or Korean producer of autos not presently invested in Mexico, many with plans for expansion, at least prior to the arrival of President Trump.

Special rules of origin under USMCA 2020 are discussed in my *Free Trade Agreements* Concise Hornbook, Chapter 6. These rules tighten North American trade in autos and auto parts. They are likely to adversely impact auto industry investments in Mexico. On the other hand, USMCA rules expanding cross-border internet commerce have created opportunities for Mexican maquiladoras to become fulfillment centers.

§ 6.5   Mexican Free Trade Treaties as an Investment Incentive

Many foreign investors from the United States, Japan, Korea, and Europe have established assembly plants (maquiladoras) in Mexico. Increasingly, these investors are using Mexico as an export platform, particularly to those markets covered by Mexican free trade agreements (FTA). A list of these agreements is reproduced below. European Union and Japanese investors, following in the wake of the EU-Mexico FTA (2000, expanded in 2019) and the Japan-Mexico FTA (2004), likewise have taken advantage of Mexico's free trade treaties, as well as NAFTA 1994 and USMCA 2020.

United States and Asian producers in Mexico are especially interested in the possibility of shipping their goods to the European Union on a duty-free basis, something they cannot typically do by exporting from their home countries, though Canada and Japan have FTAs with the EU. Mexico's free trade treaties include:

- The U.S. and Canada (NAFTA 1994 and USMCA 2020);

- Columbia and Venezuela (G-3 FTA, 1995); (Venezuela terminated, 2006);

- Costa Rica (FTA, 1995);

- Bolivia (FTA, 1995);

- Nicaragua (FTA, 1998);

- Chile (FTA 1999);

- Israel (FTA, 2000);

- EFTA (FTA, 2000);

- The EU (FTA, 2000 and 2019);

- Guatemala, Honduras and El Salvador (FTA, Northern Triangle, 2001);

- Peru (2002);

- Uruguay (2002);

- Japan (2004);

- Panama (2006) and

- The Comprehensive and Progressive Trans-Pacific Partnership Agreement (TPP-11, 2018) (ratified by Japan, Canada, Mexico, Vietnam, South Korea, Australia, New Zealand, Peru, Chile, and Singapore).

§ 6.6   Foreign Investment in the United States

The United States has proven to be one of the most desirable locations for direct and indirect (portfolio) investment by foreign persons. It is by far the largest recipient of foreign direct investment in the world, much of that coming from European nations and Japan. These investors employ over 12 million U.S. workers. Under U.S. law, "foreign direct investment" means ownership or control, directly or indirectly by one person of ten percent or more of the voting securities of an incorporated, business enterprise or an equivalent interest in an unincorporated business enterprise. "Portfolio investment" means any international investment that is not direct.

The United States is viewed as a relatively risk-free environment which welcomes foreign as well as domestic investment and imposes relatively few controls on foreign investment that are not also imposed on domestic investment. This view is merited, but foreign investors under many laws and regulations do not have the same standing as domestic U.S. investors.

As is the case in any nation, these restrictions may constitute obstacles to the entry and formation of an investment, or they may constitute restrictions during the operation of the investment. An example of the former is a limitation on the percentage of permissible foreign ownership, while an example of the latter is taxation. The termination of a foreign investment in the United States through bankruptcy may present some additional concerns.

Furthermore, the federal government may choose to block or even divest a foreign investment for vague national security reasons. Free trade agreements such as NAFTA1994/USMCA2020 tend to reduce restrictions on foreign investment but have little effect on restrictions based on national-security grounds.

Certificates of public convenience and necessity to engage in air transportation may be held only by U.S. citizens because Congress wanted to safeguard national security by assuring U.S. air carriers would provide aircraft to the armed forces in times of war or national emergency. This theme of control is also reflected in the aviation regulations. For example, although the law requires the president and two-thirds of the board of directors of an air carrier to be U.S. citizens, and at least 75 percent ownership of voting equity be held by U.S. citizens, the agencies charged with enforcing that mandate have interpreted the law broadly to require the carrier to be controlled by U.S. citizens.

The concept of reciprocity is a continually recurring theme in attitudes toward regulating foreign investment. A foreign firm in the United States is often accorded the same treatment as U.S. firms receive in that firm's home country. For example, the government will not allow foreign companies to acquire federal lands for rights-of-way gas pipelines or leases for mining certain minerals and fuels on those lands, if the foreign investor's home-country denies similar rights to U.S. corporations.

Despite a general policy of openness, the United States has maintained a variety of restrictions on foreign investment that tend to reflect three themes: National security, foreign control, and reciprocity. The main deviation from the policies of national treatment and an open-door investment policy is based on grounds of national security, detailed below.

§ 6.7   The United States as a Host Nation

The 1980s saw a major shift in the United States from an exporter of investment to becoming a host to foreign investment. Yet the relative value of foreign investment in the United States remains low when compared to other industrialized countries, excepting Japan.

Two general theories seek to explain why multinationals invest in foreign countries: The cost-of-capital theory, which is based on responses to real interest rate differentials, and the industrial-organization theory, which focuses on the internal advantages of firms within certain countries and industries and includes strategies to avoid import restrictions and tariffs. For example, Japanese firms invest in electronics because of advantages their organizations possess in that industry.

Despite the political conflicts at various levels of U.S. government over the value and problems associated with foreign direct investment, the trend in the early 1990s nullified much of the concern about foreign acquisitions of U.S. companies. Foreign direct investment in the United States decreased, including substantial decreases in investment from France and Japan. This decrease contributed to a shift in capital flows from a net inward flow to a net outflow from the United States.

When foreign firms invest, the overwhelming method of establishing new operations in the United States is by acquiring existing firms. This pattern has led to a variety of concerns reflected in policy debates in the United States about whether or how to further regulate foreign investment. Perhaps the greatest concern is that foreign parents may reduce or curtail research and development by their newly acquired U.S. affiliates and transfer "American" technology abroad.

A second concern is that foreign owned investments in the United States use imported rather than domestic components in their production process. That appears less the case with European-owned investments in the United States, many of which have been in the United States for decades, than with Japanese-owned and Chinese-owned investments, nearly all of which are relatively recent arrivals in the U.S. market. This fear did not stop, however, Lenovo of China's acquisition of IBM's personal computer business.

A third concern regarding foreign investment in the United States is that foreign governments may provide support in targeting the acquisition of U.S. companies. Although there is little evidence of any "plan" to bring foreign-government control to U.S. companies, such fears remain, especially regarding China, which has attempted or made U.S. acquisitions in recent years. That said, China's acquisitions in America have risen, *e.g.*, Smithfield Ham with its agro-tech skills. When proposed Chinese investments are greenfields, for example development of a high-speed rail system between Southern California and Las Vegas, state ownership of the Chinese party seems less of a concern.

These U.S. concerns have led to new attempts to regulate foreign investment. Many proponents of a free trade and investment policy concluded that the government should intervene as the trade balance deteriorated and inbound foreign investment increased. A popular solution proposed by some federal policymakers supported a broad interpretation of regulations based on national security to include economic security. It is perhaps noteworthy that Chinese national security regulations include protection of its economy.

Contrasting U.S. Federal Goals Affecting Foreign Investment

Foreign direct investment is often subject to U.S. legislative enactments based as much on political as economic goals. These goals may be general or country specific. How the political goals are expressed within the federal government depends on the perspectives of the sector of the government attempting to achieve such goals. The President and the Congress may have different goals, or they may have similar goals but different views on where the power to control ought to be. Even within the same branch of the federal government there may be different goals. The House may have a view quite different from the Senate, and the various parts of the Executive Branch may disagree over policy.

But the general attitude in both the Legislative and Executive branches has for the most part been receptive of foreign investment, or it at least is viewed from abroad as being receptive when contrasted with other potential host nations. Where differences begin to arise is often related to the nature of technology to which foreign companies may gain access. This is particularly true when a foreign company wishes to acquire a U.S. company that owns advanced technology, notably technology used or adaptable for military purposes.

Attitudes change as political alignments change. For example, the Department of Defense (DOD) approved production of F-16 military aircraft by an offspring of the same Japanese company that built the Zeros which bombed Hawaii in World War II. Furthermore, the DOD eased restrictions on foreign-controlled firms gaining DOD contracts, reversing a historic pattern of opposition to such contractors because of access to key technology.

The Department of Commerce presents the most inconsistent policies on foreign investment, advocating a mix of open investment and industrial protection which does not always appear to have a rational basis. At one time, Commerce may oppose any new legal restrictions on direct investment for fear of chilling foreign-investment inflows, suggesting that U.S. industries' expressions of concern regarding national security are merely cries for unmerited government protection, but at another time Commerce may step in and block a planned acquisition of a U.S. firm by foreign interests. Congressional hearings on proposed legislation, such as Exon-Florio discussed below, often expose the lack of cohesion within the Department of Commerce.

The Department of Treasury has historically promoted an open-door investment policy and has been the chief advocate within the cabinet of foreign investors' interests, to the dismay of Treasury's critics, who believe its view too solicitous of foreign investment. Those fears increased when, in 1988, Treasury was designated the chair of the interdepartmental Committee on Foreign Investment in the United States (CFIUS), playing a central role under the Exon-Florio law (below).

§ 6.8   U.S. Securities Registration, Disclosure, and Bans on Foreign Issuers

The general rule is that any public offering by foreign issuers in the United States is subject to the Securities Exchange Act of 1933 Act registration requirements. That means registration and full disclosure or being exempt. Such a rule appears logical when the foreign issuer wishes to come to the U.S. and issue its securities to United States citizens, or even when it remains abroad in its home nation but addresses the issuance to U.S. citizens. But such regulation becomes increasingly extraterritorial and subject to foreign challenge when the links with the United States further diminish.

Acknowledging the problem, the United States has developed some special rules to address foreign issuers selling to United States citizens or residents. Schedule B to the 1933 Act includes requirements for the registration of securities issued by foreign *governments*. There are special forms for registration and disclosure applicable to foreign issuers. Foreign issuers generally enjoy the same exemptions as domestic issuers. An offering by a foreign issuer is considered in its entirety, not only that part which affects United States purchasers.

The private offering exemption has not been very useful to foreign issuers. A private offering exemption is not generally available to a foreign issuer when all the issuance is made abroad, except for that to a single United States purchaser who falls within the statutory qualifications. But these relatively minor variants affecting foreign issuers do not address the real issue, the extent to which a foreign issuer must register when there is some offering in the United States. Several approaches adopted by the SEC have attempted to address this issue.

Regulations for Foreign Issuers

The Securities and Exchange Commission has issued regulations which attempt to reach some compromise where foreign issuances reach more than a few United States purchasers. Rule 12g3–2(b) and its regulations essentially allow foreign issuers to satisfy United States disclosure requirements by reliance on home nation disclosure.

The biggest problem with these regulations for the foreign issuer is how to limit the number of United States residents to below 300. If a foreign issuer sells its shares exclusively through a national securities market and has tens of thousands of shareholders, it may not believe that the incidental share ownership by 300 United States owners should bring the company within the United States requirements. If it does not comply with United States securities laws, the next step is the extent to which the United States courts will apply the law extraterritorially.

Rule 144A was enacted as recognition of the increasing globalization of the securities market, and to address both the private placement market and purchases by institutional investors. The rule was intended to encourage foreign issuers to raise capital in the United States. Some issuers did use the reporting exemption provisions of Rule 12g3–2(b), but it was not viewed as helpful in certain markets. Rule 144A was designed to create a new market (for secondary trading only) with limited disclosure to attract foreign issuers, and to liberalize the privately placed securities market.

Rule 144A has been used with American Depositary Receipts (ADRs). It has also been used with Regulation S, which limits registration requirements where the offers and sales are outside the United States. The result appears to be the use of two-stage transactions by foreign issuers. First is a listing on a foreign exchange, and second a sale in the United States. The ADRs are denominated in United States dollars rather than the issuer's nation's currency. Dividends are paid in dollars. Changes in the exchange rate of the dollar and the issuer nation's currency obviously affect the value of the security, but the United States investor is not burdened by having to constantly make exchange calculations.

In recent years, China has issued billions of U.S. dollar bonds of short and long maturities under Rule 144a. They have been well received in the U.S. market.

U.S. Securities Controls over Chinese Firms

Commencing Jan. 11, 2021, President Trump's Executive Order 13959 prohibits U.S. persons from purchasing publicly traded debt or equity securities tied to or "linked to" over 30 designated "Communist Chinese military companies", notably including Huawei, CNOOC, SMIC, COMAC and Xiaomi (later dropped). This Order also was issued under the rarely used International Emergency Economic Powers Act (IEEPA, P.L. 95-223 (1977)) administered by OFAC. The list of banned Chinese companies is called the Non-SDN Chinese Military-Industrial Complex Companies (NS-CMIC). In 2022, President Biden added Chinese surveillance and tracking companies assertedly used against China's religious minorities, particularly the Muslim Uyghur minority in Xinjiang, to this list. This addition followed shortly after U.S. adoption of The Uyghur Forced Labor Prevention Act late in 2021.

As a result of Trump's Executive Order, NYSE-listed China Mobile, China Telecom and China Unicom Hong Kong were de-listed along with numerous other Chinese firms registered on NASDAQ. This ban covers Chinese controlled subsidiaries and embraces derivatives, American depository receipts, exchange-traded funds, index funds and mutual funds within its scope. President Biden has embraced Trump's IEEPA order and de-listing policy.

In addition, the Holding Foreign Companies Act of 2020 requires delisting in the future of Chinese firms in U.S. financial markets (*e.g.*, Alibaba, Baidu) that repeatedly fail to comply with U.S. accounting and auditing standards. Chinese firms cannot easily comply without risking violations of PRC laws regarding "state secrets". Owners of Chinese ADRs have been swapping their shares for Hong Kong or Shanghai listings where possible. The market value of Chinese ADRs exceeded $2 trillion dollars in 2020 but has been declining since then.

President Biden has continued Trump's securities controls focused on Chinese listings in U.S. markets. To a degree, China has joined in this de-coupling. For example, rapidly ordered its ride-sharing star Didi to withdraw its 2021 NYSE listing citing Didi's alleged "national security" violations. Chinese IPOs in the USA may be coming to an end, an outcome giving still more control to PRC officials. If foreigners and their funds want to buy Chinese stocks or bonds, they will increasingly need to do so in the Hong Kong, Shanghai, and Shenzhen markets.

§ 6.9   Specific Federal Prohibitions or Limitations on Foreign Investment

Federal law includes few absolute prohibitions on foreign ownership of U.S. means of production and distribution. Some industries are more strictly regulated regarding permissible levels of foreign ownership than others.

Atomic Energy

Foreign ownership or control is not permitted for commercial licensees of atomic energy. The Nuclear Regulatory Commission is prohibited from issuing a license to any person "for activities which are not under or within the jurisdiction of the United States" or to an alien or any corporation or other entity "if the Commission knows or has reason to believe it is owned, controlled, or dominated, by an alien, a foreign corporation, or a foreign government." The broad concluding phrase discloses the intent of the statute, that in any event, "no license may be issued to any person within the United States if, in the opinion of the Commission, the issuance of a license to such person would be inimical to the common defense and security, or to the health and safety of the public."

Merchant Marine

A similar policy justification is in the Jones Act statutes governing the merchant marine. Stating that it is "necessary for the national defense and for the proper growth of its foreign and domestic commerce," the merchant marine must serve as a naval or military auxiliary in time of war or national emergency. Merchant marine vessels are "ultimately to be owned and operated privately by citizens of the United States."

To enforce that policy, no merchandise may be transported by water, or by land and water, between points in the United States, in any other vessel than one built in and documented under the laws of the United States and owned by U.S. citizens. Control extends to the transfer of ownership of U.S.-owned vessels. A U.S. owner is prohibited from selling any interest in a vessel (other than certain pleasure and fishing vessels) to a non-citizen of the United States without approval of the Department of Transportation.

Airlines

The airlines rules were developed in the 1920s and 1930s, when airlines were subsidized, and U.S. airspace was rigidly protected. The industry has changed, but the foreign investment rules have not. Concerns now seem focused on reciprocity: Access to foreign routes in exchange for domestic routes, with airline ownership of necessary determination to understand who has what rights.

Current laws follow outmoded justifications, but with new considerations of a "managed" balance in access apparently being the reason for limiting foreign ownership. These limitations may well place U.S. airlines in a disadvantageous position. They are denied foreign equity and must turn to less favorable domestic debt financing, which in turn may cause their demise.

United States citizens must own 75 percent of the voting shares of an air carrier, as well as constitute two-thirds or more of the board of directors and managing officers, and specifically the presidency. Voting equity remains the key focus of Department of Transportation (DOT) investigations concerning control by foreigners. But combined with other factors of control, an extensive foreign total-equity ownership, absent voting powers may result in denial of participation. Under policies of the DOT, a foreign airline may be allowed up to 49 percent of the total equity, but the limit of 25 percent of the voting equity remains.

For example, the Dutch airline KLM planned to acquire up to 57 percent of the total equity of Northwest, with its ownership of *voting* equity remaining under the limit. The DOT concluded that the high percentage of total foreign equity ownership, along with other relationships between the two airlines, created a potential for control and influence inconsistent with the law.

DOT and KLM eventually concluded a consent agreement that reduced KLM's total planned equity stake and limited KLM's participation on Northwest's board of directors. Its participation could only be what was necessary to protect its interest, and its appointed members would have to excuse themselves from discussion of any bilateral issues between the companies. The DOT, after the KLM case, indicated a desire to balance the benefits of foreign investment without imposing arbitrary obstacles, as successful investments by British Air in US Air and Air Canada in Continental appear to demonstrate.

Banking

Regulation of the foreign participation in banking has changed because in several instances foreign participation was not disclosed until losses were incurred. After the Bank of Credit and Commerce International (BCCI) and Banca Nazionale de Lavorro (BNL) scandals involving the operations of foreign banks in the United States, Congress enacted new legislation, particularly the Foreign Bank Supervision Enhancement Act of 1991 (FBSEA).

The FBSEA mandated that the Federal Reserve approve establishment of U.S. offices by foreign banks only if the bank is under comprehensive and consolidated regulation by its home country's authorities. The role of foreign direct investment is more significant in banking than most other sectors of the economy. United States affiliates of foreign banks account for roughly 20 percent of the total assets of all banks in America.

Mineral Leases and Timber Rights

The laws governing interests in mineral leases involve more direct reciprocity. Deposits of natural resources and the lands containing them owned by the United States are available for exploitation by U.S. citizens, but not to foreigners of any country that does not grant comparable rights to Americans. The United States formerly maintained a list of "reciprocal" nations, but since 1982 administrative procedures have been used to make such determinations.

Current law traces to the 1920 Mineral Lands Leasing Act. The regulations reflect a policy of reciprocity, stating that foreigners may hold mineral leases through their interests in U.S. corporations provided that their home country does not deny similar rights to citizens and corporations of the United States. Under this law, the state-owned Kuwaiti Petroleum Corp. (KPC), which owned Santa Fe Petroleum and other U.S. corporations, was barred from obtaining further oil and gas leases on public lands.

Timber rights are also restricted. United States citizens have various rights to use timber on federal lands. Aliens who are bona fide residents may also obtain such access.

Outer-Continental Shelf Activities

Federal law governs foreign ownership of offshore leases on the outer-continental shelf. The federal government has control beyond the three-mile limit which defines the outer reach of state authority. Federal regulations govern both the outer continental shelf and offshore leases. There is no statutory prohibition of foreign access because there is no citizenship requirement. But Department of Interior regulations have limited the access. Aliens are allowed access when admitted for permanent residence. There is no reciprocity requirement.

What is important are the restrictions on aliens working on the outer-continental shelf. U.S. immigration rules apply. The statutory provisions essentially limit the manning of outer-continental shelf rigs, vessels, and platforms to U.S. citizens, with some special exceptions.

Communications

The laws governing the communications industry remain a key area of federal foreign investment regulation. The principal law governing electromagnetic media is the Federal Communications Act (FCA) of 1934. Of particular concern is the television industry, part of the "wireless communication" industry. For example, during the 1980s, Australian media owner Rupert Murdoch became a U.S. citizen to acquire a U.S. television station. Foreign investment in U.S. communication companies holding licenses issued by the Federal Communications Commission (FCC) is not totally prohibited.

The FCC may not grant a station license to any foreign government or representative, or to an alien or alien corporation, but the law does allow for less than 20 percent of the shares to be foreign owned. The reason for the restrictions is to maintain control by U.S. citizens. The FCC will not grant licenses to "any corporation directly or indirectly controlled" by any corporation where 25 percent or more of the directors and officers are aliens or where 25 percent or more of the shares are owned of record or voted by aliens, their representatives, or a foreign government or corporation. Cable television is considered to come under this provision because it uses microwave stations.

Wire communications are also governed by the same FCA. There is no citizenship requirement for this industry, but because states retain considerable control over telephone service they may have restrictions. These restrictions are usually applied to all out-of-state, vice truly foreign, persons. A special area, satellite communications, is subject to the Communications Satellite Act of 1962, which prohibits more than 20 percent of the shares of a satellite corporation to be owned by aliens.

Acquisitions by foreigners of U.S. common carrier, broadcast and submarine cable licenses must obtain FCC approval acting, after a multi-agency review, under a public interest standard. If permitted, such acquisitions are often subject to National Security Agreements. Such "Team Telecom" reviews and Agreements differ from more common CFIUS national security reviews of foreign investments in the USA (discussed below).

Real Estate

There are four principal federal laws of the United States that mandate disclosure when aliens purchase U.S. realty. These are the International Investment and Trade in Services Survey Act of 1976, the Agricultural Foreign Investment Disclosure Act of 1978, the Foreign Investment in Real Property Tax Act of 1980 (reduced taxation was adopted in 2015), and the Tax Equity and Fiscal Responsibility Act of 1982.

These laws particularly impact foreign pension funds, which are major investors in U.S. commercial real estate. Restrictions on foreign investment in United States real estate at the federal level concern U.S. government-owned public lands. Most of these public lands are located in Alaska and the Western states. Federal statutes regulating grazing, mining, and energy resources are uniquely relevant to the foreign investor.

§ 6.10   U.S. State Regulation of Foreign Investment

Unlike the merchant marine or airline regulations at the federal level, most state regulations governing foreign investment do not have national security as their justification. State laws that seek to review foreign investments are essentially state versions of federal Exon-Florio/FINSA/FIRRMA rules (below) without the national security justification.

These state laws often prove to be unconstitutional. They frequently violate the commerce clause as well as the doctrine of uniformity, meaning that the United States ought to speak with one voice where foreign investment is concerned. But the laws buy time and send a message to the foreign investor that it is unwelcome and likely to be subject to harassment at the state level, notwithstanding federal rejection of successive state attempts to regulate.

One example of the barriers a state may create to block foreign investors was Ohio's attempt to block a foreign corporate raider acting by means of a Canadian corporation and its wholly owned New York subsidiary, CRTF Corporation, to acquire Federal Department Stores, Inc. (Federated), a Delaware corporation. Ohio quickly enacted the Ohio Foreign Business Acquisitions Act to regulate control of a "resident business" by a "foreign business." On the same day, the foreign investor filed suit challenging the constitutionality of the Act, which required foreign businesses to file an "application for approval of acquisition" with the state.

The restrictions on establishing businesses in Ohio by foreign persons did not apply to U.S. firms incorporated in the United States, or to foreign businesses that already maintained "substantial interests" in Ohio. The federal district court held the act to be discriminatory on its face and granted a motion for a preliminary injunction. The court concluded that although a state may enact laws pursuant to its police powers that have the purpose and effect of encouraging domestic industry, a state may not enact laws which discriminate against foreign commerce, or which create the risk of inconsistent state regulation.

Notwithstanding the experience of state statutes like that in Ohio, many states continue to maintain statutes governing foreign investment in *real estate*. States restrict the real property rights of aliens and alien corporations in a variety of ways. Some states have onerous restrictions, and others have no restrictions.

Those states whose laws are essentially restraint-free regarding real estate include Alabama, Arizona, Colorado, Delaware, the District of Columbia, Florida, Georgia, Maine, Maryland, Massachusetts, Michigan, Nevada, New Hampshire, New Mexico, Rhode Island, Tennessee, Texas, Utah, Vermont, Washington, and West Virginia.

Banking regulation also has a state level that foreign investors must consider. For example, New York has considered adopting banking regulations like those at the federal level requiring home-country supervision and cooperation. The state regulatory board has also suggested that foreign banks without offices incorporated in New York should obtain approval for changes in control of 25 percent or more.

§ 6.11   Franchising in the United States

Franchising is an important sector in the United States economy. Thousands of franchisors have created and administer franchise systems throughout the nation. United States franchisees number in the hundreds of thousands. These franchisees are typically independent businesspersons, and their local franchise outlets employ millions of people. It has been estimated that approximately one-third of all retail sales in the United States take place through franchised outlets. Just as United States franchisors have found franchising particularly effective for market penetration abroad, Canadian, European, and Japanese companies are increasingly penetrating the United States market through franchising.

Franchising is a business technique that permits rapid and flexible penetration of markets, growth, and capital development. In the United States, there are traditional distinctions between product franchises and business format franchises. Product franchises involve manufacturers who produce the goods that are distributed through franchise agreements. For example, ice cream stores, soft drink bottling companies and gasoline retailers are often the subject of product franchises.

Business format franchises are more common. These do not involve the manufacture by the franchisor of the product being sold by the franchisee. More typically, the franchisor licenses intellectual property rights in conjunction with a particular "formula for success" of the business. Fast food establishments, hotels, and a variety of service franchises are examples of business format franchising.

United States regulation of franchise relationships occurs at both the federal and state levels of government. Such regulation can be as specific as the Federal Trade Commission Franchising Rule or as amorphous as the ever-present dangers of state and federal antitrust law. The latter can particularly impact the drafting of United States franchise agreements to avoid potential liabilities for *per se* unlawful resale price maintenance, unreasonable market division or customer restraints, Robinson-Patman Act price discrimination violations, and heavily litigated "tying arrangements" (coercive purchasing requirements).

State Franchise Disclosure Requirements and Regulations

The most obvious form of governmental regulation of franchising occurs through disclosure statutes enacted by some U.S. states. These disclosure statutes resemble those commonly found when securities are offered for sale. At least fifteen states have such franchise disclosure laws, using the Uniform Franchise Offering Circular (UFOC) of the North American Securities Administrators Association (NASAA). See discussion of the UFOC in Section 6.21.

The typical franchise disclosure statute adopted at the state level in the United States, and through the Franchises Act of Alberta Canada, creates criminal penalties for material misrepresentations or omissions in the franchise circular. It also ordinarily permits withdrawal from any franchise agreement if the franchisee did not receive a copy of the prospectus. Moreover, if there has been a misstatement or omission of material facts, the franchisees may rescind the agreement.

Most franchise disclosure laws require the franchisor to register with a state agency by filing a proposed prospectus for the franchise offering. Such a prospectus is often called a franchise offering circular. The state agency then reviews the circular to ensure that it meets the necessary disclosure requirements. Once the franchise offering is registered with the state, the franchisor is effectively licensed to sell franchises in that state.

One issue in connection with these disclosure statutes is what constitutes a "franchise." A franchise normally exists when one person grants another the right to distribute goods or services using the trademark of the grantor under a marketing plan created substantially by that person and in return the franchisee pays a fee to maintain the franchise relationship.

In some jurisdictions, franchises are said to exist whenever there is a community of interest between the franchisor and the franchisee in the distribution of goods or services. Such a community of interest would typically be found when the franchisor controls the site or territory of the franchisee, tells the franchisee what hours to operate or in what manner to operate the local premises, or generally controls how the franchisee's business or marketing is conducted.

Practically speaking, many state registration agencies also review the capitalization of franchisors before permitting the sale of franchises. This is done notwithstanding the fact that few state laws or regulations specify what constitutes adequate capitalization for a franchisor. A general review of the franchisor's financial statements is typically undertaken. This scrutiny may call into question the solvency of the franchisor, as for example where loans to officers are on the books as an asset. A franchisor's net worth generally should exceed the initial capital investment that is being requested of a franchisee.

States that actively regulate the sale of franchises have developed a "coordinated review" process working through a lead state. This "one-stop" regulatory process is expected to significantly reduce inconsistent results as well as costs and expenses.

Wisconsin State Franchise Disclosure Law

The authority of state agencies to regulate franchises is not unlimited. In one decision, for example, a manufacturer of photo processing machinery (KIS) was ordered *ex parte* to stop selling its equipment in Wisconsin. The Commissioner of Securities claimed that the manufacturer was a franchisor because it offered suggestions and advice to equipment purchasers.

In a lengthy decision, an administrative law judge held that mere suggestions do not amount to a prescribed marketing plan or system constituting a franchise. KIS was therefore not required to register as a franchisor under the Wisconsin disclosure statutes. If the suggestions made by KIS had been combined with penalties or sanctions for failing to follow them, or it could have been otherwise shown that as a practical reality the purchaser did not have unrestricted autonomy in operating the photo finishing business, then KIS would have been a franchisor subject to Wisconsin registration requirements.

States may require disclosure if there is a community of (financial) interest between the parties. The basic question is whether there is a manufacturer/distributor relationship or a franchise. In this area, Wisconsin law is again prominent. A Wisconsin Supreme Court decision emphasizes that the test is not merely percentages of business time or revenues devoted to the products in question.

Rather, the finder of fact must also review a range of factors in making community of interest determinations: (1) Length of dealing; (2) extent of obligations; (3) territorial scope; (4) use of trademarks; (5) financial investments; (6) personnel commitments; (7) advertising and promotions; and (8) supplementary services.

Under these criteria, a community of interest amounting to a franchise existed where a sales representative had been the manufacturer's sole Midwest stocking inventory dealer for five years, devoted 70 percent of his time to that effort and derived 60 percent of his income there from, and had invested $15,000 in developing the business.

Termination of the Franchise Relationship

Another variety of state regulation of franchising is more intrusive than disclosure requirements. Approximately half of the states regulate the franchise relationship over its life. States have enacted legislation which deals with the termination of franchisees. These laws ordinarily prohibit a franchisor from undertaking termination before the ordinary end of the franchise contract unless there is "good cause."

Good cause is frequently defined to mean a breach by the franchisee of a material provision of the franchise agreement that has not been cured. Good cause typically does not include the relevant business needs of the franchisor. Some of these laws also require renewal of the franchise agreement unless there is "good cause" for nonrenewal. In some jurisdictions, this provision may not apply to a franchise which has a fixed term as opposed to a franchise which creates by contract a right of renewal or option for a successor.

There is relatively little case law elaborating upon what constitutes good cause to terminate franchisees. However, the following have been recognized as good cause for such terminations:

(1) Failure to meet sales goals;

(2) Health and safety violations by the franchisee;

(3) Breach of implied covenants; and

(4) Verbal customer abuse.

If there is good cause for franchisee termination, the fact of economic hardship to the franchisee may not override the franchisor's right of termination.

Ending franchise relationships can sometimes be tumultuous. Texas franchisees who set up a directly competing business one month before the termination of their muffler franchise even using the same phone number were ultimately held liable for actual and punitive damages of $10,000 plus $560,000 in attorneys' fees on breach of contract and civil conspiracy claims. The general trend in the courts is against finding any fiduciary duties as between franchisor and franchisee. But the duty to act in good faith in connection with termination of franchisees has been affirmed in leading opinions.

FTC Franchising Rule

Federal law may also concurrently regulate franchising in the United States. In particular, the U.S. Federal Trade Commission has issued a Trade Regulation Rule on Franchising and Business Opportunity Ventures (16 C.F.R. Part 436). See Section 6.21 for an FTC overview of this Rule as amended.

This Rule applies to continuing business relationships such as package franchises (business format), product franchises (distribution systems) and business opportunity ventures involving significant financial risks for the franchisee and subject to significant assistance or control by the franchisor. In addition, the franchise must involve the distribution of goods or services associated with the franchisor's trademark. Employer-employee, retail cooperative, single license and general partnership relationships are excluded from coverage under the FTC Rule.

Individuals and groups may petition for exemption from the FTC Rule on the grounds that unfairness and deceptive practices are not issues requiring its applicability, for example when the franchisees are sophisticated businesspersons.

The FTC Rule requires disclosure in advance to prospective franchisees. However, unlike state law, the FTC Rule does not require a filing of an offering circular with the Federal Trade Commission. If the necessary disclosures are not undertaken, the Commission may enforce the rule through cease-and-desist order proceedings. The FTC Franchising Rule can also be enforced through civil penalty actions in the federal district courts. In such actions, the FTC may seek up to $10,000 per violation of the rule as well as a permanent injunction against future violations. There is no private right of action in connection with the FTC Trade Regulation Rule on Franchising and Business Opportunity Ventures.

The FTC Rule mandates a thorough description of the franchise system, and detailed biographies of the persons who are principally responsible for that system. Any civil or criminal litigation involving the franchise or any officers of the franchisor must be revealed. The rule also requires disclosure of costs at the front end to the franchisee, royalties that must be paid, any advertising or promotional payments by the franchisee, and inventory purchasing requirements.

The net effect of these duties is to give the franchisee a reasonably clear picture of the financial commitments that flow from the franchise agreement. If the franchisor wishes to represent the likely success or earnings schedule of the franchise, a separate earnings document must be released. The disclosure notice must also clearly indicate what are the terms and conditions of termination or non-renewal.

A common way in which states enforce the Federal Trade Commission Rule on Franchising and Business Opportunities is through what are known as Little FTC Acts. Under these statutes, many states have held that a violation of the Federal Trade Commission Rule constitutes an unfair or deceptive act or practice for purposes of state law. Any such holding typically results in injunctive or public civil penalty relief through actions by local prosecutors.

Unlike federal law, state Little FTC Acts sometimes permit private parties to obtain relief, including in some cases damages relief. The FTC Rule in the franchising area has a broader remedial scope than that which is provided in the FTC Act.

Evaluating the FTC Disclosure Rule

The Federal Trade Commission has undertaken evaluative studies of its franchise rule. These studies were conducted by independent research organizations. The first study examined the utility of disclosure to purchasers and those who did not purchase a franchise. The second study examined the costs and benefits to franchisors in complying with the FTC Rule. Some broad conclusions were reached in these studies. Roughly two-thirds of all franchisees indicated that they used the FTC disclosure document in making their purchasing decision. A significant number of franchisees found that the disclosure document was helpful in obtaining financing.

After reading the disclosure document, roughly three-quarters of all prospective franchisees contacted other existing franchisees. About half of all the prospective franchisees also sought professional advice. The franchisees indicated that the disclosure document was most useful because it created an awareness of the information necessary to make an intelligent purchasing decision. Many indicated that it revealed information that they had not previously known and that it saved them time in their information search.

Among the franchisors contacted in the second study, the most important disclosures were the necessary initial investment to be made by franchisees, the franchisor's obligations, earnings claims and renewal and termination details. Many franchisors believed that the disclosure document contained information that franchisees otherwise would not have had and that it added credibility to their franchise proposal. They not only thought that disclosure protected franchisees from fraudulent sales practices, but they recognized that franchisors were less likely to be subject to claims of misrepresentation by franchisees. Franchisors also felt that the disclosure statement helped them qualify prospective franchisees.

A variety of other uses for the disclosure information was found. Franchisors often used the same documents in reporting to their banks, in assisting franchisees to obtain financing, in reporting to stockholders or potential investors and in federal or state tax returns or securities filings. On the negative side, franchisors noted the administrative time and expense in complying with disclosure laws, including legal and accounting fees. Some objected to the difficulty in making earnings claims under existing disclosure criteria.

§ 6.12 Labor Law Rules for Foreign Investors in the United States

Businesses operated in the United States by foreign investors remain subject to the same laws regarding the operation of a business as those owned by domestic investors. This is true generally regarding taxation of foreign controlled companies operating within the United States. However, such companies may retain more flexibility to employ and dismiss employees than companies controlled by U.S. investors.

Generally, foreign companies with operations in the United States remain subject to U.S. civil rights laws affecting the employment relationship. But a possible exception may exist, even for subsidiaries incorporated in the United States, under commercial treaty protections, provided that the employment decisions were directed or controlled by the foreign parent. Two cases suggest an exception: *Sumitomo Shoji America, Inc. v. Avagliano*, 457 U.S. 176 (1982) and *Fortino v. Quasar Co.*, 950 F.2d 389 (7th Cir. 1991).

The Sumitomo Case

In *Sumitomo*, Avagliano and other female secretarial employees brought a class-action suit against Sumitomo, a New York corporation and wholly owned subsidiary of a Japanese trading company. They alleged violation of 42 U.S.C.A. § 1981 and Title VII of the Civil Rights Act because of the company's practice of hiring only male Japanese citizens to fill executive, managerial, and sales positions. Sumitomo moved to dismiss the suit because first, any discrimination based on Japanese citizenship does not violate those provisions, and second, Sumitomo's practices were protected under the Treaty of Friendship, Commerce, and Navigation between Japan and the United States.

The trial court agreed with Sumitomo on the § 1981 claim and dismissed it because neither sex nor national-origin discrimination were covered by the provision. The court refused to dismiss the Title VII claim because, although Sumitomo was a wholly owned Japanese subsidiary, it was incorporated in the United States and not covered by the treaty. The Second Circuit Court of Appeals reversed in part, stating that the treaty did cover locally incorporated subsidiaries, although that would not end the Title VII analysis.

The Supreme Court agreed with the trial court and vacated the Circuit Court's decision. It held that the intent of the United States and Japan in concluding the FCN treaty was not to include subsidiaries regardless of their place of incorporation. The Court stated that the treaty's provision giving companies of each country the right to hire, within the other country, certain managerial and support staff of their choice, applied only to companies from the other country.

Rejecting Sumitomo's claim that the U.S. entity was a Japanese company, the Court held that the treaty's definition looked to the place of incorporation, in Sumitomo's case, New York—an interpretation that both the U.S. and Japanese governments supported.

While Sumitomo failed in its attempt to assert FCN privileges, Quasar succeeded. Quasar is an unincorporated division of a U.S. company wholly owned by the Japanese firm Matsushita Electric Industrial Company Ltd. Matsushita assigned several financial and marketing executives to Quasar, who remained under Quasar's day-to-day control, but they retained their status as Matsushita employees. The executives' temporary work visas pursuant to the FCA treaty offered further evidence of the employees' temporary status at Quasar. The meaning of temporary or expatriate employment is not fully settled, since some such employees remain as managers of the foreign plant for many years.

The Fortino *Case*

When Quasar lost $20 million in 1985, Matsushita assigned one of these expatriate executives to reorganize the company. He reduced the managing employees by half, discharging Fortino and others who sued Quasar. None of the "temporary" executives were among those discharged, and though two were rotated back to Japan, those who remained received pay increases, while the remaining American management staff did not.

Fortino's suit charged that Quasar's behavior violated the Age Discrimination in Employment Act and Title VII of the Civil Rights Act because of discrimination based on national origin. The suit succeeded at the trial court level because of the different treatment of the remaining Japanese and U.S. executives.

On appeal, Quasar argued that the national origin discrimination claim was not supportable because the discrimination was in favor of foreigners employed temporarily in the United States in accordance with the FCN treaty that permits Japanese firms to employ executives of their own choice.

Fortino argued that by failing to bring the treaty to the attention of the trial court, Quasar had waived the defense. The Seventh Circuit decided that it would hear the appeal, not only because of interests in international comity, amity, and commerce, but also because the issue was not so much a defense, but part of the background argument for why Title VII should not apply at all. To the court the essence of the case was the distinction between discrimination based on national origin, which Title VII forbids, and discrimination based on citizenship, which the treaty allows.

The court found that the better treatment Quasar afforded the remaining foreign executives constituted favoritism, and although it might have appeared to be discrimination based on national origin because of the apparent homogeneity of the Japanese people involved, it was discrimination based upon citizenship allowed by the treaty. The court saw Quasar's firing of some Japanese Americans as evidence of citizenship discrimination rather than Title VII national origin discrimination. In dismissing the Title VII claim, it stated that the "exercise of a treaty right may not be made the basis for inferring a violation of Title VII."

One difference between *Quasar* and *Sumitomo* pertains to who directed the allegedly discriminatory behavior. In *Sumitomo* there was no contention that the parent dictated the discriminatory behavior of the subsidiary, as Matsushita did with Quasar. But a subsidiary ought to have the capacity to assert the parent's FCN rights if the parent could have been sued.

The Quasar court concluded with one final reciprocity policy rationale. Observing that the United States, not Japan, had wanted the inclusion of a treaty provision allowing each nation's companies to select their employees, the court stated that American jobs in Japan would be jeopardized by reciprocal decisions of Japan's courts, should Fortino's argument have won.

This reciprocity argument may be used by counsel attempting to argue the non-application of the U.S. laws governing employment discrimination. Such an argument weakens when the decision is made by a U.S. incorporated but foreign owned company.

§ 6.13   U.S. Immigrant Investor EB-5 Visas

A popular United States employment-based immigrant visa is the Fifth Preference Employment Based (EB-5) category, renewed in 2015. While it is referred to as an employment category, it is an *investment*-based classification. This category, commonly referred to as the "Million Dollar Green Card," offers the only option to aliens who wish to petition for an immigrant visa based on an investment made in the United States. A maximum number of EB-5 visas may be issued annually to alien investors. A petition for classification as an EB-5 "alien entrepreneur" may only be filed by the alien on the alien's own behalf.

To qualify for an EB-5 visa the alien must establish and engage in a new commercial enterprise by investing $1,000,000 in that enterprise and create ten *new* full-time jobs for United States workers. In certain circumstances the required investment may be increased to as much as $3,000,000, or in "high unemployment areas" (sometimes gerrymandered by local officials to achieve this status) decreased to as little as $500,000. Amendments to increase this minimum amount to $900,000 are pending in the courts.

Only active investments will qualify an alien in the EB-5 category. Passive investments such as ownership of real estate or stocks would not qualify even if the job creation criteria are somehow satisfied. Not only must the investment be active, but it also must be invested in a *new business*. And it must create ten new full-time jobs for United States workers. The purpose of this requirement is to ensure that an alien is not just "buying" lawful permanent resident status but is creating something that will benefit the country.

In most cases purchasing an existing enterprise will not fulfill the "new business" requirement. However, the regulations have defined when this is permissible. The establishment of a new commercial enterprise may consist of:

1.   The creation of an original business;

2.   The purchase of an existing business and simultaneous or subsequent restructuring or reorganization such that a new organization results; or

3.   The expansion of an existing business through the investment of the required amount, so that a substantial change in the net worth or number of employees results from the investment of capital.

Substantial change means a 40 percent increase either in the net worth, or in the number of employees, so that the new net worth, or number of employees amounts to at least 140 percent of the pre-expansion net worth or number of employees.

Establishment of a new commercial enterprise in this manner does not exempt the petitioner from the required amount of capital investment and the creation of full-time employment for ten qualifying employees. In the case of a capital investment in a troubled business, employment creation may meet separate criteria.

The EB-5 visa is issued on a two-year conditional basis. Ninety days prior to the end of the two years the alien investor must apply to have the condition lifted. To qualify for removal of the condition the investor must establish that the business is still operating according to the stipulated guidelines and is still employing at least ten full-time United States workers. If these criteria are met the condition will be lifted and the alien and the alien's family will become *lawful permanent residents, unconditionally*. However, if the business is no longer in operation the alien and accompanying family members will lose their immigrant status—no waiver is permitted.

Utilizing EB-5 Visas

By 2021, many thousands of foreign nationals had applied for EB-5 visas. A majority were from China, with many Chinese parents hoping to help their children stay in the USA after college. Wealthy Indians from Dubai, not entitled to citizenship there, are also active pursuers of EB-5 visas. Construction and the film industry account for the lion's share of EB-5 investments. Marriot, Sony, and the Barclays Center developers have tapped hundreds of EB-5 investors to fund huge projects.

On a more modest scale, U.S. franchisors are also obtaining EB-5 franchisees, including McDonald's, Subway and Burger King. All of them benefit from inexpensive financing under the EB-5 program, whose foreign investors are ready to take well below market returns.

The SEC monitors EB-5 programs and has terminated several fraudulent operations.

Under fire from many directions, and riddled with failed investment projects, visa delays, and outright fraud, the EB-5 program may be more restricted in the future. The number of Chinese applicants has dropped dramatically in the past few years. Vietnamese applicants are on the rise.

My thanks to San Diego Attorney and Adjunct USD Professor of Law, Geoffrey Leibl Esq., for his contribution to this coverage of EB-5 investor visas.

§ 6.14 Mergers and Acquisitions

U.S. federal merger and acquisition law rests principally on the Clayton Antitrust Act of 1914, as amended. Since 1975, this includes "premerger notification" requirements (sometimes known as "Hart-Scott-Rodino" notifications) stipulating that parties to large mergers and acquisitions must give the Department of Justice *and* the Federal Trade Commission advance notice of their intentions. This advance notice allows the government antitrust authorities to review proposed mergers and acquisitions for their potential to violate Section 7 of the Clayton Act and the desirability of challenging them in court.

Of all the mergers that take place in the United States annually, including those involving takeovers by foreign firms, probably less than 1 percent are required to be notified to the federal antitrust authorities.

A second statute, the Federal Trade Commission Act (FTC Act), enacted in 1913, established the Federal Trade Commission (FTC) as an independent agency with broad regulatory and enforcement powers. Section 5 of the FTC Act prohibits "unfair methods of competition." As interpreted by the U.S. Supreme Court, Section 5 covers all types of activities prohibited by the Sherman and Clayton Acts as well as anticompetitive methods that are not clearly prohibited by those statutes but which the FTC determines to be unfair. The FTC Act is said to fill in the gaps of federal antitrust law.

Over the years, the FTC has had a sporadic record in accomplishing its mission. It is composed of five persons nominated by the President and confirmed by the Senate, no more than three of whom can be from the same political party. Despite the political nature of the appointment process, the FTC is supposed to exercise its statutory authority to act against unfair methods of competition without influence from the President or Congress. However, Presidents (through appointments) and Congress (through the budgetary process) have increasingly involved themselves in FTC policy and enforcement decisions.

The FTC is authorized to issue cease and desist orders against parties found to violate Section 5 of the FTC Act. Additional remedies can follow, including civil penalties and restitution, if there is noncompliance with such orders. The FTC can also enforce the prohibitions found in the Clayton Act. In the modern era, the FTC's primary merger-related activity is evaluating transactions under the premerger notification rules of Section 7 of the Clayton Act.

A waiting period after filing notification of the planned acquisition or merger allows the U.S. agencies time to investigate for possible antitrust implications, sometimes in cooperation with merger authorities elsewhere (the EU for example, see Chapter 5), thus avoiding the later dismemberment of a completed transaction.

A decision to challenge the transaction by either the DOJ or FTC typically kills the deal. For example, in 2015 the DOJ rejected on anticompetitive grounds the acquisition of GE's appliance business by Sweden's Electrolux. GE quickly sold that business to Haier of China.

Private challenges to mergers and acquisitions, including cross-border transactions involving foreign companies, can also be brought under the Clayton Act. A notable example involved the hostile takeover of British Consolidated Gold Fields by Minorco (a Luxembourg company controlled by the two leading South African gold producers). Gold Fields sought to block the takeover on antitrust grounds in the United States, Britain, South Africa, Australia, and the EU. These efforts failed everywhere except in a private action in the United States, where a U.S. federal district court judge enjoined the takeover.

U.S. states also have antitrust laws that may restrict mergers and acquisitions. Some mergers approved by the federal authorities have been subsequently challenged by a state attorney general. The states have, in general, become quite active in the mergers area and have adopted their own set of Horizontal Merger Guidelines through the National Association of Attorneys General (NAAG).

Mergers and acquisitions are the primary way foreign parties invest in the USA. When there are national security implications, as frequently is the case with Chinese buyers, special CFIUS national security scrutiny and clearance procedures (below) apply.

§ 6.15 National Security Regulation of Foreign Investments in the USA

Before the enactment of Exon-Florio, when the concern for widespread Arab buyouts of American businesses in the 1970s was perceived as a threat to national security, the U.S. executive, seeking a compromise with the Congress, agreed to create the Committee on Foreign Investment in the United States (CFIUS) as an interagency, interdepartmental group to investigate inward foreign direct investment and recommend policy. CFIUS, which would have no real screening or review power, would serve at the President's discretion. For example, President Carter's administration investigated only one transaction.

During President Reagan's second term, the concern turned more toward the increasing trade deficit and the "Japanese threat." There were large inflows of foreign investment in the 1980s, although they were not limited to Japanese investors. The administration began to intervene in these inflows more frequently, especially when they constituted planned acquisitions of U.S. companies.

The policy of open versus controlled investment seemed most confused when the Japanese electronics conglomerate Fujitsu sought to acquire an 80 percent share in Fairchild Semiconductor. Fairchild had openly solicited the bid. Even though the French concern Schlumberger already owned Fairchild, the Commerce, Defense and Justice Departments all joined to oppose the proposed acquisition. The Department of Justice was concerned with antitrust implications, while the departments of Commerce and Defense appeared to object primarily to force Japanese markets to open more. Because of the extensive concern, Fujitsu withdrew its proposed acquisition even though CFIUS at the time lacked the power to block the sale.

By 1988, Congress seemed intent on creating some mechanism to review proposed foreign investment in the United States. The determination was increased when the proposed foreign purchase of Phoenix Steel was announced. Phoenix Steel was a producer of many items procured by the Department of Defense. The purchaser, represented by a Hong Kong agent, was to obtain financing for the acquisition from the People's Republic of China. CFIUS had no authority to block the sale, but it nevertheless began an investigation because many of Phoenix's products were subject to U.S. export controls.

Representative Florio of New Jersey proposed foreign-investment control legislation which would allow the President to block the sale of a U.S.-owned company to any entity with financing by a potential enemy, to ensure that the U.S. controlled technology would not be acquired by the foreign nation. The administration accepted the Exon-Florio proposal as a compromise because competing proposals would have imposed even greater reporting and disclosure requirements on foreign investors, which the administration opposed. For example, one proposal required any foreign investor acquiring a five percent or greater interest to report to the Department of Commerce certain information which would become available to the public.

Exon-Florio National Security Controls (1988)

The Exon-Florio amendment to the Defense Production Act of 1950 passed as part of the Omnibus Trade and Competitiveness Act of 1988. It grants the President the authority to investigate and suspend or prohibit mergers, acquisitions or other transactions leading to the "control" of existing American firms by foreign persons, based on national-security, critical infrastructure (virtual or physical), or critical technology concerns.

The main point of contact in the United States for inquiries about the Exon-Florio law is the Committee on Foreign Investment in the United States (CFIUS), located in the Office of International Investment, Department of the Treasury. CFIUS is comprised of nine U.S. departments or agencies (*e.g.*, State, DOD, Justice, Homeland Security) along with other ex officio members. Exon-Florio is the only U.S. law that broadly regulates foreign investment.

There were two basic problems that Exon-Florio presented to foreign investors. The first was that Exon-Florio issues may arise throughout the investment process. Foreign acquisitions that could affect national security could be reported to CFIUS at the outset. Otherwise, the government may be prompted to investigate on its own initiative and possibly order divestment. The result could be that foreign investors acquired property that lacks clear title.

The second problem was the uncertainty about the definition of national security under Exon-Florio. The Exon-Florio Regulations offer few bright-line tests. That confirms CFIUS, the President's designated center of investigation, as the omnipotent reviewer of foreign acquisitions. Exon-Florio initially earned the nickname "Lawyers Full Employment Act" because of the potentially broad scope of national security.

CFIUS interpreted national security on a case-by-case basis, leaving other companies, even in similar industries, somewhat baffled about the criteria used to evaluate the transaction. But Exon-Florio did include a list of factors to be considered in the evaluation of a transaction's national-security implications. There nevertheless remained concern about the potential abuse of the broad language and consequent wide scope of Exon-Florio's national-security language.

Foreign Investment and National Security Act Of 2007 (FINSA)

In 2005, CNOOC, a state-owned Chinese oil company, sought to buy Unocal Corp. Congressional opposition was so fierce this proposed acquisition was withdrawn. In 2006, responding to the proposed purchase by Dubai Ports World of a British operator of six American ports, a concerned Congress amended the Exon-Florio provisions by the Foreign Investment and National Security Act of 2007 (FINSA). Well before Congress acted, Dubai Ports World removed the controversy by selling its U.S. ports to an American company.

The FINSA amendments:

(1) Allow the President to intervene in transactions perceived to be a national security risk;

(2) Establish a mandatory 45-day investigation period for acquiring companies owned by foreign governments;

(3) Require high level U.S. agency approvals;

(4) Reinforce the role of the National Intelligence Director in CFIUS reviews;

(5) Mandate tracking of withdrawn transactions; and

(6) Create a flexible definition of national security that includes foreign acquisition of "critical infrastructure" and "critical technology", both broadly defined.

FINSA tightened national security review of foreign investment, notably by clarifying examination of less than 10 percent shareholdings, by treating sovereign wealth funds as state-owned enterprises subject to strict scrutiny, and by detailing when U.S. investments are "controlled" by foreigners. It also mandates monitoring of CFIUS mitigation agreements undertaken by foreign investors.

In general, a pattern exists that if a foreign government plays a role in a foreign investment, CFIUS, or perhaps its apparent watchdog, the Congress, will examine the proposal very carefully. Exon-Florio/FINSA proved to be a law the operation of which Congress follows closely, ready to enter the review of a proposed acquisition with the threat of amendments that would undo any CFIUS or presidential approval.

After the Thomson-CSF attempted merger, other sensitive cases have been heard by CFIUS. When China or Mid-East countries are involved there seems to be immediate suspicion of the intention of the proposed acquisition. In 2010, for example, Huawei Technologies of China, was "asked" by CFIUS to apply for approval of the acquisition of 3Leaf Systems, a U.S. cloud computing tech firm. Huawei applied, but when informed that CFIUS intended to recommend divestiture to the President, threatened to go through with the transaction before quickly backing out of it.

Foreign Investment Risk Review Modernization Act of 2018 (FIRRMA)

Building on Exon-Florio and FINSA, FIRRMA 2018 expands CFIUS applicability to "Covered Transactions" including:

1. Real estate transactions of a foreign person leasing or purchasing real estate in close proximity to U.S. military or other sensitive U.S. government locations that could reasonably facilitate the collection of intelligence, expose the property to the risk of foreign surveillance, or otherwise expose national security activities;

2. Non-controlling foreign investments in *critical technology* (expanded to include "emerging and foundational technologies" per the Export Control Reform Act of 2018) *critical infrastructure* or *sensitive personal data* allowing access to material nonpublic technical information.

   Such transactions may involve minority-share investments that do not convey investment control, including tech start-ups, an area where for example Chinese funds have notably supported Lyft, Uber, Unify Technologies' virtual reality, cancer-testing Grail, the fin-tech Sofi. Also covered are transactions exposing substantive decision making related to sensitive personal data of U.S. persons, critical technologies, or critical infrastructure; and

3. Changes resulting in control of a U.S. business or critical technology and critical infrastructure companies. Any transaction designed or intended to evade or circumvent CFIUS jurisdiction.

Other important changes modified CFIUS timelines to expedite certain reviews while strategically targeting others for more in-depth review (*e.g.*, Chinese transactions). Filing fees up to $300,000 per transaction and potential "fast track" fees apply. CFIUS is granted increased authority to investigate transactions not notified to it.

CFIUS filings are *mandatory* when a foreign government obtains a substantial interest (more than 10%) in critical infrastructure or critical technology or a company that maintains sensitive data about U.S. persons. *This change (effective October 15, 2020) made the applicability of U.S. export license controls under its Export Administration Regulations (EAR) and International Traffic in Arms Regulations (ITAR) a trigger for CFIUS filings.* Failure to file penalties may be up to and including the amount of the investment.

For detailed coverage of U.S. export controls, see my Concise Hornbook on *International Trade Beyond Trump*, Chapter 5.

CFIUS is also instructed to review the foreign person's history of compliance with U.S. laws and evaluate whether the proposed transaction could create cybersecurity risks for the United States.

FIRRMA further requires CFIUS to monitor mitigation plans imposed on approved transactions and is now empowered to impose penalties if the parties fail to comply with conditions imposed by the CFIUS clearance process. FIRRMA allows civil actions by parties denied CFIUS clearance or wishing to challenge outcomes on due process grounds. But Presidential determinations under CFIUS remain outside judicial scrutiny.

CFIUS may effectively waive filing requirements for NATO countries as well as Korea, Japan, Australia, and New Zealand.

Excerpts from FIRRMA are reproduced in Section 6.20.

§ 6.16 CFIUS Reviews of Proposed Foreign Investments

Exon-Florio/FINSA/FIRRMA authorizes the President or President's designee to investigate the national-security impact of "mergers, acquisitions, and takeovers" by or with foreign persons that could result in control by foreign persons. In other words, CFIUS regulates inbound foreign investment, not outbound investments. Since 1992, CFIUS investigations are mandatory when the entity seeking control over a U.S. firm is itself controlled or acting on behalf of a foreign government. This requirement was part of the 1992 Byrd Amendment resulting from the Thomson/LTV case discussed below.

Most investigations are at the discretion of CFIUS after receipt of written notification by the parties. Notice may be submitted and CFIUS review commenced at any time while the transaction is pending or after it is completed. But there is a three-year limitation after the transaction is completed, unless the CFIUS chairman, consulting with other members, requests an investigation.

To avoid the possibility of having a completed transaction questioned, companies frequently submit a voluntary notice to commence review before completing the transaction. Any transaction which has been the subject of CFIUS review or investigation is not subject to later Presidential action. Thus, even when there seems to be little apparent impact on national security, a review request might be useful.

Presidential Powers

CFIUS has 30 days after notification to decide whether to investigate, and 45 days after that to investigate and make a recommendation to the President. The President has 15 days to either suspend or prohibit the acquisition, merger, or takeover, or seek divestiture for an already completed transaction. The President may direct the Attorney General to seek appropriate relief in U.S. district courts to enforce his decision.

The President must make two findings to exercise his authority. First, he must believe that there is "credible evidence" that the foreign interest would exercise "control" which might threaten "national security." Second, he must believe that other provisions of law, aside from the International Emergency Economic Powers Act, provide inadequate authority to safeguard national security. Although these two findings remain prerequisites to presidential action, they are not subject to judicial review.

Although considerable debate occurred, "national security" remains undefined in either the law or regulations. The Exon-Florio/FINSA provisions suggest that the President consider several factors in evaluating national security concerns. These are mainly directed to the capacity of domestic industry to meet national-defense requirements in view of the proposed takeover. Amendments to Exon-Florio have added as factors for presidential consideration both the potential for proliferation of missiles and nuclear and biological weapons, as well as the potential effect of the transaction on U.S. leadership in technology that affects national security.

CFIUS Procedures

Any information filed with CFIUS is largely confidential, although some releases of information may be made to authorized members of Congress. Critics have charged that CFIUS has abused the confidentiality provisions in some cases and has left important players out of the investigation process until after CFIUS has made its decisions. The confidentiality provision has made official reports of cases impossible but has protected both the interests of foreign investors and national security.

How CFIUS and the President have applied the law, and the criticism generated from such application, have focused on the proper meaning of three terms: "Mergers, Acquisitions, and Takeovers," "Control", and "National Security."

The regulations consider devices created to avoid Exon-Florio review, such as foreign-controlled corporations seeking to purchase U.S. businesses using American agents supposedly acting independently. As Treasury drafted the regulations, Rep. Florio and other commentators wondered about the applicability of the law toward other types of transactions, such as proxy solicitations which might lead to foreign control, foreign bank financing which might lead to control by default, joint ventures, and "greenfield" investments. The regulations address most of those issues, although they include few "bright-line tests."

Exon-Florio/FINSA/FIRRMA does *not* apply to portfolio investments where the foreigner obtains ten percent or less of voting securities solely for investment purposes, where the foreign buyer has the same parent as the target, or the foreign investor does not acquire managerial control of a U.S. business. Joint ventures, originally thought to be exempt from CFIUS review, are included.

Foreign persons soliciting proxies to obtain control are also covered. The regulations do not subject lending transactions by foreign persons to CFIUS review unless the lender assumes some degree of control, at either the time that the loan is made or when default appears imminent.

Control by Foreign Persons

As these comments suggest, what *control* would be exercised by the foreign person is the key to determining whether a transaction is within the scope of Exon-Florio/FINSA/FIRRMA. The regulations define "control" without limitation on voting percentages or majority ownership, but as "the power, direct or indirect, whether or not exercised. . .to determine, direct, take, reach or cause decisions" in a series of key areas. These areas include the transfer (sale, lease, mortgage, or pledge) of assets, the dissolution of the business, the closing or relocation of research and development facilities, terminating or not fulfilling the business contracts, and amending the Articles of Incorporation of the business regarding any of these matters.

In addition, when examining control, if more than one foreign person is involved, CFIUS may consider the possibility of their acting in concert. However, an *unrelated* group of foreign investors holding majority shares in a U.S. company will not be assumed to control that company.

"National Security"

In contrast with the attempt to define "control," Exon-Florio/ FINSA/FIRRMA and its associated regulations still do *not* define "national security." Many of the public comments during Treasury's drafting of the regulations urged a specific definition, but the statute and regulations consciously leave the determination of a national-security concern to the President's discretion. Few involved in regulating foreign investment outside the administration were satisfied with that result. Some in Congress thought that the White House interpreted "national security" too narrowly, equating it only with military security.

The General Accounting Office (GAO) criticized CFIUS for not determining if anti-competitive behavior by foreign firms might jeopardize national security. A former Attorney General and Secretary of Defense, speaking for a segment of the foreign-investment regulatory community, criticized the rules lack of national-security criteria because more mergers and acquisitions may fall under review than Congress intended. Nevertheless, administration officials stressed the need for "national security" to have a broad scope and not be confined to specific industries should the target company provide products or technologies essential to the U.S. defense industrial base.

§ 6.17 CFIUS Cases

The application of Exon-Florio/FINSA/FIRRMA in real situations resolves some of the apparent ambiguity to the meaning of "national security" and the other important statutory and regulatory terms. CFIUS has reviewed thousands of proposed acquisitions. Some detailed investigations lead to withdrawals, but rarely a presidential order of divestment. Because of CFIUS' confidentiality requirements, no official reports or summaries of its investigations exist for lawyers or investors to consult.

Instead, secondary sources must be used to draw meanings given to the statute and regulations. The cases when the President chose not to act, when the parties themselves withdrew, and the few cases when the President has ordered divestment present some general patterns of what foreign investors may expect from a CFIUS investigation. Here are some case examples:

Huels AG of Germany/Monsanto

The Department of Defense prompted one of the first investigations under Exon-Florio/FINSA because the U.S. semiconductor research consortium that the DOD sponsors, SEMATECH, wanted guaranteed access to silicon wafers manufactured by Monsanto Electronic Materials Co., which was about to be sold to Huels AG, a German company.

Although CFIUS recommended that the President allow the transaction to go forward, notwithstanding the objections of 29 congressmen, CFIUS obtained as part of its approval written assurances that SEMATECH would retain access and no technology would transfer for five years. There appeared to be a quid pro quo that CFIUS would not disapprove the takeover in return for Huels' assurances, creating a performance requirement for foreign investment.

Matra SA of France/Fairchild

CFIUS apparently imposed a similar requirement on Matra SA of France when it sought to purchase Fairchild industries, requiring a restructured export-control system as a condition for CFIUS approval. Foreign investors therefore may have to agree to government-imposed conditions on their transactions, with CFIUS approval received only after an Exon-Florio/FINSA/FIRRMA investigation is conducted as a bargaining tool.

British Tire & Rubber (UK)/Norton

U.S. administrations are not alone in using Exon-Florio/FINSA/ FIRRMA as a bargaining tool. United States companies which are targets of hostile takeovers by foreign investors have used CFIUS as one method to oppose proposed takeovers. Within two months of passage of the law, companies began to invoke Exon-Florio to delay or discourage takeovers.

A good example of an American firm using political pressure on a foreign buyer through Exon-Florio and other mechanisms is the attempted purchase of the Norton Company of Worcester, Mass., by British Tire and Rubber, PLC (BTR). Norton manufactured ceramic ball bearings used in the space shuttle. More than 200 congressmen urged an investigation, including Senator Kerry of Massachusetts, who noted Norton's role in the Massachusetts economy as justification for an investigation in addition to national security reasons. The Massachusetts state legislature soon enacted a law depriving BTR of control should the purchase succeed, leading BTR to pull out, and a French buyer to make a friendly offer at a much higher price.

No security concerns were raised when the friendly French buyer appeared offering a better price, even though Norton had earlier argued that BTR planned to dismember Norton and reduce its research and development budgets to the detriment of national security. This led many to conclude that the CFIUS process was easily abused. Critics argued that existing DOD regulations could handle true national-security concerns, and that Exon-Florio only added a political element to the ability of foreign investors to acquire U.S. companies.

China National Aero Tech/MAMCO

While some firms use a CFIUS investigation to scare away hostile foreign investors, one transaction that the President decided to reject had already been finalized at the time of the order. The order forced the foreign entity to divest. The target was MAMCO Manufacturing, Inc., a U.S. company in Seattle that manufactured metal parts for commercial aircraft made by Boeing. MAMCO mainly supplied Boeing, and although some of its products were subject to export controls, MAMCO had no contracts involving classified information. The buyer was China National Aero-Technology Import and Export Corp. (CATIC), owned by the People's Republic of China.

During the investigation, it appeared that CATIC had previously violated export-control laws concerning aircraft engines purchased from General Electric. But concerns about CATIC went beyond export-control problems with China. Administration sources revealed that CATIC had been trying to obtain technology to build jet fighters capable of refueling during flight. In addition, there were concerns by the administration and Congress that the Chinese government used CATIC as a base for covert operations in the United States.

The Executive Order directing CATIC to divest itself of MAMCO contained none of the above concerns or information, but simply stated that the two requirements of Exon-Florio had been satisfied: Credible evidence existed of a threat to national security, and no other provision of law could protect the national-security interest.

Considering the relatively low level of technology involved, however, the President's action on CFIUS' unanimous recommendation to terminate the investment surprised many observers, leading some to believe that the national-security concern was a pretext for other political motives. Foreign-investor lobbying organizations agreed with this perception, fearing that CFIUS would become a foreign-policy tool.

But the administration stressed that the order did not constitute a change in America's general policy of openness toward investment from foreigners or reflect upon the PRC. That said, the order seemed to indicate that investment owned or supported by foreign governments would receive special scrutiny under Exon-Florio.

Nakamichi/Applied Magnetics

MOST, a United States incorporated subsidiary of Nakamichi Corp. of Japan, agreed to purchase the Optical Products Division of United States Applied Magnetics Corporation. Although about 98 percent of OPD's sales were optical heads for computers the products have application in some weapons systems. CFIUS reviewed the application and approved the sale one day before the inauguration of President Clinton.

Congress was unaware of the ongoing review until the announced approval. But some members quickly intervened and produced evidence allegedly showing that the CFIUS review was based on misleading and incomplete information. That would allow reopening of the review process. Although much publicity followed there was no further review, but a clear warning sounded that a clearance by CFIUS may lead to public outcry if the process remains silent until the CFIUS decision.

Thomson/LTV and 1992 Exon-Florio Amendments

By 1992, Congressional dissatisfaction with how the President and CFIUS had interpreted Exon-Florio led to proposals for new and stricter controls. The circumstances that led to the first substantive amendments to the Exon-Florio law involved foreign-government participation in a proposed acquisition, the attempted purchase of the missile division of LTV Corp. by Thomson-CSF, a conglomerate partially owned (58 percent) and financed by the French government.

LTV, a defense contractor, had been operating under bankruptcy protection since 1986. Thomson made a bid for $450 million in association with an American investment bank and Northrop, the U.S. aircraft company, to buy LTV's aircraft and missile business. The bankruptcy court approved the sale. Thomson outbid the U.S. defense contractor Martin Marietta by nearly $100 million. Martin Marietta was the buyer LTV favored because of the prospective problems Thomson would have with CFIUS.

Thomson filed the notice for review under Exon-Florio. To diminish concerns regarding national security, Thomson initially proposed to the DOD to structure its purchase of LTV through an agreement that would allow some control over LTV. As pressure increased, Thomson withdrew that proposal and stated that a proxy agreement would suffice, with the proxies being U.S. citizens who had no prior connection to the parties. But Thomson was unable to satisfy DOD demands to protect classified information. The DOD has separate authority under the Industrial Security Regulations to protect classified information, including the ability to block an acquisition.

There was immediate adverse Congressional reaction, acknowledging that the United States and France were allies, but noting that French interests have not always been the same as those of America. The Senate even passed a non-binding resolution (vote of 93–4) finding the proposed acquisition to be harmful to national security. Administration officials were reluctant to discuss even the general policy of allowing a foreign government-owned or-controlled company to purchase a U.S. defense contractor while the investigation was in process.

Because the DOD apparently did not at first intend to object to the sale, it was criticized for failing to consider the questionable record of Thomson and the French government in exporting weapons to countries with which the United States did not have good relations, such as Iran, Libya, and Iraq. And criticized for ignoring a Defense Intelligence Agency warning of extensive technology leakage. The lesson is that even "friendly" nations may have skeletons in the closet which the DOD and other critics of a proposed investment will quickly make public. France's military policy, which was made independently of NATO, did not help.

Other commentators remained equally critical of Thomson's proposal suggesting that although an open-door policy makes sense for *private* foreign investors, that policy should be reexamined where foreign *governments* are involved, especially in this case, where LTV's products could not be replaced by another domestic firm. Exon-Florio (as it then existed) did not seem an appropriate vehicle to carry out a policy intended to prevent foreign-government ownership of defense contractors.

It became apparent during the controversy over LTV that the CFIUS was almost certain to recommend that the President block the transaction. Consequently, Thomson first withdrew its bid to restructure the deal and ultimately withdrew completely, leading to a suit by LTV for breach of contract. Martin Marietta soon submitted a higher bid, justified because it would not have to compete with the inexhaustible resources of a government-assisted competitor.

During and following the Thomson-LTV attempted merger, Congress, not the President and CFIUS, assumed the lead role. Congress led the effort to gain more information on Thomson, and during its hearings to reconsider the policy of open direct investment involving foreign governments, Thomson's bid was withdrawn.

Because of the perception that the administration took up the case only with prompting by Congress, amendments to Exon-Florio soon appeared on Capitol Hill.

The committee working on what would become the Byrd Amendment to Exon-Florio identified three factors of greatest concern in the attempted merger. First, LTV was a substantial contractor with the DOD and NASA and was the largest contractor ever for sale to a foreign firm. Second, as much as 75 percent of the work LTV did for the DOD required access to highly classified information that is generally prohibited for foreign nationals or representatives of foreign interests. Third, the French government owned 58 percent of Thomson's stock. Of considerable concern to the committee was that government ownership would introduce into the company's decision-making process the foreign government's political and diplomatic interests, which may contrast with those of the United States.

Exon-Florio Amendments

Two major amendments to Exon-Florio are directly attributable to the experience of the failed Thomson purchase of LTV. When Congress assumed the lead in that investigation, the President appeared to be slow to react to the attempted takeover involving a foreign government. The first change sought by Congress was to remove any presidential and CFIUS reticence in carrying out their responsibilities under Exon-Florio.

The Byrd Amendment *requires* the President or his designee to investigate if the purchasing foreigner is "controlled by or acting on behalf of a foreign government." The "acting on behalf" language is not without some ambiguity. It remains unclear whether this would include a lesser form of control as defined in the regulations (issued before the Byrd Amendment), consequently increasing Exon-Florio's coverage when a foreign government is involved. But the Byrd Amendment did add a new concept of "effective control" by a foreign government, which may increase the ambiguity of the meaning of "control by a foreign government."

The second important amendment forbids the sale of some U.S. companies to certain foreign investors, principally those involved with foreign governments. In a separate statutory section, entities controlled by a foreign government are prohibited from acquiring certain Department of Energy or Defense contractors. Such contractors may not be acquired by entities controlled by or acting on behalf of foreign governments if they work under a national-security program that cannot be done without access to a "proscribed category of information."

Furthermore, any firm awarded at least $500 million in prime DOD contracts or at least $500 million in prime Department of Energy contracts under national-security programs may not be acquired. There may be an escape clause, however. Section 2170a(b) suggests that if foreign investors are patient and go through an investigation that ends without suspension or prohibition, the acquisition restraints may not apply.

There was an additional 1992 amendment which requires the President to report to Congress his national decision, including a detailed explanation of how the decision was reached. These reports are not disclosed to the public under an exemption to the Freedom of Information Act.

§ 6.18   Foreign Investments Blocked Under CFIUS

Commercial airlines

The first presidentially blocked deal came from President George H.W. Bush in 1990. MAMCO Manufacturing, a Seattle-based aircraft parts maker had been sold to the China National Aero-Technology Import and Export Corporation (CATIC), a Chinese state-owned aviation company. President Bush used his authority to retroactively undo the deal, requesting that CATIC divest its acquisition of MAMCO. President Bush cited concerns of CATIC gaining access to technology through the ownership of MAMCO that it otherwise wouldn't have access to absent an export license.

The second block came from President Barack Obama in 2012, when he ordered Ralls Corporation, a Chinese-owned electric company, to divest its acquisition of Oregon wind farm assets from Terna Energy SA, citing national security concerns.

President Obama also blocked a deal on the recommendation of CFIUS in 2016. This time he prevented the takeover of the US assets of the German-based semiconductor company Aixtron. The prospective buyer, Fujian Grand Chip Investment Fund, was a Chinese firm with ties to the Chinese Government. This transaction was blocked due to national security risks stemming from Aixtron's technical knowledge and the military applications possible with that knowledge.

In 2016, President Donald Trump blocked the acquisition of Lattice Semiconductor, a US chipmaker, by the Chinese investment firm Canyon Bridge Capital Partners where the deal was partially financed by Chinese state-owned capital. After CFIUS referred the $1.3 billion deal to the president, recommending the president block it on the grounds of national security, the parties appealed to President Trump to overrule CFIUS's recommendation. After the formal block, the Chinese Ministry of Commerce issued a statement that countries should not push protectionism through national security reviews.

Finally, in 2018, President Trump blocked the attempted takeover of Qualcomm, a U.S. semiconductor chipmaker telecom leader and the U.S. leading firm in the 5G race, by a Singaporean-based competitor, Broadcom. Broadcom even took steps in anticipation of a CFIUS review of the $117 billion deal and moved its headquarters to the U.S. to mitigate potential national security risks, but to no avail. President Trump blocked the deal on national security grounds, and there was additional concern that this deal would reduce U.S. technological competitiveness, particularly in the emerging 5G field where China is the U.S.'s largest competitor.

In its recommendation to President Trump, CFIUS members cited Broadcom's plans to take a "private equity style" approach if it acquired Qualcomm. Private equity investors typically have a lifespan of 5–10 years, and thus are concerned with a company's short-term performance to maximize financial gain at a deemed liquidation event, such as a sale, merger, or an IPO. Broadcom's plans suggested to CFIUS that long-term research and development investment in Qualcomm would be sacrificed for a focus on short-term profits. In addition to being the largest technology-related foreign investment transaction in the world, this deal was far and wide the largest deal to be blocked by presidential order on CFIUS's recommendation.

However, it is not just a presidential order that can kill deals. Although CFIUS can refer a deal to the President with a recommendation to block, CFIUS investigation and mitigation orders alone can cause parties to abandon a deal before it is ever sent to the president for review. In fact, the potentially negative publicity associated with a CFIUS investigation has had a major effect on transactions that CFIUS has investigated. Nearly half of transactions investigated by CFIUS since 1990 were terminated by the parties due to a preference to withdraw from the transaction rather than face a negative determination or mitigation orders by CFIUS.

In 2006, the possibility of a CFIUS investigation was reportedly a significant reason the Israeli firm Check Point Software Technologies withdrew its proposed $225 million acquisition of Sourcefire, a U.S. firm that specializes in security appliances for protecting a corporation's internal computer networks. Additionally, the China National Offshore Oil Company (CNOOC) decided to drop its proposed $18 billion acquisition of Unocal oil in 2005 partly because of concerns by CNOOC about an impending CFIUS investigation of the transaction.

Additionally, the deal for Ant Financial, a Chinese electronic payments company, to purchase MoneyGram, a Dallas-based money transfer company, for $1.2 billion collapsed after CFIUS refused to approve it. The Trump administration's concerns about Chinese acquisitions of American knowhow were too strong for Chinese tycoon Jack Ma, to overcome through a direct appeal to President-elect Trump and a pledge to create one million American jobs.

The author thanks Kayla Brennan, Esq. for her assistance on CFIUS blocks by U.S. presidents.

§ 6.19 China Invests in the USA

Since 2007, CFIUS has reviewed numerous transactions, investigating roughly half of them. Some foreign buyers of U.S. companies have agreed to CFIUS mitigation measures related to U.S. national security. For example, China's state-owned CNOOC was notably cleared to acquire Canada's Nexen subject to alterations in Nexen's control over U.S. oil and gas drilling leases.

Moreover, some 98 percent of proposed acquisitions since 1988 that have been notified under the law have been approved without a full investigation under "no action" letters. Chinese, British, and Canadian firms have filed the largest number of notices for CFIUS review. Chinese investments blocked or withdrawn under Presidents George H. W. Bush, Obama and Trump are noted above.

China's investments in the United States have grown, by and large through mergers and acquisitions: AMC Entertainment Holdings in 2012, Smithfield Foods in 2013, Motorola Mobility in 2014, and Legendary Entertainment, Carmike Cinemas and GE's appliance business in 2016. All these investments survived CFIUS review.

However, there was a notable "extraterritorial" CFIUS rejection in 2016 of an attempt by a Chinese venture capital company to buy Lumaleds from Royal Philips NV of The Netherlands. CFIUS was concerned that Lumaleds has extensive U.S. assets and patent holdings in the LED lighting field. Similarly, a Chinese investor withdrew from a multi-billion-dollar deal to acquire a stake in Western Digital, a California disk-drive maker, when CFIUS commenced an investigation.

Other Chinese acquisitions have completed CFIUS review. These include: The HNA Group of China's acquisition of technology distributor Ingram Micro (denied), Chinese attempts to buy the Chicago Stock Exchange (denied), and China National Chemical's purchase of Syngenta AG of Switzerland, which has substantial U.S.

agricultural chemical and seed interests (cleared). The latter is part of a pattern of Chinese goals to achieve "food security".

In 2019, acting on its own initiative, CFIUS ordered a Chinese company to divest its majority ownership Grindr, a gay-dating app. CFIUS asserted that Grindr's collection of personal data could be exploited by the PRC to blackmail individuals with U.S. security clearances. In 2020, President Trump ordered the Chinese Shiji Group to divest itself of StayNTouch, a U.S. cloud-based hotel management system using facial recognition to authenticate guest identities.

In 2021, in another example of the extraterritorial application of U.S. national security foreign investment law, CFIUS ordered a hold pending its review of an attempt by a private Chinese investor to acquire South Korean chipmaker Magnachip Semiconductor, listed on the NYSE.

By 2022, Chinese efforts to buy American firms had declined, in part due to PRC capital export restraints and in part to added CFIUS scrutiny.

§ 6.20   Text of the Foreign Investment Risk Review Modernization Act (2018) (FIRRMA)

SEC. 1701. SHORT TITLE: FOREIGN INVESTMENT RISK REVIEW MODERNIZATION ACT OF 2018.

This subtitle may be cited as the "Foreign Investment Risk Review Modernization Act of 2018".

SEC. 1702. FINDINGS; SENSE OF CONGRESS.

(a)   FINDINGS. Congress makes the following findings:

(1) According to a February 2016 report by the International Trade Administration of the Department of Commerce, 12,000,000 United States workers, equivalent to 8.5 percent of the labor force, have jobs resulting from foreign investment, including 3,500,000 jobs in the manufacturing sector alone.

(2)   In 2016, new foreign direct investment in United States manufacturing totaled $129,400,000,000.

(3)   The Bureau of Economic Analysis of the Department of Commerce concluded that, in 2015—

(A)   foreign-owned affiliates in the United States—

(i) contributed $894,500,000,000 in value added to the United States economy;

(ii) exported goods valued at $352,800,000,000, accounting for nearly a quarter of total exports of goods from the United States; and

(iii) undertook $56,700,000,000 in research and development; and H. R. 5515–540

(B) the 7 countries investing the most in the United States, all of which are United States allies (the United Kingdom, Japan, Germany, France, Canada, Switzerland, and the Netherlands) accounted for 72.1 percent of the value added by foreign-owned affiliates in the United States and more than 80 percent of research and development expenditures by such entities.

(4) According to the Government Accountability Office, from 2011 to 2016, the number of transactions reviewed by the Committee on Foreign Investment in the United States (commonly referred to as "CFIUS") grew by 55 percent, while the staff of the Committees assigned to the reviews increased by 11 percent.

(5) According to a February 2018 report of the Government Accountability Office on the Committee on Foreign Investment in the United States (GAO-18-249): "Officials from Treasury and other member agencies are aware of pressures on their CFIUS staff given the current workload and have expressed concerns about possible workload increases.". The Government Accountability Office concluded: "Without attaining an understanding of the staffing levels needed to address the current and future CFIUS workload, particularly if legislative changes to CFIUS's authorities further expand its workload, CFIUS may be limited in its ability to fulfill its objectives and address threats to the national security of the United States.".

(6) On March 30, 1954, Dwight David Eisenhower—five-star general, Supreme Allied Commander, and 34th President of the United States—in his "Special Message to the Congress on Foreign Economic Policy", counseled: "Great mutual advantages to buyer and seller, to producer and consumer, to investor and to the community where investment is made, accrue from high levels of trade and investment.". President Eisenhower continued: "The internal strength of the American economy has evolved from such a system of mutual advantage. In the press of other problems and in the haste to meet emergencies, this

nation—and many other nations of the free world—have all too often lost sight of this central fact.". President Eisenhower concluded: "If we fail in our trade policy, we may fail in all. Our domestic employment, our standard of living, our security, and the solidarity of the free world—all are involved.".

(b) SENSE OF CONGRESS. It is the sense of Congress that—

(1) foreign investment provides substantial economic benefits to the United States, including the promotion of economic growth, productivity, competitiveness, and job creation, thereby enhancing national security;

(2) maintaining the commitment of the United States to an open investment policy encourages other countries to reciprocate and helps open new foreign markets for United States businesses;

(3) it should continue to be the policy of the United States to enthusiastically welcome and support foreign investment, consistent with the protection of national security;

(4) at the same time, the national security landscape has shifted in recent years, and so has the nature of the investments that pose the greatest potential risk to national security, which warrants an appropriate modernization of the processes and H. R. 5515–541 authorities of the Committee on Foreign Investment in the United States and of the United States export control system;

(5) the Committee on Foreign Investment in the United States plays a critical role in protecting the national security of the United States, and, therefore, it is essential that the member agencies of the Committee are adequately resourced and able to hire appropriately qualified individuals in a timely manner, and that those individuals' security clearances are processed as a high priority;

(6) the President should conduct a more robust international outreach effort to urge and help allies and partners of the United States to establish processes that are similar to the Committee on Foreign Investment in the United States to screen foreign investments for national security risks and to facilitate coordination;

(7) the President should lead a collaborative effort with allies and partners of the United States to strengthen the multilateral export control regime;

(8) any penalties imposed by the United States Government with respect to an individual or entity pursuant to

a determination that the individual or entity has violated sanctions imposed by the United States or the export control laws of the United States should not be reversed for reasons unrelated to the national security of the United States; and

(9) the Committee on Foreign Investment in the United States should continue to review transactions for the purpose of protecting national security and should not consider issues of national interest absent a national security nexus.

(c) SENSE OF CONGRESS ON CONSIDERATION OF COVERED TRANSACTIONS. It is the sense of Congress that, when considering national security risks, the Committee on Foreign Investment in the United States may consider—

(1) whether a covered transaction involves a country of special concern that has a demonstrated or declared strategic goal of acquiring a type of critical technology or critical infrastructure that would affect United States leadership in areas related to national security;

(2) the potential national security-related effects of the cumulative control of, or pattern of recent transactions involving, any one type of critical infrastructure, energy asset, critical material, or critical technology by a foreign government or foreign person;

(3) whether any foreign person engaging in a covered transaction with a United States business has a history of complying with United States laws and regulations;

(4) the control of United States industries and commercial activity by foreign persons as it affects the capability and capacity of the United States to meet the requirements of national security, including the availability of human resources, products, technology, materials, and other supplies and services, and in considering "the availability of human resources", should construe that term to include potential losses of such availability resulting from reductions in the employment of United States persons whose knowledge or skills are critical to national security, including the continued production in the United States of items that are likely to be acquired by the H. R. 5515–542 Department of Defense or other Federal departments or agencies for the advancement of the national security of the United States;

(5) the extent to which a covered transaction is likely to expose, either directly or indirectly, personally identifiable information, genetic information, or other sensitive data of

United States citizens to access by a foreign government or foreign person that may exploit that information in a manner that threatens national security; and

(6) whether a covered transaction is likely to have the effect of exacerbating or creating new cybersecurity vulnerabilities in the United States or is likely to result in a foreign government gaining a significant new capability to engage in malicious cyber-enabled activities against the United States, including such activities designed to affect the outcome of any election for Federal office.

SEC. 1703. DEFINITIONS.

* * *

"(5) CRITICAL INFRASTRUCTURE.—The term 'critical infrastructure' means, subject to regulations prescribed by the Committee, systems and assets, whether physical or virtual, so vital to the United States that the incapacity or destruction of such systems or assets would have a debilitating impact on national security.

"(6) CRITICAL TECHNOLOGIES.—H. R. 5515–547

"(A) IN GENERAL.—The term 'critical technologies' means the following:

"(i) Defense articles or defense services included on the United States Munitions List set forth in the International Traffic in Arms Regulations under subchapter M of chapter I of title 22, Code of Federal Regulations.

"(ii) Items included on the Commerce Control List set forth in Supplement No. 1 to part 774 of the Export Administration Regulations under subchapter C of chapter VII of title 15, Code of Federal Regulations, and controlled—

"(I) pursuant to multilateral regimes, including for reasons relating to national security, chemical and biological weapons proliferation, nuclear nonproliferation, or missile technology; or

"(II) for reasons relating to regional stability or surreptitious listening.

"(iii) Specially designed and prepared nuclear equipment, parts and components, materials, software, and technology covered by part 810 of title

10, Code of Federal Regulations (relating to assistance to foreign atomic energy activities).

"(iv) Nuclear facilities, equipment, and material covered by part 110 of title 10, Code of Federal Regulations (relating to export and import of nuclear equipment and material).

"(v) Select agents and toxins covered by part 331 of title 7, Code of Federal Regulations, part 121 of title 9 of such Code, or part 73 of title 42 of such Code.

"(vi) Emerging and foundational technologies controlled pursuant to section 1758 of the Export Control Reform Act of 2018.

* * *

"(7) FOREIGN GOVERNMENT-CONTROLLED TRANSACTION.—The term 'foreign government-controlled transaction' means any covered transaction that could result in the control of any United States business by a foreign government or an entity controlled by or acting on behalf of a foreign government covered transaction may submit to the Committee a declaration with basic information regarding the transaction instead of a written notice under clause.

* * *

SEC. 1706. DECLARATIONS FOR CERTAIN COVERED TRANSACTIONS.

* * *

"(IV) MANDATORY DECLARATIONS.—

"(aa) REGULATIONS.—The Committee shall prescribe regulations specifying the types of H. R. 5515–550 covered transactions for which the Committee requires a declaration under this subclause.

"(bb) CERTAIN COVERED TRANSACTIONS WITH FOREIGN GOVERNMENT INTERESTS.—

"(AA) IN GENERAL.—Except as provided in subitem (BB), the parties to a covered transaction shall submit a declaration described in subclause (I) with respect to the transaction if the transaction involves an investment that results in the acquisition, directly or indirectly, of a substantial interest in a United States business described in subsection (a)(4)(B)(iii) by a foreign person in which a foreign government has, directly or indirectly, a substantial interest.

"(BB) SUBSTANTIAL INTEREST DEFINED.—In this item, the term 'substantial interest' has the meaning given that term in regulations which the Committee shall prescribe. In developing those regulations, the Committee shall consider the means by which a foreign government could influence the actions of a foreign person, including through board membership, ownership interest, or shareholder rights. An interest that is excluded under subparagraph (D) of subsection (a)(4) from the term 'other investment' as used in subparagraph (B)(iii) of that subsection or that is less than a 10 percent voting interest shall not be considered a substantial interest.

"(CC) WAIVER.—The Committee may waive, with respect to a foreign person, the requirement under subitem (AA) for the submission of a declaration described in subclause (I) if the Committee determines that the foreign person demonstrates that the investments of the foreign person are not directed by a foreign government and the foreign person has a history of cooperation with the Committee. person with membership as a limited partner on an advisory board or a committee of the fund, the criteria specified in items (cc) and (dd) of subsection (a)(4)(D)(iv).

"(ee) SUBMISSION OF WRITTEN NOTICE AS AN ALTERNATIVE.—Parties to a covered transaction for which a declaration is required under this subclause may instead elect to submit a written notice under clause (i).["]

* * *

SEC. 1708. AUTHORITY FOR UNILATERAL INITIATION OF REVIEWS.

Section 721(b)(1) of the Defense Production Act of 1950 (50 U.S.C. 4565(b)(1)) is amended—

* * *

SEC. 1719. MODIFICATION OF ANNUAL REPORT AND OTHER REPORTING REQUIREMENTS.

* * *

(b) REPORT ON CHINESE INVESTMENT.—

(1) IN GENERAL.—Not later than 2 years after the date of the enactment of this Act, and every 2 years thereafter through 2026, the Secretary of Commerce shall submit to Congress and the Committee on Foreign Investment in the United States a report on foreign direct investment transactions made by entities of the People's Republic of China in the United States.

§ 6.21 Text of FTC Overview of the Amended Franchise Rule (16 C.F.R. 436) (2007)

The final amended Rule maintains the benefits of the original Rule, preventing deceptive and unfair practices identified in the original rulemaking through presale disclosure of material information necessary to make an informed purchasing decision and prohibition of specified misrepresentations. At the same time, part 436 of the final amended Rule reduces unnecessary compliance costs. First, part 436 covers only the sale of franchises to be located in the United States and its territories. Second, based upon the record, the Commission also has created several new exemptions for sophisticated franchise purchasers, including exemptions for large investments and large franchisees with sufficient net worth and prior experience.

Part 436 of the final amended Rule also reduces inconsistencies between federal and state pre-sale disclosure requirements. Since the original Rule was promulgated, NASAA, which represents the 15 states with pre-sale franchise disclosure laws, has developed a standard disclosure document, the UFOC. The Commission, as a matter of policy, has in the past permitted franchisors to comply with the Franchise Rule by furnishing prospective franchisees with a UFOC, even in the 35 states without franchise disclosure laws. The Commission found that the UFOC Guidelines, taken as a whole, offer consumers the same or greater consumer protection as that provided by the original Rule. As a result, the UFOC Guidelines already are used by the vast majority of franchisors to comply with the Rule 47 and, in fact, the UFOC Guidelines have become the national franchise industry standard. Further, as NASAA noted, the UFOC Guidelines were developed with significant input from franchisors, franchisees, and franchise administrators, and were subject to public hearings and notice and comment.49 Therefore, the UFOC Guidelines, like the Franchise Rule, reflect a balance of interests among all affected parties.

Overwhelmingly, franchisors, franchisees, and franchise regulators urged the Commission throughout the Rule amendment proceeding to adopt the UFOC Guidelines disclosure format. These commenters include a broad range of interests, such as NASAA, the International Franchise Association ("IFA"), the American Bar Association's Antitrust Section, the American Franchisee Association, the State Bar of California Business Law Section, and major franchisors, such as Cendant, Marriott, YUM! Brands, 7-Eleven, Arby's, and Starwood Hotels and Resorts.

Accordingly, part 436 of the final amended Rule closely tracks the UFOC Guidelines. Nevertheless, part 436 is not identical to the UFOC Guidelines. In a few instances, part 436 omits or streamlines a UFOC Guidelines disclosure requirement that the Commission believes is unnecessary or is overly burdensome—for example, mandatory cover page risk factors, broker disclosures, and detailed computer equipment disclosures. As explained in greater detail below, part 436 of the final amended Rule also avoids problems with Item 20 of the UFOC Guidelines (the disclosure of statistical information on franchisees in the system) that were revealed during the proceeding and that were examined in detail by a number of commenters, including NASAA.

Part 436 of the final amended Rule also retains a few provisions from the original Rule that are not in the UFOC Guidelines, because the Commission believes they are necessary to prevent deception. For example, part 436 of the final amended Rule retains the original Rule's requirement that, in some instances, franchisors disclose information about a parent. Similarly, part 436 retains the original

Rule's phase-in of audited financial statements, thereby preserving flexibility not present in the UFOC Guidelines.

At the same time, part 436 of the final amended Rule adds to the UFOC Guidelines a few narrowly tailored disclosures based upon the Commission's law enforcement experience and the rulemaking record, mostly to prevent deception involving the nature of the franchise relationship.[51] For example, as explained in greater detail below, part 436 of the final amended Rule expands the UFOC Guidelines' Item 3 litigation disclosure requirements to include the disclosure of franchisor-initiated litigation. In addition, part 436 of the final amended Rule goes beyond the UFOC Guidelines' Item 20 franchisee statistics disclosures to require disclosure of information about the franchisor's use of confidentiality clauses and the existence of trademark specific franchisee associations. In addition, in a few instances, part 436 of the final amended Rule requires franchisors to make prescribed statements to clarify issues that the record established are often misinterpreted by prospective franchisees, particularly in the area of protected territories and financial performance representations.

Further, part 436 of the final amended Rule updates the original Rule and UFOC Guidelines by addressing changes in the marketplace and new technologies. For example, as explained below, part 436 of the final amended Rule permits franchisors to furnish disclosures electronically and enables franchisees to use electronic signatures. Part 436 of the final amended Rule also updates the original Rule and UFOC Guidelines to address the impact of the Internet on a franchisor's business operations. Specifically, part 436 requires more disclosure about the affect of the Internet on sales restrictions imposed on franchisees and any right of franchisors to compete online. It also addresses financial performance representations made on the Internet.

Finally, part 436 of the final amended Rule contains a few provisions and prohibitions that are necessary to make the Rule effective, to facilitate compliance, and to prevent deception. For example, part 436 of the final amended Rule prohibits a franchisor from unilaterally altering the material terms and conditions of its franchise agreements, unless the franchise seller informs the prospective franchisee about the changes within a reasonable time before execution. Part 436 of the final amended Rule also prohibits

---

[51]   A decision to retain any portion of the original Rule may be based upon evidence gathered during the original rulemaking and the Commission's subsequent enforcement experience, as well as evidence adduced during the current rulemaking. Indeed, to the extent that nothing supplements evidence from the initial rulemaking, there is a presumption that the existing rule should be retained. *See* Motor Vehicle Mfrs. Ass'n v. State Farm Mut. Auto. Ins. Co., 463 U.S. 29, 42 (1983).

the use of shills, who are persons paid or otherwise given consideration to provide a false favorable report about the franchisor's performance history.

Chapter 7

INVESTOR-STATE ARBITRATIONS UNDER BITs AND FTAs

Given the absence of a cohesive body of widely accepted foreign investment law, and notably the failure of the Multilateral Agreement of Investment (MAI), nations have turned to negotiation of bilateral foreign investment treaties (BITs) and/or free trade agreements (FTAs) that contain foreign investment chapters. For detailed NAFTA 1994 and USMCA 2020 coverage of foreign investor-host state rules and arbitration examples, see Chapter 8.

From the perspective of capital exporting countries, BITs and FTAs offer protection from host state actions that violate the foreign investor rights contained therein. From the perspective of capital importing countries, investment treaties and FTAs create incentives to invest in what may be high-risk markets.

There is a long history of foreign investors' purchasing political-risk insurance against expropriation, civil unrest, and the like, sometimes from their home governments. See Chapter 3. In Latin America, the spread of "Calvo Doctrine" rules designed to limit foreign investors to host nations' judicial and administrative remedies increased the desire for protection. Investor-state dispute settlement (ISDS) by arbitration first appeared in a 1959 BIT between Germany and Pakistan. The creation of BITs and FTAs with investment arbitration provisions has proliferated, but there are signs of a retreat underway. India, for example, has withdrawn from 73 BITs, including with Britain and The Netherlands.

§ 7.1   The Proliferation of Investor-State Arbitrations

Bilateral Investment Treaties (BITs)

The principal focus of BITs and FTAs covering foreign investment dispute settlement is the protection and promotion of foreign investment. It is not only the United States, which has emphasized these treaties. They are common features of most developed nations in their relations with developing host nations.

Tracking its rise as a capital exporter, China has over 100 investment protection agreements, mostly with emerging economies, but also with such nations as Australia, Austria, Belgium/Luxembourg, Denmark, France, Germany, Japan, the Netherlands, the United Kingdom, and the PRC signed a major agreement with the EU late in 2020. A benefit of such an agreement is that its provisions prevail over domestic law and remedies, although the agreements usually allow for exceptions to investment protection in the interests of national security.

Approximately 3,000 bilateral investment treaties (BITs) lattice the globe. Germany and China have well over 100 BITs, France, Britain, and the Netherlands about 100, Romania, Italy, The Czech Republic, Belgium/Luxembourg 75 to 85, Russia, Sweden, Poland 65, while Brazil has none, Pakistan has dropped 23 BITs, and South Africa has said it will withdraw from all its ISDS treaty obligations.

Singapore has BITs that seem designed to attract foreign investors to incorporate there to take advantage of Singaporean subsidiaries as foreign investment vehicles in the likes of India, Jordan, and Egypt. Investment arbitrations administered by the Singapore International Arbitration Center have skyrocketed.

The United States has nearly 50 BITs, mostly with developing nations, in addition to comparable coverage of foreign investment under its 12 free trade agreements (below). However, the 2020 United States-Mexico-Canada FTA USMCA notably eliminated ISDS as between Canada and the USA, while retaining ISDS (subject to limitations discussed below) as between the U.S. and Mexico.

U.S. FTAs, undertaken as executive agreements, need implementing legislation approved by both houses of Congress. U.S. BITs, as treaties of the United States, only require ratification by the Senate.

In 2012, the United States issued a revised Model BIT, usually employed as a starting point in its BIT negotiations. This Model BIT includes a definition of "foreign investment" that reaches broadly to sovereign obligations and intellectual property rights, expressly covers indirect expropriations, and omits any balance of payments safeguard escape clause.

The United States has considered a BIT with China, which inked a BIT with Canada in 2012 that does not cover regulatory controls over permissions to invest ("pre-investment" rules). In other words, the Canada-China BIT only concerns operational and disposal aspects of foreign investment law. This approach is common in European-based BITs, which are the most prevalent around the globe. Late in 2020, the European Union (despite delay requests from the incoming Biden team) signed an historic BIT with the PRC.

The EU-China 2020 Bilateral Investment Treaty (BIT)

China and the European Union finalized very late in December 2020 a bilateral foreign investment agreement, the EU-China Comprehensive Agreement on Investment (CAI). Led by Germany, this agreement was undertaken despite requests by the incoming Biden administration to delay and organize a transatlantic U.S.-EU strategy for dealing with China. Once ratified by the European Parliament, this treaty will replace 26 existing bilateral investment treaties (BITs) between China and individual EU Member States.

The CAI outlines two-way "rules of the road" for foreign investment between the EU and China. Foreign investors will obtain better access on fairer terms. The CAI opens markets with Beijing making concessions on financial services, manufacturing, real estate, construction, advertising, air transport, maritime services, telecom and, to a limited extent, cloud computing.

In turn, China secured the EU's agreement to open its renewable energy sector to Chinese investment. The CAI also prohibits forced tech transfer by EU firms that establish themselves in China and includes provisions to enhance the transparency of state subsidies for Chinese state-owned companies. On the human rights side, Beijing pledged to adhere to International Labor Organization's rules on forced labor in Xinjiang.

Commenced in 2014, the Trump trade war gave Beijing a sense of urgency to cut a deal with Brussels, particularly as U.S.-China BIT negotiations had been going nowhere. Of critical importance to Beijing is a desire to stave off any anti-China alliance. Politically symbolic, CAI represents rejection of the Trump administration's aggressive, disruptive, trade policy against both China *and* Europe. Indeed, a U.S.-led containment strategy for China may be the biggest loser.

The CAI demonstrates that Europe can take the lead on negotiations and stand up to China, a position that the U.S. forfeited when it abandoned U.S.-China BIT negotiations and multilateral platforms such as the TPP, TTIP and WTO. Having piled on sanctions against Chinese companies and investors in the USA, the silence on CAI from the outgoing Trump Administration on the deal was deafening.

Some observers feared CAI would tie the hands of the incoming Biden Administration. Other observers believe the Biden administration should not fret over CAI since much of its content aligns with U.S. interests. CAI could possibly turn out to be a foundational document and benchmark for follow-up BIT negotiations by the Biden team with the PRC.

Excerpts from the EU-China BIT are reproduced at the end of Chapter 4.

I am grateful to USD alumnus Attorney James Zimmerman of Perkins Coie for his reporting and analysis regarding CAI.

BIT Treaty Shopping

The Netherlands is known for allowing "mailbox" companies to utilize their network of BITs by making foreign investments through them. Critics assert that this lattice allows foreign investors to engage in "treaty shopping", the making of investments to raise arbitral challenges to national laws. A prominent example is the Phillip Morris (Asia) acquisition of a Hong Kong firm to facilitate challenge of Australia's 2011 plain packaging (no brand) cigarette law under the British-era 1993 Hong Kong-Australia BIT. This arbitration was dismissed by the arbitrators in 2015 for lack of jurisdiction as an abuse of process.

Treaty shopping inside the European Union to avoid the dubious legitimacy of national courts in Poland, Hungary, Romania, Bulgaria, and other EU states has been undertaken by making investments in those countries via U.K., Dutch and German "mailbox" or "shell" companies benefiting from *intra-EU* BITs. Intra-EU BIT arbitration provisions have been declared invalid by the European Court of Justice in its landmark 2018 *Slovak Republic v. Achmea* (Case 284/16) decision. The logic of the Court's reasoning is that such provisions interfere with the autonomy, effectiveness, and primacy of the EU legal regime.

As such, awards rendered thereunder are arguably unenforceable. This decision raises questions as to whether *extra-EU* member state BIT arbitration decisions, which are numerous, may also be unenforceable. Energy Charter ISDS provisions as applied to EU states have also been declared invalid by the European Court of

Justice. *Republic of Moldova v. Komstroy LLC* (Case C-741/19) (2021).

It is an open question as to whether ICSID investment arbitrations (below) are suspect under the *Achmea* precedent. Several ICSID arbitration panels have *refused* to deny awards based upon *Achmea*. These tribunals cite the treaty termination provisions of the Vienna Convention on the Law of Treaties as controlling support of their decisions.

Free Trade Agreements (FTAs) with Investment Coverage

NAFTA 1994 was a watershed event. In its wake, hundreds of free trade agreements (FTAs) proliferated around the world. These include, for examples, FTAs between the European Union and South Africa, Canada and Costa Rica, China and Chile, and Japan and Singapore. Mexico has dozens of bilateral free trade agreements.

The worldwide array of FTAs includes agreements between developed countries (such as between the United States and Australia), agreements between developed and developing countries (such as between Japan and Vietnam), and agreements between developing nations (such as between India and Sri Lanka).

Leading nations have established networks of free trade agreements under various titles, some with investor-state dispute settlement (ISDS) by arbitration, and some not:

(1) *Japan* has "Economic Partnership Agreements" (free trade agreements) with Mexico, Chile, Thailand, the Philippines, Malaysia, Vietnam, Switzerland, India, Indonesia, Brunei, Singapore, Peru, Mongolia, and the Association of Southeast Asian Nations (ASEAN). Japan negotiated a major 2018 FTA with the European Union (no investment coverage).

Japan is a leader in the Comprehensive and Progressive Trans-Pacific Partnership (TPP-11) (investment and ISDS included). TPP-11 took effect in 2019 after President Trump rejected the TPP-12 agreement negotiated by President Obama. TPP-11 embraces Japan, Canada, Mexico, Australia, New Zealand, Singapore, Peru, Chile, and Vietnam. Britain, China, and Taiwan are seeking to join this FTA.

(2) *China* has free trade agreements with its own Hong Kong and Macau Special Administrative Regions, Chile, Pakistan, Costa Rica, Peru, Singapore, New Zealand, Australia, South Korea, Iceland, Maldives, and ASEAN. Like Japan, China and its firms have only been involved in

a few ISDS arbitrations, initiated under its very large number of BITs (above).

(3) The *European Union* has numerous free trade agreements, including with Algeria, Chile, Egypt, Iceland, Israel, Jordan, Lebanon, Mexico, Morocco, Norway, Serbia, South Africa, Vietnam, Singapore, Japan, Canada, Tunisia, and a customs union agreement with Turkey. Many EU FTAs have been rolled over to apply the *UK post-BREXIT* Britain's first independently negotiated FTA (Australia 2021) does *not* provide for ISDS by arbitration.

Traditionally, EU FTAs included foreign investment law rules and dispute settlement exclusively by arbitration. Recent EU FTAs with Vietnam, Singapore, Canada (below), MERCOSUR, and Mexico, under a "new generation" policy for foreign investment dispute settlement, anticipate creating an Investment Court system to review ISDS arbitrations.

(4) The *United States* has 12 bilateral free trade agreements with Australia (2004), Bahrain (2006), Chile (2004), Colombia (2012), Israel and the Palestinian Authority (1985), Jordan (2001), South Korea (KORUS I 2012 and II 2018), Morocco (2006), Oman (2006), Panama (2012), Peru (2012) and Singapore (2004).

The U.S. also has two multilateral agreements: The USMCA 2020 agreement replacing NAFTA 1994 with Canada and Mexico, and the Central America Free Trade Agreement (CAFTA-DR 2015) which includes the Dominican Republic, Guatemala, Honduras, El Salvador, Nicaragua, and Costa Rica.

All U.S. FTAs include foreign investment dispute settlement by arbitration *except* those with Israel, Australia, and Canada under the USMCA 2020. For examples of NAFTA investor-state arbitrations, the text of NAFTA Chapter 11 covering investment, and post-NAFTA foreign investment rules in later U.S. FTAs, see Chapter 8.

(5) *India* has free trade agreements with ASEAN, Sri Lanka, Malaysia, the Gulf Cooperation Council (GCC), Singapore, Korea, Japan, Afghanistan, Chile, MERCOSUR, and leads the 7-nation South Asian FTA. Foreign investment arbitration coverage is limited.

(6) *South Korea* has free trade agreements with ASEAN, India, Australia, Canada, the United States (KORUS I and

II), China, Chile, Colombia, EFTA, the European Union (KOREU), Turkey, Vietnam, Peru, and Singapore. Some of these FTAs cover foreign investment arbitrations, including KORUS I and II, but some do not.

(7) *Canada* has free trade agreements (in addition to the USMCA of 2020) with Korea, the EU (CETA 2017), Chile, Peru, Colombia, Costa Rica, Israel, EFTA, Jordan, Panama, Honduras, and Ukraine, and is a leader in the TPP-11. All have foreign investment arbitration coverage except as between Canada and U.S. under the USMCA. Canada did participate in ISDS under NAFTA 1994. See Chapter 8.

Ratification of the Canada-EU Comprehensive Economic and Trade Agreement of 2014 (CETA) was delayed primarily due foreign investor-host state issues. These were resolved by agreeing to significant upgrades for ISDS proceedings, and agreement to create a new Investment Court comprised of Canadian, European, and other jurists to review ISDS arbitrations. Other EU free trade agreements (above) follow this "new generation" course for ISDS.

The USMCA of 2020 raised a fundamental question: Is ISDS by arbitration needed or desirable when both parties have sophisticated judicial systems and/or good diplomatic relations capable of handling foreign investor disputes? *Under the USMCA, Canada and the United States eliminated ISDS arbitrations.* Australia and the UK did likewise in their 2021 FTA.

(8) *Mexico* has free trade agreements, in addition to the USMCA, with Chile, Colombia, Venezuela (dormant), Costa Rica, Bolivia, Nicaragua, Guatemala, Honduras, El Salvador, Peru, Uruguay, the European Union, Japan and Israel. It also has an enhanced Pacific Alliance with Chile, Peru, and Colombia, and participates in the TPP-11. All Mexican FTAs embrace investor-state dispute settlement by arbitration.

Under NAFTA's successor, the USMCA Agreement of 2020, Mexico-Canada ISDS by arbitration is governed by TPP-11. U.S.-Mexico investor-state arbitrations under the USMCA are restricted. For USMCA arbitration rules and NAFTA arbitration examples involving Mexico, see Chapter 8.

For global, detailed FTA coverage, see my Concise Hornbook on *Free Trade Agreements.*

§ 7.2   Foreign Investor Rights

Bilateral investment treaties and FTAs with investment coverage traditionally provide foreign investors with certain core rights:

(1) "National treatment";

(2) "Most-favored-nation treatment";

(3) "Fair and equitable treatment" (known as the "minimum standard");

(4) "Full protection and security"; and

(5) Direct and indirect expropriation rules.

Some BIT agreements also require host governments to comply with obligations undertaken with foreign investors, often via foreign investment agreements, including for example *"umbrella or stabilization clauses"* intended to stabilize or even freeze the law of the host country at the time of the signing of the agreement. If the investor-state agreement contains such a clause promising that no significant change in the host state's law will adversely affect the investment, such clauses may give rise to breach of contract claims.

These claims may also be used to assert BIT/FTA violations subject to arbitration. Veolia (a French utility), for example, commenced arbitration proceedings against Egypt for raising the minimum wage.

National and Most-Favored-Nation Treatment

National treatment promises nondiscriminatory, equal treatment with domestic investors. *Most-favored-nation treatment* means foreign investors from different nations will be treated equally, sometimes allowing investors to claim more generous benefits provided in *other* agreements. In one such dispute, an Argentinian investor in Spain obtained the benefit of a Chile-Spain BIT dispute resolution provision that did not require prior exhaustion of local judicial remedies. *See Maffeni v. Spain*, ICSID Case No. ARB/97/7 (2000).

General exception clauses in some investment protection agreements, notably the Canada-EU Comprehensive Economic and Trade Agreement (CETA 2017), tend to mirror Article XX of the GATT and Article XIV of the GATS. Such clauses create state immunities for permissible policy objectives and acts, such as for the protection of human, animal or plant life or health, national security, and the conservation of natural resources.

Fair and Equitable Treatment

Fair and equitable treatment, and *full protection and security,* are notably open-ended "minimum standards" derived from customary international law. In determining fair and equitable treatment, the investor's legitimate expectations and the transparency, predictability, consistency, and denial of justice under state rules have been treated as appropriate criteria. *See, e.g., Tecmed v. Mexico,* 10 ICSID Reports 133 (2004) and *OEPC v. Ecuador,* Case No. UN 3467 (London Court Intl Arbitration 2004).

The duty of fair and equitable treatment has frequently been construed by arbitrators as protecting the stability of the legal and business framework under which the foreign investor operates. *Id.* Fair and equitable treatment has been interpreted as requiring that the host state respect the basic expectations of the investor at the time of the investment. In other words, the host state may not unilaterally alter rules and decisions upon which the investor relied in planning its investment. *Id.* Some investor-state agreements make this duty explicit under what are called *"umbrella or stabilization clauses".*

Unilateral changes in the legal and contractual framework existing at the time of the original investment, frustrating the investor's legitimate expectations, have been deemed unfair and inequitable. For example, a recent series of ISDS arbitrations against Spain after it changed the regulated feed-in-tariff for investors in renewable energy resulted in very substantial damages awards.

Unfair and inequitable treatment has become the primary violation found by foreign investment arbitration tribunals. For an informative review of "unfair and inequitable" conduct by Argentina in connection with emergency financial measures and judicial access to remedies, see the U.S. Supreme Court case *BG Group PLC v. Argentina,* 572 U.S. 25 (2014) ("litigate first" requirement in UK-Argentina BIT excused in New York Convention recognition and enforcement proceedings in the USA).

If the investor obtained investment rights by unlawful means, for example corruption, dismissal of its claims is appropriate as a matter of international public policy. *See World Duty Free v. Kenya,* ICSID Case No. ARB/00/07 (2006). Beyond core foreign investor rights, some agreements broadly allow arbitration of "other claims" related to the investment.

Expropriation

Almost all BITs and FTAs with investment coverage cover expropriation. Most rules on *expropriation* require valid public purposes and prompt, adequate, and effective compensation. See Chapter 3. NAFTA rules protected foreign investors from governmental acts "tantamount to expropriation", an ambiguous term. See Chapter 8.

In addition, BITs and FTAs may also protect capital movement and limit performance requirements. Foreign investor rights may extend beyond the life of a BIT or FTA and cannot be retroactively revoked. This may allow for investor claims against states under "tails."

§ 7.3   Foreign Investor-Host State Dispute Settlement

BITs and FTAs providing foreign investors with designated rights typically establish investor-state dispute settlement procedures (ISDS) to resolve alleged violations of those rights. These may involve state-to-state dispute settlement negotiations (SSDS). Exhaustion or at least attempted utilization of host state national legal remedies (courts, agencies) may first be required, a requirement found for example in the Trans-Pacific Partnership Agreement (TPP-12), its TPP-11 successor, and the USMCA 2020 Agreement. In some jurisdictions, notably under Calvo Clauses in Latin America, foreign investor-host state disputes can proceed only pursuant to local remedies.

A highlight of many BIT and FTA foreign investment agreements is the consent in advance of host sovereign states to arbitration of foreign investor disputes. No separate consent is required. ISDS arbitrations are subject to review in the place or "seat" of arbitration, *and* wherever enforcement is sought.

Investor-State Arbitrations for Damages

Foreign investment provisions frequently establish mandatory, binding dispute settlement procedures allowing foreign investors to invoke arbitration procedures by filing claims for *damages* against host nations. Acts of sub-central government authorities or state-owned companies may be attributed to the state for liability purposes. *See Salini Costruttori v. Morocco*, ICSID Case No. ARB00/04 (2001) (state-owned company). Recovery of damages is normally limited to actual, not punitive, damages.

The procedures and venues for BIT and FTA ISDS differ. Many agreements channel investor-state disputes to the World Bank's International Centre for Settlement of Investment Disputes (ICSID) in Washington, D.C., discussed below. Some BIT arbitrations have gone to the Stockholm Chamber of Commerce, the Permanent Court of Arbitration in The Hague, the U.N. Commission on International

Trade Law (UNCITRAL), and the International Chamber of Commerce (ICC) in Paris.

Thousands of investor-state arbitration claims have been filed. The largest number have been against Argentina (many arising out of its sovereign debt repudiations and emergency economic measures affecting utilities). The mere filing of such claims by foreign investors facilitates leverage in renegotiation of investment contracts as well as compensation.

ISDS claims have been lodged against the United States, and U.S. investors abroad have very actively pursued claims under U.S. BIT and free trade agreements. Exxon Mobil obtained a $1.6 billion expropriation award in ICSID proceedings under the U.S.-Venezuela BIT. Dow Chemical received a $2.2 billion award in ICC proceedings against Kuwait. Under the U.S.-Ecuador BIT, in ICSID proceedings, Occidental Petroleum won a $2.3 billion award against Ecuador for termination of an oil-concession contract.

Some investor-state claims are settled, others dismissed on technical grounds. UNCTAD data indicates that arbitrated investment disputes reaching final awards favor the state by close to two to one. Investors from the developed world (notably the United States, the Netherlands, the United Kingdom and Germany) comprise a large majority of the claimants against developing nations (notably Argentina, Venezuela, Ecuador, and Mexico).

Investment arbitration awards can generally be recognized and enforced in foreign courts under the 1958 New York Convention on the Recognition and Enforcement of Arbitral Awards. See my Concise Hornbook on *International Arbitration and Litigation,* Chapter 3.

The growth of foreign investment arbitration has in many instances overrun contract-based choice of forum clauses, including alternative arbitral proceedings. When "parallel proceedings" exist, arbitrators have often declined to defer to party autonomy. For example, U.S. investors in an Argentine port terminal agreed "for all purposes" in their concession contract to the jurisdiction of Argentinian courts.

The investors invoked instead the U.S.-Argentina BIT arbitration procedures under ICSID. The arbitrators upheld their "jurisdiction" to hear the dispute. *See generally,* Gus Van Harten, *Sovereign Choices and Sovereign Constraints: Judicial Restraint in Investment Treaty Arbitration* (2013).

Investor-State Arbitration Critiques

Critics of ISDS arbitrations broadly decry the creation of a private system of justice for foreign investors. Even the U.S.

Congress has frequently expressed concern that ISDS arbitrations may provide foreign investors in the United States with greater remedies than U.S. investors enjoy in their home country.

Critics focus particularly on the fair and equitable treatment obligation, which has been increasingly construed by arbitrators to create "legitimate expectations" (future profits), and "specific commitments" that host governments will compensate foreign investors for changes in law, notably regulatory law. This has created a degree of foreign investment "regulatory chill."

Investors have been arguing that they are entitled to the legitimate expectation that governments will adhere to their international treaty obligations, notably under the WTO TRIPs agreement concerning intellectual property rights. See Chapter 9. Investors have also used BIT and FTA provisions to influence, and challenge, proposed host state regulations.

Additional criticisms assert there is something of a "good old boy" network of inherently biased ISDS arbitrators drawn significantly from corporate legal worlds operating with relatively little transparency. Arbitrators who simultaneously act as counsel in other ongoing arbitrations, or repeat as arbitrators for the same parties, have been particularly critiqued. Most NAFTA 1994 and ICSID awards and related documents are published, and greater transparency should be forthcoming under the UNCITRAL Mauritius Convention (2015).

Treaty Shopping

"Treaty shopping" to access investor-state arbitration remedies occurs, notably in connection with the formation of "mailbox" or "shell" companies for that purpose. Romanian and other companies have been reported using Dutch mailbox shell companies as the vehicle for investments in their *own home countries* to avoid local law and assertedly corrupt local courts.

As noted above, Philip Morris made a strategic investment in Hong Kong to be able to challenge anticipated (but not yet enacted) Australian no-brand, plain packaging cigarette rules under a Hong Kong-Australia BIT dating from the British era. Philip Morris feared losing Marlboro Man and other trademarked brand names. In 2015, the arbitrators dismissed this proceeding for lack of jurisdiction on abuse of process grounds.

Philip Morris also utilized the Swiss-Uruguay BIT to challenge Uruguay's comparable plain packaging cigarette rules. In the first "jurisdictional" round of this ICSID dispute, Philip Morris persuaded the arbitrators that an "investment" had indeed been made in

Uruguay based on its economic contribution to development, despite smoking's adverse effects on the people and economy of that country. This dispute was eventually settled after Philip Morris lost its treaty shopping attempt at overcoming Australian tobacco packaging rules. *See generally,* J. Chaisse, *The Treaty Shopping Practice: Corporate Structuring and Restructuring to Gain Access to Investment Treaties and Arbitration,* 11 Hastings Bus. L.J. 225 (2015).

Some recent BITs allow host countries to deny benefits to claimants that are owned or controlled by a party in a third country (often shell companies) lacking substantial business activities in their jurisdiction.

Rejection or Limitation of Investor-State Arbitration

Reacting negatively to investor-state arbitrations, some developing world BITs, for example the Indian Model BIT and the Southern African Development Community (SADC) Model BIT, require foreign investors to first exhaust local remedies. The Trans-Pacific Partnership Agreements (TPP-12 and TPP-11) as well as the USMCA 2020 successor to NAFTA do likewise. See Chapter 8.

South Africa, Pakistan and India are actively terminating their BITs in favor of national investment code rules. Indonesia, Brazil, Bolivia, Ecuador, Nicaragua, Venezuela, and others have started moving away from investor-state arbitrations under ICSID (below), replacing arbitrations with local remedies or state-to-state dispute settlement (SSDS). SSDS includes use of the World Court and Permanent Court of Arbitration in The Hague, Ombudsmen, conciliation, and diplomatic remedies. State-to-state remedies force foreign investors to seek remedies via their home governments, very different from investor-state arbitration mechanisms.

Foreign investors should take note that the Canada-EU FTA of 2017 (CETA) anticipates utilizing traditional ISDS arbitrators supervised by an Investment Court comprised of judges from both sides. Recent EU FTAs with Singapore, Vietnam, MERCOSUR, and Mexico do likewise. See Chapter 5.

Under the USMCA, Canada and the United States eliminated ISDS arbitrations. They are retained, subject to limitations, for U.S.-Mexico and Canada-Mexico ISDS. See Chapter 8.

At Australia's insistence, the United States-Australia free trade agreement does NOT contain investor-state arbitration procedures, though the Trans-Pacific Partnership (TPP-12) vetoed by President Trump would have altered that result. The 2021 UK-Australia FTA does not enable ISDS arbitrations.

Reform of ISDS

Growing rejection and criticism of ISDS by party-selected arbitrators has led to tune ups of procedures and rules related to them. For example, TPP-12 and TPP-11 (to which the United States is not a party) undertake material ISDS arbitration reforms. These reforms include, for example:

(1)   Mandating that financial stability regulation falls outside indirect expropriation claims;

(2)   Providing that tobacco regulation may not be challenged;

(3)   Indicating that mere frustration of profit expectations is insufficient to pursue investor-state arbitrations;

(4)   Placing the burden of proof on investor claimants;

(5)   Barring use of shell companies to access investor-state arbitral remedies;

(6)   Stipulating that state-owned enterprises along with authorized government agents are subject to the agreement's dispute settlement regime;

(7)   Public access to hearings and documents;

(8)   Allowance of amicus briefs;

(9)   Facilitation of expedited dismissals of frivolous claims;

(10) Greater transparency;

(11) Challenge procedures against arbitrator bias; and

(12) Protection of existing intellectual property license royalties and durations from alteration.

All these reforms represent an effort to respond to ISDS critics and rehabilitate use of investor-state arbitrations.

§ 7.4   United States BITs and Model BIT

To promote national treatment and protect U.S. investors abroad, the United States embarked on a BIT program in the early 1980s. The BIT program followed earlier extensive use of Friendship, Commerce, and Navigation (FCNs) treaties, some of which provided for diplomatic state-to-state protection for U.S. foreign investors, notably regarding expropriation. Some U.S. FCNs remain in effect, *e.g.*, the U.S.-Japan FCN.

Unlike the FCNs, the Model U.S. BIT distinguishes treatment of foreign owned, domestically incorporated subsidiaries and branches of foreign firms for some provisions, particularly employment. The Japan-U.S. FCN treaty afforded no protection to a foreign company using its nationals in hiring inside the United States. See Chapter 6. Under the typical U.S. BIT, explicit freedom to hire nationals exists in a narrow range of management provisions.

Most U.S. BITs have been negotiated with small developing countries, though the United States has signed a BIT with Argentina, Egypt, Turkey, and several Eastern European countries such as Poland. Most U.S. BITs preceded NAFTA 1994 and the 1995 WTO TRIMs Agreement regarding foreign investor performance requirements.

Early U.S. BITs placed particular emphasis on reducing performance requirements. Later U.S. BIT agreements generally reflect the foreign investor rights and investor-state arbitration claims procedures found in NAFTA 1994. The NAFTA agreement generated a substantial number of ISDS arbitrations. NAFTA arbitrations were influenced by official interpretations (particularly regarding indirect expropriations), and post-NAFTA U.S. FTAs. See Chapter 8.

Most U.S. BITs and FTAs do not include provisions for consultations when investment differences arise. The Argentina-United States and Sri Lanka-United States BITs are exceptions. U.S. BITs and FTAs typically provide for investor-state arbitration, sometimes with no necessary recourse to prior exhaustion of local remedies. The 2012 Model U.S. BIT, reproduced in Section 7.8 of this chapter, is thought to have reduced the scope of foreign investor protections, but it appears only two U.S. BITs, with Rwanda and Uruguay, have been negotiated under the 2012 Model.

Numerous U.S. investors have filed and frequently won arbitration awards for damages against Argentina. Under U.S. law, ICSID awards (below) are given full faith and credit in federal courts. The Federal Arbitration Act does not apply, and reliance on the New York Convention is not needed. Hence the enforcement rate of ICSID awards in U.S. courts is high. Argentina has as a rule unsuccessfully defended itself on foreign sovereign immunity grounds. One court held that Argentina waived its immunity by becoming a party to ICSID, and further noted that the U.S. Foreign Sovereign Immunities Act exempts arbitration awards. *See Blue Ridge Investments v. Argentina,* 902 F. Supp.2d 367 (S.D.N.Y. 2012) affirmed 735 F.3d 72 (2d Cir. 2013).

United States BITs do *not* prohibit nations from enacting foreign investment control laws. Such laws are common in developing nations, notably in Latin America. Some developed nations, such as Canada, also screen foreign investments, particularly mergers and acquisitions. For coverage of Mexican and Canadian foreign investment law, see Chapter 6. Most U.S. BIT agreements provide that pre-investment laws should not interfere with any rights in the treaty, but since no rights to avoid national foreign investment controls are created, challenges to foreign investment control laws are generally not possible under U.S. BITs and FTAs.

One important provision the United States seeks to include in its BITs and FTAs is the "prompt, adequate and effective" concept of compensation for expropriations. For example, the 1994 Argentina-United States BIT uses language referring to compensation for the "fair market value. . . immediately before the expropriatory action." Many of the nations that agreed to this language disputed its appropriateness during the nationalistic North-South dialogue of the 1960s and 1970s. But as they began to promote rather than restrict investment, those nations had to accept the idea that expropriated investment had to be compensated reasonably soon after the taking ("prompt"), based on a fair valuation ("adequate"), and in a realistic form ("effective").

U.S. BITs

The United States has approximately 40 bilateral investment treaties (BITs).

Agreement Title

Agreement Title
Albania Bilateral Investment Treaty
Argentina Bilateral Investment Treaty
Armenia Bilateral Investment Treaty
Azerbaijan Bilateral Investment Treaty
Bahrain Bilateral Investment Treaty
Bangladesh Bilateral Investment Treaty
Bolivia Bilateral Investment Treaty
Bulgaria Bilateral Investment Treaty
Cameroon Bilateral Investment Treaty
Congo, Democratic Republic Of (Kinshasa) Bilateral Investment Treaty
Congo, Republic Of (Brazzaville) Bilateral Investment Treaty
Croatia Bilateral Investment Treaty

Czech Republic Bilateral Investment Treaty

Ecuador Bilateral Investment Treaty

Egypt Bilateral Investment Treaty

Estonia Bilateral Investment Treaty

Georgia Bilateral Investment Treaty

Grenada Bilateral Investment Treaty

Honduras Bilateral Investment Treaty

Jamaica Bilateral Investment Treaty

Jordan Bilateral Investment Treaty

Kazakhstan Bilateral Investment Treaty

Kyrgyzstan Bilateral Investment Treaty

Latvia Bilateral Investment Treaty

Lithuania Bilateral Investment Treaty

Moldova Bilateral Investment Treaty

Mongolia Bilateral Investment Treaty

Morocco Bilateral Investment Treaty

Mozambique Bilateral Investment Treaty

Panama Bilateral Investment Treaty

Poland Bilateral Investment Treaty

Poland Business and Economic Relations Treaty

Romania Bilateral Investment Treaty

Rwanda Bilateral Investment Treaty

Senegal Bilateral Investment Treaty

Slovakia Bilateral Investment Treaty

Sri Lanka Bilateral Investment Treaty

Trinidad And Tobago Bilateral Investment Treaty

Tunisia Bilateral Investment Treaty

Turkey Bilateral Investment Treaty

Ukraine Bilateral Investment Treaty

Uruguay Bilateral Investment Treaty

§ 7.5   ICSID Foreign Investment Arbitrations

Arbitration rules were adopted under the 1966 Convention on the Settlement of Investment Disputes between States and Nationals of Other States (ICSID). The text of the ICSID Convention is reproduced at the end of this chapter. Over 150 countries are parties to this Convention, but Brazil, Canada (until 2013), Mexico, Russia, Thailand, and Vietnam have notably not joined the ICSID Convention. In recent years, Bolivia, Ecuador, and Venezuela have withdrawn from ICSID, asserting it is biased toward investors and undermines national sovereignty. After a change in regime, Ecuador rejoined ICSID.

The Convention was implemented in the United States by 22 U.S.C.A. § 1650 and § 1650a. The text of ICSID is reproduced in Section 7.9. An arbitral money award, rendered pursuant to the Convention, is entitled to the same full faith and credit in the United States as a final judgment of a court of general jurisdiction in a State of the United States (22 U.S.C.A. § 1650a).

The 1966 Convention provides for the establishment of an International Center for the Settlement of Investment Disputes (ICSID), as a non-financial organ of the World Bank (the International Bank for Reconstruction and Development). The ICSID Convention is reproduced in Section 7.9 of this chapter.

ICSID is designed to serve as a forum for both conciliation and arbitration of disputes between private investors and host governments. It provides an institutional framework within which arbitrators, selected by the disputing parties from an ICSID Panel of Arbitrators or from elsewhere, conduct arbitration in accordance with ICSID Rules of Procedure for Arbitration Proceedings. Arbitrations are held in Washington D.C. unless agreed otherwise.

Under the 1966 Convention (Article 25), ICSID's jurisdiction extends only "to any legal dispute arising directly out of an investment, between a Contracting State or... any subdivision... and a national of another Contracting State, which the parties to the dispute consent in writing to submit to the Centre. Where the parties have given their consent, either in respect of future disputes or in respect of existing disputes, no party may withdraw its consent unilaterally." Consent by signatory states cannot unilaterally be withdrawn so long as that state is still a member of ICSID.

ICSID is an attempt to institutionalize dispute resolution between States and non-State foreign investors. The disputes often arise under contracts between foreign investors and member states. Many sovereign consents to ICSID arbitrations are found in bilateral investment treaties (BITs, see above) and free trade agreements (see for example NAFTA 1994 in Chapter 8).

Unlike international commercial arbitrations, the law of the place of arbitration generally has no influence over ICSID arbitrations, which are said to be "delocalized." If one party questions such jurisdiction (predicated upon disputes arising "directly out of" an investment, between a Contracting Party and the national of another, and written consent to submission), the issue may be decided by the arbitration tribunal (Rule 41).

Annulment and Enforcement

A party may seek annulment of any award only by an appeal to an ad hoc committee of persons drawn by the Administrative Council of ICSID from the Panel of Arbitrators under the Convention (Article 52). Annulment is available only if the ICSID Tribunal was not properly constituted, exceeded its powers, seriously departed from a fundamental procedural rule, failed to state the reasons for its award, or included a member who practiced corruption. An ICSID award cannot be set aside by national courts or in any other way.

Divergent ad hoc Annulment Committee decisions, particularly those known as the "Argentine Gas Sector Cases", have cast doubt on the legitimacy of ICSID annulment proceedings. Those cases concern challenges by foreign investors to emergency measures converting U.S. dollar bank deposits to pesos after Argentina's sovereign default in 2001. Depending on the Committee, with nearly identical facts, some investors have prevailed, and others have lost arguments centered on whether Argentina was entitled to invoke public order or necessity defenses.

Similar inconsistencies in essentially identical fact patterns emerged in UNCITRAL arbitration proceedings involving investments in The Czech Republic, and on umbrella clause interpretations by ICSID panels involving investments in Pakistan and The Philippines.

Enforcement of the award (with attachment of assets if needed) is automatically possible within ICSID signatory state courts, including those of the host state, without further review or consideration of setting aside the award. All member states must enforce ICSID awards as if they were final, binding judgments of their national courts. There is no need to go through the New York Convention procedures associated with international commercial arbitration awards.

§ 7.6   ICSID Additional Facility Arbitrations

The Convention's 1966 jurisdictional limitations prompted the ICSID Administrative Counsel to establish an Additional Facility for conducting conciliations and arbitrations for disputes that do not arise directly out of an investment, and for investment disputes in which one party is not a Contracting State to the Convention or the national of a Contracting State.

The Additional Facility is intended for use by parties having long-term relationships of special economic importance to the State party to the dispute and which involve the commitment of substantial resources on the part of either party. The Facility is not designed to service disputes which fall within the 1966 Convention, or which are "ordinary commercial transaction" disputes. ICSID's Secretary General must give advance approval of an agreement contemplating use of the Additional Facility.

Because the Additional Facility operates outside the scope of the 1966 Convention, the Facility has its own Arbitration Rules. Under them, ICSID Convention rules regarding exclusion of other remedies, denial of provisional relief in national courts, internal annulment review, and recognition and enforcement do not apply. Additional Facility awards are subject to the set aside rules of the arbitral seat, and enforceable under the New York Convention.

The ICSID Convention has been used under numerous bilateral investment treaties (BITs). Because neither Canada (until December 2013) nor Mexico are ICSID signatories, the Additional Facility Rules were employed in most NAFTA investor-state arbitrations. Mexican-U.S. investor-state arbitrations under the USMCA 2020 Agreement are likely to follow this pattern.

§ 7.7 Energy Charter Treaty Arbitrations

Some 60 nations have signed the Energy Charter Treaty of 1991. Article 26 permits foreign investors to take to arbitration disputes with signatory states concerning investment treatment rights contained in the Charter. These rights focus on national treatment, protection from direct or indirect expropriation, and contract adherence duties of the host state. Such arbitrations can be conducted before the Permanent Court of Arbitration in The Hague under ICSID, UNCITRAL or Stockholm Chamber of Commerce rules.

In 2009, the Permanent Court of Arbitration held that Russia's signing of the Charter, without subsequent ratification, was sufficient to confer jurisdiction. In 2014, that body ordered Russia to pay billions to the shareholders of Yukos for what it described as Russia's "devious and calculated expropriation" of assets designed to bankrupt Yukos, which happened. Because Yukos had unclean hands after tax abuses, the arbitrators reduced the award by 25% to roughly $50 billion. In 2020, this decision was upheld by the Hague Court of Appeal.

Collection efforts have been centered on Russian state assets and Rosneft, the Russian company that gained control of most of these assets in a series of politically driven bankruptcy proceedings.

As of 2021, limited success has been had in Dutch, French and Belgian courts. Seizure of the well-known Stolichnaya and Moskovskaya vodka trademarks owned by Russia in the Netherlands was successful. In general, state assets are only available for execution of awards if they are commercial assets.

Another controversial invocation of ISDS before the Permanent Court of Arbitration occurred in 2011 when Germany, following the Fukushima disaster, decided to close its nuclear power industry. Vattenfall, a Swedish operator of two nuclear power plants in Germany, demanded billions in expropriation compensation under the Energy Charter Treaty. This dispute was settled confidentially.

Whether allowance of Energy Charter Treaty dispute settlement arbitrations is incompatible with the Paris Accord and the global climate agenda is disputed. See the analysis of Di Salvatore et al., *Investment Treaty News* (Oct. 8, 2021).

§ 7.8　Text of United States Model BIT (2012)

CONCERNING THE ENCOURAGEMENT AND RECIPROCAL PROTECTION OF INVESTMENT

The Government of the United States of America and the Government of [Country] (hereinafter the "Parties");

Desiring to promote greater economic cooperation between them with respect to investment by nationals and enterprises of one Party in the territory of the other Party;

Recognizing that agreement on the treatment to be accorded such investment will stimulate the flow of private capital and the economic development of the Parties;

Agreeing that a stable framework for investment will maximize effective utilization of economic resources and improve living standards;

Recognizing the importance of providing effective means of asserting claims and enforcing rights with respect to investment under national law as well as through international arbitration;

Desiring to achieve these objectives in a manner consistent with the protection of health, safety, and the environment, and the promotion of internationally recognized labor rights;

Having resolved to conclude a Treaty concerning the encouragement and reciprocal protection of investment;

Have agreed as follows:

SECTION A

Article 1: Definitions

For purposes of this Treaty:

"central level of government" means:

    (a) for the United States, the federal level of government; and

    (b) for [Country],

"Centre" means the International Centre for Settlement of Investment Disputes ("ICSID") established by the ICSID Convention.

"claimant" means an investor of a Party that is a party to an investment dispute with the other Party.

"covered investment" means, with respect to a Party, an investment in its territory of an investor of the other Party in existence as of the date of entry into force of this Treaty or established, acquired, or expanded thereafter.

"disputing parties" means the claimant and the respondent.

"disputing party" means either the claimant or the respondent.

"enterprise" means any entity constituted or organized under applicable law, whether or not for profit, and whether privately or governmentally owned or controlled, including a corporation, trust, partnership, sole proprietorship, joint venture, association, or similar organization; and a branch of an enterprise.

"enterprise of a Party" means an enterprise constituted or organized under the law of a Party, and a branch located in the territory of a Party and carrying out business activities there.

"existing" means in effect on the date of entry into force of this Treaty.

"freely usable currency" means "freely usable currency" as determined by the International Monetary Fund under its *Articles of Agreement*.

"GATS" means the *General Agreement on Trade in Services*, contained in Annex 1B to the WTO Agreement.

"government procurement" means the process by which a government obtains the use of or acquires goods or services, or any combination thereof, for governmental purposes and not with a view to commercial sale or resale, or use in the production or supply of goods or services for commercial sale or resale.

"ICSID Additional Facility Rules" means the *Rules Governing the Additional Facility for the Administration of Proceedings by the*

Secretariat of the International Centre for Settlement of Investment Disputes.

"ICSID Convention" means the *Convention on the Settlement of Investment Disputes between States and Nationals of Other States*, done at Washington, March 18, 1965.

[**"Inter-American Convention"** means the *Inter-American Convention on International Commercial Arbitration*, done at Panama, January 30, 1975.]

"investment" means every asset that an investor owns or controls, directly or indirectly, that has the characteristics of an investment, including such characteristics as the commitment of capital or other resources, the expectation of gain or profit, or the assumption of risk. Forms that an investment may take include:

(a)   an enterprise;

(b)   shares, stock, and other forms of equity participation in an enterprise;

(c)   bonds, debentures, other debt instruments, and loans;[1]

(d)   futures, options, and other derivatives;

(e)   turnkey, construction, management, production, concession, revenue-sharing, and other similar contracts;

(f)   intellectual property rights;

(g)   licenses, authorizations, permits, and similar rights conferred pursuant to domestic law;[2, 3] and

(h)   other tangible or intangible, movable or immovable property, and related property rights, such as leases, mortgages, liens, and pledges.

---

[1]   Some forms of debt, such as bonds, debentures, and long-term notes, are more likely to have the characteristics of an investment, while other forms of debt, such as claims to payment that are immediately due and result from the sale of goods or services, are less likely to have such characteristics.

[2]   Whether a particular type of license, authorization, permit, or similar instrument (including a concession, to the extent that it has the nature of such an instrument) has the characteristics of an investment depends on such factors as the nature and extent of the rights that the holder has under the law of the Party. Among the licenses, authorizations, permits, and similar instruments that do not have the characteristics of an investment are those that do not create any rights protected under domestic law. For greater certainty, the foregoing is without prejudice to whether any asset associated with the license, authorization, permit, or similar instrument has the characteristics of an investment.

[3]   The term "investment" does not include an order or judgment entered in a judicial or administrative action.

"**investment agreement**" means a written agreement[4] between a national authority[5] of a Party and a covered investment or an investor of the other Party, on which the covered investment or the investor relies in establishing or acquiring a covered investment other than the written agreement itself, that grants rights to the covered investment or investor:

(a) with respect to natural resources that a national authority controls, such as for their exploration, extraction, refining, transportation, distribution, or sale;

(b) to supply services to the public on behalf of the Party, such as power generation or distribution, water treatment or distribution, or telecommunications; or

(c) to undertake infrastructure projects, such as the construction of roads, bridges, canals, dams, or pipelines, that are not for the exclusive or predominant use and benefit of the government.

"**investment authorization**"[6] means an authorization that the foreign investment authority of a Party grants to a covered investment or an investor of the other Party.

"**investor of a non-Party**" means, with respect to a Party, an investor that attempts to make, is making, or has made an investment in the territory of that Party, that is not an investor of either Party.

"**investor of a Party**" means a Party or state enterprise thereof, or a national or an enterprise of a Party, that attempts to make, is making, or has made an investment in the territory of the other Party; provided, however, that a natural person who is a dual national shall be deemed to be exclusively a national of the State of his or her dominant and effective nationality.

"**measure**" includes any law, regulation, procedure, requirement, or practice.

---

4   "Written agreement" refers to an agreement in writing, executed by both parties, whether in a single instrument or in multiple instruments, that creates an exchange of rights and obligations, binding on both parties under the law applicable under Article 30[Governing Law](2). For greater certainty, (a) a unilateral act of an administrative or judicial authority, such as a permit, license, or authorization issued by a Party solely in its regulatory capacity, or a decree, order, or judgment, standing alone; and (b) an administrative or judicial consent decree or order, shall not be considered a written agreement.

5   For purposes of this definition, "national authority" means (a) for the United States, an authority at the central level of government; and (b) for [Country], [ ].

6   For greater certainty, actions taken by a Party to enforce laws of general application, such as competition laws, are not encompassed within this definition.

"national" means:

(a)   for the United States, a natural person who is a national of the United States as defined in Title III of the Immigration and Nationality Act; and

(b)   for [Country], [___]

"New York Convention" means the *United Nations Convention on the Recognition and Enforcement of Foreign Arbitral Awards*, done at New York, June 10, 1958.

"non-disputing Party" means the Party that is not a party to an investment dispute.

"person" means a natural person or an enterprise.

"person of a Party" means a national or an enterprise of a Party.

"protected information" means confidential business information or information that is privileged or otherwise protected from disclosure under a Party's law.

"regional level of government" means:

(a)   for the United States, a state of the United States, the District of Columbia, or Puerto Rico; and

(b)   for [Country],

"respondent" means the Party that is a party to an investment dispute.

"Secretary-General" means the Secretary-General of ICSID.

"state enterprise" means an enterprise owned, or controlled through ownership interests, by a Party.

"territory" means:

(a)   with respect to the United States,

(i)   the customs territory of the United States, which includes the 50 states, the District of Columbia, and Puerto Rico;

(ii)   the foreign trade zones located in the United States and Puerto Rico.

(b)   with respect to [Country,] [___].

(c)   with respect to each Party, the territorial sea and any area beyond the territorial sea of the Party within which, in accordance with customary international law as reflected in the United Nations Convention on the Law of the Sea, the Party may exercise sovereign rights or jurisdiction.

"TRIPS Agreement" means the *Agreement on Trade-Related Aspects of Intellectual Property Rights*, contained in Annex 1C to the WTO Agreement.[7]

"UNCITRAL Arbitration Rules" means the arbitration rules of the United Nations Commission on International Trade Law.

"WTO Agreement" means the *Marrakesh Agreement Establishing the World Trade Organization*, done on April 15, 1994.

Article 2: Scope and Coverage

1.   This Treaty applies to measures adopted or maintained by a Party relating to:

(a)   investors of the other Party;

(b)   covered investments; and

(c)   with respect to Articles 8 [Performance Requirements], 12 [Investment and Environment], and 13 [Investment and Labor], all investments in the territory of the Party.

2.   A Party's obligations under Section A shall apply:

(a)   to a state enterprise or other person when it exercises any regulatory, administrative, or other governmental authority delegated to it by that Party;[8] and

(b)   to the political subdivisions of that Party.

3.   For greater certainty, this Treaty does not bind either Party in relation to any act or fact that took place or any situation that ceased to exist before the date of entry into force of this Treaty.

Article 3: National Treatment

1.   Each Party shall accord to investors of the other Party treatment no less favorable than that it accords, in like circumstances, to its own investors with respect to the establishment, acquisition, expansion, management, conduct, operation, and sale or other disposition of investments in its territory.

2.   Each Party shall accord to covered investments treatment no less favorable than that it accords, in like circumstances, to investments in its territory of its own investors with respect to the

---

7   For greater certainty, "TRIPS Agreement" includes any waiver in force between the Parties of any provision of the TRIPS Agreement granted by WTO Members in accordance with the WTO Agreement.

8   For greater certainty, government authority that has been delegated includes a legislative grant, and a government order, directive or other action transferring to the state enterprise or other person, or authorizing the exercise by the state enterprise or other person of, governmental authority.

establishment, acquisition, expansion, management, conduct, operation, and sale or other disposition of investments.

3.   The treatment to be accorded by a Party under paragraphs 1 and 2 means, with respect to a regional level of government, treatment no less favorable than the treatment accorded, in like circumstances, by that regional level of government to natural persons resident in and enterprises constituted under the laws of other regional levels of government of the Party of which it forms a part, and to their respective investments.

Article 4: Most-Favored-Nation Treatment

1.   Each Party shall accord to investors of the other Party treatment no less favorable than that it accords, in like circumstances, to investors of any non-Party with respect to the establishment, acquisition, expansion, management, conduct, operation, and sale or other disposition of investments in its territory.

2.   Each Party shall accord to covered investments treatment no less favorable than that it accords, in like circumstances, to investments in its territory of investors of any non-Party with respect to the establishment, acquisition, expansion, management, conduct, operation, and sale or other disposition of investments.

Article 5: Minimum Standard of Treatment[9]

1.   Each Party shall accord to covered investments treatment in accordance with customary international law, including fair and equitable treatment and full protection and security.

2.   For greater certainty, paragraph 1 prescribes the customary international law minimum standard of treatment of aliens as the minimum standard of treatment to be afforded to covered investments. The concepts of "fair and equitable treatment" and "full protection and security" do not require treatment in addition to or beyond that which is required by that standard, and do not create additional substantive rights. The obligation in paragraph 1 to provide:

(a)   "fair and equitable treatment" includes the obligation not to deny justice in criminal, civil, or administrative adjudicatory proceedings in accordance with the principle of due process embodied in the principal legal systems of the world; and

(b)   "full protection and security" requires each Party to provide the level of police protection required under customary international law.

---

⁹   Article 5 [Minimum Standard of Treatment] shall be interpreted in accordance with Annex A.

3.   A determination that there has been a breach of another provision of this Treaty, or of a separate international agreement, does not establish that there has been a breach of this Article.

4.   Notwithstanding Article 14 [Non-Conforming Measures] (5)(b) [subsidies and grants], each Party shall accord to investors of the other Party, and to covered investments, non-discriminatory treatment with respect to measures it adopts or maintains relating to losses suffered by investments in its territory owing to armed conflict or civil strife.

5.   Notwithstanding paragraph 4, if an investor of a Party, in the situations referred to in paragraph 4, suffers a loss in the territory of the other Party resulting from:

    (a)   requisitioning of its covered investment or part thereof by the latter's forces or authorities; or

    (b)   destruction of its covered investment or part thereof by the latter's forces or authorities, which was not required by the necessity of the situation, the latter Party shall provide the investor restitution, compensation, or both, as appropriate, for such loss. Any compensation shall be prompt, adequate, and effective in accordance with Article 6 [Expropriation and Compensation] (2) through (4), *mutatis mutandis*.

6.   Paragraph 4 does not apply to existing measures relating to subsidies or grants that would be inconsistent with Article 3 [National Treatment] but for Article 14 [Non-Conforming Measures] (5)(b) [subsidies and grants].

Article 6: Expropriation and Compensation[10]

1.   Neither Party may expropriate or nationalize a covered investment either directly or indirectly through measures equivalent to expropriation or nationalization ("expropriation"), except:

    (a)   for a public purpose;

    (b)   in a non-discriminatory manner;

    (c)   on payment of prompt, adequate, and effective compensation; and

    (d)   in accordance with due process of law and Article 5 [Minimum Standard of Treatment] (1) through (3).

2.   The compensation referred to in paragraph 1(c) shall:

    (a)   be paid without delay;

---

[10]   Article 6 [Expropriation] shall be interpreted in accordance with Annexes A and B.

(b) be equivalent to the fair market value of the expropriated investment immediately before the expropriation took place ("the date of expropriation");

(c) not reflect any change in value occurring because the intended expropriation had become known earlier; and

(d) be fully realizable and freely transferable.

3. If the fair market value is denominated in a freely usable currency, the compensation referred to in paragraph 1(c) shall be no less than the fair market value on the date of expropriation, plus interest at a commercially reasonable rate for that currency, accrued from the date of expropriation until the date of payment.

4. If the fair market value is denominated in a currency that is not freely usable, the compensation referred to in paragraph 1(c)— converted into the currency of payment at the market rate of exchange prevailing on the date of payment—shall be no less than:

(a) the fair market value on the date of expropriation, converted into a freely usable currency at the market rate of exchange prevailing on that date, plus

(b) interest, at a commercially reasonable rate for that freely usable currency, accrued from the date of expropriation until the date of payment.

5. This Article does not apply to the issuance of compulsory licenses granted in relation to intellectual property rights in accordance with the TRIPS Agreement, or to the revocation, limitation, or creation of intellectual property rights, to the extent that such issuance, revocation, limitation, or creation is consistent with the TRIPS Agreement.

Article 7: Transfers

1. Each Party shall permit all transfers relating to a covered investment to be made freely and without delay into and out of its territory. Such transfers include:

(a) contributions to capital;

(b) profits, dividends, capital gains, and proceeds from the sale of all or any part of the covered investment or from the partial or complete liquidation of the covered investment;

(c) interest, royalty payments, management fees, and technical assistance and other fees;

(d) payments made under a contract, including a loan agreement;

(e)   payments made pursuant to Article 5 [Minimum Standard of Treatment] (4) and (5) and Article 6 [Expropriation and Compensation]; and

(f)   payments arising out of a dispute.

2.   Each Party shall permit transfers relating to a covered investment to be made in a freely usable currency at the market rate of exchange prevailing at the time of transfer.

3.   Each Party shall permit returns in kind relating to a covered investment to be made as authorized or specified in a written agreement between the Party and a covered investment or an investor of the other Party.

4.   Notwithstanding paragraphs 1 through 3, a Party may prevent a transfer through the equitable, non-discriminatory, and good faith application of its laws relating to:

(a)   bankruptcy, insolvency, or the protection of the rights of creditors;

(b)   issuing, trading, or dealing in securities, futures, options, or derivatives;

(c)   criminal or penal offenses;

(d)   financial reporting or record keeping of transfers when necessary to assist law enforcement or financial regulatory authorities; or

(e)   ensuring compliance with orders or judgments in judicial or administrative proceedings.

Article 8: Performance Requirements

1.   Neither Party may, in connection with the establishment, acquisition, expansion, management, conduct, operation, or sale or other disposition of an investment of an investor of a Party or of a non-Party in its territory, impose or enforce any requirement or enforce any commitment or undertaking:[11]

(a)   to export a given level or percentage of goods or services;

(b)   to achieve a given level or percentage of domestic content;

(c)   to purchase, use, or accord a preference to goods produced in its territory, or to purchase goods from persons in its territory;

---

[11]   For greater certainty, a condition for the receipt or continued receipt of an advantage referred to in paragraph 2 does not constitute a "commitment or undertaking" for the purposes of paragraph 1.

(d)   to relate in any way the volume or value of imports to the volume or value of exports or to the amount of foreign exchange inflows associated with such investment;

(e)   to restrict sales of goods or services in its territory that such investment produces or supplies by relating such sales in any way to the volume or value of its exports or foreign exchange earnings;

(f)   to transfer a particular technology, a production process, or other proprietary knowledge to a person in its territory;

(g)   to supply exclusively from the territory of the Party the goods that such investment produces or the services that it supplies to a specific regional market or to the world market; or

(h)   (i)   to purchase, use, or accord a preference to, in its territory, technology of the Party or of persons of the Party;[12] or

(ii)   that prevents the purchase or use of, or the according of a preference to, in its territory, particular technology, so as to afford protection on the basis of nationality to its own investors or investments or to technology of the Party or of persons of the Party.

2.   Neither Party may condition the receipt or continued receipt of an advantage, in connection with the establishment, acquisition, expansion, management, conduct, operation, or sale or other disposition of an investment in its territory of an investor of a Party or of a non-Party, on compliance with any requirement:

(a)   to achieve a given level or percentage of domestic content;

(b)   to purchase, use, or accord a preference to goods produced in its territory, or to purchase goods from persons in its territory;

(c)   to relate in any way the volume or value of imports to the volume or value of exports or to the amount of foreign exchange inflows associated with such investment; or

(d)   to restrict sales of goods or services in its territory that such investment produces or supplies by relating such sales in any way to the volume or value of its exports or foreign exchange earnings.

3.   (a)   Nothing in paragraph 2 shall be construed to prevent a Party from conditioning the receipt or continued receipt of an advantage, in connection with an investment in its territory of an investor of a Party or of a non-Party, on compliance with a requirement to locate production, supply a service, train or employ

---

[12]   For purposes of this Article, the term "technology of the Party or of persons of the Party" includes technology that is owned by the Party or persons of the Party, and technology for which the Party holds, or persons of the Party hold, an exclusive license.

workers, construct or expand particular facilities, or carry out research and development, in its territory.

(b)   Paragraphs 1(f) and (h) do not apply:

(i)   when a Party authorizes use of an intellectual property right in accordance with Article 31 of the TRIPS Agreement, or to measures requiring the disclosure of proprietary information that fall within the scope of, and are consistent with, Article 39 of the TRIPS Agreement; or

(ii)   when the requirement is imposed or the commitment or undertaking is enforced by a court, administrative tribunal, or competition authority to remedy a practice determined after judicial or administrative process to be anticompetitive under the Party's competition laws.[13]

(c)   Provided that such measures are not applied in an arbitrary or unjustifiable manner, and provided that such measures do not constitute a disguised restriction on international trade or investment, paragraphs 1(b), (c), (f), and (h), and 2(a) and (b), shall not be construed to prevent a Party from adopting or maintaining measures, including environmental measures:

(i)   necessary to secure compliance with laws and regulations that are not inconsistent with this Treaty;

(ii)   necessary to protect human, animal, or plant life or health; or

(iii)   related to the conservation of living or non-living exhaustible natural resources.

(d)   Paragraphs 1(a), (b), and (c), and 2(a) and (b), do not apply to qualification requirements for goods or services with respect to export promotion and foreign aid programs.

(e)   Paragraphs 1(b), (c), (f), (g), and (h), and 2(a) and (b), do not apply to government procurement.

(f)   Paragraphs 2(a) and (b) do not apply to requirements imposed by an importing Party relating to the content of goods necessary to qualify for preferential tariffs or preferential quotas.

4.   For greater certainty, paragraphs 1 and 2 do not apply to any commitment, undertaking, or requirement other than those set out in those paragraphs.

5.   This Article does not preclude enforcement of any commitment, undertaking, or requirement between private parties, where a Party

---

[13]   The Parties recognize that a patent does not necessarily confer market power.

did not impose or require the commitment, undertaking, or requirement.

Article 9: Senior Management and Boards of Directors

1.   Neither Party may require that an enterprise of that Party that is a covered investment appoint to senior management positions natural persons of any particular nationality.

2.   A Party may require that a majority of the board of directors, or any committee thereof, of an enterprise of that Party that is a covered investment, be of a particular nationality, or resident in the territory of the Party, provided that the requirement does not materially impair the ability of the investor to exercise control over its investment.

Article 10: Publication of Laws and Decisions Respecting Investment

1.   Each Party shall ensure that its:

    (a)   laws, regulations, procedures, and administrative rulings of general application; and

    (b)   adjudicatory decisions respecting any matter covered by this Treaty are promptly published or otherwise made publicly available.

2.   For purposes of this Article, "administrative ruling of general application" means an administrative ruling or interpretation that applies to all persons and fact situations that fall generally within its ambit and that establishes a norm of conduct but does not include:

    (a)   a determination or ruling made in an administrative or quasi-judicial proceeding that applies to a particular covered investment or investor of the other Party in a specific case; or

    (b)   a ruling that adjudicates with respect to a particular act or practice.

Article 11: Transparency

1.   The Parties agree to consult periodically on ways to improve the transparency practices set out in this Article, Article 10 and Article 29.

2.   Publication

    To the extent possible, each Party shall:

    (a)   publish in advance any measure referred to in Article 10(1)(a) that it proposes to adopt; and

    (b)   provide interested persons and the other Party a reasonable opportunity to comment on such proposed measures.

3.   With respect to proposed regulations of general application of its central level of government respecting any matter covered by this Treaty that are published in accordance with paragraph 2(a), each Party:

(a)   shall publish the proposed regulations in a single official journal of national circulation and shall encourage their distribution through additional outlets;

(b)   should in most cases publish the proposed regulations not less than 60 days before the date public comments are due;

(c)   shall include in the publication an explanation of the purpose of and rationale for the proposed regulations; and

(d)   shall, at the time it adopts final regulations, address significant, substantive comments received during the comment period and explain substantive revisions that it made to the proposed regulations in its official journal or in a prominent location on a government Internet site.

4.   With respect to regulations of general application that are adopted by its central level of government respecting any matter covered by this Treaty, each Party:

(a)   shall publish the regulations in a single official journal of national circulation and shall encourage their distribution through additional outlets; and

(b)   shall include in the publication an explanation of the purpose of and rationale for the regulations.

5.   Provision of Information

(a)   On request of the other Party, a Party shall promptly provide information and respond to questions pertaining to any actual or proposed measure that the requesting Party considers might materially affect the operation of this Treaty or otherwise substantially affect its interests under this Treaty.

(b)   Any request or information under this paragraph shall be provided to the other Party through the relevant contact points.

(c)   Any information provided under this paragraph shall be without prejudice as to whether the measure is consistent with this Treaty.

6.   Administrative Proceedings

With a view to administering in a consistent, impartial, and reasonable manner all measures referred to in Article 10(1)(a), each Party shall ensure that in its administrative proceedings applying such measures to particular covered investments or investors of the other Party in specific cases:

(a) wherever possible, covered investments or investors of the other Party that are directly affected by a proceeding are provided reasonable notice, in accordance with domestic procedures, when a proceeding is initiated, including a description of the nature of the proceeding, a statement of the legal authority under which the proceeding is initiated, and a general description of any issues in controversy;

(b) such persons are afforded a reasonable opportunity to present facts and arguments in support of their positions prior to any final administrative action, when time, the nature of the proceeding, and the public interest permit; and

(c) its procedures are in accordance with domestic law.

7.   Review and Appeal

(a) Each Party shall establish or maintain judicial, quasi-judicial, or administrative tribunals or procedures for the purpose of the prompt review and, where warranted, correction of final administrative actions regarding matters covered by this Treaty. Such tribunals shall be impartial and independent of the office or authority entrusted with administrative enforcement and shall not have any substantial interest in the outcome of the matter.

(b) Each Party shall ensure that, in any such tribunals or procedures, the parties to the proceeding are provided with the right to:

(i) a reasonable opportunity to support or defend their respective positions; and

(ii) a decision based on the evidence and submissions of record or, where required by domestic law, the record compiled by the administrative authority.

(c) Each Party shall ensure, subject to appeal or further review as provided in its domestic law, that such decisions shall be implemented by, and shall govern the practice of, the offices or authorities with respect to the administrative action at issue.

8.   Standards-Setting

(a) Each Party shall allow persons of the other Party to participate in the development of standards and technical regulations by its central government bodies.[14] Each Party shall

---

14   A Party may satisfy this obligation by, for example, providing interested persons a reasonable opportunity to provide comments on the measure it proposes to develop and taking those comments into account in the development of the measure.

allow persons of the other Party to participate in the development of these measures, and the development of conformity assessment procedures by its central government bodies, on terms no less favorable than those it accords to its own persons.

(b) Each Party shall recommend that non-governmental standardizing bodies in its territory allow persons of the other Party to participate in the development of standards by those bodies. Each Party shall recommend that non-governmental standardizing bodies in its territory allow persons of the other Party to participate in the development of these standards, and the development of conformity assessment procedures by those bodies, on terms no less favorable than those they accord to persons of the Party.

(c)   Subparagraphs 8(a) and 8(b) do not apply to:

(i)   sanitary and phytosanitary measures as defined in Annex A of the World Trade Organization (WTO) Agreement on the Application of Sanitary and Phytosanitary Measures; or

(ii) purchasing specifications prepared by a governmental body for its production or consumption requirements.

(d) For purposes of subparagraphs 8(a) and 8(b), "central government body", "standards", "technical regulations" and "conformity assessment procedures" have the meanings assigned to those terms in Annex 1 of the WTO Agreement on Technical Barriers to Trade. Consistent with Annex 1, the three latter terms do not include standards, technical regulations or conformity assessment procedures 'for the supply of a service.

Article 12: Investment and Environment

1.   The Parties recognize that their respective environmental laws and policies, and multilateral environmental agreements to which they are both party, play an important role in protecting the environment.

2.   The Parties recognize that it is inappropriate to encourage investment by weakening or reducing the protections afforded in domestic environmental laws. Accordingly, each Party shall ensure that it does not waive or otherwise derogate from or offer to waive or otherwise derogate from its environmental laws[15] in a manner that weakens or reduces the protections afforded in those laws, or fail to effectively enforce those laws through a sustained or recurring course of action or inaction, as an encouragement for the establishment, acquisition, expansion, or retention of an investment in its territory.

---

[15]   Paragraph 2 shall not apply where a Party waives or derogates from an environmental law pursuant to a provision in law providing for waivers or derogations.

3.   The Parties recognize that each Party retains the right to exercise discretion with respect to regulatory, compliance, investigatory, and prosecutorial matters, and to make decisions regarding the allocation of resources to enforcement with respect to other environmental matters determined to have higher priorities. Accordingly, the Parties understand that a Party is in compliance with paragraph 2 where a course of action or inaction reflects a reasonable exercise of such discretion, or results from a *bona fide* decision regarding the allocation of resources.

4.   For purposes of this Article, "environmental law" means each Party's statutes or regulations,[16] or provisions thereof, the primary purpose of which is the protection of the environment, or the prevention of a danger to human, animal, or plant life or health, through the:

   (a)   prevention, abatement, or control of the release, discharge, or emission of pollutants or environmental contaminants;

   (b)   control of environmentally hazardous or toxic chemicals, substances, materials, and wastes, and the dissemination of information related thereto; or

   (c)   protection or conservation of wild flora or fauna, including endangered species, their habitat, and specially protected natural areas, in the Party's territory, but does not include any statute or regulation, or provision thereof, directly related to worker safety or health.

5.   Nothing in this Treaty shall be construed to prevent a Party from adopting, maintaining, or enforcing any measure otherwise consistent with this Treaty that it considers appropriate to ensure that investment activity in its territory is undertaken in a manner sensitive to environmental concerns.

6.   A Party may make a written request for consultations with the other Party regarding any matter arising under this Article. The other Party shall respond to a request for consultations within thirty days of receipt of such request. Thereafter, the Parties shall consult and endeavor to reach a mutually satisfactory resolution.

7.   The Parties confirm that each Party may, as appropriate, provide opportunities for public participation regarding any matter arising under this Article.

---

[16]   For the United States, "statutes or regulations" for the purposes of this Article means an act of the United States Congress or regulations promulgated pursuant to an act of the United States Congress that is enforceable by action of the central level of government.

Article 13: Investment and Labor

1.   The Parties reaffirm their respective obligations as members of the International Labor Organization ("ILO") and their commitments under the *ILO Declaration on Fundamental Principles and Rights at Work and its Follow-Up.*

2.   The Parties recognize that it is inappropriate to encourage investment by weakening or reducing the protections afforded in domestic labor laws. Accordingly, each Party shall ensure that it does not waive or otherwise derogate from or offer to waive or otherwise derogate from its labor laws where the waiver or derogation would be inconsistent with the labor rights referred to in subparagraphs (a) through (e) of paragraph 3, or fail to effectively enforce its labor laws through a sustained or recurring course of actions or inaction, as an encouragement for the establishment, acquisition, expansion, or retention of an investment in its territory.

3.   For purposes of this Article, "labor laws" means each Party's statutes or regulations,[17] or provisions thereof, that are directly related to the following:

(a)   freedom of association;

(b)   the effective recognition of the right to collective bargaining;

(c)   the elimination of all forms of forced or compulsory labor;

(d)   the effective abolition of child labor and a prohibition on the worst forms of child labor;

(e)   the elimination of discrimination in respect of employment and occupation; and

(f)   acceptable conditions of work with respect to minimum wages, hours of work, and occupational safety and health.

4.   A Party may make a written request for consultations with the other Party regarding any matter arising under this Article. The other Party shall respond to a request for consultations within thirty days of receipt of such request. Thereafter, the Parties shall consult and endeavor to reach a mutually satisfactory resolution.

5.   The Parties confirm that each Party may, as appropriate, provide opportunities for public participation regarding any matter arising under this Article.

---

[17]   For the United States, "statutes or regulations" for purposes of this Article means an act of the United States Congress or regulations promulgated pursuant to an act of the United States Congress that is enforceable by action of the central level of government.

Article 14: Non-Conforming Measures

1.   Articles 3 [National Treatment], 4 [Most-Favored-Nation Treatment], 8 [Performance Requirements], and 9 [Senior Management and Boards of Directors] do not apply to:

(a)   any existing non-conforming measure that is maintained by a Party at:

(i)   the central level of government, as set out by that Party in its Schedule to Annex I or Annex III,

(ii)   a regional level of government, as set out by that Party in its Schedule to Annex I or Annex III, or

(iii)   a local level of government;

(b)   the continuation or prompt renewal of any non-conforming measure referred to in subparagraph (a); or

(c)   an amendment to any non-conforming measure referred to in subparagraph (a) to the extent that the amendment does not decrease the conformity of the measure, as it existed immediately before the amendment, with Article 3 [National Treatment], 4 [Most Favored-Nation Treatment], 8 [Performance Requirements], or 9 [Senior Management and Boards of Directors].

2.   Articles 3 [National Treatment], 4 [Most-Favored-Nation Treatment], 8 [Performance Requirements], and 9 [Senior Management and Boards of Directors] do not apply to any measure that a Party adopts or maintains with respect to sectors, subsectors, or activities, as set out in its Schedule to Annex II.

3.   Neither Party may, under any measure adopted after the date of entry into force of this Treaty and covered by its Schedule to Annex II, require an investor of the other Party, by reason of its nationality, to sell or otherwise dispose of an investment existing at the time the measure becomes effective.

4.   Articles 3 [National Treatment] and 4 [Most-Favored-Nation Treatment] do not apply to any measure covered by an exception to, or derogation from, the obligations under Article 3 or 4 of the TRIPS Agreement, as specifically provided in those Articles and in Article 5 of the TRIPS Agreement.

5.   Articles 3 [National Treatment], 4 [Most-Favored-Nation Treatment], and 9 [Senior Management and Boards of Directors] do not apply to:

(a)   government procurement; or

(b)   subsidies or grants provided by a Party, including government-supported loans, guarantees, and insurance.

Article 15: Special Formalities and Information Requirements

1.   Nothing in Article 3 [National Treatment] shall be construed to prevent a Party from adopting or maintaining a measure that prescribes special formalities in connection with covered investments, such as a requirement that investors be residents of the Party or that covered investments be legally constituted under the laws or regulations of the Party, provided that such formalities do not materially impair the protections afforded by a Party to investors of the other Party and covered investments pursuant to this Treaty.

2.   Notwithstanding Articles 3 [National Treatment] and 4 [Most-Favored-Nation Treatment], a Party may require an investor of the other Party or its covered investment to provide information concerning that investment solely for informational or statistical purposes. The Party shall protect any confidential business information from any disclosure that would prejudice the competitive position of the investor or the covered investment. Nothing in this paragraph shall be construed to prevent a Party from otherwise obtaining or disclosing information in connection with the equitable and good faith application of its law.

Article 16: Non-Derogation

This Treaty shall not derogate from any of the following that entitle an investor of a Party or a covered investment to treatment more favorable than that accorded by this Treaty:

1.   laws or regulations, administrative practices or procedures, or administrative or adjudicatory decisions of a Party;

2.   international legal obligations of a Party; or

3.   obligations assumed by a Party, including those contained in an investment authorization or an investment agreement.

Article 17: Denial of Benefits

1.   A Party may deny the benefits of this Treaty to an investor of the other Party that is an enterprise of such other Party and to investments of that investor if persons of a non-Party own or control the enterprise and the denying Party:

(a)   does not maintain diplomatic relations with the non-Party; or

(b)   adopts or maintains measures with respect to the non-Party or a person of the non-Party that prohibit transactions with the enterprise or that would be violated or circumvented if the benefits of this Treaty were accorded to the enterprise or to its investments.

2.   A Party may deny the benefits of this Treaty to an investor of the other Party that is an enterprise of such other Party and to investments of that investor if the enterprise has no substantial business activities in the territory of the other Party and persons of a non-Party, or of the denying Party, own or control the enterprise.

Article 18: Essential Security

Nothing in this Treaty shall be construed:

1.   to require a Party to furnish or allow access to any information the disclosure of which it determines to be contrary to its essential security interests; or

2.   to preclude a Party from applying measures that it considers necessary for the fulfillment of its obligations with respect to the maintenance or restoration of international peace or security, or the protection of its own essential security interests.

Article 19: Disclosure of Information

Nothing in this Treaty shall be construed to require a Party to furnish or allow access to confidential information the disclosure of which would impede law enforcement or otherwise be contrary to the public interest, or which would prejudice the legitimate commercial interests of particular enterprises, public or private.

Article 20: Financial Services

1.   Notwithstanding any other provision of this Treaty, a Party shall not be prevented from adopting or maintaining measures relating to financial services for prudential reasons, including for the protection of investors, depositors, policy holders, or persons to whom a fiduciary duty is owed by a financial services supplier, or to ensure the integrity and stability of the financial system.[18] Where such measures do not conform with the provisions of this Treaty, they shall not be used as a means of avoiding the Party's commitments or obligations under this Treaty.

2.   (a) Nothing in this Treaty applies to non-discriminatory measures of general application taken by any public entity in pursuit of monetary and related credit policies or exchange rate policies. This paragraph shall not affect a Party's obligations under Article 7 [Transfers] or Article 8 [Performance Requirements].[19]

---

[18]   It is understood that the term "prudential reasons" includes the maintenance of the safety, soundness, integrity, or financial responsibility of individual financial institutions, as well as the maintenance of the safety and financial and operational integrity of payment and clearing systems.

[19]   For greater certainty, measures of general application taken in pursuit of monetary and related credit policies or exchange rate policies do not include measures

(b) For purposes of this paragraph, "public entity" means a central bank or monetary authority of a Party.

3. Where a claimant submits a claim to arbitration under Section B [Investor-State Dispute Settlement], and the respondent invokes paragraph 1 or 2 as a defense, the following provisions shall apply:

(a) The respondent shall, within 120 days of the date the claim is submitted to arbitration under Section B, submit in writing to the competent financial authorities[20] of both Parties a request for a joint determination on the issue of whether and to what extent paragraph 1 or 2 is a valid defense to the claim. The respondent shall promptly provide the tribunal, if constituted, a copy of such request. The arbitration may proceed with respect to the claim only as provided in subparagraph (d).

(b) The competent financial authorities of both Parties shall make themselves available for consultations with each other and shall attempt in good faith to make a determination as described in subparagraph (a). Any such determination shall be transmitted promptly to the disputing parties and, if constituted, to the tribunal. The determination shall be binding on the tribunal.

(c) If the competent financial authorities of both Parties, within 120 days of the date by which they have both received the respondent's written request for a joint determination under subparagraph (a), have not made a determination as described in that subparagraph, the tribunal shall decide the issue or issues left unresolved by the competent financial authorities. The provisions of Section B shall apply, except as modified by this subparagraph.

(i) In the appointment of all arbitrators not yet appointed to the tribunal, each disputing party shall take appropriate steps to ensure that the tribunal has expertise or experience in financial services law or practice. The expertise of particular candidates with respect to the particular sector of financial services in which the dispute arises shall be taken into account in the appointment of the presiding arbitrator.

(ii) If, before the respondent submits the request for a joint determination in conformance with subparagraph (a), the presiding arbitrator has been appointed pursuant to Article 27(3), such arbitrator shall be replaced on the request of either

---

that expressly nullify or amend contractual provisions that specify the currency of denomination or the rate of exchange of currencies.

20   For purposes of this Article, "competent financial authorities" means, for the United States, the Department of the Treasury for banking and other financial services, and the Office of the United States Trade Representative, in coordination with the Department of Commerce and other agencies, for insurance; and for [Country].

disputing party and the tribunal shall be reconstituted consistent with subparagraph (c)(i). If, within 30 days of the date the arbitration proceedings are resumed under subparagraph (d), the disputing parties have not agreed on the appointment of a new presiding arbitrator, the Secretary-General, on the request of a disputing party, shall appoint the presiding arbitrator consistent with subparagraph (c)(i).

(iii) The tribunal shall draw no inference regarding the application of paragraph 1 or 2 from the fact that the competent financial authorities have not made a determination as described in subparagraph (a).

(iv) The non-disputing Party may make oral and written submissions to the tribunal regarding the issue of whether and to what extent paragraph 1 or 2 is a valid defense to the claim. Unless it makes such a submission, the non-disputing Party shall be presumed, for purposes of the arbitration, to take a position on paragraph 1 or 2 not inconsistent with that of the respondent.

(d) The arbitration referred to in subparagraph (a) may proceed with respect to the claim:

(i) 10 days after the date the competent financial authorities' joint determination has been received by both the disputing parties and, if constituted, the tribunal; or

(ii) 10 days after the expiration of the 120-day period provided to the competent financial authorities in subparagraph (c).

(e) On the request of the respondent made within 30 days after the expiration of the 120-day period for a joint determination referred to in subparagraph (c), or, if the tribunal has not been constituted as of the expiration of the 120-day period, within 30 days after the tribunal is constituted, the tribunal shall address and decide the issue or issues left unresolved by the competent financial authorities as referred to in subparagraph (c) prior to deciding the merits of the claim for which paragraph 1 or 2 has been invoked by the respondent as a defense. Failure of the respondent to make such a request is without prejudice to the right of the respondent to invoke paragraph 1 or 2 as a defense at any appropriate phase of the arbitration.

4. Where a dispute arises under Section C and the competent financial authorities of one Party provide written notice to the competent financial authorities of the other Party that the dispute involves financial services, Section C shall apply except as modified by this paragraph and paragraph (a).

(a) The competent financial authorities of both Parties shall make themselves available for consultations with each other regarding the dispute, and shall have 180 days from the date such notice is received to transmit a report on their consultations to the Parties. A Party may submit the dispute to arbitration under Section C only after the expiration of that 180-day period.

(b) Either Party may make any such report available to a tribunal constituted under Section C to decide the dispute referred to in this paragraph or a similar dispute, or to a tribunal constituted under Section B to decide a claim arising out of the same events or circumstances that gave rise to the dispute under Section C.

5. Where a Party submits a dispute involving financial services to arbitration under Section C in conformance with paragraph 4, and on the request of either Party within 30 days of the date the dispute is submitted to arbitration, each Party shall, in the appointment of all arbitrators not yet appointed, take appropriate steps to ensure that the tribunal has expertise or experience in financial services law or practice. The expertise of particular candidates with respect to financial services shall be taken into account in the appointment of the presiding arbitrator.

6. Notwithstanding Article 11(2)–(4) [Transparency-Publication], each Party, to the extent practicable,

(a) shall publish in advance any regulations of general application relating to financial services that it proposes to adopt and the purpose of the regulation;

(b) shall provide interested persons and the other Party a reasonable opportunity to comment on such proposed regulations; and

(c) should at the time it adopts final regulations, address in writing significant substantive comments received from interested persons with respect to the proposed regulations.

7. The terms "financial service" or "financial services" shall have the same meaning as in subparagraph 5(a) of the Annex on Financial Services of the GATS.

8. For greater certainty, nothing in this Treaty shall be construed to prevent the adoption or enforcement by a party of measures relating to investors of the other Party, or covered investments, in financial institutions that are necessary to secure compliance with laws or regulations that are not inconsistent with this Treaty, including those related to the prevention of deceptive and fraudulent practices or that deal with the effects of a default on financial services contracts, subject to the requirement that such measures are not

applied in a manner which would constitute a means of arbitrary or unjustifiable discrimination between countries where like conditions prevail, or a disguised restriction on investment in financial institutions.

Article 21: Taxation

1.   Except as provided in this Article, nothing in Section A shall impose obligations with respect to taxation measures.

2.   Article 6 [Expropriation] shall apply to all taxation measures, except that a claimant that asserts that a taxation measure involves an expropriation may submit a claim to arbitration under Section B only if:

(a)   the claimant has first referred to the competent tax authorities[21] of both Parties in writing the issue of whether that taxation measure involves an expropriation;

and

(b)   within 180 days after the date of such referral, the competent tax authorities of both Parties fail to agree that the taxation measure is not an expropriation.

3.   Subject to paragraph 4, Article 8 [Performance Requirements] (2) through (4) shall apply to all taxation measures.

4.   Nothing in this Treaty shall affect the rights and obligations of either Party under any tax convention. In the event of any inconsistency between this Treaty and any such convention, that convention shall prevail to the extent of the inconsistency. In the case of a tax convention between the Parties, the competent authorities under that convention shall have sole responsibility for determining whether any inconsistency exists between this Treaty and that convention.

Article 22: Entry into Force, Duration, and Termination

1.   This Treaty shall enter into force thirty days after the date the Parties exchange instruments of ratification. It shall remain in force for a period of ten years and shall continue in force thereafter unless terminated in accordance with paragraph 2.

2.   A Party may terminate this Treaty at the end of the initial ten-year period or at any time thereafter by giving one year's written notice to the other Party.

---

[21]   For purposes of this Article, the "competent tax authority" means: (a) for the United States, the Assistant Secretary of Treasury (Tax Policy), Department of Treasury; (b) for [Country].

3.   For ten years from the date of termination, all other Articles shall continue to apply to covered investments established or acquired prior to the date of termination, except insofar as those Articles extend to the establishment or acquisition of covered investments.

SECTION B

Article 23: Consultation and Negotiation

In the event of an investment dispute, the claimant and the respondent should initially seek to resolve the dispute through consultation and negotiation, which may include the use of non-binding, third-party procedures.

Article 24: Submission of a Claim to Arbitration

1.   In the event that a disputing party considers that an investment dispute cannot be settled by consultation and negotiation:

(a)   the claimant, on its own behalf, may submit to arbitration under this Section a claim

(i)   that the respondent has breached

(A)   an obligation under Articles 3 through 10,

(B)   an investment authorization, or

(C)   an investment agreement;

and

(ii)   that the claimant has incurred loss or damage by reason of, or arising out of, that breach; and

(b)   the claimant, on behalf of an enterprise of the respondent that is a juridical person that the claimant owns or controls directly or indirectly, may submit to arbitration under this Section a claim

(i)   that the respondent has breached

(A)   an obligation under Articles 3 through 10,

(B)   an investment authorization, or

(C)   an investment agreement;

and

(ii)   that the enterprise has incurred loss or damage by reason of, or arising out of, that breach, provided that a claimant may submit pursuant to subparagraph (a)(i)(C) or (b)(i)(C) a claim for breach of an investment agreement only if the subject matter of the claim and the claimed damages directly relate to the covered investment that was established or acquired, or sought to be established or acquired, in reliance on the relevant investment agreement.

2.   At least 90 days before submitting any claim to arbitration under this Section, a claimant shall deliver to the respondent a written notice of its intention to submit the claim to arbitration ("notice of intent"). The notice shall specify:

(a)   the name and address of the claimant and, where a claim is submitted on behalf of an enterprise, the name, address, and place of incorporation of the enterprise;

(b)   for each claim, the provision of this Treaty, investment authorization, or investment agreement alleged to have been breached and any other relevant provisions;

(c)   the legal and factual basis for each claim; and

(d)   the relief sought and the approximate amount of damages claimed.

3.   Provided that six months have elapsed since the events giving rise to the claim, a claimant may submit a claim referred to in paragraph 1:

(a)   under the ICSID Convention and the ICSID Rules of Procedure for Arbitration Proceedings, provided that both the respondent and the non-disputing Party are parties to the ICSID Convention;

(b)   under the ICSID Additional Facility Rules, provided that either the respondent or the non-disputing Party is a party to the ICSID Convention;

(c)   under the UNCITRAL Arbitration Rules; or

(d)   if the claimant and respondent agree, to any other arbitration institution or under any other arbitration rules.

4.   A claim shall be deemed submitted to arbitration under this Section when the claimant's notice of or request for arbitration ("notice of arbitration"):

(a)   referred to in paragraph 1 of Article 36 of the ICSID Convention is received by the Secretary-General;

(b)   referred to in Article 2 of Schedule C of the ICSID Additional Facility Rules is received by the Secretary-General;

(c)   referred to in Article 3 of the UNCITRAL Arbitration Rules, together with the statement of claim referred to in Article 20 of the UNCITRAL Arbitration Rules, are received by the respondent; or

(d)   referred to under any arbitral institution or arbitral rules selected under paragraph 3(d) is received by the respondent.

A claim asserted by the claimant for the first time after such notice of arbitration is submitted shall be deemed submitted to arbitration under this Section on the date of its receipt under the applicable arbitral rules.

5.   The arbitration rules applicable under paragraph 3, and in effect on the date the claim or claims were submitted to arbitration under this Section, shall govern the arbitration except to the extent modified by this Treaty.

6.   The claimant shall provide with the notice of arbitration:

(a)   the name of the arbitrator that the claimant appoints; or

(b)   the claimant's written consent for the Secretary-General to appoint that arbitrator.

Article 25: Consent of Each Party to Arbitration

1.   Each Party consents to the submission of a claim to arbitration under this Section in accordance with this Treaty.

2.   The consent under paragraph 1 and the submission of a claim to arbitration under this Section shall satisfy the requirements of:

(a)   Chapter II of the ICSID Convention (Jurisdiction of the Centre) and the ICSID Additional Facility Rules for written consent of the parties to the dispute; [and]

(b)   Article II of the New York Convention for an "agreement in writing[."] [;" and

(c)   Article I of the Inter-American Convention for an "agreement."]

Article 26: Conditions and Limitations on Consent of Each Party

1.   No claim may be submitted to arbitration under this Section if more than three years have elapsed from the date on which the claimant first acquired, or should have first acquired, knowledge of the breach alleged under Article 24(1) and knowledge that the claimant (for claims brought under Article 24(1)(a)) or the enterprise (for claims brought under Article 24(1)(b)) has incurred loss or damage.

2.   No claim may be submitted to arbitration under this Section unless:

(a)   the claimant consents in writing to arbitration in accordance with the procedures set out in this Treaty; and

(b)   the notice of arbitration is accompanied,

(i)   for claims submitted to arbitration under Article 24(1)(a), by the claimant's written waiver, and

(ii)   for claims submitted to arbitration under Article 24(1)(b), by the claimant's and the enterprise's written waivers of any right to initiate or continue before any administrative tribunal or court under the law of either Party, or other dispute settlement procedures, any proceeding with respect to any measure alleged to constitute a breach referred to in Article 24.

3.   Notwithstanding paragraph 2(b), the claimant (for claims brought under Article 24(1)(a)) and the claimant or the enterprise (for claims brought under Article 24(1)(b)) may initiate or continue an action that seeks interim injunctive relief and does not involve the payment of monetary damages before a judicial or administrative tribunal of the respondent, provided that the action is brought for the sole purpose of preserving the claimant's or the enterprise's rights and interests during the pendency of the arbitration.

Article 27: Selection of Arbitrators

1.   Unless the disputing parties otherwise agree, the tribunal shall comprise three arbitrators, one arbitrator appointed by each of the disputing parties and the third, who shall be the presiding arbitrator, appointed by agreement of the disputing parties.

2.   The Secretary-General shall serve as appointing authority for an arbitration under this Section.

3.   Subject to Article 20(3), if a tribunal has not been constituted within 75 days from the date that a claim is submitted to arbitration under this Section, the Secretary-General, on the request of a disputing party, shall appoint, in his or her discretion, the arbitrator or arbitrators not yet appointed.

4.   For purposes of Article 39 of the ICSID Convention and Article 7 of Schedule C to the ICSID Additional Facility Rules, and without prejudice to an objection to an arbitrator on a ground other than nationality:

(a)   the respondent agrees to the appointment of each individual member of a tribunal established under the ICSID Convention or the ICSID Additional Facility Rules;

(b)   a claimant referred to in Article 24(1)(a) may submit a claim to arbitration under this Section, or continue a claim, under the ICSID Convention or the ICSID Additional Facility Rules, only on condition that the claimant agrees in writing to the appointment of each individual member of the tribunal; and

(c)   a claimant referred to in Article 24(1)(b) may submit a claim to arbitration under this Section, or continue a claim, under the ICSID Convention or the ICSID Additional Facility Rules, only on condition that the claimant and the enterprise agree in writing to the appointment of each individual member of the tribunal.

Article 28: Conduct of the Arbitration

1.   The disputing parties may agree on the legal place of any arbitration under the arbitral rules applicable under Article 24(3). If the disputing parties fail to reach agreement, the tribunal shall determine the place in accordance with the applicable arbitral rules, provided that the place shall be in the territory of a State that is a party to the New York Convention.

2.   The non-disputing Party may make oral and written submissions to the tribunal regarding the interpretation of this Treaty.

3.   The tribunal shall have the authority to accept and consider *amicus curiae* submissions from a person or entity that is not a disputing party.

4.   Without prejudice to a tribunal's authority to address other objections as a preliminary question, a tribunal shall address and decide as a preliminary question any objection by the respondent that, as a matter of law, a claim submitted is not a claim for which an award in favor of the claimant may be made under Article 34.

(a)   Such objection shall be submitted to the tribunal as soon as possible after the tribunal is constituted, and in no event later than the date the tribunal fixes for the respondent to submit its counter-memorial (or, in the case of an amendment to the notice of arbitration, the date the tribunal fixes for the respondent to submit its response to the amendment).

(b)   On receipt of an objection under this paragraph, the tribunal shall suspend any proceedings on the merits, establish a schedule for considering the objection consistent with any schedule it has established for considering any other preliminary question, and issue a decision or award on the objection, stating the grounds therefor.

(c)   In deciding an objection under this paragraph, the tribunal shall assume to be true claimant's factual allegations in support of any claim in the notice of arbitration (or any amendment thereof) and, in disputes brought under the UNCITRAL Arbitration Rules, the statement of claim referred to in Article 20 of the UNCITRAL Arbitration Rules. The tribunal may also consider any relevant facts not in dispute.

(d) The respondent does not waive any objection as to competence or any argument on the merits merely because the respondent did or did not raise an objection under this paragraph or make use of the expedited procedure set out in paragraph 5.

5.   In the event that the respondent so requests within 45 days after the tribunal is constituted, the tribunal shall decide on an expedited basis an objection under paragraph 4 and any objection that the dispute is not within the tribunal's competence. The tribunal shall suspend any proceedings on the merits and issue a decision or award on the objection(s), stating the grounds therefor, no later than 150 days after the date of the request. However, if a disputing party requests a hearing, the tribunal may take an additional 30 days to issue the decision or award. Regardless of whether a hearing is requested, a tribunal may, on a showing of extraordinary cause, delay issuing its decision or award by an additional brief period, which may not exceed 30 days.

6.   When it decides a respondent's objection under paragraph 4 or 5, the tribunal may, if warranted, award to the prevailing disputing party reasonable costs and attorney's fees incurred in submitting or opposing the objection. In determining whether such an award is warranted, the tribunal shall consider whether either the claimant's claim or the respondent's objection was frivolous, and shall provide the disputing parties a reasonable opportunity to comment.

7.   A respondent may not assert as a defense, counterclaim, right of set-off, or for any other reason that the claimant has received or will receive indemnification or other compensation for all or part of the alleged damages pursuant to an insurance or guarantee contract.

8.   A tribunal may order an interim measure of protection to preserve the rights of a disputing party, or to ensure that the tribunal's jurisdiction is made fully effective, including an order to preserve evidence in the possession or control of a disputing party or to protect the tribunal's jurisdiction. A tribunal may not order attachment or enjoin the application of a measure alleged to constitute a breach referred to in Article 24. For purposes of this paragraph, an order includes a recommendation.

9.   (a) In any arbitration conducted under this Section, at the request of a disputing party, a tribunal shall, before issuing a decision or award on liability, transmit its proposed decision or award to the disputing parties and to the non-disputing Party. Within 60 days after the tribunal transmits its proposed decision or award, the disputing parties may submit written comments to the tribunal concerning any aspect of its proposed decision or award. The tribunal

shall consider any such comments and issue its decision or award not later than 45 days after the expiration of the 60-day comment period.

(b) Subparagraph (a) shall not apply in any arbitration conducted pursuant to this Section for which an appeal has been made available pursuant to paragraph 10.

10.   In the event that an appellate mechanism for reviewing awards rendered by investor-State dispute settlement tribunals is developed in the future under other institutional arrangements, the Parties shall consider whether awards rendered under Article 34 should be subject to that appellate mechanism. The Parties shall strive to ensure that any such appellate mechanism they consider adopting provides for transparency of proceedings similar to the transparency provisions established in Article 29.

Article 29: Transparency of Arbitral Proceedings

1.   Subject to paragraphs 2 and 4, the respondent shall, after receiving the following documents, promptly transmit them to the non-disputing Party and make them available to the public:

(a)   the notice of intent;

(b)   the notice of arbitration;

(c)   pleadings, memorials, and briefs submitted to the tribunal by a disputing party and any written submissions submitted pursuant to Article 28(2) [Non-Disputing Party submissions] and (3) [*Amicus* Submissions] and Article 33 [Consolidation];

(d)   minutes or transcripts of hearings of the tribunal, where available; and

(e)   orders, awards, and decisions of the tribunal.

2.   The tribunal shall conduct hearings open to the public and shall determine, in consultation with the disputing parties, the appropriate logistical arrangements. However, any disputing party that intends to use information designated as protected information in a hearing shall so advise the tribunal. The tribunal shall make appropriate arrangements to protect the information from disclosure.

3.   Nothing in this Section requires a respondent to disclose protected information or to furnish or allow access to information that it may withhold in accordance with Article 18 [Essential Security Article] or Article 19 [Disclosure of Information Article].

4.   Any protected information that is submitted to the tribunal shall be protected from disclosure in accordance with the following procedures:

(a) Subject to subparagraph (d), neither the disputing parties nor the tribunal shall disclose to the non-disputing Party or to the public any protected information where the disputing party that provided the information clearly designates it in accordance with subparagraph (b);

(b) Any disputing party claiming that certain information constitutes protected information shall clearly designate the information at the time it is submitted to the tribunal;

(c) A disputing party shall, at the time it submits a document containing information claimed to be protected information, submit a redacted version of the document that does not contain the information. Only the redacted version shall be provided to the non-disputing Party and made public in accordance with paragraph 1; and

(d) The tribunal shall decide any objection regarding the designation of information claimed to be protected information. If the tribunal determines that such information was not properly designated, the disputing party that submitted the information may (i) withdraw all or part of its submission containing such information, or (ii) agree to resubmit complete and redacted documents with corrected designations in accordance with the tribunal's determination and subparagraph (c). In either case, the other disputing party shall, whenever necessary, resubmit complete and redacted documents which either remove the information withdrawn under (i) by the disputing party that first submitted the information or re-designate the information consistent with the designation.

5.   Nothing in this Section requires a respondent to withhold from the public information required to be disclosed by its laws.

Article 30: Governing Law

1.   Subject to paragraph 3, when a claim is submitted under Article 24(1)(a)(i)(A) or Article 24(1)(b)(i)(A), the tribunal shall decide the issues in dispute in accordance with this Treaty and applicable rules of international law.

2.   Subject to paragraph 3 and the other terms of this Section, when a claim is submitted under Article 24(1)(a)(i)(B) or (C), or Article 24(1)(b)(i)(B) or (C), the tribunal shall apply:

(a) the rules of law specified in the pertinent investment authorization or investment agreement, or as the disputing parties may otherwise agree; or

(b) if the rules of law have not been specified or otherwise agreed:

(i)   the law of the respondent, including its rules on the conflict of laws;[22] and

(ii) such rules of international law as may be applicable.

3.   A joint decision of the Parties, each acting through its representative designated for purposes of this Article, declaring their interpretation of a provision of this Treaty shall be binding on a tribunal, and any decision or award issued by a tribunal must be consistent with that joint decision.

Article 31: Interpretation of Annexes

1.   Where a respondent asserts as a defense that the measure alleged to be a breach is within the scope of an entry set out in Annex I, II, or III, the tribunal shall, on request of the respondent, request the interpretation of the Parties on the issue. The Parties shall submit in writing any joint decision declaring their interpretation to the tribunal within 90 days of delivery of the request.

2.   A joint decision issued under paragraph 1 by the Parties, each acting through its representative designated for purposes of this Article, shall be binding on the tribunal, and any decision or award issued by the tribunal must be consistent with that joint decision. If the Parties fail to issue such a decision within 90 days, the tribunal shall decide the issue.

Article 32: Expert Reports

Without prejudice to the appointment of other kinds of experts where authorized by the applicable arbitration rules, a tribunal, at the request of a disputing party or, unless the disputing parties disapprove, on its own initiative, may appoint one or more experts to report to it in writing on any factual issue concerning environmental, health, safety, or other scientific matters raised by a disputing party in a proceeding, subject to such terms and conditions as the disputing parties may agree.

Article 33: Consolidation

1.   Where two or more claims have been submitted separately to arbitration under Article 24(1) and the claims have a question of law or fact in common and arise out of the same events or circumstances, any disputing party may seek a consolidation order in accordance with the agreement of all the disputing parties sought to be covered by the order or the terms of paragraphs 2 through 10.

2.   A disputing party that seeks a consolidation order under this Article shall deliver, in writing, a request to the Secretary-General

---

[22]   The "law of the respondent" means the law that a domestic court or tribunal of proper jurisdiction would apply in the same case.

and to all the disputing parties sought to be covered by the order and shall specify in the request:

(a)   the names and addresses of all the disputing parties sought to be covered by the order;

(b)   the nature of the order sought; and

(c)   the grounds on which the order is sought.

3.   Unless the Secretary-General finds within 30 days after receiving a request under paragraph 2 that the request is manifestly unfounded, a tribunal shall be established under this Article.

4.   Unless all the disputing parties sought to be covered by the order otherwise agree, a tribunal established under this Article shall comprise three arbitrators:

(a)   one arbitrator appointed by agreement of the claimants;

(b)   one arbitrator appointed by the respondent; and

(c)   the presiding arbitrator appointed by the Secretary-General, provided, however, that the presiding arbitrator shall not be a national of either Party.

5.   If, within 60 days after the Secretary-General receives a request made under paragraph 2, the respondent fails or the claimants fail to appoint an arbitrator in accordance with paragraph 4, the Secretary-General, on the request of any disputing party sought to be covered by the order, shall appoint the arbitrator or arbitrators not yet appointed. If the respondent fails to appoint an arbitrator, the Secretary-General shall appoint a national of the disputing Party, and if the claimants fail to appoint an arbitrator, the Secretary-General shall appoint a national of the non-disputing Party.

6.   Where a tribunal established under this Article is satisfied that two or more claims that have been submitted to arbitration under Article 24(1) have a question of law or fact in common, and arise out of the same events or circumstances, the tribunal may, in the interest of fair and efficient resolution of the claims, and after hearing the disputing parties, by order:

(a)   assume jurisdiction over, and hear and determine together, all or part of the claims;

(b)   assume jurisdiction over, and hear and determine one or more of the claims, the determination of which it believes would assist in the resolution of the others; or

(c)   instruct a tribunal previously established under Article 27 [Selection of Arbitrators] to assume jurisdiction over, and hear and determine together, all or part of the claims, provided that

(i) that tribunal, at the request of any claimant not previously a disputing party before that tribunal, shall be reconstituted with its original members, except that the arbitrator for the claimants shall be appointed pursuant to paragraphs 4(a) and 5; and

(ii) that tribunal shall decide whether any prior hearing shall be repeated.

7. Where a tribunal has been established under this Article, a claimant that has submitted a claim to arbitration under Article 24(1) and that has not been named in a request made under paragraph 2 may make a written request to the tribunal that it be included in any order made under paragraph 6, and shall specify in the request:

(a) the name and address of the claimant;

(b) the nature of the order sought; and

(c) the grounds on which the order is sought.

The claimant shall deliver a copy of its request to the Secretary-General.

8. A tribunal established under this Article shall conduct its proceedings in accordance with the UNCITRAL Arbitration Rules, except as modified by this Section.

9. A tribunal established under Article 27 [Selection of Arbitrators] shall not have jurisdiction to decide a claim, or a part of a claim, over which a tribunal established or instructed under this Article has assumed jurisdiction.

10. On application of a disputing party, a tribunal established under this Article, pending its decision under paragraph 6, may order that the proceedings of a tribunal established under Article 27 [Selection of Arbitrators] be stayed, unless the latter tribunal has already adjourned its proceedings.

Article 34: Awards

1. Where a tribunal makes a final award against a respondent, the tribunal may award, separately or in combination, only:

(a) monetary damages and any applicable interest; and

(b) restitution of property, in which case the award shall provide that the respondent may pay monetary damages and any applicable interest in lieu of restitution.

A tribunal may also award costs and attorney's fees in accordance with this Treaty and the applicable arbitration rules.

2.   Subject to paragraph 1, where a claim is submitted to arbitration under Article 24(1)(b):

(a)   an award of restitution of property shall provide that restitution be made to the enterprise;

(b)   an award of monetary damages and any applicable interest shall provide that the sum be paid to the enterprise; and

(c)   the award shall provide that it is made without prejudice to any right that any person may have in the relief under applicable domestic law.

3.   A tribunal may not award punitive damages.

4.   An award made by a tribunal shall have no binding force except between the disputing parties and in respect of the particular case.

5.   Subject to paragraph 6 and the applicable review procedure for an interim award, a disputing party shall abide by and comply with an award without delay.

6.   A disputing party may not seek enforcement of a final award until:

(a)   in the case of a final award made under the ICSID Convention,

(i)   120 days have elapsed from the date the award was rendered and no disputing party has requested revision or annulment of the award; or

(ii)   revision or annulment proceedings have been completed; and

(b)   in the case of a final award under the ICSID Additional Facility Rules, the UNCITRAL Arbitration Rules, or the rules selected pursuant to Article 24(3)(d),

(i)   90 days have elapsed from the date the award was rendered and no disputing party has commenced a proceeding to revise, set aside, or annul the award; or

(ii)   a court has dismissed or allowed an application to revise, set aside, or annul the award and there is no further appeal.

7.   Each Party shall provide for the enforcement of an award in its territory.

8.   If the respondent fails to abide by or comply with a final award, on delivery of a request by the non-disputing Party, a tribunal shall be established under Article 37 [State-State Dispute Settlement]. Without prejudice to other remedies available under applicable rules

of international law, the requesting Party may seek in such proceedings:

(a) a determination that the failure to abide by or comply with the final award is inconsistent with the obligations of this Treaty; and

(b) a recommendation that the respondent abide by or comply with the final award.

9. A disputing party may seek enforcement of an arbitration award under the ICSID Convention or the New York Convention [or the Inter-American Convention] regardless of whether proceedings have been taken under paragraph 8.

10. A claim that is submitted to arbitration under this Section shall be considered to arise out of a commercial relationship or transaction for purposes of Article I of the New York Convention [and Article I of the Inter-American Convention].

Article 35: Annexes and Footnotes

The Annexes and footnotes shall form an integral part of this Treaty.

Article 36: Service of Documents

Delivery of notice and other documents on a Party shall be made to the place named for that Party in Annex C.

SECTION C

Article 37: State-State Dispute Settlement

1. Subject to paragraph 5, any dispute between the Parties concerning the interpretation or application of this Treaty, that is not resolved through consultations or other diplomatic channels, shall be submitted on the request of either Party to arbitration for a binding decision or award by a tribunal in accordance with applicable rules of international law. In the absence of an agreement by the Parties to the contrary, the UNCITRAL Arbitration Rules shall govern, except as modified by the Parties or this Treaty.

2. Unless the Parties otherwise agree, the tribunal shall comprise three arbitrators, one arbitrator appointed by each Party and the third, who shall be the presiding arbitrator, appointed by agreement of the Parties. If a tribunal has not been constituted within 75 days from the date that a claim is submitted to arbitration under this Section, the Secretary-General, on the request of either Party, shall appoint, in his or her discretion, the arbitrator or arbitrators not yet appointed.

3.   Expenses incurred by the arbitrators, and other costs of the proceedings, shall be paid for equally by the Parties. However, the tribunal may, in its discretion, direct that a higher proportion of the costs be paid by one of the Parties.

§ 7.9   Text of the ICSID Convention (1966)

CHAPTER I
International Centre for Settlement of Investment Disputes

Article 1

(1)   There is hereby established the International Centre for Settlement of Investment Disputes (hereinafter called the Centre).

(2)   The purpose of the Centre shall be to provide facilities for conciliation and arbitration of investment disputes between Contracting States and nationals of other Contracting States in accordance with the provisions of this Convention.

Article 2

The seat of the Centre shall be at the principal office of the International Bank for Reconstruction and Development (hereinafter called the Bank). The seat may be moved to another place by decision of the Administrative Council adopted by a majority of two-thirds of its members.

Article 3

The Centre shall have an Administrative Council and a Secretariat and shall maintain a Panel of Conciliators and a Panel of Arbitrators.

Article 4

(1)   The Administrative Council shall be composed of one representative of each Contracting State. An alternate may act as representative in case of his principal's absence from a meeting or inability to act.

(2)   In the absence of a contrary designation, each governor and alternate governor of the Bank appointed by a Contracting State shall be *ex officio* its representative and its alternate respectively.

Article 5

The President of the Bank shall be *ex officio* Chairman of the Administrative Council (hereinafter called the Chairman) but shall have no vote. During his absence or inability to act and during any vacancy in the office of President of the Bank, the person for the time being acting as President shall act as Chairman of the Administrative Council.

Article 6

(1) Without prejudice to the powers and functions vested in it by other provisions of this Convention, the Administrative Council shall:

(a) adopt the administrative and financial regulations of the Centre;

(b) adopt the rules of procedure for the institution of conciliation and arbitration proceedings;

(c) adopt the rules of procedure for conciliation and arbitration proceedings (hereinafter called the Conciliation Rules and the Arbitration Rules);

(d) approve arrangements with the Bank for the use of the Bank's administrative facilities and services;

(e) determine the conditions of service of the Secretary-General and of any Deputy Secretary-General;

(f) adopt the annual budget of revenues and expenditures of the Centre;

(g) approve the annual report on the operation of the Centre.

The decisions referred to in sub-paragraphs (a), (b), (c) and (f) above shall be adopted by a majority of two-thirds of the members of the Administrative Council.

(2) The Administrative Council may appoint such committees as it considers necessary.

(3) The Administrative Council shall also exercise such other powers and perform such other functions as it shall determine to be necessary for the implementation of the provisions of this Convention.

Article 7

(1) The Administrative Council shall hold an annual meeting and such other meetings as may be determined by the Council, or convened by the Chairman, or convened by the Secretary-General at the request of not less than five members of the Council.

(2) Each member of the Administrative Council shall have one vote and, except as otherwise herein provided, all matters before the Council shall be decided by a majority of the votes cast.

(3)   A quorum for any meeting of the Administrative Council shall be a majority of its members.

(4)   The Administrative Council may establish, by a majority of two-thirds of its members, a procedure whereby the Chairman may seek a vote of the Council without convening a meeting of the Council. The vote shall be considered valid only if the majority of the members of the Council cast their votes within the time limit fixed by the said procedure.

Article 8

Members of the Administrative Council and the Chairman shall serve without remuneration from the Centre.

Article 9

The Secretariat shall consist of a Secretary-General, one or more Deputy Secretaries-General and staff.

Article 10

(1)   The Secretary-General and any Deputy Secretary-General shall be elected by the Administrative Council by a majority of two-thirds of its members upon the nomination of the Chairman for a term of service not exceeding six years and shall be eligible for re-election. After consulting the members of the Administrative Council, the Chairman shall propose one or more candidates for each such office.

(2)   The offices of Secretary-General and Deputy Secretary-General shall be incompatible with the exercise of any political function. Neither the Secretary-General nor any Deputy Secretary-General may hold any other employment or engage in any other occupation except with the approval of the Administrative Council.

(3)   During the Secretary-General's absence or inability to act, and during any vacancy of the office of Secretary-General, the Deputy Secretary-General shall act as Secretary-General. If there shall be more than one Deputy Secretary-General, the Administrative Council shall determine in advance the order in which they shall act as Secretary-General.

Article 11

The Secretary-General shall be the legal representative and the principal officer of the Centre and shall be responsible for its administration, including the appointment of staff, in accordance with the provisions of this Convention and the rules adopted by the Administrative Council. He shall perform the function of registrar and shall have the power to authenticate arbitral awards rendered pursuant to this Convention, and to certify copies thereof.

Article 12

The Panel of Conciliators and the Panel of Arbitrators shall each consist of qualified persons, designated as hereinafter provided, who are willing to serve thereon.

Article 13

(1) Each Contracting State may designate to each Panel four persons who may but need not be its nationals.

(2) The Chairman may designate ten persons to each Panel. The persons so designated to a Panel shall each have a different nationality.

Article 14

(1) Persons designated to serve on the Panels shall be persons of high moral character and recognized competence in the fields of law, commerce, industry or finance, who may be relied upon to exercise independent judgment. Competence in the field of law shall be of particular importance in the case of persons on the Panel of Arbitrators.

(2) The Chairman, in designating persons to serve on the Panels, shall in addition pay due regard to the importance of assuring representation on the Panels of the principal legal systems of the world and of the main forms of economic activity.

Article 15

(1) Panel members shall serve for renewable periods of six years.

(2) In case of death or resignation of a member of a Panel, the authority which designated the member shall have the right to designate another person to serve for the remainder of that member's term.

(3) Panel members shall continue in office until their successors have been designated.

Article 16

(1) A person may serve on both Panels.

(2) If a person shall have been designated to serve on the same Panel by more than one Contracting State, or by one or more Contracting States and the Chairman, he shall be deemed to have been designated by the authority which first designated him or, if one such authority is the State of which he is a national, by that State.

(3)   All designations shall be notified to the Secretary-General and shall take effect from the date on which the notification is received.

Article 17

If the expenditure of the Centre cannot be met out of charges for the use of its facilities, or out of other receipts, the excess shall be borne by Contracting States which are members of the Bank in proportion to their respective subscriptions to the capital stock of the Bank, and by Contracting States which are not members of the Bank in accordance with rules adopted by the Administrative Council.

Article 18

The Centre shall have full international legal personality. The legal capacity of the Centre shall include the capacity:

(a)   to contract;

(b)   to acquire and dispose of movable and immovable property;

(c)   to institute legal proceedings.

Article 19

To enable the Centre to fulfil its functions, it shall enjoy in the territories of each Contracting State the immunities and privileges set forth in this Section.

Article 20

The Centre, its property and assets shall enjoy immunity from all legal process, except when the Centre waives this immunity.

Article 21

The Chairman, the members of the Administrative Council, persons acting as conciliators or arbitrators or members of a Committee appointed pursuant to paragraph (3) of Article 52, and the officers and employees of the Secretariat

(a)   shall enjoy immunity from legal process with respect to acts performed by them in the exercise of their functions, except when the Centre waives this immunity;

(b)   not being local nationals, shall enjoy the same immunities from immigration restrictions, alien registration requirements and national service obligations, the same facilities as regards exchange restrictions and the same treatment in respect of travelling facilities as are accorded by Contracting States to the representatives, officials and employees of comparable rank of other Contracting States.

Article 22

The provisions of Article 21 shall apply to persons appearing in proceedings under this Convention as parties, agents, counsel, advocates, witnesses or experts; provided, however, that sub-paragraph (b) thereof shall apply only in connection with their travel to and from, and their stay at, the place where the proceedings are held.

Article 23

(1) The archives of the Centre shall be inviolable, wherever they may be.

(2) With regard to its official communications, the Centre shall be accorded by each Contracting State treatment not less favorable than that accorded to other international organizations.

Article 24

(1) The Centre, its assets, property and income, and its operations and transactions authorized by this Convention shall be exempt from all taxation and customs duties. The Centre shall also be exempt from liability for the collection or payment of any taxes or customs duties.

(2) Except in the case of local nationals, no tax shall be levied on or in respect of expense allowances paid by the Centre to the Chairman or members of the Administrative Council, or on or in respect of salaries, expense allowances or other emoluments paid by the Centre to officials or employees of the Secretariat.

(3) No tax shall be levied on or in respect of fees or expense allowances received by persons acting as conciliators, or arbitrators, or members of a Committee appointed pursuant to paragraph (3) of Article 52, in proceedings under this Convention, if the sole jurisdictional basis for such tax is the location of the Centre or the place where such proceedings are conducted or the place where such fees or allowances are paid.

CHAPTER II
Jurisdiction of the Centre

Article 25

(1) The jurisdiction of the Centre shall extend to any legal dispute arising directly out of an investment, between a Contracting State (or any constituent subdivision or agency of a Contracting State designated to the Centre by that State) and a national of another Contracting State, which the parties to the dispute consent in writing to submit to the Centre. When the parties have given their consent, no party may withdraw its consent unilaterally.

(2) "National of another Contracting State" means:

(a) any natural person who had the nationality of a Contracting State other than the State party to the dispute on the date on which the parties consented to submit such dispute to conciliation or arbitration as well as on the date on which the request was registered pursuant to paragraph (3) of Article 28 or paragraph (3) of Article 36, but does not include any person who on either date also had the nationality of the Contracting State party to the dispute; and

(b) any juridical person which had the nationality of a Contracting State other than the State party to the dispute on the date on which the parties consented to submit such dispute to conciliation or arbitration and any juridical person which had the nationality of the Contracting State party to the dispute on that date and which, because of foreign control, the parties have agreed should be treated as a national of another Contracting State for the purposes of this Convention.

(3) Consent by a constituent subdivision or agency of a Contracting State shall require the approval of that State unless that State notifies the Centre that no such approval is required.

(4) Any Contracting State may, at the time of ratification, acceptance or approval of this Convention or at any time thereafter, notify the Centre of the class or classes of disputes which it would or would not consider submitting to the jurisdiction of the Centre. The Secretary-General shall forthwith transmit such notification to all Contracting States. Such notification shall not constitute the consent required by paragraph (1).

Article 26

Consent of the parties to arbitration under this Convention shall, unless otherwise stated, be deemed consent to such arbitration to the exclusion of any other remedy. A Contracting State may require the exhaustion of local administrative or judicial remedies as a condition of its consent to arbitration under this Convention.

Article 27

(1) No Contracting State shall give diplomatic protection, or bring an international claim, in respect of a dispute which one of its nationals and another Contracting State shall have consented to submit or shall have submitted to arbitration under this Convention, unless such other Contracting State shall have failed to abide by and comply with the award rendered in such dispute.

(2) Diplomatic protection, for the purposes of paragraph (1), shall not include informal diplomatic exchanges for the sole purpose of facilitating a settlement of the dispute.

CHAPTER III
Conciliation

Article 28

(1) Any Contracting State or any national of a Contracting State wishing to institute conciliation proceedings shall address a request to that effect in writing to the Secretary-General who shall send a copy of the request to the other party.

(2) The request shall contain information concerning the issues in dispute, the identity of the parties and their consent to conciliation in accordance with the rules of procedure for the institution of conciliation and arbitration proceedings.

(3) The Secretary-General shall register the request unless he finds, on the basis of the information contained in the request that the dispute is manifestly outside the jurisdiction of the Centre. He shall forthwith notify the parties of registration or refusal to register.

Article 29

(1) The Conciliation Commission (hereinafter called the Commission) shall be constituted as soon as possible after registration of a request pursuant to Article 28.

(2) (a) The Commission shall consist of a sole conciliator or any uneven number of conciliators appointed as the parties shall agree.

(b) Where the parties do not agree upon the number of conciliators and the method of their appointment, the Commission shall consist of three conciliators, one conciliator appointed by each party and the third, who shall be the president of the Commission, appointed by agreement of the parties.

Article 30

If the Commission shall not have been constituted within 90 days after notice of registration of the request has been dispatched by the Secretary-General in accordance with paragraph (3) of Article 28, or such other period as the parties may agree, the Chairman shall, at the request of either party and after consulting both parties as far as possible, appoint the conciliator or conciliators not yet appointed.

Article 31

(1)   Conciliators may be appointed from outside the Panel of Conciliators, except in the case of appointments by the Chairman pursuant to Article 30.

(2)   Conciliators appointed from outside the Panel of Conciliators shall possess the qualities stated in paragraph (1) of Article 14.

Article 32

(1)   The Commission shall be the judge of its own competence.

(2)   Any objection by a party to the dispute that that dispute is not within the jurisdiction of the Centre, or for other reasons is not within the competence of the Commission, shall be considered by the Commission which shall determine whether to deal with it as a preliminary question or to join it to the merits of the dispute.

Article 33

Any conciliation proceeding shall be conducted in accordance with the provisions of this Section and, except as the parties otherwise agree, in accordance with the Conciliation Rules in effect on the date on which the parties consented to conciliation. If any question of procedure arises which is not covered by this Section or the Conciliation Rules or any rules agreed by the parties, the Commission shall decide the question.

Article 34

(1)   It shall be the duty of the Commission to clarify the issues in dispute between the parties and to endeavor to bring about agreement between them upon mutually acceptable terms. To that end, the Commission may at any stage of the proceedings and from time to time recommend terms of settlement to the parties. The parties shall cooperate in good faith with the Commission in order to enable the Commission to carry out its functions, and shall give their most serious consideration to its recommendations.

(2)   If the parties reach agreement, the Commission shall draw up a report noting the issues in dispute and recording that the parties have reached agreement. If, at any stage of the proceedings, it appears to the Commission that there is no likelihood of agreement between the parties, it shall close the proceedings and shall draw up a report noting the submission of the dispute and recording the failure of the parties to reach agreement. If one party fails to appear or participate in the proceedings the Commission shall close the proceedings and shall draw up a report noting that party's failure to appear or participate.

Article 35

Except as the parties to the dispute shall otherwise agree, neither party to a conciliation proceeding shall be entitled in any other proceeding, whether before arbitrators or in a court of law or otherwise, to invoke or rely on any views expressed or statements or admissions or offers of settlement made by the other party in the conciliation proceedings, or the report or any recommendations made by the Commission.

CHAPTER IV
Arbitration

Article 36

(1) Any Contracting State or any national of a Contracting State wishing to institute arbitration proceedings shall address a request to that effect in writing to the Secretary-General who shall send a copy of the request to the other party.

(2) The request shall contain information concerning the issues in dispute, the identity of the parties and their consent to arbitration in accordance with the rules of procedure for the institution of conciliation and arbitration proceedings.

(3) The Secretary-General shall register the request unless he finds, on the basis of the information contained in the request that the dispute is manifestly outside the jurisdiction of the Centre. He shall forthwith notify the parties of registration or refusal to register.

Article 37

(1) The Arbitral Tribunal (hereinafter called the Tribunal) shall be constituted as soon as possible after registration of a request pursuant to Article 36.

(2) (a) The Tribunal shall consist of a sole arbitrator or any uneven number of arbitrators appointed as the parties shall agree.

(b) Where the parties do not agree upon the number of arbitrators and the method of their appointment, the Tribunal shall consist of three arbitrators, one arbitrator appointed by each party and the third, who shall be the president of the Tribunal, appointed by agreement of the parties.

Article 38

If the Tribunal shall not have been constituted within 90 days after notice of registration of the request has been dispatched by the Secretary-General in accordance with paragraph (3) of Article 36, or such other period as the parties may agree, the Chairman shall, at the request of either party and after consulting both parties as far as possible, appoint the arbitrator or arbitrators not yet appointed. Arbitrators appointed by the Chairman pursuant to this Article shall not be nationals of the Contracting State party to the dispute or of the Contracting State whose national is a party to the dispute.

Article 39

The majority of the arbitrators shall be nationals of States other than the Contracting State party to the dispute and the Contracting State whose national is a party to the dispute; provided, however, that the foregoing provisions of this Article shall not apply if the sole arbitrator or each individual member of the Tribunal has been appointed by agreement of the parties.

Article 40

(1)   Arbitrators may be appointed from outside the Panel of Arbitrators, except in the case of appointments by the Chairman pursuant to Article 38.

(2)   Arbitrators appointed from outside the Panel of Arbitrators shall possess the qualities stated in paragraph (1) of Article 14.

Article 41

(1)   The Tribunal shall be the judge of its own competence.

(2)   Any objection by a party to the dispute that that dispute is not within the jurisdiction of the Centre, or for other reasons is not within the competence of the Tribunal, shall be considered by the Tribunal which shall determine whether to deal with it as a preliminary question or to join it to the merits of the dispute.

Article 42

(1)   The Tribunal shall decide a dispute in accordance with such rules of law as may be agreed by the parties. In the absence of such agreement, the Tribunal shall apply the law of the Contracting State party to the dispute (including its rules on the conflict of laws) and such rules of international law as may be applicable.

(2)   The Tribunal may not bring in a finding of *non liquet* on the ground of silence or obscurity of the law.

(3)   The provisions of paragraphs (1) and (2) shall not prejudice the power of the Tribunal to decide a dispute *ex aequo et bono* if the parties so agree.

Article 43

Except as the parties otherwise agree, the Tribunal may, if it deems it necessary at any stage of the proceedings,

(a) call upon the parties to produce documents or other evidence, and

(b) visit the scene connected with the dispute, and conduct such inquiries there as it may deem appropriate.

Article 44

Any arbitration proceeding shall be conducted in accordance with the provisions of this Section and, except as the parties otherwise agree, in accordance with the Arbitration Rules in effect on the date on which the parties consented to arbitration. If any question of procedure arises which is not covered by this Section or the Arbitration Rules or any rules agreed by the parties, the Tribunal shall decide the question.

Article 45

(1) Failure of a party to appear or to present his case shall not be deemed an admission of the other party's assertions.

(2) If a party fails to appear or to present his case at any stage of the proceedings the other party may request the Tribunal to deal with the questions submitted to it and to render an award. Before rendering an award, the Tribunal shall notify, and grant a period of grace to, the party failing to appear or to present its case, unless it is satisfied that that party does not intend to do so.

Article 46

Except as the parties otherwise agree, the Tribunal shall, if requested by a party, determine any incidental or additional claims or counterclaims arising directly out of the subject-matter of the dispute provided that they are within the scope of the consent of the parties and are otherwise within the jurisdiction of the Centre.

Article 47

Except as the parties otherwise agree, the Tribunal may, if it considers that the circumstances so require, recommend any provisional measures which should be taken to preserve the respective rights of either party.

Article 48

(1) The Tribunal shall decide questions by a majority of the votes of all its members.

(2) The award of the Tribunal shall be in writing and shall be signed by the members of the Tribunal who voted for it.

(3) The award shall deal with every question submitted to the Tribunal, and shall state the reasons upon which it is based.

(4)   Any member of the Tribunal may attach his individual opinion to the award, whether he dissents from the majority or not, or a statement of his dissent.

(5)   The Centre shall not publish the award without the consent of the parties.

Article 49

(1)   The Secretary-General shall promptly dispatch certified copies of the award to the parties. The award shall be deemed to have been rendered on the date on which the certified copies were dispatched.

(2)   The Tribunal upon the request of a party made within 45 days after the date on which the award was rendered may after notice to the other party decide any question which it had omitted to decide in the award, and shall rectify any clerical, arithmetical or similar error in the award. Its decision shall become part of the award and shall be notified to the parties in the same manner as the award. The periods of time provided for under paragraph (2) of Article 51 and paragraph (2) of Article 52 shall run from the date on which the decision was rendered.

Article 50

(1)   If any dispute shall arise between the parties as to the meaning or scope of an award, either party may request interpretation of the award by an application in writing addressed to the Secretary-General.

(2)   The request shall, if possible, be submitted to the Tribunal which rendered the award. If this shall not be possible, a new Tribunal shall be constituted in accordance with Section 2 of this Chapter. The Tribunal may, if it considers that the circumstances so require, stay enforcement of the award pending its decision.

Article 51

(1)   Either party may request revision of the award by an application in writing addressed to the Secretary-General on the ground of discovery of some fact of such a nature as decisively to affect the award, provided that when the award was rendered that fact was unknown to the Tribunal and to the applicant and that the applicant's ignorance of that fact was not due to negligence.

(2)   The application shall be made within 90 days after the discovery of such fact and in any event within three years after the date on which the award was rendered.

(3)   The request shall, if possible, be submitted to the Tribunal which rendered the award. If this shall not be possible, a new

Tribunal shall be constituted in accordance with Section 2 of this Chapter.

(4) The Tribunal may, if it considers that the circumstances so require, stay enforcement of the award pending its decision. If the applicant requests a stay of enforcement of the award in his application, enforcement shall be stayed provisionally until the Tribunal rules on such request.

Article 52

(1) Either party may request annulment of the award by an application in writing addressed to the Secretary-General on one or more of the following grounds:

(a) that the Tribunal was not properly constituted;

(b) that the Tribunal has manifestly exceeded its powers;

(c) that there was corruption on the part of a member of the Tribunal;

(d) that there has been a serious departure from a fundamental rule of procedure; or

(e) that the award has failed to state the reasons on which it is based.

(2) The application shall be made within 120 days after the date on which the award was rendered except that when annulment is requested on the ground of corruption such application shall be made within 120 days after discovery of the corruption and in any event within three years after the date on which the award was rendered.

(3) On receipt of the request the Chairman shall forthwith appoint from the Panel of Arbitrators an *ad hoc* Committee of three persons. None of the members of the Committee shall have been a member of the Tribunal which rendered the award, shall be of the same nationality as any such member, shall be a national of the State party to the dispute or of the State whose national is a party to the dispute, shall have been designated to the Panel of Arbitrators by either of those States, or shall have acted as a conciliator in the same dispute. The Committee shall have the authority to annul the award or any part thereof on any of the grounds set forth in paragraph (1).

(4) The provisions of Articles 41–45, 48, 49, 53 and 54, and of Chapters VI and VII shall apply *mutatis mutandis* to proceedings before the Committee.

(5) The Committee may, if it considers that the circumstances so require, stay enforcement of the award pending its decision. If the

applicant requests a stay of enforcement of the award in his application, enforcement shall be stayed provisionally until the Committee rules on such request.

(6)   If the award is annulled the dispute shall, at the request of either party, be submitted to a new Tribunal constituted in accordance with Section 2 of this Chapter.

Article 53

(1)   The award shall be binding on the parties and shall not be subject to any appeal or to any other remedy except those provided for in this Convention. Each party shall abide by and comply with the terms of the award except to the extent that enforcement shall have been stayed pursuant to the relevant provisions of this Convention.

(2)   For the purposes of this Section, "award" shall include any decision interpreting, revising or annulling such award pursuant to Articles 50, 51 or 52.

Article 54

(1)   Each Contracting State shall recognize an award rendered pursuant to this Convention as binding and enforce the pecuniary obligations imposed by that award within its territories as if it were a final judgment of a court in that State. A Contracting State with a federal constitution may enforce such an award in or through its federal courts and may provide that such courts shall treat the award as if it were a final judgment of the courts of a constituent state.

(2)   A party seeking recognition or enforcement in the territories of a Contracting State shall furnish to a competent court or other authority which such State shall have designated for this purpose a copy of the award certified by the Secretary-General. Each Contracting State shall notify the Secretary-General of the designation of the competent court or other authority for this purpose and of any subsequent change in such designation.

(3)   Execution of the award shall be governed by the laws concerning the execution of judgments in force in the State in whose territories such execution is sought.

Article 55

Nothing in Article 54 shall be construed as derogating from the law in force in any Contracting State relating to immunity of that State or of any foreign State from execution.

CHAPTER V
Replacement and Disqualification of Conciliators and Arbitrators

Article 56

(1) After a Commission or a Tribunal has been constituted and proceedings have begun, its composition shall remain unchanged; provided, however, that if a conciliator or an arbitrator should die, become incapacitated, or resign, the resulting vacancy shall be filled in accordance with the provisions of Section 2 of Chapter III or Section 2 of Chapter IV.

(2) A member of a Commission or Tribunal shall continue to serve in that capacity notwithstanding that he shall have ceased to be a member of the Panel.

(3) If a conciliator or arbitrator appointed by a party shall have resigned without the consent of the Commission or Tribunal of which he was a member, the Chairman shall appoint a person from the appropriate Panel to fill the resulting vacancy.

Article 57

A party may propose to a Commission or Tribunal the disqualification of any of its members on account of any fact indicating a manifest lack of the qualities required by paragraph (1) of Article 14. A party to arbitration proceedings may, in addition, propose the disqualification of an arbitrator on the ground that he was ineligible for appointment to the Tribunal under Section 2 of Chapter IV.

Article 58

The decision on any proposal to disqualify a conciliator or arbitrator shall be taken by the other members of the Commission or Tribunal as the case may be, provided that where those members are equally divided, or in the case of a proposal to disqualify a sole conciliator or arbitrator, or a majority of the conciliators or arbitrators, the Chairman shall take that decision. If it is decided that the proposal is well-founded the conciliator or arbitrator to whom the decision relates shall be replaced in accordance with the provisions of Section 2 of Chapter III or Section 2 of Chapter IV.

CHAPTER VI
Cost of Proceedings

Article 59

The charges payable by the parties for the use of the facilities of the Centre shall be determined by the Secretary-General in accordance with the regulations adopted by the Administrative Council.

Article 60

(1)   Each Commission and each Tribunal shall determine the fees and expenses of its members within limits established from time to time by the Administrative Council and after consultation with the Secretary-General.

(2)   Nothing in paragraph (1) of this Article shall preclude the parties from agreeing in advance with the Commission or Tribunal concerned upon the fees and expenses of its members.

Article 61

(1)   In the case of conciliation proceedings the fees and expenses of members of the Commission as well as the charges for the use of the facilities of the Centre, shall be borne equally by the parties. Each party shall bear any other expenses it incurs in connection with the proceedings.

(2)   In the case of arbitration proceedings the Tribunal shall, except as the parties otherwise agree, assess the expenses incurred by the parties in connection with the proceedings, and shall decide how and by paid. Such decision shall form part of the award.

CHAPTER VII
Place of Proceedings

Article 62

Conciliation and arbitration proceedings shall be held at the seat of the Centre except as hereinafter provided.

Article 63

Conciliation and arbitration proceedings may be held, if the parties so agree,

(a)   at the seat of the Permanent Court of Arbitration or of any other appropriate institution, whether private or public, with which the Centre may make arrangements for that purpose; or

(b)   at any other place approved by the Commission or Tribunal after consultation with the Secretary-General.

CHAPTER VIII
Disputes between Contracting States

Article 64

Any dispute arising between Contracting States concerning the interpretation or application of this Convention which is not settled by negotiation shall be referred to the International Court of Justice by the application of any party to such dispute, unless the States concerned agree to another method of settlement.

CHAPTER IX
Amendment
Article 65

Any Contracting State may propose amendment of this Convention. The text of a proposed amendment shall be communicated to the Secretary-General not less than 90 days prior to the meeting of the Administrative Council at which such amendment is to be considered and shall forthwith be transmitted by him to all the members of the Administrative Council.

Article 66

(1)   If the Administrative Council shall so decide by a majority of two-thirds of its members, the proposed amendment shall be circulated to all Contracting States for ratification, acceptance or approval. Each amendment shall enter into force 30 days after dispatch by the depositary of this Convention of a notification to Contracting States that all Contracting States have ratified, accepted or approved the amendment.

(2)   No amendment shall affect the rights and obligations under this Convention of any Contracting State or of any of its constituent subdivisions or agencies, or of any national of such State arising out of consent to the jurisdiction of the Centre given before the date of entry into force of the amendment.

CHAPTER X
Final Provisions
Article 67

This Convention shall be open for signature on behalf of States members of the Bank. It shall also be open for signature on behalf of any other State which is a party to the Statute of the International Court of Justice and which the Administrative Council, by a vote of two-thirds of its members, shall have invited to sign the Convention.

Chapter 8

NAFTA 1994 AND USMCA 2020 FOREIGN INVESTMENT LAW AND ARBITRATIONS

The North American Free Trade Agreement of 1994 (NAFTA 1994) broke new ground on foreign investment law and dispute settlement. Drawing from bilateral investment treaty precedents (BITs, see Chapter 7), NAFTA expanded the scope of foreign investor rights and the use of arbitration to resolve investor-state disputes. It is presented here as a richly revealing and controversial case study, one which had a substantial impact on subsequent BITs and free trade agreements covering investment.

For a detailed review of NAFTA 1994 and USMCA 2020, see my Concise Hornbook on *Free Trade Agreements*.

§ 8.1   NAFTA and Mexican Foreign Investment Law

NAFTA placed special emphasis on relaxation of Mexico's foreign investment controls. As outlined in Chapter 6, these controls find their roots in the revolutionary 1917 Mexican Constitution and the nationalization of foreign oil and gas interests in 1937, as well as the widespread adoption of foreign investment control commissions throughout Latin America during the 1970s.

Under Mexican regulation of foreign investment since the 1940s, some industries were reserved for state ownership while others could only be owned by Mexicans. Foreigners were ordinarily allowed to invest in less sensitive industries, but often subject to mandatory joint venture requirements with majority Mexican ownership and "Calvo Clause" rules limiting foreign investor dispute remedies to those available under Mexican law.

In 1973, Mexico promulgated an Investment Law that mandated more use of joint ventures if approved by the National Foreign Investment Commission. This Law was the most restrictive of its kind in Mexican history. By the 1980s, after years of mismanagement and corruption while awash in petroleum dollars, Mexico had a massive national debt problem. Foreign investment regulations issued by Presidential decree in 1989 shifted significantly towards allowance of wholly owned subsidiaries. However, these regulations conflicted with the 1973 Investment Law. These uncertainties were finally resolved in 1993 as a direct consequence of NAFTA 1994 when Mexico adopted a new Law on Foreign Investment.

The 1993 Law is much more permissive of foreign investment without prior approval of by the Mexican Investment Commission. Although adopted on the eve of NAFTA, the 1993 Law opens many of the same doors to all investors, not just those from NAFTA. Investment opportunities based upon the NAFTA agreement that are not generally available include the suspension of many performance requirements, the phased removal of market share caps on financial services, and reduced thresholds triggering Investment Commission review. In addition, NAFTA investors were not subject to Mexico's mandatory joint venture rule, nor its "Calvo Clause" remedies. Removal of these restrictions represented a major concession on the part of Mexico.

Acquisitions or sales of existing Mexican companies were generally subject to Commission review if exceeding $25 million U.S. This threshold increased to $150 million for NAFTA 1994 investors in 2003. For NAFTA investors, no permission from the National Commission was required to invest on a wholly owned basis or acquire or sell Mexican companies whose values fell below this threshold.

§ 8.2   NAFTA Foreign Investment Coverage

In an unusual provision, Article 1112 subordinated all of Chapter 11 on investment to the rest of the NAFTA agreement. In other words, if there were inconsistencies between Chapter 11 and other parts of the NAFTA agreement, those other parts are supreme. That said, NAFTA provided investors and their investments with important rights.

Canadian, Mexican and United States citizens, permanently resident aliens, and other designated persons were eligible to benefit from NAFTA's investment rules. In addition, most private and public, profit and nonprofit businesses "constituted or organized" under Canadian, Mexican or United States law also qualified. This coverage specifically included businesses operating as corporations, partnerships, trusts, sole proprietorships, joint ventures, and business associations.

Furthermore, it was not necessary for such businesses to be owned or controlled by Canadian, Mexican or U.S. nationals or enterprises. As with services, this meant that businesses owned by anyone which were "constituted or organized" in Mexico, Canada or the USA benefitted from the agreement *provided* they carried on substantial business activities in North America. *Asians, Europeans, and Latin Americans (for example) could invest in North America and benefit from NAFTA investment law and remedies.* See the *Corn Syrup Sweeteners* dispute in Section 8.10.

Exceptions were made for NAFTA businesses owned or controlled by third parties from countries lacking diplomatic relations with or economically embargoed by Canada, Mexico, or the United States.

Beneficiaries of NAFTA 1994 rights enjoyed a broad definition of "investment." This definition includes most stocks, bonds, loans, and income, profit, or asset interests. Real estate, tangible or intangible (intellectual) business property, turnkey or construction contracts, concessions, and licensing and franchising contracts are also generally included.

However, under Annex III, each member state reserved certain economic activities to its state or domestic investors. Mexico has done so under its 1993 Foreign Investment Law. For purposes of Chapter 11, investment was defined to exclude claims to money arising solely from commercial contracts for the sale of goods or services, or trade financing, and claims for money that do not involve the interests noted above.

§ 8.3   NAFTA Foreign Investor Rights

Minimum Standard of Treatment

The NAFTA agreement established a so-called "minimum standard of treatment" for NAFTA investors and investments. *This minimum was "treatment in accordance with international law," including "fair and equitable treatment and full protection and security" (Article 1105).* For example, if losses occurred due to armed conflict or civil strife, NAFTA investors and investments had to be accorded nondiscriminatory treatment in response.

An official 2001 NAFTA interpretative ruling indicates that Article 1105 embraces treatment in accordance with *"customary"* international law, a ruling intended to limit the scope of protection afforded to foreign investors. Subsequent NAFTA arbitral bodies consequently limited claims of unfair and inequitable treatment to state conduct that is arbitrary, grossly unfair, unjust, or idiosyncratic, discriminatory, or lacking in due process offending judicial or administrative propriety.

Refinements of the customary international law standard in arbitral decisions under NAFTA Chapter 11 refer to "sufficiently egregious and shocking" state acts that amount to gross denials of justice, manifest arbitrariness, blatant unfairness, a complete lack of due process, evident discrimination, or a manifest lack of reasons. In addition, limiting definitions of "fair and equitable treatment" and "full protection and security" were established in subsequent U.S. free trade agreements. See Chapter 7.

National and Most-Favored Nation Treatment

Beyond this minimum, NAFTA investors and their investments were entitled to the better of national or most-favored-nation treatment from federal governments. Such treatment rights extended to establishing, acquiring, expanding, managing, conducting, operating, and selling or disposing of investments. From state or provincial governments, NAFTA investors and their investments were entitled to receive the most-favored treatment those governments grant their own investors and investments.

Along these lines, United Parcel Service found Mexico lacking when it was initially limited to using smaller vans than Mexican competitors. UPS persuaded the United States to lodge a complaint under Chapter 20, which led to intergovernmental consultations followed by NAFTA Commission mediation. These efforts lasted many months but eventually UPS got permission to use larger vans.

Mandatory Joint Ventures and Managers

Article 1102 of NAFTA prohibited requiring minimum levels of equity holdings by nationals of the host government. Hence the historic bias in Mexican law towards mandatory joint ventures was overcome by NAFTA. No investor could be forced on grounds of nationality to sell or dispose of a qualified investment.

Mandatory appointment of senior managers based on nationality was also contrary to NAFTA. However, it was permissible to require boards of directors and corporate committees with majorities from one nationality or residence, provided this did not materially impair the investor's ability to exercise control. Canadian law often makes such stipulations.

Residency requirements were generally authorized if there was no impairment of the treaty rights of NAFTA investors.

Regulatory Rules

Article 1106 of NAFTA prohibited various investment performance obligations, including tax-related measures, in a scope that surpasses the WTO Agreement on Trade-Related Investment Measures (TRIMs, see Chapter 1). Requirements relating to exports, domestic content, domestic purchases, trade balancing of foreign exchange inflows or earnings, import/export ratios, technology transfers, and regional or global sales exclusivity ("product mandates") were broadly prohibited. All other types of investment-related performance requirements, such as employment and research and development obligations, were not prohibited and therefore presumably lawful.

Article 1106.3 of NAFTA further prohibited conditioning the receipt or continued receipt of "an advantage" (*e.g.*, a government subsidy or tax benefit) on compliance with requirements relating to domestic content, domestic purchases, domestic sales restraints, or trade balancing. But "advantages" could be given when the requirements concerned production location, provision of services, training or employing workers, constructing, or expanding facilities, or carrying out research and development locally.

By way of exception, domestic content or purchase requirements *and* advantages could be linked to investor compliance with:

> (1) Laws and regulations that are consistent with NAFTA;

> (2) Laws necessary to protect human, animal or plant life or health; or

(3) Laws needed to conserve living or non-living exhaustible natural resources.

However, such requirements could not be applied arbitrarily or unjustifiably, and could not constitute a disguised restraint on trade or investment.

Monetary Transfers

All monetary transfers relating to NAFTA investments were to be allowed "freely and without delay." (Article 1109) Such transfers had to be possible in a "freely usable currency" at the market rate of exchange prevailing in spot transactions on the transfer date. For these purposes, monetary transfers specifically included profits, dividends, interest, capital gains, royalties, management, technical assistance, and other fees, returns in kind, and funds derived from the investment. Sale or liquidation proceeds, contract payments, compensatory payments for expropriation and NAFTA dispute settlement payments were also encompassed.

Requiring investment-related monetary transfers or penalizing them was prohibited. However, such transfers could be controlled in an equitable, nondiscriminatory, and good faith application of bankruptcy, insolvency, creditors' rights, securities, criminal, currency reporting and satisfaction of judgment laws. Tax withholding was *not* a justifiable basis for restricting monetary transfers under NAFTA. However, special restraints could arise in connection with balance of payments problems and taxation laws.

§ 8.4   Expropriation

Article 1110 of NAFTA generally prohibited direct or indirect nationalization or expropriation of NAFTA investments. Measures *"tantamount to"* nationalization or expropriation, such as creeping expropriation or confiscatory taxation, were also prohibited.

Expropriation, nationalization, or tantamount measures could occur for public purposes on a nondiscriminatory basis in accordance with due process of law and NAFTA's "minimum level of treatment" (above). Post-NAFTA U.S. free trade agreements expressly limited the possibility of succeeding with "indirect" regulatory taking expropriation claims (see below).

Any authorized expropriation had to result in payment of compensation without delay. The amount of payment had to be equivalent to the fair market value of the investment immediately prior to expropriation. In valuing the investment, going concern value, asset value (including declared tax values of tangible property) and other appropriate factors had to be considered.

Payment had to be made in a manner that is fully realizable, such as in a "G7" currency (U.S. dollars, Canadian dollars, EUROS, British pounds sterling, Japanese yen). Interest at a commercially reasonable rate must also be included. If payment was made in Mexican pesos, this amount must be calculated as of the expropriation date in a G7 currency plus interest.

Certain governmental acts were not treated as expropriations. For example, NAFTA specified that nondiscriminatory measures of general application that impose costs on defaulting debtors are not tantamount to expropriation of a bond or loan *solely* for that reason. Compulsory licensing of intellectual property rights was not an expropriation. Revocation, limitation, or creation of such rights as allowed by Chapter 17 of NAFTA was also deemed not an expropriation.

In one Chapter 11 proceeding, lawful, court-approved annulment of a Mexican concession contract with a U.S. firm was determined by NAFTA arbitrators not to amount to an act of expropriation. No denial of justice in the Mexican courts was alleged. (*Azinian v. Mexico*, 1999).

The NAFTA provisions embodied an historic change in Mexico's position on expropriation law. Without explicitly saying so, Mexico essentially embraced the U.S. position that under "international law" expropriation of foreign investments requires "prompt, adequate and effective" compensation.

Mexico had specifically rejected this standard in negotiating a settlement of its oil and gas (and land) expropriations in the 1930s. Down through the years Mexico adamantly clung to its view that compensation would only be paid according to Mexican law. For investors protected under NAFTA (which were not just Canadian and U.S. investors), Chapter 11 represented the dawn of a new era.

Chapter 11 is reproduced at the end of this chapter.

§ 8.5   Exceptions and Reservations, the Environment

Annexes I–IV of NAFTA reveal a host of investment-related reservations and exceptions. Many pre-existing, non-conforming regulations were grandfathered though most (not including basic telecommunications, social services, and maritime services) were subject to a standstill agreement intended to avoid relapses into greater protection. In contrast, regulations promoting investment "sensitive to environmental concerns" were expressly authorized. Mexico's tradition of assessing the environmental impact of foreign investments therefore continued.

There was also a formal recognition that creating exceptions to environmental laws to encourage NAFTA investors to establish, acquire, expand, or retain their investments is inappropriate. However, NAFTA's Chapter 20 dispute settlement mechanism could not be invoked concerning this "commitment." Only intergovernmental consultations were mandatory.

Other investment related exceptions concerned government procurement, subsidies, export promotion, foreign aid, and preferential trade arrangements. These exceptions applied mostly to the rules on nondiscriminatory treatment and performance requirements.

Most general exceptions to NAFTA, such as for Canadian cultural industries, also applied to its investment rules. The general national security exception, for example, allowed the United States to block the acquisition of U.S. companies by foreigners (including Canadians and Mexicans) under CFIUS regulations (see Chapter 6).

§ 8.6   Motor Vehicles Under NAFTA

Canada and the United States had a long tradition of free automotive trade and investment under their 1965 Auto Pact and the Canada-U.S. FTA of 1989. NAFTA made only a few changes to this relationship. The more demanding NAFTA rules of origin were substituted, notably the 62.5 percent regional value content requirement for passenger autos and light trucks (60 percent for other vehicles and parts). These content rules took full effect in 2002 and were calculated on a net cost basis traced back through suppliers.

NAFTA continued the preferential trade terms of the Canada-U.S. Auto Pact, but only for Auto Pact beneficiaries. Toyota and Honda Canada were not such beneficiaries but had been receiving duty drawback and production-based customs duty remissions on auto parts which effectively matched Auto Pact benefits. When NAFTA required the elimination of these duty drawback and remission programs at the end of 1995, Honda and Toyota faced a 2.5 percent tariff on auto parts imported for assembly in Canada. The Canadian government, shortly after Honda and Toyota announced plans for expanded assembly plants, removed the 2.5 percent tariff in an effort at maintaining the costs of assembly in Canada.

Automotive investment and trade had been controlled by the Mexican federal government for many years. Prior to NAFTA, Mexico imposed tariffs as high as 20% on automobile imports and required up to 80% local content for producers based in Mexico. Not a lot of cars or car parts entered Mexico under these restrictive rules, which also discouraged foreign investment to produce automobiles in Mexico.

The 1989 presidential Decree for Development and Modernization of the Automotive Industry and related 1990 implementing regulations were in place as NAFTA was negotiated. Mexico kept this Decree in force until 2003. Mexico's refusal to allow importation of used vehicles remained effective until 2009. Thereafter used auto imports (known in Mexico as "chocolates" when still bearing U.S. plates) were phased in over ten years based on the age of the vehicle.

Pre-NAFTA auto manufacturers in Mexico included Ford, General Motors, Chrysler, Volkswagen, and Nissan. These producers were gradually relieved of "trade balancing" export obligations as a precondition to importing but retained their exclusive import rights until 2003. Mexico also gradually reduced the percentage of Mexican value that auto manufacturers must add to vehicles. Since 2003, there has been no Mexican value-added requirement. As a result, fewer auto parts needed to be purchased from Mexican "national suppliers."

In addition, auto components manufactured in Mexican maquiladoras were treated as Mexican in origin and United States and Canadian investors could wholly own Mexican auto parts suppliers. All limits on the importation of autos tied to sales volumes in Mexico were removed.

Other Mexican automotive trade and investment restraints were altered by NAFTA. The Auto Transportation Decree of 1989 regulating the production and importation of buses and trucks has been repealed. Since 1999 Mexico no longer requires its manufacturers to limit imports to 50 percent of Mexican production. Non-manufacturers have been able to import more buses and trucks under quotas auctioned by the Mexican government. These quotas corresponded to progressively higher percentages of Mexican production. Since 1999 they too disappeared.

Mexico and the United States had different auto tariff obligations. Mexico reduced its passenger automobile tariffs by 50 percent in 1994 and phased out the remainder by 2003. On light trucks, it cut tariffs immediately by 50 percent, phasing out the remainder by 1998. For all other vehicles, Mexico phased out its tariffs by 2003.

In contrast, the United States immediately removed all tariffs on Mexican passenger automobiles. The United States also phased out tariffs on Mexican light trucks. All other United States tariffs on motor vehicles from Mexico were phased out after 2003. On auto parts, Mexico and the U.S. removed certain tariffs in 1994. They phased out most others over five years and eliminated all tariffs on auto parts after 2003.

The United States minimum corporate fuel average economy rules (CAFE rules) provide a good example of United States regulations with trade restraining potential. No alteration in these standards was required by NAFTA. However, the United States agreed to permit inclusion of Mexican auto parts and vehicles under its CAFE regulations. Canadian parts and autos with at least 75 percent of their value added in Canada were classified as domestic and included under CAFE. Mexican goods have been equally treated since 2004.

Motor vehicles and their components were by far the most significant trade sector under NAFTA. This significance helps explain the level of detail in the NAFTA agreement concerning motor vehicles, especially their rules of origin. Despite Mexico's financial crisis and ensuing recession, U.S. and Canadian exports of motor vehicles exploded. Shipments of completed vehicles to Mexico increased over 500 percent in the first three years of NAFTA.

New investment in auto production facilities after 1994 significantly increased south of the border. Toyota, Audi, Daimler-Benz, Hyundai, Kia, BMW, and Honda commenced production in Mexico, and pre-NAFTA auto plants (above) expanded. Investment in auto parts production in Mexico skyrocketed.

A large share of the production of auto parts is being done by Mexican industrial conglomerates. Supply chains for auto production were greatly integrated, with parts often moving back and forth repeatedly. Auto exports from Mexico to destinations other than Canada and the United States also rose notably, so much so that in 2012 Mexico agreed to voluntarily limit auto exports to Brazil.

Overall, the integration of the auto parts and production markets under NAFTA enhanced the ability of North America to compete with Asian and European producers. For example, BMW in South Carolina and Mercedes-Benz in Alabama have risen to the top of the U.S. list of auto exporters. Both firms are also producing in China for its massive and growing internal market. Despite shipping costs to North America, rising Chinese labor costs and Trump tariffs, Ford, BMW, Tesla, and others expect to join GM (Buick) in exporting cars made in China to the USA.

§ 8.7   NAFTA Trader and Investor Visas

NAFTA traders and investors enjoyed preferential temporary entry visas. "Traders" were defined as persons employed to carry on substantial trade in goods or services principally between NAFTA countries. "Investors" were defined person employed to establish, develop, administer, or provide advice or key technical services to the operation of an investment to which a substantial amount of capital has been or is in the process of being committed. For both categories, preferential NAFTA treatment was available only if the person concerned acted in a capacity that was supervisory, executive, or involved essential skills.

In practice, these provisions chiefly benefited Canadians and Mexicans entering the United States. NAFTA gave treaty trader and investor status to Mexicans for the first time.

Standard public safety and national security exceptions applied to NAFTA traders and investors. Pre-entry labor certification screening was not necessary, and there were no numerical limits to these temporary entry visas (E-1 and E-2 visas in the United States). However, by special provision, such visas could be denied if settlement of a current labor dispute or employment of persons involved in the dispute would be adversely affected.

Intra-Company Transferees

NAFTA further benefitted executives, managers, or employees with specialized knowledge rendering services to their employer, its subsidiary or affiliate in another NAFTA country. Such persons could obtain special "intra-company transferee" temporary entry visas. Public safety, national security and labor dispute reviews applied.

There were no pre-entry labor certification screens, nor any numerical limits to intra-company transferee visas. In the United States these are known as L-1 visas. The United States, but not Canada and Mexico, required proof of employment for the same or a related employer during one of the three prior years.

§ 8.8   Arbitration of Foreign Investor-Host State Disputes Under NAFTA

NAFTA created a highly innovative and increasingly controversial investment dispute settlement system. This system provided a way for foreign investors to challenge governmental and state enterprise acts and recover damages for violation of rights established in Chapter 11. Remarkably, investors could not only assert claims as individuals, but also on behalf of NAFTA enterprises they own or control directly or indirectly (Article 1117). This authorization avoids one of international law's most famous problems. . . "standing to sue" when the investor's only loss or damage is injury to its investment abroad.

Chapter 20 NAFTA dispute settlement did not apply to "investor-state disputes." Such disputes were instead subject to binding arbitration, another major concession on the part of Mexico which has always adhered to the "Calvo Doctrine." That doctrine (widely followed in Latin America) requires foreign investors to forego protection by their home governments, be treated as Mexican nationals, and pursue legal remedies exclusively in Mexico. See Article 27 of the Mexican Constitution.

Individual investors claiming that a government breached NAFTA investment or state enterprise obligations, or that one of its monopolies had done so, commenced the dispute resolution process. All claims were filed against the federal government even when it is state, provincial, or local government action that was being challenged. This d placed Canada, Mexico, and the United States in the awkward position of defending sub-central governmental acts. See the *Metalclad* and *Loewen* disputes in Section 8.10.

The investor had to allege that the breach of NAFTA caused loss or damage. Such claims had to be asserted no later than three years after the date when knowledge of the alleged breach and knowledge of the loss or damage was first acquired or should have been first acquired. However, decisions by the Canadian or Mexican foreign investment control commissions, national security actions, and Canadian cultural industry reservations could not be the basis for such a claim.

Moreover, a host of reservations and exceptions contained in Chapter 11B deny access to NAFTA's investor-state arbitration remedy. Even so, as outlined below, the number of claims was substantial, and some claims produced unexpected results. The process itself, though quite transparent, fell under dispute.

Before submitting a claim to arbitration, individual investors had to give 90 days' advance notice to the host country. Such notice included an explanation of the issues, their factual basis and remedies sought. Claimants also consented in writing to arbitrate under the procedures established in the NAFTA agreement. They had to *waive* in writing their rights to initiate or continue any other damages proceedings.

Individual investors did not need to waive their rights to injunctive, declaratory, or other extraordinary relief (not involving damages). Such remedies could not be awarded through NAFTA arbitration of investor-state disputes.

§ 8.9   NAFTA Arbitration Procedures, Appeals and Remedies

The NAFTA nations consented unconditionally in advance to the submission of investor claims to arbitration under NAFTA procedures. Furthermore, they agreed not to assert insurance payments or other investor indemnification rights as a defense, counterclaim, right of setoff or otherwise. *Arbitration of investor-state disputes continues in a more limited way as between Mexico and the United States under the USMCA 2020 (discussed below in Section 8.13). It is eliminated as between the United States and Canada.*

The investor submitting a claim to arbitration against a NAFTA state ordinarily could elect between the following arbitration rules:

(1)   The ICSID Convention (see Chapter 7) if both member states adhere. (At present the United States and Canada have ratified ICSID);

(2)   The Additional Facility Rules of ICSID provided one member state adheres to the ICSID Convention; or

(3)   The U.N.-derived UNCITRAL Arbitration Rules.

Until Canada's ratification of ICSID in 2013, joining the United States but not Mexico, opened the door to investor-state claims under ICSID or the UNCITRAL Rules. The key difference between them is that ICSID has its own annulment procedures, which exclude use of the New York Convention on Enforcement of Arbitral Awards.

NAFTA investor-state tribunals had three panelists. The investor and the state each chose one arbitrator. If possible, the third presiding panelist was chosen by agreement. The ICSID Secretary-General selected the presiding arbitrator if agreement was not reached within 90 days. That person was chosen from a consensus roster of acceptable names but could not be a national from either side of the dispute.

Investor-state tribunals had to decide the dispute in accordance with the NAFTA agreement and "applicable rules of international law." The responding state could raise defenses based upon reservations or exceptions contained in Annexes I–IV to the NAFTA agreement. In such instances, the NAFTA Commission (not the arbitration panel) generally issued a binding ruling on the validity of such a defense. Defenses based upon permissible regulation of monetary transfers by financial institutions were generally decided by the NAFTA Financial Services Committee.

By agreement of the parties, the investor-state arbitration tribunal could obtain expert reports on factual issues concerning environmental, health, safety, or other scientific matters. The tribunal could also order temporary relief measures to preserve rights or the full effectiveness of its jurisdiction. It could, for example, order the preservation of evidence. The tribunal could not, however, order attachment or enjoin governmental regulations that were being challenged.

Damages Awards

NAFTA investor-state tribunals were authorized to award investors or NAFTA enterprises actual *damages* and interest, or restitution of property, or both. Damages were awarded against and paid by Canada and Mexico, but not the United States. See *Metalclad* and *S.D. Myers* in Section 8.10.

If the award was to an enterprise, any person could *also* pursue relief under "applicable domestic law." If restitution was ordered, the responsible member state could provide monetary damages and interest instead. NAFTA tribunals could apportion legal fees between the parties at their discretion. Such fees routinely ran into hundreds of thousands, if not millions, of dollars. The costs of administering Chapter 11 tribunals, including generous fees for the arbitrators, often exceeded $500,000. The losing party was typically required to pay these costs.

Appeals and Enforcement

The award of the tribunal was binding on the parties, but subject to revision or annulment in the courts of the arbitration's *situs*. See *Metalclad* and *S.D. Myers* in Section 8.10. Absent agreement, the arbitrators determined *situs*. Professor Brower and others have argued that a standing appellate body not unlike that of the WTO or proposed by the EU would provide greater legitimacy and uniformity to Chapter 11 arbitrations.

Awards were specifically not "precedent" in future NAFTA arbitrations (Article 1136), yet routinely cited and argued in Chapter 11 proceedings and decisions. NAFTA investor-state arbitration awards were supposed to be honored. If this did not occur, the investor could seek enforcement of the award. NAFTA nations agreed to provide the means for such enforcement.

The NAFTA investor-state dispute settlement system met the various requirements of the ICSID Convention, its Additional Facility Rules, the New York Convention on Recognition and Enforcement of Foreign Arbitral Awards (1958), and the Inter-American Convention on International Commercial Arbitration (1975).

If it became necessary to judicially enforce an investor-state arbitration award, the New York Convention provided a likely recourse as all three nations adhere to it. However, U.S. courts held the grounds for denying enforcement of NAFTA awards under the New York Convention limited strictly to its provisions. The longstanding U.S. doctrine of denying enforcement when arbitrators "manifestly disregard the law", a doctrine not incorporated in the New York Convention, was not applicable in a NAFTA award enforcement proceeding.

If there was no compliance with the award and enforcement proceedings fail, the investor's government could as a last recourse commence intergovernmental dispute settlement under Chapter 20 of NAFTA. This panel ruled on whether noncompliance inconsistent with the NAFTA agreement occurred and could recommend compliance. If compliance still did not follow, benefits granted under NAFTA to the noncomplying nation could be suspended.

§ 8.10 Arbitrated Foreign Investor Claims Against NAFTA Host States

Foreign investors did not hesitate to invoke the innovative investor-state arbitration procedures authorized under Section B of Chapter 11 of NAFTA. After 2001, in an official Interpretation, Chapter 11 was construed as not imposing a general duty of confidentiality. The NAFTA governments therefore released all documents submitted to or issued by Chapter 11 arbitration tribunals. A particularly good collection of these materials can be found at http://www.naftaclaims.com. Moreover, since late 2003, open Chapter 11 hearings became the rule, as did permissive procedures for non-party submissions (amicus curiae).

Many investors alleged state action that was "tantamount to expropriation." This was a claim that Article 1110 authorized and one which could be construed to fit many fact patterns. National treatment and the NAFTA minimum standard of treatment (fair and equitable treatment, see above) were also commonly disputed. Some examples of these disputes follow:

Metalclad v. Mexico

A prominent dispute involved Metalclad Corp. of California, which had acquired a hazardous waste site operated by a Mexican company in Guadalcazar, San Luis Potosi subject to various federal approvals, all of which were obtained. State and local opposition to opening the site after an expensive cleanup resulted in the denial of a building permit in a newly created "ecological zone." Metalclad claimed these acts were tantamount to expropriation, and denial of national and the NAFTA 1994 minimum standards of treatment.

It sought $90 million in damages from the Mexican federal government, which despite having supported the Metalclad contract was obliged to defend the hostile local and state actions. Metalclad received an award of $16 million under NAFTA Chapter 11 in 2000. The arbitration was conducted under the ICSID Additional Facility rules.

Mexico instituted judicial proceedings to set aside the award in British Columbia, the arbitration's legal *situs*. Canada intervened in support of Mexico. The arbitrators had found the Mexican regulatory action a breach of NAFTA's minimum standard based on a lack of "transparency," and regulatory acts tantamount to expropriation without adequate compensation.

Despite a Canadian brief in support of Mexico, the British Columbia Supreme Court, ruling under the B.C. International Arbitration Act, agreed that the expropriation decision fell within the scope of the dispute submitted and was therefore valid. It rejected, however, the transparency decision as beyond the scope of the submission. The court found no transparency obligations in Chapter 11, and none as a matter of *customary* international law (which traditionally bars only "egregious," "outrageous" or "shocking" conduct).

Mexico subsequently paid Metalclad approximately $16 million U.S., the first payment by a state to an investor under Chapter 11.

Ethyl v. Canada and Methanex v. United States

A second prominent dispute involved Ethyl Corp. of the USA, which claimed $250 million U.S. damages against the Canadian government following 1997 federal legislation banning importation or interprovincial trade of the gasoline additive, MMT. Canada was the first country to ban MMT as a pollution and health hazard, although California has also done so. MMT is a manganese-based octane enhancer alleged to interfere with the proper functioning of catalytic converters.

Ethyl Corp. is the sole producer of MMT in North America. Ethyl claimed that the new law was tantamount to expropriation, violated NAFTA's national treatment standards and constituted an unlawful Canadian-content performance requirement (because the ban would favor Canadian ethanol as a substitute for MMT).

A dispute resolution panel under Canada's Agreement on Internal Trade struck down the interprovincial trade ban. In 1998, Canada withdrew its ban on MMT and paid $13 million to Ethyl

Corp. Ethyl then withdrew its $250 million arbitration claim. Canada noted the current lack of scientific evidence documenting MMT harm, an apparent abandonment of the "precautionary principle."

Environmentalists decried evidence of NAFTA's negative impact, and Europeans cited *Ethyl* as good reason to reject multilateral investment guarantee agreements in the OECD (Organization for Economic Cooperation and Development). Both groups believe Chapter 11 has created a privileged class of "super-citizens" who are a threat to state sovereignty,

Methanex Corp. of Canada submitted a claim that was in some ways the reverse of *Ethyl*. Methanex claimed that California's ban of the MTBE gasoline additive (for which it makes feedstock) amounted to an expropriation of its business interests and violated its minimum treatment rights. It sought $970 million in damages and simultaneously filed a petition under the North American Environmental Cooperation Agreement asserting that California failed to enforce its gasoline storage regulations, which Methanex saw as the source of MTBE water pollution.

In 2002, the *Methanex* panel working under the UNCITRAL Rules largely rejected the complaint on jurisdictional grounds, allowing a limited re-filing on the question of intentional injury. The *Methanex* panel notably ruled that it would accept NGO amicus briefs, in this instance from the International Institute for Sustainable Development. This position was subsequently ratified for all Chapter 11 arbitrations by the NAFTA Free Trade Commission in 2003.

Loewen v. United States

The Loewen Group of Canada was held liable by a jury in 1995 to $500 million in a Mississippi breach of a funeral home contract suit. The case was settled for $150 million after the Mississippi Supreme Court required posting a $625 million bond prior to appealing the jury's verdict, a sum exceeding Loewen's net worth.

In 1998, Loewen filed a claim under NAFTA alleging discrimination, denial of the minimum NAFTA standard of treatment, and uncompensated expropriation. This claim, like that of Ethyl Corp., was destined for controversy. Among other things, it challenged the discretion of American juries in awarding punitive damages. Note that it does so in a forum that does not give the American Trial Lawyers Association an opportunity to respond.

In 2003, the *Loewen* panel, calling the Mississippi decision "a disgrace," nevertheless ruled heavily against the bankrupt funeral home giant because its status as a Canadian (versus U.S.) company entitled to NAFTA foreign investor rights was in doubt.

Loewen had consolidated its numerous U.S. funeral home subsidiaries into a Delaware holding company, and hence its "foreign" status was not continuous. In a later clarification, the panel stressed that Loewen's failure to appeal or seek review of the judgment was critical to their denial of its claim.

Pope & Talbot v. Canada

Pope & Talbot, Inc. of Portland, Oregon claimed that the 1996 U.S.-Canada Softwood Lumber Agreement violated the national treatment, most-favored-nation treatment, minimum treatment, and performance requirements rules of NAFTA. The claim asserted that the company's British Columbia subsidiary was the victim of discrimination in that the Canadian export restraints required under that Agreement applied only to four Canadian provinces. Pope & Talbot sought $20 million in compensation from the Canadian government.

Rejecting most of the claims, the Pope & Talbot panel found Canada did violate the NAFTA minimum standard of treatment in denying export authorization to the company's B.C. subsidiary.

Although the award was only about $460,000 U.S., the panel's reasoning set off fireworks. In its view, Article 1105 demanded something more than the level of treatment commanded by customary international law. "Fair and equitable treatment" and "full protection and security" were perceived to be "additive" new and expansive norms created by NAFTA's novel investor protection regime.

The additive reading of Pope & Talbot was subsequently rejected by the British Columbia Supreme Court in Metalclad (above), and collectively negated by a binding interpretation of Article 1105 issued by the three NAFTA parties in 2001. This controversial, defensive interpretation "clarifies" that Article 1105 corresponds to and thus does not expand the customary international law standard of minimum treatment, and that breach of a NAFTA obligation does not ipso facto constitute a breach of that Article.

S.D. Myers v. Canada

S.D. Myers is an Ohio company specializing in hazardous waste management of PCBs. Its Canadian affiliate imported PCBs from Ontario, to the consternation of the only Canadian PCB remediation company, Chem-Security of Alberta. In 1995, Canada banned PCB exports, intentionally giving Chem-Security a monopoly. S.D. Myers asserted this export ban violated the national treatment, performance requirements, expropriation, and fair and equitable treatment provisions of Chapter 11.

The arbitrators found in favor of S.D. Myers on the national treatment and fair and equitable treatment claims, awarding over $6,000,000 CDN in damages. Canada appealed to the courts of Ontario, the situs of the arbitration, and lost. In Ontario, at least, considerable deference is given to arbitral decisions. Compare British Columbia in *Metalclad* above. Subsequently, S.D. Myers and Canada settled the dispute.

Mondev v. United States

Mondev is a Canadian company engaged in commercial real estate development. It pursued various claims against the City of Boston and the Boston Redevelopment Authority in the Massachusetts courts, which were denied on sovereign immunity grounds. Mondev then filed a Chapter 11 claim arguing primarily unfair and inequitable treatment in the Massachusetts courts.

In its complaint, Mondev directly challenged the 2001 Interpretation of Article 1105, arguing it was de facto an amendment of the NAFTA agreement. Mondev also argued that customary international law should be construed in light of conclusions reached under hundreds of bilateral investment treaties and modern judgments.

The tribunal recognized that fair and equitable treatment had evolved by 1994 (NAFTA's effective date) beyond what is "egregious" or "outrageous" (a frequently cited standard derived from *Neer v. Mexico*, 21 Am. J. Intl. L. 555 (1927) (U.S. and Mexico General Claims Commission), and that bad faith on the part of states need not be shown. It then ruled against Mondev's denial of justice claims.

Waste Management v. Mexico

Waste Management, through its Mexican subsidiary, contracted for waste disposal, street cleaning and landfill services with the city of Acapulco. When Acapulco allegedly failed to honor various contract terms, Waste Management asserted unfair and inequitable treatment in its Chapter 11 claim.

Under customary international law, the tribunal held Acapulco would be liable if its conduct was "arbitrary, grossly unfair, unjust or idiosyncratic . . . [or] discriminatory . . . exposing the claimant to sectional or racial prejudice or involves a lack of due process leading to an outcome that offends judicial propriety." In applying this standard, the tribunal deemed breach of representations by Acapulco reasonably relied upon by Waste Management "relevant" to its denial of unfair and inequitable treatment findings.

Glamis v. United States

A Canadian mining company, Glamis, alleged that government regulations limiting the impact of open pit mining and protecting indigenous peoples' religious sites made its *proposed* California gold mine unprofitable. Under Chapter 11, it asserted violations of the NAFTA rules against government acts tantamount to expropriation, and denial of fair and equitable treatment.

In June of 2009, a Chapter 11 tribunal accepted, in principle, that "regulatory taking" measures could amount to "creeping expropriation." That said, the tribunal undertook a detailed accounting of Glamis' alleged losses and found the mine project still had a net positive value of $20 million U.S. Hence it concluded Glamis was not impacted sufficiently to support a NAFTA expropriation claim.

While the outcome once again allowed the United States to avoid paying Chapter 11 damages, the willingness of the tribunal to entertain a regulatory taking claim was controversial (to put it mildly) and once again raised concerns that foreign investors may have greater rights under NAFTA than U.S. investors possess under United States law. *Glamis* continued the trend in NAFTA arbitrations of treating fair and equitable treatment as an evolving customary international law standard, referencing *inter alia* BIT arbitration decisions. See Chapter 7.

Chemtura v. Canada

Crompton (Chemtura) Corp. of the USA filed a "tantamount to expropriation" Chapter 11 complaint against Canada after it banned lindane-based pesticides. The arbitral tribunal, in 2010, unanimously noted that this ban had been undertaken in a non-discriminatory manner motivated by human health and environmental concerns. As such, it was a valid exercise of Canada's police powers and did not constitute expropriation.

Corn Syrup Sweeteners v. Mexico

Late in 2009, a third Chapter 11 tribunal ruled against Mexico concerning its 20% tax from 2002 to 2007 on the production and sale of soft drinks using High Fructose Corn Syrup (HFCS). This tax was imposed in the context of a trade dispute between the U.S. and Mexico over HFCS exports south of the border and Mexican sugar exports headed north.

U.S. agribusiness giants Cargill, Corn Products International and Archer Daniels Midlands, along with British Tate and Lyle's U.S. subsidiary, successfully argued that the tax constituted a "performance requirement" in violation of NAFTA Article 1106. The

Mexican government was ordered to pay a total of $170 million plus interest.

AbitibiBowater v. Canada

In August 2010, the Canadian federal government agreed to pay $130 million CDN to settle a Chapter 11 claim by a U.S. pulp and paper multinational, Abitibi Bowater (AB). In 2008, AB closed a longstanding mill in Newfoundland via bankruptcy, terminating 800 workers without severance. Newfoundland passed a law returning, without compensation, the company's water and timber rights to the crown, and expropriating with compensation AB lands, buildings and dams in the province. AB asserted NAFTA expropriation violations.

This settlement, along with the *Glamis* decision (above), raised concerns that resource-related NAFTA investor claims may increase. For example, a Brazilian company with a U.S. subsidiary received a $15 million settlement form Canada after alleging permit delays for rock quarrying.

Apotex v. United States

Apotex is a Canadian manufacturer of generic pharmaceuticals. It has filed at least three Chapter 11 claims against the United States. These filings challenge U.S. federal court decisions denying its efforts to obtain "patent certainty" for drugs (to allow its generic versions to proceed), FDA denial of approval for another Apotex generic drug, and FDA import inspection practices for drugs.

Exxon/Mobil v. Canada

Exxon/Mobil challenged Canadian Petroleum Board rules mandating fees to support R & D in Newfoundland and Labrador. Nearby, Exxon/Mobil has developed oil fields offshore. A Chapter 11 panel affirmed in 2012 that these fees amounted to NAFTA-prohibited "performance requirements."

Bilcon v. Canada

Bilcon of Delaware sought to develop a quarry and marine terminal in Nova Scotia, subject to environmental review. A joint federal/province review denied approval based upon "incompatibility with community core values". Bilcon alleged NAFTA Chapter 11 violations of the national and minimum treatment standards (the latter claim focused on fair and equitable treatment). By agreement, the UNCITRAL Rules controlled before the Permanent Court of Arbitration.

In a split 2015 decision, the arbitrators held in favor of Bilcon, noting particularly an absence of fair notice and treatment in the environmental review process, and a fundamental departure from the "likely significant adverse effects after mitigation" standard of evaluation required by Canadian law.

Eli Lilly v. Canada

Eli Lilly filed a claim for damages under Chapter 11 after Canadian courts invalidated patents on two of its blockbuster drugs on grounds that their utility was not shown. Eli Lilly argued unfair, inequitable, and discriminatory treatment. A 2017 arbitration panel rejected these arguments, noting that the "promise of utility" doctrine developed by Canadian courts was well established, putting Eli Lilly on notice prior to its patent claims.

This dispute was unusual because it asserted violation of NAFTA Chapter 11 by Canadian *courts*, not by Canadian legislation or regulation. Subsequently, in June of 2017, the Canadian Supreme Court overturned the "promise doctrine" under its patent law

Windstream Energy v. Canada and Mesa Power Group v. Canada

Windstream Energy of the USA sought to participate in Ontario's green energy program and obtained a contract to build an offshore wind farm. Subsequently, Ontario imposed a moratorium on offshore wind projects pending further scientific study. This had the effect of suspending but not terminating the Windstream contract. Other participants in the program were offered alternative opportunities to join the green energy program, but Windstream was not.

Windstream filed a Chapter 11 complaint before the Permanent Court of Arbitration arguing discrimination, indirect expropriation, and unfair and inequitable treatment.

A 2017 arbitration panel rejected all but the unfair and inequitable treatment claim, recognizing that Ontario had not within a reasonable time clarified the relevant science or the status of the contract, leaving Windstream in legal limbo. It assessed 21 million Euros damages, minus certain adjustments, based upon the value of comparable transactions in Europe.

Mesa Power challenged Ontario's award of power purchase contracts under its green energy program as discriminatory and unfair under Chapter 11 before the Permanent Court of Arbitration in The Hague. In a split decision, the arbitrators rejected Mesa' claims of unfair bidding rules and procedures for power contracts.

Other Foreign Investor Claims of Note

Several U.S. companies commenced Chapter 11 proceedings against Canada asserting damages based on Quebec's moratorium on "fracking", the use of water and chemicals to release sub-surface oil and gas reserves.

After President Obama's rejection in 2015 of the Keystone Pipeline from Alberta's tar sands to Texas, Trans Canada has filed a Chapter 11 claim against the United States alleging discriminatory (non-national) treatment, breach of the duty of most-favored-nation treatment, U.S. governmental acts tantamount to expropriation, and unfair and inequitable treatment. Trans Canada sought more than $15 billion in damages but withdrew its claim after President Trump approved the pipeline. President Biden later reversed Trump's decision.

The United States, unlike Mexico and Canada, never lost an investment arbitration nor paid damages under NAFTA 1994.

§ 8.11   Post-NAFTA Investor-State Arbitration Developments

These examples of investor-state claims under NAFTA 1994 represent only the tip of the iceberg. Lawyers learned that U.S. FTA investor-state provisions could be used to challenge or threaten to challenge all sorts of existing or proposed government actions, particularly regulatory decisions. There was leverage in the broad investor rights, and in its mandatory arbitral procedures. No wonder Australia refused to allow investor-state arbitrations in its free trade agreement with the United States.

Whether, and if so in what form, NAFTA 1994 investor-state rules might be replicated in future U.S. free trade agreements was hotly contested. Mutations on the law of investor-state claims appeared in subsequent the U.S. free trade agreements noted in Chapter 7.

Regarding investor-state claims, for example, post-NAFTA U.S. free trade agreements insert the word "customary" before international law in defining the minimum standard of treatment to which foreign investors are entitled. This insertion tracks the official 2001 Interpretation issued in that regard under NAFTA 1994. Further, the contested terms "fair and equitable treatment" and "full protection and security" do not require treatment in addition to or beyond that customary standard, and do not create additional substantive rights. This language was defined for the first time:

> *"fair and equitable treatment"* includes the obligation not to deny justice in criminal, civil, or administrative adjudicatory proceedings in accordance with the principle of due process embodied in the principal legal systems of the world; and

"full protection and security" requires each Party to provide
the level of police protection required under *customary*
international law.

More significantly perhaps, starting with the U.S.-Chile FTA, these
agreements contain an Annex restricting the scope of *"indirect
expropriation"* claims:

> Except in rare circumstances, nondiscriminatory regulatory
> actions by a Party that are designed and applied to protect
> legitimate public welfare objectives, such as public health,
> safety, and the environment, do not constitute indirect
> expropriations.

Hence the potential for succeeding with "regulatory takings"
investor-state claims has been reduced.

These mutations were in part a response to Congressional
concerns expressed in the Trade Promotion Authority (fast track) Act
of 2002 that Chapter 11 of NAFTA 1994 may accord "greater
substantive rights" to foreigners with respect to investment
protection than enjoyed by U.S. investors in the United States.

Similar concerns were raised by Congress in adopting fast track
in 2015, targeting U.S. participation in the Trans- Pacific
Partnership (TPP-12) and Transatlantic Trade and Investment
Partnership (TTIP) negotiations.

§ 8.12 Investor-State Arbitrations Under TPP-12

The Trans-Pacific Partnership Agreement (TTP-12) agreement,
signed by President Obama but not implemented by President
Trump, contained attempts at investor-state dispute settlement
reform. For example, under TPP-12 financial stability regulation fell
outside indirect expropriation claims, tobacco regulation could not be
challenged, and mere frustration of profit expectations was
insufficient to pursue investor-state arbitrations. The burden of proof
fell on investor claimants, no shell companies could be used to access
investor-state arbitral remedies, and state-owned enterprises along
with authorized government agents were made subject to the TPP-
12 regime.

In addition, the TPP-12 agreement mandated public access to
hearings and documents, allowed amicus briefs, facilitated expedited
dismissals of frivolous claims, and generally protected existing IP
license royalties and durations from alteration.

Most of these arbitration law upgrades were retained in the
TPP-11 agreement that went into effect Jan. 1, 2019 for the remaining
TPP-12 partners. Likewise, most of these upgrades found their way

into the investment provisions of NAFTA re-negotiated, the USMCA 2020 agreement.

§ 8.13 Investor-State Arbitrations Under USMCA 2020

Investor-state arbitration of disputes for damages continues in full as between Mexico and Canada under the TPP-11 effective Jan. 1, 2019. Such arbitrations continue under revised terms as between Mexico and the United States but are eliminated as between the U.S. and Canada under

U.S.-Mexico claims involving *government contracts* are limited to specified capital-intensive sectors (oil and gas, telecommunications, power generation, and contracts for roads, railways, bridges, or canals but not apparently dams, seaports and airports). Such government contract disputes may assert the full range of NAFTA 1994 investor rights (direct and indirect expropriation, fair and equitable treatment (minimum standard), national and MFN treatment, and other rights noted above).

For claims *not* involving government contracts, limitations are placed on ISDS by USMCA 2020. Such claims are limited to national and most-favored nation treatment, and expropriation grounds, notably dropping out fair and equitable treatment claims. In addition, borrowing from post-NAFTA U.S. free trade agreements (above) and TPP-12, "indirect" expropriation claims are also limited.

Indirect expropriations are defined as situations "in which an action or series of actions by a Party has an effect equivalent to direct expropriation without formal transfer of title or outright seizure". Further, "non-discriminatory regulatory actions by a Party that are designed and applied to protect legitimate public welfare objectives, such as health, safety and the environment, do *not* constitute indirect expropriations, except in rare circumstances." This language addresses criticisms of NAFTA investor-state arbitrations challenging environmental measures as regulatory takings and/or indirect expropriations. For examples, see Section 8.10 above.

Furthermore, borrowing a TPP-12 rule, investor claimants under USMCA must first exhaust local remedies or attempt to do so for 30 months prior to seeking arbitration. This rule does not appear to apply to the select Mexican or U.S. government contract claimants noted above.

Claimants owned or controlled by non-market economy states are barred from using USMCA ISDS, and establishment claims prior to actual foreign investment are generally excluded.

By agreement in USMCA Chapter 14, apart from legacy NAFTA 1994 claims (presented no later than three years after the USMCA entered into force), *Canada and the United States completely removed the availability of arbitrations to resolve investor-state disputes.* Presumably, in the future, such disputes will be resolved by state-to-state negotiations (SSDS), or the courts and agencies of either nation.

Chapter 14 of the USMCA on Investment is reproduced in Section 8.15 of this chapter.

§ 8.14 Text of NAFTA Chapter 11 on Investment

SECTION A—INVESTMENT

Article 1101: Scope and Coverage

1.   This Chapter applies to measures adopted or maintained by a Party relating to:

(a)   investors of another Party;

(b)   investments of investors of another Party in the territory of the Party; and

(c)   with respect to Article 1106, all investments in the territory of the Party.

2.   A Party has the right to perform exclusively the economic activities set out in Annex III and to refuse to permit the establishment of investment in such activities.

3.   This Chapter does not apply to measures adopted or maintained by a Party to the extent that they are covered by Chapter Fourteen (Financial Services).

4.   Nothing in this Chapter shall be construed to prevent a Party from providing a service or performing a function such as law enforcement, correctional services, income security or insurance, social security or insurance, social welfare, public education, public training, health, and child care, in a manner that is not inconsistent with this Chapter.

Article 1102: National Treatment

1.   Each Party shall accord to investors of another Party treatment no less favorable than that it accords, in like circumstances, to its own investors with respect to the establishment, acquisition, expansion, management, conduct, operation, and sale or other disposition of investments.

2.   Each Party shall accord to investments of investors of another Party treatment no less favorable than that it accords, in like circumstances, to investments of its own investors with respect to the

establishment, acquisition, expansion, management, conduct, operation, and sale or other disposition of investments.

3.   The treatment accorded by a Party under paragraphs 1 and 2 means, with respect to a state or province, treatment no less favorable than the most favorable treatment accorded, in like circumstances, by that state or province to investors, and to investments of investors, of the Party of which it forms a part.

4.   For greater certainty, no Party may:

(a)   impose on an investor of another Party a requirement that a minimum level of equity in an enterprise in the territory of the Party be held by its nationals, other than nominal qualifying shares for directors or incorporators of corporations; or

(b)   require an investor of another Party, by reason of its nationality, to sell or otherwise dispose of an investment in the territory of the Party.

Article 1103: Most-Favored-Nation Treatment

1.   Each Party shall accord to investors of another Party treatment no less favorable than that it accords, in like circumstances, to investors of another Party or of a non-Party with respect to the establishment, acquisition, expansion, management, conduct, operation, and sale or other disposition of investments.

2.   Each Party shall accord to investments of investors of another Party treatment no less favorable than that it accords, in like circumstances, to investments of investors of another Party or of a non-Party with respect to the establishment, acquisition, expansion, management, conduct, operation, and sale or other disposition of investments.

Article 1104: Standard of Treatment

Each Party shall accord to investors of another Party and to investments of investors of another Party the better of the treatment required by Articles 1102 and 1103.

Article 1105: Minimum Standard of Treatment

1.   Each Party shall accord to investments of investors of another Party treatment in accordance with international law, including fair and equitable treatment and full protection and security.

2.   Without prejudice to paragraph 1 and notwithstanding Article 1108(7)(b), each Party shall accord to investors of another Party, and to investments of investors of another Party, non-

discriminatory treatment with respect to measures it adopts or maintains relating to losses suffered by investments in its territory owing to armed conflict or civil strife.

3.   Paragraph 2 does not apply to existing measures relating to subsidies or grants that are inconsistent with Article 1102.

Article 1106: Performance Requirements

1.   No Party may impose or enforce any of the following requirements, or enforce any commitment or undertaking, in connection with the establishment, acquisition, expansion, management, conduct or operation of an investment of an investor of a Party or of a non-Party in its territory:

(a)   to export a given level or percentage of goods or services;

(b)   to achieve a given level or percentage of domestic content;

(c)   to purchase, use or accord a preference to goods produced or services provided in its territory, or to purchase goods or services from persons in its territory;

(d)   to relate in any way the volume or value of imports to the volume or value of exports or to the amount of foreign exchange inflows associated with such investment;

(e)   to restrict sales of goods or services in its territory that such investment produces or provides by relating such sales in any way to the volume or value of its exports or foreign exchange earnings;

(f)   to transfer technology, a production process or other proprietary knowledge to a person in its territory, except when the requirement is imposed or the 4 commitment or undertaking is enforced by a court, administrative tribunal or competition authority to remedy an alleged violation of competition laws or to act in a manner not inconsistent with other provisions of this Agreement; or

(g)   to act as the exclusive supplier of the goods it produces or services it provides to a specific region or world market.

2.   A measure that requires an investment to use a technology to meet generally applicable health, safety or environmental requirements shall not be construed to be inconsistent with paragraph (1)(f). For greater certainty, Articles 1102 and 1103 apply to the measure.

3.   No Party may condition the receipt or continued receipt of an advantage, in connection with an investment in its territory of an investor of a Party or of a non-Party, on compliance with any of the following requirements:

(a)   to purchase, use or accord a preference to goods produced in its territory, or to purchase goods from producers in its territory;

(b)   to achieve a given level or percentage of domestic content;

(c)   to relate in any way the volume or value of imports to the volume or value of exports or to the amount of foreign exchange inflows associated with such investment; or

(d)   to restrict sales of goods or services in its territory that such investment produces or provides by relating such sales in any way to the volume or value of its exports or foreign exchange earnings.

4.   Nothing in paragraph 3 shall be construed to prevent a Party from conditioning the receipt or continued receipt of an advantage, in connection with an investment in its territory of an investor of a Party or of a non-Party, on compliance with a requirement to locate production, provide a service, train or employ workers, construct or expand particular facilities, or carry out research and development, in its territory.

5.   Paragraphs 1 and 3 do not apply to any requirement other than the requirements set out in those paragraphs.

6.   Provided that such measures are not applied in an arbitrary or unjustifiable manner, or do not constitute a disguised restriction on international trade or investment, nothing in 5 paragraph 1(b) or (c) or 3(a) or (b) shall be construed to prevent any Party from adopting or maintaining measures, including environmental measures:

(a)   necessary to secure compliance with laws and regulations that are not inconsistent with the provisions of this Agreement;

(b)   necessary to protect human, animal or plant life or health; or

(c)   necessary for the conservation of living or non-living exhaustible natural resources.

Article 1107: Senior Management
and Boards of Directors

1.   No Party may require that an enterprise of that Party that is an investment of an investor of another Party appoint to senior management positions individuals of any particular nationality.

2.   A Party may require that a majority of the board of directors, or any committee thereof, of an enterprise of that Party that is an investment of an investor of another Party, be of a particular nationality, or resident in the territory of the Party, provided that the requirement does not materially impair the ability of the investor to exercise control over its investment.

Article 1108: Reservations and Exceptions

1.   Articles 1102, 1103, 1106 and 1107 do not apply to:

(a) any existing non-conforming measure that is maintained by

(i) a Party at the federal level, as set out in its Schedule to Annex I or III,

(ii) a state or province, for two years after the date of entry into force of this Agreement, and thereafter as set out by a Party in its Schedule to Annex I, in accordance with paragraph 2, or

(iii) a local government;

(b) the continuation or prompt renewal of any non-conforming measure referred to in subparagraph (a); or

(c) an amendment to any non-conforming measure referred to in subparagraph (a) to the extent that the amendment does not decrease the conformity of the measure, as it existed immediately before the amendment, with Articles 1102, 1103, 1106 and 1107.

2.   Each Party may set out in its Schedule to Annex I any existing non-conforming measure maintained by a state or province, not including a local government, within two years of the date of entry into force of this Agreement.

3.   Articles 1102, 1103, 1106 and 1107 do not apply to any measure that a Party adopts or maintains with respect to sectors, subsectors or activities, as set out in its Schedule to Annex II.

4.   No Party may, under any measure adopted after the date of entry into force of this Agreement and covered by its Schedule to Annex II, require an investor of another Party, by reason of its

nationality, to sell or otherwise dispose of an investment existing at the time the measure becomes effective.

5.   Articles 1102 and 1103 do not apply to any measure that is an exception to, or derogation from, the obligations under Article 1703 (Intellectual Property—National Treatment) as specifically provided for in that Article.

6.   Article 1103 does not apply to treatment accorded by a Party pursuant to agreements, or with respect to sectors, set out in its Schedule to Annex IV.

7.   Articles 1102, 1103 and 1107 do not apply to:

(a) procurement by a Party or a state enterprise; or

(b) subsidies or grants provided by a Party or a state enterprise, including government-supported loans, guarantees and insurance.

8.   The provisions of:

(a) Article 1106(1)(a), (b) and (c), and (3)(a) and (b) do not apply to qualification requirements for goods or services with respect to export promotion and foreign aid programs;

(b) Article 1106(1)(b), (c), (f) and (g), and (3)(a) and (b) do not apply to procurement by a Party or a state enterprise; and

(c) Article 1106(3)(a) and (b) do not apply to requirements imposed by an importing Party relating to the content of goods necessary to qualify for preferential tariffs or preferential quotas.

Article 1109: Transfers

1.   Each Party shall permit all transfers relating to an investment of an investor of another Party in the territory of the Party to be made freely and without delay. Such transfers include:

(a) profits, dividends, interest, capital gains, royalty payments, management fees, technical assistance and other fees, returns in kind and other amounts derived from the investment;

(b) proceeds from the sale of all or any part of the investment or from the partial or complete liquidation of the investment;

(c) payments made under a contract entered into by the investor, or its investment, including payments made pursuant to a loan agreement;

(d)   payments made pursuant to Article 1110; and

(e)   payments arising under Section B.

2.   Each Party shall permit transfers to be made in a freely usable currency at the market rate of exchange prevailing on the date of transfer with respect to spot transactions in the currency to be transferred.

3.   No Party may require its investors to transfer, or penalize its investors that fail to transfer, the income, earnings, profits or other amounts derived from, or attributable to, investments in the territory of another Party.

4.   Notwithstanding paragraphs 1 and 2, a Party may prevent a transfer through the equitable, non-discriminatory and good faith application of its laws relating to:

(a)   bankruptcy, insolvency or the protection of the rights of creditors;

(b)   issuing, trading or dealing in securities;

(c)   criminal or penal offenses;

(d)   reports of transfers of currency or other monetary instruments; or

(e)   ensuring the satisfaction of judgments in adjudicatory proceedings.

5.   Paragraph 3 shall not be construed to prevent a Party from imposing any measure through the equitable, non-discriminatory and good faith application of its laws relating to the matters set out in subparagraphs (a) through (e) of paragraph 4.

6.   Notwithstanding paragraph 1, a Party may restrict transfers of returns in kind in circumstances where it could otherwise restrict such transfers under this Agreement.

Article 1110: Expropriation and Compensation

1.   No Party may directly or indirectly nationalize or expropriate an investment of an investor of another Party in its territory or take a measure tantamount to nationalization or expropriation of such an investment ("expropriation"), except:

(a)   for a public purpose;

(b)   on a non-discriminatory basis;

(c)   in accordance with due process of law and Article 1105(1); and

(d) on payment of compensation in accordance with paragraphs 2 through 6.

2.   Compensation shall be equivalent to the fair market value of the expropriated investment immediately before the expropriation took place ("date of expropriation"), and shall not reflect any change in value occurring because the intended expropriation had become known earlier. Valuation criteria shall include going concern value, asset value including declared tax value of tangible property, and other criteria, as appropriate, to determine fair market value.

3.   Compensation shall be paid without delay and be fully realizable.

4.   If payment is made in a G7 currency, compensation shall include interest at a commercially reasonable rate for that currency from the date of expropriation until the date of actual payment.

5.   If a Party elects to pay in a currency other than a G7 currency, the amount paid on the date of payment, if converted into a G7 currency at the market rate of exchange prevailing on that date, shall be no less than if the amount of compensation owed on the date of expropriation had been converted into that G7 currency at the market rate of exchange prevailing on that date, and interest had accrued at a commercially reasonable rate for that G7 currency from the date of expropriation until the date of payment.

6.   On payment, compensation shall be freely transferable as provided in Article 1109.

7.   This Article does not apply to the issuance of compulsory licenses granted in relation to intellectual property rights, or the revocation, limitation or creation of intellectual property rights, to the extent that such issuance, revocation, limitation or creation is consistent with Chapter Seventeen (Intellectual Property).

8.   For purposes of this Article and for greater certainty, a non-discriminatory measure of general application shall not be considered a measure tantamount to an expropriation of a debt security or loan covered by this Chapter solely on the ground that the measure imposes costs on the debtor that cause it to default on the debt.

Article 1111: Special Formalities and Information Requirements

1.   Nothing in Article 1102 shall be construed to prevent a Party from adopting or maintaining a measure that prescribes special formalities in connection with the establishment of investments by investors of another Party, such as a requirement that investors be residents of the Party or that investments be legally

constituted under the laws or regulations of the Party, provided that such formalities do not materially impair the protections afforded by a Party to investors of another Party and investments of investors of another Party pursuant to this Chapter.

2.   Notwithstanding Articles 1102 or 1103, a Party may require an investor of another Party, or its investment in its territory, to provide routine information concerning that investment solely for informational or statistical purposes. The Party shall protect such business information that is confidential from any disclosure that would prejudice the competitive position of the investor or the investment. Nothing in this paragraph shall be 10 construed to prevent a Party from otherwise obtaining or disclosing information in connection with the equitable and good faith application of its law.

Article 1112: Relation to Other Chapters

1.   In the event of any inconsistency between a provision of this Chapter and a provision of another Chapter, the provision of the other Chapter shall prevail to the extent of the inconsistency.

2.   A requirement by a Party that a service provider of another Party post a bond or other form of financial security as a condition of providing a service into its territory does not of itself make this Chapter applicable to the provision of that cross-border service. This Chapter applies to that Party's treatment of the posted bond or financial security.

Article 1113: Denial of Benefits

1.   A Party may deny the benefits of this Chapter to an investor of another Party that is an enterprise of such Party and to investments of such investor if investors of a non-Party own or control the enterprise and the denying Party:

(a)   does not maintain diplomatic relations with the non-Party; or

(b)   adopts or maintains measures with respect to the non-Party that prohibit transactions with the enterprise or that would be violated or circumvented if the benefits of this Chapter were accorded to the enterprise or to its investments.

2.   Subject to prior notification and consultation in accordance with Articles 1803 (Notification and Provision of Information) and 2006 (Consultations), a Party may deny the benefits of this Chapter to an investor of another Party that is an enterprise of such Party and to investments of such investors if investors of a non-Party own or control the enterprise and the enterprise has no substantial business activities in the territory of the Party under whose law it is constituted or organized.

Article 1114: Environmental Measures

1.   Nothing in this Chapter shall be construed to prevent a Party from adopting, maintaining or enforcing any measure otherwise consistent with this Chapter that it considers appropriate to ensure that investment activity in its territory is undertaken in a manner sensitive to environmental concerns.

2.   The Parties recognize that it is inappropriate to encourage investment by relaxing domestic health, safety or environmental measures. Accordingly, a Party should not waive or otherwise derogate from, or offer to waive or otherwise derogate from, such measures as an encouragement for the establishment, acquisition, expansion or retention in its territory of an investment of an investor. If a Party considers that another Party has offered such an encouragement, it may request consultations with the other Party and the two Parties shall consult with a view to avoiding any such encouragement.

SECTION B—SETTLEMENT OF DISPUTES BETWEEN A PARTY AND AN INVESTOR OF ANOTHER PARTY

Article 1115: Purpose

Without prejudice to the rights and obligations of the Parties under Chapter Twenty (Institutional Arrangements and Dispute Settlement Procedures), this Section establishes a mechanism for the settlement of investment disputes that assures both equal treatment among investors of the Parties in accordance with the principle of international reciprocity and due process before an impartial tribunal.

Article 1116: Claim by an Investor of a Party on Its Own Behalf

1.   An investor of a Party may submit to arbitration under this Section a claim that another Party has breached an obligation under:

(a)   Section A or Article 1503(2) (State Enterprises); or

(b)   Article 1502(3)(a) (Monopolies and State Enterprises) where the monopoly has acted in a manner inconsistent with the Party's obligations under Section A, and that the investor has incurred loss or damage by reason of, or arising out of, that breach.

2.   An investor may not make a claim if more than three years have elapsed from the date on which the investor first acquired, or should have first acquired, knowledge of the alleged breach and knowledge that the investor has incurred loss or damage.

Article 1117: Claim by an Investor of a
Party on Behalf of an Enterprise

1.   An investor of a Party, on behalf of an enterprise of another Party that is a juridical person that the investor owns or controls directly or indirectly, may submit to arbitration under this Section a claim that the other Party has breached an obligation under:

(a)   Section A or Article 1503(2) (State Enterprises); or

(b)   Article 1502(3)(a) (Monopolies and State Enterprises) where the monopoly has acted in a manner inconsistent with the Party's obligations under Section A, and that the enterprise has incurred loss or damage by reason of, or arising out of, that breach.

2.   An investor may not make a claim on behalf of an enterprise described in paragraph 1 if more than three years have elapsed from the date on which the enterprise first acquired, or should have first acquired, knowledge of the alleged breach and knowledge that the enterprise has incurred loss or damage.

3.   Where an investor makes a claim under this Article and the investor or a non-controlling investor in the enterprise makes a claim under Article 1116 arising out of the same events that gave rise to the claim under this Article, and two or more of the claims are submitted to arbitration under Article 1120, the claims should be heard together by a Tribunal established under Article 1126, unless the Tribunal finds that the interests of a disputing party would be prejudiced thereby.

4.   An investment may not make a claim under this Section.

Article 1118: Settlement of a Claim through
Consultation and Negotiation

The disputing parties should first attempt to settle a claim through consultation or negotiation.

Article 1119: Notice of Intent to
Submit a Claim to Arbitration

The disputing investor shall deliver to the disputing Party written notice of its intention to submit a claim to arbitration at least 90 days before the claim is submitted, which notice shall specify:

(a)   the name and address of the disputing investor and, where a claim is made under Article 1117, the name and address of the enterprise;

(b)   the provisions of this Agreement alleged to have been breached and any other relevant provisions;

(c)   the issues and the factual basis for the claim; and

(d)   the relief sought and the approximate amount of damages claimed.

Article 1120: Submission of a Claim to Arbitration

1.   Except as provided in Annex 1120.1, and provided that six months have elapsed since the events giving rise to a claim, a disputing investor may submit the claim to arbitration under:

(a)   the ICSID Convention, provided that both the disputing Party and the Party of the investor are parties to the Convention;

(b)   the Additional Facility Rules of ICSID, provided that either the disputing Party or the Party of the investor, but not both, is a party to the ICSID Convention; or

(c)   the UNCITRAL Arbitration Rules.

2.   The applicable arbitration rules shall govern the arbitration except to the extent modified by this Section.

Article 1121: Conditions Precedent to Submission of a Claim to Arbitration

1.   A disputing investor may submit a claim under Article 1116 to arbitration only if:

(a)   the investor consents to arbitration in accordance with the procedures set out in this Agreement; and

(b)   both the investor and an enterprise of another Party that is a juridical person that the investor owns or controls directly or indirectly, waive their right to initiate or continue before any administrative tribunal or court under the law of any Party any proceedings with respect to the measure of the disputing Party that is alleged to be a breach referred to in Article 1116, except for proceedings for injunctive, declaratory or other extraordinary relief, not involving the payment of damages, before an administrative tribunal or court under the law of the disputing Party.

2.   A disputing investor may submit a claim under Article 1117 to arbitration only if both the investor and the enterprise: (a) consent to arbitration in accordance with the procedures set out in this Agreement; and (b) waive their right to initiate or continue before any administrative tribunal or court under the law of any Party any proceedings with respect to the measure of the disputing Party that is alleged to be a breach referred to in Article 1117, except for

proceedings for injunctive, declaratory or other extraordinary relief, not involving the payment of damages, before an administrative tribunal or court under the law of the disputing Party.

3.   A consent and waiver required by this Article shall be in writing, shall be delivered to the disputing Party and shall be included in the submission of a claim to arbitration.

Article 1122: Consent to Arbitration

1.   Each Party consents to the submission of a claim to arbitration in accordance with the procedures set out in this Agreement.

2.   The consent given by paragraph 1 and the submission by a disputing investor of a claim to arbitration shall satisfy the requirement of:

(a)   Chapter II of the ICSID Convention (Jurisdiction of the Centre) and the Additional Facility Rules for written consent of the parties;

(b)   Article II of the New York Convention for an agreement in writing; and

(c)   Article I of the Inter-American Convention for an agreement.

Article 1123: Number of Arbitrators and Method of Appointment

Except in respect of a Tribunal established under Article 1126, and unless the disputing parties otherwise agree, the Tribunal shall comprise three arbitrators, one arbitrator appointed by each of the disputing parties and the third, who shall be the presiding arbitrator, appointed by agreement of the disputing parties.

Article 1124: Constitution of a Tribunal When a Party Fails to Appoint an Arbitrator or the Disputing Parties Are Unable to Agree on a Presiding Arbitrator

1.   The Secretary-General shall serve as appointing authority for an arbitration under this Section.

2.   If a Tribunal, other than a Tribunal established under Article 1126, has not been constituted within 90 days from the date that a claim is submitted to arbitration, the Secretary-General, on the request of either disputing party, shall appoint, in his discretion, the arbitrator or arbitrators not yet appointed, except that the presiding arbitrator shall be appointed in accordance with paragraph 3.

3. The Secretary-General shall appoint the presiding arbitrator from the roster of presiding arbitrators referred to in paragraph 4, provided that the presiding arbitrator shall not be a national of the disputing Party or a national of the Party of the disputing investor. In the event that no such presiding arbitrator is available to serve, the Secretary-General shall appoint, from the ICSID Panel of Arbitrators, a presiding arbitrator who is not a national of any of the Parties.

4. On the date of entry into force of this Agreement, the Parties shall establish, and thereafter maintain, a roster of 45 presiding arbitrators meeting the qualifications of the Convention and rules referred to in Article 1120 and experienced in international law and investment matters. The roster members shall be appointed by consensus and without regard to nationality.

Article 1125: Agreement to Appointment of Arbitrators

For purposes of Article 39 of the ICSID Convention and Article 7 of Schedule C to the ICSID Additional Facility Rules, and without prejudice to an objection to an arbitrator based on Article 1124(3) or on a ground other than nationality:

(a) the disputing Party agrees to the appointment of each individual member of a Tribunal established under the ICSID Convention or the ICSID Additional Facility Rules;

(b) a disputing investor referred to in Article 1116 may submit a claim to arbitration, or continue a claim, under the ICSID Convention or the ICSID Additional Facility Rules, only on condition that the disputing investor agrees in writing to the appointment of each individual member of the Tribunal; and

(c) a disputing investor referred to in Article 1117(1) may submit a claim to arbitration, or continue a claim, under the ICSID Convention or the ICSID Additional Facility Rules, only on condition that the disputing investor and the enterprise agree in writing to the appointment of each individual member of the Tribunal.

Article 1126: Consolidation

1. A Tribunal established under this Article shall be established under the UNCITRAL Arbitration Rules and shall conduct its proceedings in accordance with those Rules, except as modified by this Section.

* * *

Article 1128: Participation by a Party

On written notice to the disputing parties, a Party may make submissions to a Tribunal on a question of interpretation of this Agreement.

Article 1129: Documents

1. A Party shall be entitled to receive from the disputing Party, at the cost of the requesting Party a copy of:

(a) the evidence that has been tendered to the Tribunal; and

(b) the written argument of the disputing

2. A Party receiving information pursuant to paragraph 1 shall treat the information as if it were a disputing Party.

Article 1130: Place of Arbitration

Unless the disputing parties agree otherwise, a Tribunal shall hold an arbitration in the territory of a Party that is a party to the New York Convention, selected in accordance with:

(a) the ICSID Additional Facility Rules if the arbitration is under those Rules or the ICSID Convention; or

(b) the UNCITRAL Arbitration Rules if the arbitration is under those Rules.

Article 1131: Governing Law

1. A Tribunal established under this Section shall decide the issues in dispute in accordance with this Agreement and applicable rules of international law.

2. An interpretation by the Commission of a provision of this Agreement shall be binding on a Tribunal established under this Section.

Article 1132: Interpretation of Annexes

1. Where a disputing Party asserts as a defense that the measure alleged to be a breach is within the scope of a reservation or exception set out in Annex I, Annex II, Annex III or Annex IV, on request of the disputing Party, the Tribunal shall request the interpretation of the Commission on the issue. The Commission, within 60 days of delivery of the request, shall submit in writing its interpretation to the Tribunal.

2. Further to Article 1131(2), a Commission interpretation submitted under paragraph 1 shall be binding on the Tribunal. If the Commission fails to submit an interpretation within 60 days, the Tribunal shall decide the issue.

Article 1133: Expert Reports

Without prejudice to the appointment of other kinds of experts where authorized by the applicable arbitration rules, a Tribunal, at the request of a disputing party or, unless the disputing parties disapprove, on its own initiative, may appoint one or more experts to report to it in writing on any factual issue concerning environmental, health, safety or other scientific matters raised by a disputing party in a proceeding, subject to such terms and conditions as the disputing parties may agree.

Article 1134: Interim Measures of Protection

A Tribunal may order an interim measure of protection to preserve the rights of a disputing party, or to ensure that the Tribunal's jurisdiction is made fully effective, including an order to preserve evidence in the possession or control of a disputing party or to protect the Tribunal's jurisdiction. A Tribunal may not order attachment or enjoin the application of the measure alleged to constitute a breach referred to in Article 1116 or 1117. For purposes of this paragraph, an order includes a recommendation.

Article 1135: Final Award

1.   Where a Tribunal makes a final award against a Party, the Tribunal may award only:

(a)   monetary damages and any applicable interest; or

(b)   restitution of property, in which case the award shall provide that the disputing Party may pay monetary damages and any applicable interest in lieu of restitution.

A tribunal may also award costs in accordance with the applicable arbitration rules.

2.   Subject to paragraph 1, where a claim is made under Article 1117(1):

(a)   an award of restitution of property shall provide that restitution be made to the enterprise;

(b)   an award of monetary damages and any applicable interest shall provide that the sum be paid to the enterprise; and

(c)   the award shall provide that it is made without prejudice to any right that any person may have in the relief under applicable domestic law.

3.   A Tribunal may not order a Party to pay punitive damages.

Article 1136: Finality and Enforcement of an Award

1.   An award made by a Tribunal shall have no binding force except between the disputing parties and in respect of the particular case.

2.   Subject to paragraph 3 and the applicable review procedure for an interim award, a disputing party shall abide by and comply with an award without delay.

3.   A disputing party may not seek enforcement of a final award until:

(a)   in the case of a final award made under the ICSID Convention

(i)   120 days have elapsed from the date the award was rendered and no disputing party has requested revision or annulment of the award, or

(ii)   revision or annulment proceedings have been completed; and

(b)   in the case of a final award under the ICSID Additional Facility Rules or the UNCITRAL Arbitration Rules

(i)   three months have elapsed from the date the award was rendered and no disputing party has commenced a proceeding to revise, set aside or annul the award, or

(ii)   a court has dismissed or allowed an application to revise, set aside or annul the award and there is no further appeal.

4.   Each Party shall provide for the enforcement of an award in its territory.

5.   If a disputing Party fails to abide by or comply with a final award, the Commission, on delivery of a request by a Party whose investor was a party to the arbitration, shall establish a panel under Article 2008 (Request for an Arbitral Panel). The requesting Party may seek in such proceedings:

(a)   a determination that the failure to abide by or comply with the final award is inconsistent with the obligations of this Agreement; and

(b)   a recommendation that the Party abide by or comply with the final award.

6.   A disputing investor may seek enforcement of an arbitration award under the ICSID Convention, the New York Convention or the Inter-American Convention regardless of whether proceedings have been taken under paragraph 5.

7.   A claim that is submitted to arbitration under this Section shall be considered to arise out of a commercial relationship or transaction for purposes of Article I of the New York Convention and Article I of the Inter-American Convention.

* * *

Article 1138: Exclusions

1.   Without prejudice to the applicability or non-applicability of the dispute settlement provisions of this Section or of Chapter Twenty (Institutional Arrangements and Dispute Settlement Procedures) to other actions taken by a Party pursuant to Article 2102 (National Security), a decision by a Party to prohibit or restrict the acquisition of an investment in its territory by an investor of another Party, or its investment, pursuant to that Article shall not be subject to such provisions.

2.   The dispute settlement provisions of this Section and of Chapter Twenty shall not apply to the matters referred to in Annex 1138.2.

Article 1139: Definitions

For purposes of this Chapter:

disputing investor means an investor that makes a claim under Section B;

disputing parties means the disputing investor and the disputing Party;

disputing party means the disputing investor or the disputing Party;

disputing Party means a Party against which a claim is made under Section B;

enterprise means an "enterprise" as defined in Article 201, and a branch of an enterprise;

enterprise of a Party means an enterprise constituted or organized under the law of a Party, and a branch located in the territory of a Party and carrying out business activities there;

equity or debt securities includes voting and non-voting shares, bonds, convertible debentures, stock options and warrants;

G7 Currency means the currency of Canada, France, Germany, Italy, Japan, the United Kingdom of Great Britain and Northern Ireland or the United States;

ICSID means the International Centre for Settlement of Investment Disputes;

ICSID Convention means the Convention on the Settlement of Investment Disputes between States and Nationals of other States, done at Washington, March 18, 1965;

Inter-American Convention means the Inter-American Convention on International Commercial Arbitration, done at Panama, January 30, 1975;

investment means:

(a)   an enterprise;

(b)   an equity security of an enterprise;

(c)   a debt security of an enterprise

(i)   where the enterprise is an affiliate of the investor, or

(ii)   where the original maturity of the debt security is at least three years, but does not include a debt security, regardless of original maturity, of a state enterprise;

(d)   a loan to an enterprise

(i)   where the enterprise is an affiliate of the investor, or

(ii)   where the original maturity of the loan is at least three years, but does not include a loan, regardless of original maturity, to a state enterprise;

(e)   an interest in an enterprise that entitles the owner to share in income or profits of the enterprise;

(f)   an interest in an enterprise that entitles the owner to share in the assets of that enterprise on dissolution, other than a debt security or a loan excluded from subparagraph (c) or (d);

(g)   real estate or other property, tangible or intangible, acquired in the expectation or used for the purpose of economic benefit or other business purposes; and

(h)   interests arising from the commitment of capital or other resources in the territory of a Party to economic activity in such territory, such as under

(i)   contracts involving the presence of an investor's property in the territory of the Party, including turnkey or construction contracts, or concessions, or

(ii)   contracts where remuneration depends substantially on the production, revenues or profits of an enterprise;

but investment does not mean,

    (i)   claims to money that arise solely from

        (i)   commercial contracts for the sale of goods or services by a national or enterprise in the territory of a Party to an enterprise in the territory of another Party, or

        (ii)   the extension of credit in connection with a commercial transaction, such as trade financing, other than a loan covered by subparagraph (d); or

    (j)   any other claims to money,

that do not involve the kinds of interests set out in subparagraphs (a) through (h);

investment of an investor of a Party means an investment owned or controlled directly or indirectly by an investor of such Party;

investor of a Party means a Party or state enterprise thereof, or a national or an enterprise of such Party, that seeks to make, is making or has made an investment;

investor of a non-Party means an investor other than an investor of a Party, that seeks to make, is making or has made an investment;

New York Convention means the United Nations Convention on the Recognition and Enforcement of Foreign Arbitral Awards, done at New York, June 10, 1958;

Secretary-General means the Secretary-General of ICSID;

transfers means transfers and international payments;

Tribunal means an arbitration tribunal established under Article 1120 or 1126; and

UNCITRAL Arbitration Rules means the arbitration rules of the United Nations Commission on International Trade Law, approved by the United Nations General Assembly on December 15, 1976.

Annex 1120.1
Submission of a Claim to Arbitration

Mexico

With respect to the submission of a claim to arbitration:

    (a)   an investor of another Party may not allege that Mexico has breached an obligation under:

        (i)   Section A or Article 1503(2) (State Enterprises), or

(ii) Article 1502(3)(a) (Monopolies and State Enterprises) where the monopoly has acted in a manner inconsistent with the Party's obligations under Section A,

both in an arbitration under this Section and in proceedings before a Mexican court or administrative tribunal; and

(b) where an enterprise of Mexico that is a juridical person that an investor of another Party owns or controls directly or indirectly alleges in proceedings before a Mexican court or administrative tribunal that Mexico has breached an obligation under:

(i) Section A or Article 1503(2) (State Enterprises), or

(ii) Article 1502(3)(a) (Monopolies and State Enterprises) where the monopoly has acted in a manner inconsistent with the Party's obligations under Section A, the investor may not allege the breach in an arbitration under this Section.

* * *

Annex 1138.2
Exclusions from Dispute Settlement

Canada

A decision by Canada following a review under the Investment Canada Act, with respect to whether or not to permit an acquisition that is subject to review, shall not be subject to the dispute settlement provisions of Section B or of Chapter Twenty (Institutional Arrangements and Dispute Settlement Procedures).

Mexico

A decision by the National Commission on Foreign Investment ("Comision Nacional de Inversiones Extranjeras") following a review pursuant to Annex I, page I-M-4, with respect to whether or not to permit an acquisition that is subject to review, shall not be subject to the dispute settlement provisions of Section B or of Chapter Twenty (Institutional Arrangements and Dispute Settlement Procedures).

§ 8.15   Text of USMCA Chapter 14 on Investment

Article 14.1: Definitions

For the purposes of this Chapter:

covered investment means, with respect to a Party, an investment in its territory of an investor of another Party in existence as of the date of entry into force of this Agreement or established, acquired, or expanded thereafter;

enterprise means an enterprise as defined in Article 1.4 (General Definitions), and a branch of an enterprise;

enterprise of a Party means an enterprise constituted or organized under the law of a Party, or a branch located in the territory of a Party and carrying out business activities there;

freely usable currency means "freely usable currency" as determined by the International Monetary Fund under its *Articles of Agreement*;

investment means every asset that an investor owns or controls, directly or indirectly, that has the characteristics of an investment, including such characteristics as the commitment of capital or other resources, the expectation of gain or profit, or the assumption of risk. An investment may include:

(a)   an enterprise;

(b)   shares, stock and other forms of equity participation in an enterprise;

(c)   bonds, debentures, other debt instruments, and loans;[1]

(d)   futures, options, and other derivatives;

(e)   turnkey, construction, management, production, concession, revenue-sharing, and other similar contracts;

(f)   intellectual property rights;

(g)   licenses, authorizations, permits, and similar rights conferred pursuant to a Party's law;[2] and

(h)   other tangible or intangible, movable or immovable property, and related property rights, such as liens, mortgages, pledges, and leases,

but investment does not mean:

(i)   an order or judgment entered in a judicial or administrative action;

---

[1]   Some forms of debt, such as bonds, debentures, and long-term notes or loans, are more likely to have the characteristics of an investment, while other forms of debt, such as claims to payment that are immediately due, are less likely to have these characteristics.

[2]   Whether a particular type of license, authorization, permit, or similar instrument (including a concession to the extent that it has the nature of such an instrument) has the characteristics of an investment depends on such factors as the nature and extent of the rights that the holder has under a Party's law. For greater certainty, among such instruments that do not have the characteristics of an investment are those that do not create any rights protected under the Party's law. For greater certainty, the foregoing is without prejudice to whether any asset associated with such instruments has the characteristics of an investment.

(j)   claims to money that arise solely from:

(i)   commercial contracts for the sale of goods or services by a natural person or enterprise in the territory of a Party to an enterprise in the territory of another Party, or

(ii) the extension of credit in connection with a commercial contract referred to in subparagraph (j)(i);

investor of a non-Party means, with respect to a Party, an investor that attempts to make,[3] is making, or has made an investment in the territory of that Party, that is not an investor of a Party; and

investor of a Party means a Party, or a national or an enterprise of a Party, that attempts to make, is making, or has made an investment in the territory of another Party, provided however that:

(a)   a natural person who is a dual citizen is deemed to be exclusively a national of the State of his or her dominant and effective citizenship; and

(b)   a natural person who is a citizen of a Party and a permanent resident of another Party is deemed to be exclusively a national of the Party of which that natural person is a citizen.

Article 14.2: Scope

1.   This Chapter applies to measures adopted or maintained by a Party relating to:

(a)   investors of another Party;

(b)   covered investments; and

(c)   with respect to Article 14.10 (Performance Requirements) and Article 14.16 (Investment and Environmental, Health, Safety, and other Regulatory Objectives), all investments in the territory of that Party.

2.   A Party's obligations under this Chapter apply to measures adopted or maintained by:

(a)   the central, regional, or local governments or authorities of that Party;[4] and

---

[3]   For greater certainty, the Parties understand that, for the purposes of the definitions of "investor of a non-Party" and "investor of a Party", an investor "attempts to make" an investment when that investor has taken concrete action or actions to make an investment, such as channeling resources or capital in order to set up a business, or applying for a permit or license.

[4]   For greater certainty, the term "governments or authorities" means the organs of a Party, consistent with the principles of attribution under customary international law.

(b)   a person, including a state enterprise or another body, when it exercises any governmental authority delegated to it by central, regional, or local governments or authorities of that Party.[5]

3.   For greater certainty, this Chapter, except as provided for in Annex 14-C (Legacy Investment Claims and Pending Claims) does not bind a Party in relation to an act or fact that took place or a situation that ceased to exist before the date of entry into force of this Agreement.

4.   For greater certainty, an investor may only submit a claim to arbitration under this Chapter as provided under Annex 14-C (Legacy Investment Claims and Pending Claims), Annex 14-D (Mexico-United States Investment Disputes), or Annex 14-E (Mexico-United States Investment Disputes Related to Covered Government Contracts).

Article 14.3: Relation to Other Chapters

1.   In the event of any inconsistency between this Chapter and another Chapter of this Agreement, the other Chapter shall prevail to the extent of the inconsistency.

2.   This Chapter does not apply to measures adopted or maintained by a Party to the extent that they are covered by Chapter 17 (Financial Services).

3.   A requirement of a Party that a service supplier of another Party post a bond or other form of financial security as a condition for the cross-border supply of a service does not of itself make this Chapter applicable to measures adopted or maintained by the Party relating to the cross-border supply of the service. This Chapter applies to measures adopted or maintained by the Party relating to the posted bond or financial security, to the extent that the bond or financial security is a covered investment.

4.   For greater certainty, consistent with Article 15.2.2(a) (Scope), Article 15.5 (Market Access), and Article 15.8 (Development and Administration of Measures) apply to measures adopted or maintained by a Party relating to the supply of a service in its territory by a covered investment.

Article 14.4: National Treatment

1.   Each Party shall accord to investors of another Party treatment no less favorable than that it accords, in like circumstances, to

---

[5]   For greater certainty, governmental authority is delegated to any person under the Party's law, including through a legislative grant or a government order, directive, or other act transferring or authorizing the exercise **of** governmental authority.

its own investors with respect to the establishment, acquisition, expansion, management, conduct, operation, and sale or other disposition of investments in its territory.

2. Each Party shall accord to covered investments treatment no less favorable than that it accords, in like circumstances, to investments in its territory of its own investors with respect to the establishment, acquisition, expansion, management, conduct, operation, and sale or other disposition of investments.

3. The treatment accorded by a Party under paragraphs 1 and 2 means, with respect to a government other than at the central level, treatment no less favorable than the most favorable treatment accorded, in like circumstances, by that government to investors, and to investments of investors, of the Party of which it forms a part.

4. For greater certainty, whether treatment is accorded in "like circumstances" under this Article depends on the totality of the circumstances, including whether the relevant treatment distinguishes between investors or investments on the basis of legitimate public welfare objectives.

Article 14.5: Most-Favored-Nation Treatment

1. Each Party shall accord to investors of another Party treatment no less favorable than the treatment it accords, in like circumstances, to investors of any other Party or of any non-Party with respect to the establishment, acquisition, expansion, management, conduct, operation, and sale or other disposition of investments in its territory.

2. Each Party shall accord to covered investments treatment no less favorable than that it accords, in like circumstances, to investments in its territory of investors of any other Party or of any non-Party with respect to the establishment, acquisition, expansion, management, conduct, operation, and sale or other disposition of investments.

3. The treatment accorded by a Party under paragraphs 1 and 2 means, with respect to a government other than at the central level, treatment no less favorable than the most favorable treatment accorded, in like circumstances, by that government to investors in its territory, and to investments of those investors, of any other Party or of any non-Party.

4. For greater certainty, whether treatment is accorded in "like circumstances" under this Article depends on the totality of the circumstances, including whether the relevant treatment

distinguishes between investors or investments on the basis of legitimate public welfare objectives.

Article 14.6: Minimum Standard of Treatment[6]

1. Each Party shall accord to covered investments treatment in accordance with customary international law, including fair and equitable treatment and full protection and security.

2. For greater certainty, paragraph 1 prescribes the customary international law minimum standard of treatment of aliens as the standard of treatment to be afforded to covered investments. The concepts of "fair and equitable treatment" and "full protection and security" do not require treatment in addition to or beyond that which is required by that standard, and do not create additional substantive rights. The obligations in paragraph 1 to provide:

   (a) "fair and equitable treatment" includes the obligation not to deny justice in criminal, civil, or administrative adjudicatory proceedings in accordance with the principle of due process embodied in the principal legal systems of the world; and

   (b) "full protection and security" requires each Party to provide the level of police protection required under customary international law.

3. A determination that there has been a breach of another provision of this Agreement, or of a separate international agreement, does not establish that there has been a breach of this Article.

4. For greater certainty, the mere fact that a Party takes or fails to take an action that may be inconsistent with an investor's expectations does not constitute a breach of this Article, even if there is loss or damage to the covered investment as a result.

Article 14.7: Treatment in Case of Armed Conflict or Civil Strife

1. Notwithstanding Article 14.12.5(b) (Non-Conforming Measures), each Party shall accord to investors of another Party and to covered investments non-discriminatory treatment with respect to measures it adopts or maintains relating to losses suffered by investments in its territory owing to armed conflict or civil strife.

---

6   This Article shall be interpreted in accordance with Annex 14-A (Customary International Law).

2.   Notwithstanding paragraph 1, if an investor of a Party, in a situation referred to in paragraph 1, suffers a loss in the territory of another Party resulting from:

(a)   requisitioning of its covered investment or part thereof by the latter's forces or authorities; or

(b)   destruction of its covered investment or part thereof by the latter's forces or authorities, which was not required by the necessity of the situation,

the latter Party shall provide the investor restitution, compensation, or both, as appropriate, for that loss.

3.   Paragraph 1 does not apply to existing measures relating to subsidies or grants that would be inconsistent with Article 14.4 (National Treatment) but for Article 14.12.5(b) (Non-Conforming Measures).

Article 14.8: Expropriation and Compensation[7]

1.   No Party shall expropriate or nationalize a covered investment either directly or indirectly through measures equivalent to expropriation or nationalization (expropriation), except:

(a)   for a public purpose;

(b)   in a non-discriminatory manner;

(c)   on payment of prompt, adequate, and effective compensation in accordance with paragraphs 2, 3, and 4; and

(d)   in accordance with due process of law.

2.   Compensation shall:

(a)   be paid without delay;

(b)   be equivalent to the fair market value of the expropriated investment immediately before the expropriation took place (the date of expropriation);

(c)   not reflect any change in value occurring because the intended expropriation had become known earlier; and

(d)   be fully realizable and freely transferable.

3.   If the fair market value is denominated in a freely usable currency, the compensation paid shall be no less than the fair market value on the date of expropriation, plus interest at a commercially reasonable rate for that currency, accrued from the date of expropriation until the date of payment.

---

[7]   This Article shall be interpreted in accordance with Annex 14-B (Expropriation).

4. If the fair market value is denominated in a currency that is not freely usable, the compensation paid—converted into the currency of payment at the market rate of exchange prevailing on the date of payment[8]—shall be no less than:

    (a) the fair market value on the date of expropriation, converted into a freely usable currency at the market rate of exchange prevailing on that date; plus

    (b) interest, at a commercially reasonable rate for that freely usable currency, accrued from the date of expropriation until the date of payment.

5. For greater certainty, whether an action or series of actions by a Party constitutes an expropriation shall be determined in accordance with paragraph 1 of this Article and Annex 14-B (Expropriation).

6. This Article does not apply to the issuance of compulsory licenses granted in relation to intellectual property rights in accordance with the TRIPS Agreement, or to the revocation, limitation, or creation of intellectual property rights, to the extent that the issuance, revocation, limitation, or creation is consistent with Chapter 20 (Intellectual Property) and the TRIPS Agreement.[9]

Article 14.9: Transfers

1. Each Party shall permit all transfers relating to a covered investment to be made freely and without delay into and out of its territory. These transfers include:

    (a) contributions to capital;[10]

    (b) profits, dividends, interest, capital gains, royalty payments, management fees, technical assistance, and other fees;

    (c) proceeds from the sale of all or any part of the covered investment or from the partial or complete liquidation of the covered investment;

    (d) payments made under a contract entered into by the investor, or the covered investment, including payments made pursuant to a loan agreement or employment contract; and

---

[8] For greater certainty, for the purposes of this paragraph, the currency of payment may be the same as the currency in which the fair market value is denominated.

[9] For greater certainty, the Parties recognize that, for the purposes of this Article, the term "revocation" of an intellectual property right includes the cancellation or nullification of that right, and the term "limitation" of an intellectual property right includes exceptions to that right.

[10] For greater certainty, contributions to capital include the initial contribution.

(e) payments made pursuant to Article 14.7 (Treatment in Case of Armed Conflict or Civil Strife) and Article 14.8 (Expropriation and Compensation).

2. Each Party shall permit transfers relating to a covered investment to be made in a freely usable currency at the market rate of exchange prevailing at the time of transfer.

3. A Party shall not require its investors to transfer, or penalize its investors that fail to transfer, the income, earnings, profits, or other amounts derived from, or attributable to, investments in the territory of another Party.

4. Each Party shall permit returns in kind relating to a covered investment to be made as authorized or specified in a written agreement between the Party and a covered investment or an investor of another Party.

5. Notwithstanding paragraphs 1, 2, and 4, a Party may prevent or delay a transfer through the equitable, non-discriminatory, and good faith application of its laws[11] relating to:

(a) bankruptcy, insolvency, or the protection of the rights of creditors;

(b) issuing, trading, or dealing in securities or derivatives;

(c) criminal or penal offenses;

(d) financial reporting or record keeping of transfers when necessary to assist law enforcement or financial regulatory authorities; or

(e) ensuring compliance with orders or judgments in judicial or administrative proceedings.

6. Notwithstanding paragraph 4, a Party may restrict transfers of returns in kind in circumstances where it could otherwise restrict those transfers under this Agreement, including as set out in paragraph 5.

Article 14.10: Performance Requirements

1. No Party shall, in connection with the establishment, acquisition, expansion, management, conduct, operation, or sale or other disposition of an investment of an investor of a Party or

---

[11] For greater certainty, this Article does not preclude the equitable, non-discriminatory, and good faith application of a Party's laws relating to its social security, public retirement, or compulsory savings programs.

of a non-Party in its territory, impose or enforce any requirement, or enforce any commitment or undertaking:[12]

(a)   to export a given level or percentage of goods or services;

(b)   to achieve a given level or percentage of domestic content;

(c)   to purchase, use, or accord a preference to a good produced or a service supplied in its territory, or to purchase a good or a service from a person in its territory;

(d)   to regulate in any way the volume or value of imports to the volume or value of exports or to the amount of foreign exchange inflows associated with the investment;

(e)   to restrict sales of a good or a service in its territory that the investment produces or supplies by relating those sales in any way to the volume or value of its exports or foreign exchange earnings;

(f)   to transfer a technology, a production process, or other proprietary knowledge to a person in its territory;

(g)   to supply exclusively from the territory of the Party a good that the investment produces or a service that it supplies to a specific regional market or to the world market;

(h)   (i)   to purchase, use, or accord a preference to, in its territory, technology of the Party or of a person of the Party,[13] or

(ii)   that prevents the purchase or use of, or the according of a preference to, in its territory, a technology; or

(i)   to adopt:

(i)   a given rate or amount of royalty under a license contract, or

(ii)   a given duration of the term of a license contract,

in regard to any license contract in existence at the time the requirement is imposed or enforced, or any commitment or undertaking is enforced, or any future license contract[14] freely entered into between the investor and a person in its territory, provided that the requirement is imposed or the commitment or

---

[12]   For greater certainty, a condition for the receipt or continued receipt of an advantage referred to in paragraph 2 does not constitute a "requirement" or a "commitment or undertaking" for the purposes of paragraph 1.

[13]   For the purposes of this Article, the term "technology of the Party or of a person of the Party" includes technology that is owned by the Party or a person of the Party, and technology for which the Party or a person of the Party holds an exclusive license.

[14]   A "license contract" referred to in this subparagraph means a contract concerning the licensing of technology, a production process, or other proprietary knowledge.

undertaking is enforced in a manner that constitutes direct interference with that license contract by an exercise of non-judicial governmental authority of a Party. For greater certainty, paragraph 1(i) does not apply when the license contract is concluded between the investor and a Party.

2.   No Party shall condition the receipt or continued receipt of an advantage, in connection with the establishment, acquisition, expansion, management, conduct, operation, or sale or other disposition of an investment of an investor of a Party or of a non-Party in its territory, on compliance with any requirement:

(a)   to achieve a given level or percentage of domestic content;

(b)   to purchase, use, or accord a preference to a good produced in its territory, or to purchase a good from a person in its territory;

(c)   to relate in any way the volume or value of imports to the volume or value of exports or to the amount of foreign exchange inflows associated with the investment;

(d)   to restrict sales of goods or services in its territory that the investment produces or supplies by relating those sales in any way to the volume or value of its exports or foreign exchange earnings; or

(e)   (i)   to purchase, use or accord a preference to, in its territory, technology of the Party or of a person of the Party, or

(ii)   that prevents the purchase or use of, or the according of a preference to, in its territory, a technology.

3.   In relation to paragraphs 1 and 2:

(a)   Nothing in paragraph 2 shall be construed to prevent a Party from conditioning the receipt or continued receipt of an advantage, in connection with an investment of an investor of a Party or of a non-Party in its territory, on compliance with a requirement to locate production, supply a service, train or employ workers, construct or expand particular facilities, or carry out research and development, in its territory.

(b)   Paragraphs 1(f), 1(h), 1(i), and 2(e) do not apply:

(i)   if a Party authorizes use of an intellectual property right in accordance with Article 31[15] of the TRIPS Agreement, or to a measure requiring the disclosure of

---

[15]   The reference to "Article 31" includes any waiver or amendment to the TRIPS Agreement implementing paragraph 6 of the *Doha Declaration on the TRIPS Agreement and Public Health* (WT/MIN (01)/DEC/2).

proprietary information that fall within the scope of, and is consistent with, Article 39 of the TRIPS Agreement, or

(ii) if the requirement is imposed or the commitment or undertaking[16] is enforced by a court, administrative tribunal, or competition authority, after judicial or administrative process, to remedy an alleged violation of competition laws.[17]

(c) Provided that such measures are not applied in an arbitrary or unjustifiable manner, or do not constitute a disguised restriction on international trade or investment, paragraphs 1(b), 1(c), 1(f), 2(a), and 2(b) shall not be construed to prevent a Party from adopting or maintaining measures:

(i) necessary to secure compliance with laws and regulations that are not inconsistent with this Agreement,

(ii) necessary to protect human, animal or plant life or health, or

(iii) related to the conservation of living or non-living exhaustible natural resources.

(d) Paragraphs 1(a), 1(b), 1(c), 2(a), and 2(b) do not apply to qualification requirements for a good or a service with respect to export promotion and foreign aid programs.

(e) Paragraphs 1(b), 1(c), 1(f), 1(g), 1(h), 1(i), 2(a), 2(b), and 2(e) do not apply to government procurement.

(f) Paragraphs 2(a) and 2(b) do not apply to requirements imposed by an importing Party relating to the content of a good necessary to qualify for preferential tariffs or preferential quotas.

(g) Paragraphs 1(h), 1(i), and 2(e) shall not be construed to prevent a Party from adopting or maintaining measures to protect legitimate public welfare objectives, provided that such measures are not applied in an arbitrary or unjustifiable manner, or in a manner that constitutes a disguised restriction on international trade or investment.

4. For greater certainty, paragraphs 1 and 2 do not apply to any commitment, undertaking, or requirement other than those set out in those paragraphs.

---

[16] For greater certainty, for the purposes of this subparagraph, a commitment or undertaking includes a consent agreement.

[17] The Parties recognize that a patent does not necessarily confer market power.

5.   This Article does not preclude enforcement of any commitment, undertaking, or requirement between private parties, if a Party did not impose or require the commitment, undertaking, or requirement.

Article 14.11: Senior Management and Boards of Directors

1.   No Party shall require that an enterprise of that Party that is a covered investment appoint to senior management positions a natural person of a particular nationality.

2.   A Party may require that a majority of the board of directors, or any committee thereof, of an enterprise of that Party that is a covered investment, be of a particular nationality, or resident in the territory of the Party, provided that the requirement does not materially impair the ability of the investor to exercise control over its investment.

Article 14.12: Non-Conforming Measures

1.   Article 14.4 (National Treatment), Article 14.5 (Most-Favored-Nation Treatment), Article 14.10 (Performance Requirements), and Article 14.11 (Senior Management and Boards of Directors) do not apply to:

(a)   any existing non-conforming measure that is maintained by a Party at:

(i)   the central level of government, as set out by that Party in its Schedule to Annex I,

(ii)   a regional level of government, as set out by that Party in its Schedule to Annex I, or

(iii)   a local level of government;

(b)   the continuation or prompt renewal of any non-conforming measure referred to in subparagraph (a); or

(c)   an amendment to any non-conforming measure referred to in subparagraph (a) to the extent that the amendment does not decrease the conformity of the measure, as it existed immediately before the amendment, with Article 14.4 (National Treatment), Article 14.5 (Most-Favored-Nation Treatment), Article 14.10 (Performance Requirements), or Article 14.11 (Senior Management and Boards of Directors).

2.   Article 14.4 (National Treatment), Article 14.5 (Most-Favored-Nation Treatment), Article 14.10 (Performance Requirements), and Article 14.11 (Senior Management and Boards of Directors) do not apply to any measure that a Party adopts or maintains

with respect to sectors, sub-sectors, or activities, as set out by that Party in its Schedule to Annex II.

3. No Party shall, under any measure adopted after the date of entry into force of this Agreement and covered by its Schedule to Annex II, require an investor of another Party, by reason of its nationality, to sell or otherwise dispose of an investment existing at the time the measure becomes effective.

4. (a) Article 14.4 (National Treatment) does not apply to any measure that falls within an exception to, or derogation from, the obligations imposed by:

(i) Article 20.8 (National Treatment), or

(ii) Article 3 of the TRIPS Agreement, if the exception or derogation relates to matters not addressed by Chapter 20 (Intellectual Property Rights);

(b) Article 14.5 (Most-Favored-Nation Treatment) does not apply to any measure that falls within Article 5 of the TRIPS Agreement, or an exception to, or derogation from, an obligation imposed by:

(i) Article 20.8 (National Treatment), or

(ii) Article 4 of the TRIPS Agreement.

5. Article 14.4 (National Treatment), Article 14.5 (Most-Favored-Nation Treatment), and Article 14.11 (Senior Management and Boards of Directors) do not apply to:

(a) government procurement; or

(b) subsidies or grants provided by a Party, including government-supported loans, guarantees, and insurance.

Article 14.13: Special Formalities
and Information Requirements

1. Nothing in Article 14.4 (National Treatment) shall be construed to prevent a Party from adopting or maintaining a measure that prescribes special formalities in connection with covered investments, such as a requirement that investors be residents of the Party or that covered investments be legally constituted under the laws or regulations of the Party, provided that these formalities do not materially impair the protections afforded by the Party to investors of another Party and covered investments pursuant to this Chapter.

2. Notwithstanding Article 14.4 (National Treatment) and Article 14.5 (Most-Favored-Nation Treatment), a Party may require an investor of another Party or its covered investment to provide

information concerning that investment solely for informational or statistical purposes. The Party shall protect such information that is confidential from any disclosure that would prejudice the competitive position of the investor or its covered investment. Nothing in this paragraph shall be construed to prevent a Party from otherwise obtaining or disclosing information in connection with the equitable and good faith application of its law.

Article 14.14: Denial of Benefits

1. A Party may deny the benefits of this Chapter to an investor of another Party that is an enterprise of that other Party and to investments of that investor if the enterprise:

    (a) is owned or controlled by a person of a non-Party or of the denying Party; and

    (b) has no substantial business activities in the territory of any Party other than the denying Party.

2. A Party may deny the benefits of this Chapter to an investor of another Party that is an enterprise of that other Party and to investments of that investor if persons of a non-Party own or control the enterprise and the denying Party adopts or maintains measures with respect to the non-Party or a person of the non-Party that prohibit transactions with the enterprise or that would be violated or circumvented if the benefits of this Chapter were accorded to the enterprise or to its investments.

Article 14.15: Subrogation

If a Party, or an agency of a Party, makes a payment to an investor of the Party under a guarantee, a contract of insurance, or other form of indemnity that it has entered into with respect to a covered investment, the other Party in whose territory the covered investment was made shall recognize the subrogation or transfer of any right the investor would have possessed with respect to the covered investment but for the subrogation, and the investor shall be precluded from pursuing that right to the extent of the subrogation, unless a Party or an agency of a Party authorizes the investor to act on its behalf.

Article 14.16: Investment and Environmental, Health, Safety, and other Regulatory Objectives

Nothing in this Chapter shall be construed to prevent a Party from adopting, maintaining, or enforcing any measure otherwise consistent with this Chapter that it considers appropriate to ensure that investment activity in its territory is undertaken in a manner sensitive to environmental, health, safety, or other regulatory objectives.

Article 14.17: Corporate Social Responsibility

The Parties reaffirm the importance of each Party encouraging enterprises operating within its territory or subject to its jurisdiction to voluntarily incorporate into their internal policies those internationally recognized standards, guidelines, and principles of corporate social responsibility that have been endorsed or are supported by that Party, which may include the OECD Guidelines for Multinational Enterprises. These standards, guidelines, and principles may address areas such as labor, environment, gender equality, human rights, indigenous and aboriginal peoples' rights, and corruption.

ANNEX 14-A
CUSTOMARY INTERNATIONAL LAW

The Parties confirm their shared understanding that "customary international law" generally and as specifically referenced in Article 14.6 (Minimum Standard of Treatment) results from a general and consistent practice of States that they follow from a sense of legal obligation. The customary international law minimum standard of treatment of aliens refers to all customary international law principles that protect the investments of aliens.

ANNEX 14-B
EXPROPRIATION

The Parties confirm their shared understanding that:

1. An action or a series of actions by a Party cannot constitute an expropriation unless it interferes with a tangible or intangible property right[18] or property interest in an investment.

2. Article 14.8.1 (Expropriation and Compensation) addresses two situations. The first is direct expropriation, in which an investment is nationalized or otherwise directly expropriated through formal transfer of title or outright seizure.

3. The second situation addressed by Article 14.8.1 (Expropriation and Compensation) is indirect expropriation, in which an action or series of actions by a Party has an effect equivalent to direct expropriation without formal transfer of title or outright seizure.

    (a) The determination of whether an action or series of actions by a Party, in a specific fact situation, constitutes an indirect expropriation, requires a case-by-case, fact-based inquiry that considers, among other factors:

---

[18] For greater certainty, the existence of a property right is determined with reference to a Party's law.

(i)   the economic impact of the government action, although the fact that an action or series of actions by a Party has an adverse effect on the economic value of an investment, standing alone, does not establish that an indirect expropriation has occurred,

(ii) the extent to which the government action interferes with distinct, reasonable investment-backed expectations,[19] and

(iii) the character of the government action, including its object, context, and intent.

(b)   Non-discriminatory regulatory actions by a Party that are designed and applied to protect legitimate public welfare objectives, such as health, safety and the environment, do not constitute indirect expropriations, except in rare circumstances.

ANNEX 14-C
LEGACY INVESTMENT CLAIMS
AND PENDING CLAIMS

1.   Each Party consents, with respect to a legacy investment, to the submission of a claim to arbitration in accordance with Section B of Chapter 11 (Investment) of NAFTA 1994 and this Annex alleging breach of an obligation under:

(a)   Section A of Chapter 11 (Investment) of NAFTA 1994;

(b)   Article 1503(2) (State Enterprises) of NAFTA 1994; and

(c)   Article 1502(3)(a) (Monopolies and State Enterprises) of NAFTA 1994 where the monopoly has acted in a manner inconsistent with the Party's obligations under Section A of Chapter 11 (Investment) of NAFTA 1994.[20, 21]

2.   The consent under paragraph 1 and the submission of a claim to arbitration in accordance with Section B of Chapter 11

---

[19]   For greater certainty, whether an investor's investment-backed expectations are reasonable depends, to the extent relevant, on factors such as whether the government provided the investor with binding written assurances and the nature and extent of governmental regulation or the potential for government regulation in the relevant sector.

[20]   For greater certainty, the relevant provisions in Chapter 2 (General Definitions), Chapter 11 (Section A) (Investment), Chapter 14 (Financial Services), Chapter 15 (Competition Policy, Monopolies and State Enterprises), Chapter 17 (Intellectual Property), Chapter 21 (Exceptions), and Annexes I-VII (Reservations and Exceptions to Investment, Cross-Border Trade in Services and Financial Services Chapters) of NAFTA 1994 apply with respect to such a claim.

[21]   Mexico and the United States do not consent under paragraph 1 with respect to an investor of the other Party that is eligible to submit claims to arbitration under paragraph 2 of Annex 14-E (Mexico-United States Investment Disputes Related to Covered Government Contracts).

(Investment) of NAFTA 1994 and this Annex shall satisfy the requirements of:

(a) Chapter II of the ICSID Convention (Jurisdiction of the Centre) and the ICSID Additional Facility Rules for written consent of the parties to the dispute;

(b) Article II of the New York Convention for an "agreement in writing"; and

(c) Article I of the Inter-American Convention for an "agreement".

3. A Party's consent under paragraph 1 shall expire three years after the termination of NAFTA 1994.

4. For greater certainty, an arbitration initiated pursuant to the submission of a claim under paragraph 1 may proceed to its conclusion in accordance with Section B of Chapter 11 (Investment) of NAFTA 1994, the Tribunal's jurisdiction with respect to such a claim is not affected by the expiration of consent referenced in paragraph 3, and Article 1136 (Finality and Enforcement of an Award) of NAFTA 1994 (excluding paragraph 5) applies with respect to any award made by the Tribunal.

5. For greater certainty, an arbitration initiated pursuant to the submission of a claim under Section B of Chapter 11 (Investment) of NAFTA 1994 while NAFTA 1994 is in force may proceed to its conclusion in accordance with Section B of Chapter 11 (Investment) of NAFTA 1994, the Tribunal's jurisdiction with respect to such a claim is not affected by the termination of NAFTA 1994, and Article 1136 of NAFTA 1994 (excluding paragraph 5) applies with respect to any award made by the Tribunal.

6. For the purposes of this Annex:

(a) "legacy investment" means an investment of an investor of another Party in the territory of the Party established or acquired between January 1, 1994, and the date of termination of NAFTA 1994, and in existence on the date of entry into force of this Agreement;

(b) "investment", "investor", and "Tribunal" have the meanings accorded in Chapter 11 (Investment) of NAFTA 1994; and

(c) "ICSID Convention", "ICSID Additional Facility Rules", "New York Convention", and "Inter-American Convention" have the meanings accorded in Article 14.D.1 (Definitions).

ANNEX 14-D
MEXICO-UNITED STATES INVESTMENT DISPUTES
Article 14.D.1: Definitions

For the purposes of this Annex:

Annex Party means Mexico or the United States;

Centre means the International Centre for Settlement of Investment Disputes (ICSID) established by the ICSID Convention;

claimant means an investor of an Annex Party that is a party to a qualifying investment dispute, excluding an investor that is owned or controlled by a person of a non-Annex Party that, on the date of signature of this Agreement, the other Annex Party has determined to be a non-market economy for purposes of its trade remedy laws and with which no Party has a free trade agreement;

disputing parties means the claimant and the respondent;

disputing party means either the claimant or the respondent;

ICSID Additional Facility Rules means the *Rules Governing the Additional Facility for the Administration of Proceedings by the Secretariat of the International Centre for Settlement of Investment Disputes;*

ICSID Convention means the *Convention on the Settlement of Investment Disputes between States and Nationals of other States,* done at Washington, March 18, 1965;

Inter-American Convention means the *Inter-American Convention on International Commercial Arbitration,* done at Panama, January 30, 1975;

New York Convention means the *Convention on the Recognition and Enforcement of Foreign Arbitral Awards,* done at New York, June 10, 1958;

non-disputing Annex Party means the Annex Party that is not a party to a qualifying investment dispute;

protected information means confidential business information or information that is privileged or otherwise protected from disclosure under a Party's law, including classified government information;

qualifying investment dispute means an investment dispute between an investor of an Annex Party and the other Annex Party;

respondent means the Annex Party that is a party to a qualifying investment dispute;

Secretary-General means the Secretary-General of ICSID; and

UNCITRAL Arbitration Rules means the arbitration rules of the United Nations Commission on International Trade Law.

Article 14.D.2: Consultation and Negotiation

1. In the event of a qualifying investment dispute, the claimant and the respondent should initially seek to resolve the dispute through consultation and negotiation, which may include the use of non-binding, third party procedures, such as good offices, conciliation, or mediation.

2. For greater certainty, the initiation of consultations and negotiations shall not be construed as recognition of the jurisdiction of the tribunal.

Article 14.D.3: Submission of a Claim to Arbitration

1. In the event that a disputing party considers that a qualifying investment dispute cannot be settled by consultation and negotiation:

    (a) the claimant, on its own behalf, may submit to arbitration under this Annex a claim:

        (i) that the respondent has breached:

            (A) Article 14.4 (National Treatment) or Article 14.5 (Most-Favored-Nation Treatment),[22] except with respect to the establishment or acquisition of an investment, or

            (B) Article 14.8 (Expropriation and Compensation), except with respect to indirect expropriation, and

        (ii) that the claimant has incurred loss or damage by reason of, or arising out of, that breach; and

    (b) the claimant, on behalf of an enterprise of the respondent that is a juridical person that the claimant owns or controls directly or indirectly, may submit to arbitration under this Annex a claim:

        (i) that the respondent has breached:

            (A) Article 14.4 (National Treatment) or Article 14.5 (Most-Favored-Nation Treatment), except with respect

---

[22] For the purposes of this paragraph: (i) the "treatment" referred to in Article 14.5 (Most-Favored-Nation Treatment) excludes provisions in other international trade or investment agreements that establish international dispute resolution procedures or impose substantive obligations; and (ii) the "treatment" referred to in Article 14.5 only encompasses measures adopted or maintained by the other Annex Party, which for greater clarity may include measures adopted in connection with the implementation of substantive obligations in other international trade or investment agreements.

to the establishment or acquisition of an investment, or

(B) Article 14.8 (Expropriation and Compensation), except with respect to indirect expropriation, and

(ii) that the enterprise has incurred loss or damage by reason of, or arising out of, that breach.[23]

2. At least 90 days before submitting any claim to arbitration under this Annex, the claimant shall deliver to the respondent a written notice of its intention to submit a claim to arbitration (notice of intent). The notice shall specify:

(a) the name and address of the claimant and, if a claim is submitted on behalf of an enterprise, the name, address, and place of incorporation of the enterprise;

(b) for each claim, the provision of this Agreement alleged to have been breached and any other relevant provisions;

(c) the legal and factual basis for each claim; and

(d) the relief sought and the approximate amount of damages claimed.

3. The claimant may submit a claim referred to in paragraph 1 under one of the following alternatives:

(a) the ICSID Convention and the ICSID *Rules of Procedure for Arbitration Proceedings*, provided that both the respondent and the Party of the claimant are parties to the ICSID Convention;[24]

(b) the ICSID Additional Facility Rules, provided that either the respondent or the Party of the claimant is a party to the ICSID Convention;

(c) the UNCITRAL Arbitration Rules; or

(d) if the claimant and respondent agree, any other arbitral institution or any other arbitration rules.

4. A claim shall be deemed submitted to arbitration under this Annex when the claimant's notice of or request for arbitration (notice of arbitration):

---

[23] For greater certainty, in order for a claim to be submitted to arbitration under subparagraph (b), an investor of the Party of the claimant must own or control the enterprise on the date of the alleged breach and the date on which the claim is submitted to arbitration.

[24] For greater certainty, if a claimant submits a claim under this subparagraph, any award made by the tribunal under Article 14.D.13 (Awards) constitutes an award under Chapter IV of the ICSID Convention (Arbitration).

(a) referred to in the ICSID Convention is received by the Secretary-General;

(b) referred to in the ICSID Additional Facility Rules is received by the Secretary-General;

(c) referred to in the UNCITRAL Arbitration Rules, together with the statement of claim referred to therein, are received by the respondent; or

(d) referred to under any arbitral institution or arbitration rules selected under paragraph 3(d) is received by the respondent.

A claim asserted by the claimant for the first time after such notice of arbitration is submitted shall be deemed submitted to arbitration under this Annex on the date of its receipt under the applicable arbitration rules.

5. The arbitration rules applicable under paragraph 3 that are in effect on the date the claim or claims were submitted to arbitration under this Annex shall govern the arbitration except to the extent modified by this Agreement.

6. The claimant shall provide with the notice of arbitration:

(a) the name of the arbitrator that the claimant appoints; or

(b) the claimant's written consent for the Secretary-General to appoint that arbitrator.

Article 14.D.4: Consent to Arbitration

1. Each Annex Party consents to the submission of a claim to arbitration under this Annex in accordance with this Agreement.

2. The consent under paragraph 1 and the submission of a claim to arbitration under this Annex shall be deemed to satisfy the requirements of:

(a) Chapter II of the ICSID Convention (Jurisdiction of the Centre) and the ICSID Additional Facility Rules for written consent of the parties to the dispute;

(b) Article II of the New York Convention for an "agreement in writing"; and

(c) Article I of the Inter-American Convention for an "agreement".

Article 14.D.5: Conditions and Limitations on Consent

1. No claim shall be submitted to arbitration under this Annex unless:

(a)   the claimant (for claims brought under Article 14.D.3.1(a) (Submission of a Claim to Arbitration)) and the claimant or the enterprise (for claims brought under Article 14.D.3.1(b)) first initiated a proceeding before a competent court or administrative tribunal of the respondent with respect to the measures alleged to constitute a breach referred to in Article 14.D.3;

(b)   the claimant or the enterprise obtained a final decision from a court of last resort of the respondent or 30 months have elapsed from the date the proceeding in subparagraph (a) was initiated;[25]

(c)   no more than four years have elapsed from the date on which the claimant first acquired, or should have first acquired, knowledge of the breach alleged under Article 14.D.3.1 (Submission of a Claim to Arbitration) and knowledge that the claimant (for claims brought under Article 14.D.3.1(a)) or the enterprise (for claims brought under Article 14.D.3.1(b)) has incurred loss or damage;

(d)   the claimant consents in writing to arbitration in accordance with the procedures set out in this Agreement; and

(e)   the notice of arbitration is accompanied:

(i)   for claims submitted to arbitration under Article 14.D.3.1(a) (Submission of a Claim to Arbitration), by the claimant's written waiver, and

(ii)   for claims submitted to arbitration under Article 14.D.3.1(b) (Submission of a Claim to Arbitration), by the claimant's and the enterprise's written waivers,

of any right to initiate or continue before any court or administrative tribunal under the law of an Annex Party, or any other dispute settlement procedures, any proceeding with respect to any measure alleged to constitute a breach referred to in Article 14.D.3 (Submission of a Claim to Arbitration).

2.   Notwithstanding paragraph 1(e), the claimant (for claims brought under Article 14.D.3.1(a) (Submission of a Claim to Arbitration)) and the claimant or the enterprise (for claims brought under Article 14.D.3.1(b)) may initiate or continue an action that seeks interim injunctive relief and does not involve the payment of monetary damages before a judicial or administrative tribunal of the respondent, provided that the action is brought for the sole purpose of preserving the

---

[25]   The provisions in subparagraphs (a) and (b) do not apply to the extent recourse to domestic remedies was obviously futile.

claimant's or the enterprise's rights and interests during the pendency of the arbitration.

Article 14.D.6: Selection of Arbitrators

1. Unless the disputing parties agree otherwise, the tribunal shall comprise three arbitrators, one arbitrator appointed by each of the disputing parties and the third, who shall be the presiding arbitrator, appointed by agreement of the disputing parties.

2. The Secretary-General shall serve as appointing authority for an arbitration under this Annex.

3. If a tribunal has not been constituted within a period of 75 days after the date that a claim is submitted to arbitration under this Annex, the Secretary-General, on the request of a disputing party, shall appoint, in his or her discretion, the arbitrator or arbitrators not yet appointed. The Secretary-General shall not appoint a national of either the respondent or the Party of the claimant as the presiding arbitrator unless the disputing parties agree otherwise.

4. For the purposes of Article 39 of the ICSID Convention and Article 7 of Schedule C to the ICSID Additional Facility Rules, and without prejudice to an objection to an arbitrator on a ground other than nationality:

    (a) the respondent agrees to the appointment of each individual member of a tribunal established under the ICSID Convention or the ICSID Additional Facility Rules;

    (b) a claimant referred to in Article 14.D.3.1(a) (Submission of a Claim to Arbitration) may submit a claim to arbitration under this Annex, or continue a claim, under the ICSID Convention or the ICSID Additional Facility Rules, only on condition that the claimant agrees in writing to the appointment of each individual member of the tribunal; and

    (c) a claimant referred to in Article 14.D.3.1(b) (Submission of a Claim to Arbitration) may submit a claim to arbitration under this Annex, or continue a claim, under the ICSID Convention or the ICSID Additional Facility Rules, only on condition that the claimant and the enterprise agree in writing to the appointment of each individual member of the tribunal.

5. Arbitrators appointed to a tribunal for claims submitted under Article 14.D.3.1 shall:

    (a) comply with the International Bar Association Guidelines on Conflicts of Interest in International Arbitration, including guidelines regarding direct or indirect conflicts of interest, or

any supplemental guidelines or rules adopted by the Annex
Parties;

(b)   not take instructions from any organization or government
regarding the dispute; and not, for the duration of the
proceedings, act as counsel or as party-appointed expert or
witness in any pending arbitration under the annexes to this
Chapter.

6.   Challenges to arbitrators shall be governed by the procedures in
the UNCITRAL Arbitration Rules.

Article 14.D.7: Conduct of the Arbitration

1.   The disputing parties may agree on the legal place of any
arbitration under the arbitration rules applicable under Article
14.D.3.3 (Submission of a Claim to Arbitration). If the disputing
parties fail to reach agreement, the tribunal shall determine the
place in accordance with the applicable arbitration rules,
provided that the place shall be in the territory of a State that is
a party to the New York Convention.

2.   The non-disputing Annex Party may make oral and written
submissions to the tribunal regarding the interpretation of this
Agreement.

3.   After consultation with the disputing parties, the tribunal may
accept and consider written *amicus curiae* submissions
regarding a matter of fact or law within the scope of the dispute
that may assist the tribunal in evaluating the submissions and
arguments of the disputing parties from a person or entity that
is not a disputing party but has a significant interest in the
arbitral proceedings. Each submission shall identify the author;
disclose any affiliation, direct or indirect, with any disputing
party; and identify any person, government, or other entity that
has provided, or will provide, any financial or other assistance
in preparing the submission. Each submission shall be in a
language of the arbitration and comply with any page limits and
deadlines set by the tribunal. The tribunal shall provide the
disputing parties with an opportunity to respond to such
submissions. The tribunal shall ensure that the submissions do
not disrupt or unduly burden the arbitral proceedings, or
unfairly prejudice any disputing party.

4.   Without prejudice to a tribunal's authority to address other
objections as a preliminary question, such as an objection that a
dispute is not within the competence of the tribunal, including
an objection to the tribunal's jurisdiction, a tribunal shall
address and decide as a preliminary question any objection by

the respondent that, as a matter of law, a claim submitted is not a claim for which an award in favor of the claimant may be made under Article 14.D.13 (Awards) or that a claim is manifestly without legal merit.

(a) An objection under this paragraph shall be submitted to the tribunal as soon as possible after the tribunal is constituted, and in no event later than the date the tribunal fixes for the respondent to submit its counter-memorial or, in the case of an amendment to the notice of arbitration, the date the tribunal fixes for the respondent to submit its response to the amendment.

(b) On receipt of an objection under this paragraph, the tribunal shall suspend any proceedings on the merits, establish a schedule for considering the objection consistent with any schedule it has established for considering any other preliminary question, and issue a decision or award on the objection, stating the grounds therefor.

(c) In deciding an objection under this paragraph that a claim submitted is not a claim for which an award in favor of the claimant may be made under Article 14.D.13 (Awards), the tribunal shall assume to be true the claimant's factual allegations in support of any claim in the notice of arbitration (or any amendment thereof) and, in disputes brought under the UNCITRAL Arbitration Rules, the statement of claim referred to in the relevant article of the UNCITRAL Arbitration Rules. The tribunal may also consider any relevant facts not in dispute.

(d) The respondent does not waive any objection as to competence, including an objection to jurisdiction, or any argument on the merits merely because the respondent did or did not raise an objection under this paragraph or make use of the expedited procedure set out in paragraph 5.

5. In the event that the respondent so requests within 45 days after the tribunal is constituted, the tribunal shall decide on an expedited basis an objection under paragraph 4 or any objection that the dispute is not within the tribunal's competence, including an objection that the dispute is not within the tribunal's jurisdiction. The tribunal shall suspend any proceedings on the merits and issue a decision or award on the objection, stating the grounds therefor, no later than 150 days after the date of the request. However, if a disputing party requests a hearing, the tribunal may take an additional 30 days to issue the decision or award. Regardless of whether a hearing is requested, a tribunal may, on a showing of extraordinary

cause, delay issuing its decision or award by an additional brief
period, which may not exceed 30 days.

6.   When the tribunal decides a respondent's objection under
      paragraph 4 or 5, it may, if warranted, award to the prevailing
      disputing party reasonable costs and attorney's fees incurred in
      submitting or opposing the objection. In determining whether
      such an award is warranted, the tribunal shall consider whether
      either the claimant's claim or the respondent's objection was
      frivolous, and shall provide the disputing parties a reasonable
      opportunity to comment.

7.   For greater certainty, if an investor of an Annex Party submits
      a claim under this Annex, the investor has the burden of proving
      all elements of its claims, consistent with general principles of
      international law applicable to international arbitration.

8.   A respondent may not assert as a defense, counterclaim, right of
      set-off, or for any other reason, that the claimant has received or
      will receive indemnification or other compensation for all or part
      of the alleged damages pursuant to an insurance or guarantee
      contract.

9.   A tribunal may order an interim measure of protection to
      preserve the rights of a disputing party, or to ensure that the
      tribunal's jurisdiction is made fully effective, including an order
      to preserve evidence in the possession or control of a disputing
      party or to protect the tribunal's jurisdiction. A tribunal may not
      order attachment or enjoin the application of a measure alleged
      to constitute a breach referred to in Article 14.D.3 (Submission
      of a Claim to Arbitration). For the purposes of this paragraph,
      an order includes a recommendation.

10.   The tribunal and the disputing parties shall endeavor to conduct
      the arbitration in an expeditious and cost-effective manner.

11.   Following the submission of a claim to arbitration under this
      Annex, if the disputing parties fail to take any steps in the
      proceedings for more than 150 days, or such period as they may
      agree with the approval of the tribunal, the tribunal shall notify
      the disputing parties that they shall be deemed to have
      discontinued the proceedings if the parties fail to take any steps
      within 30 days after the notice is received. If the parties fail to
      take any steps within that time period, the tribunal shall take
      note of the discontinuance in an order. If a tribunal has not yet
      been constituted, the Secretary-General shall assume these
      responsibilities.

12. In any arbitration conducted under this Annex, at the request of a disputing party, a tribunal shall, before issuing a decision or award on liability, transmit its proposed decision or award to the disputing parties. Within 60 days after the tribunal transmits its proposed decision or award, the disputing parties may submit written comments to the tribunal concerning any aspect of its proposed decision or award. The tribunal shall consider any comments and issue its decision or award no later than 45 days after the expiration of the 60-day comment period.

Article 14.D.8: Transparency of Arbitral Proceedings

1. Subject to paragraphs 2 and 4, the respondent shall, after receiving the following documents, promptly transmit them to the non-disputing Annex Party and make them available to the public:

   (a) the notice of intent;

   (b) the notice of arbitration;

   (c) pleadings, memorials, and briefs submitted to the tribunal by a disputing party and any written submissions submitted pursuant to Article 14.D.7.2 and 14.D.7.3 (Conduct of the Arbitration), and Article 14.D.12 (Consolidation);

   (d) minutes or transcripts of hearings of the tribunal, if available; and

   (e) orders, awards, and decisions of the tribunal.

2. The tribunal shall conduct hearings open to the public and shall determine, in consultation with the disputing parties, the appropriate logistical arrangements. If a disputing party intends to use information in a hearing that is designated as protected information or otherwise subject to paragraph 3 it shall so advise the tribunal. The tribunal shall make appropriate arrangements to protect such information from disclosure which may include closing the hearing for the duration of the discussion of that information.

3. Nothing in this Annex, including paragraph 4(d), requires a respondent to make available to the public or otherwise disclose during or after the arbitral proceedings, including the hearing, protected information, or to furnish or allow access to information that it may withhold in accordance with Article 32.2 (Essential Security) or Article 32.5 (Disclosure of Information).[26]

---

[26] For greater certainty, when a respondent chooses to disclose to the tribunal information that may be withheld in accordance with Article 32.2 (Essential Security)

4.   Any protected information that is submitted to the tribunal shall
be protected from disclosure in accordance with the following
procedures:

(a)   subject to subparagraph (d), neither the disputing parties
nor the tribunal shall disclose to the non-disputing Annex Party
or to the public any protected information if the disputing party
that provided the information clearly designates it in accordance
with subparagraph (b);

(b)   any disputing party claiming that certain information
constitutes protected information shall clearly designate the
information according to any schedule set by the tribunal;

(c)   a disputing party shall, according to any schedule set by the
tribunal, submit a redacted version of the document that does
not contain the protected information. Only the redacted version
shall be disclosed in accordance with paragraph 1; and

(d)   the tribunal, subject to paragraph 3, shall decide any
objection regarding the designation of information claimed to be
protected information. If the tribunal determines that the
information was not properly designated, the disputing party
that submitted the information may:

(i)   withdraw all or part of its submission containing that
information, or

(ii)   agree to resubmit complete and redacted documents
with corrected designations in accordance with the
tribunal's determination and subparagraph (c).

In either case, the other disputing party shall, whenever
necessary, resubmit complete and redacted documents which
either remove the information withdrawn under subparagraph
(d)(i) by the disputing party that first submitted the information
or redesignate the information consistent with the designation
under subparagraph (d)(ii) of the disputing party that first
submitted the information.

5.   Nothing in this Annex requires a respondent to withhold from
the public information required to be disclosed by its laws. The
respondent should endeavor to apply those laws in a manner
sensitive to protecting from disclosure information that has been
designated as protected information.

---

or Article 32.5 (Disclosure of Information), the respondent may still withhold that
information from disclosure to the public.

Article 14.D.9: Governing Law

1. Subject to paragraph 2, when a claim is submitted under Article 14.D.3.1 (Submission of a Claim to Arbitration), the tribunal shall decide the issues in dispute in accordance with this Agreement and applicable rules of international law.

2. A decision of the Commission on the interpretation of a provision of this Agreement under Article 30.2 (Functions of the Commission) shall be binding on a tribunal, and any decision or award issued by a tribunal must be consistent with that decision.

Article 14.D.10: Interpretation of Annexes

1. If a respondent asserts as a defense that the measure alleged to be a breach is within the scope of a non-conforming measure set out in Annex I or Annex II, the tribunal shall, on request of the respondent, request the interpretation of the Commission on the issue. The Commission shall submit in writing any decision on its interpretation under Article 30.2 (Functions of the Commission) to the tribunal within 90 days of delivery of the request.

2. A decision issued by the Commission under paragraph 1 shall be binding on the tribunal, and any decision or award issued by the tribunal must be consistent with that decision. If the Commission fails to issue such a decision within 90 days, the tribunal shall decide the issue.

Article 14.D.11: Expert Reports

Without prejudice to the appointment of other kinds of experts when authorized by the applicable arbitration rules, a tribunal, on request of a disputing party or, unless the disputing parties disapprove, on its own initiative, may appoint one or more experts to report to it in writing on any factual issue concerning scientific matters raised by a disputing party in a proceeding, subject to any terms and conditions that the disputing parties may agree.

Article 14.D.12: Consolidation

1. If two or more claims have been submitted separately to arbitration under Article 14.D.3.1 (Submission of a Claim to Arbitration) and the claims have a question of law or fact in common and arise out of the same events or circumstances, any disputing party may seek a consolidation order in accordance with the agreement of all the disputing parties sought to be covered by the order or the terms of paragraphs 2 through 10.

2.   A disputing party that seeks a consolidation order under this
     Article shall deliver, in writing, a request to the Secretary-
     General and to all the disputing parties sought to be covered by
     the order and shall specify in the request:

     (a)   the names and addresses of all the disputing parties sought
     to be covered by the order;

     (b)   the nature of the order sought; and

     (c)   the grounds on which the order is sought.

3.   Unless the Secretary-General finds within a period of 30 days
     after the date of receiving a request under paragraph 2 that the
     request is manifestly unfounded, a tribunal shall be established
     under this Article.

4.   Unless all the disputing parties sought to be covered by the order
     agree otherwise, a tribunal established under this Article shall
     comprise three arbitrators:

     (a)   one arbitrator appointed by agreement of the claimants;

     (b)   one arbitrator appointed by the respondent; and

     (c)   the presiding arbitrator appointed by the Secretary-
     General, provided that the presiding arbitrator is not a national
     of the respondent or of the Party of the claimants.

5.   If, within a period of 60 days after the date when the Secretary-
     General receives a request made under paragraph 2, the
     respondent fails or the claimants fail to appoint an arbitrator in
     accordance with paragraph 4, the Secretary-General, on request
     of any disputing party sought to be covered by the order, shall
     appoint, in his or her discretion, the arbitrator or arbitrators not
     yet appointed.

6.   If a tribunal established under this Article is satisfied that two
     or more claims that have been submitted to arbitration under
     Article 14.D.3.1 (Submission of a Claim to Arbitration) have a
     question of law or fact in common, and arise out of the same
     events or circumstances, the tribunal may, in the interest of fair
     and efficient resolution of the claims, and after hearing the
     disputing parties, by order:

     (a)   assume jurisdiction over, and hear and determine together,
     all or part of the claims;

     (b)   assume jurisdiction over, and hear and determine one or
     more of the claims, the determination of which it believes would
     assist in the resolution of the others; or

(c) instruct a tribunal previously established under Article 14.D.6 (Selection of Arbitrators) to assume jurisdiction over, and hear and determine together, all or part of the claims, provided that:

> (i) that tribunal, on request of a claimant that was not previously a disputing party before that tribunal, shall be reconstituted with its original members, except that the arbitrator for the claimants shall be appointed pursuant to paragraphs 4(a) and 5, and

> (ii) that tribunal shall decide whether a prior hearing shall be repeated.

7. If a tribunal has been established under this Article, a claimant that has submitted a claim to arbitration under Article 14.D.3.1 (Submission of a Claim to Arbitration) and that has not been named in a request made under paragraph 2 may make a written request to the tribunal that it be included in any order made under paragraph 6. The request shall specify:

(a) the name and address of the claimant;

(b) the nature of the order sought; and

(c) the grounds on which the order is sought.

The claimant shall deliver a copy of its request to the Secretary-General.

8. A tribunal established under this Article shall conduct its proceedings in accordance with the UNCITRAL Arbitration Rules, except as modified by this Annex.

9. A tribunal established under Article 14.D.6 (Selection of Arbitrators) shall not have jurisdiction to decide a claim, or a part of a claim, over which a tribunal established or instructed under this Article has assumed jurisdiction.

10. On the application of a disputing party, a tribunal established under this Article, pending its decision under paragraph 6, may order that the proceedings of a tribunal established under Article 14.D.6 (Selection of Arbitrators) be stayed, unless the latter tribunal has already adjourned its proceedings.

Article 14.D.13: Awards

1. When a tribunal makes a final award, the tribunal may award, separately or in combination, only:

(a) monetary damages and any applicable interest; and

(b) restitution of property, in which case the award shall provide that the respondent may pay monetary damages and any applicable interest in lieu of restitution.[27]

2. For greater certainty, if an investor of an Annex Party submits a claim to arbitration under Article 14.D.3.1 (Submission of a Claim to Arbitration), it may recover only for loss or damage that is established on the basis of satisfactory evidence and that is not inherently speculative.

3. For greater certainty, if an investor of an Annex Party submits a claim to arbitration under Article 14.D.3.1(a) (Submission of a Claim to Arbitration), it may recover only for loss or damage incurred in its capacity as an investor of an Annex Party.

4. A tribunal may also award costs and attorney's fees incurred by the disputing parties in connection with the arbitral proceedings, and shall determine how and by whom those costs and attorney's fees shall be paid, in accordance with this Annex and the applicable arbitration rules.

5. Subject to paragraph 1, if a claim is submitted to arbitration under Article 14.D.3.1(b) (Submission of a Claim to Arbitration) and an award is made in favor of the enterprise:

(a) an award of restitution of property shall provide that restitution be made to the enterprise;

(b) an award of monetary damages and any applicable interest shall provide that the sum be paid to the enterprise; and

(c) the award shall provide that it is made without prejudice to any right that any person may have under applicable domestic law with respect to the relief provided in the award.

6. A tribunal shall not award punitive damages.

7. An award made by a tribunal has no binding force except between the disputing parties and in respect of the particular case.

8. Subject to paragraph 9 and the applicable review procedure for an interim award, a disputing party shall abide by and comply with an award without delay.

9. A disputing party shall not seek enforcement of a final award until:

---

[27] For greater certainty, in the final award the tribunal may not order the respondent to take or not to take other actions, including the amendment, repeal, adoption, or implementation of a law or regulation.

(a)   in the case of a final award made under the ICSID Convention:

> (i)   120 days have elapsed from the date the award was rendered and no disputing party has requested revision or annulment of the award, or

> (ii) revision or annulment proceedings have been completed; and

(b)   in the case of a final award under the ICSID Additional Facility Rules, the UNCITRAL Arbitration Rules, or the rules selected pursuant to Article 14.D.3.3(d) (Submission of a Claim to Arbitration):

> (i)   90 days have elapsed from the date the award was rendered and no disputing party has commenced a proceeding to revise, set aside or annul the award, or

> (ii) a court has dismissed or allowed an application to revise, set aside or annul the award and there is no further appeal.

10.   Each Annex Party shall provide for the enforcement of an award in its territory.

11.   If the respondent fails to abide by or comply with a final award, on delivery of a request by the Party of the claimant, a panel shall be established under Article 31.6 (Establishment of a Panel). The requesting Party may seek in those proceedings:

(a)   a determination that the failure to abide by or comply with the final award is inconsistent with the obligations of this Agreement; and

(b)   in accordance with Article 31.17 (Panel Report), a recommendation that the respondent abide by or comply with the final award.

12.   A disputing party may seek enforcement of an arbitration award under the ICSID Convention, the New York Convention, or the Inter-American Convention regardless of whether proceedings have been taken under paragraph 11.

13.   A claim that is submitted to arbitration under this Annex shall be considered to arise out of a commercial relationship or transaction for the purposes of Article I of the New York Convention and Article I of the Inter-American Convention.

Article 14.D.14: Service of Documents

Delivery of notice and other documents to an Annex Party shall be made to the place named for that Annex Party in Appendix 1

(Service of Documents on an Annex Party). An Annex Party shall promptly make publicly available and notify the other Annex Party of any change to the place referred to in that Appendix.

* * *

APPENDIX 2
PUBLIC DEBT

1. For greater certainty, no award shall be made in favor of a claimant for a claim under Article 14.D.3.1 (Submission of a Claim to Arbitration) with respect to default or non-payment of debt issued by a Party[28] unless the claimant meets its burden of proving that such default or non-payment constitutes a breach of a relevant obligation in the Chapter.

2. No claim that a restructuring of debt issued by a Party, standing alone, breaches an obligation in this Chapter shall be submitted to arbitration under Article 14.D.3.1 (Submission of a Claim to Arbitration), provided that the restructuring is effected as provided for under the debt instrument's terms, including the debt instrument's governing law.

APPENDIX 3
SUBMISSION OF A CLAIM TO ARBITRATION

An investor of the United States may not submit to arbitration a claim that Mexico has breached an obligation under this Chapter either:

(a) on its own behalf under Article 14.D.3.1(a) (Submission of a Claim to Arbitration); or

(b) on behalf of an enterprise of Mexico that is a juridical person that the investor owns or controls directly or indirectly under Article 14.D.3.1(b) (Submission of a Claim to Arbitration),

if the investor or the enterprise, respectively, has alleged that breach of an obligation under this Chapter, as distinguished from breach of other obligations under Mexican law, in proceedings before a court or administrative tribunal of Mexico.

ANNEX 14-E
MEXICO-UNITED STATES INVESTMENT DISPUTES RELATED TO COVERED GOVERNMENT CONTRACTS

1. Annex 14-D (Mexico-United States Investment Disputes) applies as modified by this Annex to the settlement of a

---

[28]   For purposes of this Annex, "debt issued by a Party" includes, in the case of Mexico, "public debt" of Mexico as defined in Article 1 of the Federal Law on Public Debt (*Ley Federal de Deuda Pública*).

qualifying investment dispute under this Chapter in the circumstances set out in paragraph 2.[29]

2.   In the event that a disputing party considers that a qualifying investment dispute cannot be settled by consultation and negotiation:

(a)   the claimant, on its own behalf, may submit to arbitration under Annex 14-D (Mexico-United States Investment Disputes) a claim:

(i)   that the respondent has breached any obligation under this Chapter,[30] provided that:

(A)   the claimant is:

(1)   a party to a covered government contract, or

(2)   engaged in activities in the same covered sector in the territory of the respondent as an enterprise of the respondent that the claimant owns or controls directly or indirectly and that is a party to a covered government contract, and

(B)   the respondent is a party to another international trade or investment agreement that permits investors to initiate dispute settlement procedures to resolve an investment dispute with a government, and

(ii)   that the claimant has incurred loss or damage by reason of, or arising out of, that breach;

(b)   the claimant, on behalf of an enterprise of the respondent that is a juridical person that the claimant owns or controls directly or indirectly, may submit to arbitration under Annex 14-D (Mexico-United States Investment Disputes) a claim:

(i)   that the respondent has breached any obligation under this Chapter, provided that:

(A)   the enterprise is:

(1)   a party to a covered government contract,

---

[29]   For greater certainty, Annex 14-D (Mexico-United States Investment Disputes) includes its appendices.

[30]   For the purposes of this paragraph: (i) the "treatment" referred to in Article 14.5 (Most-Favored-Nation Treatment) excludes provisions in other international trade or investment agreements that establish international dispute resolution procedures or impose substantive obligations; (ii) the "treatment" referred to in Article 14.5 only encompasses measures adopted or maintained by the other Annex Party, which for greater clarity may include measures adopted in connection with the implementation of substantive obligations in other international trade or investment agreements.

(2) engaged in activities in the same covered sector in the territory of the respondent as the claimant and the claimant is a party to a covered government contract, or

(3) engaged in activities in the same covered sector in the territory of the respondent as another enterprise of the respondent that the claimant owns or controls directly or indirectly and that is a party to a covered government contract, and

(B) the respondent is a party to another international trade or investment agreement that permits investors to initiate dispute settlement procedures to resolve an investment dispute with a government, and

(ii) that the enterprise has incurred loss or damage by reason of, or arising out of, that breach.[31]

3.   For the purposes of paragraph 2, if a covered government contract is terminated in a manner inconsistent with an obligation under this Chapter, the claimant or enterprise that was previously a party to the contract shall be deemed to remain a party for the duration of the contract, as if it had not been terminated.

4.   No claim shall be submitted to arbitration under paragraph 2 if:

(a) less than six months have elapsed from the events giving rise to the claim; and

(b) more than three years have elapsed from the date on which the claimant first acquired, or should have first acquired, knowledge of the breach alleged under paragraph 2 and knowledge that the claimant (for claims brought under paragraph 2(a)) or the enterprise (for claims brought under paragraph 2(b)) has incurred loss or damage.[32]

5.   For greater certainty, the Annex Parties may agree to modify or eliminate this Annex.

6.   For the purposes of this Annex:

(a) "covered sector" means:

---

[31]   For greater certainty, in order for a claim to be submitted to arbitration under subparagraph (b), an investor of the Party of the claimant must own or control the enterprise on the date of the alleged breach and the date on which the claim is submitted to arbitration.

[32]   For greater certainty, Article 14.D.5.1(a)–(c) does not apply to claims under paragraph 2.

(i)   activities with respect to oil and natural gas that a national authority of an Annex Party controls, such as exploration, extraction, refining, transportation, distribution, or sale,

(ii) the supply of power generation services to the public on behalf of an Annex Party,

(iii) the supply of telecommunications services to the public on behalf of an Annex Party,

(iv) the supply of transportation services to the public on behalf of an Annex Party, or

(v)   the ownership or management of roads, railways, bridges, or canals that are not for the exclusive or predominant use and benefit of the government of an Annex Party;

(b) "national authority" means an authority at the central level of government;[33] and

(c) "written agreement" means an agreement in writing, negotiated, and executed by two or more parties, whether in a single instrument or in multiple instruments.[34]

CHAPTER 15
CROSS-BORDER TRADE IN SERVICES
Article 15.1: Definitions

For the purposes of this Chapter:

cross-border trade in services or **cross-border supply of services** means the supply of a service:

(a) from the territory of a Party into the territory of another Party;

(b) in the territory of a Party by a person of that Party to a person of another Party; or

(c) by a national of a Party in the territory of another Party,

---

[33]   For greater certainty, an authority at the central level of government includes any person, including a state enterprise or another body, when it exercises governmental authority delegated to it by an authority at the central level of government.

[34]   For greater certainty, (a) a unilateral act of an administrative or judicial authority, such as a permit, license, certificate, approval, or similar instrument issued by an Annex Party in its regulatory capacity, or a subsidy or grant, or a decree, order or judgment, standing alone; and (b) an administrative or judicial consent decree or order, shall not be considered a written agreement.

but does not include the supply of a service in the territory of a Party by a covered investment;

enterprise means an enterprise as defined in Article 1.4 (General Definitions), or a branch of an enterprise;

professional service means a service, the supply of which requires specialized post-secondary education, or equivalent training or experience, and for which the right to practice is granted or restricted by a Party, but does not include a service provided by a tradesperson, or a vessel or aircraft crew member;

service supplied in the exercise of governmental authority means, for a Party, a service that is supplied neither on a commercial basis nor in competition with one or more service suppliers;

service supplier of another Party means a person of a Party that seeks to supply or supplies a service; and

specialty air service means a specialized commercial operation using an aircraft whose primary purpose is not the transportation of goods or passengers, such as aerial fire-fighting, flight training, sightseeing, spraying, surveying, mapping, photography, parachute jumping, glider towing, and helicopter-lift for logging and construction, and other airborne agricultural, industrial, and inspection services.

Article 15.2: Scope

1. This Chapter applies to measures adopted or maintained by a Party relating to cross-border trade in services by a service supplier of another Party, including a measure relating to:

    (a) the production, distribution, marketing, sale or delivery of a service;[1]

    (b) the purchase or use of, or payment for, a service;[2]

    (c) the access to or use of distribution, transport, or telecommunications networks or services in connection with the supply of a service;

    (d) the presence in the Party's territory of a service supplier of another Party; or

    (e) the provision of a bond or other form of financial security as a condition for the supply of a service.

---

[1] For greater certainty, subparagraph (a) includes the production, distribution, marketing, sale or delivery of a service by electronic means.

[2] For greater certainty, subparagraph (b) includes the purchase or use of, or payment for, a service by electronic means.

2.   In addition to paragraph 1:

(a)   Article 15.5 (Market Access) and Article 15.8 (Development and Administration of Measures) apply to measures adopted or maintained by a Party relating to the supply of a service in its territory by a covered investment; and

(b)   Annex 15-A (Delivery Services) applies to measures adopted or maintained by a Party relating to the supply of delivery services, including by a covered investment.

3.   This Chapter does not apply to:

(a)   a financial service as defined in Article 17.1 (Definitions), except that paragraph 2(a) applies if the financial service is supplied by a covered investment that is not a covered investment in a financial institution as defined in Article 17.1 (Definitions) in the Party's territory;

(b)   government procurement;

(c)   a service supplied in the exercise of governmental authority; or

(d)   a subsidy or grant provided by a Party or a state enterprise, including government-supported loans, guarantees, or insurance.

4.   This Chapter does not apply to air services, including domestic and international air transportation services, whether scheduled or non-scheduled, or to related services in support of air services, other than the following:

(a)   aircraft repair or maintenance services during which an aircraft is withdrawn from service, excluding so-called line maintenance; and

(b)   specialty air services.

5.   This Chapter does not impose an obligation on a Party with respect to a national of another Party who seeks access to its employment market or who is employed on a permanent basis in its territory, and does not confer any right on that national with respect to that access or employment.

6.   Annex 15-B (Committee on Transportation Services) and Annex 15-D (Programming Services) include additional provisions related to this Chapter.

Article 15.3: National Treatment

1.   Each Party shall accord to services or service suppliers of another Party treatment no less favorable than that it accords, in like circumstances, to its own services and service suppliers.

2. The treatment to be accorded by a Party under paragraph 1
    means, with respect to a government other than at the central
    level, treatment no less favorable than the most favorable
    treatment accorded, in like circumstances, by that government
    to services and service suppliers of the Party of which it forms a
    part.

3. For greater certainty, whether treatment referred to in
    paragraph 1 is accorded in "like circumstances" depends on the
    totality of the circumstances, including whether the relevant
    treatment distinguishes between services or service suppliers on
    the basis of legitimate public welfare objectives.

Article 15.4: Most-Favored-Nation Treatment

1. Each Party shall accord to services or service suppliers of
    another Party treatment no less favorable than that it accords,
    in like circumstances, to services and service suppliers of
    another Party or a non-Party.

2. The treatment to be accorded by a Party under paragraph 1
    means, with respect to a government other than at the central
    level, treatment no less favorable than the most favorable
    treatment accorded, in like circumstances, by that government
    to services and service suppliers of another Party or a non-Party.

3. For greater certainty, whether treatment referred to in
    paragraph 1 is accorded in "like circumstances" depends on the
    totality of the circumstances, including whether the relevant
    treatment distinguishes between services or services suppliers
    on the basis of legitimate public welfare objectives.

Article 15.5: Market Access

1. No Party shall adopt or maintain, either on the basis of a
    regional subdivision or on the basis of its entire territory, a
    measure that:

    (a) imposes a limitation on:

        (i) the number of service suppliers, whether in the form of
        a numerical quota, monopoly, exclusive service suppliers, or
        the requirement of an economic needs test,

        (ii) the total value of service transactions or assets in the
        form of a numerical quota or the requirement of an
        economic needs test,

        (iii) the total number of service operations or the total
        quantity of service output expressed in terms of a

designated numerical unit in the form of a quota or the requirement of an economic needs test,[3] or

(iv) the total number of natural persons that may be employed in a particular service sector or that a service supplier may employ and who are necessary for, and directly related to, the supply of a specific service in the form of a numerical quota or the requirement of an economic needs test; or

(b)   restricts or requires a specific type of legal entity or joint venture through which a service supplier may supply a service.

Article 15.6: Local Presence

No Party shall require a service supplier of another Party to establish or maintain a representative office or an enterprise, or to be resident, in its territory as a condition for the cross-border supply of a service.

Article 15.7: Non-Conforming Measures

1.   Article 15.3 (National Treatment), Article 15.4 (Most-Favored-Nation Treatment), Article 15.5 (Market Access), and Article 15.6 (Local Presence) do not apply to:

(a)   an existing non-conforming measure that is maintained by a Party at:

(i)   the central level of government, as set out by that Party in its Schedule to Annex I,

(ii)   a regional level of government, as set out by that Party in its Schedule to Annex I, or

(iii)   a local level of government;

(b)   the continuation or prompt renewal of a non-conforming measure referred to in subparagraph (a); or

(c)   an amendment to a non-conforming measure referred to in subparagraph (a), to the extent that the amendment does not decrease the conformity of the measure, as it existed immediately before the amendment, with Article 15.3 (National Treatment), Article 15.4 (Most-Favored-Nation Treatment), Article 15.5 (Market Access), or Article 15.6 (Local Presence).

2.   Article 15.3 (National Treatment), Article 15.4 (Most-Favored-Nation Treatment), Article 15.5 (Market Access), and Article 15.6 (Local Presence) do not apply to a measure that a Party

---

[3]   Subparagraph (a)(iii) does not cover measures of a Party which limit inputs for the supply of services.

adopts or maintains with respect to sectors, sub-sectors or activities, as set out by that Party in its Schedule to Annex II.

3.   If a Party considers that a non-conforming measure applied by a regional level of government of another Party, as referred to in sub-paragraph 1(a)(ii), creates a material impediment to the cross-border supply of services in relation to the former Party, it may request consultations with regard to that measure. These Parties shall enter into consultations with a view to exchanging information on the operation of the measure and to considering whether further steps are necessary and appropriate.

4.   For greater certainty, a Party may request consultations with another Party regarding non-conforming measures applied by the central level of government, as referred to in subparagraph 1(a)(i).

Article 15.8: Development and Administration of Measures

1.   Each Party shall ensure that a measure of general application affecting trade in services is administered in a reasonable, objective, and impartial manner.

2.   If a Party adopts or maintains a measure relating to licensing requirements and procedures, or qualification requirements and procedures, affecting trade in services, the Party shall, with respect to that measure:

(a)   ensure that the requirement or procedure is based on criteria that are objective and transparent. For greater certainty, these criteria may include competence or ability to supply a service, or potential health or environmental impacts of an authorization, and competent authorities may assess the weight given to such criteria;

(b)   ensure that the competent authority reaches and administers a decision in an independent manner;

(c)   ensure that the procedure does not in itself prevent fulfilment of a requirement; and

(d)   to the extent practicable, avoid requiring an applicant to approach more than one competent authority for each application for authorization.[4]

3.   If a Party requires an authorization for the supply of a service, it shall ensure that each of its competent authorities:

---

[4]   For greater certainty, a Party may require multiple applications for authorization if a service is within the jurisdiction of multiple competent authorities.

(a)   to the extent practicable, permits an applicant to submit an application at any time;

(b)   if a specific time period for applications exists, allows a reasonable period for the submission of an application;

(c)   if an examination is required, schedules the examination at reasonably frequent intervals and provides a reasonable period of time to enable an applicant to request to take the examination;

(d)   endeavors to accept an application electronically;

(e)   to the extent practicable, provides an indicative timeframe for processing an application;

(f)   to the extent practicable, ascertains without undue delay the completeness of an application for processing under the Party's law;

(g)   accepts copies of documents that are authenticated in accordance with the Party's law, in place of original documents, unless the competent authority requires original documents to protect the integrity of the authorization process;

(h)   at the request of the applicant, provides without undue delay information concerning the status of the application;

(i)   if an application is considered complete under the Party's law, within a reasonable period of time after the submission of the application, ensures that the processing of the application is completed, and that the applicant is informed of the decision concerning the application, to the extent possible in writing;[5]

(j)   if an application is considered incomplete for processing under the Party's law, within a reasonable period of time, to the extent practicable:

> (i)   informs the applicant that the application is incomplete,

> (ii)   if the applicant requests, provides guidance on why the application is considered incomplete,

---

[5]   A competent authority can meet this requirement by informing an applicant in advance in writing, including through a published measure, that lack of response after a specified period of time from the date of submission of the application indicates either acceptance or rejection of the application. For greater certainty, "in writing" includes in electronic form.

(iii) provides the applicant with an opportunity[6] to provide the additional information that is required for the application to be considered complete, and

if none of the above is practicable, and the application is rejected due to incompleteness, ensures that the applicant is informed of the rejection within a reasonable period of time;

(k) if an application is rejected, to the extent possible, either upon its own initiative or upon the request of the applicant, informs the applicant of the reasons for rejection and, if applicable, the timeframe for an appeal or review of the decision to reject the application and the procedures for resubmission of an application; and

(*l*) ensures that authorization, once granted, enters into effect without undue delay, subject to the applicable terms and conditions.

4.   Each Party shall ensure that any authorization fee charged by any of its competent authorities is reasonable, transparent, and does not, in itself, restrict the supply of the relevant service. For the purposes of this paragraph, an authorization fee does not include a fee for the use of natural resources, payments for auction, tendering, or other non-discriminatory means of awarding concessions, or mandated contributions to the provision of universal service.

5.   Each Party shall encourage its competent authorities, when adopting a technical standard, to adopt technical standards developed through an open and transparent process, and shall encourage a body designated to develop a technical standard to use an open and transparent process.

6.   If a Party requires authorization for the supply of a service, the Party shall provide to a service supplier or person seeking to supply a service the information necessary to comply with requirements or procedures for obtaining, maintaining, amending, and renewing that authorization. That information must include:

(a)   any fee;

(b)   the contact information of a relevant competent authority;

(c)   any procedure for appeal or review of a decision concerning an application;

---

[6]   For greater certainty, providing this opportunity does not require a competent authority to provide extensions of deadlines.

(d) any procedure for monitoring or enforcing compliance with the terms and conditions of licenses;

(e) any opportunities for public involvement, such as through hearings or comments;

(f) any indicative timeframe for processing of an application;

(g) any requirement or procedure; and

(h) any technical standard.

7. Paragraphs 1 through 6 do not apply to the aspects of a measure set out in an entry to a Party's Schedule to Annex I, or to a measure that a Party adopts or maintains with respect to sectors, sub-sectors, or activities as set out by that Party in its Schedule to Annex II.

Article 15.9: Recognition

1. For the purposes of the fulfilment, in whole or in part, of a Party's standards or criteria for the authorization, licensing, or certification of a service supplier, and subject to the requirements of paragraph 4, a Party may recognize any education or experience obtained, requirements met, or licenses or certifications granted, in the territory of another Party or a non-Party. That recognition, which may be achieved through harmonization or otherwise, may be based on an agreement or arrangement with the Party or non-Party concerned, or may be accorded autonomously.

2. If a Party recognizes, autonomously or by agreement or arrangement, the education or experience obtained, requirements met, or licenses or certifications granted, in the territory of another Party or a non-Party, Article 15.4 (Most-Favored-Nation Treatment) does not require the Party to accord recognition to the education or experience obtained, requirements met, or licenses or certifications granted, in the territory of another Party.

3. If a Party is a party to an agreement or arrangement of the type referred to in paragraph 1, whether existing or future, the Party shall afford adequate opportunity to another Party, on request, to negotiate its accession to that agreement or arrangement, or to negotiate a comparable agreement or arrangement. If a Party accords recognition of the type referred to in paragraph 1 autonomously, the Party shall afford adequate opportunity to another Party to demonstrate that education or experience obtained, requirements met, or licenses or certifications granted, in that other Party's territory should be recognized.

4.   A Party shall not accord recognition in a manner that would
      constitute a means of discrimination between Parties or between
      a Party and a non-Party in the application of its standards or
      criteria for the authorization, licensing, or certification of a
      service supplier, or a disguised restriction on trade in services.

5.   The Parties shall endeavor to facilitate trade in professional
      services as set out in Annex 15-C (Professional Services).

Article 15.10: Small and Medium-Sized Enterprises

1.   With a view to enhancing commercial opportunities in services
      for SMEs, and further to Chapter 25 (Small and Medium-Sized
      Enterprises), each Party shall endeavor to support the
      development of SME trade in services and SME-enabling
      business models, such as direct selling services,[7] including
      through measures that facilitate SME access to resources or
      protect individuals from fraudulent practices.

2.   Further to Chapter 28 (Good Regulatory Practices), each Party
      shall endeavor to adopt or maintain appropriate mechanisms
      that consider the effects of regulatory actions on SME service
      suppliers and that enable small businesses to participate in
      regulatory policy development.

3.   Further to Article 15.8 (Development and Administration of
      Measures), each Party shall endeavor to ensure that
      authorization procedures for a service sector do not impose
      disproportionate burdens on SMEs.

Article 15.11: Denial of Benefits

1.   A Party may deny the benefits of this Chapter to a service
      supplier of another Party if the service supplier is an enterprise
      owned or controlled by a person of a non-Party, and the denying
      Party adopts or maintains a measure with respect to the non-
      Party or a person of the non-Party that prohibits a transaction
      with that enterprise or that would be violated or circumvented
      if the benefits of this Chapter were accorded to that enterprise.

2.   A Party may deny the benefits of this Chapter to a service
      supplier of another Party if the service supplier is an enterprise
      owned or controlled by a person of a non-Party, or by a person of

---

[7]   Direct selling is the retail distribution of goods by an independent sales
representative, and for which the representative is compensated based exclusively on
the value of goods sold either by the representative or additional representatives
recruited, trained, or otherwise supported by the representative. These goods include
any product that may be distributed by other retail distribution service suppliers
without a prescription or other special authorization, and may include food products,
such as food and nutritional supplements in tablet, powder, or liquid capsule form;

the denying Party, that has no substantial business activities in the territory of any Party other than the denying Party.

Article 15.12: Payments and Transfers

1. Each Party shall permit all transfers and payments that relate to the cross-border supply of services to be made freely and without delay into and out of its territory.

2. Each Party shall permit transfers and payments that relate to the cross-border supply of services to be made in a freely usable currency at the market rate of exchange that prevails at the time of transfer.

3. Notwithstanding paragraphs 1 and 2, a Party may prevent or delay a transfer or payment through the equitable, non-discriminatory, and good faith application of its laws that relate to:

   (a)   bankruptcy, insolvency, or the protection of the rights of creditors;

   (b)   issuing, trading, or dealing in securities or derivatives;[8]

   (c)   financial reporting or record keeping of transfers when necessary to assist law enforcement or financial regulatory authorities;

   (d)   criminal or penal offenses; or

   (e)   ensuring compliance with orders or judgments in judicial or administrative proceedings.

4. For greater certainty, this Article does not preclude the equitable, non-discriminatory, and good faith application of a Party's laws relating to its social security, public retirement, or compulsory savings programs.

ANNEX 15-A
DELIVERY SERVICES

1. For the purposes of this Annex:

   delivery services means the collection, sorting, transport, and delivery of documents, printed matter, parcels, goods, or other items;

---

8   cosmetics; common consumer products for which medical expertise is not required, such as cotton swabs; and other hygiene and cleaning products. The term "nutritional supplement" applies to all health-maintenance products not intended to cure or treat a disease, and that are sold without prescription or other special authorization.

postal monopoly means the exclusive right accorded to an operator within a Party's territory to supply specified delivery services pursuant to a measure of the Party; and

universal service means a delivery service that is made available to all users in a designated territory in accordance with standards of price and quality as defined by each Party.

2.   For greater certainty, this Annex does not apply to maritime, internal waterway, air, rail, or road transportation services, including cabotage.

3.   Each Party that maintains a postal monopoly shall define the scope of the monopoly on the basis of objective criteria, including quantitative criteria such as price or weight thresholds.

4.   For greater certainty, each Party has the right to define the kind of universal service obligation it wishes to adopt or maintain. Each Party that maintains a universal service obligation shall administer it in a transparent, non-discriminatory, and impartial manner with regard to all service suppliers subject to the obligation.

5.   No Party shall allow a supplier of a delivery service covered by a postal monopoly to:

(a)   use revenues derived from the supply of such services to cross-subsidize the supply of a delivery service not covered by a postal monopoly;[8] or

(b)   unjustifiably differentiate among mailers in like circumstances or consolidators in like circumstances with respect to tariffs or other terms and conditions for the supply of a delivery service covered by a postal monopoly.

6.   Each Party shall ensure that a supplier of services covered by a postal monopoly does not abuse its monopoly position to act in the Party's territory in a manner inconsistent with the Party's commitments under Article 14.4 (National Treatment), Article 15.3 (National Treatment), or Article 15.5 (Market Access) with respect to the supply of delivery services outside of the postal monopoly.

---

[8]   A Party shall be deemed in compliance with this paragraph if an independent audit (which, for greater certainty, means for the United States a finding by the Postal Regulatory Commission) determines on an annual basis that the Party's supplier of a delivery service covered by a postal monopoly has not used revenues derived from that monopoly to cross-subsidize its delivery services not covered by a postal monopoly. For greater certainty, this paragraph does not require a Party to ensure that a supplier of a delivery service covered by a postal monopoly maintain accounts in a sufficiently detailed manner to show the costs and revenues of each of its delivery services.

7.   No Party shall:

(a)   require the supply of a delivery service on a universal basis as a condition for an authorization or license to supply a delivery service not covered by a postal monopoly; or

(b)   assess fees or other charges exclusively on the supply of any delivery service that is not a universal service for the purpose of funding the supply of a universal service.

8.   Each Party shall ensure that the authority primarily responsible for regulating delivery services is not accountable to any supplier of delivery services, and that the decisions and procedures that the authority adopts are impartial, non-discriminatory, and transparent with respect to all delivery services not covered by a postal monopoly in its territory.[9]

9.   No Party may require a supplier of a delivery service not covered by a postal monopoly to contract, or prevent such a supplier from contracting, with another service supplier to supply a segment of the delivery service.

ANNEX 15-B
COMMITTEE ON TRANSPORTATION
SERVICES [Omitted]

ANNEX 15-C
PROFESSIONAL SERVICES [Omitted]

APPENDIX 1
GUIDELINES FOR MUTUAL RECOGNITION
AGREEMENTS OR ARRANGEMENTS FOR
THE PROFESSIONAL SERVICES SECTOR

Introductory Notes

This Appendix provides practical guidance for governments, negotiating entities or other entities entering into mutual recognition negotiations for the professional services sector. These guidelines are non-binding and are intended to be used by the Parties on a voluntary basis. They do not modify or affect the rights and obligations of the Parties under this Agreement.

The objective of these guidelines is to facilitate the negotiation of mutual recognition agreements or arrangements (MRAs).

The examples listed under this Appendix are provided by way of illustration. The listing of these examples is indicative and is

---

[9]   For greater certainty, and for the purposes of this paragraph, an "authority responsible for regulating delivery services" does not mean a customs administration.

intended neither to be exhaustive, nor as an endorsement of the application of such measures by the Parties.

Section A: Conduct of Negotiations and Relevant Obligations

Opening of Negotiations

1.   Parties intending to enter into negotiations towards an MRA are encouraged to inform the Professional Services Working Group established under Annex 15-C. The following information may be supplied:

(a) the entities involved in discussions (for example, governments, national organizations in the professional services sector or institutes which have authority, statutory or otherwise, to enter into such negotiations);

(b)   a contact point to obtain further information;

(c)   the subject of the negotiations (specific activity covered); and

(d)   the expected time of the start of negotiations.

Single Negotiating Entity

2.   If no single negotiating entity exists, the Parties are encouraged to establish one.

Results

3.   Upon the conclusion of an MRA, parties to the MRA are encouraged to inform the Professional Services Working Group, and may supply the following information in its notification:

(a)   the content of a new MRA; or

(b)   the significant modifications to an existing MRA.

Follow-up Actions

4.   As a follow-up action to a conclusion of an MRA, parties to the MRA are encouraged to inform the Professional Services Working Group of the following:

(a)   that the MRA comply with the provisions of this Chapter;

(b)   measures and actions taken regarding the implementation and monitoring of the MRA; and

(c)   that the text of the MRA is publicly available.

Section B: Form and Content of MRAs

Introductory Note

This Section sets out various issues that may be addressed in MRA negotiations and, if so agreed during the negotiations, included in the MRA. It includes some basic ideas on what a Party might require of foreign professionals seeking to take advantage of an MRA.

Participants

5.   The MRA should identify clearly:

(a)   the parties to the MRA (for example, governments, national professional organisations, or institutes);

(b)   competent authorities or organizations other than the parties to the MRA, if any, and their position in relation to the MRA; and

(c)   the status and area of competence of each party to the MRA.

Purpose of the MRA

6.   The purpose of the MRA should be clearly stated.

Scope of the MRA

7.   The MRA should set out clearly:

(a)   its scope in terms of the specific profession or titles and professional activities it covers in the territories of the parties;

(b)   who is entitled to use the professional titles concerned;

(c)   whether the recognition mechanism is based on qualifications, on the license obtained in the country of origin or on some other requirement; and

(d)   whether it covers temporary access, permanent access, or both, to the profession concerned.

MRA Provisions

8.   The MRA should clearly specify the conditions to be met for recognition in the territories of each Party and the level of equivalence agreed between the parties to the MRA. The precise terms of the MRA depend on the basis on which the MRA is founded, as discussed above. If the requirements of the various sub-national jurisdictions of a party to an MRA are not identical, the difference should be clearly presented. The MRA should address the applicability of the recognition granted by one sub-national jurisdiction in the other sub-national jurisdictions of the party to the MRA.

9.   The Parties should seek to ensure that recognition does not require citizenship or any form of residency, or education, experience, or training in the territory of the host jurisdiction.

Eligibility for Recognition—Qualifications

10. If the MRA is based on recognition of qualifications, then it should, where applicable, state:

(a) the minimum level of education required (including entry requirements, length of study, and subjects studied);

(b) the minimum level of experience required (including location, length, and conditions of practical training or supervised professional practice prior to licensing, and framework of ethical and disciplinary standards);

(c) examinations passed, especially examinations of professional competence;

(d) the extent to which home country qualifications are recognised in the host country; and

(e) the qualifications which the parties to the MRA are prepared to recognize, for instance, by listing particular diplomas or certificates issued by certain institutions, or by reference to particular minimum requirements to be certified by the authorities of the country of origin, including whether the possession of a certain level of qualification would allow recognition for some activities but not others.

Eligibility for Recognition—Registration

11. If the MRA is based on recognition of the licensing or registration decision made by regulators in the country of origin, it should specify the mechanism by which eligibility for such recognition may be established.

12. If it is considered necessary to provide for additional requirements in order to ensure the quality of the service, the MRA should set out the conditions under which those requirements may apply, for example, in case of shortcomings in relation to qualification requirements in the host country or knowledge of local law, practice, standards, and regulations. This knowledge should be essential for practice in the host country or required because there are differences in the scope of licensed practice.

13. If additional requirements are deemed necessary, the MRA should set out in detail what they entail (for example, examination, aptitude test, additional practice in the host country or in the country of origin, practical training, and language used for examination).

Mechanisms for Implementation

14. The MRA could state:

(a) the rules and procedures to be used to monitor and enforce the provisions of the MRA;

(b) the mechanisms for dialogue and administrative cooperation between the parties to the MRA; and

(c) the means of arbitration for disputes under the MRA.

15. As a guide to the treatment of individual applicants, the MRA could include details on:

(a) the focal point of contact in each party to the MRA for information on all issues relevant to the application (such as the name and address of competent authorities, licensing formalities, and information on additional requirements which need to be met in the host country);

(b) the duration of procedures for the processing of applications by the relevant authorities of the host country;

(c) the documentation required of applicants and the form in which it should be presented and any time limits for applications;

(d) acceptance of documents and certificates issued in the country of origin in relation to qualifications and licensing;

(e) the procedures of appeal to or review by the relevant authorities; and

(f) the fees that might be reasonably required.

16. The MRA could also include the following commitments:

(a) that requests about the measures will be promptly dealt with;

(b) that adequate preparation time will be provided where necessary;

(c) that any exams or tests will be arranged with reasonable periodicity;

(d) that fees to applicants seeking to take advantage of the terms of the MRA will be in proportion to the cost to the host country or organisation; and

(e) that information on any assistance programmes in the host country for practical training, and any commitments of the host country in that context, be supplied.

Licensing and Other Provisions in the Host Country

17. If applicable:

(a) the MRA could also set out the means by which, and the conditions under which, a license is actually obtained following the establishment of eligibility, and what such license entails (such as a license and its content, membership of a professional body, and use of professional or academic titles);

(b) a licensing requirement, other than qualifications, should include, for example:

(i) an office address, an establishment requirement, or a residency requirement,

(ii) a language requirement,

(iii) proof of good conduct and financial standing,

(iv) professional indemnity insurance,

(v) compliance with host country's requirements for use of trade or firm names, and

(vi) compliance with host country ethics, for instance independence and incompatibility.

Revision of the MRA

18. If the MRA includes terms under which it can be reviewed or revoked, the details of such terms should be clearly stated.

ANNEX 15-D
PROGRAMMING SERVICES

Simultaneous Substitution

1. Canada shall rescind Broadcasting Regulatory Policy CRTC 2016-334 and Broadcasting Order CRTC 2016-335. With respect to simultaneous substitution of signals during the retransmission in Canada of the program referenced in those measures, Canada may not accord the program treatment less favorable than the treatment accorded to other programs originating in the United States retransmitted in Canada.

2. The United States and Canada shall each provide in its copyright law that:

(a) retransmission to the public of program signals not intended in the original transmission for free, over-the-air reception by the general public shall be permitted only with the authorization of the holder of the copyright in the program; and

(b) if the original transmission of the program is carried in signals intended for free, over-the-air reception by the general public, willful retransmission in altered form or non-simultaneous retransmission of signals carrying a copyright holder's program shall be permitted only with the authorization of the holder of the copyright in the program.

3.   Other than as provided for in paragraph 1, nothing in subparagraph 2 (b) shall be construed to prevent a Party from maintaining existing measures relating to retransmission of a program carried in signals intended for free, over-the-air reception by the general public; or introducing measures to enable the local licensee of the copyrighted program to exploit fully the commercial value of its license.

Home Shopping Programming Services

4.   Canada shall ensure that U.S. programming services specializing in home shopping, including modified versions of these U.S. programming services for the Canadian market, are authorized for distribution in Canada and may negotiate affiliation agreements with Canadian cable, satellite, and IPTV distributors.

ANNEX 15-E
MEXICO'S CULTURAL EXCEPTIONS

Recognizing that culture is an important component of the creative, symbolic and economic dimension of human development,

Affirming the fundamental right of freedom of expression and the right to plural and diverse information,

Recognizing that states have the sovereign right to preserve, develop and implement their cultural policies, to support their cultural industries for the purpose of strengthening the diversity of cultural expressions, and to preserve their cultural identity, and

In order to preserve and promote the development of Mexican culture, Mexico has negotiated reservations in its schedules to Annex I and Annex II for certain obligations in Chapter 14 (Investment) and Chapter 15 (Cross-Border Trade in Services), which are summarized below.

In Annex I:

Broadcasting (radio and free-to-air television):

Reservations taken against:

•   National Treatment obligations for Investment and Cross-Border Trade in Services Chapters

- Local Presence obligation for Cross-Border Trade in Services Chapter

  - Sole concessions and frequency band concessions will be granted only to Mexican nationals or enterprises constituted under Mexican laws and regulations.

  - Investors of a Party or their investments may participate up to 49 per cent in concessionaire enterprises providing broadcasting services. This maximum foreign investment will be applied according to the reciprocity existent with the country in which the investor or trader who ultimately controls it, directly or indirectly, is constituted.

  - Concessions for indigenous social use shall be granted to indigenous people and indigenous communities of Mexico, with the objective to promote, develop and preserve languages, culture, knowledge, traditions, identity and their internal rules that, under principles of gender equality, enable the integration of indigenous women in the accomplishment of the purposes for which the concession is granted.

  - Under no circumstances may a concession, the rights conferred therein, facilities, auxiliary services, offices or accessories and properties affected thereto, be assigned, encumbered, pledged or given in trust, mortgaged, or transferred totally or partially to any foreign government or state.

  - The State shall guarantee that broadcasting promotes the values of national identity.

  - The broadcasting concessionaires shall use and stimulate local and national artistic values and expressions of Mexican culture, according to the characteristics of its programming.

  - The daily programming with personal performances shall include more time covered by Mexicans.

Newspaper publishing

Reservation taken against:

- National Treatment obligation for Investment Chapter

  - Investors of another Party or their investments may only own, directly or indirectly, up to 49 per cent of the ownership interest in an enterprise established or to be established in the territory of Mexico engaged in the printing or publication of daily newspapers written primarily for a Mexican audience and distributed in the territory of Mexico.

Cinema services

Reservation taken against:

- National Treatment obligation for Investment Chapter
- Most-Favored-Nation Treatment obligation for Investment and Cross-Border Trade in Services Chapters

  - Exhibitors shall reserve 10 per cent of the total screen time to the projection of national films.

In Annex II:

Audiovisual services

Reservation taken against:

- Market Access obligation for Cross-Border Trade in Services Chapter

  - Mexico is taking only limited commitments in the Market Access obligation with respect to the audiovisual services sectors.

Chapter 9

TECHNOLOGY TRANSFERS

For coverage of PRC technology transfers, tech piracy, Made in China 2025, and responses thereto, see Chapter 4.

For coverage of EU regulation of technology transfers, see Chapter 5.

For coverage of global tech piracy and related U.S. remedies, see Folsom et al., *International Business Transactions 5th* Concise Hornbook, Chapter 13.

Licensing on its own is a middle ground alternative to exporting from the owner's home country and direct investment in host markets. It can often produce, with relatively little cost, immediate positive cash flows. Licensing agreements routinely accompany foreign investment transactions.

After a brief introduction to patents and knowhow, the main themes are standard licensing contract terms and the regulation of international licensing agreements.

Licensing on its own is a middle ground alternative to exporting from the owner's home country and direct investment in host markets. It can often produce, with relatively little cost, immediate positive cash flows. After a brief introduction to patents and knowhow, the main themes are standard licensing contract terms and the regulation of international licensing agreements.

Issues surrounding the transfer of knowledge across national borders have provoked intense discussions during the last decade. The discussions promise to continue unabated. At the core is the desire of developing countries (often advanced developing countries such as China, Brazil, and India) to obtain protected information quickly and affordably irrespective of the proprietary rights and profit motives of current holders (usually persons from the most developed countries).

Developing countries want production processes which maximize inexpensive labor, but which result in products that are competitive in the international marketplace. Capital intensive production processes (*e.g.*, robot production of automobiles) may be of less interest. Multinational enterprises (MNEs) may be willing to share (by way of license or sale) a good deal of proprietary information but are reluctant to part with their "core technology."

Among the industrialized countries, efforts often occur to acquire (even by way of stealing) "leading edge" technology. One example involved attempted theft of IBM computer technology by Japanese companies ultimately caught by the FBI. In the United States, the Office of Export Administration uses the export license procedure to control strategic technological "diversions." See my Concise Hornbook on *International Trade Beyond Trump*, Chapter 10.

Falsification of licensing documents by prominent Norwegian and Japanese companies allowed the Soviets to obtain the technology for making vastly quieter submarine propellers. In the ensuing scandal, "anti-Toshiba" legislation was adopted in the U.S. Congress. See Section 2443 of the 1988 Omnibus Trade and Competitiveness Act. Leading Japanese executives resigned their positions, which is considered the highest form of apology in Japanese business circles.

The predominant vehicle for controlling technology transfers across national borders is the "license" or "franchise" contract. Some $180 billion in licensing royalties flow annually across borders. The holder of information in one country first acquires the legally protected right to own the information in another country. With few exceptions, intellectual property (IP) rights are national in origin, products of territorial domestic regimes. This makes the acquisition of IP rights around the globe remarkably expensive.

Once acquired, the holder then licenses the right, usually for a fee, to a person in the other country. This sharing of information raises a risk that proprietary control of the technology may be lost or, at a minimum, that a competitor will be created. Absent authorized transfers, piracy of intellectual property is increasingly commonplace. Indeed, in some countries such theft has risen to the height of development strategy.

The developing nations (as a "Group of 77"), the industrialized nations and the nonmarket economy nations tried to agree in the U.N. Conference on Trade and Development (UNCTAD) upon an international "Code of Conduct" for the transfer of technology. Wide disparities in attitudes toward such a Code were reflected by the developing nations' insistence that it be an "internationally legally binding Code," and the industrialized nations' position that it consist of "guidelines for the international transfer of technology."

Some economics of the debate are illustrated by the fact that persons in the United States pay about one-tenth in royalties for use of imported technology than they receive in royalty payments from technology sent abroad. Many considered development of an international technology transfer Code the most important feature of the North-South dialogue. But it was not to be. Instead, to some degree, the TRIPs Agreement of the World Trade Organization functions as such a code.

§ 9.1   The TRIPs Agreement

The World Trade Organization (WTO) agreements, effective January 1995, include an Agreement on Trade-Related Intellectual Property Rights (TRIPs). This agreement is binding upon the approximately 165 nations that are members of the WTO. In the United States, the TRIPs agreement was approved and implemented by Congress in December 1994 under the Uruguay Round Agreements Act. There is a general requirement of national and most-favored-nation treatment among the parties.

The TRIPs Code covers the gamut of intellectual property. On copyrights, there is protection for computer programs and databases, rental authorization controls for owners of computer software and sound recordings, a 50-year motion picture and sound recording copyright term, and a general obligation to comply with the Berne Convention (except for its provisions on moral rights).

On patents, the Paris Convention (1967 version) prevails, 20-year product and process patents are available "in all fields of technology," including pharmaceuticals and agricultural chemicals. However, patents can be denied when necessary to protect public morals or order, to protect human, animal or plant life or health, and to avoid serious environmental prejudice. The TRIPs provisions did not stop the Indian Supreme Court in 2013 from denying Novartis a patent on its cancer drug, Gleevac. The court took the view that

Novartis was engaged in "ever-greening," i.e., making small, inconsequential changes to existing patents and that Indian law could require proof of "improved therapeutic efficacy" before a patent grant.

Article 31 of the TRIPs permits compulsory licensing of patents in national emergencies or other circumstances of extreme urgency, subject to a duty to reasonably compensate the patent owner. Thailand has issued compulsory licenses on a range of cancer, heart disease and AIDS drugs. There is considerable controversy over pharmaceutical patents based on traditional medicines of indigenous peoples, which some see as bio-piracy. Proposals have been made to amend TRIPs to require disclosure of the origins of bio-patents, obtain informed consent from the indigenous communities involved, and share the benefits of such patents.

For trademarks, internationally prominent marks receive enhanced protection, the linking of local marks with foreign trademarks is prohibited, service marks are registrable, and compulsory licensing is banned. Geographical indicators of origin (Feta cheese, Bordeaux wines, Tennessee whiskey) must be protected. In addition, trade secret protection is assisted by TRIPs rules enabling owners to prevent unauthorized use or disclosure. Integrated circuits are covered by rules intended to improve upon the Washington Treaty. Lastly, industrial designs are also part of the TRIPs regime.

Infringement and anti-counterfeiting remedies are included in the TRIPs, for both domestic and international trade protection. There are specific provisions governing injunctions, damages, customs seizures, and discovery of evidence.

Pharmaceuticals

Late in 2001, the Doha Round of WTO negotiations was launched. These negotiations have reconsidered the TRIPs agreement, particularly as it applies to developing nations. In addition, a Declaration on the TRIPs Agreement and Public Health was issued at the Qatar Ministerial Conference. This Declaration includes the following statement:

We agree that the TRIPs Agreement does not prevent Members from taking measures to protect public health. Accordingly, while reiterating our commitment to the TRIPs Agreement, we affirm that the Agreement can and should be interpreted and implemented in a manner supportive of WTO Members' right to protect public health and, to promote access to medicines for all.

A "Medicines Agreement" waiver (2003) and amendment to TRIPs (2005) implement this Declaration.

Compulsory Patent Licensing, COVID

Article 31 of the WTO TRIPs agreement permits compulsory licensing of patents in national emergencies or other circumstances of extreme urgency, subject to a duty to reasonably compensate the patent owner. Such activities may not pursue industrial or commercial policy objectives, and different packaging and labeling must be used in an effort at minimizing the risk of diversion of the generics to developed country markets.

Under pressure from the United States, more advanced developing nations (such as Mexico, Singapore, and Qatar) agreed not to employ compulsory licensing except in situations of national emergency or extreme urgency. Canada, China, the European Union (EU), India, South Korea, and other WTO members, on the other hand, have licensed production of drugs to countries incapable of pharmaceutical production.

Thailand, Brazil, and other countries have issued compulsory licenses on a range of cancer, heart disease and AIDS drugs. In most cases, compulsory licenses only enable making products for domestic markets.

Does the Medicines Agreement cover COVID vaccines and medicines? India and South Africa have pushed this issue within the WTO, and the United States under the Biden administration has joined others in supporting a waiver of IP vaccine rights. Compulsory IP rights alone without a substantial dose of the related technical trade secrets and know-how necessary to make COVID vaccines and treatments might not suffice.

TRIPs Disputes

TRIPs disputes decided by WTO Panels or the Appellate Body have, for examples, required:

- India to reform its "mailbox rule" for pharmaceutical and agricultural chemical patent applications (patentable since 2005);

- Canada to give 20-year terms to pre-TRIPs patents and limit its generic pharmaceutical regulatory review and stockpiling patent rights' exceptions;

- The European Union to remove information technology tariffs and amend discriminatory regulations regarding geographical indicators;

- The United States to pay for small "business use" of copyrighted music and to remove a prohibition against registration of Cuban confiscated trademarks without the original owner's consent (HAVANA CLUB rum); and

- China to extend copyright coverage and entertainment product restraints.

§ 9.2 Patent Protection

For the most part, patents are granted to inventors according to national law. Thus, patents represent *territorial* grants of exclusive rights. The inventor receives Canadian patents, U.S. patents, Mexican patents, and so on. The EU, however, has recently created a Unitary EU Patent that provides an alternative to 27-member state patents obtained individually or en masse via the longstanding European Patent Convention (a non-EU agreement). See Chapter 5.

Since over one hundred countries have laws regulating patents, there are relatively few jurisdictions without some form of patent protection. Approximately 2 million patents are issued around the world each year. However, legally protected intellectual property in one country may not be protected similarly in another country. For example, some developing nations refuse to grant patents on pharmaceuticals. These countries often assert that their public health needs require such a policy. Thailand was traditionally one such country and unlicensed or compulsory licensed "generics" have been a growth industry there, and in Brazil and India.

Nominal patent protection in some developing nations may lack effective forms of relief-giving the appearance but not the reality of legal rights. Since international patent protection is expensive to obtain, some holders take a chance and limit their applications to those markets where they foresee demand or competition for their product. Nevertheless, U.S. nationals continue to receive tens of thousands of patents in other countries. But the reverse is also increasingly true. Residents of foreign countries now receive over 50 percent of the patents issued under U.S. law. In many countries, persons who deal with the issuance and protection of patents are called patent agents. In the United States, patent practice is a specialized branch of the legal profession. Obtaining international patent protection often involves retaining the services of specialists in each country.

What constitutes a "patent" and how it is protected in any country depends upon domestic law. In the United States, a patent issued by the U.S. Patent Office grants the right for 20 years to exclude everyone from making, using, or selling the patented invention without the permission of the patentee. The United States traditionally granted patents to the "first to invent," not (as in many other countries) the "first to file."

In 2011, the United States switched to first to file rules. Patent infringement, including the supply of "components" for patented inventions, can result in injunctive and damages relief in the U.S. courts. "Exclusion orders" against foreign-made patent-infringing goods are also available. Such orders are frequently issued by the International Trade Commission under Section 337 of the Tariff Act of 1930 and are enforced by the U.S. Customs Service.

A U.S. patent thus provides a short-term legal, but not necessarily economic, monopoly. For example, the exclusive legal rights conveyed by the patents held by Xerox on its photocopying machines have not given it a monopoly in the marketplace. There are many other producers of non-infringing photocopy machines with whom Xerox competes.

Patent Systems

There are basically two types of patent systems in the world community, registration, and examination. Some countries (*e.g.,* France) grant a patent upon "registration" accompanied by appropriate documents and fees, without making an inquiry about the patentability of the invention. The validity of such a patent grant is most difficult to gauge until a time comes to defend the patent against alleged infringement in an appropriate tribunal.

In other countries, the patent grant is made following a careful "examination" of the prior art and statutory criteria on patentability or a "deferred examination" is made following public notice given to permit an "opposition." The odds are increased that the validity of such a patent will be sustained in the face of an alleged infringement. The United States and Germany have examination systems.

To obtain U.S. patents, applicants must demonstrate to the satisfaction of the U.S. Patent Office that their inventions are novel, useful, and nonobvious. Nevertheless, a significant number of U.S. patents have been subsequently held invalid in the courts and the Patent Office has frequently been criticized for a lax approach to issuance of patents. Much of this growth is centered in high-tech industries, including computer software and business methods patents. The United States also been criticized for sometimes allowing patents on "traditional knowledge" (*e.g.*, Mexican Enola Beans) found primarily in the developing world.

The terms of a patent grant vary from country to country. For example, local law may provide for "confirmation," "importation," "introduction" or "revalidation" patents (which serve to extend limited protection to patents already existing in another country). "Inventor's certificates" and rewards are granted in some socialist countries where private ownership of the means of production is discouraged. The state owns the invention. This was the case in China, for example, but inventors now may obtain patents and exclusive private rights under the 1984 Patent Law.

Some countries, such as Britain, require that a patent be "worked" (commercially applied) within a designated period. This requirement is so important that the British mandate a "compulsory license" to local persons if a patent is deemed unworked. Many developing nations have similar provisions in their patent laws: the patent owner must use it or lose it.

§ 9.3   International Recognition of Patents

The principal treaties regarding patents are the 1970 Patent Cooperation Treaty and the 1883 Convention of the Union of Paris, frequently revised and amended. To some extent, the Paris Convention also deals with trademarks, service marks, trade names, industrial designs, and unfair competition. Other treaties dealing with patents are the European Patent Convention (designed to permit a single office at Munich and The Hague to issue patents of 35 countries party to the treaty), and the proposed European Union Patent Convention (intended to create a single patent valid throughout the EU).

Paris Convention

The Paris Convention, to which over 170 countries including the United States are parties, remains the basic international agreement dealing with treatment of foreigners under national patent laws. It is administered by the International Bureau of the World Intellectual Property Organization (WIPO) at Geneva. The "right of national treatment" prohibits discrimination against foreign holders of local patents and trademarks. Thus, for example, a foreigner granted a Canadian patent must receive the same legal rights and remedies accorded Canadian nationals.

Furthermore, important "rights of priority" are granted to patent holders provided they file in foreign jurisdictions within twelve months of their home country patent applications. But such rights may not overcome prior filings by others in "first to file" jurisdictions.

Patent applications in foreign jurisdictions are not dependent upon success in the home country. Patentability criteria vary from country to country. Nevertheless, the Paris Convention obviates the need to file simultaneously in every country where intellectual property protection is sought. If an inventor elects not to obtain patent protection in other countries, anyone may make, use, or sell the invention in that territory. The Paris Convention does not attempt to reduce the need for individual patent applications in all jurisdictions where patent protection is sought. Nor does it alter the various domestic criteria on patentability.

Patent Cooperation Treaty

The Patent Cooperation Treaty (PCT), to which about 140 countries including the United States are parties, is designed to achieve greater uniformity and less cost in the international patent filing process, and in the examination of prior art. Instead of filing patent applications individually in each nation, filings under the PCT are done in selected countries. The national patent offices of Japan, Sweden, Russia, and the United States have been designated International Searching Authorities (ISA), as has the European Patent Office at Munich and The Hague.

The international application, together with the international search report, is communicated by an ISA to each national patent office where protection is sought. Nothing in this Treaty limits the freedom of each nation to require expensive translations, establish substantive conditions of patentability and determine infringement remedies.

However, the Patent Cooperation Treaty also provides that the applicant may arrange for an international preliminary examination to formulate a non-binding opinion on whether the claimed invention is novel, involves an inventive step (non-obvious) and is industrially applicable. In a country without sophisticated search facilities, the report of the international preliminary examination may largely determine whether a patent will be granted. For this reason alone, the Patent Cooperation Treaty may generate considerable uniformity in world patent law.

§ 9.4 Knowhow

Knowhow is commercially valuable knowledge. It may or may not be a trade secret and may or may not be patentable. Though often technical or scientific, *e.g.*, engineering services, knowhow can also be more general in character. Marketing and management skills as well as simply business advice can constitute knowhow. If someone is willing to pay for the information, it can be sold or licensed internationally.

Legal protection for knowhow varies from country to country and is, at best, limited. Unlike patents, copyrights and trademarks, exclusive legal rights to knowhow cannot be obtained by registration. Knowledge, like the air we breathe, is a public good. Once released in the community, knowhow can generally be used by anyone and is almost impossible to retrieve.

In the absence of exclusive legal rights, preserving the confidentiality of knowhow becomes an important business strategy. If everyone knows it, who will pay for it? If competitors have access to the knowledge, a company's market position is at risk. It is for these reasons that only a few people on earth ever know the Coca Cola formula, which is perhaps the world's best kept knowhow secret.

Protecting knowhow is mostly a function of contract, tort, and trade secrets law. Employers will surround their critical knowhow with employees bound by contract to confidentiality. But some valuable knowledge leaks from or moves with these employees, *e.g.*, when a disgruntled retired or ex-employee sells or goes public with the knowhow. The remedies at law or in equity for breach of contract are unlikely to render the employer whole.

Neither is torts relief likely to be sufficient since most employees are essentially judgment proof, though they may be of more use if a competitor induced the breach of contract. Likewise, even though genuine trade secrets are protected by criminal statutes in a few jurisdictions, persuading the prosecutor to take up your business problem is not easy and criminal penalties will not recoup the trade secrets (though they may make the revelation of others less likely in the future).

The U.S. Economic Espionage Act of 1996 creates *criminal* penalties for misappropriation of trade secrets for the benefit of foreign governments or anyone. For these purposes, a "trade secret" is defined as "financial, business, scientific, technical, economic or engineering information" that the owner has taken reasonable measures to keep secret and whose "independent economic value derives from being closely held." In addition to criminal fines, forfeitures and jail terms, the Act authorizes seizure of all proceeds from the theft of trade secrets as well as property used or intended for use in the misappropriation (*e.g.*, buildings and capital equipment).

Despite these legal hazards, even when certain knowhow is patentable, a desire to prolong the commercial exploitation of that knowledge may result in no patent registrations. The international chemicals industry, for example, is said to prefer trade secrets to public disclosure and patent rights with time limitations. Licensing or selling such knowhow around the globe is risky, but lucrative.

§ 9.5   Trademark Protection

Virtually all countries offer some legal protection to trademarks, even when they do not have trademark registration systems. Trademark rights derived from the use of marks on goods in commerce have long been recognized at common law and remain so today in countries as diverse as the United States and the United Arab Emirates. The latter nation, for example, had no trademark registration law in 1986, but this did not prevent McDonald's from obtaining an injunction against a local business using its famous name and golden arches without authorization. However, obtaining international trademark protection requires separate registration under the law of each nation.

Over three million trademarks are registered around the globe each year. In the United States, trademarks are protected at common law and by state and federal registrations. Federal registration is permitted by the U.S. Trademark Office for all marks capable of distinguishing the goods on which they appear from other goods. U.S. law notably allows trademarks on distinct smells, colors, sounds and tastes. Unless the mark falls within a category of forbidden registrations (*e.g.*, those that offend socialist morality in the People's Republic of China), a mark becomes valid for a term of years following registration.

In some countries (like the United States prior to 1989), marks must be used on goods before registration. In others, like France, use is not required, and speculative registration of marks can occur. It is said that ESSO was obliged to purchase French trademark rights from such a speculator when it switched to EXXON in its search for the perfect global trademark.

Since 1989, U.S. law has allowed applications when there is a bona fide intent to use a trademark within 12 months and, if there is good cause for the delay in actual usage, up to 24 additional months. Such filings in effect reserve the mark for the applicant. The emphasis on bona fide intent and good cause are an attempt to control any speculative use of U.S. trademark law.

The scope of trademark protection may differ substantially from country to country. Under U.S. federal trademark law, injunctions, damages, and seizures of goods by customs officials may follow infringement. Other jurisdictions may provide similar remedies on their law books but offer little practical enforcement.

Thus, trademark registration is no guarantee against trademark piracy. A pair of blue jeans labeled "Levi Strauss made in San Francisco" may have been counterfeited in Israel or Paraguay without the knowledge or consent of Levi Strauss and despite its trademark registrations in those countries. Trademark counterfeiting is not just a developing country problem, as any visitor to a U.S. "flea market" can tell. Congress created criminal offenses and private treble damages remedies for the first time in the Trademark Counterfeiting Act of 1984.

In many countries, trademarks (appearing on goods) may be distinguished from "service marks" used by providers of services (*e.g.*, The Law Store), "trade names" (business names), "collective marks" (marks used by a group or organization), and "certification marks" (marks which certify a certain quality, origin, or other fact). Although national trademark schemes differ, it can be said generally that a valid trademark (*e.g.*, a mark not "canceled," "renounced," "abandoned," "waived" or "generic") will be protected against infringing use. A trademark can be valid in one country (ASPIRIN brand tablets in Canada), but invalid because generic in another (BAYER brand aspirin in the United States).

Unlike patents and copyrights, trademarks may be renewed continuously. A valid mark may be licensed, perhaps to a "registered user" or it may be assigned, in some cases only with the sale of the goodwill of a business. A growing example of international licensing of trademarks can be found in franchise agreements taken abroad. And national trademark law sometimes accompanies international licensing. The principal U.S. trademark law, the Lanham Act of 1946, has been construed to apply extraterritorially (much like the Sherman Antitrust Act) to foreign licensees engaging in deceptive practices with effects in the United States.

Foreigners who seek a registration may be required to prove a prior and valid "home registration," and a new registration in another country may not have an existence "independent" of the continuing validity of the home country registration. Foreigners are often assisted in their registration efforts by international and regional trademark treaties.

§ 9.6   International Recognition of Trademarks

The premium placed on priority of use of a trademark is reflected in several international trademark treaties. These include the Paris Convention, the 1957 Arrangement of Nice Concerning the International Classification of Goods and Services, and the 1973 Trademark Registration Treaty done at Vienna. The treaties of widest international application are the Paris Convention and the Arrangement of Nice, as revised to 1967, to which the United States is signatory. The International Bureau of WIPO plays a central role in the administration of arrangements contemplated by these agreements.

The Paris Convention reflects an effort to internationalize some trademark rules. In addition to extending the principle of national treatment in Article 2 and providing for a right of priority of six months for trademarks (see patent discussion above), the Convention mitigates the frequent national requirement that foreigners seeking trademark registration prove a pre-existing, valid, and continuing home registration. This makes it easier to obtain foreign trademark registrations, avoids the possibility that a lapse in registration at home will cause all foreign registrations to become invalid, and allows registration abroad of entirely different (and perhaps culturally adapted) marks.

Article 6bis of the Paris Convention gives owners of "well known" trademarks the right to block or cancel the unauthorized registration of their marks. One issue that frequently arises under this provision is whether the mark needs to be well known locally or just internationally to obtain protection.

The Nice Agreement addresses the question of registration by "class" or "classification" of goods. To simplify internal administrative procedures relating to marks, many countries classify and thereby identify goods (and sometimes services) which have the same or similar attributes. An applicant seeking registration of a mark often is required to specify the class or classes to which the product mark belongs. However, not all countries have the same classification system and some lack any such system. Article 1 of the Nice Agreement adopts, for the purposes of the registration of marks, a single classification system for goods and services. This has brought order out of chaos in the field.

The 1973 Vienna Trademark Registration Treaty (to which the United States is a signatory) contemplates an international filing and examination scheme like that in force for patents under the Patent Cooperation Treaty. This treaty has not yet been fully implemented but holds out the promise of reduced costs and greater uniformity when obtaining international trademark protection.

Numerous European and Mediterranean countries are parties to the Madrid Agreement for International Registration of Marks (1891, as amended). Since 2002, the United States has joined in the Madrid Protocol of 1989. This Protocol permits international filings to obtain about 60 national trademark rights and is administered by WIPO. A Common Market trademark has been developed by the EU, an alternative to national trademark registrations and the "principle of territoriality" underlying IP laws.

§ 9.7 Copyright Protection

Nearly one hundred nations recognize some form of copyright protection for "authors' works." The scope of this coverage and available remedies varies from country to country, with some uniformity established in the roughly 80 nations participating in the Berne and Universal Copyright Conventions (below). In the United States, for example, the Copyright Act of 1976 protects all original expressions fixed in a tangible medium (now known or later developed), including literary works, musical works, dramatic works, choreographic works, graphic works, audiovisual works, sound recordings, computer programs and selected databases.

It is not necessary to publish a work to obtain a U.S. copyright. It is sufficient that the work is original and fixed in a tangible medium of expression. Prior to 1989, to retain a U.S. copyright, the author had to give formal notice of a reservation of rights when publishing the work. Publication of the work without such notice no longer dedicates it to free public usage.

U.S. copyright protection now extends from creation of the work to 70 years after the death of the author. The author also controls "derivative works," such as movies made from books. Only the author (or her assignees or employer in appropriate cases) may make copies, display, perform, and first sell the work. Registration with the U.S. Copyright Office is not required to obtain copyright rights but is important to federal copyright infringement remedies. Infringers are subject to criminal penalties, injunctive relief, and civil damages. Infringing works are impounded pending trial and ultimately destroyed. But educators, critics and news reporters are allowed "fair use" of the work, a traditional common law doctrine now codified in the 1976 Copyright Act.

The marketing of copyrights is sometimes accomplished through agency "clearinghouses." This is especially true of musical compositions because the many authors and potential users are dispersed. In the United States, the American Society of Composers, Authors and Publishers (ASCAP) and Broadcast Music, Inc. (BMI) are the principal clearinghouses for such rights. Thousands of these rights are sold under "blanket licenses" for fees established by the clearinghouses and later distributed to their members. Similar organizations exist in most European states. Their activities have repeatedly been scrutinized under U.S. and EU antitrust law.

A Joint International Copyright Information Service run since 1981 by WIPO and UNESCO is designed to promote licensing of copyrights in developing countries. This Service does not act as an agency clearinghouse for authors' rights, a deficiency sometimes said to promote copyright piracy.

Copyright protection in other countries may be less comprehensive or capable of adaptation to modern technologies. Copyrights on computer programs, for example, are less certain in many jurisdictions. In some developing countries, "fair use" is a theme which is expansively construed to undermine copyright protection. But these differences seem less significant when contrasted with the worldwide problem of copyright piracy, ranging from satellite signal poaching to unlicensed music and books.

In the United States, the Copyright Felony Act of 1992 criminalized all copyright infringements. The No Electronic Theft Act of 1997 (NET) removed the need to prove financial gain as element of copyright infringement law, thus ensuring coverage of copying done with intent to harm copyright owners or copying simply for personal use.

The Digital Millennium Copyright Act of 1998 (DMCA) brought the United States into compliance with WIPO treaties and created two new copyright offenses: one for circumventing technological measures used by copyright owners to protect their works ("hacking") and a second for tampering with copyright management information (encryption). The DMCA also made it clear that "webmasters" digitally broadcasting music on the internet must pay performance royalties.

§ 9.8   International Recognition of Copyrights

Absent an appropriate convention, copyright registrations must be tediously acquired in each country recognizing such rights. However, copyright holders receive national treatment, translation rights and other benefits under the Universal Copyright Convention (UCC) of 1952 (to which the United States adheres). Most importantly, the UCC *excuses* foreigners from registration requirements provided notice of a claim of copyright is adequately given (*e.g.*, Copyright R. Folsom, 2022). Some countries like the United States took advantage of an option *not* to excuse registration requirements. The exercise of this option had the effect at that time of reinforcing the U.S. "manufacturing clause" requiring local printing of U.S. copyrighted books and prohibiting importation of foreign copies. This protectionist clause finally expired under U.S. copyright law in 1986.

The UCC establishes a minimum term for copyright protection: 25 years after publication, prior registration, or death of the author. It also authorizes compulsory license schemes for translation rights in all states and compulsory reprint rights and instructional usage in developing countries.

National treatment and a release from registration formalities (subject to copyright notice requirements) can be obtained in Pan-American countries under the Mexico City Convention of 1902 and the Buenos Aires Convention of 1911, the United States adhering to both. Various benefits can be had in many other countries through the Berne Convention of 1886 (as revised). Like the UCC, the Berne Convention suspends registration requirements for copyright holders from participating states. Unlike the UCC, it allows for local copyright protection independent of protection granted in the country of origin and does not require copyright notice.

The Berne Convention establishes a minimum copyright term of the life of the author plus 50 years, a more generous minimum copyright than that of the UCC. It also recognizes the exclusive translation rights of authors. The Berne Convention does not contemplate compulsory licensing of translation rights. Most U.S. copyright holders previously acquired Berne Convention benefits by simultaneously publishing their works in Canada, a member country.

In 1989, the United States ratified the Berne Convention. U.S. ratification of the Berne Convention created copyright relations with an additional 25 nations. Ratification eliminated U.S. registration requirements (reserved under the UCC) for foreign copyright holders and required protection of the "moral rights" of authors, i.e., the rights of integrity and paternity. The right of paternity insures acknowledgment of authorship. The right of integrity conveys the ability to object to distortion, alteration, or other derogation of the work. It is generally thought that unfair competition law at the federal and state levels will provide the legal basis in U.S. law for these moral rights. A limited class of visual artists explicitly receives these rights under the Visual Artists Rights Act of 1990.

§ 9.9   International Patent and Knowhow Licensing

This section concerns the most common form of lawful international technology transfer—patent and knowhow licensing. Before any patent licensing can take place, patents must be acquired in all countries in which the owner hopes there will be persons interested in purchasing the technology. Even in countries where the owner has no such hope, patent rights may still be obtained to foreclose future unlicensed competitors. Licensing is a middle ground alternative to exporting from the owner's home country and direct investment in host markets. It can often produce, with relatively little cost, immediate positive cash flows.

International patent and knowhow licensing is the most critical form of technology transfer to developing countries. From the owner's standpoint, it presents an alternative to and sometimes a first step towards foreign investment. Such licensing involves a transfer of patent rights or knowhow (commercially valuable knowledge, often falling short of a patentable invention) in return for payments, usually termed royalties. Unlike foreign investment, licensing does not have to involve a capital investment in a host jurisdiction. However, licensing of patents and knowhow is not without legal risks.

From the licensee's standpoint, and the perspective of its government, there is the risk that the licensed technology may be old or obsolete, not "state of the art." Goods produced under old technology will be hard to export and convey a certain "second class" status. On the other hand, older more labor-intensive technologies may be sought (as sometimes done by China) in the early stages of development. Excessive royalties may threaten the economic viability of the licensee and drain hard currencies from the country. The licensee typically is not in a sufficiently powerful position to bargain away restrictive features of standard international licenses.

For all these reasons, and more, developing countries frequently regulate patent and knowhow licensing agreements. Such law is found in the Brazilian Normative Act No. 17 (1976) and the Mexican Technology Transfer Law (1982, repealed 1991), among others. Royalty levels will be limited, certain clauses prohibited (*e.g.*, export restraints, resale price maintenance, mandatory grant-backs to the licensor of improvements), and the desirability of the technology evaluated. See Section 9.10 below.

Regulation of patent and knowhow licensing agreements is hardly limited to the third world. The EU, for example, after several test cases before the European Court of Justice, issued a "block exemption" controlling patent licensing agreements. Many of the licensing agreement clauses controlled by this 1984 Regulation were the same as those covered by developing countries' technology transfer legislation. Its successors, Regulations 240 of 1996, 772 of 2004 and 316 of 2014, broadly cover technology transfer agreements (including, since 2004, software copyright licensing). See Chapter 5.

EU regulation prohibits production restraints, forbids the fixing of retail prices for the licensed product by the licensor, limits the licensor's power to select to whom the licensee may sell, controls the "grant back" of product improvements and determines the licensee's right to challenge the validity of intellectual property. It also affects exclusive licensing arrangements, the allocation of geographic territories among licensees, trademark usage, tying arrangements, fields of use, duration of the license, quality controls, and discrimination between licensees by the licensor. Regulation of patent, knowhow and software copyright licensing in the United States is less direct and predominantly the concern of patent and antitrust law (*e.g.*, tying practices).

The licensor also faces legal risks. The flow of royalty payments may be stopped, suspended, or reduced by currency exchange regulations. The taxation of the royalties, if not governed by double taxation treaties, may be confiscatory. The licensee may produce "gray market" goods that eventually compete for sales in markets exclusively intended for the licensor. In the end, patents expire and become part of the world domain. At that point, the licensee has effectively purchased the technology and becomes an independent competitor (though not necessarily an effective competitor if the licensor has made new technological advances).

Licensing is a kind of partnership. If the licensee succeeds, the licensor's royalties (often based on sales volumes) will increase and a continuing partnership through succeeding generations of technology may evolve. If not, the dispute settlement provisions of the agreement may be called upon as either party withdraws from the partnership. Licensing of patents and knowhow often is combined with, indeed essential to, foreign investments. A foreign subsidiary or joint venture will need technical assistance and knowhow to commence operations. When this occurs, the licensing terms are usually a part of the basic joint venture or investment agreement.

Licensing may also be combined with a trade agreement, as where the licensor ships necessary supplies to the licensee, joint venture partner, or subsidiary. Such supply agreements have sometimes been used to overcome royalty limitations through a form of "transfer pricing," the practice of marking up or down the price of goods to allocate revenues to preferred parties and preferred jurisdictions such as tax havens.

§ 9.10 Regulation of Technology Transfers, Developing World

Technology Transfer Agreements

There are many variations of technology transfer agreements. But they all in some way address the transfer of intellectual property. The agreement may be exclusively for that purpose, or the transfer may be part of a larger agreement, such as the creation of a joint venture. What is included within the definition of intellectual property or technology transfers tends to be quite broad. The transfer may involve property which is granted protection under such laws as those protecting and regulating patents, copyrights and trademarks, or the transfer may involve property, which is not granted such protection, but where some protection is maintained by controlling who obtains the knowledge.

A comparatively new form of transferring technology is by way of a strategic alliance. It is a kind of joint venture where two firms (or more) from different nations agree to jointly exploit technology. The participants often make different contributions to the alliance-one may contribute technology, another capital, or a distribution network, or service facilities, etc. Perhaps the most important part of a strategic alliance is the technology license agreement. It is not always clear whether the alliance structure also transfers enforcement rights to the licensee of the technology.

The process of transferring technology involves an agreement which outlines the relationship between the transferor and the transferee. The extent to which the agreement is detailed may depend upon the character of the transferee.

Even when the technology is transferred to a wholly owned subsidiary in a foreign nation, there is almost always some agreement, at the very least for tax purposes. The corporate structure using a parent and subsidiary (the latter being an entity incorporated under the laws of the foreign host nation) demands that the separate nature of the two entities be maintained. If not, the parent may be held responsible for the debts of the subsidiary under veil piercing theory. Consequently, the transfer of technology from a parent to a subsidiary should be at arms-length to avoid transfer pricing allegations and represented by a written agreement. But if the parent is convinced that there is little likelihood that the subsidiary's management will adversely affect the value of the technology, or produce poor quality goods using the technology, there are likely to be fewer provisions in the agreement than where the transferee is an independent entity, unrelated to the transferor.

When the agreement is to transfer technology to an entity which is not part of the transferor's corporate structure, such as a subsidiary or affiliate, there will be a sense that more detail ought to appear in the technology agreement. For example, disputes will not be settled "within" the company, as they may when the transfer of technology is to a subsidiary, but by judicial or arbitral tribunals. A transfer within a corporate structure is usually easily worked out, but a transfer to an independent transferee may involve considerable negotiation of many details.

Transfers may assume other functions or address other matters than noted above. They sometimes apply to a particular area because of the frequent use of licensing in that area.

Computer Software

The laws of some nations do not recognize computer software as protectable property by copyright or as a trade secret, thus making a transfer particularly risky. It may be recognized as property protected by copyright or patent law. Even when there is legal recognition of computer software as protectable property, however, it may be best not to transfer it if the risk of loss is high. Where computer technology is in the final product, such as the bar-coding process for retail products, the software technology may be protected by retaining it in the home country and only transferring the end use product.

Management Contracts. Many enterprises, especially in the hotel industry, function by means of management contracts. The transfer usually involves knowhow, the knowledge of how to operate a facility. Often the most important aspect of the transfer is the experience of the manager of the management company. That experience is reflected in the manager's day to day decisions. It is an experience which has proven that it has value. For example, many Cuban government organizations attempted to manage hotels to develop tourism beginning in the mid-1980s. But the hotels were inefficiently managed until foreign management was obtained.

Training Contracts. Knowledge of how to undertake a particular function or functions has value. That knowledge may be transferred as any other knowhow. The management contract noted above may include training of host nation persons in hotel management. Even if the management contract is not also a training contract, there will be a certain amount of transfer of training involved simply by other employees viewing how a well-managed unit functions.

For extensive coverage of intellectual property licensing law and sample international licensing agreements, see R. Folsom, *International Business Transactions Practitioner Treatise*, Chapter 23.

Developing World Regulation of Technology Transfers (TT)

When transfer of technology rules do not exist in the recipient country, the technology transfer agreement is the conclusion of the bargaining of the two parties. The agreement will not be public; it will not be registered. But in some nations, especially developing nations and nonmarket economy nations, the government may be involved in the determination and regulation of the technology transfer agreement. Typically, without approval from a technology transfer commission, the TT agreement is void and unenforceable. In such jurisdictions, the parties end up negotiating terms for their agreement that are acceptable to the TT Commission.

During the 1970s developing nations enacted transfer of technology laws. In Latin America, Decision No. 24 of the ANCOM group pioneered the use of regulatory TT Commissions. The ANCOM approach spread like wildfire throughout Latin America. The laws were adopted both as part of the general attempt to control foreign investment and technology transfers, but also to preserve scarce hard currency at a time of severe balance of payment problems. The developing nations viewed technology transfer agreements as an area where there were serious abuses and believed that their laws would adequately address these issues. The principal abuses were thought to include the following:

1.   Transfer of obsolete technology;

2.   Excessive price paid for the technology;

3.   Limitations on use of new developments by the transferee by grant back provisions;

4.   Little research performed by the transferee;

5.   Too much intervention by the transferor in transferee activities;

6.   Limitations on where the transferee may market the product;

7.   Requirements for components be purchased from the transferor which are available locally or could be obtained from other foreign sources more cheaply;

8.   Inadequate training of transferee's personnel to do jobs performed by personnel of the transferor;

9.   Transfer of technology which has adequate domestic substitutes and is therefore not needed;

10. Too long a duration of the agreement; and

11. Application of foreign law and use of foreign tribunals for dispute resolution.

These do not establish an exclusive list. Some nations had different reasons wishing for more closely governed technology transfers. But these reasons provide an outline of what areas transfer of technology laws in the 1970s attempted to govern.

The result of these restrictive laws was the transfer of less technology, and of technology less valuable to the source. It was often older technology over which the company was willing to relinquish some control. The bureaucracies established to register and approve or disapprove the agreements were often staffed with persons who knew little about technology. The laws did not bring in more technology, but less. The consequence was that they did not serve the purpose of helping the balance of payments. Furthermore, the nations which adopted strict rules regulating the transfer of technology often did not have laws which protected intellectual property.

In the 1980s and 1990s, some of these restrictive laws were dismantled, whether by formal repeal or replacement by more transfer encouraging and intellectual property protecting laws, or by a relaxed interpretation of the laws and a general automatic approval of what the transferor and transferee agreed upon. Mexico, for example, eliminated its Technology Transfer Commission in 1991. Ironically, some technology agreements which were used in the 1960s before the enactment of the strict laws, and which became unusable after such enactments, are now once again being used in the developing world but regulated in the European Union. See Section 15.24.

That said, a substantial number of "technology transfer" control laws remain in force in Latin America, China and elsewhere.

§ 9.11 Tech Transfers and Foreign Investment

Any foreign direct investment which includes the transfer of some technology may include the transfer in an agreement which also includes the direct investment, quite possibly in a joint venture contract. Whether there is such an agreement will depend on the laws of the host nation. China, for example, regularly requires technology transfers to obtain foreign investment permits.

In many nations which restrict foreign investment, there may be an agreement which expresses the total relationship, including the transfer of technology. For example, foreign investments established in Cuba must comply with the broad and often vague provisions of the out-of-date 1982 joint venture law. That law notes the need for foreign technology and that a formal agreement with the government for an investment must also outline the nature of any technology transfers. Little technology is being transferred because there is little protection of technology under Cuban law.

Investment in nations which mandate joint ventures are the most likely situations where the investment agreement will also include the technology transfer provisions. There is nothing wrong with combining transfer of technology provisions in a larger scope agreement, but the agreement ought to be just as detailed regarding technology provisions as it would standing alone as a separate agreement.

Where technology is transferred within the context of a joint venture or other form of investment agreement, the agreement ought to be clear as to the access of the host nation joint venture partner to any sensitive technology. Particularly where there is knowhow transferred, the foreign investor may wish to control the local party's access to the technology. Unless there are restrictions on the transfer of ownership interests, the foreign party may change and bringing in persons less trusted.

India demanded in the 1970s that the Coca-Cola Company alter its structure from a wholly foreign owned investment to a joint venture. While the Indian government did not expressly state that the foreign parent would have to share the secret formula, the government did say that such sharing would be the natural consequence of the partnership sense of the joint venture. Coca-Cola would not disclose the technology, and withdrew from India, not to return until the 1990s, when India had relaxed its previously strict foreign investment rules.

§ 9.12 Impact of U.S. Antitrust Law on Tech Transfers

United States export controls, covered in Chapter 10, directly regulate the transfer of technology and technical data from the U.S. to the rest of the world. United States antitrust law impacts such exports more obliquely. A good example is U.S. antitrust law governing "tying arrangements" in franchising and licensing contracts, discussed in Section 15.7. Likewise, European Union business competition law is also concerned with such arrangements. Microsoft, for example, paid a considerable fine under EU law for "bundling" (tying) a media player with its Windows operating system. For coverage of EU competition law's impact on technology transfers, see my Concise Hornbook on *The European Union Beyond BREXIT*, Chapter 7.

Antitrust law is a distinctly United States subject. It is a body of law that reflects United States economic history and perspectives. Antitrust is one of the relatively few areas of U.S. law that has been exported to foreign jurisdictions, albeit with many local variations. The European Union, Canada, China, Australia, Germany, Brazil, Japan, Britain and (since 1993) Mexico have notably developed such law. Global, co-operative antitrust enforcement can and frequently does result in multiple liabilities, for example via the U.S.-EU Agreement on Cooperation in Antitrust Matters.

United States antitrust law is often of intense interest to foreigners because of its reputation for severity and incomprehensibility, particularly when applied "extraterritorially" to persons and actions located outside the United States. EU competition law also has an extraterritorial component. Unlike most jurisdictions, the U.S. assesses *criminal* antitrust fines, penalties, and jail terms. The U.S., for example, extradited an Italian business executive from Germany to face criminal charges under the Sherman Act. The U.S. used Interpol's red notice system to capture him. Dozens of Japanese executives have voluntarily served prison terms for U.S. antitrust violations.

A vast majority of all U.S. antitrust litigation involves private actions for the punitive remedy of *treble damages*. This remedy is unavailable in any other jurisdiction around the globe. The United States does not principally rely upon public law enforcement in the antitrust field. When the incentive of the automatic treble damages remedy is mixed with the allowance of contingency fee arrangements between U.S. lawyers and their clients (a litigation financing device), the successful plaintiffs' ability to recover attorneys' fees and legal costs from defendants (but not vice-versa), and the extensive array of pre-trial private discovery rights accorded civil litigants in the United States, the intense interest of foreigners in antitrust law usually rises to a high level of fear and disbelief. Dealing with these reactions often falls to U.S. counsel.

A less visible but more pervasive aspect of U.S. antitrust law is its influence upon business practices and the terms of business agreements. For example, most licensing, distributorship, and sales representatives' agreements are drafted to minimize the risk of treble damages. This can be done by creating geographic "areas of primary responsibility," a technique specifically approved by the U.S. Supreme Court. *See United States v. Topco Associates*, 1973 WL 805 (N.D. Ill. 1973), affirmed per curiam 414 U.S. 801 (1973).

Many clauses in typical U.S. agreements will reflect calculated antitrust risk assessments in their design. Clauses governing exclusive dealing, full-line coverage, covenants not to compete, purchase requirements, grant-backs of new patents, resale prices and termination are likely to be subjected to such assessments.

In addition, many U.S. companies employ counsel to conduct antitrust "compliance reviews" of their entire business conduct. It is through the advice of business counsel, drawing upon the myriad of reported antitrust cases, that U.S. antitrust law often has its greatest (and often silent) impact on technology transfers.

For detailed coverage of extraterritorial U.S. antitrust jurisdiction and procedure, see my Concise Hornbook on *International Litigation and Arbitration*, Chapters 5 and 6.

§ 9.13   Text of WTO TRIPs Agreement (1995)

WTO AGREEMENT ON TRADE-RELATED ASPECTS OF INTELLECTUAL PROPERTY RIGHTS (TRIPs) (1995)

(Selected Provisions)

Table of Contents

AGREEMENT ON TRADE-RELATED ASPECTS OF
INTELLECTUAL PROPERTY RIGHTS

Members,

Desiring to reduce distortions and impediments to international trade, and taking into account the need to promote effective and adequate protection of intellectual property rights, and to ensure that measures and procedures to enforce intellectual property rights do not themselves become barriers to legitimate trade;

Recognizing, to this end, the need for new rules and disciplines concerning:

(a)   the applicability of the basic principles of GATT 1994 and of relevant international intellectual property agreements or conventions;

(b)   the provision of adequate standards and principles concerning the availability, scope and use of trade-related intellectual property rights;

(c)   the provision of effective and appropriate means for the enforcement of trade-related intellectual property rights, taking into account differences in national legal systems;

(d)   the provision of effective and expeditious procedures for the multilateral prevention and settlement of disputes between governments; and

(e)   transitional arrangements aiming at the fullest participation in the results of the negotiations;

Recognizing the need for a multilateral framework of principles, rules and disciplines dealing with international trade in counterfeit goods;

Recognizing that intellectual property rights are private rights;

Recognizing the underlying public policy objectives of national systems for the protection of intellectual property, including developmental and technological objectives;

Recognizing also the special needs of the least-developed country Members in respect of maximum flexibility in the domestic implementation of laws and regulations in order to enable them to create a sound and viable technological base;

Emphasizing the importance of reducing tensions by reaching strengthened commitments to resolve disputes on trade-related intellectual property issues through multilateral procedures;

Desiring to establish a mutually supportive relationship between the WTO and the World Intellectual Property Organization (referred to in this Agreement as "WIPO") as well as other relevant international organizations;

Hereby agree as follows:

PART I
GENERAL PROVISIONS AND BASIC PRINCIPLES

Article 1
Nature and Scope of Obligations

1.   Members shall give effect to the provisions of this Agreement. Members may, but shall not be obliged to, implement in their law more extensive protection than is required by this Agreement, provided that such protection does not contravene the provisions of this Agreement. Members shall be free to determine the appropriate method of implementing the provisions of this Agreement within their own legal system and practice.

2.   For the purposes of this Agreement, the term "intellectual property" refers to all categories of intellectual property that are the subject of Sections 1 through 7 of Part II.

3.   Members shall accord the treatment provided for in this Agreement to the nationals of other Members.[1] In respect of the relevant intellectual property right, the nationals of other Members shall be understood as those natural or legal persons that would meet the criteria for eligibility for protection provided for in the Paris Convention (1967), the Berne Convention (1971), the Rome Convention and the Treaty on Intellectual Property in Respect of Integrated Circuits, were all Members of the WTO members of those conventions.[2] Any Member availing itself of the possibilities provided in paragraph 3 of Article 5 or paragraph 2 of Article 6 of the Rome Convention shall make a notification as foreseen in those provisions to the Council for Trade-Related Aspects of Intellectual Property Rights (the "Council for TRIPS").

---

[1]   When "nationals" are referred to in this Agreement, they shall be deemed, in the case of a separate customs territory Member of the WTO, to mean persons, natural or legal, who are domiciled or who have a real and effective industrial or commercial establishment in that customs territory.

[2]   In this Agreement, "Paris Convention" refers to the Paris Convention for the Protection of Industrial Property; "Paris Convention (1967)" refers to the Stockholm Act of this Convention of 14 July 1967. "Berne Convention" refers to the Berne Convention for the Protection of Literary and Artistic Works; "Berne Convention (1971)" refers to the Paris Act of this Convention of 24 July 1971. "Rome Convention" refers to the International Convention for the Protection of Performers, Producers of Phonograms and Broadcasting Organizations, adopted at Rome on 26 October 1961. "Treaty on Intellectual Property in Respect of Integrated Circuits" (IPIC Treaty) refers to the Treaty on Intellectual Property in Respect of Integrated Circuits, adopted at Washington on 26 May 1989. "WTO Agreement" refers to the Agreement Establishing the WTO.

Article 2
Intellectual Property Conventions

1.   In respect of Parts II, III and IV of this Agreement, Members shall comply with Articles 1 through 12, and Article 19, of the Paris Convention (1967).

2.   Nothing in Parts I to IV of this Agreement shall derogate from existing obligations that Members may have to each other under the Paris Convention, the Berne Convention, the Rome Convention and the Treaty on Intellectual Property in Respect of Integrated Circuits.

Article 3
National Treatment

1.   Each Member shall accord to the nationals of other Members treatment no less favourable than that it accords to its own nationals with regard to the protection[3] of intellectual property, subject to the exceptions already provided in, respectively, the Paris Convention (1967), the Berne Convention (1971), the Rome Convention or the Treaty on Intellectual Property in Respect of Integrated Circuits. In respect of performers, producers of phonograms and broadcasting organizations, this obligation only applies in respect of the rights provided under this Agreement. Any Member availing itself of the possibilities provided in Article 6 of the Berne Convention (1971) or paragraph 1(b) of Article 16 of the Rome Convention shall make a notification as foreseen in those provisions to the Council for TRIPS.

2.   Members may avail themselves of the exceptions permitted under paragraph 1 in relation to judicial and administrative procedures, including the designation of an address for service or the appointment of an agent within the jurisdiction of a Member, only where such exceptions are necessary to secure compliance with laws and regulations which are not inconsistent with the provisions of this Agreement and where such practices are not applied in a manner which would constitute a disguised restriction on trade.

Article 4
Most-Favoured-Nation Treatment

With regard to the protection of intellectual property, any advantage, favour, privilege or immunity granted by a Member to the nationals of any other country shall be accorded immediately and unconditionally to the nationals of all other Members. Exempted

---

[3]   For the purposes of Articles 3 and 4, "protection" shall include matters affecting the availability, acquisition, scope, maintenance and enforcement of intellectual property rights as well as those matters affecting the use of intellectual property rights specifically addressed in this Agreement.

from this obligation are any advantage, favour, privilege or immunity accorded by a Member:

(a) deriving from international agreements on judicial assistance or law enforcement of a general nature and not particularly confined to the protection of intellectual property;

(b) granted in accordance with the provisions of the Berne Convention (1971) or the Rome Convention authorizing that the treatment accorded be a function not of national treatment but of the treatment accorded in another country;

(c) in respect of the rights of performers, producers of phonograms and broadcasting organizations not provided under this Agreement;

(d) deriving from international agreements related to the protection of intellectual property which entered into force prior to the entry into force of the WTO Agreement, provided that such agreements are notified to the Council for TRIPS and do not constitute an arbitrary or unjustifiable discrimination against nationals of other Members.

Article 5
Multilateral Agreements on Acquisition
or Maintenance of Protection

The obligations under Articles 3 and 4 do not apply to procedures provided in multilateral agreements concluded under the auspices of WIPO relating to the acquisition or maintenance of intellectual property rights.

Article 6
Exhaustion

For the purposes of dispute settlement under this Agreement, subject to the provisions of Articles 3 and 4 nothing in this Agreement shall be used to address the issue of the exhaustion of intellectual property rights.

Article 7
Objectives

The protection and enforcement of intellectual property rights should contribute to the promotion of technological innovation and to the transfer and dissemination of technology, to the mutual advantage of producers and users of technological knowledge and in a manner conducive to social and economic welfare, and to a balance of rights and obligations.

Article 8
Principles

1.   Members may, in formulating or amending their laws and regulations, adopt measures necessary to protect public health and nutrition, and to promote the public interest in sectors of vital importance to their socio-economic and technological development, provided that such measures are consistent with the provisions of this Agreement.

2.   Appropriate measures, provided that they are consistent with the provisions of this Agreement, may be needed to prevent the abuse of intellectual property rights by right holders or the resort to practices which unreasonably restrain trade or adversely affect the international transfer of technology.

PART II
STANDARDS CONCERNING THE AVAILABILITY, SCOPE AND USE OF INTELLECTUAL PROPERTY RIGHTS

SECTION 1: COPYRIGHT AND RELATED RIGHTS

Article 9
Relation to the Berne Convention

1.   Members shall comply with Articles 1 through 21 of the Berne Convention (1971) and the Appendix thereto. However, Members shall not have rights or obligations under this Agreement in respect of the rights conferred under Article 6 *bis* of that Convention or of the rights derived therefrom.

2.   Copyright protection shall extend to expressions and not to ideas, procedures, methods of operation or mathematical concepts as such.

Article 10
Computer Programs and Compilations of Data

1.   Computer programs, whether in source or object code, shall be protected as literary works under the Berne Convention (1971).

2.   Compilations of data or other material, whether in machine readable or other form, which by reason of the selection or arrangement of their contents constitute intellectual creations shall be protected as such. Such protection, which shall not extend to the data or material itself, shall be without prejudice to any copyright subsisting in the data or material itself.

Article 11
Rental Rights

In respect of at least computer programs and cinematographic works, a Member shall provide authors and their successors in title the right to authorize or to prohibit the commercial rental to the public of originals or copies of their copyright works. A Member shall be excepted from this obligation in respect of cinematographic works unless such rental has led to widespread copying of such works which is materially impairing the exclusive right of reproduction conferred in that Member on authors and their successors in title. In respect of computer programs, this obligation does not apply to rentals where the program itself is not the essential object of the rental.

Article 12
Term of Protection

Whenever the term of protection of a work, other than a photographic work or a work of applied art, is calculated on a basis other than the life of a natural person, such term shall be no less than 50 years from the end of the calendar year of authorized publication, or, failing such authorized publication within 50 years from the making of the work, 50 years from the end of the calendar year of making.

Article 13
Limitations and Exceptions

Members shall confine limitations or exceptions to exclusive rights to certain special cases which do not conflict with a normal exploitation of the work and do not unreasonably prejudice the legitimate interests of the right holder.

Article 14
Protection of Performers, Producers of Phonograms
(Sound Recordings) and Broadcasting Organizations

1.   In respect of a fixation of their performance on a phonogram, performers shall have the possibility of preventing the following acts when undertaken without their authorization: the fixation of their unfixed performance and the reproduction of such fixation. Performers shall also have the possibility of preventing the following acts when undertaken without their authorization: the broadcasting by wireless means and the communication to the public of their live performance.

2.   Producers of phonograms shall enjoy the right to authorize or prohibit the direct or indirect reproduction of their phonograms.

3.   Broadcasting organizations shall have the right to prohibit the following acts when undertaken without their authorization: the

fixation, the reproduction of fixations, and the rebroadcasting by wireless means of broadcasts, as well as the communication to the public of television broadcasts of the same. Where Members do not grant such rights to broadcasting organizations, they shall provide owners of copyright in the subject matter of broadcasts with the possibility of preventing the above acts, subject to the provisions of the Berne Convention (1971).

4.   The provisions of Article 11 in respect of computer programs shall apply *mutatis mutandis* to producers of phonograms and any other right holders in phonograms as determined in a Member's law. If on 15 April 1994 a Member has in force a system of equitable remuneration of right holders in respect of the rental of phonograms, it may maintain such system provided that the commercial rental of phonograms is not giving rise to the material impairment of the exclusive rights of reproduction of right holders.

5.   The term of the protection available under this Agreement to performers and producers of phonograms shall last at least until the end of a period of 50 years computed from the end of the calendar year in which the fixation was made or the performance took place. The term of protection granted pursuant to paragraph 3 shall last for at least 20 years from the end of the calendar year in which the broadcast took place.

6.   Any Member may, in relation to the rights conferred under paragraphs 1, 2 and 3, provide for conditions, limitations, exceptions and reservations to the extent permitted by the Rome Convention. However, the provisions of Article 18 of the Berne Convention (1971) shall also apply, *mutatis mutandis,* to the rights of performers and producers of phonograms in phonograms.

SECTION 2: TRADEMARKS

Article 15
Protectable Subject Matter

1.   Any sign, or any combination of signs, capable of distinguishing the goods or services of one undertaking from those of other undertakings, shall be capable of constituting a trademark. Such signs, in particular words including personal names, letters, numerals, figurative elements and combinations of colours as well as any combination of such signs, shall be eligible for registration as trademarks. Where signs are not inherently capable of distinguishing the relevant goods or services, Members may make registrability depend on distinctiveness acquired through use. Members may require, as a condition of registration, that signs be visually perceptible.

2.   Paragraph 1 shall not be understood to prevent a Member from denying registration of a trademark on other grounds, provided that they do not derogate from the provisions of the Paris Convention (1967).

3.   Members may make registrability depend on use. However, actual use of a trademark shall not be a condition for filing an application for registration. An application shall not be refused solely on the ground that intended use has not taken place before the expiry of a period of three years from the date of application.

4.   The nature of the goods or services to which a trademark is to be applied shall in no case form an obstacle to registration of the trademark.

5.   Members shall publish each trademark either before it is registered or promptly after it is registered and shall afford a reasonable opportunity for petitions to cancel the registration. In addition, Members may afford an opportunity for the registration of a trademark to be opposed.

Article 16
Rights Conferred

1.   The owner of a registered trademark shall have the exclusive right to prevent all third parties not having the owner's consent from using in the course of trade identical or similar signs for goods or services which are identical or similar to those in respect of which the trademark is registered where such use would result in a likelihood of confusion. In case of the use of an identical sign for identical goods or services, a likelihood of confusion shall be presumed. The rights described above shall not prejudice any existing prior rights, nor shall they affect the possibility of Members making rights available on the basis of use.

2.   Article 6 *bis* of the Paris Convention (1967) shall apply, *mutatis mutandis,* to services. In determining whether a trademark is well-known, Members shall take account of the knowledge of the trademark in the relevant sector of the public, including knowledge in the Member concerned which has been obtained as a result of the promotion of the trademark.

3.   Article 6 *bis* of the Paris Convention (1967) shall apply, *mutatis mutandis,* to goods or services which are not similar to those in respect of which a trademark is registered, provided that use of that trademark in relation to those goods or services would indicate a connection between those goods or services and the owner of the registered trademark and provided that the interests of the owner of the registered trademark are likely to be damaged by such use.

Article 17
Exceptions

Members may provide limited exceptions to the rights conferred by a trademark, such as fair use of descriptive terms, provided that such exceptions take account of the legitimate interests of the owner of the trademark and of third parties.

Article 18
Term of Protection

Initial registration, and each renewal of registration, of a trademark shall be for a term of no less than seven years. The registration of a trademark shall be renewable indefinitely.

Article 19
Requirement of Use

1. If use is required to maintain a registration, the registration may be cancelled only after an uninterrupted period of at least three years of non-use, unless valid reasons based on the existence of obstacles to such use are shown by the trademark owner. Circumstances arising independently of the will of the owner of the trademark which constitute an obstacle to the use of the trademark, such as import restrictions on or other government requirements for goods or services protected by the trademark, shall be recognized as valid reasons for non-use.

2. When subject to the control of its owner, use of a trademark by another person shall be recognized as use of the trademark for the purpose of maintaining the registration.

Article 20
Other Requirements

The use of a trademark in the course of trade shall not be unjustifiably encumbered by special requirements, such as use with another trademark, use in a special form or use in a manner detrimental to its capability to distinguish the goods or services of one undertaking from those of other undertakings. This will not preclude a requirement prescribing the use of the trademark identifying the undertaking producing the goods or services along with, but without linking it to, the trademark distinguishing the specific goods or services in question of that undertaking.

Article 21
Licensing and Assignment

Members may determine conditions on the licensing and assignment of trademarks, it being understood that the compulsory licensing of trademarks shall not be permitted and that the owner of a registered trademark shall have the right to assign the trademark with or without the transfer of the business to which the trademark belongs.

SECTION 3: GEOGRAPHICAL INDICATIONS [omitted]

* * *

SECTION 4: INDUSTRIAL DESIGNS [omitted]

* * *

SECTION 5: PATENTS

Article 27
Patentable Subject Matter

1.   Subject to the provisions of paragraphs 2 and 3, patents shall be available for any inventions, whether products or processes, in all fields of technology, provided that they are new, involve an inventive step and are capable of industrial application.[5] Subject to paragraph 4 of Article 65, paragraph 8 of Article 70 and paragraph 3 of this Article, patents shall be available and patent rights enjoyable without discrimination as to the place of invention, the field of technology and whether products are imported or locally produced.

2.   Members may exclude from patentability inventions, the prevention within their territory of the commercial exploitation of which is necessary to protect *ordre public* or morality, including to protect human, animal or plant life or health or to avoid serious prejudice to the environment, provided that such exclusion is not made merely because the exploitation is prohibited by their law.

3.   Members may also exclude from patentability:

(a)   diagnostic, therapeutic and surgical methods for the treatment of humans or animals;

(b)   plants and animals other than micro-organisms, and essentially biological processes for the production of plants or animals other than non-biological and microbiological processes. However, Members shall provide for the protection of plant varieties either by patents or by an effective *sui generis* system or by any combination thereof. The provisions of this subparagraph shall be reviewed four years after the date of entry into force of the WTO Agreement.

---

[5]   For the purposes of this Article, the terms "inventive step" and "capable of industrial application" may be deemed by a Member to be synonymous with the terms "non-obvious" and "useful" respectively.

Article 28
Rights Conferred

1.   A patent shall confer on its owner the following exclusive rights:

(a)   where the subject matter of a patent is a product, to prevent third parties not having the owner's consent from the acts of: making, using, offering for sale, selling, or importing[6] for these purposes that product;

(b)   where the subject matter of a patent is a process, to prevent third parties not having the owner's consent from the act of using the process, and from the acts of: using, offering for sale, selling, or importing for these purposes at least the product obtained directly by that process.

2.   Patent owners shall also have the right to assign, or transfer by succession, the patent and to conclude licensing contracts.

Article 29
Conditions on Patent Applicants

1.   Members shall require that an applicant for a patent shall disclose the invention in a manner sufficiently clear and complete for the invention to be carried out by a person skilled in the art and may require the applicant to indicate the best mode for carrying out the invention known to the inventor at the filing date or, where priority is claimed, at the priority date of the application.

2.   Members may require an applicant for a patent to provide information concerning the applicant's corresponding foreign applications and grants.

Article 30
Exceptions to Rights Conferred

Members may provide limited exceptions to the exclusive rights conferred by a patent, provided that such exceptions do not unreasonably conflict with a normal exploitation of the patent and do not unreasonably prejudice the legitimate interests of the patent owner, taking account of the legitimate interests of third parties.

Article 31
Other Use Without Authorization of the Right Holder

Where the law of a Member allows for other use[7] of the subject matter of a patent without the authorization of the right holder,

---

[6]   This right, like all other rights conferred under this Agreement in respect of the use, sale, importation or other distribution of goods, is subject to the provisions of Article 6.

[7]   "Other use" refers to other than that allowed under Article 30.

including use by the government or third parties authorized by the government, the following provisions shall be respected:

(a)   authorization of such use shall be considered on its individual merits;

(b)   such use may only be permitted if, prior to such use, the proposed user has made efforts to obtain authorization from the right holder on reasonable commercial terms and conditions and that such efforts have not been successful within a reasonable period of time. This requirement may be waived by a Member in the case of a national emergency or other circumstances of extreme urgency or in cases of public non-commercial use. In situations of national emergency or other circumstances of extreme urgency, the right holder shall, nevertheless, be notified as soon as reasonably practicable. In the case of public non-commercial use, where the government or contractor, without making a patent search, knows or has demonstrable grounds to know that a valid patent is or will be used by or for the government, the right holder shall be informed promptly;

(c)   the scope and duration of such use shall be limited to the purpose for which it was authorized, and in the case of semi-conductor technology shall only be for public non-commercial use or to remedy a practice determined after judicial or administrative process to be anti-competitive;

(d)   such use shall be non-exclusive;

(e)   such use shall be non-assignable, except with that part of the enterprise or goodwill which enjoys such use;

(f)   any such use shall be authorized predominantly for the supply of the domestic market of the Member authorizing such use;

(g)   authorization for such use shall be liable, subject to adequate protection of the legitimate interests of the persons so authorized, to be terminated if and when the circumstances which led to it cease to exist and are unlikely to recur. The competent authority shall have the authority to review, upon motivated request, the continued existence of these circumstances;

(h)   the right holder shall be paid adequate remuneration in the circumstances of each case, taking into account the economic value of the authorization;

(i)   the legal validity of any decision relating to the authorization of such use shall be subject to judicial review or other independent review by a distinct higher authority in that Member;

(j)   any decision relating to the remuneration provided in respect of such use shall be subject to judicial review or other independent review by a distinct higher authority in that Member;

(k) Members are not obliged to apply the conditions set forth in subparagraphs (b) and (f) where such use is permitted to remedy a practice determined after judicial or administrative process to be anti-competitive. The need to correct anti-competitive practices may be taken into account in determining the amount of remuneration in such cases. Competent authorities shall have the authority to refuse termination of authorization if and when the conditions which led to such authorization are likely to recur;

(l)   where such use is authorized to permit the exploitation of a patent ("the second patent") which cannot be exploited without infringing another patent ("the first patent"), the following additional conditions shall apply:

(i)   the invention claimed in the second patent shall involve an important technical advance of considerable economic significance in relation to the invention claimed in the first patent;

(ii) the owner of the first patent shall be entitled to a cross-licence on reasonable terms to use the invention claimed in the second patent; and

(iii) the use authorized in respect of the first patent shall be non-assignable except with the assignment of the second patent.

Article 32
Revocation / Forfeiture

An opportunity for judicial review of any decision to revoke or forfeit a patent shall be available.

Article 33
Term of Protection

The term of protection available shall not end before the expiration of a period of twenty years counted from the filing date.[8]

---

[8]   It is understood that those Members which do not have a system of original grant may provide that the term of protection shall be computed from the filing date in the system of original grant.

Article 34
Process Patents: Burden of Proof

1.   For the purposes of civil proceedings in respect of the infringement of the rights of the owner referred to in paragraph 1(b) of Article 28, if the subject matter of a patent is a process for obtaining a product, the judicial authorities shall have the authority to order the defendant to prove that the process to obtain an identical product is different from the patented process. Therefore, Members shall provide, in at least one of the following circumstances, that any identical product when produced without the consent of the patent owner shall, in the absence of proof to the contrary, be deemed to have been obtained by the patented process:

(a)   if the product obtained by the patented process is new;

(b)   if there is a substantial likelihood that the identical product was made by the process and the owner of the patent has been unable through reasonable efforts to determine the process actually used.

2.   Any Member shall be free to provide that the burden of proof indicated in paragraph 1 shall be on the alleged infringer only if the condition referred to in subparagraph (a) is fulfilled or only if the condition referred to in subparagraph (b) is fulfilled.

3.   In the adduction of proof to the contrary, the legitimate interests of defendants in protecting their manufacturing and business secrets shall be taken into account.

SECTION 6: LAYOUT-DESIGNS (TOPOGRAPHIES)
OF INTEGRATED CIRCUITS [omitted]

* * *

SECTION 7: PROTECTION OF
UNDISCLOSED INFORMATION

Article 39

1.   In the course of ensuring effective protection against unfair competition as provided in Article 10 *bis* of the Paris Convention (1967), Members shall protect undisclosed information in accordance with paragraph 2 and data submitted to governments or governmental agencies in accordance with paragraph 3.

2.   Natural and legal persons shall have the possibility of preventing information lawfully within their control from being disclosed to, acquired by, or used by others without their consent in

a manner contrary to honest commercial practices[10] so long as such information:

(a) is secret in the sense that it is not, as a body or in the precise configuration and assembly of its components, generally known among or readily accessible to persons within the circles that normally deal with the kind of information in question;

(b) has commercial value because it is secret; and

(c) has been subject to reasonable steps under the circumstances, by the person lawfully in control of the information, to keep it secret.

3.   Members, when requiring, as a condition of approving the marketing of pharmaceutical or of agricultural chemical products which utilize new chemical entities, the submission of undisclosed test or other data, the origination of which involves a considerable effort, shall protect such data against unfair commercial use. In addition, Members shall protect such data against disclosure, except where necessary to protect the public, or unless steps are taken to ensure that the data are protected against unfair commercial use.

SECTION 8: CONTROL OF ANTI-COMPETITIVE PRACTICES IN CONTRACTUAL LICENSES

Article 40

1.   Members agree that some licensing practices or conditions pertaining to intellectual property rights which restrain competition may have adverse effects on trade and may impede the transfer and dissemination of technology.

2.   Nothing in this Agreement shall prevent Members from specifying in their legislation licensing practices or conditions that may in particular cases constitute an abuse of intellectual property rights having an adverse effect on competition in the relevant market. As provided above, a Member may adopt, consistently with the other provisions of this Agreement, appropriate measures to prevent or control such practices, which may include for example exclusive grantback conditions, conditions preventing challenges to validity and coercive package licensing, in the light of the relevant laws and regulations of that Member.

3.   Each Member shall enter, upon request, into consultations with any other Member which has cause to believe that an

---

[10] For the purpose of this provision, "a manner contrary to honest commercial practices" shall mean at least practices such as breach of contract, breach of confidence and inducement to breach, and includes the acquisition of undisclosed information by third parties who knew, or were grossly negligent in failing to know, that such practices were involved in the acquisition.

intellectual property right owner that is a national or domiciliary of the Member to which the request for consultations has been addressed is undertaking practices in violation of the requesting Member's laws and regulations on the subject matter of this Section, and which wishes to secure compliance with such legislation, without prejudice to any action under the law and to the full freedom of an ultimate decision of either Member. The Member addressed shall accord full and sympathetic consideration to, and shall afford adequate opportunity for, consultations with the requesting Member, and shall cooperate through supply of publicly available non-confidential information of relevance to the matter in question and of other information available to the Member, subject to domestic law and to the conclusion of mutually satisfactory agreements concerning the safeguarding of its confidentiality by the requesting Member.

4.   A Member whose nationals or domiciliaries are subject to proceedings in another Member concerning alleged violation of that other Member's laws and regulations on the subject matter of this Section shall, upon request, be granted an opportunity for consultations by the other Member under the same conditions as those foreseen in paragraph 3.

PART III
ENFORCEMENT OF INTELLECTUAL PROPERTY RIGHTS
SECTION 1: GENERAL OBLIGATIONS

Article 41

1.   Members shall ensure that enforcement procedures as specified in this Part are available under their law so as to permit effective action against any act of infringement of intellectual property rights covered by this Agreement, including expeditious remedies to prevent infringements and remedies which constitute a deterrent to further infringements. These procedures shall be applied in such a manner as to avoid the creation of barriers to legitimate trade and to provide for safeguards against their abuse.

2.   Procedures concerning the enforcement of intellectual property rights shall be fair and equitable. They shall not be unnecessarily complicated or costly, or entail unreasonable time-limits or unwarranted delays.

3.   Decisions on the merits of a case shall preferably be in writing and reasoned. They shall be made available at least to the parties to the proceeding without undue delay. Decisions on the merits of a case shall be based only on evidence in respect of which parties were offered the opportunity to be heard.

4.   Parties to a proceeding shall have an opportunity for review by a judicial authority of final administrative decisions and, subject to jurisdictional provisions in a Member's law concerning the importance of a case, of at least the legal aspects of initial judicial decisions on the merits of a case. However, there shall be no obligation to provide an opportunity for review of acquittals in criminal cases.

5.   It is understood that this Part does not create any obligation to put in place a judicial system for the enforcement of intellectual property rights distinct from that for the enforcement of law in general, nor does it affect the capacity of Members to enforce their law in general. Nothing in this Part creates any obligation with respect to the distribution of resources as between enforcement of intellectual property rights and the enforcement of law in general.

SECTION 2: CIVIL AND ADMINISTRATIVE PROCEDURES AND REMEDIES

Article 42
Fair and Equitable Procedures

Members shall make available to right holders[11] civil judicial procedures concerning the enforcement of any intellectual property right covered by this Agreement. Defendants shall have the right to written notice which is timely and contains sufficient detail, including the basis of the claims. Parties shall be allowed to be represented by independent legal counsel, and procedures shall not impose overly burdensome requirements concerning mandatory personal appearances. All parties to such procedures shall be duly entitled to substantiate their claims and to present all relevant evidence. The procedure shall provide a means to identify and protect confidential information, unless this would be contrary to existing constitutional requirements.

Article 43
Evidence

1.   The judicial authorities shall have the authority, where a party has presented reasonably available evidence sufficient to support its claims and has specified evidence relevant to substantiation of its claims which lies in the control of the opposing party, to order that this evidence be produced by the opposing party, subject in appropriate cases to conditions which ensure the protection of confidential information.

---

[11]   For the purpose of this Part, the term "right holder" includes federations and associations having legal standing to assert such rights.

2.   In cases in which a party to a proceeding voluntarily and without good reason refuses access to, or otherwise does not provide necessary information within a reasonable period, or significantly impedes a procedure relating to an enforcement action, a Member may accord judicial authorities the authority to make preliminary and final determinations, affirmative or negative, on the basis of the information presented to them, including the complaint or the allegation presented by the party adversely affected by the denial of access to information, subject to providing the parties an opportunity to be heard on the allegations or evidence.

Article 44
Injunctions

1.   The judicial authorities shall have the authority to order a party to desist from an infringement, *inter alia* to prevent the entry into the channels of commerce in their jurisdiction of imported goods that involve the infringement of an intellectual property right, immediately after customs clearance of such goods. Members are not obliged to accord such authority in respect of protected subject matter acquired or ordered by a person prior to knowing or having reasonable grounds to know that dealing in such subject matter would entail the infringement of an intellectual property right.

2.   Notwithstanding the other provisions of this Part and provided that the provisions of Part II specifically addressing use by governments, or by third parties authorized by a government, without the authorization of the right holder are complied with, Members may limit the remedies available against such use to payment of remuneration in accordance with subparagraph (h) of Article 31. In other cases, the remedies under this Part shall apply or, where these remedies are inconsistent with a Member's law, declaratory judgments and adequate compensation shall be available.

Article 45
Damages

1.   The judicial authorities shall have the authority to order the infringer to pay the right holder damages adequate to compensate for the injury the right holder has suffered because of an infringement of that person's intellectual property right by an infringer who knowingly, or with reasonable grounds to know, engaged in infringing activity.

2.   The judicial authorities shall also have the authority to order the infringer to pay the right holder expenses, which may include appropriate attorney's fees. In appropriate cases, Members may authorize the judicial authorities to order recovery of profits

and/or payment of pre-established damages even where the infringer did not knowingly, or with reasonable grounds to know, engage in infringing activity.

Article 46
Other Remedies

In order to create an effective deterrent to infringement, the judicial authorities shall have the authority to order that goods that they have found to be infringing be, without compensation of any sort, disposed of outside the channels of commerce in such a manner as to avoid any harm caused to the right holder, or, unless this would be contrary to existing constitutional requirements, destroyed. The judicial authorities shall also have the authority to order that materials and implements the predominant use of which has been in the creation of the infringing goods be, without compensation of any sort, disposed of outside the channels of commerce in such a manner as to minimize the risks of further infringements. In considering such requests, the need for proportionality between the seriousness of the infringement and the remedies ordered as well as the interests of third parties shall be taken into account. In regard to counterfeit trademark goods, the simple removal of the trademark unlawfully affixed shall not be sufficient, other than in exceptional cases, to permit release of the goods into the channels of commerce.

Article 47
Right of Information

Members may provide that the judicial authorities shall have the authority, unless this would be out of proportion to the seriousness of the infringement, to order the infringer to inform the right holder of the identity of third persons involved in the production and distribution of the infringing goods or services and of their channels of distribution.

Article 48
Indemnification of the Defendant

1.   The judicial authorities shall have the authority to order a party at whose request measures were taken and who has abused enforcement procedures to provide to a party wrongfully enjoined or restrained adequate compensation for the injury suffered because of such abuse. The judicial authorities shall also have the authority to order the applicant to pay the defendant expenses, which may include appropriate attorney's fees.

2.   In respect of the administration of any law pertaining to the protection or enforcement of intellectual property rights, Members shall only exempt both public authorities and officials from liability

to appropriate remedial measures where actions are taken or intended in good faith in the course of the administration of that law.

Article 49
Administrative Procedures

To the extent that any civil remedy can be ordered as a result of administrative procedures on the merits of a case, such procedures shall conform to principles equivalent in substance to those set forth in this Section.

SECTION 3: PROVISIONAL MEASURES

Article 50

1.   The judicial authorities shall have the authority to order prompt and effective provisional measures:

(a)   to prevent an infringement of any intellectual property right from occurring, and in particular to prevent the entry into the channels of commerce in their jurisdiction of goods, including imported goods immediately after customs clearance;

(b)   to preserve relevant evidence in regard to the alleged infringement.

2.   The judicial authorities shall have the authority to adopt provisional measures *inaudita altera parte* where appropriate, in particular where any delay is likely to cause irreparable harm to the right holder, or where there is a demonstrable risk of evidence being destroyed.

3.   The judicial authorities shall have the authority to require the applicant to provide any reasonably available evidence in order to satisfy themselves with a sufficient degree of certainty that the applicant is the right holder and that the applicant's right is being infringed or that such infringement is imminent, and to order the applicant to provide a security or equivalent assurance sufficient to protect the defendant and to prevent abuse.

4.   Where provisional measures have been adopted *inaudita altera parte,* the parties affected shall be given notice, without delay after the execution of the measures at the latest. A review, including a right to be heard, shall take place upon request of the defendant with a view to deciding, within a reasonable period after the notification of the measures, whether these measures shall be modified, revoked or confirmed.

5.   The applicant may be required to supply other information necessary for the identification of the goods concerned by the authority that will execute the provisional measures.

6. Without prejudice to paragraph 4, provisional measures taken on the basis of paragraphs 1 and 2 shall, upon request by the defendant, be revoked or otherwise cease to have effect, if proceedings leading to a decision on the merits of the case are not initiated within a reasonable period, to be determined by the judicial authority ordering the measures where a Member's law so permits or, in the absence of such a determination, not to exceed 20 working days or 31 calendar days, whichever is the longer.

7. Where the provisional measures are revoked or where they lapse due to any act or omission by the applicant, or where it is subsequently found that there has been no infringement or threat of infringement of an intellectual property right, the judicial authorities shall have the authority to order the applicant, upon request of the defendant, to provide the defendant appropriate compensation for any injury caused by these measures.

8. To the extent that any provisional measure can be ordered as a result of administrative procedures, such procedures shall conform to principles equivalent in substance to those set forth in this section.

Table of Cases

Table of CFIUS Investment in USA Decisions

Table of NAFTA Investor-State Arbitration Tribunal Decisions